SAFE BOAT

By Brayton Harris and Jerry Kirschenbaum

THE U.S. NAVY DIVING MANUAL (1972)

By Brayton Harris

THE AGE OF THE BATTLESHIP: 1890–1922 (1965)
JOHANN GUTENBERG AND THE INVENTION OF PRINTING (1970)
THE ROLE OF THE PRESS IN THE CIVIL WAR (1988)

W · W · NORTON & COMPANY

New York   London

SAFE BOAT

A Comprehensive Guide to the Purchase, Equipping, Maintenance, and Operation of a Safe Boat

JERRY KIRSCHENBAUM
and
BRAYTON HARRIS

The text of this book is composed in Aster,
with the display set in Spectra Medium.
Composition by Com Com.
Manufacturing by R.R. Donnelley & Sons.
Book design by Jacques Chazaud.

FIRST EDITION

Library of Congress Cataloging-in-Publication Data
Kirschenbaum, Jerome M.
    Safe boat : a comprehensive guide to the purchase, equipping,
  maintenance, and operation of a safe boat / Jerome M. Kirschenbaum
  and Brayton Harris.
          p.   cm.
    Includes index.
    ISBN 0-393-02910-7
    1. Boats and boating—Safety measures.   2. Boats and boating—
  Equipment and supplies.   I. Harris, Brayton.   II. Title.
  GV777.55.K57   1990
  797.1'028'9—dc20   90-2365
                                                        CIP

W. W. Norton & Company Inc., 500 Fifth Avenue, New York, N.Y. 10110
W. W. Norton & Company Ltd., 10 Coptic Street, London WC1A 1PU

For Charlie Martin,
who taught me how to sail;

Lt. Jim Storms, USN,
who taught me how to handle a ship and men;

Captain Giffy Full,
who taught me quality and discipline at sea;

and Lois,
who teaches me every day.

—Jerry Kirschenbaum

For K.K.

—F. Brayton Harris

Contents

Part III　Facing Problems and Handling Emergencies　*277*

Appendixes　*371*

Foreword

By purchasing this book, you've made a wise investment—not only in the maintenance of your boat, but also in the safety of you and your family.

Every year, the Coast Guard answers more than 60,000 calls for assistance and saves about 6,000 lives. Tragically, there are nearly 1,000 lives lost in boating mishaps.

While I am proud of the hard work of my crews, I'm also concerned that much of the boating public just isn't prepared to handle emergencies. No matter how hard we try, the Coast Guard and other rescue agencies can't be everywhere at once. So until we arrive, the best way to help us is first to help yourself.

Before you get underway, make sure you are thoroughly familiar with your boat and its safety equipment. When an engine catches fire, you don't have time to learn how to operate the fire extinguisher. If the boat capsizes, it's too late to get the life preservers out of the plastic wrapper.

Knowing navigation rules can prevent you from getting into trouble in the first place. So I encourage boaters to **study this book thoroughly,** take a boating safety course, and ask for a Courtesy Marine Examination from the Coast Guard Auxiliary.

Have fun, but remember, it's best to know before you go.

Wishing you years of safe boating.

—Paul A. Yost
Commandant
United States Coast Guard

PAUL A. YOST, Commandant, United States Coast Guard. (Courtesy United States Coast Guard)

Acknowledgments

A book like this really has more than two authors.

First, there are all the men and women with whom we have sailed and powered. There is the friend of the family who provided that first boat—a flat-bottomed dory on Long Island's Great South Bay. And there is Charlie Martin in New York's Adirondacks, who explained the mysteries of the Adirondack Guide Boat and the straight-eight 1929 Chris-Craft motor launches. There are all of those deck officers, bosun's mates, snipes, and chief quartermasters on the bridges of U.S. Navy tankers, oceangoing tugs, rescue vessels, and submarines who brought two inexperienced naval officers along. There are all of the professional yacht captains, marine surveyors, crew members, other skippers, shipyard foremen, boatbuilders, and other lovers of boats and the sea who helped us find and buy boats, stood our watches with us, tolerated and survived our mistakes, and repaired the results.

They all should be considered as co-authors of this book.

However, there are a few individuals who stood fast on the voyage of this book and they bear special mention. Candace Maté, our editor at Norton, has always kept the vision of this book clear—even in the fog of our writing. If this book speaks widely to the boating audience, it is because of her intelligence, experience, and guidance. Kathleen Brandes did a superlative job of copyediting this odyssey. If you find yourself easily carried from one paragraph to another with your thoughts intact, then credit her hand on the helm.

Finally, we would like to thank Perry Knowlton, our literary agent, for his calm and firm advice; and Eric Swenson of W. W. Norton for his initial confidence in the idea of this book, and his great patience in awaiting its arrival in safe harbor.

—Jerry Kirschenbaum and Brayton Harris

Introduction

We are a nation that loves boating; 25 percent of us participate, for an average of almost ten days a year each, aboard 10 million registered and 6 million unregistered boats, supported by more than 27,500 manufacturers, dealers, and suppliers.

But, in spite of our love for boats, many of us don't know very much *about* boats. More people are killed each year in boating accidents than in airplane crashes; perhaps 5,000 are seriously injured, with the annual property damage running to several hundred million dollars. Very few of these accidents are as spectacular as those featured in the movies—explosions or splintering collisions. Most are far less dramatic: tipping over when overloaded; getting a hand crushed between the boat and the pier; being caught unprepared in a sudden storm.

And, while we'd probably like to think that only reckless rednecks and rambunctious teenagers cause most of the accidents, for most of us the truth comes much closer to home. From Coast Guard reports, we could draw this statistical portrait of the average boater involved in a fatal accident: a mature family man, perhaps sharing a few beers with a friend in familiar waters on a clear, pleasant summer's day, who had *no* formal training in boat operation.

We don't offer this book as a substitute for that formal training; of necessity, it only touches upon many topics on which many volumes could be written. It is, rather, a guidebook along the path to boating safety—and, like any good guidebook, it points out the highlights, warns of the hazards, and gives you lists of things to think about.

Our goal is simple: to help you choose a safe boat, equip her properly, and keep her safe; to help you avoid the hidden traps of maritime law and insurance; to help you understand the hazards of naive guests and curious children, sudden storms and pea-soup fogs, mechanical breakdown and physical injury—how to avoid them if possible and how to deal with them if you must.

In covering a topic as vital as *safety*, we can assume no common baseline of knowledge among our readers. To the experienced boater, much of what follows may seem basic and to the beginner contemplating the purchase of a first boat, much of this may seem overwhelming. We hope, however, that within these pages, the old hand will find new information and the neophyte will find confidence.

PART I

You and
Your Boat

When we stroll through the local marina and admire the assembled boats, we are likely to view them in terms of hopes, dreams, and the romance of the sea—transport to exotic climes and new friends.

However, since we want a boat that will transport us *safely* and at a cost we can afford, we need to cut through the romantic haze and take a closer look.

No manufacturer sets out deliberately to make an unsafe boat, yet unsafe boats there are: boats with dangerously slick decks, boats with massive instrument consoles that are designed to appeal to the eye but block visibility for all but the tallest helmsmen, boats with steering sheaves and deck hardware screwed into flimsy fiberglass, ready to pop out with the first real strain.

There are boats that once were safe, but that now carry the cumulative sins of past owners, each of whom may have added unsafe or improper equipment. The harsh marine environment will quickly weaken or destroy materials that are perfectly suited for your home or automobile. Materials that are "certified for marine use" are not a luxury of the wealthy— they are mandatory aboard a safe boat.

There are boats that display the ignorance and laziness of present owners: boats with gasoline stored in picnic jugs, rat's-nest wiring, grease-covered galley curtains, and useless fire extinguishers—floating time bombs waiting for a signal.

Having said all that, we should emphasize that *most* boats are safe boats when designed according to accepted standards, built and used according to the designer's intentions, and then maintained according to the manufacturer's specifications.

The basic standards for safe boats have been developed over the years by such organizations as the American Boat and Yacht Council (ABYC) and the U.S. Coast Guard (USCG). The ABYC continually analyzes and periodically issues guidelines on such topics as flotation, visibility from the helm, and electrical wiring. However, a caution: ABYC standards are voluntary; a boat manufacturer is not required to follow any of them. A manufacturer can ignore suggestions for color-coded wiring, for example, with impunity. On the other hand, the U.S. Coast Guard's regulations on safe design, operation, and equipment (such as fire extinguishers, life jackets, signaling devices) are mandatory. For most of them, compliance is under *your* control: It is your responsibility to carry the right equipment and keep it in proper working order, and it is your responsibility to operate your boat in a safe manner.

Part I of this book focuses first on a safe boat for you, then on each of the major sections and systems of a boat: the hull, deck, rig and helm, accommodations, and the mechanical and electrical systems that keep everything going. Next we'll walk through a Boat Buyer's Checklist, examine the important role of the marine surveyor in helping you make your decision, discuss some legal and financial aspects of boat ownership, and offer suggestions for equipping your boat with safety in mind. To finish Part I, we will describe the various maintenance procedures you must follow regularly to keep your boat safe.

CHAPTER ONE

The Boat

THE RIGHT BOAT FOR YOU

We can begin with a bold statement: Unless your choice of boat is well matched to your needs, expectations, and capabilities, it probably is *not* a safe boat.

Your choice should be rational, not emotional. Don't be so carried away with dreams of tropical sunsets that you ignore the realities of boating: often cold, often wet, often frustrating, sometimes hazardous. If you are not psychologically prepared for the down side, you will not enjoy boating and there may be no "right" boat for you after all.

Start by analyzing your boating needs. Somewhere between the extremes of a dinghy and a world cruiser, there are a lot of boats. And there are a lot of boat owners who either buy more boat than they can handle or buy less boat than they need.

Ponder the following questions:

• Are you a loner or will you sail with your family or do you want to be able to take along the whole neighborhood?

• Are you happy when puttering around, rebuilding pumps, and sanding the varnish . . . or do you just want to step aboard and turn the key and spend little time working on your boat?

• Do you enjoy physical challenges or do you prefer relaxed comfort?

• Is your sense of worth and well-being associated with the social status of things you own?

The answers to such questions are not as important as the time you take to think about the answers; you need to select a boat that suits you and not your neighbors or the guy who writes interesting travel articles for a yachting magazine. If you're a happy handyman, you're a candidate for an older boat; if not, you should stick with the latest models and probably should add the cost of hired maintenance to your budget. If you enjoy a physical challenge, you are more likely to find satisfaction with a sailboat or a deep-sea sportfisherman than a houseboat or a trawler.

But those comments are more philosophical than specific; having determined the general type of boating that most appeals to you, you must seek a boat to match your requirements—by size, power, capacity—and your capabilities, financial and physical. For example:

• Size governs the type of water in which you'll operate, the number of people you can carry, how far you can travel; it also defines your requirements for mooring space. Small boats stick to quiet, sheltered waters; if you intend to go off-shore, you'll need something larger, certainly above 22 feet and preferably above 30 feet. If you have a family of five, a 16-foot runabout rated for four passengers probably will not work out.

• Financial considerations go beyond your ability to make the down payment and keep up the monthlies. You'll need insurance, a place to keep your boat, money for maintenance and repairs and for operating costs.

• Your level of skill and experience (coupled with your willingness to study and practice to increase both) will govern both the size and the type of boat you can handle safely.

If you are at all uncertain—or if you don't have much experience with the type of boat in which you're interested—look into chartering a similar boat for at least a few days, preferably for a week. Find one with a paid, qualified captain to show you the ropes and keep you out of trouble. How much will this cost? Perhaps $200 a day for a run-

---

Organized Ownership

In chapter 10, we describe a thorough, detailed, self-created Owner's Notebook. In truth, the review and collection of information for this invaluable tool should begin well before you decide on a specific boat. Start with a simple file or loose-leaf binder and put into it photographs and specification sheets on every boat in which you might be interested; test reports from boating magazines; copies of related articles on equipment; copies of for-sale ads; manufacturers' brochures. The information you compile not only will aid you in your search for the right boat, but also will provide a database for future sales and purchases.

---

about, $2,000 a week for a cruising sailboat, captain included. If $2,000 seems like a lot of money for a trial run, consider this: The cost of owning such a boat might run $2,000 a month (payments, insurance, slip, maintenance), and it's too late to discover that you don't enjoy this type of boat after you're committed to spending all that money. Besides, that one-week charter is, after all, a vacation. Enjoy it!

The next safety step: Determine whether the boat you have in mind is the right boat. Examine every line and bilge, every blower and pump, every engine and sail. Consider both appropriateness and condition. In doing this with boats of any appreciable size, you should have the assistance of a professional marine surveyor (see chapter 6). Then you must make sure that the boat is properly equipped for safe operations.

The last step—the step that never ends—is to keep learning the arts of the mariner: how to handle the boat in fair weather or foul, how to maintain it in safe condition, how to handle—with skill and confidence—the myriad emergencies that can strike anywhere, at any time.

A Note of Introduction: The Language of Sailing

The language of sailing is both a frustration and a delight. It is a frustration until you understand it—at which point it becomes a delight because you now understand that it means exactly what it says and helps you communicate with your crew to ensure safety and comfort. It also helps the authors of books on sailing to explain how it all works. Thus, we direct your attention, as necessary, to appendix VII, A Working Glossary of Sailing Terms.

How Big a Boat Can You Handle Alone?

Your level of skill and your overall physical condition play a major role, of course, but there are two main considerations:

1. For any boat, how large an anchor can you handle by yourself? If you are uncertain, try lifting aboard the boat's largest anchor. Then try it with one hand. If the boat is equipped with such laborsaving features as a bow roller and an anchor windlass, these devices will reduce the required level of effort to launch and recover the anchor, but . . . if the windlass is powered by electricity, you may not be able to count on it in an emergency.

2. For a sailboat, can you furl the largest sail without assistance? Raising a heavy mainsail is not all that difficult, given the proper winch. The problem is to get it under control in a brisk breeze. As with the anchor, the addition of appropriate accessories might help. In this case, return to yesteryear—when all sails were too large even for several people to handle easily—and install lazyjacks to catch the billowing cloth as it descends from the masthead.

As a practical matter, these factors suggest a boat—for a reasonably healthy man or woman—of 45 feet or less.

CHAPTER TWO

Hull, Deck, Helm, and Accommodations

THE HULL

The hull is basic: It *is* the boat, and the other components and systems are what make it mobile and habitable. Most of them can be modified or replaced; the hull cannot. When you choose a boat, you may be dazzled by the exterior design and the interior decor—but you need to take a close, hard look at the size, type, or design of the hull; the type of materials used in construction; and the quality of the materials and construction.

SIZE

The size of a boat is usually defined by length. Length overall (LOA) is the measurement from one end to the other, usually including the bow pulpit or bowsprit; length on the waterline (LWL) is the measurement from bow to stern at the waterline—where the boat sits in the water. Another measure might be called the "marketing length" of the boat: The Federal Trade Commission (FTC) requires that "Any representation as to the length of a boat either direct, or indirect by

use of model numbers suggesting length, or otherwise, must state the exact distance measured end to end over the deck of such boat, excluding sheer." This does *not* include a pulpit or bowsprit.

LOA is most important when trailering or berthing the boat in a marina; LWL is significant in determining performance characteristics of a boat. The FTC length is the one used in its model name—a Deepwater 30, for example, or a Gofast 243 (24 feet 3 inches).

Other hull measurements include beam, draft, freeboard, and displacement. The beam is the width of the boat at the widest point; the draft is the amount of water depth required to float the boat. Boats equipped with centerboards will have two draft measurements: board up and board down, which might vary by four or five feet. Freeboard is the height from the load waterline (where a fully loaded boat will float in calm water) to the lowest point of the deck edge. This is an indicator of how seaworthy a boat might be before it begins taking water aboard, and this measurement is especially critical in small, open boats. (See of Special Considerations for Small Boats at the end of this chapter.)

Displacement is a measure of the weight of water displaced by the floating hull. In boats of similar size, it is a pretty good indication of the quality of construction and the handling characteristics. A light boat is more maneuverable and faster; a heavy boat, more comfortable and essentially safer. Lightweight boats are fine for inshore club racing and weekend cruising, but they lack the capacity to carry the additional weight of food, fuel, and supplies for ocean passages. A lightweight boat will bounce around more, at sea and at anchor (which can make for some uncomfortable sleeping).

The displacement of a sailboat in the 36-to-37-foot range might vary from under 10,000 pounds to more than 36,000 pounds: on the light end, a fast, tricky racing boat; on the heavy end, a solid (and stolid) long-range cruiser.

The displacement-to-length ratio of any boat is useful in making general comparisons; it is computed as follows:

$$\text{D/L} = \frac{\text{weight in long tons (2,240 lb)}}{(.01 \times \text{waterline length})^3}$$

For an ultralight boat, the D/L will be under 100; a light boat, under 200; a medium boat, under 300. A heavy boat is anything with a D/L over 300.

With the exception of very sophisticated lightweight racers made of high-technology, high-strength, low-weight materials, lighter boats are less costly to make and therefore more plentiful in the marketplace.

STABILITY

Stability might be defined as the tendency of a boat to return to the original, upright position after being inclined away from that position by wind or wave. A boat is considered very stable, or "stiff," when the center of gravity (CG) is relatively far beneath the center of buoyancy (CB),

and "tender" (or tippy) when those two centers are relatively close together. Stability (or lack thereof) is created by a combination of hull shape, topside weight (such as masts or fishing towers), deep-in-the-hull weight (such as engines), and ballast. Stability tends to be designed in, and what you get is what you get—unless the boat has been dangerously modified with too much topside architecture or you violate safe loading practices (and the Coast Guard–certified load limit for your boat) and try to take your entire neighborhood for a spin.

The most stable boats—heavy, full-displacement, deep-keeled sailboats—will take you around the world in all kinds of weather. A very stable boat, tightly closed against the weather, can be knocked down on her beam ends (that is, forced over until the deck is perpendicular) and still return to a vertical floating position. Some boats are so stable that they can survive a 360-degree roll. The voyage plans of the least stable boats—say, an unballasted sailing dinghy or a shallow-draft bass fisherman—should be confined to sheltered lakes or rivers.

HULL TYPES

As a general rule, there are two basic types of hull, displacement and planing, with a range of modifications and combinations between. A displacement boat—typically, a trawler or a cruising sailboat with a wide, deep, and rounded hull—moves through the water, actually pushing aside a volume of water equal to its underwater body. A planing hull—found on speedboats and most small-to-medium-sized powerboats—tends to ride on top of the water when it reaches cruising speed.

The top speed of most boats is a function more of hull design than of power. The speed of a displacement boat is generally limited to a hull speed that is directly proportional to the length of the waterline. This may be computed simply as 1.34 times the square root of the waterline, in feet. In other words, a 25-foot waterline (*not* length overall) would produce a hull speed of 6.7

knots; a 36-foot waterline, 8.04 knots; a 49-foot waterline, 9.38 knots.

You can turn on the engine, hoist all sail, and be blessed with a spanking fresh breeze—but you won't get much past 7 or 8 knots on any typical displacement sailboat on the market today. You can put big twin diesels in a displacement-hull trawler, cruise at 2000 rpm—and you'll lumber along at about the same 7 or 8 knots that you'd get with a single engine. With a strong following sea, any boat may go surfing down the crest of a wave, at a rate above hull speed—but that's a hazard to be avoided, not bragged about; see chapter 20.

Another factor in the speed of a displacement hull is the wetted area of the hull—that is, the underwater surface area producing constant drag. The more drag, the lower the top speed no matter what you compute as the theoretical hull speed. Sailboats designed for racing sacrifice the stability of the deep underwater body (with greater wetted area) in favor of a very shallow hull with fin keels and spade rudders. (Think of a shark swimming upside down.) Multihull sailboats such as catamarans and trimarans offer some advantages in speed, because their long, narrow hulls provide little resistance and their wide stance (between the hulls) lets them carry inordinately large sail area. However, many tend to be marginally seaworthy, too easily flipped over in moderate weather and broken apart in heavy weather. In port, their extreme width makes maneuvering difficult, and adequate dock space is rare.

A displacement hull is more efficient than a planing hull: Less power is needed to keep it moving along at cruising speed. A single-engine powerplant may use one or two gallons an hour. Even a displacement boat as large as 65 feet may burn not much more than four gallons an hour at 9 or 10 knots.

So-called modified trawlers, which reach speeds of 12 to 14 knots, put trawler-style accommodations on a powerboat hull that may be described as "semidisplacement." This has full-bodied roundness forward, giving good buoyancy and stability, with a flatter, shallow aft section that provides some of the attributes of a planing hull.

If you want speed—for racing or simply to get places faster—you want a different type of hull. In most cases, that will be a planing-hull powerboat with sufficient power to get the boat up "on the step" quickly. The boat might be a 22-foot open fisherman with a pair of 200 hp outboards, or a 65-foot sportfisherman with enough power to drive it at 35 knots. Fuel consumption will rise dramatically, since those big engines burn one or two gallons a *mile*.

If you want real speed, you will need to explore such exotica as hydroplanes—which, with the ultimate planing hull, act like stones skipping along the surface—and hydrofoils—designed more like airplanes than boats.

OTHER FACTORS

The lines of the bow and stern will influence seakeeping qualities. The bow should be sharp enough to provide good entry through the water but should have enough flare to provide quick buoyancy as the bow digs into a wave. The stern of most boats is flat, which adds to buoyancy aft and overall stability but may be a liability in slow offshore cruising boats, which face the possibility of powerful following seas. Such boats do better with a rounded or canoe-type stern design, which splits the seas while still giving good buoyancy.

Many racing sailboats sacrifice the buoyancy of a flared bow in favor of a sharp, narrow entry that will cut through the waves. This helps keep the boat moving forward at the best speed but also makes for a very wet foredeck. Not only do flared bows add forward buoyancy; they also direct the force of the waves out to the side. As a general rule, sailboats designed only for racing can be tricky to handle and should be used only for racing, with a qualified and experienced skipper and crew.

HULL MATERIALS AND CONSTRUCTION

Hull material is a matter of aesthetics, convenience, and cost. Any of the commonly used materials—ferrocement, steel, aluminum, wood, and fiberglass—can provide a safe hull. They can be made watertight; they hold up under the pounding of wind, waves, and (occasionally) the bottom; they can be maintained to last for many years.

However, each has some special considerations.

Ferrocement once was a favorite of backyard boatbuilders, largely because the construction technique uses easily obtained and easily worked materials: iron rods and a wire mesh to form the shape, troweled-on cement to flesh it out. Cement is strong—it becomes even stronger under water and might, if given the chance, last forever. Along parts of the New Jersey shore, for example, the remnants of World War I cement-hulled barges still rise above the tidal flow.

Unfortunately, building a ferrocement hull falls somewhere between obtaining the materials and dreaming about the result. Rust-streaked gray hulks are scattered all over the backyards of America, destined never to feel the kiss of salt water. Of the boats that were finished, most show the clumsy touch of the amateur and few will ever be treated with respect in the marketplace.

Steel is the material of choice for large commercial vessels and large yachts. In a medium-sized pleasure boat, steel may become more of a liability than an asset. Maintenance problems will grow over time and will not be solved as easily as those in wood or fiberglass hulls. Few boatyards are equipped to make repairs on a steel hull, and the cost to tow an out-of-commission boat to a distant, qualified yard can be excessive.

Aluminum is strong, flexible, and lightweight; resists corrosion; and is the most common hull material for rowboats, canoes, and small outboards. However, in the present state of the art of boatbuilding, aluminum construction is too expensive for all but these smallest recreational hulls—and for the largest, where cost takes second place to strength and weight factors. New techniques for welding aluminum are beginning to bring down the cost for larger boats, but practical results have yet to be realized. And, as with steel, few yard workers are skilled in the repair of aluminum. In addition, an aluminum hull is vulnerable to the electrolytic action that might be found in a crowded marina (see chapter 3).

Wood has been with us since the beginning of maritime history—and for good reasons. It is in plentiful supply in most parts of the world, is not very expensive, can be worked by anyone with basic carpentry tools and skills, and produces a safe and seaworthy hull.

Wood has the look, the feel, the sense of being linked with seafarers through the ages. Unfortunately, if not properly maintained, a wooden hull will leak like a sieve; the fastenings will crumble and fall out; and the topsides, stem, frame, and stern will turn to soft, mushy, rotten fibers. Wood requires more day-to-day care than other hull materials, and over the past twenty years, with the rise of fiberglass hull construction, it almost seemed that wood might disappear from the boating scene.

However, thanks in part to dramatic increases in the price of fiberglass and the growing realization that fiberglass is not a maintenance-free miracle material, wooden boats are with us yet. Today, new techniques involving cold-molded

---

Rot, Rust, Rodents and Other Natural Enemies of Boats

Rot attacks certain kinds of wood under certain conditions; rust and other forms of electrolytic corrosion attack metals—almost all metals, with the probable exception of gold and platinum. Animals ranging from mice to mollusks can damage the various materials of which a boat and its accessories are made. We have assembled data on a wide range of such natural enemies. (See App. IV)

epoxy-fastened laminates are producing some beautiful hulls that may begin to find even broader markets in the years to come.

Fiberglass has become *the* hull material for recreational boats. It provides a strong, watertight shell; unlike steel and aluminum, it is easily fabricated (particularly with mass-production techniques); unlike wood, it doesn't dry out when hauled and doesn't need caulking or periodic refastening.

When fiberglass first appeared on the boating horizon, doomsayers prophesied a short life and a dramatic end for fiberglass hulls, perhaps destined to crack in half when a presumed limiting age of ten years arrived. That was more than thirty-five years ago, and very few fiberglass boats have disintegrated—far fewer, we think, than improperly maintained wooden boats.

In an ironic footnote to maritime history, the onetime president of a major recreational boat-building firm vowed that if his company ever built a fiberglass boat, it would be over his dead body. That day did come, but it was over the almost-bankrupt body of a boatbuilder that once led the industry.

Does fiberglass have problems? Certainly, but most of them can be attributed to poor or corner-cutting construction and not the material. If the hull is not fully cured—that is, if the resins used with the glass fiber material have not solidified—water may be absorbed into the hull, resulting in delamination of the glass layers and underwater surface blisters. If the core materials used for stiffness are not fully sealed, they may absorb water; if the core is of balsa, it may rot.

But not all fiberglass problems involve construction. Fiberglass is not as flexible as wood, and it does not as easily absorb an impact with a pier or a semisubmerged log. The impact energy may be transmitted through the material to a weak spot at some distance from the point of contact; one result might be microscopic cracks, which become pathways for the migration of water into the core.

A Quick Look at Fiberglass

The methods and materials used in fiberglass construction vary widely, and, as with most things maritime, cost is a reasonable indicator of quality.

In construction of a typical hull, a gelcoat of liquid resin is sprayed into a hull-shaped mold. When the hull is finished, this will be the outer layer, playing both a cosmetic and a therapeutic role: smooth and shiny, the gelcoat enhances appearance; watertight, it prevents water from being absorbed into any of the fiberglass materials.

Next, layers of pressed fiberglass mat or loose-weave roving are laid in by hand, or short pieces of glass fiber are blown in with a chopper gun, alternating with layers of laminating resin.

The resin—usually a polyester compound—soaks into the glass material, quickly jells, and then becomes increasingly hard as the resin cures.

Hand-laid mat and roving and machine-laid chop may all be used in the same hull, although the hand work takes more time and more skill, costs more, and therefore is less often used on less expensive boats. Hand-laid hulls are heavier, stronger, and better, but for small, lightweight boats, a properly handled chopper gun can do a credible job.

Other materials may be used:

• Tightly woven glass cloth is used for decks and other exposed areas where a smooth finish is desired.
• Manmade fibers such as Kevlar are 50 percent stronger and 50 percent lighter in weight than glass, but they also are harder to work with and higher in cost than glass and therefore are most often used on exotic ultralightweight ocean racers.
• Epoxy resins replace polyester in some applications but are more expensive; today these are finding a special niche in the production of cold-molded wood hulls.

Few fiberglass hulls rely solely on the glass material for strength; most have some form of longitudinal stiffening laid in; many use a core material of balsa or foam plastic to provide strength at reduced weight.

Inflatables may be constructed of various combinations of rubber, cloth, and plastic, as long as these are resistant to sunlight, salt and fresh water, and motor fuels.

QUALITY

In general, all materials and construction share a common characteristic: "You get what you pay for." First-class materials and first-class workmanship should result in a first-class hull, of whatever material.

Three examples:

1. A hatch frame can be made of wood, plastic, aluminum, fiberglass, stainless steel, or bronze—with a wide range of durability and price. A plastic frame is least expensive and easy to manufacture, but it is lightweight and short-lived compared to bronze.

2. Deck fittings such as cleats and lifeline stanchions can be held down with screws—easy and cheap—but they will quickly pull loose under strain (particularly in fiberglass boats). They might be bolted down, with holes drilled through the deck and nuts and washers on the underside—which is better, but not quite strong enough. They *should* be through-bolted, with a backing block or plate on the underside to spread the load. In addition, they must be laid in a waterproof bedding compound to minimize leaks.

3. Bulkheads—which divide the hull interior into compartments—provide strength to the hull and support for the deck. In fiberglass boats, the bulkheads are the substitute for ribs and frames. A well-installed bulkhead will help absorb an impact; a poorly installed bulkhead (merely held in place, for example, with fiberglass strips) is likely to pop loose, letting the hull take the full and damaging force of the blow. In cheaper construction, the bulkhead often is fitted tight against the hull and deck to aid in stiffening, but that provides a "hard spot" over which the fiberglass will flex and possibly fail. Better is a hard foam buffer between the bulkhead and the hull, with the joint well sealed with resin and glass.

How else do you judge quality? By the look and feel of the work; by the fit and finish; by the reputation of the builder; and by hiring the services of a professional marine surveyor, as described in chapter 6.

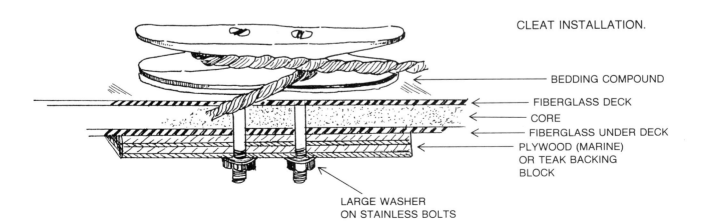

CLEAT INSTALLATION.

— BEDDING COMPOUND
— FIBERGLASS DECK
— CORE
— FIBERGLASS UNDER DECK
— PLYWOOD (MARINE) OR TEAK BACKING BLOCK

LARGE WASHER ON STAINLESS BOLTS

THE DECK

The deck is more than just an area for sunbathing and fishing; it must provide protection for the accommodations below and safe working space for handling sails, mooring lines, and the anchor.

MATERIALS

The deck itself may be constructed of the same material as the hull (fiberglass, steel, aluminum, ferrocement, or wood); the deck surface may be the same as the hull, or it may be wood, fiberglass, or canvas laid over wood and painted. There are advantages and disadvantages for each.

Wood decks are traditional, and common—for good reason. They look good and provide good footing. Teak is the most popular wood, both for appearance and because it resists rot. Teak is frequently used to cover the deck of a fiberglass boat. Oak and mahogany have also been used for decking, but too often they are coated with varnish. Avoid the temptation to varnish *any* wood used as deck planking. It may look slick, reminiscent of the glory days of classic boating, but it is "slick" in the most hazardous sense. On the downside, wood decks easily develop leaks.

Fiberglass decks and cabintops are generally watertight, but they become slippery when wet. Most fiberglass decks have a built-in textured surface in walkways and work areas, but the texture often is easily worn away—or barely useful in the first place. Nonskid material should be added—either in the form of screwed-down or glued-down treads of molded plastic or a sandpaperlike material, or painted on with brush or roller. Glued-down treads have a tendency to come loose, curl at the edges, and thus create a hazard. Traditional (i.e., old-fashioned) painted-on nonskid surfaces are created by sprinkling sand or crushed walnut shells on wet paint, or premixing them into the paint. The latter lasts longer.

Canvas —now seen primarily on home-built and older boats—provides an inexpensive cover-ing for inexpensive plywood decking, in much the same manner as wall-to-wall carpeting is a standard item in houses lacking hardwood floors. It enhances the appearance while providing protection. On a boat, the canvas is glued in place and painted. It can be painted a number of times, but eventually the paint will build up, lose flexibility (needed to accommodate weather-induced expansion and contraction), and start cracking. At that point, the waterproof quality is lost and the canvas must be ripped up and replaced. The owners of many older wooden boats have replaced the canvas with a layer of fiberglass.

CONSTRUCTION

The deck must feel solid and secure, be properly integrated with the hull, and be well supported from below. On some lightly built fiberglass boats, the foredeck has an annoying tendency to pop up and down like the bottom of an oil can. This "oilcanning" effect can lead to material fatigue or can cause a crew member to lose footing. It's easily detected, usually by walking on the deck. In some boats, the problem can be corrected by installing underdeck supports and stiffeners; it can be avoided by buying a better-built boat.

The deck-to-hull attachment is particularly important in fiberglass boats, where the deck and hull are constructed of two separate pieces that are then joined together. The junction of deck and hull is always under stress, whether from the "working" of the hull in a seaway or the pull of rigging.

If the joint is inadequate, it may fail—with very unpleasant results. Decks have been known literally to pop loose from the hull; less spectacularly, but with long-term serious consequences, the joint may become one big constant leak. On well-constructed boats, the deck will be joined to a molded-in horizontal flange on the hull, with sturdy through-bolts and generous use of bedding compound between them. On lower-quality (and typically less expensive) boats, the deck may be fastened down with screws, or fastened only with resin and glass, or fastened with machine-set pop rivets, which pop *out* almost as easily as they go *in*. One construction shortcut frequently used on smaller boats: Rather than having a flange molded with the hull, the deck is fashioned much like the lid of a shoebox, fitting down over the hull. This often-inadequate joint is then concealed with a glued-on rubber rubrail.

DECK LAYOUT

The deck layout should provide a certain logical arrangement of structure and control stations, define the work areas, and enhance safe operation. "Work" may be defined as fishing, handling the anchor, changing sails. In any topside activity, you must have adequate space, secure footing, and grabrails or other appropriate handholds.

On many powerboats today, "the deck" refers to multiple decks, levels, and connecting ladders. On a sailboat, deck layout is largely dictated by the rig and sail plan, and—particularly on boats designed primarily for racing—safety may be relegated to second place.

All-too-common hazards found in today's typical deck layouts include travelers bolted down in the middle of a walkway, ventilators scattered about without regard to clear-deck working areas, anchors positioned in the middle of the foredeck, chainplates and shrouds sprouting from the middle of a walkway. We prefer shrouds mounted at the deck edge: This provides a stronger rig, gives you something to hold onto along the sides, and keeps the walkways clear. The disadvantage: The boat won't sail as close to the wind, a factor when racing. If racing is your primary pursuit, then you'll learn to live with inboard shrouds. But watch your head when walking the deck on a dark night!

On older boats, where the rig may have been modified several times, you are likely to find runners and fairleads that go nowhere. These have neither antique nor sentimental value and should be removed.

On most boats, side decks have been sacrificed to interior headroom and accommodations; on some boats—notably small-to-medium cabin cruisers—they have disappeared. Well, almost disappeared: We have seen some designs that have left a four-inch-wide strip as "footing" for moving forward and aft past the cabin. Using that walkway, particularly when in a hurry, is asking for trouble. On such boats, the best access to the foredeck is through the foredeck hatch.

On many of those same boats, foredeck design will win no prize for safety. The deck has a sharp slant, the surface is slick, and the bowrails are about a foot high. On these boats, you must crawl along the foredeck and work while sitting down.

The deck edge should be fitted with a toerail or bulwark, which rises above the deck to provide safe footing when the boat is heeled. It also helps you find the deck edge on dark nights. A toerail may be four or five inches high, a bulwark higher. A toerail also provides a more secure mounting for lifeline stanchions than a flat deck edge; a bulwark itself may serve as a substitute for lifelines. Bulwarks are more common on large ships and workboats than on recreational boats, although many of the larger trawler-type yachts offer bulwarks around the foredeck.

A waterway should run along the deck edge, between the toerail (or bulwark) and the deck surface. This channels rain and spray to the scuppers—openings through which the water drains overboard. If this drainage system is inadequate or becomes blocked, water will pool on the deck and seriously impede safe footing. Unwanted water may also find its way under the deck or down along the fastenings, eventually resulting in undetected damage below.

Deck Openings accommodate skylights, hatches, and ventilators, which are intended to improve living conditions below. However, they impose two major penalties topside: They become trippers and leakers. The tripping impact will be minimized if the boat designer arranged for thoughtful placement—out of the way of work and normal passage—and if the edges are rounded and beveled. Leaking is harder to control. On a wooden boat, the joint between the cabin structure and the deck—to take one example—is an opening just waiting for a leak. Topside leaks from rain and spray are not merely annoyances; they can lead to serious electrical problems, hidden damage, and rot.

A WELL-EQUIPPED MAST SETUP. There is lots to see here. A pair of effective spreader lights gives good on-deck illumination and there is good chafe protection on the spreader tips. The high-performance radar reflector is securely mounted well out of the way of the roller-furling jib and the mainsail. The custom-built radar mount incorporates a protective ring above and below to prevent fouling by sails or rigging.

Mooring Hardware includes cleats for tying off a mooring line, chocks to provide a channel for mooring lines through or over the toerail, and a samson post on the foredeck for snubbing off the anchor line (see chapter 15) or for towing (see chapter 22).

A well-equipped boat will have at least four sturdy cleats and chocks on each side. The cleats must be solidly through-bolted to the deck. However, cleats are designed to take a lateral rather than a vertical pull: When setting the mooring lines, you must make allowance for the tide, lest the settling hull and a taut line combine to pull the cleats out of the deck.

Topside Stowage keeps tools, equipment, and lines out of the way, yet handy when needed. For some items—such as life rafts—it is the only acceptable stowage (see chapter 9).

Underseat Lockers and Deck Boxes hold the spare anchor, life jackets, mooring lines, cleaning gear, and extra cushions, but they too easily become junk boxes. That's a matter of housekeeping, not marine architecture, and it is totally under your control.

Lockers and deck boxes should have lids designed to keep out water. Each lid needs a lip that fits into a water channel, a sturdy hasp, and some means of keeping the hasp closed when underway. One heavy wave breaking over the stern, for example, can open an unfastened lid and wash overboard the contents of the locker. Deck boxes are even more vulnerable—not so much to being cleaned out by an errant wave, but to being taken clean off the boat.

The most difficult stowage problem may be where to keep the dinghy. Some are lashed upside down on the foredeck or the cabintop; some are slung out from stern davits; some are deflated and stuffed into a locker; some are towed astern when underway and stored ashore when in home port. Advantages and disavantages of each option are listed in chapter 8.

Deck Lighting provides illumination for necessary deckwork at night and can be particularly helpful when trying to correct a fouled rig or to clean up after a long voyage. Sealed-beam lights mounted on the spreaders (for a sailboat), the cabintop, or a tuna tower, pointed straight down, give good light and do not interfere with night vision as much as portable lights, or lights mounted nearer the deck. (The level of illumination on the work area is not as much of a problem as being hit in the face with the beam.) The best arrangement would include matched pairs of lights—one with low wattage for use while underway, one with higher wattage for use while moored.

Working lights should be rigged with parallel switches so they can be controlled from on deck as well as from the pilothouse or helm. The switches might also include a push-button feature, allowing the lights to double as an emergency signal apparatus. (See chapter 9.)

Other sources of topside illumination include fixed or portable searchlights (plugged into cigarette lighter–type outlets) and flashlights—several of which should be ready at hand throughout the boat.

It's quite useful—but rare—to have lights installed inside stowage lockers to help locate important tools and equipment quickly. Lights in the less-accessible parts of the bilge are useful for scouting out—and repairing—damage.

Running Lights are required, not optional, for nighttime operation; the specific color, intensity, and placement are spelled out by law (see appendix I). For most boats, the basic lights include port (red) and starboard (green) sidelights, a white stern light, and a white masthead light. The pattern of running lights displayed helps all mariners to determine the general size and type of vessel; whether the boat is anchored or underway; whether the boat is under power or sail; the general heading; and whether or not the boat is engaged in a special activity such as fishing, dredging, or towing.

The Cockpit is an exposed area that is lower than the deck, that has space for crew to sit, and that may receive great quantities of water. The seating may be comfortable or marginal; at best, it should provide some back support (preferably at about a 15-degree angle from the vertical—

sitting bolt upright gets to be very old, very fast) and offer something to hold onto or to brace against in heavy weather.

The flow of water may be controlled in part by a deflecting coaming around the edge; cockpit drains should get most of the water out almost as fast as it comes in—except when a large wave breaks over the boat or into the cockpit itself. In this extreme condition, the drains should be able

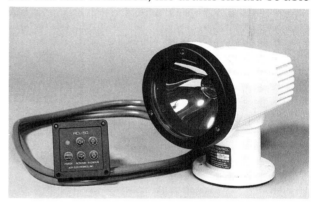

REMOTE-CONTROL SEARCHLIGHT can be useful for night navigation, low-light entries to marinas or harbors, and emergency situations such as man-overboard search and recovery. (ACR Electronics)

PORTABLE NAVIGATION LIGHTS. No matter what your boat's electrical system (or lack thereof), there is no excuse for not carrying proper navigation lights—even on a small, rented fishing dory. These battery-operated lights cure the problem. (Plastimo)

to remove water from the cockpit quickly before the next oncoming wave and thus keep up the buoyancy of the after part of the boat to prevent swamping. The sizes of the cockpit drains relate to the overall size of the cockpit. Here are two useful formulas from the American Boat and Yacht Council used to determine sizes of the drains based upon cockpit volume. (No matter what the outcome of these formulas, each drain should be no smaller than one inch in cross section.)

Watertight Cockpits	Weathertight Cockpits
$A = \dfrac{C \times W}{15} \dfrac{4C}{L} 1.5$	$A = \dfrac{C \times W}{30}$
A = Total drain area in square inches.	A = Total drain area in square inches.
C = Cockpit length in feet	C = Cockpit length in feet
W = Cockpit width in feet	W = Cockpit width in feet
L = Length of boat	L = Length of boat

On sailboats, cockpit drains are installed in pairs, with the port drain discharging to starboard, and vice versa, to avoid any backflow into the cockpit when well heeled over. Invariably, the cockpit is the location of at least one helm station.

LIFELINES

Lifelines take their name from their purpose: to save your life by preventing you from falling—or being washed—overboard. They must, therefore, be sturdy, securely mounted, and made of a material that resists deterioration.

The best material is stainless steel wire. A less expensive material is galvanized wire, which has two distinct disadvantages: (1) It will rust and lose strength, and (2) individual strands will break and create sharp burrs. If you ever have to grab for a lifeline, you will be far happier grabbing a smooth stainless one than a burred galvanized one. The galvanized wire can be (and often is) coated with plastic or slipped into a plastic tube to eliminate the hazards of burrs, but the

A SOLID STANCHION INSTALLATION.

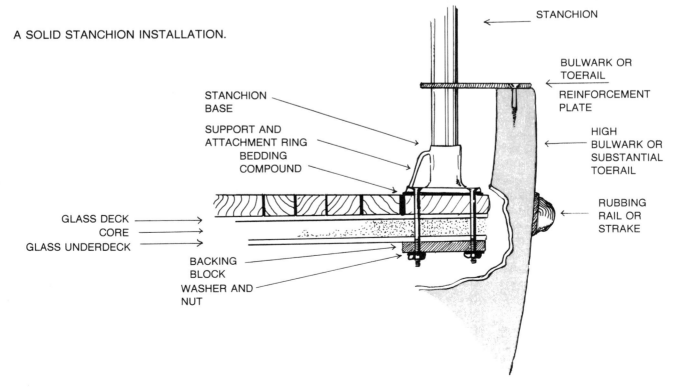

covering increases the likelihood of hidden corrosion.

Lifelines should be installed in pairs—people have been washed under a single line. The top lifeline should be high enough to block a fall overboard. That doesn't mean waist high, but it does mean high enough to hit above the average knee height—preferably about midthigh—on you or your tallest crew member.

The vertical stanchions that support the horizontal lifelines must be able to withstand the weight of a heavy adult falling against them, so they should be firmly secured at the base—through-bolted to a backing block, not just screwed into fiberglass. The preferred method for mounting stanchions is to through-bolt them to the deck (and substantial underdeck backing blocks) and also to bolt or screw them sideways to the toerail. All fastenings must also be secured well with a bedding compound. Otherwise, water leaking down around the bolts may settle in the wood of the backing block, which then slowly rots away, out of sight, only to be discovered when someone leans too heavily against the stanchion and the fittings give way.

Other deck safety hardware includes bow and stern railings, or pulpits. A proper pulpit should be stainless steel or aluminum tubing, with the top rail at least 30 inches above the deck. The structure should be through-bolted to the deck and welded, rather than bolted together with pipe fittings. Bolts and setscrews will loosen up over time, and a rickety set of rails soon becomes unsafe.

AN EFFICIENT FOREDECK FOR HANDLING ANCHORS. The powerful chain windlass is topped by a line-handling drum with an integral brake. The chain heads forward, through a custom chain stopper, and then fairleads over a substantial bow pulpit. The windlass operates through a foot button (with its own on/off switch to prevent inadvertent operation of the windlass). Note substantial pulpit to protect crew members in heavy weather, and substantial chocks to fairlead docklines and anchor rodes. The toerail, another important safety feature, is not as effective as a bulwark.

A SECURE STANCHION shows the addition of an L-shaped side-brace plate to a weaker type of deck-supported stanchion base. New stanchion installations should incorporate bases that fasten both through the deck and into the toerail or bulwark.

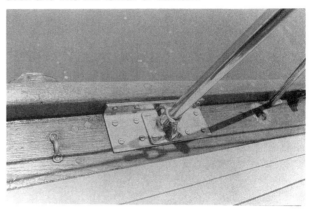

THE HELM

While the term *helm* comes from the name of the instrument used in steering (from the ancient Greek *helm,* or handle), in general usage today it also refers to any of the locations from which the boat is steered.

A motorsailer with a pilothouse may have two helms—one interior and one exterior. A powerboat may have as many as four: inside the cabin, on the flying bridge (i.e., the roof of the cabin), in the tuna tower (many feet up in the air), and in the cockpit (which, in this case, means the place where you stand for fishing and from which you can maneuver the boat when landing a Big One).

However many helms there may be, wherever located, they must be adequate to the task of controlling the boat. A proper helm must have excellent visibility all around, should be convenient to the engine controls and protected from the weather, and should offer secure seating for the helmsman.

A GOOD HELM POSITION on this cruising powerboat shows an efficient grouping of all vital instruments and navigation gear. Note ease of access and vision for vital engine controls and gauges. The radar can be easily seen in both day and night (note sun and light/glare shroud on radar), as can the Loran.

VISIBILITY

Go aboard some of the new midsize sport boats, in which the helm is configured like that of an airliner; sit in the helmsman's seat and try to figure out just how far in front of the bow you could see an object floating in the water. On some of these boats, particularly if you are a bit shorter than average, you won't even be able to see the *horizon* over the bow.

A lower helm or an interior drive station may be an advantage in stormy weather and for long night passages, but it may also be barely useful. Stand up to the wheel and make sure that you can see where you would be steering. We have been aboard one boat on which the visibility over the bow was so poor that, unless furnished with a radar display, you would have to run up on deck every few minutes to make sure you were not about to run into something.

Some aft-helm sailboats have a similar problem: When sitting down, you can't even see the *bow.*

Of particular concern, especially on high-powered cigarette-type boats, is visibility over the bow when at speed. As proven by several recent fatal accidents, where the big boat has sliced through small runabouts loaded with families out for a weekend frolic, there is *none.*

ENGINE CONTROLS AND INSTRUMENTS

Controls should be logical and well located. That is usually not a problem with engine controls, which are basically simple and typically located within easy reach (see chapter 3). but switches and gauges may be scattered all over the place—often, many feet from the helm. They should be grouped for quick comprehension: all engine readouts in one section, navigation information (speed, wind speed and direction, depth of water) in another. From each helm, you should be able to listen to (and operate) the radio, monitor all cruising functions, start and stop the engine, and shut off the fuel supply.

Lighting at the helm should be adequate for monitoring instruments, reading the compass, and, on occasion, checking the chart. To protect your night vision, such lighting should be red in color, or very dim—or both.

SEATING

The helmsman's seat should be high enough to give a clear range of vision over the bow and all around, and comfortable enough to permit many hours of operation. Beware of seats that are merely benches, without back support, or seats lacking foot support. On some medium-sized sailboats, there is no adequate seat for the helmsman. One long day standing at the wheel of such a boat will drive any sailor to the local marine supply store in search of relief.

PROTECTION

Protection from the weather is not vital, but advisable. The alertness and quick reaction of a cold, wet helmsman is soon diminished, and too much exposure to the sun induces both fatigue and potentially serious sunburn. If the helm position is not already under cover, an awning will help reduce sun exposure and keep the helmsman drier during rain showers; a dodger (a canvas and plastic windshield) will help block the spray.

NAVIGATION NIGHT LIGHT. This is an aircraft-type variable-shade light suitable for both white and red (night) lighting. Not only is the shade adjustable, but the circle of light can be changed to provide spotlighting.

Health and medical considerations are covered more fully in chapter 18.

ACCOMMODATIONS

Almost any boat, other than a sailboard, will have some sort of accommodations for the crew and guests. At the low end, they may be limited to a couple of seats for the captain and copilot; at the high end, where the boats become floating mansions, there seems to be no practical limit. However, interior decorators are not necessarily safety engineers, and the push for style may set safety adrift. On older boats, the owner's innocence or a mechanic's convenience may have resulted in the installation of unsafe materials—for example, non-safety glass in a door or mirror (see below).

Below are some considerations related to accommodations.

VENTILATION (SAILBOAT). (Nicro-Fico)

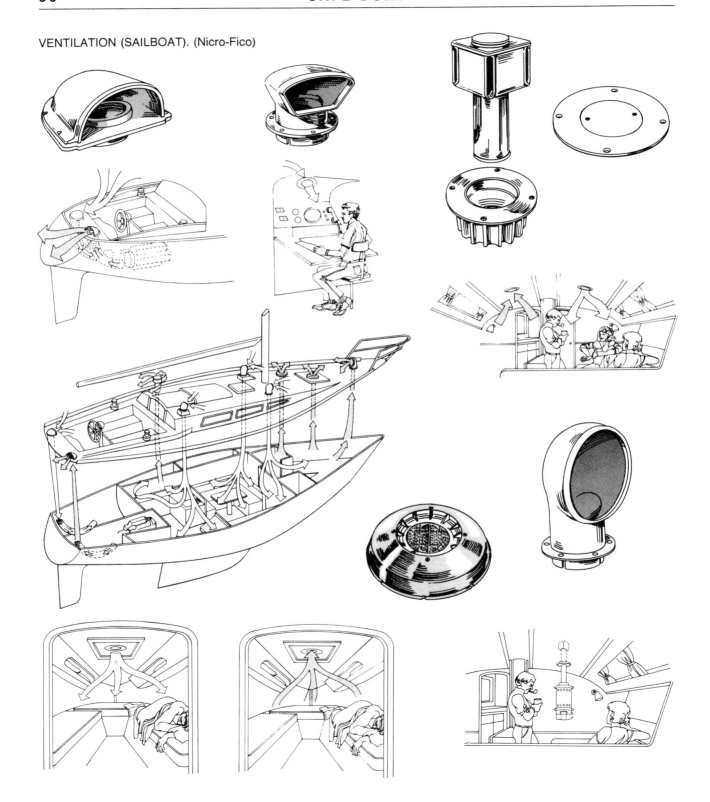

VENTILATION (POWERBOAT). (Nicro-Fico)

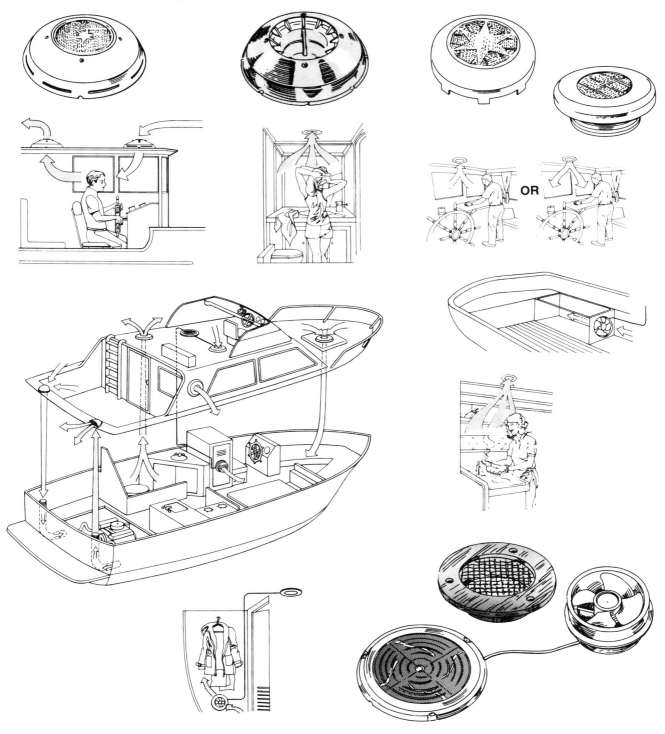

ACCESS

In an emergency, we are not so much concerned with getting *in* as with getting *out*. A boat's living spaces should have at least two means of entrance and exit. On most vessels, one of these will be a forward hatch. On some boats, however, you'd have to be a gymnast to hoist your body through the hatch. If the hatch is high and not over a bunk, you may need to install some well-founded footholds or steps, or have a special ladder standing by.

SAFETY has to be a major consideration for the well-planned galley layout. In this Hinckley 51, note how the fine galley tends to contain the cook and offer plenty of safe handholds. Note also the carefully curved partitions and absence of sharp surfaces. (Hinckley)

VENTILATION

Ventilation is critical in the engine room for proper engine operation and for removal of explosive vapors (see chapter 3); good ventilation is also vital for keeping a decent flow of fresh air moving through the living spaces. This provides comfort and also limits rot and mildew in upholstery, bedding, and clothing. You will be able to spot—or, rather, smell—ventilation problems when you first step below. Even if the boat is unused for months, a well-designed natural ventilation system will keep the inside air fresh and clean. A Dorade box or commercial ventilator will allow fresh air to enter while trapping and draining rain and spray. All deck hatches, skylights, and opening portholes must close tightly to prevent leaks from rain and spray.

SECURITY

Wherever you walk or sit, you should have handholds—something to hold onto—the edge of a counter, grabrails overhead, grabrails alongside any set of steps or ladder. When grabrails are installed in an area where the crew normally will be sitting, they should be able to withstand a load of 200 pounds in any direction. In any other location, the designed load should be 400 pounds.

Wooden grabrails or handholds should be seasoned, sanded smooth, and free of knots.

There should be *no* sharp corners; all must be rounded. Sharp corners can become painful and possibly lethal when the boat takes a violent roll.

The galley stove should be on gimbals so that it will swing with the roll of the boat. To prevent pots from sliding off, there should be a fiddle rail around the burners, and fiddle rails around the countertops for the same purpose. There must be handholds for the cook in the galley, and there should also be a safety strap or bar to help keep the cook's hands free for food preparation. A U-shaped layout helps the cook to wedge in during a heavy sea.

Cabinet latches should be sturdy, and drawers must remain closed in a seaway. On the other hand, how easy will it be to open one in a heavy blow? The latches on some cabinets are manipulated by sticking a finger through a small hole to the latch inside; if the hole is too small (as many are), it could be an invitation to a broken finger.

Bulkheads and the overhead near the galley stove should be lined with metal or other fireproof sheathing as protection from a stove flareup; a porthole above the stove is no place for decorative curtains, even if the material is fireproof. They become grease-catchers, losing any fireproof quality.

GIMBALED STOVE. (Richmond Stove Co.)

LARGE STOVE WITH OVEN AND BURNER RETAINER RAILS (FIDDLES). (Richmond Stove Co.)

GALLEY SAFETY. This is a "long" layout in the same Hinckley 51, but this galley runs aft along the companionway. Again, the galley tends to "contain the cook" and make for efficient work. (Hinckley)

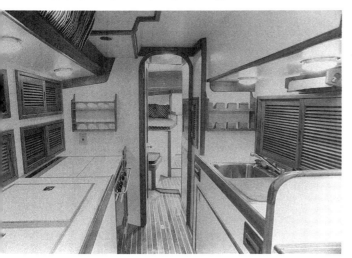

MATERIALS

All thermal, acoustic and, decorative sheathing should be noncombustible; fabric in upholstery, curtains, and wall coverings should be fireproof or fire retardant (as should all paint used on machinery and fuel tanks and in machinery spaces). Materials and coatings should not emit toxic gases when exposed to heat or flame. The adhesives or fastenings used in mounting these materials should be corrosion and solvent resistant. Equipment or materials used in the engine compartment must be able to withstand temperatures of at least 122°F (50°C) while the engine is running, with possibly higher temperatures for a time following shutdown. It may be impossible to verify these matters in an older boat; with a new boat, if the manufacturer's brochure isn't specific on these points, ask.

Carpeting is a welcome addition to cold-morning starts; reduces the danger of slipping on wet, slick wood; and helps dampen the racket from the engine compartment, thus reducing noise-induced fatigue. It also traps lint and dust where it can be vacuumed up before migrating down into the bilges. All carpeting must have a nonskid backing or be fully fastened down.

Glazing materials for windshields, side windows, portholes, tabletops, shower doors, mirrors—in other words, for *any* boating application—must be specifically manufactured for safety, as with the materials used in automobile windows. Ordinary window or plate glass breaks into dangerous, daggerlike shards; safety glass does not. Three basic types of safety glass normally are used in boating:

1. Laminated safety glass, with a sheet of clear plastic sandwiched between two panes of glass. if broken, the glass remains attached to the plastic.
2. Heat- or chemically tempered glass; if broken, it shatters into hundreds of small pieces.
3. Wired glass: a wire mesh is embedded in the glass. Wired glass should not be used for windshields or side windows.

Rigid safety plastic and flexible plastic sheeting are also acceptable in some applications, with the understanding that all plastics—even those treated for abrasion resistance—eventually will become scratched and scuffed, greatly hampering vision. If rigid plastic is used for a windshield, powered windshield wipers should not be used. Flexible plastic should not be used for portholes (which must be able to withstand the force of breaking waves).

Glazing materials used in windshields can be tinted and curved, but they must meet light-transmission and optical deviation standards established by the American National Standards Institute (ANSI) for motor vehicle windshields. For example, the material must transmit at least 70 percent of the light. Materials used in other areas need not meet these standards.

SPECIAL CONSIDERATIONS FOR SMALL BOATS

Because small boats can be dangerously unstable when overloaded or operated beyond safe limits, federal law mandates capacity limits, flotation characteristics, and safe maneuvering limits for small boats, as described below.

CAPACITY

The capacity of any boat less than 20 feet in length must be determined by the manufacturer and posted clearly; different methods are used for rigid-hull and inflatable boats.

Here's a basic method the manufacturer may use for a rigid hull:

1. Establish the static float plane of the boat. This is the point of submersion just past which water will pour into the boat over the side rails or transom or any large, uncovered opening in the hull.

2. Calculate the capacity below that static float plane, in cubic feet.

3. Multiply by 62.4 pounds (the weight of a cubic foot of fresh water); this is the amount of water the boat would displace if submerged to the static float plane—in other words, the point at which water would pour into the boat in absolutely calm water.

4. Subtract the weight of the boat (including engines, fuel, batteries, and installed equipment).

5. Determine the useful portion of the remaining capacity depending on the type of boat:

• Manually propelled boats, or boats rated for outboard engines of 2 hp or less: three pounds of capacity for each 10 pounds of remaining displacement;

• Outboard boats rated for more than 2 hp (including sailboats): one pound of capacity for each five pounds of remaining displacement;

• Inboard and inboard/outboard engine installations (including sailboats): one pound of capacity for each seven pounds of remaining displacement.

6. The capacity in pounds is converted to capacity in persons by adding 32 and dividing by 141.

CHECK THE CAPACITY PLATE. Every boat currently in production is required to have a capacity plate giving the boat's engine and carrying capacity. This should never be exceeded.

Capacity information—the maximum number of persons or total number of pounds allowed—must be posted on a permanent label, where it is clearly visible to the boat operator.

While the federal regulations apply only to boats up to 20 feet in length, the American Boat and Yacht Council recommends these standards for boats up to 26 feet.

For an inflatable, the ABYC–recommended weight capacity is three-fourths of the total volume of the main buoyancy chambers in cubic feet, times 62.4, less the weight of the boat (including floorboards).

The persons capacity in pounds is the lower of:

• The above weight capacity, reduced by the additional weight of any motors, fuel tanks, and batteries, or

• The cockpit area times 150, divided by four.

The actual number of persons depends upon the individual weights of the passengers.

FLOTATION

Federal regulations require that most boats less than 20 feet in length must have sufficient flotation to support the weight of a swamped hull, all installed machinery, and fuel, with the rated number of passengers hanging on in the water. This regulation does not apply to canoes, kayaks, sailboats, inflatables, surface-effect vessels, submersibles, amphibious boats, and race boats. However, the prudent boat owner will consider the boat's basic flotation characteristics and modify them as feasible.

Flotation can be added to the hull by installing watertight air compartments (with some provision for draining any water that does seep in, over time) or by using cellular foam—plastic with thousands of tiny trapped air cells, similar to that used for drinking cups or packaging materials. The foam may be in blocks, cut to fit, or foamed in place by pouring the liquid foaming material into a compartment or void and letting it expand to fill the space. However, the foam used in landbound applications frequently will melt when exposed to gasoline fumes; foam material for marine flotation should be impervious to fuel or oil. You can make an exception for foam installed on manually propelled boats or installed outside the engineroom and well above the bilgewater level, but a few moments of thought might conjure up conditions—especially in the midst of a disaster—under which any foam anywhere in a boat hull might come in contact with fuel or oil, and dissolve.

Inflatables under 12.5 feet in length should have at least two separate inflation chambers; boats 12.5 feet or longer should have at least three chambers. Any size of inflatable must be capable of supporting at least 50 percent of the maximum weight capacity with its largest chamber deflated.

SAFE MANEUVERING SPEED

By law, manufacturers must determine a safe maneuvering speed for boats capable of reaching 35 mph if under 20 feet in length, or 40 mph if 20 feet or longer. A prescribed 400-foot test course laid between marker floats is used for most boats.

Boats with remote steering may use a "quick-turn test," and boats capable of more than 50 mph must be tested by the quick-turn method. In the test, the boat is run straight ahead at a given throttle setting; the wheel is turned 180 degrees in a half-second or less. If the boat completes a 90-degree course change safely—in the opinion of the driver—it has passed the test at that throttle setting. The test is repeated at increasingly higher speeds until the boat does not pass or until maximum throttle has been tested.

The highest speed at which the boat maneuvers safely is the rated maneuvering speed. If this is less than the top speed of which the boat is capable, it must be posted near the operator's position in this format:

WARNING

Maneuverability above XX mph is limited
Sudden turns may cause loss of control

READ OWNER'S MANUAL

Any boat capable of higher speed than the rated maneuvering speed should also be equipped with a speedometer.

CHAPTER THREE

Marine Mechanical Systems

FIRST CHOICES

The engines and sails that power a boat, the various motors and pumps, and rigging and environmental controls that keep it (and the crew) all in comfortable balance, come in a wide variety of available choices, many of which are described in this chapter.

From the standpoint of safety, the two most important choices are the fuels for propulsion and for cooking. For engine fuel, the options are diesel and gasoline. Gasoline is a more efficient fuel, packed with energy and widely available. Diesel is a less efficient fuel; to obtain equivalent power, diesel engines must be larger, heavier, and more costly than gasoline engines. This tends to limit them to use in larger cruisers or as sailboat auxiliaries, where high power is largely irrelevant and a small, low-power engine will suffice. But diesel fuel is infinitely safer than gasoline, unlikely to explode, and can be handled with greater ease.

For stove fuel, the choice is wider—including alcohol; compressed natural gas (methane); kerosene; wood, coal, or coke; and liquid petroleum gas (LPG—propane or butane). They're all effective, although some are more cumbersome to use (for details, see Galley Equipment, later in this chapter), but again, the most efficient fuel—LPG—is the most hazardous.

In addition to high energy content, gasoline and LPG share one other characteristic that contributes to a high fire-hazard level: Their fumes, which are heavier than air, are likely to sink to the bottom of the bilge in explosive concentrations and remain unnoticed until ignited accidentally. These two characteristics influence all standards and practices applied to the installation, maintenance, and use of gasoline and LPG fuel systems.

POWERPLANTS AND INSTALLATION

ENGINES

Inboard engines may be adapted from automobile or truck engines, or may be designed specifically for marine use. Whatever their parentage, they must be marinized for operation in a watery environment. Essentially, this involves the replacement of all aluminum castings with aluminum alloy, and the replacement or modification of pumps, the gearbox, the carburetor or injectors, the cooling system, and the exhaust system.

Your boat's engine size (by horsepower rating) will be determined by the size and shape of the hull, the desired operating characteristics, and cost. To some degree, larger is better (to provide reserve power for handling difficult maneuvering situations or getting out of trouble), but the price of power may guide the final selection.

ENGINE ACCESSIBILITY is a continuing problem in most sailboat designs. This engine has better accessibility than most at the front, and easy access from above through the cockpit hatch. However, oil changes and adjustments at the side and lower sections of the engine are still difficult. An oil-change access tube and valve would be a valuable addition.

Gasoline engines tend to be roughly equivalent to intermediate-to-large automobile engines in size and horsepower; diesel engines range from compact car to earthmover size. Diesel engines might be described as light, medium, and heavy, with the following general characteristics:

Size	HP per LB.	Cruise RPM	Reduction Gear
Light	1:8	3000–4000	3:1
Medium	1:15	2000–2500	2:1
Heavy	1:20	800–1200	1:1

How much power do you really need? Setting aside any discussion of boats built for speed—where it's all relative—a displacement hull powered by a medium or small diesel will reach economical cruising speed (about 0.8 of hull speed, or about 5 to 6 knots) with an engine sized at 1.25 hp per ton of displacement and burn perhaps three-fourths gallon of fuel per hour. To reach hull speed—2 hp per ton, 1.5 gallons per hour consumption. However, to provide some reserve, the engine should be sized at 3 to 4 hp per ton; if the engine will be driving any auxiliary equipment such as pumps or compressors, it should not in any event be below 50 hp.

Engines and associated accessories should be arranged for easy maintenance. You should be able to change a drive belt without dismantling any part of the engine; oil changes and draining of coolant should be as convenient as possible. With some engines in some installations, any of these maintenance actions may be considerably more difficult than with others. This is a matter that requires careful review before you choose a boat. If you can't take care of it easily, you probably won't often try—with potentially disastrous results.

ENGINE MOUNTING

Inboard The engine bed should be built solidly into the hull. With the mounting hardware, it must be able to support the engine weight and keep the engine and prop shaft in alignment in spite of torque, propeller thrust, and the forces created by rolling at least 45 degrees to a side and pitching 15 degrees up and down—all at the same time. In any boat designed for offshore work, the engine mounting must be able to keep the engine in place even through a 360-degree roll.

Inboard/outboard The inboard unit should be mounted as above. The mounting for the outdrive must support the unit against thrust, torque, and lateral forces while keeping a tight seal against the transom.

Outboard Motor Limits for Small Boats

Small boats can easily be overwhelmed with engines that are too heavy and deliver too much power; the stern squats lower and lower until water flows in over the transom and the boat sinks. Accordingly, just as noted earlier in the discussion of capacity and flotation, safety standards have been established with outboard motor limits for small rigid hulls, inflatables, and sailboats. The limits are posted on each boat. Here's how they are determined:

For rigid-hull boats less than 20 feet in length, multiply the overall boat length (in feet) by the maximum transom width (in feet), to the nearest whole number.

Factor	35 or less	36–39	40–42	43–45	46–49	50–52
HP capacity	3	5	7.5	10	15	20

For a flat-bottomed, hard-chine boat, the capacity is reduced by one increment.

If the factor is greater than 52:
• For boats with remote wheel steering and at least 20-inch transom height, the HP capacity is equal to two times the factor, minus 90;
• For boats without remote wheel steering or with transom height less than 20 inches: flat-bottomed, hard-chine boats, .5 times the factor minus 15; all other boats, .8 times the factor minus 25.

For rigid-hull boats of 20 feet or longer, the safe limits are to be determined and posted by the manufacturer.

For inflatables equipped with a motor mount but no transom, the HP ratings shall not exceed:
• 3 HP for boats less than nine feet in length;
• 5 HP for boats from nine to 12 feet;
• 7.5 HP for boats 12 feet and over.

Inflatables with a transom may carry power as determined by the following formula: boat length (in feet) times beam (in feet) to the nearest whole number. Then:
• For a factor under 42, maximum HP is 7.5;
• For a factor between 43 and 80, maximum HP is 10/9 × the factor minus 40;
• For a factor above 80, maximum HP is .5 times the factor plus 10.

If the result of the above calculation is not an exact multiple of 5, it may be rounded up to the next multiple of 5.

For sailboats, the listed size of outboard motor, by horsepower, will propel a sailboat at approximately 6 knots in calm conditions:

8–12-foot waterline:	3 HP
12–15-foot waterline:	4 HP
15–17-foot waterline:	5 HP
17–18-foot waterline:	6 HP
18-foot waterline:	7 HP
19-foot waterline:	8 HP
20-foot waterline:	10 HP

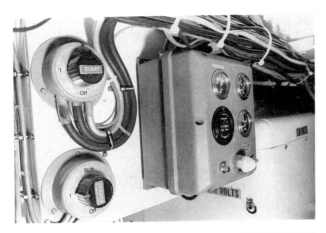

AN ENGINE-SPACE 110V AC AND 12V GENERATOR CONTROL PANEL. The box at the right contains the diesel generator oil pressure, temperature, and output voltage gauges. The push button is used to start the generator. The large indicator light shows that the unit is on, and the partially hidden toggle switch is used to preheat the generator prior to start. The two large switches to the left control the 12V batteries used to start the generator and to provide 12V service to the boat's accessories.

CRITICAL FUEL-SYSTEM DETAILS. Gasoline engines need special attention regarding fuel-system components. This older Graymarine engine has had several upgrades. (1) Note Coast Guard–approved flame arrester on the updraft carburetor. (2) Fuel lines are aircraft-quality Teflon-lined stainless steel braid. (3) Fuel sediment bowl/filter, previously glass, has been replaced by metal type. Note also the direct-reading oil pressure gauge as a backup for the panel-mounted unit.

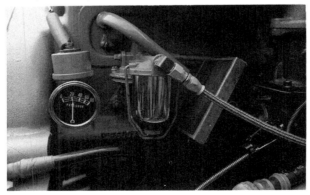

Outboard The motor may clamp onto a built-in transom mounting plate, or (for some inflatables and small sailboats) be mounted on a bracket. (Advice on getting the motor onto the mount appears in chapter 17.)

INSTRUMENTS

At a minimum, the operator control panel must include instruments to monitor engine speed (in revolutions per minute, rpm), temperature, oil pressure, and the proper operation of the generator or alternator.

Other instruments might include transmission-oil pressure and temperature, exhaust or manifold pressure, fuel tank levels, seawater temperature, and alarms for high temperature, low oil pressure, and clogged fuel filter.

CONTROLS

Engine throttle and transmission controls may be either two-lever or single-lever for each engine. The two-lever controls include a throttle with a red knob and a shift lever with a black knob. Forward movement of the throttle increases engine speed and backward movement decreases it. Forward movement of the shift lever puts the transmission "ahead" and backward movement produces "reverse."

Single-lever controls first engage the transmission, forward or reverse, and then increase engine speed. This offers one advantage: You cannot reverse direction with the engine running at high rpm, thereby avoiding possibly severe damage to the transmission.

With either type of control, neutral is between forward and reverse. The neutral position should be linked to a cutoff switch to prevent the engine from being started with the transmission in gear.

CARBURETORS

Marine gasoline engines require carburetors specifically designed to minimize the possibility of fire and explosion. These must be constructed of corrosion-resistant materials and either be fitted with a Coast Guard–approved backfire flame arrester or be designed and approved for use without one. Carburetors other than the downdraft type must be fitted with a drip collector or other device for accommodating any fuel that accumulates after the engine is shut off. This device cannot be open to the atmosphere, but it must provide a means for a controlled return of fuel to the intake manifold when the engine is restarted.

FUEL TANKS

A proper fuel tank is more than just a tank cobbled together by a local tinsmith. It must meet standards for pressure, fire resistance, and material. Tanks may be made of a number of materials, including built-in-place fiberglass, and tanks being manufactured today are most likely all in compliance with current standards. However, *older* tanks are quite likely *not* in compliance, and the owner of an antique boat must exercise due diligence. We saw one 200-gallon iron tank filled with gasoline leaking slowly through the rusting-out bottom. Why would the bottom of a fuel tank rust through? Because the lighter-than-water fuel always floats on top, and any entrapped water sinks to the bottom of the tank, there to remain perhaps for many years, working on the unprotected iron.

All connections should be made through the *top* of the tank; there should be no drain plugs or fittings at the bottom. You empty the tank for cleaning or to replace contaminated fuel through the top. While that's more of a hassle than merely opening a drain plug in the bottom, it's nothing compared to the hassle and hazard should that bottom plug start leaking—or give way altogether.

Any fuel-filter bowl should be made of shatterproof and fire-resistant plastic, not glass. Any sight glass mounted on the tank (a violation of the comment above, but nonetheless common on

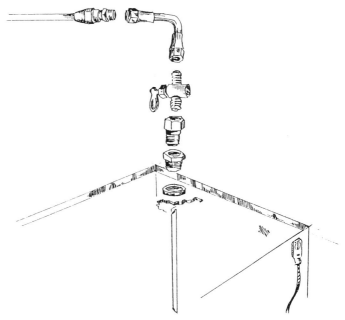

FUEL-TANK CONNECTORS.

FUEL-TANK MONITOR. A rather elegant way of solving the fuel-gauge problem. Most marine tanks are too large to be read effectively. However, this device can monitor four tanks with the use of a pressure-created column of water to measure the equivalent volume of fuel in the tank. (Hart Systems)

CRITICAL CHAFE PROTECTION ON MARINE ENGINE. The constant vibration can chafe vital lines, so this waterline crossing the transmission has been protected with a length of heater hose.

DOUBLE STRAINERS increase protection of the vital fuel supply (particularly in diesel engines). A valving connection between the strainers permits switchover to clear a strainer without interrupting engine power. (Vetus)

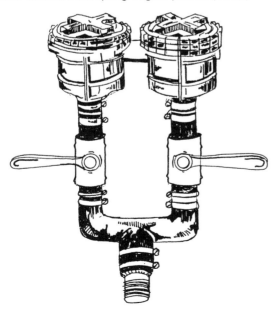

older tanks) should likewise be of shatterproof and fire-resistant plastic.

In-line gasoline filters must be certified for marine use; automobile filters are not acceptable.

Tanks should be equipped with a shutoff valve that can be operated from outside the engine compartment. If the tank and the engine are more than 12 feet apart, there should be another shutoff valve at the engine.

If the tank top is higher than the fuel filter or pump—frequently the case, especially in sailboats—an antisiphon valve should be installed. Otherwise, should the fuel line break, the siphon action could drain the tank into the bilge. An antisiphon valve is not needed if the fuel tank level is below the carburetor intake, or if an electrically operated valve is installed in the line and is open only when the engine ignition circuit is energized and the engine is running.

Fuel lines should include a flexible section between any rigid lines. You don't want an installation in which engine vibration or a shifting fuel tank will cause a fuel-line failure. Fuel lines for gasoline should be of heavy-gauge seamless copper or approved flexible tubing. Fuel lines for diesel may be of iron or steel pipe, or copper, aluminum, or flexible tubing. The line must be supported along its length, and rubber or plastic grommets should line any hole through which a fuel line passes.

Fill pipes for fuel tanks should be as straight as possible and extend to the bottom of the tank, where the fuel level will block the escape of vapor back up the pipe. The fill pipe should be made of flexible material, or there should be a flexible section inserted at some point between the deck fill pipe and the tank. However, any nonmetallic section of hose should be bridged with a ground wire of at least 8 gauge: The rush of fuel through the line can cause a buildup of static electricity. Any spillage or overfilling should drain directly overboard, not into the bilge.

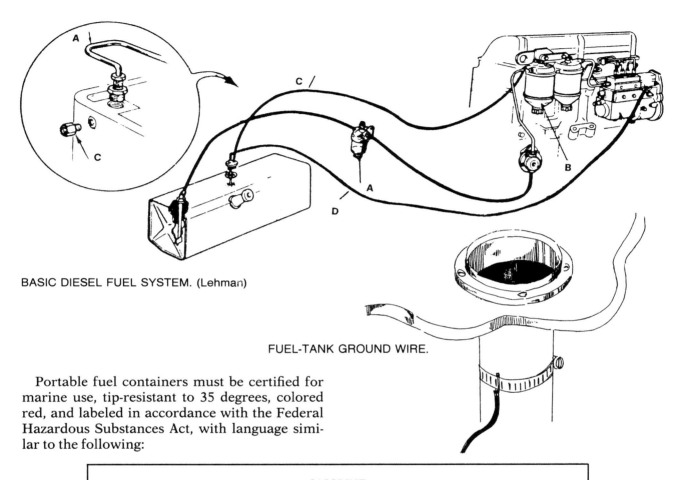

BASIC DIESEL FUEL SYSTEM. (Lehman)

FUEL-TANK GROUND WIRE.

Portable fuel containers must be certified for marine use, tip-resistant to 35 degrees, colored red, and labeled in accordance with the Federal Hazardous Substances Act, with language similar to the following:

> GASOLINE
>
> DANGER
>
> EXTREMELY FLAMMABLE—HARMFUL OR FATAL IF SWALLOWED
>
> IF SWALLOWED, DO NOT INDUCE VOMITING. CALL A PHYSICIAN IMMEDIATELY.
>
> KEEP CLOSED WHEN NOT IN USE.
>
> KEEP AWAY FROM HEAT, SPARKS, AND OPEN FLAME.
>
> SECURE IN A WELL-VENTILATED SPACE, AWAY FROM DIRECT SUNLIGHT.
>
> REMOVE FROM BOAT WHEN FILLING.
>
> KEEP OUT OF REACH OF CHILDREN.

Do not use noncertified, shore-type gasoline cans. If metal, they will soon rust away; if plastic, they are not likely to measure up to the standards, which include testing for resistance to sunlight, alcohol, detergents, and lubricants, and two drop tests. In the first test, a full tank is dropped six feet onto a flat concrete surface; in the second, the tank is filled with an antifreeze solution, cooled to 0°F, and dropped from a height of four feet.

VENTILATION

For gasoline engines, the engine spaces should have both natural and power ventilation, unless already fully open to the atmosphere. Natural ventilation—which should keep the engine compartment free of fumes while the boat is moving at or near cruising speed—will have forward-facing intakes and an aft-facing exhaust. (See discussion of ventilation in chapter 2.)

In addition, there should be at least one intake and one exhaust duct for use with the power ventilation system. These should be separated by a minimum of 24 inches (if compartment size permits); two of each is recommended. The intake duct should extend to the lower one-third of the compartment and end below the carburetor intake. The exhaust duct should begin low in the bilge, but not below normal bilgewater level. Ducts may be made of noncollapsible flexible hose but must be installed without S-curves, which might trap rainwater, blocking the flow of air.

The bilge blowers mounted with this system should be running whenever the boat is not at cruising speed. These blowers must have non-sparking motors certified for marine use and must be installed as high as possible in the ex-

AN ENGINE COMPARTMENT AND BILGE BLOWER is an absolute requirement for any safe boat with an enclosed engine or fuel compartment. (Jabsco)

haust duct. The engine ignition switch should be wired to prevent engine start until the blowers have been activated.

A warning label near the engine starter switch should read:

WARNING

GASOLINE VAPORS CAN EXPLODE.

BEFORE STARTING ENGINE,

CHECK ENGINE COMPARTMENT FOR GASOLINE OR VAPORS,

OPERATE BLOWER FOR 4 MINUTES, AND

RUN BLOWER BELOW CRUISING SPEED.

It's a good idea to put a warning label in any unventilated space into which someone might be tempted to put a can of gasoline or cleaning solvents:

WARNING

DO NOT STORE FUEL OR FLAMMABLE LIQUIDS HERE.

VENTILATION HAS NOT BEEN PROVIDED FOR EXPLOSIVE VAPORS.

For diesel engines, the air intake provided for combustion normally satisfies ventilation requirements. However, additional ventilation, natural or power, may be helpful in controlling compartment temperature and odor.

ENGINE COOLING SYSTEMS

Water-Cooled Engines In general, cooling systems may either use raw water directly from the water in which the boat is floating, or have a closed system in which a coolant solution is circulated around the engine and into a heat exchanger through which is also flowing raw water. This is similar to an automobile cooling system, in which air flows through a radiator to carry away the heat. A closed system often is called a freshwater cooling system, even though a chemical coolant solution normally is used.

Engine cooling should be set to maintain a minimum of 135°F to minimize oil sludging, with a maximum of 165°F for raw water and 185°F for a closed system. Raw-water systems must operate at a lower temperature—with some loss of engine efficiency—to limit the precipitation of salt and other minerals, which would soon clog the engine passages through which the water must flow.

The amount of cooling flow will be specified by the engine manufacturer, and the intake should be sized accordingly. In addition, the raw-water intake must be controlled by a seacock (see Seacocks, later in this chapter) and protected by two strainers: one on the inlet, with a surface area at least 50 percent greater than the area of the inlet; the other, in-line, easily accessible for opening and cleaning. The strainers prevent such outside debris as plastics, paper, seaweed, and other marine life from blocking cooling flow. Any blockage can quickly result in an overheated and inoperable engine.

Air-Cooled Engines are most commonly used in small auxiliary applications, such as generators. Cautions for mounting, carburetors, and exhaust are the same as those for inboard water-cooled engines, with special consideration for removal of cooling air: Because of the possibility of carbon monoxide contamination, it must be ducted directly overboard and not diverted for use in cabin heating.

EXHAUST SYSTEMS

Engine exhaust systems and any installed silencers must be sized to minimize back pressure—that is, they must allow a free and proper flow of exhaust away from the engine, with no sharp bends and a minimum of elbows that might impede that flow. They must be installed with hangers that will not transmit excessive heat from the exhaust system to any combustible material and that are galvanically compatible to minimize deterioration. The exhaust system itself must be made of material that will withstand the marine environment, heat, and the additionally corrosive by-products of combustion. For example, copper and brass—which might be used with gasoline engines—are not suitable for diesel engines because of the high sulfur content of the exhaust.

The system may be dry—like an automobile exhaust—or wet—cooled by water either injected into the exhaust or wrapped around it in a water jacket.

Dry Systems are very hot; surrounding combustible materials must be protected by a nine-inch clearance, all around, or shielded by suitable insulation. A dry exhaust usually is vented through a vertical stack that is cooled by a surrounding air duct or jacket. A spark arrester must be installed to capture burning soot or other discharge, and there should be some provision for draining off rainwater or spray that might enter the stack.

Wet Systems need a source of cooling water. This water may be part of the engine cooling system or furnished separately; if separate, there should be a warning alarm to signal loss of flow. The rate of flow is based on the size of the engine and the speed of operation. For an average gasoline engine of 325 cubic inches, running at 3000

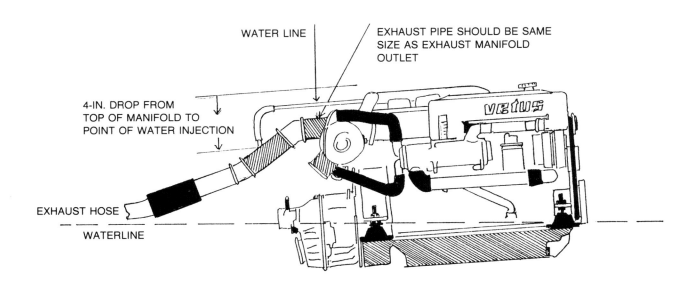

WATER LINE

EXHAUST PIPE SHOULD BE SAME
SIZE AS EXHAUST MANIFOLD
OUTLET

4-IN. DROP FROM
TOP OF MANIFOLD TO
POINT OF WATER INJECTION

EXHAUST HOSE

WATERLINE

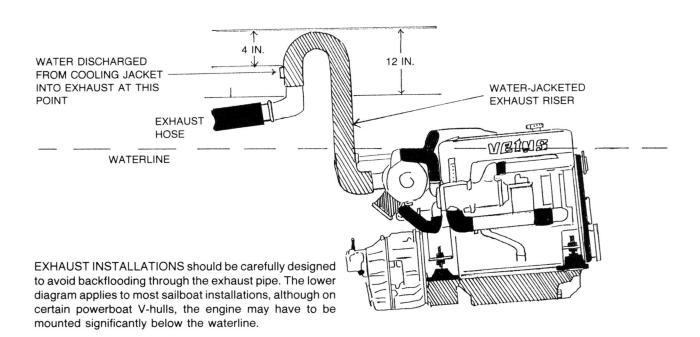

WATER DISCHARGED
FROM COOLING JACKET
INTO EXHAUST AT THIS
POINT

4 IN.

12 IN.

WATER-JACKETED
EXHAUST RISER

EXHAUST
HOSE

WATERLINE

EXHAUST INSTALLATIONS should be carefully designed
to avoid backflooding through the exhaust pipe. The lower
diagram applies to most sailboat installations, although on
certain powerboat V-hulls, the engine may have to be
mounted significantly below the waterline.

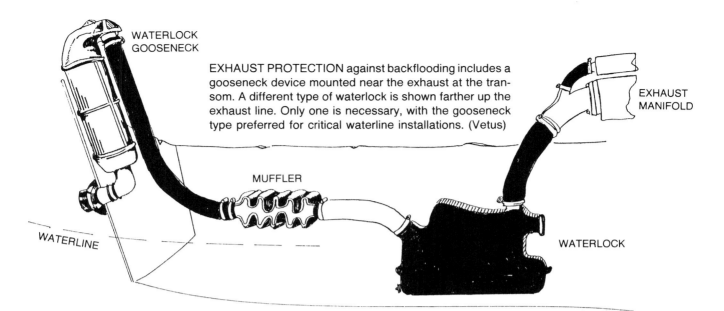

WATERLOCK GOOSENECK

EXHAUST PROTECTION against backflooding includes a gooseneck device mounted near the exhaust at the transom. A different type of waterlock is shown farther up the exhaust line. Only one is necessary, with the gooseneck type preferred for critical waterline installations. (Vetus)

EXHAUST MANIFOLD

MUFFLER

WATERLINE

WATERLOCK

rpm, the required water flow is about 1.5 gallons per minute. Since a wet system runs cooler than a dry system, combustible-material clearance requirements are reduced to two inches.

A wet exhaust system must be installed to prevent water from backing up into the engine manifolds. On a typical powerboat, the cooling water should be injected at least four inches below the manifold level and the exhaust duct should run aft with a drop of at least one-half inch per foot.

The end of the line—if located at the transom—should be as far outboard as possible, to minimize the backup of exhaust gas into the cockpit. Flapper valves will prevent the backflow of water from a following sea.

On a typical sailboat—where the engine may be installed at or below the waterline—a water-jacketed riser should take the exhaust well above the waterline. The line should be fitted with an antisiphon valve to prevent water from being drawn back into the line.

Engine Safety Checklist

☐ All exposed belt drives, rotating parts, and other moving components should be covered with protective guards or shields.

☐ Ventilation should provide an adequate air supply for optimal operation of the engine. Ventilation in a gasoline installation must be augmented by exhaust blowers designed to clear explosive fumes from the compartment before engine operation.

☐ Engines designed for automatic operation, such as an auxiliary electrical generator, should be equipped with a temperature-sensitive automatic shutdown.

☐ To forestall electrolytic damage within the engine, sacrificial zinc anodes should be installed in the cooling system.

☐ Beneath the engine there should be a full-length, rigid drip pan of sufficient capacity to hold the engine *and* transmission oil.

☐ There must be an approved-type backflame arrester on the air intake of any gasoline engine carburetor.

☐ All exposed hot surfaces on exhaust lines should have protective shields or wrappings.

☐ Exhaust outlets should be as far outboard of centerline as possible, to minimize backup of exhaust gas into the cockpit.

☐ Exhaust outlets should be fitted with flapper valves to minimize backflow of water from a following sea.

PROPELLER

With most engines, power is transmitted through a reduction gear to drive a propeller to drive the boat. Propellers may be made of cast iron or steel, aluminum alloy, plastic, or—the best—manganese bronze.

The diameter of the propeller and the pitch (angle) of the blades are directly related to such factors as the power output of the engine, the speed at which the shaft will be turning, and the speed at which the boat will be expected to operate. These should be determined in conjunction with a marine architect or powerplant specialist.

On sailboats under sail, propeller drag can be reduced by allowing the shaft to freewheel with the transmission in neutral. On smaller boats—for which a two-bladed prop is adequate under power—a folding propeller is a good solution. When not spinning, the hinged blades streamline into the water flow; when the shaft is engaged, centrifugal action throws the blades into position. On larger boats, a variable-pitch propeller will reduce drag but also introduces another piece of mechanical equipment that may break down.

PROPELLER SHAFT

Propeller shafts generally are made of naval brass, nickel-copper or nickel-copper-aluminum alloy, and certain types of steel; the diameter of the shaft is determined by engine power and operating speed (in rpm), the length of the shaft, and the material used. As above, selection is best determined by specialists.

The shaft will be supported between the engine and the propeller by one or more bearings—the number and spacing determined by shaft diameter, length, material, and operating speed. The last bearing should be no more than one shaft diameter from the propeller hub. A long stern tube—which might tend to trap water next to the shaft—should include some means to keep the water circulating; stagnant water can be corrosive.

Seals that keep water from running in along the shaft may incorporate O-rings or similar devices, or use some type of stuffing material. In this case, graphite-impregnated packing should not be used—it may cause galvanic reaction with the shaft material; wax-impregnated flax is recommended.

Most propellers are installed with a key, a propeller nut, a jam nut, and a cotter key to ensure that they *stay* installed. Other positive-locking systems may be used, but are not common. For all shaft materials other than naval brass, a protective coating must be used between the shaft and the propeller hub to guard against galvanic corrosion.

SAILING RIGS AND RIGGING

RIG TYPES

The more commonly found sailing rigs include ketch, yawl, schooner, cutter, and sloop. Each has its attributes and advocates, and each—if well installed and properly maintained—is safe enough under most sailing conditions. The split-rig designs, with more than one mast, offer some advantages in their wider variety of sail choices and smaller, more easily handled sails; the cutter rig originally was designed for heavy weather and is quite stable in a blow; the sloop tends to be faster than the others, is simple to use, and is the most popular rig on the market.

THE MAST(S)

Whatever the rig, the main structure holding up the sails, and transmitting the motive power of the wind to the hull, is the mast. The mast may be made of wood or be an aluminum tube; the reason for choosing one or the other may be for style or for cost. (Wood usually is cheaper, but heavier and harder to maintain.) The mast may be stepped (mounted) on deck, held up by the standing rigging, or it may extend down through the deck and be stepped at the keel (but still supported topside by the rigging).

Many small sailboats are equipped with folding, deck-stepped masts, for easy transportability and storage. On larger boats, deck-stepped masts allow for more open space below and avoid a most common source of topside leaks with keel-stepped masts: water running down along the mast and through the mast hole in deck. Needless to say, the deck supports for a deck-stepped mast must be extra-sturdy, and, all things considered, a keel-stepped mast will be stronger.

THE BOOM

The boom helps transmit the power from the sail to the mast, and it provides directional control of the sail. Like the mast, the boom may be either wood or aluminum.

A boom gallows (or crutch) holds the boom securely in place when the sail is down—a job that rigging will not do very well under most conditions and not at all when the boat really gets rocking. The most useful type of gallows will accommodate the boom to port, amidships, or starboard—a nice touch that lets you keep this head-knocker on the side of the boat opposite the boarding area. The gallows also is useful for keeping various lines and bits of gear off the deck and it provides another sturdy handhold.

RIGGING

Standing Rigging includes the shrouds, stays, chainplates, and fittings that keep the mast in place against the sometimes exceptional forces of wind and weather. Look for the best materials and the best workmanship; a weakness here can bring the whole thing crashing down. All wires

and fittings should be stainless steel; the rated breaking strength of turnbuckles should be 50 percent higher than that of the wires they connect.

Table 1
Breaking Strength (Pounds) of Stainless Steel Wire Rope

Diameter (Inches)	1/8	3/16	1/4	5/16	3/8	7/16
7×7	1150	2750	4800	7500	10600	14200
7×19	1280	2900	5090	7900	11100	14700
1×19	2100	4600	8000			

On most boats, the chainplates are bolted securely to the sides of the hull—which must be strong enough, or be specially beefed up, at the points of attachment. With fiberglass, a hull thickness of one-half inch would be the minimum acceptable without reinforcement. Inboard chainplates might be anchored to a solid bulkhead below or be extended through to an attachment in the bilge. All chainplates must be installed in-line with the attached rigging, to prevent failure brought on by the torque of a misaligned rig, and all of the fittings must be accessible for examination and tightening.

Running Rigging includes the lines by which the boom and sails are controlled. These come in a variety of styles, with some better suited to one use than another. A well-planned set will have woven-in color coding for quick identification of each line.

Running rigging must be free to run—that is, to move easily through the various blocks and fairleads installed to bring the line to the adjustment control points. Frequently the hardware will be not-quite-in-line, resulting in high friction, accelerated wear, and premature failure.

WINCHES

Winches provide great mechanical advantage for handling lines, and they are important equipment for any sailboat bigger than a daysailer. They help tend any sail that is too heavy—or under too much wind pressure—to be handled barehanded.

There are one-, two-, and three-speed winches; on a typical two-speed winch, you turn the handle clockwise for one level of leverage and counterclockwise for half the speed with twice the pull.

Winches are available with gear ratios ranging from 1:1 to 9:1 and at prices that range from under $100 to many thousands of dollars. Winches are best rated by power ratio:

$$\text{Power ratio} = \frac{\text{Radius of winch handle}}{(\text{Radius of drum} + \text{Radius of line})} \times \text{Gear ratio}$$

A higher-power winch requires less effort and is safer to use; however, because of the high price of bigger winches, many small-to-medium production boats are equipped with winches a few sizes smaller than they ought to be. Here are the recommended power ratios for winches on such boats:

A sturdy winch under heavy strain may develop as much as 18,000 pounds of pull—enough to snap a worn or weakened line and enough to pull an improperly mounted winch out of the deck. Winches are best mounted on a heavy teak pad, with a backing block underneath to help spread the load. Teak is the material of choice (for this and similar applications) because it resists rot. Be wary of fiberglass boats with a winch pad molded in place: There *might* be a wood pad in there, or there may be nothing underneath to prevent the winch from pulling out.

Particularly useful is a self-tailing feature, whereby a friction plate keeps the free end of the line moving off and away from the winch drum.

Finally, winches must be mounted at a slight angle so that the incoming line will not ride up over itself—causing a tangle that often is impossible to undo without cutting the line. Winches must be so positioned that the winch handler has good footing to ensure full power and can work the handle through a full 360 degrees without banging knuckles.

Note: On some boats, halyards are rigged with wire rather than rope—or with a combination of the two—with the wire end permanently led to a windlass mounted on the mast.

BOAT LENGTH	22 Ft.	25 Ft.	28 Ft.	32 Ft.	35 Ft.
SHEETS					
Genoa	8:1	8:1/16:1	16:1/28:1	28:1/40:1	40:1
Spinnaker	8:1	8:1	8:1/16:1	16:1/28:1	28:1/40:1
Main	8:1	8:1	8:1	8:1	8:1/16:1
HALYARDS					
Genoa	8:1	8:1	8:1	8:1/16:1	8:1/16:1
Spinnaker	8:1	8:1	8:1	8:1/16:1	16:1
Main	8:1	8:1	8:1	8:1	16:1

OTHER MECHANICAL SYSTEMS

STEERING

Steering systems may include tillers (which are attached to and directly move the rudder) or steering wheels (which work through a set of wires and pulleys or a hydraulic unit to position the rudder). Any boat could be rigged with one, two, or three steering systems: tiller, wheel-controlled mechanical, or wheel-controlled hydraulic. As a practical matter, however, tillers tend to be used on smaller boats and wheel steering on larger boats. There is no particular point at which one or the other might be found. Very large traditional Arab dhows and Chinese junks have tillers, but they also usually are manned by relatively large crews. Some modern cruising sailboats in the mid-40-foot range come with tillers, and many boats in the low-30-foot range have wheel steering. A 40-foot yawl or ketch, with balanced rig, can be more easily handled with a tiller than a 40-foot sloop, which may too easily overpower the steering.

Any advantages? Tillers are quicker, more sensitive to the "feel" of the boat, and less prone to mechanical failure, but they tend to sweep the cockpit. A wheel delivers more power and can be more easily "lashed" on course with a few turns of the setscrew, but, unless wrapped with leather, canvas, or light line, it is slippery when wet. However, any boat equipped with mechanical and/or hydraulic wheel steering should also have a provision for steering with an emergency tiller.

All elements of any steering system must be able to withstand the often strong forces working against the rudder. Cables should be stainless steel; fittings must be hefty; all pulleys and sheaves must be through-bolted—not screwed—into the hull structure; the rudder and rudder-post must be joined firmly.

Small outboard motors might be turned by a handle (analogous to the tiller) or by a wheel connected through a cable-over-pulley system. Larger engines—certainly any time the total outboard power exceeds 50 hp—will be turned by a hydraulic ram (activated by the wheel). The ram may be mounted with the fixed end either on the engine or on the boat.

HYDRAULIC SYSTEMS

A hydraulic system transfers pressure through a noncompressible liquid to a power unit, where that pressure is transformed into useful work. Since they operate under pressure, all units must be mounted rigidly (with through-bolts and backing blocks, not merely screwed down). The connecting lines—typically made of copper tubing—must be mounted with galvanically compatible hardware and supported at least every 24 inches. Aircraft-type stainless teflon-lined lines may also be used. But verify all line-compatibility with hydraulic fluid. In a steel or aluminum boat, the lines and hardware must not come into direct contact with the hull. A marine hydraulic system must be operable between 0°F and 176°F and be able to withstand storage temperatures as low as −20°F.

SEACOCKS

Except in the smallest of boats, the hull will not be a total watertight envelope; it will be pierced deliberately with openings to admit seawater for engine cooling, head flushing, refrigeration and air-conditioning operation, and to discharge "used" water. In any case, the through-hull openings should be kept to a minimum.

Seacock is the generic term for any valve that controls the flow of water through the hull, and there are safety considerations in both the type of valve and the material of which it is made. While you cannot change the type or material of the hull, you do have control over the seacocks.

There are three basic types: the old-fashioned tapered-plug design and the modern ball valve—which are opened and closed by a lever—and the gate valve, like the one that controls your garden hose, which is opened by turning the handle counterclockwise and closed by screwing it down in the other direction. With the gate valve,

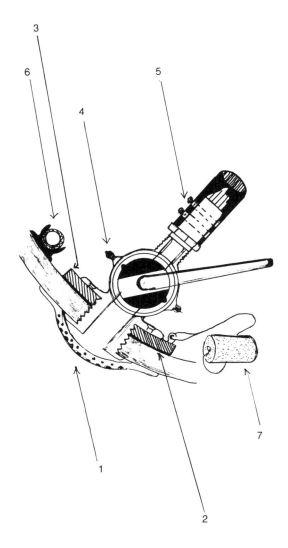

A PROPERLY MOUNTED SEACOCK. Note that the mounting includes: (1) strainer on the outside of the hull; (2) heavy bedding of sealant between the backing block and the hull; (3) substantial backing block beneath the seacock assembly; (4) grease fitting installed in one of the seacock drains for easy lubrication; (5) double hose clamps with rolled-edge stainless steel hose clamps; (6) pipe mounted in clips near the seacock for emergency (only) operation of the seacock if it is frozen; (7) tapered and correctly sized emergency wood plug fastened near the seacock with a cable tie for quick use in case of valve failure.

it may take several complete turns of the handle to go from full-open to full-closed. There are two major arguments against using gate valves as seacocks: (1) Interior marine growth or a chunk of seaweed can jam the valve in an "open" position, and (2) you can't tell by looking whether the valve is open, closed, or halfway between. On traditional seacocks and ball valves, when the handle is lined up with the plumbing, the valve is open; when set at 90 degrees, the valve is closed. The valve is positive, unambiguous, quick.

Whatever type of valve you use, it *must* be of material compatible with the marine environment and with its metallic neighbors. Some valves used in shoreside construction are made of brass or brass-and-bronze, which will corrode quickly. Valves must be all bronze or fiberglass-reinforced plastic (which is especially useful on a metal hull).

In the interests of sense and sanitation, all intakes should be on one side of the keel; all outlets should be on the other side, and farther aft whenever possible.

Finally, seacocks will be connected to some sort of hose, which directs the flow of water into or out of the boat. The hose and its connection are the weakest link in this chain. Hoses rot or otherwise deteriorate, and when they do, water might come rushing into the hull. The unrestricted flow from a broken two-inch hose may sink a typical 30-foot boat in about ninety seconds.

The best hoses are reinforced with wire; clear plastic hoses become brittle or stretch under pressure, and they should *not* be used. Hose clamps—supposed to keep tight connections at either end—will also give way unexpectedly. The best clamps are specified for marine use, made of stainless steel, and have a rolled edge to minimize cutting into the hose. Hose clamps should be used in pairs: If one fails, the other keeps the connection tight. Automobile-type clamps are not suitable; they rust.

Finally, in the event of a failure that cannot be controlled by closing the seacock, you must be able to plug the opening quickly. Soft pine tapered plugs of the right dimension should be ready for emergency use, loosely attached to each seacock by a short length of nylon line.

Other openings, not controlled by a seacock, may accommodate sensor units for the depth finder and speedometer/distance log. The sensors should have a watertight fit, with a replacement "blank" plug as a backup for each one when removed for cleaning or storage.

BILGE PUMPS

Water that gets into the boat, whether through leaks from above or from below, will collect in the lower part of the hull known as the bilge. A properly designed bilge will let the water flow freely to the deepest point of the bilge, with no trapped pools along the way. All frames or intruding bulkheads must be penetrated by a series of limber holes—about the size of your little finger—to facilitate this flow. (The worry is not so much that water will gather in puddles, but that spilled fuel might be trapped, out of sight.)

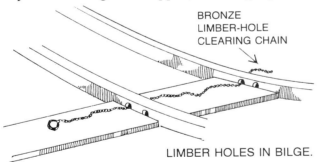

BRONZE LIMBER-HOLE CLEARING CHAIN

LIMBER HOLES IN BILGE.

Any water that gets *into* the boat needs to be pumped *out* with some regularity. In canoes or rowboats, a scoop and a big sponge may be the bailers of choice; on larger boats, a hand-operated pump (whether installed or portable) is a vital piece of emergency equipment. Any boat with a battery for power should have one or more electric bilge pumps installed.

But—what kind of pump? At every boat show, and on many counters at marine supply dealers, you will see dramatic demonstrations of high-speed, high-volume pumping by little devices

SUBMERSIBLE ELECTRIC BILGE PUMPS are pretty much standard now. They should be hooked directly to the battery through their own switch and not governed by the master battery disconnect. (Jabsco)

smaller than your fist. Some are indeed amazing—and valuable additions to your equipment list—but don't be carried away by the flash. Study the substance.

A bilge pump not only must pump water overboard, it must at the same time lift that water from the lowest point inside the hull to a place somewhat above the waterline. That lift might be three or four feet. Your pump must be able to overcome this head pressure and still deliver an acceptable discharge volume.

MANUAL BILGE PUMP definitely has its place. Whether it is for daily pumping to conserve electrical power, or for that final effort when all else fails, manual bilge pumps are basic boat gear. A strainer should be installed on the end of the pump intake line to prevent clogging from debris. (Jabsco)

There are two basic types of bilge pump: centrifugal, in which a small, spinning impeller moves the water along, and positive-displacement, in which the water is sucked along by the vacuum created when a tight-fitting diaphragm moves through a tube. This is similar to—and may be the same as—the pump used in many freshwater plumbing systems.

Centrifugal pumps can be quite small, to nestle in small niches in the bilge. In fact, they *must* nestle in the bilge, since they are not "self-priming" pumps: They do not create suction in order to draw water up through the pump. Rather, they force water up and away from the pump—but only to a point. When the head pressure is too great for a particular size of pump, it simply spins its wheel and the water goes nowhere.

Centrifugal pumps will clog or jam more easily than positive-displacement pumps, but they tend to be less expensive (perhaps a great deal less expensive) and require little or no maintenance. When one does stop working, it's usually easier just to replace it than to repair it.

PUMP STRAINER. (Jabsco)

A BILGE-PUMP SWITCH that is free of moving parts, levers, and other features that are likely to fail. The switch uses electrical capacity to sense water levels but carries no electrical current itself. If water touches the switch for twelve continuous seconds, the pump goes on and remains on for twelve seconds after water leaves the sensor. The switch can also be used to activate flooding alarms (either audio or strobe types). (Sensatron)

BILGE-PUMP ELECTRICAL INSTALLATION
WITH ALARMS.

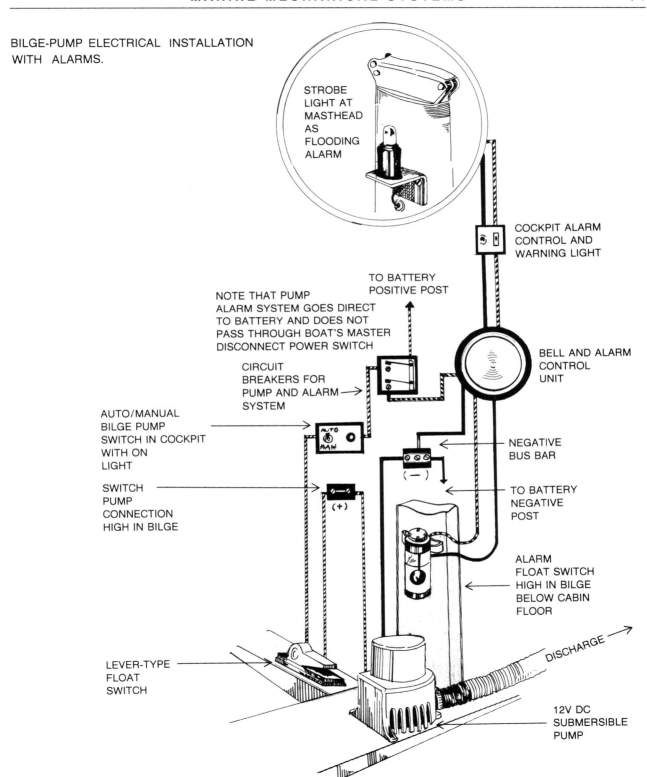

STROBE
LIGHT AT
MASTHEAD
AS
FLOODING
ALARM

COCKPIT ALARM
CONTROL AND
WARNING LIGHT

NOTE THAT PUMP
ALARM SYSTEM GOES DIRECT
TO BATTERY AND DOES NOT
PASS THROUGH BOAT'S MASTER
DISCONNECT POWER SWITCH

TO BATTERY
POSITIVE POST

CIRCUIT
BREAKERS FOR
PUMP AND ALARM
SYSTEM

BELL AND ALARM
CONTROL
UNIT

AUTO/MANUAL
BILGE PUMP
SWITCH IN COCKPIT
WITH ON
LIGHT

NEGATIVE
BUS BAR

SWITCH
PUMP
CONNECTION
HIGH IN BILGE

TO BATTERY
NEGATIVE
POST

ALARM
FLOAT SWITCH
HIGH IN BILGE
BELOW CABIN
FLOOR

DISCHARGE

LEVER-TYPE
FLOAT
SWITCH

12V DC
SUBMERSIBLE
PUMP

On the other hand, the repairability of a positive-displacement pump offers long-distance confidence; a pump rebuild kit should be one item in the spare-parts locker. In a pinch, most of the pump's parts—the gaskets and flapper valves—can be jury-rigged from rubber, leather, or plastic.

To avoid a jam from debris in the bilges, each pump intake should be protected by a screen with an area several times larger than the diameter of the pump intake. With a submerged pump, the whole unit can be surrounded by a screen.

To forestall intervening electrical problems, the bilge pump should be wired directly to the battery bank. Most pumps come with a three-position switch: off, manual, and automatic. The selector normally is left in the automatic position, energizing a float switch mounted in the bilges. When the bilgewater level lifts the float, the switch is triggered on. The switch can be set to start pumping at any predetermined level, depending on where it is mounted in the bilge.

To ensure that "automatic" peace of mind, the float switch should be checked regularly for freedom of movement. Congealed oil or other gunk may freeze the float in the down, or off, position. Or, for that matter, it may hang up in the on position, causing the pump to run indefinitely. Bilge pumps should be rated for twenty-four hours of continuous use, and they must be able to run "dry"—that is, when there is no water to be pumped—without overheating, or must be protected by an automatic cutoff.

When a centrifugal pump shuts off, the water in the line above the pump will slide back down into the bilge, possibly cycling the float switch on and off. This surging can be avoided by putting a

check valve in the line or by moving the float switch a bit higher.

If you have more than one bilge pump, each should have its own plumbing and overboard discharge, to minimize the impact of a clogged line.

CATHODIC PROTECTION

Even if you know that boats should have "zincs" installed on the propeller shaft or in other underwater places, you may not understand why. The reason is simple: to give electrolytic action something expendable to destroy, rather than attacking such underwater vitals as shaft, propeller, outdrive unit, rudder, and seacocks. (See appendix IV for a description of the electrolytic process.) The correct technical name for a zinc is *sacrificial anode*—a term commonly found in books but rarely heard on the waterfront.

A zinc is a piece of metallic zinc, magnesium, or aluminum—metals that are very low on the galvanic table and will more quickly give up molecules than common marine materials such as bronze, brass, and steel. Zincs should have a streamlined shape and be mounted so as to minimize drag; if near through-hull fittings, they should be forward of discharge ports and aft of

CORROSION-FIGHTING ZINC ANODE installed in a diesel heat exchanger on a GM-671. The zinc anode sacrifices itself over time to the corrosive effects of seawater, protecting the valuable tubes and lining of the heat exchanger. Note the dated label tape used as a reminder to change the zinc on a proper maintenance schedule.

intake ports. In general, multiple small zincs are more effective than a few large ones.

Zincs may be mounted directly on the metal they are to protect—or, for better distribution of protection, mounted equidistant from the metal parts they are protecting. If mounted directly on the rudder and propeller shaft (with care taken not to upset the balance), those units should be tied in to the overall bonding system.

Aluminum and steel-hulled boats, and boats with aluminum outdrive units, require special protection. Aluminum hulls can be left unpainted; steel hulls and aluminum outdrive units must be painted. Shore-power circuits on metal-hulled boats must be equipped with an isolation transformer or isolator.

But this is not an area for experimentation; the matter of cathodic protection is best handled by a marine architect or electrician. The boat owner's role is: (1) To inspect the installed system regularly; (2) to replace deteriorated zincs before they are too far gone to do much good; and (3) to seek professional advice if the system is not working properly.

It's not necessary to have the boat hauled out just to inspect or replace zincs. In clear water, you might be able to check the zincs merely by looking; in any event, for inspection or replace-

SACRIFICIAL ZINC ANODE placed in the outer jacket of a hammered copper exhaust riser on a marine diesel. Note the dated label as a replacement reminder. The white faucet adjusts the flow from the riser into the bypass discharge and thus controls the exhaust cooling temperature.

ment, basic snorkel or scuba gear can be used to good advantage in most boating areas during the greater part of the season.

CARING FOR THE CREW

Crew comfort is an important antidote to the fatigue that may set in after hours of standing on deck, wrestling with lines or large fish, and being exposed to sun, wind, spray, and rain. A tired sailor can be a dangerous sailor—dangerous to himself and the boat. The equipment that ensures hot food, a hot shower, and environmental heating or cooling is as related to safety as any other.

GALLEY EQUIPMENT

The galley on most boats is tucked into a corner of the main cabin and equipped with a minimal but usually effective sink, stove, and icebox or refrigerator. With most of this equipment, your choices will be based on preference and pocketbook (an icebox versus a refrigerator, a pressure water system versus a hand pump), and safety is not so much at issue.

But, as already noted, that is not the case when it comes to selecting the type of stove fuel. Of course, your choice of stove fuel often is determined when you buy the boat, and, considering the cost of the equipment and installation, you may elect to stay with it even though it would not be your first choice. Nevertheless, you should understand the advantages and disadvantages of typical stove fuels.

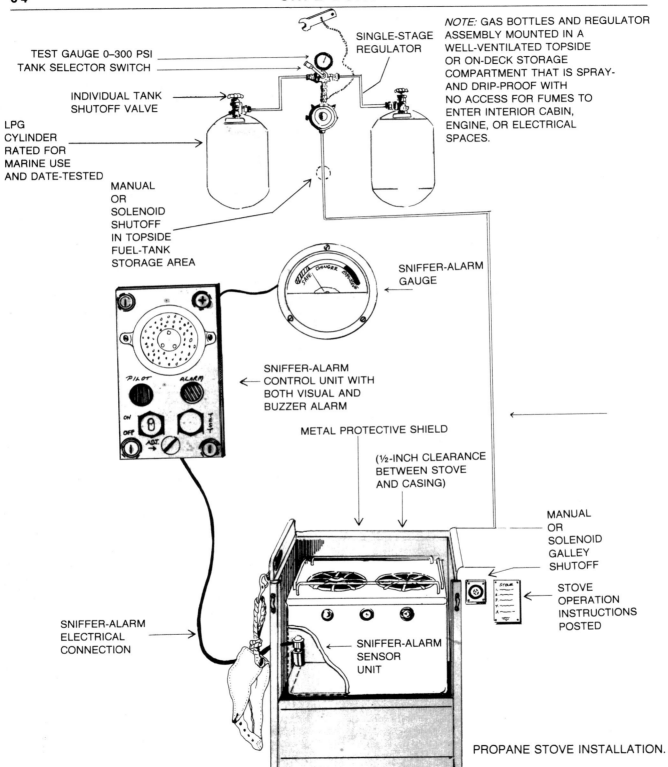

TEST GAUGE 0–300 PSI
TANK SELECTOR SWITCH

SINGLE-STAGE
REGULATOR

NOTE: GAS BOTTLES AND REGULATOR ASSEMBLY MOUNTED IN A WELL-VENTILATED TOPSIDE OR ON-DECK STORAGE COMPARTMENT THAT IS SPRAY- AND DRIP-PROOF WITH NO ACCESS FOR FUMES TO ENTER INTERIOR CABIN, ENGINE, OR ELECTRICAL SPACES.

INDIVIDUAL TANK
SHUTOFF VALVE

LPG
CYLINDER
RATED FOR
MARINE USE
AND DATE-TESTED

MANUAL
OR
SOLENOID
SHUTOFF
IN TOPSIDE
FUEL-TANK
STORAGE AREA

SNIFFER-ALARM
GAUGE

SNIFFER-ALARM
CONTROL UNIT WITH
BOTH VISUAL AND
BUZZER ALARM

METAL PROTECTIVE SHIELD

(½-INCH CLEARANCE
BETWEEN STOVE
AND CASING)

MANUAL
OR
SOLENOID
GALLEY
SHUTOFF

STOVE
OPERATION
INSTRUCTIONS
POSTED

SNIFFER-ALARM
ELECTRICAL
CONNECTION

SNIFFER-ALARM
SENSOR
UNIT

PROPANE STOVE INSTALLATION.

Propane and Butane These fuels are stored as a liquid, under pressure, which becomes a flammable gas when the pressure is released. Advantages: They burn with a clean, hot flame; are easy to light; and are commonly available in most U.S. ports. Disadvantage: The gas is heavier than air, so unless it is being consumed by a flame, it will settle to the bottom of a compartment or into the bilges, where it could explode. For this reason, the tank must be located away from any closed compartment, and, if not fully exposed to the atmosphere, must be provided with an open "drain" to the outside of the boat. That drain usually will be a hole in the bottom of the compartment connected to a length of tubing, which in turn is connected to a through-hull fitting well above the waterline.

To ensure safety, a propane or butane system should have several shutoff valves—at the least, one at the tank and one at the stove. An electrically operated tank valve with the switch panel near the galley is a convenience, and it provides an on-off light as a visual reminder that the valve is open. However—because of the high failure rate of electrical circuits in the marine environment—a manual shutoff valve is recommended. The valve handle should be painted red and should be installed to indicate "flow" or "stop" by the position of the handle. Round handles—which indicate nothing—have no place in any safety application.

The more sophisticated marine stoves have a pilot light (just as in a home gas stove) that facilitates lighting multiple burners when cooking a meal. These pilot lights are controlled by a heat-sensitive cutoff valve. Should the pilot light be accidentally extinguished, the fuel flow within the stove will be terminated. This is a mixed blessing. Over time, the pilot light may become difficult to light as the thermocouple controlling the valve becomes corroded or coated with soot from matches—and the master valve will not permit any fuel to flow to the burners unless the pilot light is on. Also, the fuel flow *to* the stove is not affected if the pilot goes out. The basic rule

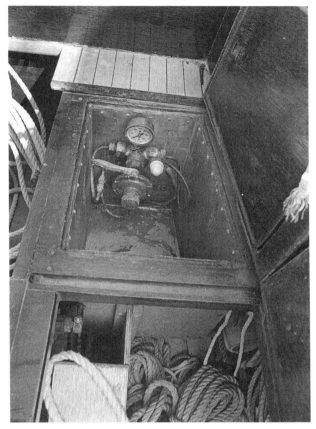

PROPANE CONTROL INSTALLATION in a cockpit locker. This is a fairly good installation incorporating a clearly readable gauge, on/off lever in a handy place, and a regulator that can be serviced easily. However, the copper lines are somewhat exposed to the weather and susceptible to corrosion, so it might be advisable to replace these lines with stainless braid/Teflon-lined lines rated for propane gas use in a marine environment.

here: Never leave a pilot light burning unattended.

A portable, camping-type unit might be used on a small boat or for cooking on the beach. The supply bottle should not be left connected to the stove when not in use; it should be stored in some fully ventilated topside location.

Compressed or **Liquid Natural Gas**   This is basically the same fuel used in a home system, but bottled under pressure for convenience. Natural gas is lighter than air—avoiding the most serious hazard of propane and butane—but it is not as efficient as a fuel and not found as commonly in boating communities. These factors raise the cost and complicate resupply.

Alcohol and **Kerosene**   These are readily available liquid fuels not likely to explode but often difficult to ignite. They may be subject to flash fires, although—if it's any comfort—*small* alcohol fires can be extinguished with water. Alcohol and kerosene stoves for marine use are small, usually well gimbaled, and may be the only practical cooking option aboard smaller boats.

On the other hand, alcohol is not very efficient (it takes a lot longer to heat a pot of soup), is expensive, and is not always available in out-of-the-way places. Kerosene is almost universally available worldwide, but it burns with an unpleasant odor—a problem for queasy stomachs.

Diesel   Diesel stoves are fine for cooking but are limited to use aboard diesel-powered boats.

Coal and **Wood**   Stoves that burn these fuels are most often found in antique boats—or boats designed to appear antique. They are not very handy for cooking (they're not handy for cooking ashore, either), but when used as space heaters, they offer the same romantic charm as a fireplace at home. A properly installed and insulated stove and chimney does not pose any exceptional fire hazard while tied up to the pier; we're not so confident this would be true in a bouncing boat. The major caution: These fuels consume large quantities of oxygen. You must provide adequate ventilation to avoid asphyxiation.

Electricity   Electric stoves are a luxury of the rich—or those rich enough to support a large generating plant aboard. Most electric stoves (if not *all* electric stoves—we've never seen one on a sailboat) are the province of large powerboats. They work just like the home units and certainly are safe enough to use. However—if the power goes out, so do the stoves.

Canned Fuel   Fuel in cans (such as Sterno) is best left ashore; it's even more noxious than kerosene and less efficient than compressed natural gas. At best, consider it an emergency backup to an electric stove.

For guidelines on cooking with the various fuels, see chapter 11.

REFRIGERATION

Refrigeration may be provided by an electrically powered refrigerator, much like the one at home, or by an icebox—much like the one that *used* to be at home (if you're old enough to remember). An icebox can be converted to mechanical refrigeration by an engine-driven compressor or by an add-on electrical unit.

Electrical units may be 120V AC (for shore power when in the marina, and for generator power when underway—if you have a generator), or 120V AC and 12V DC (shore power and battery power). Propane-powered units, such as found on recreational vehicles, may operate only in a vertical position and should be professionally installed in a boat.

Iceboxes work quite well, but the icebox must be well insulated and be top-opening (so that cold air doesn't spill out when the door is opened). If the boat is large enough, you can enjoy the convenience of two iceboxes: a large one for soft drinks and the like, which you will be opening frequently, and a smaller one for frozen foods, which probably would be opened only once or twice a day.

The major disadvantage of an icebox: You must have an occasional supply of ice; the major advantages: You don't need a steady source of electrical power, and a properly packed and carefully used icebox can keep foods cool and safe for many days, even a week (see chapter 11).

THE HEAD

The facilities in the seagoing bathroom might range from rudimentary to luxurious, but the common denominator in most systems is the marine toilet. Despite all of the technological advances in other aspects of boating, this necessary piece of equipment remains primitive and intimidating. To begin with, you have to pump it to flush it; the pump may be hand-, foot-, or electrically operated. Hand operation is most common; it also requires that you bend over the toilet when flushing, which is not pleasant and may be downright distressing under some conditions. When the gaskets start wearing out, your face may be sprayed with water from around the pump handle. Electric pumps eliminate some of this distress, but they are also prone to breakdown: Emptying a toilet that has a broken pump may be the single most unpleasant chore in boating. An electric pump is a luxury item for local cruising and a liability for any extended travel.

To meet Coast Guard requirements, the toilet must discharge waste material into a holding tank or a treatment system. The holding tank may be built into the hull or bolted in place, and it should be of sufficiently generous size to accommodate your cruising plans. How generous? Figure one gallon per flush, and then compute your own requirements.

The tank can be emptied in international waters—if you go offshore—or it must be pumped out at a commercial pumping station. With a Coast Guard–"approved" treatment system (chemical or electrical), you have the option of discharging treated waste almost anywhere. In some bodies of water, any discharge—treated or not—is prohibited. This does not prohibit the installation of a flow-through marine sanitation device (MSD), as long as it can be secured or disabled during operation in any restricted waters.

As a practical matter, most installed marine toilets include a provision, controlled by a selector valve, for discharging waste material directly overboard. This plumbing must include a vented loop well above the waterline (and above the waterline created when a sailboat is well heeled over). This prevents seawater from being siphoned back into the boat, into the bowl, and then into the bilges. Unrestrained backflow could soon enough sink the boat.

Whatever the enforcement (or lack thereof) of the waste-discharge law in *your* boating area, we encourage good, environmentally sound boating: Keep your waste in a holding tank and discharge it properly either at sea or at a pumpout station.

On a smaller boat, a self-contained Porta Potti may solve the toilet problem. One obvious advantage: You simply carry the tank ashore and dump it in a toilet. This is not much of a chore if you have been using the proper chemical treatment, give it time to work, and don't let the tank get too full.

On any boat, keep a plain, old-fashioned bucket handy as an emergency backup. Nature does not cease to call just because the toilet has ceased to function. Be prepared.

Other bathroom equipment may include a sink and a shower—with the head compartment doubling as a shower stall. Often the sink will drain directly overboard, but the shower rarely does—unless the drain is well above the waterline. On many boats, such housekeeping drains are plumbed into a gray-water sump tank. (It's called gray water because that's the color it becomes when it's loaded with dirt, soap scum, and hair.) The sump keeps this malodorous mix out of the bilge; at the same time, the gray water should be pumped overboard through a system *separate* from the bilge pump, to avoid any possibility of clogging that vital item.

WATER TANKS

Water tanks may be either built in to the hull or bolted down. Built-in tanks may carry a small penalty of a resin taste when new, but that can be controlled with a chemical additive. Bolted-in tanks need to be very securely fastened to keep them from breaking loose in a seaway. Tanks should be low in the hull and, ideally, located about two-thirds of the way back from the bow, which enhances rather than impedes stability. They must be equipped with inspection/clean-out ports large enough for practicality; even heavily treated city water may become a breeding ground for green slime after sitting too long in your tanks. The slime probably won't hurt you, but when it starts to slough away from the tank wall, it can clog the pipes and pump. Besides, it will look most unappetizing in your morning coffee.

The freshwater plumbing should lead into a central manifold, with each tank controlled by a separate valve. If you sail with all valves always open, the water level in all tanks will be equalized. That may keep the boat on an even keel, but it also may unexpectedly run the tanks dry, with no backup supply.

Your freshwater system can be pressurized by a positive-displacement pump with an accumulator or header tank, or by a combined pump and accumulator unit designed specially for the freshwater system. If you use the same model of positive-displacement pump for fresh water, the sump tank, and the bilges, your spare-parts inventory can be reduced and you'll always be able to borrow a pump from the freshwater or graywater sump if the bilge pump should fail. We would not suggest taking the bilge pump off-line to replace a "convenience" pump, nor should you put the sump pump into freshwater service, because contamination is almost certain to occur.

WATERMAKERS

Machines that take the salt out of seawater provide the ultimate in freedom from a tainted shoreside supply by producing pure water from the abundant salt water that is already around you. Capacities range from five to 50 gallons an hour. These units don't actually *make* water; they remove the salt from the water. They work by forcing water through a semipermeable membrane, under pressure. Molecules of water pass through freely, while the larger molecules of dis-

solved salt are trapped. In-line filters ahead of the membrane remove larger solids, preventing premature clogging of the membrane.

Watermakers come in two basic varieties: (1) self-contained, electrically powered units (which require an auxiliary generator) and (2) engine-driven units. Watermakers don't take up much space, and even the volume of the largest units can be more than offset by a reduction in installed water tankage. Watermakers are expensive and might be regarded as a luxury, unless your cruising plans call for many months away from civilization. (A third type of desalinator—the solar still—is a low-volume producer intended as survival equipment. It is most properly found as equipment on a life raft.)

WATER HEATERS

Water heaters come in various sizes—most of them small, six to 12 gallons—and have several modes of operation. Most of them use heated engine coolant running through a heat exchanger inside the tank. Many add an electric heating element to operate on a 110V AC generator or shore power, but they typically draw 1,500 watts and may pop the circuit breakers in an underpowered marina. Heat your water in the morning, before air conditioners and lights begin sucking up the juice. On a good heater, the insulation will keep the water quite warm for as long as twenty-four hours.

Newer models on the market are propane-fueled, flash-type heaters without storage, warming the water only while it's being used. These can be hooked into your cooking-gas supply; some have an electric ignition system and some have a pilot light, which must be extinguished before refueling a gasoline-powered boat.

Solar-powered water heaters are cheap and effective—to a point. A sturdy plastic five-gallon bag filled with water and hung up in the sun provides a hot shower—until the water runs out and a new supply needs to be heated. If you want to tinker, you might rig a solar heater patterned after a swimming-pool unit: some black plastic pipe and a small pump. A caution: If not properly set up, the pipe can become hot enough to melt. Consult a swimming-pool contractor for advice.

CABIN HEATING AND COOLING

The galley stove is useful for taking off a morning chill, but it is not very effective for overall heating. Any individual compartment can be heated with an electric space heater, provided there is a sufficient supply of 110V electricity—which will be true when underway only if you have a generator and when in port only if your marina is well wired for heavy current. Portable electric heaters should not be used afloat.

An auxiliary heating unit, taking heat from the engine cooling system, is a relatively inexpensive solution to cabin heating, but it introduces another weak link in your engine coolant system. If you use one, rig it with an isolation valve that lets you take it off-line in the event of leaking or blockage.

If your sailing plans involve chilly climes, consider investing in a small furnace or fireplace rigged to burn wood or charcoal, or a unit designed for kerosene or diesel fuel. Follow the manufacturer's instructions for placement and mounting (of course separated from any flammable materials) and be sure that the unit is vented properly through a chimney stack.

Air Conditioning runs only on electricity and therefore may not be as accessible as heating, although, if you can muster up the necessary electric power, marine air-conditioning systems can be equipped with a heating element, which provides warm-air circulation through the air-conditioning ducts.

A marine air conditioner can be placed under a cabinet in a midship head, or in any other centrally located space that provides efficient distribution of air through installed ducting. The system will require cooling water, probably adding another pair of through-hull penetrations, for inlet and overboard discharge.

A NOTE ON THE SOCIAL ASPECTS OF GENERATORS

Many of the systems described in this chapter will function only with an assured source of electrical power. In port, that's not usually much of a problem, but while underway or—especially—at anchor, an internal-combustion engine of one sort or another must remain running.

The solicitous good neighbor who would never think of running a power lawn mower early on a Sunday morning too often becomes the insensitive boat owner disturbing the quiet calm of an otherwise peaceful anchorage. Remember to be considerate.

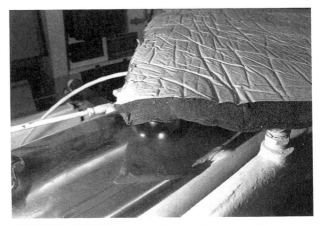

SOUNDPROOFING—consisting of layers of foam and lead sheet with a cleanable vinyl surface—can do much to reduce crew fatigue during long engine passages and can help keep the peace in quiet harbors. (Available from Soundown, Inc., of Beverly, Massachusetts)

CHAPTER FOUR

Marine Electricity

THE ELECTRICAL SYSTEM

Most of us take electricity for granted. We use it daily in our homes and automobiles, have questions only when a fuse blows or a run-down battery fails to start the car, and, once the problem has been fixed, go on about our lives. Should the problem arise again, we just call an electrician or a tow truck.

But what are your chances of finding a qualified serviceman while anchored in that secluded cove you favor for romantic weekends? Probably nil. Thus, *your* need for electrical knowledge is greater than that of most others, and you need it in three broad categories: (1) understanding and meeting your boat's electrical requirements; (2) maintaining the system in good working order; and (3) troubleshooting the system to identify—and repair—the sort of problems that might either put your boat in danger or prevent you from getting it back home after that weekend outing.

In this chapter, we examine the elements of the electrical system. Maintenance is covered in chapter 10 and troubleshooting in chapter 19.

THE SOURCE

Insofar as most boating applications are concerned, electricity is generated through one of two processes: chemical (as in a storage battery) or magnetic (as in a generator or alternator). For most of us, the primary source of electricity will be a storage battery (or, preferably, several storage batteries). A detailed discussion of the construction and operation of a marine storage battery appears in appendix III.

Other sources of DC power include engine-mounted alternators and generators, auxiliary units that produce 12V DC power from the wind

CLEARLY IDENTIFIED WIRING. The interior of this box may look intimidating, but each wire is carefully led and marked to indicate its use and proper connection. Note the special installation of the masthead stobe alarm as well as a small fuse panel for the wheelhouse panel. All wiring in the engine space has been collected in this box for ease of tracing and troubleshooting.

Useful Electrical Calculation Information

DEFINITIONS

Volts — A measurement of electrical *force,* the equivalent to water pressure in a plumbing system.

Amperes — A measurement of rate of electrical flow or current, equivalent to the rate of water flow in a pipe.

Resistance — Electrical *friction.* The opposition to current flow caused by wire size, switches, and other electrical components. Expressed in *ohms.*

Load — The use, consumption, or drain of electrical power.

Wattage — A measurement of electrical power using current (amps) and "pressure" (volts) as factors.

Ohms Law — Fundamental relationships between electrical forces (see formulas below).

CALCULATIONS

Ohms Law — To solve for volts:
E (volts) $= I$ (amps) $\times R$ (resistance/ohms)
To solve for current (amps):
I (amps) $= E$ (volts) $\div R$ (resistance in ohms)
To solve for resistance (ohms):
R (ohms) $= E$ (volts) $\div I$ (amps)

To determine wattage from amperage: W (watts) $= I \times E$ (amps) $\times$ (system voltage)

A GOOD BATTERY BOX. This box is made from marine plywood overlaid with a fiberglass liner to make it acid-proof. Note the ventilation slit at the rear. The batteries are firmly chocked. The battery on the right has hydrocaps installed to capture battery fluid vented in charging and return it to the cells as useful electrolyte. The hinged top, made from acid-proof counter material, doubles as a work surface.

or water, and solar panels that convert the sun's energy into a small but useful amount of electric current.

Shore-type 120V AC power can be produced by an auxiliary generator (which is expensive and not well suited to smaller boats), by an engine-mounted, belt-driven unit, and by a power inverter, which turns 12V DC into 120V AC at relatively low output. (Shore power is discussed later in this chapter.)

BATTERY LOCATION AND INSTALLATION

Batteries should be installed near the engine starter, providing a short path for the major current flow, but, particularly with a gasoline engine, they are best installed in a separate compartment to minimize the chance of explosion from a stray spark.

The batteries should be low in the hull (to enhance stability) but not so low that they might

Electricity: Some Basic Definitions

Electricity can be described as the movement of electrons along a conductor. There are two basic types—direct current (DC) and alternating current (AC)—and widely different levels of power: A flashlight battery may deliver 1.5V, our homes operate on 110–120 V, and industrial power (including that found in many marinas) may be 220–240V or higher. Table 4-3 provides information on electrical consumption for various types of marine equipment.

For easy visualization, think of electricity in terms of a system for moving water around a series of pipes. It starts with a reservoir or storage tank (the battery), out of which flow is controlled by a valve (the master switch). The water flows through pipes (wires) under some pressure (voltage) at a certain rate (amperage). The diameter of the pipe may impose resistance to the flow (ohms). Other valves (switches) direct the flow through the system, to the point where the water is available for use (equipment). The level in the storage tank may be replenished by a pump (alternator or battery charger).

The flow eventually reaches a point where it may be put to work (driving a water wheel, for example). The rate of doing work or expending energy (power) is measured in watts: Watts equals volts times amps. This knowledge is most useful in determining the current requirements of a piece of equipment rated in watts, because, by extension, watts (as noted on the equipment data plate) divided by volts (the known level of the system) equals amps.

There also is an interrelation among pressure, flow, and resistance—voltage, amperage, and ohms—which was first described in 1826 by high school teacher George Ohm: "Electric current is directly proportional to voltage and inversely proportional to resistance." In other words, more pressure *(volts)* means more flow *(amps)*, but higher resistance *(ohms)* reduces the flow. As a practical matter, using too small a wire for the required service will result in too little current at the end of the circuit. One result: Motors will run slowly and may overheat. Higher resistance also produces heat in the wire—a potential fire hazard.

Table 4-3.

73

Estimated Electrical Consumption Data
for Various Types of Marine Equipment

The following data is based on averaged estimates and various manufacturers' data. Actual consumption (in amps and watts) will vary according to equipment, installation, length of wire run, and age. Also, since heat has an effect on equipment consumption, more solid- *state equipment will consume less. This data is useful in planning equipment purchases and installations, choosing electrical conductors, and suitably sizing battery installations.*

Equipment	Voltage	Amperage	Wattage
Lighting			
Running light	12 DC	1.0	
Spreader light	12 DC	2.5	30
Searchlight	12 DC	8.0	100
Interior	12 DC	2.5	30
Interior	120 DC	.25	100
Interior	120 DC	.2	30
Equipment			
Galley blower	12 DC	2.0	25
Engine blower	12 DC	2.0	25
Windshield wiper	12 DC	2.0	25
Electric horn	12 DC	2.0	25
Bilge pump	12 DC	7.0	100
Engine alarm	12 DC	(negligible)	
Refrigerator	12 DC	6.0	80
Head	12 DC	18.0	200
Treatment unit	12 DC	20.0	240
Fire system	12 DC	(negligible)	
Battery charger*	120 AC (in)	9.0	
Isolation transformer		no current draw	
Battery isolator		no current draw	
Outlets			
Outlet	12 DC	20.0 max	
Outlet	120 AC	15.0 max	
Instruments			
Depth finder	12 DC	.25	
CB radio	12 DC	2.00	
VHF radio	12 DC	4.00	(transmit mode)
Radar	12 DC	4.00	
Loran	12 DC	2.00	
Alarm system	12 DC	(negligible)	
Gauges and Monitors			
Ammeter	12 DC (shunt)		
Ammeter	120 AC (coil)		
Charge indicator	12 DC	Gauge and monitor power consumption	
Voltmeter	12 DC	is negligible. Use 1 amp.	
Shore power gauge	120 AC		
Ground fault indicator	12 DC		
Pump indicator	12 DC		

*A battery charger (Constavolt or Newmar type) will draw 8 to 9 amps of AC power and put out 20 amps of charging and service power (DC). This is a rectifier type.

become submerged during flooding. And any battery compartment should be easily accessible (to encourage routine maintenance) and well ventilated (to avoid explosive concentrations of hydrogen and oxygen—see chapter 10).

Because spilled acid—even a few drops—will damage other equipment or the hull, the batteries should be contained in an acid-resistant box made of plastic or fiberglass-lined wood. The box must be strong enough to support the batteries without cracking, and it (and the batteries) must be attached firmly to the boat; don't count on gravity to keep it all in place. One quick roll could send a hundred pounds of battery smashing toward the bilges, straining at the connections and spilling acid.

The box should have a lid to shield the batteries from dropped tools or other anomalies. A big wrench hitting both terminals will elicit a magnificent and potentially hazardous spark. All

metal fuel lines or tanks within 12 inches of a mounted battery must be protected from any accidental contact that might occur while the battery is being horsed in or out of position.

Each battery has two lead terminal posts. The one of larger diameter is the positive terminal, marked with a "+" sign. The one of smaller-diameter is the negative terminal, marked with a "−" sign. The size difference prevents you from installing the battery backward; the connector for the negative terminal cannot easily be forced onto the positive terminal post. Battery power from the positive terminal will be fed directly to the main power switch (usually called the battery selector switch, described below). The negative terminal will be connected directly to the main system ground point—usually the engine block.

DISTRIBUTION

Switches control the flow of current; circuit breakers or fuses protect against current overloads and short circuits; and control panels provide a convenient mounting place for both.

SWITCHES

The main DC power switch is the master battery switch, with settings for off, battery 1, battery 2, and both (in multiple-battery installations). That's straightforward enough, but these switches come in two basic styles, and a misunderstanding of them could lead to the destruction of your alternator.

Like a fussy lady all dressed up with no place to go, an alternator may become dangerously frustrated when a master switch is turned off while the engine is running. One type of master switch has a feature that protects the alternator in such a case—by disconnecting the field current within the alternator. The other type—without this feature—should carry a warning label: STOP ENGINE BEFORE SWITCHING OFF.

Switches for multiple-battery banks should be of the "make-before-break" type, which maintain a constant battery connection during switching.

BATTERY SWITCHES set up in a variety of ways. The lower two switches direct the sources of charge (either the boat's engine or the generator/shore power 110V AC source of 12V power) to the various battery banks. The upper switches select which bank will be put on line for main engine start service and which bank will provide the boat's service supply for appliances and other uses. Note the warning to prevent cross-linking. Even without the clear labels, the neatly racked wiring gives a clear view of the switching plan. Note also the engineroom–mounted inclinometer, used for proper ballasting of the boat.

The connection to the next battery is "made" before the connection to the last battery is "broken," thus protecting the alternator.

The preferable master switch, obviously, is one that is both "make-before-break" and field-disconnecting when switched to off. Considering that well-meaning guests and helpful children may operate the switch at what might be the wrong time for the wrong switch—you should spend a few bucks to replace it if necessary.

One other point: Master switches come in several basic sizes, rated (in amps) for "continuous duty" and "momentary load." The proper size will be the one with a momentary rating higher than the engine cold cranking requirement.

Other switches may be toggles, or the "punch-on, punch-off" type mounted integral with some circuit breakers. All switches must be nonsparking and rated for marine use.

Two decades ago, there were plenty of open knife-type switches installed on older boats. They seemed ideal—contact was definite and did not work loose under vibration, and corrosion was visible and cleaned away easily. Unfortunately, the knife-type switch was prone to arc when thrown from closed to open, and the ensuing spark could be spectacular. It also proved to be deadly in an explosive concentration of gasoline or propane fumes. It's not too likely that you'll come across a knife-switch today, since all of them should have been replaced long ago, but you'll see them mentioned in older boating books urging that replacement.

OVERLOAD PROTECTION

Circuit breakers and fuses are automatic switches that protect your equipment from overloads and your boat from an electrical fire by breaking the circuit before a critical point is reached. A fuse destroys itself; a circuit breaker pops open. The most common cause for a blown fuse or a popped breaker is an overloaded circuit—too much electrical gear running at the same time. The best solution is to limit the total possible load on each circuit first by calculating

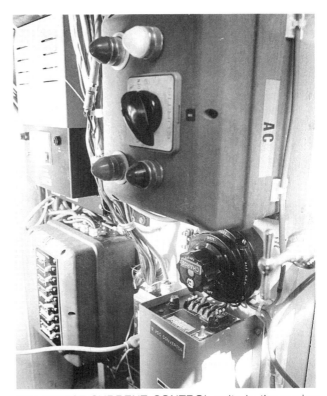

12V DIRECT-CURRENT CONTROL units in the engine spaces. The box at upper right contains a shore-power/generator selector switch with indicator lights. Below that is a battery selector switch that controls charging power as it flows to two different 12V battery banks. Below that switch is a power converter that switches 110V AC to 12V direct current for battery charging. The box at lower left contains the circuit breakers used to protect 12V direct-current circuits. The box in the upper left background converts either shore power or generator 110V AC to 32V for the boat's heavier main-engine batteries.

the power requirements of each element and then by ensuring that no more than 10 or 20 amps (or whatever the rated load for the circuit) are assigned to that circuit.

If the circuit is breaking because of faulty equipment or wiring, you will need to isolate and correct the problem before trying to operate the offending equipment. If, out of desperation, you try to install a higher-rated fuse, you may destroy

Electrical Load Factors (use) for 12-Volt
Direct Current Marine Equipment
(Wattage and Amperage also shown)

Item	Load Factor	Watts (Approx)	Amperes (Approx)	Notes
Lighting				
Cabin (small)	40%	25	2.0	Actual much lower
Cabin (large)	40%	60	5.0	
Spreader	20%	40	3.0	Use much lower
Engine space	10%	25	2.0	
Running & navigation	100%	negligible	1.0	Entire group
Searchlight (100,000 candlepower)	20%	100	8.3	actual use is
Searchlight (250,000 candlepower)	20%	250	20.0	intermittent
Equipment				
Engine gauges	100%	negligible	1.0	1 amp for calculation
Windshield wiper	10%	40	3.0	
Electric horn	10%	60	5.0	
Galley blower	20%	40	3.3	
Engine-room blower	100%	25	2.0	
Bilge pump	20%	85	7.0	
Oil-fired cabin heater	100%	100	8.3	
Refrigerator (12V DC or 12V AC)	100%	80	6.0	
Heads	10%	200	18.0	
Electric windlass	10%	200	15.0	Use calculated at
Pressure water pump	25%	84	7.0	surge power
Appliance Outlets				
Wheelhouse	10%	240	20.0	
Galley	10%	240	20.0	
Deck	10%	240	20.0	
Instruments and Navigation Gear				
Depthfinders (flasher type)	100%	3	.25	
Depthfinders (recording strip type)	100%	6	.50	
Direction finders (portable)	100%	½	.04	
Direction finders (fixed)	100%	1	.08	
Automatic pilots (small yacht type*)	100%	40 (avg)	3.30	Calculated at surge
Radar (commercial type)	100%	240	20.00	
Radar (yacht type)	100%	50	4.00	
Sonar	100%	120	10.00	
Radio (receiver only)	100%	negligible		
Radio transceiver (VHF)	100%	25	2.00	
Radio, single-sideband	100%	100	8.30	
Weather facsimile machine	100%	120	10.00	
Speed logs	100%	3	.25	
Loran C	100%	25	2.00	
Omega	100%	50	4.00	
Decca	100%	50	4.00	

*Older types of autopilots, such as earlier makes of Sperry and Bendix electrohydraulic types, tend to draw substantially more current (tubes in their amplifiers, etc). Five amperes is a normal steering consumption, with up to 10 to 12 amps going at surge points used in more radical course corrections, extreme rudder angles at higher speeds, or in difficult autopilot environments such as heavy following seas.

HEAVY-DUTY INDUSTRIAL-GRADE CIRCUIT BREAKERS provide overcurrent protection to the main boat circuits. Note the protective fiberglass electrical box, as well as the internally mounted solenoids and negative bus bar contained in the box.

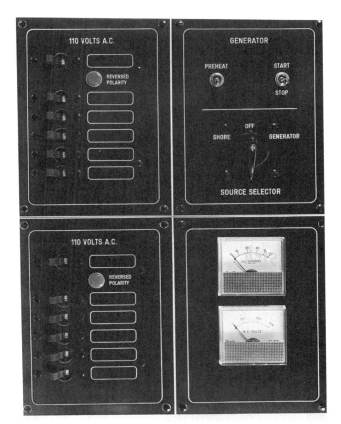

Engine Starting Amperages

(Average for yacht-size power plants, minimum of four cylinders)

DIESEL: 300 to 600 amps, momentary
GASOLINE: 100 to 300 amps, momentary
(Repeated heavy cranking or faults in starter cables and switches will result in extremely heavy battery-discharge rates.)

the equipment it was meant to protect. Circuit breakers protect you from that mistake—the "trip-free" type used on boats cannot be reclosed until the current overload has been removed.

A boat equipped with circuit breakers will most likely also have some fuses installed in-line between the control panel and some equipment, or inside some equipment (such as a Loran unit). As always, know your equipment, know what "hidden" fuses are present, and have appropriate spares on hand.

CONTROL PANELS

Control panels provide safe and convenient mounting for switches, circuit breakers, and gauges to monitor the flow of current and the state of the battery charge. Panels should be mounted in a convenient location, at eye level, and *not* on a bulkhead that encloses a fuel or engine compartment. In addition, they must be well protected from rain or spray.

MARINE ELECTRICAL PANEL COMBINATION. Upper left includes the circuit breakers and usage lights for the 110V AC service. Note the shore-power polarity-reversal warning light. Upper right panel is an onboard Generator 'start/stop panel with preheater switch—combined with a shore-power/generator selector switch. One important feature of all of these panels is the usage indicator lights. Lower right panel has the AC amperes (usage) and a gauge monitoring AC voltage. An additional useful gauge would be a Herzmeter showing the frequency of the alternating current. This is an important measurement, since a great variation in cycles between the extremes of the alternating current can cause malfunction or damage in AC-powered equipment. The U.S. standard is 60 cycles. The lower left panel contains additional 110V AC circuit breakers.

WIRING

Electrical current is distributed to the various working elements of the system through a network of wires. That may seem pretty obvious, but the nature of that network is not arbitrary.

The size of the wire is directly proportional to the amount of current it may carry safely. As already noted, resistance produces heat—usefully in an electric stove, not so usefully when an overheated wire starts a fire. Resistance depends on three factors: (1) the type of material of which the wire is made (copper or aluminum, for example), (2) the thickness of the wire, and (3) the length of the wire. All things considered, copper is better than almost anything for boat wiring and therefore is about the only material used; shorter is better and thicker is better. The wire thickness is described by the American Wire Gauge (AWG) number: the lower the number, the heavier the wire. Wire used aboard boats must be *multistranded*, not the single-stranded type used in houses ashore. Single-stranded wire too easily corrodes and breaks.

Table 4-1 lists the sizes of wire, by AWG number, required to keep voltage drop within an acceptable limit of 3 percent over the noted length of wire run. Because the current travels a round-trip route—to the electrical accessory and back to the power source—the entire route must be measured.

NAVIGATION AREA in a Hinckley 51 provides a separate and more-than-equal area for precision navigation, chart stowage, continuous reading of electronic navigation gear, monitoring of electrical system, and a lighted area away from sleeping and cockpit spaces. (Hinckley)

Table 4-1.
Wire Sizes for 3 Percent Drop in Voltage

Current (Amps)	Length (Feet) Between Power Source and Accessory, and Return									
	10	20	30	40	50	60	70	80	90	100
5	18	14	12	10	10	10	8	8	8	6
10	14	10	10	8	6	6	6	6	4	4
15	12	10	8	6	6	6	4	4	2	2
20	10	8	6	6	4	4	2	2	2	2
25	10	6	6	4	4	2	2	2	1	1
30	10	6	4	4	2	2	1	1	0	0

Connections must be absolute—that is, tight and likely to remain so. Since boats are almost always moving up, down, and sideways, and exist in a humid and corrosive atmosphere, a wire wrapped around a screw or bolted on a post is not acceptable. Screws can work loose; nuts vibrate slowly until they eventually back off from the post.

All connections must be made with an electrical wiring terminal. These come in several styles: ring, hook, captive spade, and friction. A ring terminal is the most secure—it could pop off only if a nut or screw came completely free. A hook terminal *may* remain in place; a spade will likely drop off when the connection is only slightly loosened (although the upward tilt of the ends will maintain some contact for some period of time). Some boatbuilders use hook and spade terminals to speed up installation, but they have no place on a well-built boat. Friction terminals—which are like a miniature plug-and-socket—have been approved for marine use provided that they can withstand a six-pound lateral pull.

The terminals are married to the end of the wire with a crimping tool, which squeezes the terminal shank against the wire with great pressure. A properly crimped terminal may be adequate, but well-organized marine electricians also seal the connection with solder.

Color Coding of electrical wiring provides an immediate guide for tracing circuits—provided that the wiring has been installed with scrupulous consistency. At the very least, all wires carrying current to an accessory should be one color, the return wires another color. The American Boat and Yacht Council (ABYC) coding recommendations call for red wiring for positive main-current circuits; white or black (but not both) for the return, negative main line; and green for the bonding circuits.

MATERIALS FOR BOAT WIRING. Clockwise from center top: multistrand cabling with oil-resistant rubber coating; hose clamps for non-current–carrying connections (such as in the bonding or ground systems); adhesive-backed wire markers; captivated ring terminals; vinyl electrical tape; heavy-duty battery and bonding terminal connectors; a copper bus mounted on insulated bakelite material; rubber-cushioned wire holders; shrink tubing; and base plates for adjustable plastic wire straps.

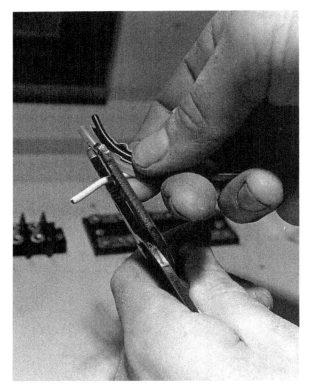

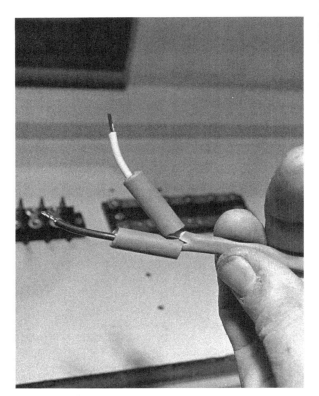

MAKING A SAFE ELECTRICAL CONNECTION, Step 1. Using a crimping/stripping tool, cut and peel back the outer protective coat on the wire.

MAKING A SAFE ELECTRICAL CONNECTION, Step 2. Slide heat shrink tubing over the wire body.

MAKING A SAFE ELECTRICAL CONNECTION, Step 3. Double-crimp a proper-sized terminal connector. Be sure these connectors are the circular, fully captivated type. Spade-type or screw-type fittings are not appropriate for marine service. Note that the connector can also be soldered for further strength.

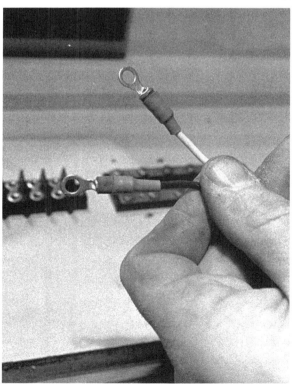

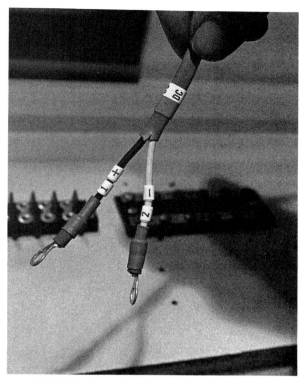

MAKING A SAFE ELECTRICAL CONNECTION, Step 4. Shrink the tubing using a high-temperature heat gun.

MAKING A SAFE ELECTRICAL CONNECTION, Step 5. Allow the shrunken tubing to cool.

MAKING A SAFE ELECTRICAL CONNECTION, Step 6. Place clear labels on the connector and wire matched to voltage and use. These labels include a number code matched to the electrical terminal strip, a positive and negative indicator, and a label indicating that the wire provides 12V direct current.

BASIC DIRECT-CURRENT ELECTRICAL SYSTEM.

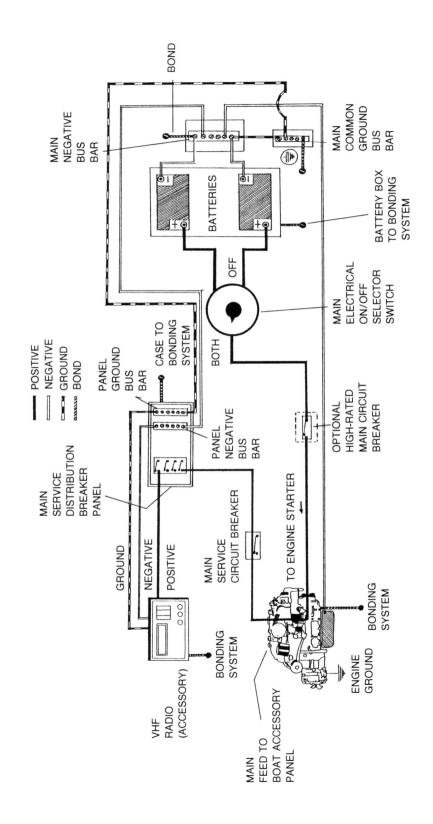

Specific color coding is recommended for certain circuits, as noted in Table 4-2, but since few marine supply stores keep such a wide range of colors in stock, the chances are great that your boat is not in compliance with this standard—even if it may have started out that way. As a substitute for colored insulation, each wire should be marked or tagged at several points.

And—to help trace any wire, whether color-coded, marked, or not—create an accurate scale diagram of your electrical system for your Owner's Notebook (see chapter 10).

Table 4-2.
Required Marine Wiring Color Code for DC Systems under 50V

Color	Use	Color	Use
Green	Ground or bond	Orange	Ammeter to alternator or generator output and accessory fuses or switches; distribution panel to accessory switch
White or Black	Return, negative main (either color may be used but must be used exclusively throughout the system)	Purple	Ignition switch to coil and electrical instruments; distribution panel to electrical instruments
Red	Positive main	Dark Blue	Fuse or switch to cabin and instrument lights
Yellow with red stripe	Starting switch to solenoid	Light Blue	Oil-pressure sender to gauge
Yellow	Generator or alternator field to regulator field terminal	Tan	Water-temperature sender to gauge
Dark Gray	Fuse or switch to navigation lights; tachometer sender to gauge	Pink	Fuel-gauge sender to gauge
Brown	Generator armature to regulator; generator terminal/alternator auxiliary terminal to light to regulator; fuse or switch to pumps		

SHORE POWER

Shore power—which usually comes aboard your boat as 110/120 or 220/240V AC (subsequently split into two 110/120V AC circuits)—is useful but potentially lethal to you and your boat. Failure to color-code the 12V system will lead to later frustration when you are trying to isolate a faulty wire or component—but you can live with frustration. Failure to observe the standard codes for 120V AC circuits can result in greatly increased shock hazards—with which you (or a visiting repairman) may not be able to live. The black wire should always be the hot, current-carrying line; the white wire, always the neutral ground return;

the green wire, always the non-current-carrying line, which is grounded to the metal cabinet or chassis of the accessory.

Do not assume that your circuits are properly wired; not everyone who has worked on your boat will have been a licensed electrician, and if your boat is old enough, the system may have been installed before the standards were established. Verify for yourself that the black wire at the incoming shore-power connection does in fact match up, in the connection, with the black "hot" wire coming aboard from the pier. Verify that the runs within your boat are consistent.

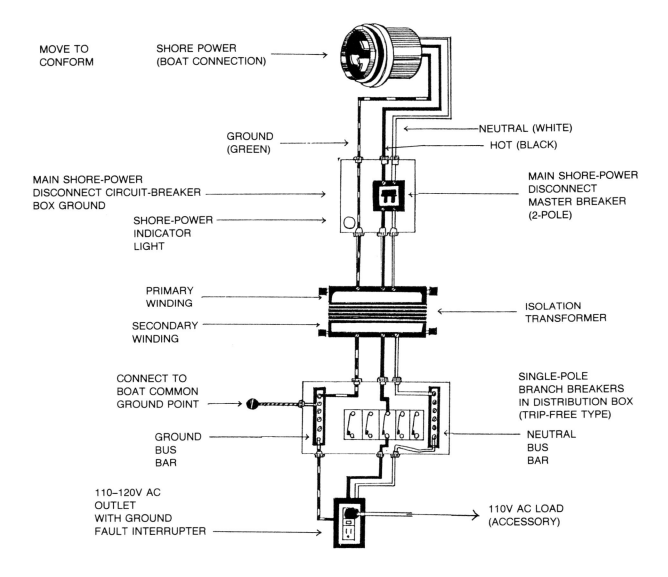

MOVE TO
CONFORM

SHORE POWER
(BOAT CONNECTION)

GROUND
(GREEN)

NEUTRAL (WHITE)

HOT (BLACK)

MAIN SHORE-POWER
DISCONNECT CIRCUIT-BREAKER
BOX GROUND

MAIN SHORE-POWER
DISCONNECT
MASTER BREAKER
(2-POLE)

SHORE-POWER
INDICATOR
LIGHT

PRIMARY
WINDING

ISOLATION
TRANSFORMER

SECONDARY
WINDING

CONNECT TO
BOAT COMMON
GROUND POINT

SINGLE-POLE
BRANCH BREAKERS
IN DISTRIBUTION BOX
(TRIP-FREE TYPE)

GROUND
BUS
BAR

NEUTRAL
BUS
BAR

110–120V AC
OUTLET
WITH GROUND
FAULT INTERRUPTER

110V AC LOAD
(ACCESSORY)

A SHORE-POWER INSTALLATION. This schematic drawing shows the full run for 110V alternating current incorporating an isolation transformer to guard against reversed potential, stray power breaks in the marina, and electrical corrosion on board. Note that the main breakers are located on board but operate in the line before the isolation transformer.

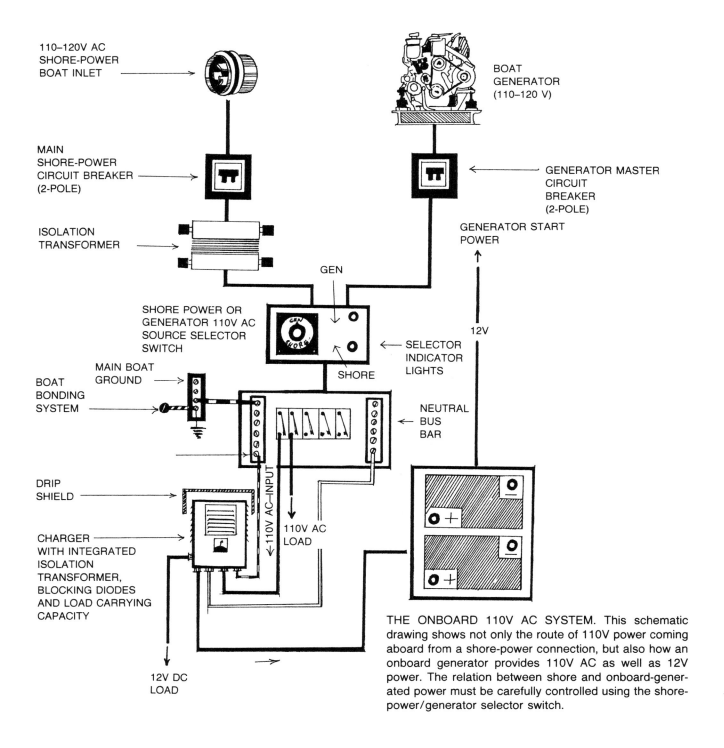

110–120V AC
SHORE-POWER
BOAT INLET

BOAT
GENERATOR
(110–120 V)

MAIN
SHORE-POWER
CIRCUIT BREAKER
(2-POLE)

GENERATOR MASTER
CIRCUIT
BREAKER
(2-POLE)

ISOLATION
TRANSFORMER

GENERATOR START
POWER

GEN

SHORE POWER OR
GENERATOR 110V AC
SOURCE SELECTOR
SWITCH

12V

SELECTOR
INDICATOR
LIGHTS

SHORE

MAIN BOAT
GROUND

BOAT
BONDING
SYSTEM

NEUTRAL
BUS
BAR

DRIP
SHIELD

110V AC-INPUT

110V AC
LOAD

CHARGER
WITH INTEGRATED
ISOLATION
TRANSFORMER,
BLOCKING DIODES
AND LOAD CARRYING
CAPACITY

12V DC
LOAD

THE ONBOARD 110V AC SYSTEM. This schematic
drawing shows not only the route of 110V power coming
aboard from a shore-power connection, but also how an
onboard generator provides 110V AC as well as 12V
power. The relation between shore and onboard-gener-
ated power must be carefully controlled using the shore-
power/generator selector switch.

Even if your boat is wired correctly, you must be prepared for the possibility that each new marina you visit may be providing power with reversed polarity.

Such is the nature of AC power that all of your 120V accessories and equipment will function just fine if the polarity is reversed (and it doesn't matter if the problem is with the marina or with your boat's own circuits). But two unpleasant results are likely to occur: (1) The potential for an electrical shock is increased if a casual worker assumes that black is hot and white is neutral, and (2) the electrolytic damage to underwater metal may be greatly accelerated—not just *your* underwater metal, but also that of other boats moored in your vicinity. And, of course, the reverse is true—an improperly wired boat nearby can cause damage to your boat.

If your boat's system is electrically isolated from the shore system by an isolation transformer, a polarity indicator would be superfluous. However, this would not protect you from damage caused by improper wiring on other boats; that's when your underwater zincs pay for themselves.

If you have an installed auxiliary generator, your AC circuit must be wired for either/or operation—either the shipboard AC generator or shore power, but not both simultaneously.

Wires should be run clear of, or protected from, any potential rubbing or chafing from equipment, control cables, and bulkhead penetrations. Access to any energized parts of electrical equipment must be guarded by enclosures or covers that can be opened only with the use of a hand tool such as a screwdriver; this prevents inadvertent or casual poking around.

A ground fault circuit interrupter provides excellent protection against electrical shock, particularly in a damp environment. These units are becoming quite common in bathrooms and kitchens ashore, and they should be installed in every 120V AC outlet aboard your boat.

The variety of available shore power—single-phase 120V AC, single-phase 120/240V AC, three-phase 120/240V AC, and three-phase 120/208V AC, with power levels ranging from 20 to 50 amps—poses some problem for the cruising boat, and one not necessarily solved merely by carrying a variety of adapters and plugs. Some systems are not interchangeable; well-equipped marinas usually are able to match the power needs of most boats.

The American Boat and Yacht Council recommends posting a warning notice near the shore-power cable storage or connection point:

WARNING: DANGER OF SHOCK OR FIRE

1. Turn off the boat's shore-power switch before connecting or disconnecting shore cable.

2. Connect shore-power cable at the boat first, then ashore.

3. Turn on the shore-power switch; if the polarity warning lights (or sounds), turn off switch immediately and disconnect cable.

4. Disconnect shore-power cable at shore outlet first.

5. Close shore-power inlet cover tightly.

BONDING

In all boats with a permanently installed electrical system, all major pieces of machinery and equipment should be connected through a bonding system. Bonding provides an easy pathway for safely carrying away electric currents generated by electrolytic action, short circuits, or lightning strikes. In principle, all exposed, metallic, non-current-carrying parts of the boat and equipment are bonded together by a network of wires, passing any current through them to the engine negative terminal. In practice, this is accomplished first by running a main common bonding conductor fore-and aft through the bilges (but above bilgewater level) and connecting it to the engine. Then branch lines are run to the non-current-carrying frames or cabinets of each of the following:

- Auxiliary engines;
- Such electrical equipment as motors, pumps, control panels, electronic devices, metal-sheathed conduits;
- Fuel tanks and fuel-fill deck fittings.

Equipment mounted on the engine—such as generators and other electrical accessories—need not otherwise be connected to the bonding network.

The common bonding conductor may be an uninsulated copper or bronze strip at least $\frac{1}{32}$ and $\frac{1}{2}$ inch in size, or copper tubing, or insulated copper wire of at least AWG number 8. Copper braid should not be used as a common bonding conductor.

The wires that tie the equipment to the common bonding conductor should each be at least as large as the wire carrying current to the equipment; if insulated, they should be green in color.

Engines—in a multiengine installation—should be bonded together with a cable the same size as the starting-current cable.

Since propeller shafts may be electrically isolated from the engine by transmissions and couplings, they should be bonded through the use of a slip ring, which keeps contact without adding much drag. Rudderposts may be connected

110V AC CONTROLS for a 7.5 kilowatt onboard diesel generator. They include an engine-room control box with temperature, oil pressure, and amperage gauges, as well as a start/stop button and on/off light indicator. Battery switches at the left select which battery bank will be on line to start the generator and which bank will be brought on line to provide 12V DC power to the boat's accessories.

through a slip ring or a flexible strap of sufficient length to allow free and full movement of the rudder.

For protection from underwater electrolysis, see chapter 3; for protection from lightning, see chapter 8).

A WORD ON STANDARD VOLTAGE

DC voltage has been standardized at 12 volts, but "standard" voltage has varied widely over the years. We have owned older boats with functioning equipment powered by 6V, 12V, and 32V DC circuits (along with 110V and 220V AC)—an uneasy jumble of wires all on the same hull. New circuits have been laid alongside the old ones, with no thought given to labeling or color coding;

old circuits have been adapted to new equipment (and new voltages), with no thought given to wire size; 6V, 8V, and 12V batteries of uncertain vintage lie side by side, deteriorating differentially to provide a recurring money trap.

When one battery gives up, do you buy a new one of the same voltage, perpetuating the problem, or do you replace the equipment it serves?

Or, conversely, when a 32V winch motor burns out just after you have replaced the 32V bank (of four 8V batteries), do you replace the motor? For that matter, can you find a 32V motor?

With the full understanding that this may pose some difficult choices, we suggest you treat this as an engineering challenge: Rewire and reequip as necessary to get everything in synchronization.

CHAPTER FIVE

The Boat Buyer's Checklist

THE ORGANIZED APPROACH TO BOAT SELECTION

As you narrow your selection to a particular boat, you need to take a hard look before you make a deposit and certainly before you go to the next step—hiring a professional surveyor.

In fact, a good surveyor will insist that you go over the boat with some care before committing to his services.

The Boat Buyer's Checklist is a distillation of the previous chapters of this book—with additional comments and suggestions. In most instances, it will not dictate absolutes but will pose some choices; if you choose a boat lacking a suggested feature (say, engine guards), at least you will know what you are dealing with.

OVERALL CONSIDERATIONS

• Does the boat suit you? Is it of the right type and size for your intended use? Given your level of experience, will you be able to handle the boat? Given your level of financial resources, will you be able to maintain the boat in a safe, seaworthy condition?

• Has the boat been designed and built by well-known and well-regarded people? This is not to imply that a one-off custom boat by a first-time builder will not be acceptable (it may even be superior), but—when the time comes to sell the boat, how will it be regarded by potential buyers?

HULL

☑ Can all parts of the hull's interior be reached for inspection in the event of grounding or a collision?

☑ Is the hull-to-deck joint solidly connected, without signs of stress? Are bulkheads well fastened to the hull and firmly in place? Is there any evidence that a bulkhead has shifted out of position?

☑ If possible, examine the keelbolts for evidence of leaking or corrosion.

☑ In the event of a person overboard, will you be able easily to get him or her back aboard? Is there an adequate boarding ladder (reaching at least two rungs below the surface)?

☑ On smaller boats (particularly below 26 feet), check for flotation. Make sure that capacity label-plates and engine size are in accordance with federal standards.

☑ Check for posted limitations on safe maneuvering speed.

☑ Check the general condition and finish for signs of damage:

Fiberglass The hull should be smooth, with no bumps, hollows, or wavy surfaces. Look for "hard spots" where bulkheads can be "read through" the surface. Check the surface gelcoat for blisters, spiderweb crazing, and other stress marks, particularly around chainplates and other points of heavy strain. The structure should be rigid, and not responsive to hand pressure.

Wood Seams should run clean, without signs of patching; fastenings should not show at all (look for rust streaks, popped covering plugs). Look for signs of rot: peeling paint, dark wet wood, dark stains. With a knife, probe for softness, particularly at the top of the stem and where the planks joint into the stem; at any junction point between cabin or hatch coamings and the deck; along the deck edge; in corners of wood paneling in the accommodation spaces; at the bottom of window frames; along the sides of the transom; around and under scupper and bilge-pump discharges.

Metal Steel and aluminum hulls pose difficulties for untrained eyes. At the least, on initial inspection, look for signs of rust or corrosion—especially in the bilge, where flaking steel or deteriorated aluminum might be noticed most easily.

☑ Check the bilges for cleanliness and water. Most boats usually will have some water in the bilges—even with a leak-free fiberglass hull, water may seep in around the propeller shaft, or come in from above as rain and spray. The quality of the water is more important than the quantity (assuming that the automatic bilge pump is doing its job). Stagnant water may smell bad but

signifies a tight hull. Clear, fresh-looking water has arrived more recently, perhaps from a rainstorm or (more likely) from a steady leak somewhere. The water remains fresh because it's constantly being replaced as the electric bilge pump cycles on and off. Clear, fresh-looking water that seems to be flowing along the bilges is the sign of a serious problem that must soon be identified and solved.

DECK

☑ Walk the deck. Can you get from stern to bow quickly and safely? If you were forced to inch along the side of the cabin, would footing and handholds be adequate? If the logical route is below, through the cabin—try it.

☑ When walking the deck, think "night" and think "heavy weather." Can you move along the walkways without stubbing your toe or bumping your head on illogically placed equipment? Are there enough objects to hold onto, and does the arrangement of rails and lifelines give you a feeling of security?

☑ For a sailboat, imagine yourself under sail in a fresh breeze, well heeled over, and work through the different sailhandling routines. Is there adequate free space in which to stuff a jib into a sail bag?

☑ For a sportfisherman, think through the process of working a big fish. Can you keep all lines clear—or clear them out of the way quickly? Is there room for several crew members to help bring the fish aboard? Is the fighting chair sturdy and well mounted?

☑ Are the lifelines rigged properly? The lines should be stainless steel; the top line should be high enough to hit you above the knee, with a second line halfway to the deck. The stanchions must be securely fastened, through-bolted, or at least mounted with a brace against the toerail.

☑ Are the lifelines and stanchions free of corrosion? Are there any signs of rot at the base or from below (you may want to remove the cabin header for a close look)?

☑ The deck surface must be nonskid in all walkways and working areas; if the nonskid pattern is molded into fiberglass, has it worn down too much to be of value? If it is painted on or glued down, is it still effective? Are treads lifting?

☑ Is the foredeck a safe place, with good footing and adequate bowrails? When handling the anchor, will you be able to stand or must you sit on deck?

☑ How about topside storage: Is it convenient and does it appear adequate for spare anchors, lines, other equipment? Are all cockpit lockers fitted with snug lids and fastened with a sturdy latch to keep them from being opened by a wave?

☑ Check visibility from the helm—from each helm. Can you see over the bow, both port and starboard?

☑ Are engine controls convenient and logically grouped? Can you start and stop the engine and shut off fuel flow from each station?

☑ Check mooring cleats (four to a side) and the trailering or towing ring for proper mounting; they should be bedded and also through-bolted with backing blocks or plates.

☑ On a sailboat, work each winch. Can you take a line to the winch easily? Can you swing the handle through a full circle without hitting an obstruction? Is there adequate footing to permit a good level of muscle power? Is there a safe place to put the winch handle when it is not in use?

☑ Sit down in every crew seat or seating area. Check the back support (often lacking on sailboats). Check for foot support—for example, when sailing well heeled over, will crew members slide off the seat and onto the deck or can they brace themselves with their legs against the opposite seat?

ACCOMMODATION

☑ Check for escape routes. Walk to the forward cabin; imagine a raging fire in the engine compartment or the galley. How will you get back on deck? If your answer is a logical, "through the forward hatch," try it.

☑ How about general room to move about? How is the headroom for you or any taller members of your family? Does the cabin layout allow you to move quickly from one end to the other without having to fold up the dining table?

☑ Can the galley be used safely when the boat is underway? The stove should be on gimbals and be fitted with fiddle rails (as should countertops and dining tables). Are there adequate handholds for the cook, and/or a safety harness? Where is the fire extinguisher mounted? Not, we trust, behind the stove. Stand in the galley area, imagine a flare-up on the stove, and reach for the fire extinguisher.

☑ Check the installation of tanks, lines, and fittings for the galley fuel system. LPG tanks must be mounted outside of the accommodation and be equipped with open drains to the exterior of the hull. There should be shutoff valves at the tank and near the stove.

☑ Is the interior free of topside leaks? Look for telltale signs: patterns of streaking along the bulkheads; dark, soft spots in the corners of cabinets; water stains along the main hull stringers, where water may have puddled and then dried. Lift up the bunk cushions and examine the undersides of the covers for the stains and mildew sure to be there if they have had repeated soakings in puddles of water. (For information on the prevention and correction of leaks, see chapter 10.)

☑ Has safety glass or plastic, as appropriate, been used in all windows, portholes, and mirrors?

☑ Is ventilation adequate? Give the boat the "sniff test." Can ventilators be sealed off, and windows protected, in heavy weather?

☑ Check the main companionway leading below for a good sill and secure closure (such as a sturdy hatch or sliding boards) to block flooding from overtaking waves in a storm.

☑ Check out the bunks for size and comfort; can they be fitted with leecloths or boards for offshore operations?

☑ Will the head be adequate to your needs? Is it well equipped with grabrails or other handholds? Is the toilet itself securely fastened down, with hoses in good condition and double clamped? Does it comply with legal requirements for holding tanks or treatment systems? If it has an overboard discharge, can it be closed when required? Is the head intake located near the discharge, or is it properly separated (intake forward or, even better, forward *and* on the other side of the keel)? If the head is below the waterline, is the discharge fitted with an antisiphon loop?

☑ Is there a gray-water sump to keep shower, sink, and galley waste out of the bilges? Is there an in-line filter to keep hair and debris from jamming the pump?

☑ Are water tanks fastened securely and fitted with clean-out ports?

☑ Look over all crew-comfort items with safety in mind: nonflammable or fire-retardant sheathing, upholstery, and accessories; nonskid carpeting.

ENGINE ROOM

☑ Is the engine accessible from all sides and above, or can you work comfortably only on one side?

☑ Is there a place to stand or sit while working on the engine, or do you have to hang down from above?

☑ Will the engine room be a safe or a hazardous place to work? Are there, for example, belt guards to keep hands, hair, and clothing from being grabbed and mangled?

☑ Will the engine room be an efficient place to work? Are there adequate lighting, electrical power, a place for the tool chest, and a place to lay out tools and spare parts? Is there a place to spread out your engine manual or a wiring diagram?

☑ What about protection from the weather? Some "engine rooms" are accessible only through hatches in the afterdeck—above which there is no overhead canopy or awning. Imagine trying to solve an electrical problem in a downpour.

☑ Will routine maintenance actions be easy, or will you postpone them too easily because of awkward access? To answer this, work through a simple series of tasks: Check the oil, the level of transmission fluid, the raw-water filter, the coolant level, the fuel filters.

☑ Are the engine spaces fitted with an automatic fire-extinguishing system? At the least, are they fitted with an access port for use with a portable extinguisher?

ENGINE

☑ Ask to see equipment manuals and maintenance logs; their absence may be an indication of a lack of proper care.

☑ For a gasoline engine installation, is the carburetor an approved type and equipped with a backfire flame arrester? Are the bilge blowers adequate and in good working condition?

☑ Check the engine mounting—is it solid? Are the rubber vibration-dampers in place and undamaged?

☑ Look over the entire engine for signs of leaking fuel or oil. Under each engine should be a full-length drip pan that is clean (and easy *to* clean) and marked with only an occasional spot of oil. Signs of excessive leaking of oil or transmission fluids are indications of trouble.

☑ Take a sample of engine oil for laboratory analysis.

☑ Examine the engine for signs of frequent repair, such as worn bolt heads, bright metal spots.

☑ Examine the cooling system. The intake strainer should be easily accessible for cleaning; all hoses should be firm and flexible and mounted with paired hose clamps; the connection to the exhaust or discharge should be tight, without signs of leaking. There should be clean coolant solution in the heat-exchanger tank (for a freshwater cooling system). Try to move the water pump—is it firm or does it wobble?

☑ Are the fuel tanks well mounted? Are all connections through the tops of the tanks? Are flexible sections installed between rigid sections of fuel line, with all hoses double-clamped? Is there an electrical bridge across nonconducting hose to carry any static charge from the fuel-fill cap to the tank? Is the overflow vented overboard and not into the cockpit or bilges?

☑ Are exhaust lines separated from flammable materials and protected from accidental contact? Are there any signs of exhaust leaks, such as carbon streaks or discolored paint?

SAILS AND RIGGING

☑ Examine all standing rigging for signs of corrosion or stress (bent or twisted fittings, broken strands, cracking at deck or hull attachment). Remove protective tape from all turnbuckles: Are the threads clean and cotter pins in place?

☑ Does the mast appear straight? If not, is the rigging overtight or is the mast itself warped or bent? Check the mast step for corrosion, cracked welds, or fractured fiberglass.

☑ Are the sails clean and in good repair, with all grommets and stitching tight? Are the sails stowed neatly or are they stuffed into lockers all over the boat?

OTHER MECHANICAL SYSTEMS

☑ Are there proper marine seacocks (*not* gate valves) on all through-hull penetrations? They should be of reinforced plastic or bronze and connected with wire-reinforced hoses that are double-clamped with rolled-edge, stainless steel hose clamps. Are all seacocks accessible? Do they work freely or are they frozen from disuse and lack of lubrication? Are there tapered wooden plugs handy in the event of seacock failure?

☑ If there are through-hull sensor units for depth and speed, are the fittings watertight? Is an appropriate replacement plug available for use while cleaning or storing the units?

☑ Are the bilge pumps in working order; hard-wired to the battery; and equipped with an automatic float switch *and* a manual override? Are pump intakes protected from debris by screens? Does each pump discharge overboard through an independent system that is not connected to any other? Is there a manual backup pump easily accessible—and easy enough to use for many hours, if need be?

☑ Rudder fittings (or the outboard motor mounting) and all connections through the steering system must be sturdy; cables must be stainless steel; pulleys must be attached firmly (and not just screwed in). Look for signs of stress, fittings pulling loose. Is there an emergency tiller? Does it work?

☑ If there are multiple steering stations, will a failure at one interfere with steering from another?

☑ Check the hydraulic systems for firm mounting and any sign of fluid leakage while at rest and also under pressure.

☑ Does the propeller shaft appear to run straight while turning over slowly? Is it free of corrosion, particularly where it is bolted to the transmission? Check for water leaking through the stuffing box; an acceptable level is four or five drops a minute.

ELECTRICAL SYSTEMS

☑ Is all wiring in accordance with ABYC standards (or an otherwise logical system) for color coding, size, and connections? Are wire runs banded together, out of the bilges, and supported every 18 inches with nonconductive clips or hangers? Is the system protected by adequate fuses or circuit breakers? Are there signs of overload (burned insulation, scorched paneling)?

☑ Check *behind* the main electrical panel. Is the wiring neatly done or is it a rat's nest? Look for signs of patchwork jumpers or jury rigs—a tipoff that past problems may have been bypassed rather than corrected.

☑ Are all major pieces of metallic equipment bonded together?

☑ Is the boat equipped with a lightning protection system?

☑ Are shore-power cables and receptacles in good repair and without signs of burning, chafing, and cuts? Does the control panel have a polarity indicator?

☑ Check batteries for adequate size; proper mounting in an acid-proof, well-ventilated box; and indications of good maintenance (clean terminals, clean tops, distilled water filled to proper level).

☑ Does the master battery switch have field-disconnect and make-before-break features?

SAFETY EQUIPMENT

The boat may or may not come with adequate and appropriate safety equipment; we suggest you use chapters 8 and 9 as a guide. In brief:

☑ Personal flotation devices (such as life jackets, vests, float coats, life rings, horseshoe buoys) should be accessible and in good repair.

☑ Electronic equipment should be installed with adequate wiring, fuses, and antennas mounted in accordance with manufacturer's instructions.

☑ Fire extinguishers should be mounted (not merely placed here and there) and appropriate to the type of fire anticipated in the area: class A in berthing, class B in the machinery spaces, class C at the electrical control panel. Extinguishers should have tags showing the most recent inspection date. There should be a means for triggering a system installed in the machinery spaces from outside the space; automatic triggering systems should be tested or replaced.

☑ Distress and warning signals should be in a convenient location (not buried in a locker); flares must be current.

☑ The first-aid kit should be complete (and not depleted through use or disuse).

CURRENT OWNER

☑ Does the boat appear to be well maintained and seaworthy?

☑ Is the installed equipment in good operating condition? With the owner's permission, check out everything—electronics, running lights, the head, the stove, the engine.

☑ Observe the general level of housekeeping. Are the bilges, the galley, and the head area clean? Any signs of vermin or insects? Are dangerous or flammable materials scattered throughout the lockers and cabinets—or are they properly confined to ventilated topside lockers?

☑ Check the gear lockers for used, worn-out, and broken bits of equipment; some people are reluctant to throw out *anything*. An assortment of chewed-up impeller wheels, corroded spark plugs, and burned-out circuit breakers may provide clues to the operating problems *you* might expect with this boat.

Let the U.S. Coast Guard Help You Choose a Boat

The Coast Guard maintains a record of deficiencies, design problems, and manufacturing defects for a wide range of boat models. They'll share the free information with you via their boating hotline:

1-800-368-5647

Also, the Coast Guard and the Coast Guard Auxiliary perform free courtesy safety inspections of any boat, upon request. Obtain permission from the owner from whom you're thinking of buying the boat, and have the safety inspection before—rather than after—you've committed any money.

Once you have bought the boat, adopt the habit of requesting a courtesy inspection at least once a year.

CHAPTER SIX

Surveying for Safety

THE MARINE SURVEY

A marine survey is a thorough inspection of the condition of a boat and installed equipment. It is prepared by a trained and experienced marine surveyor and usually ordered (and paid for) by a prospective purchaser.

The surveyor is a hard-nosed investigator who keeps his emotions and prejudices out of his work. Unlike the prospective buyer, he is not motivated or swayed by dreams of idyllic sunset sails; instead, he looks beneath the ego-enhancing, well-oiled teak and the space-age electronics for defects, design flaws, and evidence of accidents or poor maintenance.

Even the most experienced boat buyer can benefit from this objective approach: An experienced boat buyer may have dealt with a handful of boats, whereas a minimally experienced qualified surveyor will have studied hundreds.

When should you consider a survey? Anytime you think you want to buy a boat more sophisticated than an open fisherman. You probably will be required to do so if you want to finance or insure your boat. But even if you are wealthy enough to pay cash and choose to self-insure against major losses, a good survey at the least gives you a list of items needing attention and the assurance that other hidden and potentially dangerous defects are not cooking away just out of sight.

Here's a sample from the survey of a seventeen-year-old, 35-foot wood-hulled sailboat:

. . . specific items being minor repair to the top corners of the transom, refastening of two butt blocks in the forward section of the vessel, repair to partially cracked frames amidships at the outside turn of the bilge on the starboard side. The mainmast is basically sound but does require complete refinishing. Fresh water has begun to get into the planking; starboard end has small soft area. There is excessive paint buildup on deck canvas which will soon lead to cracking. Flares are outdated. The protective zinc in the heat exchanger is totally eroded. There is no anti-siphon valve on the head discharge. The fire extinguishers are not properly mounted and do not meet Coast Guard requirements.

In other words, a good survey is about the cheapest insurance you can buy.

By making your offer-to-purchase subject to a satisfactory report of survey, you can be certain that you will get the benefit of this insurance right up front. What is "satisfactory"? It's largely whatever you want it to be, should any major discrepancies be uncovered. In that event, you have the latitude to refuse to buy the boat or to negotiate for a reduced price or any other concessions.

A CRITICAL LOOK AT THE VITAL STEMHEAD. The surveyor carefully checks the stemhead fitting, forestay hardware, mounts for the pulpit, and general fairness of the forward hull sections.

TYPES OF SURVEYS

There are three basic types of marine surveys: the Survey of Condition and Value (the details of which may vary and should be negotiated in advance—see below); the more limited Insurance Survey; and an Assessment of Damage (likely for insurance purposes, but also as a guide toward making repairs). The Survey of Condition and Value—which is what most people mean when they use the term *survey*—is more thorough, detailed, and useful than an Insurance Survey and covers more ground than an Assessment of Damage.

Many people think of marine surveys only in connection with used boats. This is a mistake. Contrary to a common feeling around the waterfront (or at least the part of the waterfront that's crowded with dealers' docks and showrooms), a new boat is as much a candidate for survey as an antique. A new boat, like a new anything, can be made improperly: deck structures poorly mated to the hull, engine not well bedded down, shaft that doesn't run true, wiring of the wrong size (because the work crew ran out of the right size but was under pressure to get the boat out of the shop).

Most boats are delivered to the dealer by truck, after who-knows-how stressful a journey. Boats sometimes fall off the truck, or get clipped by a bridge or a low branch on a big tree, or get hit by other trucks maneuvering around a truck-stop parking lot. The dealer is not likely to hang a sign on the boat to advertise such experience. A survey tells you what's right and wrong and gives you a work list to hand back to the dealer with a gentle suggestion: Make it right, or no deal.

Further, should you decide upon a custom boat, the surveyor can play a role similar to that of an architect in a real estate project. Just as an architect ensures that plans are properly executed during construction, the surveyor can act as your agent to monitor the progress. He should make a visit during layup or framing of the hull; on another visit, he can inspect the ballast, the installation of the through-hull fittings, and the mating of the deck module to the hull. He will check progress against the plans and specifications and verify that substandard materials have not been substituted. He'll run a full survey on the finished boat before launching—and, finally, take the boat out for predelivery sea trials. Any discrepancies discovered, at any stage, can be brought to the attention of the builder, along with a demand for correction. This progressive construction survey should be a part of the sales contract; if the builder refuses to accept such a clause, find another builder. It's your money.

An Insurance Survey may be a complete Survey of Condition and Value, or it may be a more limited assessment that satisfies the needs of an insurance underwriter but passes over the minutiae in which the prospective owner might be interested. An Insurance Survey might be required for renewal, or change of underwriter, when there is no change of boat ownership.

An Assessment of Damage is much like what you'd need in the event of an automobile accident, but it has much greater detail, specifying the exact nature of the damage and the method and materials needed to restore the boat to "like new" condition.

SELECTING A SURVEYOR

Choosing a marine surveyor is not as straightforward as deciding to order the survey. There are no licensing requirements or codified professional qualifications for "marine surveyor," and in theory, anyone could have business cards printed and begin looking for clients. You can start, of course, by looking in the Yellow Pages, but don't limit your search to that self-selecting fraternity. The largest ads only reveal who has the largest ad budgets, and there may be no relationship whatsoever to skill and experience. Many surveyors view Yellow Pages listings as unnecessary—and *they* may well be the ones you want to find.

This is an area where "word of mouth" is indeed the best advertising. Marine surveyor Tom

Drennan, who works out of West Palm Beach, Florida, and has been around long enough, advises: "Remember the old Packard advertising? 'Ask the man who owns one.' It's the best approach to finding a surveyor." Ask for recommendations from local boatyard operators, or friends with boats. Talk with those recommended—and ask to see a copy of their survey forms. If the surveyor balks at this simple request, search elsewhere. You might also ask to see a sample, at least, of a survey summary; a survey can easily be sanitized to delete references

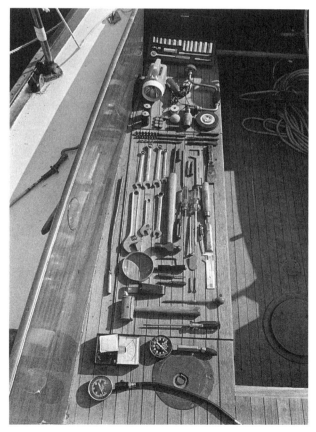

THE SURVEYOR'S SPECIALIZED TOOLKIT. With these tools, and years of experience with a wide range of boats and problems, a surveyor can give you a detailed report of boat condition and problems that no owner can hope to match.

A CHECK FOR FAIRNESS. Once the boat is secure in the Travelift and squared up on support blocks, the surveyor checks for hull fairness. Untrue lines can indicate hull twisting, repairs, or the results of impact.

THE SURVEYOR'S HAMMER, used on the port stern quarter of this boat, will sound or "feel" out any soft sections or failure points in the main hull structure.

to a particular boat or transaction. Your interest is in the style and substance of the report, not the details.

Few surveyors of our acquaintance pretend to be qualified in all respects. Determine whether the surveyor you are considering has particular areas of interest—or limitation. A man who concentrates on wooden boats, for example, may not be prepared (with either training or specialized test equipment) to survey a steel or aluminum hull. Many surveyors will suggest that you enlist an engineman or an electronics expert: They are not trying to pad the bill, they're just being honest.

Do you need to have a thorough engine or electronics check? The answer clearly depends on the age, size, complexity, and probable replacement cost of the equipment to be examined. This is more of a judgment call than the decision to order the basic survey. Your finance and insurance companies won't require this one, but keep in mind that a major overhaul on a pair of big diesel engines will cost thousands of dollars. It is useful—to say the least—to know up front what expenses you are likely to be buying along with the boat.

You might regard with caution any surveyor recommendation from the listing sales agent, or from finance or insurance agents. Not that their favored surveyor would be incompetent—rather, their particular needs may be limited, whereas your needs are broad. These agents need a survey that says the boat is in good shape and worth the asking price, and little else. No work lists, perhaps only a cursory search for hidden defects—just a marketing-oriented look at the cosmetics.

Someday we might expect to see qualifications defined and enforced by a professional association, but not today. There *is* a National Association of Marine Surveyors (NAMS), which is helpful but not necessarily definitive. Membership is open to people with demonstrated experience but not necessarily demonstrated skill. The association does, however, have a certification program, which requires an examination and is only granted to full-time surveyors.

COST

Cost should not be a major consideration; most surveyors charge by the day, and most surveys for recreational boats under, say, 50 feet in length can be completed in a day. Unless unusual travel charges are involved, the fee will be measured in hundreds, not thousands, of dollars.

Be wary of the surveyor who brags about the number of surveys he conducts every day and promises, therefore, to save you money. You're not interested in speed; you want thoroughness. You're not interested in saving money *on* the survey, but *because of* the survey.

Should you be tempted—in the interest of saving money—to accept a prior survey offered by the seller, be careful. The survey may be only a week old, but the damage inflicted in yesterday's collision won't be included.

THE SURVEY

As we have said, the survey can be as thorough, or as cursory, as you require. You may indeed want to have a surveyor run a quick look, either to eliminate a candidate boat or to validate the logic of moving to a more thorough investigation. You may or may not want to have the major items of machinery checked by the surveyor; as noted above, many will admit freely that they are not qualified engine mechanics and will suggest that you hire an engineman for that task. In any event, to avoid later misunderstanding and additional expense, know what skills and services you are buying in advance.

The survey may be conducted with the boat in the water or out of the water, but the best survey will include both—and a sea trial as well.

However, hauling the boat for a survey drives up the cost and is not a logical move unless you are reasonably certain that you'll buy the boat if it passes. In fact, it makes sense to haul the boat in that case, because you can have the bottom cleaned and painted at the same time. Make it a matter of agreement in the sales contract: You will pay for the hauling and launching of the boat

in any event; if the survey is acceptable, you've agreed to buy the boat and can go ahead with the hull work.

Running a survey only with the boat in the water leaves a lot of important hardware uninspected; we suggest you do this *only* as a preliminary look.

MASTER SURVEYOR CAPTAIN GIFFY FULL checks the fiberglass underbody of a production sailboat. He uses the worklight to spot light defects in the layup and cracks or repairs in the lower hull and keel, and to check general fairness of the structure. The man at right is the prospective owner who can observe during the survey to learn something about his future boat.

A POSSIBLE CRITICAL FAILURE POINT has attracted surveyor Giffy Full's magnifying glass. Lifted paint along this section of the boat's stem may be evidence of rot and failure in the hull structure. Here Captain Full is inspecting the critically important stemhead fitting that supports the lower attachment of the forestay after it passes through the short bowsprit. There may be corrosion in the metal fitting or attachment screws caused by water in the stem structure—or rot in the underlying stem of the boat.

A PROPELLER SHAFT CHECK shows up any slackness in the propeller mount, the securing key, or the shaft itself. The surveyor can detect any discrepancy in the shaft connection, shaft log, or various bearings in the shaft/propulsion assembly.

THE SURVEY METHOD

The method may vary with the surveyor, but not much. He should start by surveying *your* interests and needs in a boat, to ensure that *this* boat will be appropriate. Then, armed with a flashlight, a hammer, a bunch of screwdrivers, perhaps a circuit tester and some other tools, the surveyor will slowly and carefully work his way through the boat, inside and out—tapping on the hull, shining a bright light through the fiberglass,

peering up into the hidden places, poking for softness along the joints, flipping switches, and writing his findings and opinions on his series of work sheets. The details of what he inspects may well vary—as noted above—and should be discussed and agreed to in advance. If you want him to remove and inspect behind every bulkhead panel, overhead liner, bolted-in tank, or piece of equipment, you must expect to pay more—a great deal more—and probably more than is required. That's where the judgment of the surveyor comes in. Clues such as water stains or stressed fastenings clearly suggest a more thorough look. Without such signs, a random sampling might suffice: Removing and inspecting a

RUDDER ATTACHMENT is a key safety check. The surveyor checks the lower rudder mountings for corrosion or stress fractures. The fittings and attachment hardware should all be inspected carefully.

PULLING A HULL FASTENING can tell a lot about the condition of the hull of a wooden boat. Sample fastenings should be pulled from all areas of the boat. Fastenings taken from the forward section usually will show higher wear.

dozen hull-planking screws should give a good indication of the overall condition of all hull fastenings.

If at all possible, we suggest that you join the surveyor for the survey. Watching him at work should be instructive, and if he's at all sociable, he'll describe what he's doing—and why—at each stage in the effort. In addition, he can point out details of construction or materials that might not merit comment in the report but that may be of interest or value to you.

THE REPORT

The report should contain the following basic information:

• Description of the boat and equipment, including type of construction and materials, nameplate data of major elements, and general condition
• Inventory of such ancillary items as sails, lines, fenders, tools
• Evaluation of safety equipment, such as fire extinguishers, signal flares, life jackets
• Deficiencies and recommendations—in effect, a work list
• Estimate of condition and value of the boat, including both market value and replacement value
• Summary of the findings and opinion of the surveyor—the bottom line.

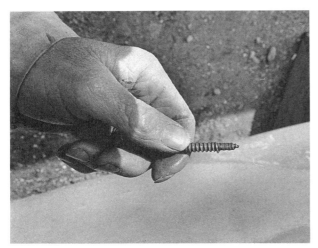

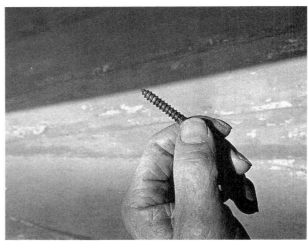

A POOR FASTENING. This bronze screw, taken from a bow section of the boat, shows deterioration and loss of thread. These fastenings should be replaced, or, failing that, one of the new owner's first yard jobs should be counterfastening the affected planks.

A HEALTHY FASTENING. This bronze screw was taken from a midship section of the boat and shows plenty of healthy thread left for fine holding power.

A CRACKED RIB. The surveyor has found this partially cracked rib behind a cabin locker. These are bent ribs, under strain, which can lead to complete rib failure. The crack has occurred at a typical weak point, right above a longitudinal stringer. The cure is either rib replacement or sister-framing with a partial rib overlaid to cover the stressed area. Since both are expensive operations, a reduced price should be negotiated for the boat. The survey has just paid for itself.

COMPRESSION TESTS are one way to measure the relative health of a marine engine. The test has to be done carefully, with the readings averaged for accuracy. The most significant aspect of the readings is relative closeness in measurements from one cylinder to the next. High pressure and small cylinder-to-cylinder differences are signs of a healthy engine.

EXAMPLES OF SURVEY REPORTS

Here are excerpts from the summary-and-opinion sections of two surveys. One of these boats had major problems:

DESCRIPTION: A 48' custom motor yacht, double-planked mahogany hull. The vessel was surveyed dockside at the owner's residence in Vero Beach, Florida.

The inside of the hull was found to have a serious problem of electrolysis. Thru-hull bolts to the struts, log shafts, rudder anchors and thru-hull transom bolts have deteriorated to the point that some have broken off. Also the wood backing plates beneath this hardware have deteriorated because of the acid created by the deteriorated bolts. This condition also exists with the thru-hull fittings and backing plates, and renders the hull unseaworthy. It is recommended that all thru-hull bolts and backing plates be replaced.

All gate valves and seacocks are frozen and should be removed and cleaned, thoroughly inspected for electrolysis damage and new backing plates installed.

It is recommended that a marine electrician inspect the wiring and circuits to determine the cause of the severe electrolysis condition.

The topside of the hull, decks, flybridge and transom were found to have serious frame and planking deterioration. The interior of the vessel also has a great deal of deteriorated wood in panels, bulkheads, and windows. These are identified in the deficiencies list.

This vessel reflects poor maintenance throughout the years, and will require extensive repair to restore it to yacht condition.

The surveyor rated the vessel as "poor" and noted an estimated replacement value of $225,000 and an estimated present-day market value of $46,000. The owner was asking $50,000 and was willing to trade for anything of value—and eventually did, for a few acres of undeveloped property. The new owner was prepared to invest a great deal of money in restoration—and did. Among other projects, the entire stern had to be removed and rebuilt.

This boat was only ten years old at the time of the survey and had spent most of its life moored in a protected canal behind the owner's residence. The two main problems—electrolysis and topside freshwater leaks—were preventable, and any incipient damage could have been corrected easily before it became a problem. The owner might be forgiven—with pity—for not noting and correcting the electrolytic problem, because he had never heard of electrolysis and had never paid any attention to the underwater through-hull bolts and fittings. One cannot be so charitable in discussing the topside rot, however, because it would be impossible not to notice that large chunks of the superstructure were beginning to break off. The owner did indeed notice, over time; his solution had been to cover the damage with a plastic sheet. This provided a stimulating hothouse environment for the rot

WATER AND POSSIBLE ROT have lifted varnish and exposed possible failure points in this section of cockpit coaming. This evidence of decay will cause the surveyor to probe more deeply in the cockpit structure.

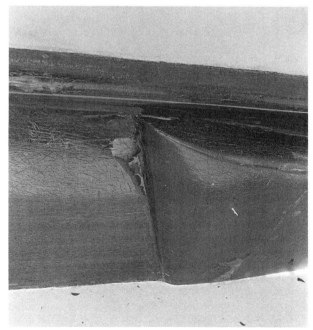

STANCHION SAFETY is an important part of the surveyor's deck safety checklist. This stanchion base is not the best, since it attaches only to the deck and has no side support meeting the toerail. The lifelines are only single strand; they should be double-strand.

DECK FASTENINGS come under close scrutiny. The surveyor has removed a few sample bungs and is withdrawing the bronze (one hopes) screws used to fasten deck planks. These will be checked for corrosion and thread holding power. This practice is not just for wooden boats, since high-quality production fiberglass boats also have screw-held teak decks.

and kept residual moisture trapped below, contributing to such other damage as corroded wiring and rusting fuel tanks. By the way, such widespread rot might be considered a clue to the quality—or, more properly, the lack of quality—of the original construction and materials.

The other sample:

DESCRIPTION: A 39' fiberglass cruising sloop, eleven years old, surveyed in a Massachusetts boatyard.
The vessel has borne some damage. There are stress cracks in the forward bow section just above the waterline and on the port side just about midships above

the waterline. The surveyor believes that the vessel has been struck in some manner on the port side amidships and that there is delamination of the fiberglass in the interior side of the hull which will require professional repair.

The water tank in the forward section has been torn loose from its tabbings and bracketing, and the tank marked as a leaking tank. It should be removed from its mounts, pressure tested, reinstalled and properly reglassed into the hull.

The forward partition in the forepeak has broken away at the bottom on both sides, requiring re-tabbing work. This is related to the foregoing item.

Taken alone, those comments might seem to disqualify the boat from further consideration, but there's one final important step in any survey—a post-report conversation with the surveyor. In this instance, surveyor Giffy Full of Marblehead, Massachusetts (whom some boat owners regard as a legend in his own time), offered the following amplification:

You might think all of this stuff is kind of grim, but it is not. She is an absolutely average boat with typical problems for her age. She hit a float or something rather hard, and the work has to be done, pure and simple. No big deal. Do it, and she will be right again. There are a lot of years of sailing in her. Just don't expect more of her than she is. I've surveyed a lot worse. Some I've left alone after the first hour; there's no sense in wasting my time and another guy's money. This boat is different. There's nothing really bad here, but you have to get it done.

The seller had been asking a price at the top of the range for that model in the BUC Guide, the national boat-pricing manual (similar to the automobile Blue Book). Armed with the survey report—and the reassurance of the surveyor—the buyer was able to negotiate a price reduction of almost $8,000. The price of the survey was $300.

MASTHEAD CHECK of upper pulleys, sheaves, and fittings. A magnifying glass emphasizes any stress cracking, halyard system failure points, or chafed sections.

THE RESULT OF IMPACT. The survey has turned up a hidden and subtle fracture in the hull structure. This mounting tab for a cabin berth has fractured and pulled away from the bulkhead. More important is the reason for the damage. To the practiced eye of the surveyor, this is possible evidence of a fairly heavy impact with a dock, another boat, or a submerged object. This kind of flaw will make the surveyor look closely for more serious damage in key hull sections or components.

THE SURVEY REPORT will give you not only a detailed report of the boat's condition and possible problems but also a list of work to be done to bring the boat to top condition, specifications of boat measurements and other vital data, a complete inventory of onboard equipment, and an accounting of the presence and state of safety equipment. A proper survey report on a 30-foot sailboat could easily exceed ten pages.

CHAPTER SEVEN

Legal and Financial Safety

LEGAL PECULIARITIES OF BOAT OWNERSHIP

Selection and survey of the boat are not the last steps before taking ownership. Next you'll need assurance that the boat is free and clear of any debts; you'll need to arrange for documentation or registration; you'll probably need financing; and you'll certainly need insurance.

In these matters, buying a boat is not as straightforward as many people assume. Maritime law, financing, and insurance are frequently quite different from the shoreside equivalents, and they provide traps easy to fall into but expensive to escape from.

The first topic: admiralty law, a little-known but potentially powerful influence upon your maritime financial safety.

ADMIRALTY LAW

"Admiralty" refers generally to a body of international maritime law and custom that, in the United States, is codified under various acts of the Congress and adjudicated by federal district courts "sitting in Admiralty."

With roots going back perhaps 3,000 years, ad-miralty may represent the oldest form of international agreement. It grew out of the experiences of those early seagoing merchant pioneers who sought to expand their fortunes by enlarging their markets. They did so at great risk—not only from the natural perils of the sea, but also from the whim and vagary of each local government where their ships might call.

Over time, those nations that most involved with international trade came to recognize the benefits to be gained from reciprocal agreements governing the rights, privileges, and obligations of seamen and shipowners. Thus arose a series of agreements known generally as the Laws of Admiralty. These have been improved and modified over the centuries but are very much in force today.

Does admiralty apply to the average U.S. pleasure boat? The answer is a qualified yes. Granting that admiralty was created for commercial vessels and crews and was intended for situations not likely to be encountered in pleasure boating, there are many holes in the coverage afforded by shoreside law that are addressed by admiralty law.

As a practical matter, bringing suit in admiralty court is an expensive, cumbersome, and lengthy process, and a litigant would resort to admiralty only if an easier solution could not be found. In recent years, the special characteristics of pleasure boating have been recognized by many state and local governments, and a growing body of law and regulation specifically for pleasure boating does provide some legal alternative to admiralty. But . . . a caution: These local statutes do not replace federal law. Unless both parties to a suit agree to submit to lower jurisdic-

tion, one or the other could invoke superior federal law and take the case to admiralty.

As a practical matter, it is in the creation and payment of debts lodged against a boat that admiralty touches many boat owners. Note well the phrase, "debts lodged against a boat." Not against an owner, past or present, but against the boat.

The origins of this are easy to trace. A voyaging merchant ship frequently would incur debts in ports far from home—debts for supplies, for wages, for repairs—that could not be covered with whatever funds the ship's captain might

BOAT DOCUMENTS are vital to any cruiser for dealing with law enforcement people or in case of accident. Proof of ownership, insurance policies, special permits, and licenses should be part of every boat's document portfolio.

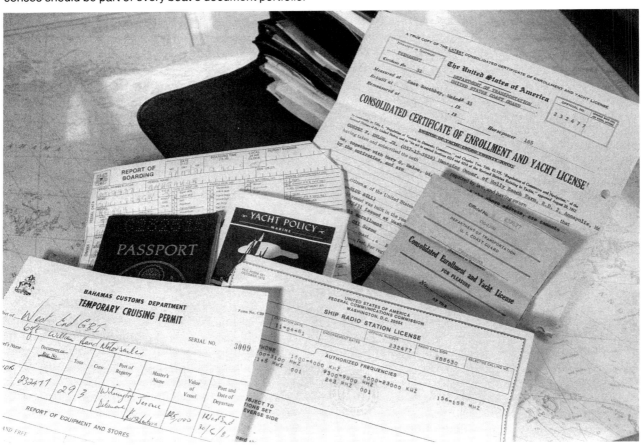

have available during the voyage. In the days before bank drafts, credit cards, and electronic fund transfers, a supplier of goods and services had limited options: He could trust the distant owner to make good on the debt or he could keep the ship from sailing until the debt was paid.

Of course, holding a ship to force payment was akin to putting a pauper in debtor's prison: Unless he could work, he could not pay his debts; unless he paid his debts, he would not be released. A ship held captive at the pier could not generate revenue—but, if allowed to sail away, it might never be seen again. A creditor might try to sue the absentee owner—but under which nation's laws, in what manner, and in what court? From this dilemma evolved the maritime lien— whereby a claim for payment could be lodged against the *ship*. The ship is permitted to continue voyaging and ownership might even change, but the liens remain. The ship is held liable.

Following some ancient logic, maritime liens are given a priority ranking. Those in the highest priority are the first to be paid—regardless of the order in which they were acquired. Within categories, the most recent claim has first priority.

The highest category is claims for wages, followed by claims for damage inflicted by the ship, salvage claims, charges for repairs, and, finally, charges for supplies. These rules still apply: highest category, first paid; last incurred in each category, first due.

Another peculiarity of the maritime lien is that it need not be recorded. This is also a carryover from ancient times, when it was impractical for a creditor to travel to the home port of a vessel to register his claim, and equally impractical to require a shipowner to search out the records in each port visited by his ships. In theory, the owner would know well what claims he owed and would undertake to pay them off in timely fashion.

Should a lien go too long unpaid, the ship can be seized whenever and wherever that action might be practical and be held hostage for the payment. The arresting authority must publish a public notice to encourage any other lienholders to come forth with their claims. If payment is still not forthcoming after a reasonable length of time, the ship will be sold at public auction. The known creditors will be paid off from the proceeds and the ship will be allowed to proceed under new ownership, unencumbered. Should the proceeds not be enough to cover the debts— or should new claimants appear later—the previous owner might be sued, but the ship sails free and clear.

By now it should be obvious that unless a ship—or boat, since admiralty makes no distinction—is purchased through a court-sponsored auction, any new owner should exercise due diligence in searching for outstanding claims.

For a 22-foot open boat on a trailer, hidden liens are not likely to be much of a problem. For a $200,000 sportfisherman, you should exercise at least as much prudence as you would in buying a house.

For example—you could check with the boatyard that performed any recent maintenance or repair work, to ensure that the yard bills were all paid. If the seller makes a point of complaining about the quality of work or service with any yard or supplier, or if the seller seems vague about just who installed that new pair of engines, take it as a warning that he may have withheld payment or partial payment. Do a more thorough job of checking.

Incidentally, claims for payment arising from the construction of a new boat cannot be lodged as maritime liens. A boat is not eligible for admiralty treatment until finished and ready for use as a boat. The person who contracted for construction, not a new owner, would be liable for payment unless these claims are specifically passed along with the bill of Sale.

FINANCING

Since few people can afford to pay cash for most boats, some form of financing usually is involved. For smaller boats, this may take the form of either a conditional sales contract, with the boat pledged as collateral for the loan, or a chattel mortgage, where the finance company owns the boat until the loan is paid in full. As a practical matter, there isn't much difference between the two—you are the registered owner and have full use of the boat as long as you are making the payments.

For larger boats, the financing may become a bit more complicated because admiralty treats a boat loan as just another piece of paper. If the finance company forecloses on a loan and takes possession of the boat, it might at the same time assume "ownership" of a string of outstanding maritime liens, which take priority. Therefore, the finance company may want to create a preferred ship's mortgage, which is a maritime lien of high standing. A preferred ship's mortgage can be enforced no matter where the boat may travel or to whom "ownership" might be transferred. The owner may make the payments, but as long as any remain outstanding, the boat can be held liable.

In addition, to ensure that their transactions are a matter of public record and to protect themselves from unpleasant legal wrangling, most lenders will require that any eligible boat be federally documented, thus opening a file in which their lien *can* be recorded.

DOCUMENTATION

Documentation is simply the process of registering a qualified boat with the Coast Guard. In the recent past, documentation gave a pleasure boat some privileges beyond those granted to state-registered boats—largely centered on simplified customs procedures when returning from a foreign voyage. That privilege no longer applies, and all pleasure boats are treated equally.

In addition to the advantage to a lender, documentation provides the owner with tangible proof of that ownership, which can be helpful when dealing with government authorities around the world. Also, on a more aesthetic level, documentation eliminates the need to display state registration numbers on the bow.

Documentation does *not*, however, relieve a boat owner of any obligation to register the boat or to pay any applicable local sales or personal property tax.

For specific information on the qualifications and application process for documentation, see appendix VI.

REGISTRATION

The Federal Boating Act (administered and enforced by the Coast Guard) requires state registration and numbering of undocumented power-driven boats. The law allows a sixty-day grace period for reregistration when a boat moves to a new state; it mandates notification within fifteen days if a boat is sold, lost, destroyed, abandoned, or stolen, or if the registration certificate is lost or the owner moves.

BILL OF SALE

Ownership is conveyed to a buyer by a seller who has the legal right to do so. This would seem obvious, but a boat may—or may not—have a document that approximates an automobile title, identifying the owner. The apparent "owner" may—or may not—have the right to sell the boat. For example, if the boat is owned by a corporation, the seller must produce written authority from the board of directors.

At the least, your bill of sale should attest to the following:

• Name and address of the owner
• Name and address of the seller (if different)
• Description of the boat, including the hull identification number (see below)
• Affirmation that the seller has the right to sell the boat
• The agreed sale price
• Conditions of payment
• Notice of any liens outstanding and an indication of how they are reflected in the sales price
• Any warranties or guarantees and the conditions under which they would be honored

• Any conditions or exclusions of the sale (e.g., "subject to a satisfactory report of survey; subject to obtaining a mortgage" of a specific amount).

HULL IDENTIFICATION NUMBER

All boats manufactured in or imported into the United States must have a permanently affixed hull identification number (HIN). This is separate from any state registration or federal documentation number and is similar to the vehicle identification number given to automobiles.

For boats built or certified on or after August 1, 1984, the HIN consists of the following:

1. a three-letter manufacturer ID code (assigned by the Coast Guard);
2. a five-character serial number that may incorporate letters, numbers, or both (but *not* the letters I, O, and Q);
3. a letter/number pair indicating the month and year of manufacture; a letter for the month (A for January, B for February, C for March, etc.), followed by a single-digit number for the year (i.e., "9" for 1989);
4. a two-number "model year."

Example: AAA23Y8UE787 = a 1987 model boat, serial number 23Y8U, built by the AAA company in May 1987.

LIABILITY

Ownership carries the responsibility for proper maintenance and safe operation—of your house, your car, or your boat. When you invite a guest into your home, you have offered an implied warranty that your home is safe; when you take to the highways, your passengers and fellow drivers should be able to assume that you know how to drive and both you and your automobile are in proper condition to do so; when you take guests out for a ride in your boat, the same assumptions apply.

At the same time, a typically knowledgeable person who willingly goes aboard a boat can be expected to realize that *some* hazard is involved; that the vagaries of wind and weather cannot always be foretold or accommodated; that mechanical things do break down; and that boats do, on occasion, sink. However, in this litigious society of ours, an injured party will often find grounds upon which to base a suit, no matter how removed from the event they might seem. To protect your family and friends from injury—and to protect yourself from suit should an injury occur—you must know your boat, know your abilities, and know how to deal with emergencies when they arise.

Recreational boating is supposed to be fun, and you don't want always to be looking aft to see what liabilities might be creeping up on you. Yet you must exercise due prudence. A leaking fuel tank cannot be ignored. A frayed line should be replaced *before* it breaks under strain—before it has a chance to whip into someone's face.

What sort of financial exposure can you face from a boating accident? There are no fixed guidelines. As a general rule, for an "act of God," your liability might be limited to the value of your boat—unless you or someone acting on your behalf (paid crew) or with your permission (your teenage son) contributed to the problem. A member of your immediate family may be assumed to have permission, in a legal sense, whether or not permission was actually granted. Make sure that your teenage son or daughter, or your spouse, has a solid base of knowledge of boat operation and the responsibilities of ownership.

Incidentally, if you hire any paid crew (whether for a chartered or a wholly owned boat), you may become liable to pay medical and living expenses should he or she become injured or incapacitated—even if you (or your boat) are not at fault. Another holdover from earlier times: Going to sea has always been a hazardous profession, and the sailor is little better than a paid slave while the ship is at sea. His schedule is totally under the control of others; his willingness to expose himself to danger in support of the ship is assumed. Law and custom hold that a sailor injured in the course of a voyage deserves support while recovering.

If you *are* at fault—if, for example, your boat is not adequately seaworthy or is not properly equipped—injured crew may bring suit in either admiralty court or civil court, or both.

How best to protect yourself from financial loss? Beyond exercising prudence and good seamanship at all times, you'll need a good marine insurance policy. Even the best of them, however, will not protect you from all hazards. Be sure you are aware of the limits of your protection *before* you sign an agreement to purchase a boat.

INSURANCE

Insurance should protect a boat owner against loss of or damage *to* his boat, and against claims for loss, damage, or injury caused by the operation *of* his boat. At first glance, a modern marine insurance policy appears to be equivalent to an automobile insurance policy: The documents are written in clear language, easily understood by the layman and apparently covering the expected range of claims and losses. However, marine insurance is *not* the same as auto insurance, and you must understand the differences.

In a typical policy, a boat owner will be protected against the normal perils of the sea—storm, fire and explosion, collision, pirates, highway perils (if trailered, or if in transit), and theft of the boat and equipment while moored. The owner should be protected against liability arising from damage or injury to others under similar conditions.

However, the owner will *not* be protected against loss arising from his own negligence—and here is a major departure from automobile coverage. If your car is totally destroyed because of a blowout, you are likely to be reimbursed even if the blowout was in a rotten tire that should long ago have been replaced.

The boat that sinks because a hose gives way is a loss charged against poor maintenance—and is not covered. The boat that sinks in heavy weather because the seams open up is also a loss charged against poor maintenance—the owner clearly was not diligent in checking the condition of hull fastenings and caulking.

For losses that are allowed, however, marine insurance provides better coverage than shoreside policies. Ashore, coverage for most losses is based on depreciated value. The majority of maritime losses, however, are treated as "new for old" (to the maximum amount of coverage). Thus, electronic equipment destroyed by lightning would be replaced with equivalent new equipment; a hull punctured by collision will be rebuilt like new and not just patched. Usual exceptions to the "new for old" rule include sails and canvas covers, which will be depreciated, and machinery that is more than seven years old, which *may* be depreciated at the discretion of the insurance agency.

Because theft of electronic or fishing equipment is relatively common, and may also be difficult to prove, insurance companies protect themselves by imposing a high deductible limit on coverage—say, $1,000. Up to that level, the owner absorbs the total loss, of whatever nature; beyond that, the insurance company covers the loss to the limits of coverage.

Coverage   Normal coverage under "hull insurance"—the major section of a policy dealing with property—will include the boat and (quoting from a typical modern yacht policy) those "spars, sails, tackle, machinery, furniture, and fittings which are part of your insured boat and which are required to be on your insured boat for its safe operation and maintenance while afloat and on shore."

Dinghies operated from the insured boat usually are covered; wearing apparel, cameras, fishing and diving equipment, water skis or other sporting equipment, portable audio equipment, fuel, and provisions are *not* covered under hull insurance. Some of these items—such as clothing and sports equipment belonging to you, your guests, and unpaid crew members—may be covered under a "personal property" clause, for an additional premium. However, payment would likely be limited to depreciated value and would not be made for losses arising from wear and tear, moths, mildew, mechanical or electrical breakdown (unless caused by lightning), and "mysterious disappearance or unexplained loss of any kind."

Valuable items such as money, business papers and documents, jewelry, watches, furs, and pets likely will not be covered. Look to your homeowner's policy for protection of these, but don't assume that it is automatically included. Talk to your insurance agent.

Other coverage will protect you from claims arising from damage caused by your boat, salvage of your boat (see chapter 22) and personal injury. You are likely to be covered for the use of a borrowed or rented boat, and for any new boat you purchase of the same general size and type, provided that you notify the insurance company within a specified period and pay any required additional premium.

Your coverage should include medical payments for persons "injured while in, upon, boarding or leaving your insured boat," but it may exclude "anyone who is an employee of yours injured in the course of employment" or "anyone while being in or upon or boarding or leaving your insured boat, who is a trespasser." Those could become expensive exclusions; make sure that your employees are covered under Worker's Compensation plans, and that a bold trespasser (bold enough, that is, to file a suit) falls under your homeowner's "umbrella" coverage.

The most common insurance claims are for petty theft; the next most frequent are those resulting from poor maintenance—neither of which, as noted above, is likely to be reimbursed. The third most commonly reported losses are those resulting from poor seamanship—storm damage to sails that were not reefed or dropped in time, or damage from a pier, pilings, or other boats caused by improper mooring. These are reimbursable.

The data base for establishing premiums for boat insurance is not as extensive or as well orga-

nized as that for automobile insurance. This is an area where it definitely pays to shop around. With any given company, the quoted rates will reflect that company's experience with similar boats in similar locations, the level of safety equipment aboard, and the experience and training of the owner. A credit—perhaps 5 or 10 percent of the premium—may be granted, for example, for an automatic fire extinguisher installed in the engine room and/or for completion of U.S. Power Squadron or maritime-school training courses. On the other hand, the base-line premium assumes an owner with some experience and knowledge appropriate to the insured boat; a first-time owner of a large powerboat may be charged an extra 10 percent.

Premiums are also affected by the location of, and operating area for, the boat. As with auto policies, higher rates are assessed for congested or high-crime areas. Auto policies, however, do not restrict the area of operation; boat policies usually do. The range of operation in which marine coverage is provided will be specified—for example, "U.S. Atlantic and Gulf coastal and navigable inland tributary waters between Eastport, Maine, and Pensacola, Florida, and the waters of the Bahamas, including voyages to and from U.S. coastal waters." That does not cover a voyage to Canada or Texas or Puerto Rico unless you make specific application and pay an additional premium.

Should you stray from the covered area, your insurance will lapse until you sail back across the line; a casual side trip could prove very expensive. An exception *may* be made in the event of an inadvertent transit caused by storm, or diversion for emergency repairs—provided that you notify your insurance agent or underwriter by radio, telephone, telegram, or FAX as soon as possible.

In those parts of the world where the boating season is limited by weather, or for long-distance seasonal commuters (who perhaps have a boat at each end), insurance premiums are reduced to compensate for a specified layup period. The boat may be hauled out and set on blocks, or kept afloat in an appropriate mooring, but it may not be operated without loss of insurance coverage.

ILLEGAL ACTIVITIES

It should be obvious that your insurance company will decline to reimburse you for the loss of a boat engaged in illegal activity—which, in this day and age, generally means a boat involved in smuggling drugs.

What is not so obvious is the fact that your boat can be seized by the Coast Guard or other law-enforcement agency for transporting drugs (or other illegal substances) *in any quantity*. They operate under a "zero-tolerance" rule, and "zero" means "zero." Boats have been seized for very small quantities, although the Coast Guard does exercise some discretion in this. If the owner has taken steps to warn crew or guests of *his* zero-tolerance policy, and he can demonstrate to the satisfaction of the Coast Guard that he had no knowledge of the presence of drugs, he may escape penalty.

A boat taken under such conditions can be kept by the government agency involved, or sold at auction with all proceeds going to the government—none to you or to the lending institution that holds your mortgage. And you still owe the mortgage balance.

Before you lost the boat permanently, you would be given formal legal notice. You have the right to contest the action, but to be successful, you must prove that the boat was not and never had been involved in drug smuggling and that any illegal substances found aboard were there without your knowledge. Depending upon the circumstances, that may be difficult or impossible; this is not a case of "innocent until proven guilty," because it is the *boat* that is the legal violator.

To make the best case, you must be able to demonstrate your commitment to "zero tolerance." As a minimum, include the following actions as part of your regular boating routine:

• Post a ZERO TOLERANCE sign in a prominent place; they are readily available in marine supply stores or you can make your own, simply stating, "The owner and operator of this vessel have a ZERO TOLERANCE to the use or possession of drugs IN ANY QUANTITY."

• Include a similar phrase in any welcome-aboard material.

• Have each salaried crew member sign a statement to the effect that he or she is aware of and will comply with your zero-tolerance policy.

• Specifically warn your guests before getting underway of your zero-tolerance policy, *and mean it.*

Coast Guard and other law-enforcement officers have the right to board your boat at any time; boarding-party practices and suggestions for your response are discussed in some detail in appendix VI.

SPECIAL SITUATION: CHARTERING

If you charter a boat, you may—or may not—acquire temporary ownership, with attendant rights and responsibilities. If the boat comes with a crew, then you and your guests are merely paying passengers; the owner and his agents—the crew—are responsible. In a bareboat charter, where you provide the crew (whether paid or volunteer), *you* are, for all intents and purposes, the owner for the period of the charter. You must maintain the boat and operate it in a safe manner; should a passenger or visitor trip over a line and fall, you are likely to be held responsible.

Should you be tempted to offer your *own* boat for charter, be careful. Make sure that your insurance will cover charter operations. Make sure that the captain who will be operating your boat is qualified and licensed to do so. And make sure that *you* are not aboard during charter operations unless you also are qualified and licensed; not only would you be held accountable for any injuries or damage, but you also could be charged by the Coast Guard for illegally carrying passengers for hire, a violation of federal law.

Table 7-1.
U.S. Coast Guard Minimum Equipment Requirements

Equipment	Boats less than 16 ft.	16 to less than 26 ft.	26 to less than 40 ft.	40 to not more than 65 ft.
Personal Flotation Devices (Life jackets)	One approved Type I, II, III, IV or V PFD for each person on board or being towed on water skis, etc.	One approved Type I, II, III, or V device for each person on board or being towed on water skis, etc. In addition, one throwable Type IV device. Type V Recreational Hybrid PFDs must be worn when the boat is underway. Other Type V PFDs must be approved for the activity in which the boat is being used.		
Fire Extinguisher* Must say Coast Guard approved	At least one B-I–type approved hand portable fire extinguisher (not required on outboard motorboats less than 26 feet in length and not carrying passengers for hire if the construction of such motorboats will not permit the entrapment of explosive or flammable gases or vapors and if fuel tanks are not permanently installed).		At least two B-I–type approved portable fire extinguishers; OR at least one B-II–type approved portable fire extinguisher.	At least three B-I–type approved portable fire extinguishers; OR at least one B-I–type **plus** one B-II–type approved portable fire extinguisher.
Visual Distress Signals (Required on coastal waters only)	Must carry approved visual distress signals for nighttime use.	Must carry visual distress signals approved for both daytime use and nighttime use.		
Bell, Whistle	Every vessel less than 12m (39.4 ft.) in length must carry an efficient sound-producing device.	Every vessel 12m (39.4 ft.) but less than 20m (65.6 ft.) in length must carry a whistle and a bell. The whistle must be audible for ½ nautical mile. The mouth of the bell must be at least 200mm (7.87 in.) in diameter.		
Ventilation Boats built before August 1, 1980	At least two ventilator ducts fitted with cowls or their equivalent for the purpose of properly and efficiently ventilating the bilges of every closed engine and fuel-tank compartment of boats constructed or decked over after April 25, 1940, using gasoline as fuel or other fuels having a flashpoint of 110°F or less.			
Ventilation Boats built on August 1, 1980, or later	At least two ventilator ducts for the purpose of efficiently ventilating every closed compartment that contains a gasoline engine and every closed compartment containing a gasoline tank, except those having permanently installed tanks that vent outside the boat and that contain no unprotected electrical devices. Also, engine compartments containing a gasoline engine having a cranking motor must contain power-operated exhaust blowers that can be controlled from the instrument panel.			
Backfire Flame Arrester	One approved device on each carburetor of all gasoline engines installed after April 25, 1940, except outboard motors.			

*When fixed fire extinguishing system is installed in machinery space(s), it will replace one B-1–type portable fire extinguisher.

Note: Coast Guard minimum equipment requirements vary with the size of the boat, type of propulsion, whether operated at night or in periods of reduced visibility, and, in some cases, the body of water on which it is used. For a more thorough discussion and complete details on how many and what types of equipment you must have aboard your boat, request a copy of the free pamphlet Federal Requirements for Recreational Boats from the Coast Guard. Many states have their own requirements that go beyond Coast Guard requirements. Contact your state boating office to learn what they are.

Marine Fire Extinguisher Classification

Coast Guard Classes	Foam (Gal.)	CO_2 (Lb.)	Dry Chem. (Lb.)	Halon (Lb.)
B-I	1.25	4	2	2.5
B-II	2.5	15	10	10
	—	10	2.5	5

OTHER LEGAL ASPECTS OF EQUIPMENT AND OPERATION

Every boat, regardless of size, must have certain safety equipment. Failure to carry the proper equipment may result in a fine and/or imprisonment. In addition, a willful failure to carry the proper equipment represents a dangerous arrogance that the recreational boating community cannot tolerate.

Equipment requirements are generally linked to the size of the boat, and they include such obvious safety-related items as lights, fire extinguishers, life jackets, and other flotation devices; for details, see chapters 8 and 9.

Boat operation is governed by the Rules of the Road (see chapter 14 and appendix I) and the Federal Boating Act. This law:

• proscribes "reckless or negligent" operation of a boat;
• requires that assistance be rendered "as may be practical and necessary" in the event of a collision, accident, or other casualty insofar as that can be provided without serious danger to one's own boat or crew;
• orders the formal reporting within forty-eight hours of any accident that results in death, disappearance under circumstances that suggest death, injury requiring medical treatment other than first aid, or property damage in excess of $200.

Various state laws supplement or amplify the Federal Boating Act, and you must be familiar with the law in your boating area. Some states have long maintained a "hands-off, look the other way" posture when it comes to boating, but this is changing—under pressure from citizens outraged at reckless behavior. Connecticut, for example, has become the first state to require a boat driver's license; proposed legislation in other states envisions mandatory training; waterway speed limits are being imposed in high-traffic areas; drinking-and-driving afloat is being given the same status it receives ashore, as are other breaches of the law. In Florida, for example, a "hit and run" boating accident is a felony.

CHAPTER EIGHT

Equipping for Safety

LEGAL AND LOGICAL PREPAREDNESS

Safety equipment is not a "nice to have" option: The law mandates such safety equipment as life jackets, fire extinguishers, and distress signals, and common sense calls for such additional items as communications gear, foul-weather protection, and equipment for dealing with a crisis.

A crisis is just that: You won't have the time to rummage around looking for emergency equipment, or the option of reviewing emergency procedures in a book. You must plan ahead. Spend time assessing the type of crisis with which you might have to deal, assemble the appropriate tools and equipment, and study and practice the procedures best suited to solving the crisis before it becomes a disaster.

Your primary safety system is your boat itself, in good repair and operational condition. To this you add:

FOR THE BOAT

• Basic electronics: a VHF radio and a depth finder;
• Detectors and alarms;
• Adequate ground tackle (anchors) to keep the boat out of danger;
• Protection from electrolysis and lightning;
• A dinghy (size of boat permitting);

• Tools, spare parts, and backup equipment for repairing broken rigs, broken-down engines, and flooding bilges.

FOR THE CREW

• Flotation and environmental protection;
• A medical kit appropriate to the type of boating (expected distance from shore and assistance; special needs of the crew).

FOR EMERGENCIES

• Flares and other signaling devices;
• Firefighting equipment;
• Damage-control gear (special tools and equipment);
• Depending on the type of boat and nature of planned operations, a fully equipped life raft might be added.

Knowledge about the location and proper use of all the above-listed equipment must be shared with, or immediately available to, other members of the crew.

Finally, you must have a clear understanding that safety equipment doesn't make your boat safe. You do.

VHF Marine Radio Channels

Channel	Description		Channel	Description
W1	NOAA Weather		27	USA Marine Operator
W2	NOAA Weather		28	USA Marine Operator
W3	NOAA Weather		60	International
W4	Canadian Weather		61	International
W5	NOAA Weather		62	International
W6	NOAA Weather		63	USA Commercial/Port Operations
W7	NOAA Weather		64	International
W8	NOAA Weather		65	USA Port Operations
W9	Canadian Weather		66	USA Port Operations
			67	USA Navigation
01	USA Commercial/Port Operations		68	USA Noncommercial
02	International		69	USA Noncommercial
03	International		70	USA Noncommercial
04	International		71	USA Noncommercial
05	USA Port Operations		72	USA Noncommercial
06	USA Intership Safety Channel		73	USA Port Operations
07	USA Commercial		74	USA Port Operations
08	USA Commercial		75	Listen Only/Guard Band
09	Commercial/Noncommercial Working		76	Listen Only/Guard Band
10	USA Commercial		77	USA Pilots Only
11	USA Commercial		78	USA Noncommercial
12	USA Port Operations		79	USA Commercial
13	USA Navigation		80	USA Commercial
14	USA Port Operations		81	USA U.S. Coast Guard Only
15	USA EPIRB		82	USA U.S. Coast Guard Only
16	EMERGENCY/SAFETY CHANNEL/CALLING		83	USA U.S. Coast Guard Only
			84	USA Marine Operator
17	USA State Government		85	USA Marine Operator
18	USA Commercial		86	USA Marine Operator
19	USA Commercial		87	USA Marine Operator
20	USA Port Operations		88	USA Marine Operator, Great Lakes
21	U.S. Coast Guard		88A	USA Commercial, except Great Lakes
22	U.S. Coast Guard and Notice to Mariners		89	Canadian
23	U.S. Coast Guard		90	Canadian
24	USA Marine Operator		91	Canadian
25	USA Marine Operator		92	Canadian
26	USA Marine Operator			

Notes on VHF Marine Radio Channels

• Channels assigned to the Canadian government require authorization prior to use.

• Certain alphabetic suffixes have been deleted from USA channels, since most VHF radios display only numeric designations.

• The majority of international channels are not shown. However, their alphanumeric designations closely follow USA designations.

SAFETY EQUIPMENT FOR THE BOAT

ELECTRONICS

VHF radio—the basic piece of electronic safety equipment—receives weather reports and Coast Guard warnings and transmits requests for assistance.

The radio must have an adequate power supply and should be hard-wired to the battery, bypassing the central control panel. The radio must be protected against a current surge by an in-line fuse. The radio should be checked for electrical interference—which should be isolated and eliminated. The antenna must be of the right size and style for the radio—as specified in the owner's manual—and mounted as high as possible for maximum range. A jury-rig emergency antenna should be made up in advance and stowed in a handy location.

The radio itself should be protected from the weather yet handy to the helmsman. Remote speakers should be mounted in various locations aboard the boat to ensure full coverage; remote microphones should be installed at each helm station.

When you buy a radio, you must obtain a license from the Federal Communications Commission (FCC), which has responsibility for the safe and equitable use of the airways, including those used in recreational and commercial boating. You must have an FCC ship radio station license, which is issued to one individual for use with one boat. The license may not be transferred or assigned. When a boat is sold (even if the radio is removed first for installation on a new boat), the license must be returned to the FCC.

Operating instructions should be posted near the radio, including easy-to-follow instructions for making an emergency transmission. They should be easy enough for a child to use—because it may be a child who has to make the call (see chapter 21).

Navigation equipment, such as depth finders, Loran, Sat-Nav, and radar—certainly part of the safety picture—is described in chapter 12.

Reducing Radio Interference

Because a clear and strong radio signal is a vital link to safety, take the steps necessary to reduce or eliminate any signal interference that may be created by such on-board sources as electrical generators/alternators, voltage regulators, gasoline engine ignition system, a spinning propeller shaft, or even the standing rigging. Here's a quick-check reference:

Symptom	Source	Fix
Snapping	Ignition	Install a shielding kit; install a suppression regulator between the coil and the distributor cap; install a rate capacitor between the ignition coil (hot primary terminal) and the ground (engine block); install resistor-type spark-plug wires; be sure ignition coil is mounted on the engine, not on a bulkhead.
Whining noise	Generator	Place a 200V capacitor between the armature terminal (battery side of generator) and the ground.
Hiss	Alternator	Place a 200V capacitor between the alternator output (the battery terminal) and the ground.
Steady bursts of noise	Propeller shaft	Place a bronze strip or brush in rubbing contact with the propeller shaft between the engine and the stuffing box; connect to the ground.
Whine	Standing rigging	Run a bronze jumper wire across turnbuckles; wrap with tape.
Static	——	Check all grounds and bonding connections.

DETECTORS AND ALARMS

Properly selected and installed detectors and alarms will help protect your boat from such unwanted intrusions as burglars on the deck and explosive vapors trapped below.

A well-thought-out alarm system will signal flooding in the bilges (with a float switch mounted above the normal bilgewater level) as well as dangerous levels of gasoline, propane, or hydrogen fumes (with sensors mounted in appropriate compartments below decks; additional

sensors can be added to warn of low oil pressure, loss of engine coolant, and fire).

The system can also warn of unauthorized attempts to start the engine (wired through a hidden manual alarm-disconnect switch) and the presence of skulking thieves (through a variety of means). However, traditional home or automobile burglar alarms may be impractical aboard an occupied boat. Switches used to signal the opening of a window, for example, are of little value on a boat hatch already left open for ventilation; ultrasonic or infrared systems used to detect movement in a room on the other side of a house are of no more use on a boat than they would be in your bedroom. The warning comes a bit too late. Intruders are best intercepted while still outside the boat.

An effective burglar alarm system can be rigged with some simple pressure-sensitive switches under a deck pad, plus fishing-line trip wires hooked up to an alarm bell (or siren) and a bright spotlight that shines on the deck.

GALLEY SWITCHES AND ALARMS. The panel at lower left controls the Halon firefighting system for the galley. The panel with the round sensor is the sniffer alarm for the propane stove system. The plate above it contains the on/off switches for the onboard diesel generator providing 110V AC power for galley equipment and refrigeration. The panel to the right mounts a ground-fault protected 110V AC outlet.

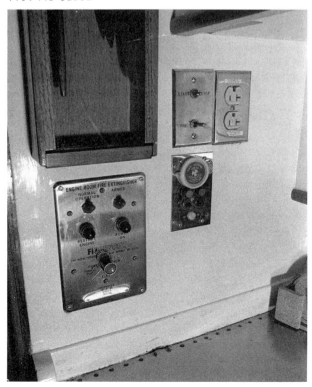

MULTIPLE ALARM UNIT. A flexible alarm system can take the outputs from a variety of sensors and trigger light and audible alarms. This system monitors fire, low oil pressure, high engine temperature, bilgewater level, cooling water flow for engines, and also includes a burglar alarm. The alarm system is available for either singles or twin-engine installations. It can also be modified to activate a strobe light mounted at the masthead (Aqualarm)

FIRE DETECTION

If you can smell the smoke, feel the heat, or see the flames, you have lost precious moments in dealing with a fire and may already be too late to save your boat. Fire-detection units, which respond to a trace of smoke or an increase in temperature, will give an early warning; many can be rigged to set off an extinguishing system. Other sensors provide timely warning of explosive vapors, to keep you from starting engines (or lighting the stove) until the vapors have been cleared away by bilge blowers or other ventilation.

Smoke and fume detectors come in several varieties, all of which can be effective. All require some electrical power (best provided by a self-contained battery), and many are multipurpose units that include flooding and burglar alarms and give warning if the battery charging or refrigeration circuits should fail.

Regardless of other features, every unit should have:

- On/off signal light;
- Built-in test circuit, with provision for calibration;
- Certification for marine use, rated for continuous operation at temperatures ranging from 0° to 150°F;
- An alarm with sufficient volume to be heard clearly above the noise of engines running at full speed.

The sensor units must be mounted where they will do the most good. Since gasoline and LPG fumes are heavier than air, the vapor sensor should be set as low as possible in the hull (but above normal bilgewater level). Smoke and heat rise, so fire sensors should be set at the top of the compartment. If fuel tanks and the engine are in separate compartments, there should be separate sensors. For boats without compartmentation, the sensor should go in the lowest part of the bilge in which fumes are likely to settle.

The control panel should be at the main helm station, with remote indicators at the secondary helm and in the galley.

PROPANE AND NATURAL GAS FUME AND VAPOR MONITOR. This system, which can monitor several sensors in different locations, incorporates a remote-control on/off valve button. (Fireboy–Xintex)

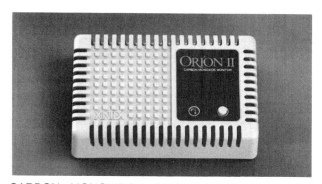

CARBON MONOXIDE MONITOR/ALARM. A useful alarm to monitor and warn of noxious gas buildup in engine spaces and bilge sections. (Fireboy–Xintex)

COOLING WATER FLOW MONITOR.

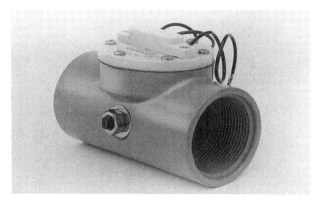

FLOODING ALARM uses a variety of systems to signal for help. The bilge-mounted sensor activates the alarm sender unit, which can be matched to a sound signal, a masthead strobe light, or a flashing panel light (or combinations of all these). (Jabsco)

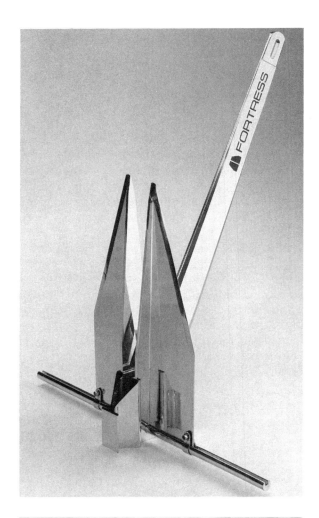

PLOW ANCHOR (CQR).

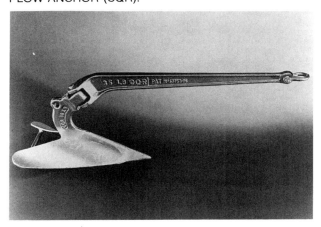

STOWABLE DANFORTH ANCHOR. The Danforth anchor provides excellent holding power far in excess of its weight-to-strength relationship, although it should not be used in grassy bottoms, as it has a tendency to skip over the bottom surface. This particular anchor is constructed of high-grade steel and has a break-apart feature for easy stowage. (Fortress)

All sensors should be checked for proper operation, using the self-test circuit, before getting underway; the units should be recalibrated every six months, or at the beginning of an extended cruise.

GROUND TACKLE

A cinder-block anchor may be adequate for a rowboat on a placid lake, but most boats in most waters need proper ground tackle—an anchor designed and sized for the purpose and selected for the particular conditions anticipated. For any type of anchor other than a cinder block, it's not the weight that holds the boat in place but the manner in which the anchor flukes work on the bottom—and there is no such thing as a truly all-purpose anchor. The traditional kedge anchor grabs well among rocks and digs into seaweed, but it usually just plows a furrow in a muddy or sandy bottom. The most popular modern anchor—the Danforth—works well in sandy or muddy bottoms, but it may slide right over heavy grass or seaweed. A well-equipped boat would carry at least two anchors, of different types.

The size of anchor must be matched to the size of the boat, but for most boats it should not be heavier than an average person can lift easily.

The anchor is attached to the boat with a length of chain or line—or a combination of the two—called the anchor rode. The rode not only holds the anchor and boat together, it also is the mechanism by which the anchor is properly set. An anchor held up-and-down won't grab; the rode, lying along the bottom for some distance before curving gently to the surface, pulls the anchor parallel to the bottom to enable the flukes to catch and dig in. A length of chain at the anchor end greatly increases that possibility. An additional factor is the length of rode in the water (known as the scope of the line); it should be seven to ten times the depth at the anchorage. It can be less in calm, sheltered waters with minimal current, but the greater the scope—offering a buffer against the shock of the waves as well as ensuring that the anchor is working parallel to

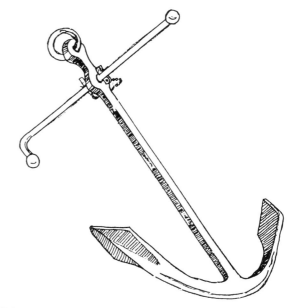

STOCK OR YACHTSMAN'S ANCHOR.

BRUCE ANCHOR. The Bruce-type anchor shown mounted on the pulpit of this Maine cruising sailboat is an extremely effective working and storm anchor in mixed or rocky bottom.

the bottom—the better the chance the anchor will hold.

A more comprehensive discussion of how and when to use anchors appears in chapter 15.

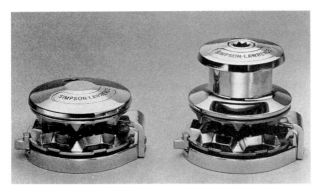

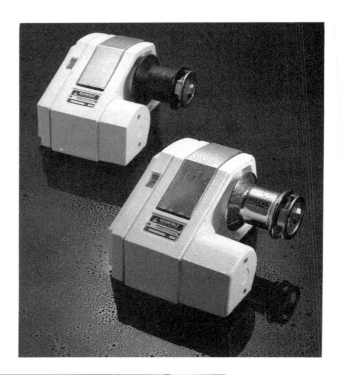

CHAIN AND ANCHOR-RODE WINCHES. Two well-designed low-profile anchor-handling winches. (Simpson-Lawrence)

DECK WINDLASSES. Two different sizes of combination rode-handling and chain windlasses for on-deck mounting. Windlasses powered by electricity should have heavy cabling to reduce resistance, as well as overcurrent protection (circuit breakers) in each leg of the direct-current circuit. (Double-pole breakers will provide this protection.) (Seawolf)

CHAIN STOPPER. This is a fairly rare piece of boat hardware, but it is easy to have custom-built if you cannot find one at a chandlery or in a specialty catalog. Many boat owners seem to shy away from full-length chain systems for anchoring, but the advantages are that it is easy to stow and hard to foul, and less rode is required because of the catenary "bow" formed by the weight of the chain. This chain stopper is placed aft of the anchor windlass and provides firm and positive locking of the chain using the insert plate.

Table 8-3.
Suggested Anchor Size,
by Type/Length of Boat

Length of Boat	21 ft.	25 ft.	30 ft.	35 ft.	42 ft.	50 ft.
Danforth	9 lb.	14 lb.	16 lb.	24 lb.	24 lb.*	39 lb.*
CQR (plow)	15 lb.	20 lb.	25 lb.	35 lb.	45 lb.	60 lb.
Fisherman	30 lb.	40 lb.	50 lb.	70 lb.	90 lb.	120 lb.
Bruce	11 lb.	22 lb.	22 lb.	44 lb.	44 lb.	65 lb.

Note: Indicated size is for a boat of average displacement; heavy-displacement boats should have the next heavier size.
*"Deepset" Danforth model for larger boats; others listed are "standard" Danforth models.

Table 8-4.
Factors for Selecting Size of Anchor Line

A. Typical Anticipated Loads on Anchor Line
(in Pounds)

LOA	Working Anchor (Average Seas)	Storm Anchor (Heavy Weather)
10	160	320
15	250	500
20	360	720
25	490	980
30	700	1400
35	900	1800
40	1200	2400
50	1600	3200

B. Working Strength (in Pounds) of Various Lines for Anchor Rode

Diameter (Inches)	3-Strand			Double-Braided		
	Nylon	Polyester	Polypropylene	Nylon	Polyester	Chain
1/4	182	182	213	420	350	1250
5/16	281	281	323	680	560	1875
3/8	407	407	459	960	750	2625
1/2	704	704	714	1630	1400	4500
5/8	1144	1100	1054	2800	2400	6800
3/4	1562	1375	1445	3600	3000	9500
7/8	2200	1980	1955	5300	4800	11375
1	2750	2420	2380	6260	5600	13950

Note: Polyester and polypropylene have very little stretch and are not recommended for anchor rodes; working loads noted above are 20 percent or less than the average breaking strength of a new rope or chain, allowing a margin of safety of at least 5:1. These figures are typical but may not necessarily represent any given brand of rope or chain; check the manufacturer's data when selecting.

SAILS FOR HEAVY WEATHER

The typical set of sails is designed for moderate wind and stress; most come with installed grommets to provide a method whereby the sail area can be decreased, or reefed, to reduce the extra pressure from higher wind. However, reefing in the traditional manner (described in chapter 14) can be cumbersome at best and difficult if attempted after the wind has already risen to hazardous levels; several alternative methods are available and should be considered when preparing your boat for safe sailing.

Jiffy (or slab) reefing incorporates a set of lines and blocks allowing relatively quick and secure sail reduction, particularly for a singlehanded sailor.

In roller reefing, the boom rotates around its axis, pulling the sail down and around like an upside-down window shade. A roller-furling rig—akin to a vertical window shade—is often found on headsails for convenience, and not especially for reefing; it is less common for mainsails, but if installed, is the only way to reef the main. Some roller-furling rigs wrap the sail around a stay; others pull it into a slot in the mast. The latter keeps the sail out of the sun and weather when not in use, but it has a greater tendency to jam than the more exposed type. (Sails used with roller furling typically have a strip of blue cloth along the luff, which is the last portion to be rolled and thus provides protection from ultraviolet rays.)

Reefing by either of these methods is a compromise—convenience weighed against efficient sail shape. But the loss of sailing efficiency is more than made up by the gain in sailing safety.

Another vital part of your safe sailing kit: stormsails. These have the same area as (or less than) a double-reefed sail (that is, a sail that has been reefed to the second stage, about as far as it can go), but they are designed especially to handle the extra pressure of high winds—heavier cloth that is strongly reinforced at stress points with extra-sturdy edge bindings. Some stormsails themselves can be reefed to further reduce the area, but these definitely should be rigged with a jiffy system. You don't want to be wrestling with traditional reefing if the wind is so high that you need to reef the stormsail.

For serious long-distance cruising or racing, you should also be equipped with a storm jib.

MODIFICATIONS TO THE SAIL RIG

• Rig at least one spare halyard. This will provide a margin of redundancy should you lose, break, or jam a halyard. It also can do double duty as a stay if one fails (see chapter 19). It is instantly available for use with a standby sail, ready to fly as you strike the drawing sail. And it is always ready to hoist a bosun's chair to carry a crew member aloft (see chapter 10).

• Carry a double forestay—even if (*especially* if) you have a roller-furling headsail. This lets you prepare the next heavier (or lighter) headsail for use while the primary sail is still working, minimizing any loss of steerageway or stability.

• Install a spur track on the mast. This lets you have another sail (such as a stormsail) in a standby position while the main is still drawing.

WINDSHIELD WIPERS

Windshield wipers are small but occasionally vital items that too often are not included as part of a boat's equipment. You know that you can't easily drive an automobile with a rain or mist-enshrouded windshield; how could you do any better in a boat where you may also have to contend with the problem of salt-covered glass?

The wipers may be operated by hand (as in the early days of automobiling) or driven by an electric motor. Many of the electric units offered for recreational boats are too flimsy; if you plan to be offshore or in marginal weather very often, you'd be better off with an expensive but sturdy commercial version—the sort used by commercial fishermen and tugboats.

An alternative: a "clear view" screen, consisting of a circular piece of glass driven at high speed by a motor in the center. Centrifugal force spins the water away. It's expensive but effective.

Worth exploring is a product called Rain-X, which often is used by racing-car drivers in lieu of windshield wipers. Rain-X coats the windshield and forces water and salt to bead up and quickly fall off the glass.

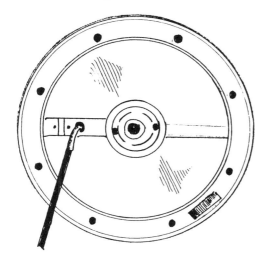

"KENT"-TYPE CLEAR-VIEW SCREEN. This unit, installed in a suitably sized windshield, consists of an inner (fixed) circle of glass and an outer glass circle that spins on a shaft driven by the center-mounted motor. The resulting centrifugal force spins rain and spray off the outer glass, affording a section of clear vision.

LIGHTNING PROTECTION

Two types of lightning protection should be installed—one to guide the charge of a main strike safely down into the water and the other to protect electronic equipment from a damaging power surge.

Metal masts or outriggers will carry the current *to* the boat, but it must be provided with a path down *through* the boat. The main conductor must be at least 8 AWG stranded (*not* solid) copper wire, or copper strip at least 1/32 inch thick, laid along as straight a path as possible. To guard against spark or side flashes, any large metal objects nearby (such as winches, guardrails and

handrails, galley stacks, and davits) that are not already part of the bonding system must be tied in with an interconnecting conductor (also of 8 AWG). On sailboats with nonmetallic hulls, all metallic standing rigging should be grounded to the system.

With a wooden mast, the securely fastened main conductor must run up the mast and extend at least 6 inches above the mast in an air terminal—a sharply pointed metal rod.

A radio antenna with conductivity equivalent to 8 AWG copper may provide lightning protection; however, the feedlines to electronic equipment should have some means for grounding during an electrical storm or be protected by designed-in lightning arresters or protective gaps. Otherwise, circuits can be destroyed by current overload.

On most powerboats, an air terminal should be installed above the boat's highest point. The best location for all-around protection would be in the middle of the boat, at a height above the waterline equal to one-half the boat's length.

The current must be directed to a lightning ground connection. On many boats, the engine block serves as the grounding connection for the electrical and bonding system, carrying the current to the ground via the shaft (with a jumper past the transmission) and propeller. However, a caution: For lightning protection, the submerged grounding surface must be at least one square foot in area, and many propellers won't measure up. The grounding surface may be *any* metal component under water, such as the rudder, the centerboard and keel, or an installed ground plate.

Properly installed, a lightning protection system will create a cone of protection for the boat and crew, extending down from the air terminal (or masthead) at a 60-degree angle.

Be aware, however, that the system will not protect a boat from accidental contact with electric power lines, nor protect it from lightning while it is out of the water.

Chapter 11 discusses rules for the crew during an electrical storm.

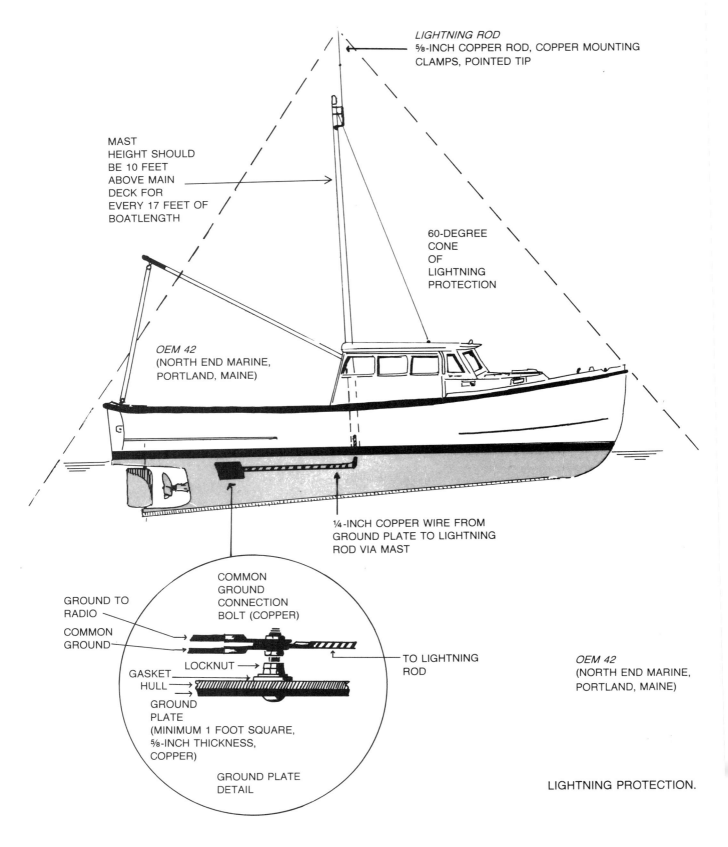

LIGHTNING ROD
⅝-INCH COPPER ROD, COPPER MOUNTING
CLAMPS, POINTED TIP

MAST
HEIGHT SHOULD
BE 10 FEET
ABOVE MAIN
DECK FOR
EVERY 17 FEET OF
BOATLENGTH

60-DEGREE
CONE
OF
LIGHTNING
PROTECTION

OEM 42
(NORTH END MARINE,
PORTLAND, MAINE)

¼-INCH COPPER WIRE FROM
GROUND PLATE TO LIGHTNING
ROD VIA MAST

COMMON
GROUND
CONNECTION
BOLT (COPPER)

GROUND TO
RADIO

COMMON
GROUND

TO LIGHTNING
ROD

LOCKNUT

GASKET
HULL

GROUND
PLATE
(MINIMUM 1 FOOT SQUARE,
⅝-INCH THICKNESS,
COPPER)

GROUND PLATE
DETAIL

OEM 42
(NORTH END MARINE,
PORTLAND, MAINE)

LIGHTNING PROTECTION.

THE DINGHY

A dinghy may be thought of as a workboat or recreation for the children, but it should also be considered part of your safety kit. You might need a dinghy to repair underwater damage, for example, or to shift an anchor in preparation for a storm. And, in the event of disaster, it can be a substitute for a life raft (see chapter 9).

Basic dinghy options include size, type, and power.

Size This is determined largely by the size and type of your boat, the size of your family or crew, and the type of boating you plan to do. This is all pretty obvious—and, just as obviously, you may have to make some compromises. Also—

INFLATABLE BOAT FEATURES: (1) V-shaped, reinforced floor for use with higher-powered motors. (2) Non-slip, draining deck surface. (3) Paddle and painter. (4) Bow-lifting handle. (5) Bow storage compartment. (6) Dinghy bailout bag containing emergency flares, safety equipment, etc. (7) Reinforced towing eye. (8) Attachment points for inflatable passenger seat. (9) Multi-inflated compartments segmented so a puncture in one section does not eliminate all buoyancy. (10) Reinforced attachment sections for transom. (11) Transom section rated for outboard attachment. (12) Safety line rigged the length of the boat for passenger security. (The line should be passed through life jackets, flippers, and other vital on-board equipment needed in the event of a capsize.) (13) Automatic bailer device integral to the transom. (14) Anti-chafe strip. (15) Lifting handles. (16) Hard rubber rubbing strake integral to the inflatable sections. (17) Rigged safety lines. (Avon)

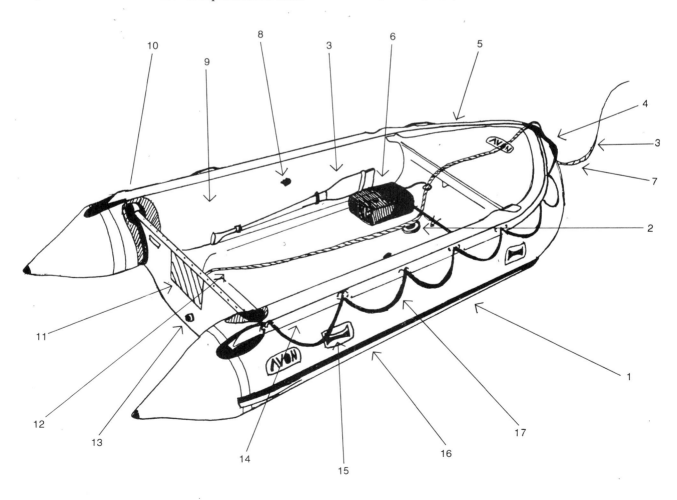

something that will become obvious the first time you have to wrestle the boat into the water—the boat will have to be of a size matched to your physical capabilities.

Type This comes down to a basic choice between a rigid hull and an inflatable.

• Rigid-hull dinghies are highly maneuverable and, if equipped with adequate floation, they remain unsinkable even when filled with water. They are, however, unstable; hard to get into and out of; and especially hard to get into from the water. Rigid dinghies are easily rowed and glide easily (we might even say effortlessly) through the water. Some can be rigged for sailing—an added advantage. For a truly efficient and attractive dinghy, check out some of the traditional designs of yesteryear that are now being reproduced in fiberglass: Whitehall pulling boats, Herreshoff yacht tenders, and Maine peapods.

• Inflatable boats are highly stable; will support passengers even if several of the chambers are punctured (although the passengers will get wet); and can be deflated for convenient storage. On the other hand, inflatables are easily cut or damaged by shells or glass or by pier and piling hardware. Large, ponderous inflatables are hard to row, glide not at all, and in fact are prone to go backward if heading into any sort of breeze.

Power Some models of either hull type may be equipped with an outboard motor. Outboards are very helpful for long hauls from shore to anchorage after a hard day on the beach—provided no one has stolen the motor. Outboards do add to the fuel-storage problem aboard your boat.

Dinghies may be stowed topside or towed. Each has its disadvantages:

• Topside, the dinghy takes up valuable space.
• Topside, launching and recovery of the dinghy is cumbersome if not difficult unless davits or a block-and-tackle has been rigged for the purpose. Even a medium-sized inflatable, with floorboards in place, weighs about 100 pounds. An outboard motor—which you would handle separately—may weigh at least half that much.
• Slung from stern davits, the dinghy is vulnerable to damage any time the boat is moored stern-to in a slip or along a quay wall.
• Deflating and stowing an inflatable boat in a storage locker gets it out of the way, but it also delays launching.
• Towed, the dinghy might founder in a rainsquall, be swamped by a passing wave, or (most likely) break loose and drift astern when no one is paying enough attention.
• Towed, when the boat slows down and the dinghy continues moving forward, the towline might settle below the surface and foul the propeller.
• A dinghy kept in the water—anytime, anywhere—is subject to the same sort of bottom growth as the boat, but it probably will not have received the same antifouling bottom protection.

SAFETY EQUIPMENT FOR THE CREW
PERSONAL FLOTATION DEVICES (PFDS)

PFDs include life jackets, water-ski vests, buoyant cushions—all items that will help keep a person afloat in the water. However, they accomplish this vital task with varying degrees of effectiveness, and merely having PFDs aboard to conform with legal requirements—without assessment of your probable actual need—is a violation of common sense.

For the record:

• Boats less than 16 feet in length must be equipped with one PFD, of any type listed below, for each person aboard;
• Boats 16 feet and larger must have one Type IV in addition to one Type I, II, III, or V, for each person aboard;

TYPE II ADULT LIFE JACKET. This personal flotation device has a synthetic outer shell and features reflective patches for high visibility in low-light situations. The jacket has more than thirty-five pounds of buoyancy and is fully reversible. It is designed to keep the wearer in an upright position and tilted so his head, nose, and mouth are clear of the water. However, it may not roll over an unconscious wearer as a Type I vest will do. This device has stainless steel closure devices and is flat for easy stowage. It meets U.S. Coast Guard and SOLAS requirements. (Stearns)

TYPE III FLOTATION VEST. This unit is a well-constructed flotation vest with flap-type, Velcro-fastened pockets. It is designed for comfort and features reflective tape sewn on the shoulder areas. While this vest is not a Type I—which will roll over an unconscious wearer and hold the head out of the water—it has a distinct advantage in that it is easy to wear and crew members will not be hampered in deck activity. The best jacket is the one that is worn and not stowed away. (Stearns)

• Canoes and kayaks, regardless of length, must carry one approved device for each person aboard;

• A water skier, while being towed, is considered to be on board the boat for purposes of compliance with the regulations;

• PFDs must be in good condition and of an appropriate size for the persons who intend to wear them; wearable PFDs must be readily accessible, and throwable devices must be immediately available for use.

All PFDs approved by the Coast Guard will bear one of the following type designations:

Type I A wearable device designed to turn an unconscious person from a face-down position in the water to a vertical or slightly backward position. The adult size provides a minimum buoyancy of 22 pounds, with some models as high as 35 pounds; the child size provides 11 pounds of buoyancy.

Type II A wearable device also *intended* to turn a person to a vertical or slightly backward position, but not as effectively under most conditions as a Type I PFD. An adult size provides a minimum buoyancy of 15.5 pounds; medium child size, 11 pounds; infant/small child size, seven pounds.

Type III A wearable device that will allow the wearer to assume a vertical or slightly backward floating position. This has the same buoyancy as the Type II but little or no turning ability. Type IIIs restrict movement less than Types I and II and come in a wide variety of styles and sizes. Many are designed for use while engaged in water sports; many are designed for people who don't want to appear to be wearing a life jacket. Type IIIs are the most widely used, despite their limited utility as life jackets. Some—such as float coats—are quite useful as foul-weather gear.

Type IV A device designed to be thrown to a person in the water and grasped and held by the user until rescued. The most common Type IV devices are buoyant cushions; the most useful are horseshoe and ring buoys.

Type V A catchall category for any device the Coast Guard approves for restricted use.

While most boaters prefer Type III PFDs for reasons of comfort and style, or they might equip their boat with Type IIs because of cost, any boat destined for serious offshore work should carry 35-pound-buoyancy Type I life jackets for each crew member. Each jacket should be equipped with:

1. A water-activated strobe light or, at the least, a small, one-celled waterproof flashlight;
2. A whistle;
3. A sailing knife in a sheath, attached by a lanyard;
4. Reflective tape, back and front at the top; and
5. A safety harness.

THE FASTNET MK II CREW VEST. This vest was developed following the high loss of life during the 1979 Fastnet Race. Lessons learned during the race showed that many of the drowned sailors were not wearing life vests, or that they delayed donning the gear because the vests restricted movement. To gain ease of movement, crew members still have to sacrifice the important lifesaving features of Type I and Type II vests—i.e., rollover to a heads-up position and the automatic upright body position in the water. However, an easily worn vest that permits free action has much to recommend it on board—particularly in singlehanded or long-distance offshore cruising.

This vest incorporates a heavy-duty and well-thought-out harness, a safety line, and storage pockets. It can be inflated by installed CO_2 cartridges or by mouth. The vest's chief failing is that it does not have inherent buoyancy, but one way around this is to mouth-inflate the vest slightly while working on deck. The vest is also available with a built-in harness or as a flotation collar. It can be used as "additional" equipment on recreational boats, but it may not be substituted for the Coast Guard–required personal flotation devices. In purely practical terms, the vest probably is one of the greatest advances in life-jacket design in the last twenty years. (Switlik)

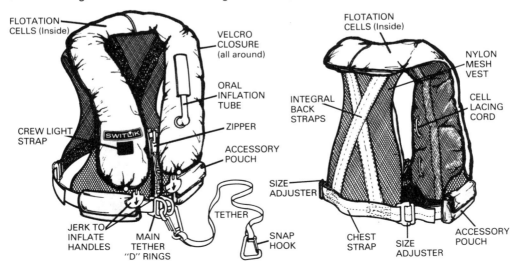

FLOTATION CELLS (Inside) — VELCRO CLOSURE (all around) — ORAL INFLATION TUBE — ZIPPER — ACCESSORY POUCH — CREW LIGHT STRAP — JERK TO INFLATE HANDLES — MAIN TETHER "D" RINGS — TETHER — SNAP HOOK — FLOTATION CELLS (Inside) — NYLON MESH VEST — CELL LACING CORD — INTEGRAL BACK STRAPS — SIZE ADJUSTER — CHEST STRAP — SIZE ADJUSTER — ACCESSORY POUCH

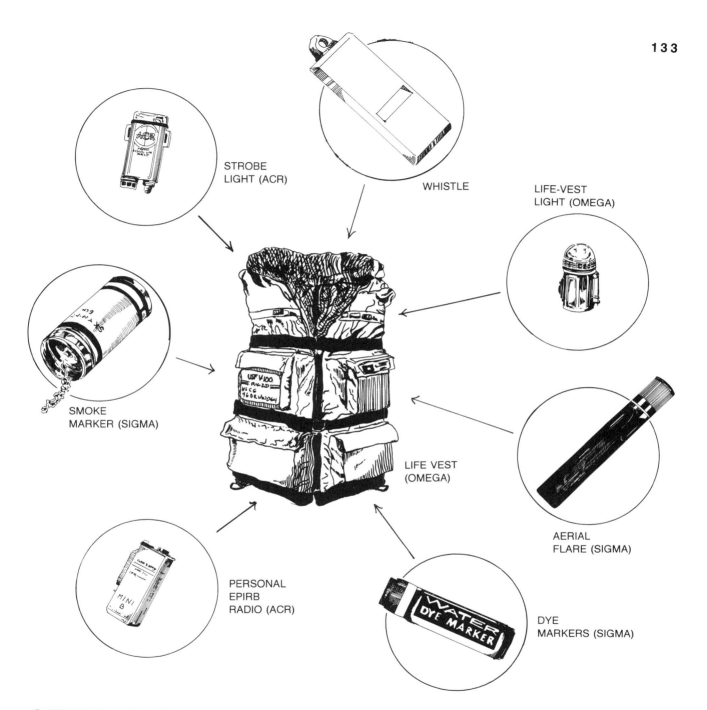

STROBE
LIGHT (ACR)

WHISTLE

LIFE-VEST
LIGHT (OMEGA)

SMOKE
MARKER (SIGMA)

LIFE VEST
(OMEGA)

AERIAL
FLARE (SIGMA)

PERSONAL
EPIRB
RADIO (ACR)

DYE
MARKERS (SIGMA)

OUTFITTING A LIFE VEST. Outfitting a life vest is a compromise between equipping for the maximum number of situations and having a jacket that is easy to wear. Most drowning victims were not wearing their life jackets. The Coast Guard is well aware that people delay putting on the jacket, often until it is too late. However, survival does not depend on flotation alone. You need the ability to alert rescuers to your problem and location, and to maintain contact—hence all the components shown in this sketch. Each item should be secured in a sealing pocket or attached with a lanyard. (Omega, ACR, Sigma, Stearns)

FLOAT COAT includes a wet-suit type of inner construction, a quick-release waist belt for further protection, storage pockets, storm flap, and drainable mesh construction at wrists and hem. (Mustang)

FLOAT COATS

While not a useful substitute for a life jacket (even though many are classed as Type III flotation aids), float coats are excellent for use as foul-weather gear. They help keep you warm and dry topside, and if you do fall overboard, they provide some degree of flotation and thermal protection.

The better models include thermal protection for the groin area (an area of rapid heat loss in water) and have a built-in safety harness for the swift attachment of safety lines.

OVERALLS

Exposure overalls—another version of foul-weather/flotation gear—cover the body from ankle to head. They also include leg and wrist tapes and a hood and provide some thermal protection and modest flotation.

SURVIVAL SUITS

A survival suit basically is a loose-fitting, foam-construction, full-body suit designed to provide flotation and thermal protection. The top-of-the-line survival suits cover all parts of the body (including feet, hands, and head), but they pretty much preclude any useful movement, such as swimming; they are cumbersome. Other models provide less protection but offer greater mobility.

Survival suits are expensive—typically, several hundred dollars—and they must be custom made for individuals not of average size, such as small women and children.

But for professionals who spend their lives in a boat, and for serious offshore cruising, particularly in colder waters such as the North Atlantic and the Pacific, they are proven lifesavers. To understand why, see chapter 18 for a discussion of hypothermia.

MUSTANG MS2175
ANTI-EXPOSURE COVERALL AND WORKSUIT

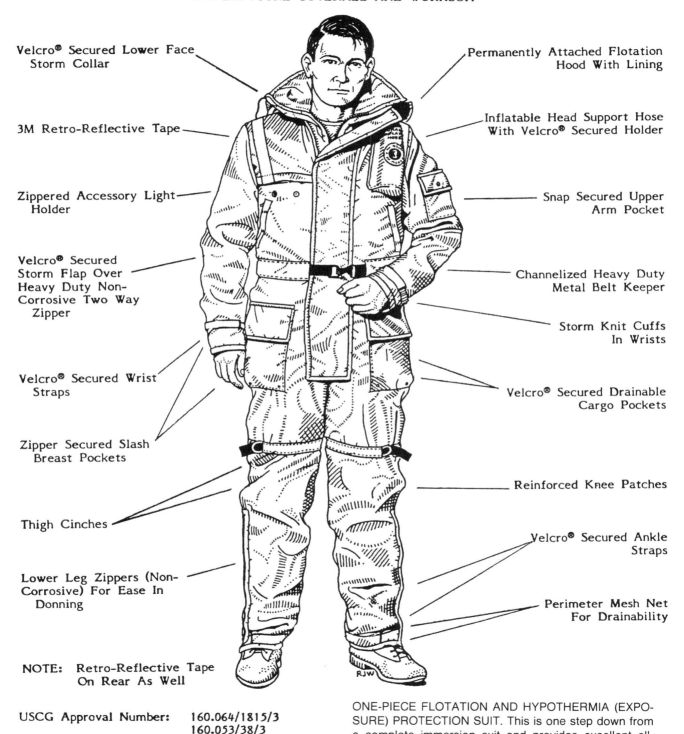

Velcro® Secured Lower Face Storm Collar

3M Retro-Reflective Tape

Zippered Accessory Light Holder

Velcro® Secured Storm Flap Over Heavy Duty Non-Corrosive Two Way Zipper

Velcro® Secured Wrist Straps

Zipper Secured Slash Breast Pockets

Thigh Cinches

Lower Leg Zippers (Non-Corrosive) For Ease In Donning

NOTE: Retro-Reflective Tape On Rear As Well

USCG Approval Number: 160.064/1815/3
                              160.053/38/3

Permanently Attached Flotation Hood With Lining

Inflatable Head Support Hose With Velcro® Secured Holder

Snap Secured Upper Arm Pocket

Channelized Heavy Duty Metal Belt Keeper

Storm Knit Cuffs In Wrists

Velcro® Secured Drainable Cargo Pockets

Reinforced Knee Patches

Velcro® Secured Ankle Straps

Perimeter Mesh Net For Drainability

RJW

ONE-PIECE FLOTATION AND HYPOTHERMIA (EXPOSURE) PROTECTION SUIT. This is one step down from a complete immersion suit and provides excellent all-weather protection as well as flotation. (Mustang)

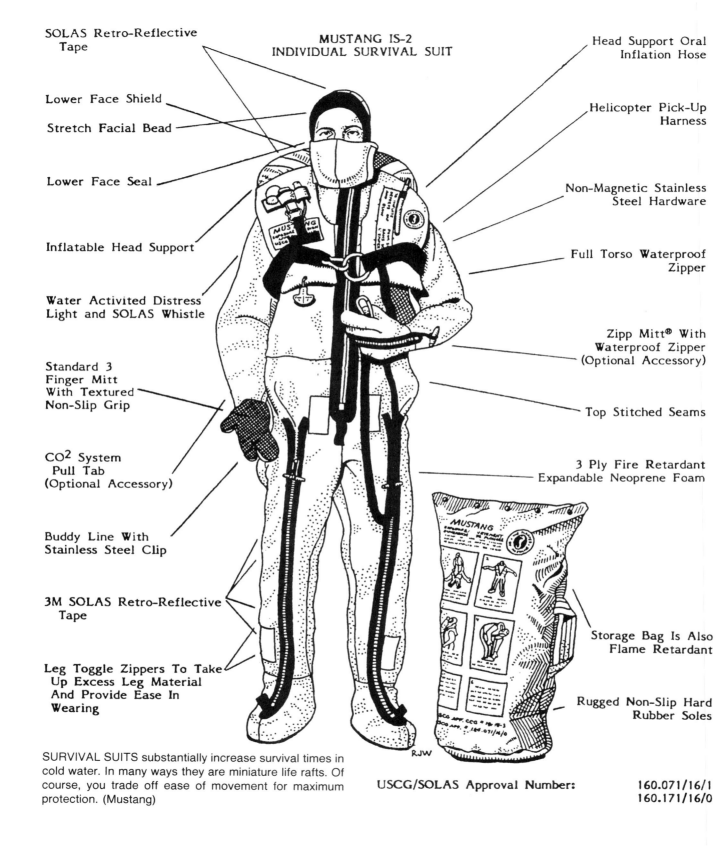

MUSTANG IS-2
INDIVIDUAL SURVIVAL SUIT

SOLAS Retro-Reflective Tape

Lower Face Shield

Stretch Facial Bead

Lower Face Seal

Inflatable Head Support

Water Activited Distress Light and SOLAS Whistle

Standard 3 Finger Mitt With Textured Non-Slip Grip

CO^2 System Pull Tab (Optional Accessory)

Buddy Line With Stainless Steel Clip

3M SOLAS Retro-Reflective Tape

Leg Toggle Zippers To Take Up Excess Leg Material And Provide Ease In Wearing

Head Support Oral Inflation Hose

Helicopter Pick-Up Harness

Non-Magnetic Stainless Steel Hardware

Full Torso Waterproof Zipper

Zipp Mitt® With Waterproof Zipper (Optional Accessory)

Top Stitched Seams

3 Ply Fire Retardant Expandable Neoprene Foam

Storage Bag Is Also Flame Retardant

Rugged Non-Slip Hard Rubber Soles

SURVIVAL SUITS substantially increase survival times in cold water. In many ways they are miniature life rafts. Of course, you trade off ease of movement for maximum protection. (Mustang)

USCG/SOLAS Approval Number: 160.071/16/1
160.171/16/0

EQUIPMENT FOR CHILDREN AND PETS

Unfortunately, the apparent market for child-size survival and foul-weather gear is too small to support much variety. Indeed, aside from small life jackets, virtually no options exist.

Children need more protection than adults; they are not strong swimmers and are more vulnerable to hypothermia, fatigue, and fear. If you take your children to sea, do your best to give them appropriate protection with custom-made or modified gear and nothing less than a Type I offshore life jacket.

Pets are best left ashore, but if included in your boating plans, they should have the same sort of flotation protection you give your children; pet vests are available at most marine supply stores.

Your dog may be a good swimmer, but you want him to do his swimming when and where *you* choose. Too often, when a pet jumps or falls overboard, the owner instinctively dives in to save him, and then you have to deal with both pet and man overboard. If the pet is wearing a life vest, you know that you can take the time to make a safe recovery.

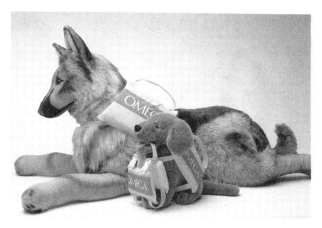

LIFE PRESERVERS FOR PETS are humane and necessary. Pets are part of the family, and when the family dog goes over the side, many people instinctively jump in right after him. Most animals can swim, but they tire easily, so a pet life preserver provides that necessary extra measure of buoyancy. Good preservers incorporate a strong lifting handle to get the animal back aboard. (Omega)

The safety of children and pets is increased greatly by rigging nylon lifeline netting all around the boat.

SAFETY NETS are particularly effective for keeping small children on board—although they are no substitute for a good life vest, a harness, and an attentive crew. This boat could also use a second lifeline mounted below the top one. This net is fine, but it compromises safety as it tapers down to the deck, leaving an unprotected foredeck area.

CHILD/INFANT VEST in floating position clearly shows that a small child's concentration of weight is in the upper body and head and requires specialized gear. All life vests used for infants should be Type I—incorporating a built-in rollover and head-support feature. (Mustang)

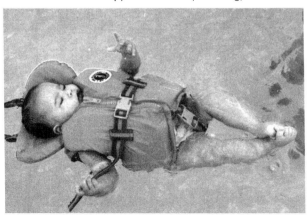

A PROPER SAFETY HARNESS. The Lirakis harness is a mainstay aboard deepwater racing vessels. The rig uses double stitching, a double-clip safety line, and well-designed shoulder supports to carry the heavy loads experienced on deck or during a man-overboard situation. (Lirakis)

JACKLINE AND SAFETY HARNESS

The jackline and safety harness are not commonly found aboard powerboats, which tend to have protected helms and limited need for a crew member to be topside in a storm. On sailboats, however, the safety of the vessel and passengers may well depend upon the ability of the crew to go out on deck to shorten or otherwise adjust or repair the sails.

The jackline should be a stainless steel wire or a good ½-inch Dacron rope, fitted for rigging from bow to stern along the centerline. Or, if the boat is too wide or the deck layout intrudes, two lines may be required. In use, a crew member (wearing a safety harness) hooks a safety line onto the jackline, which permits a full range of fore-and-aft and reasonable thwartship movement and provides safety despite the wind and waves.

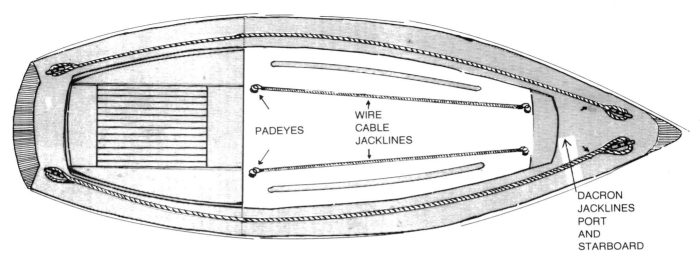

JACKLINES (TWO VERSIONS).

Use of a safety harness should not be limited to heavy-weather sailing; one should be worn:

- When sailing alone, anytime;
- When going on deck in heavy weather;
- When going on deck alone at night while underway;
- When going aloft;
- By small children.

The safety harness must have been designed and constructed for use aboard a boat and not be adapted from a mountain climber's or lineman's rig. All materials and fittings must be appropriate to the marine environment: tough, reinforced nylon webbing and stainless steel hardware.

NOTE: STRAP LENGTHS BETWEEN HOOKS SHOULD NOT BE EXCEEDED. THESE LENGTHS REDUCE CHANCE OF GOING OVERBOARD WHILE STILL TETHERED.

2 FEET
(MAXIMUM STRAP LENGTH
END HOOK TO MIDDLE HOOK)

DOUBLE
STITCHING

4 FEET
(MAXIMUM STRAP LENGTH
MID-HOOK TO END HOOK
AT HARNESS)

MOUNTAIN-CLIMBING-TYPE
CARABINER SAFETY HOOK.

MINIMUM
1-INCH
WEBBING

HARNESS
END

SAFETY LINE.

A PROPER CHILDREN'S SAFETY HARNESS features double-stitching, robust safety-line attachment point, and proper shoulder-strap load distribution. (Lirakis)

The safety harness for each crew member should be adjusted for the best fit and then *labeled* to ensure that each crew member grabs the right harness when there may be precious little time for sorting and refitting.

The harness should fasten at the chest, with a catch that requires a firm and positive action for release. The quick-release type used with a parachute harness is not acceptable; it is too vulnerable to an accidental blow to the chest or a bump against the rigging.

So that you always have a tool handy, attach a sailing knife to the harness, in a sheath and with a lanyard.

The harness should be fitted with two snap-hook-equipped safety lines. These are snapped onto the jackline, the rigging, or any strong attachment point; two lines guarantee that one will be engaged while the other is being shifted—for example, when going from one section of a jackline to another, or from the jackline to the rigging. The lines should be long enough to allow you to do useful work, but not so long that they place you in jeopardy of being hit by a big wave and left dangling over the side.

SAILING KNIFE (FIXED TYPE). A high-grade steel knife with integral shackle-opening design. Note the squared-off tip providing both safety and screw-opening capabilities. (Lirakis)

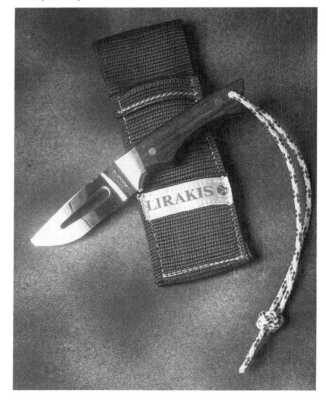

EQUIPMENT FOR MAN-OVERBOARD RECOVERY

There are three critical factors involved in recovering a man overboard:

1. You must realize that someone has fallen overboard.

2. You must be able immediately to mark the location and provide flotation by throwing over the side anything floatable.

3. You must be prepared to bring an unconscious or injured victim back aboard—without any help from the victim.

MAN-OVERBOARD HORSESHOE. This man-overboard rescue system includes a dye-marker pouch, a small drogue to keep the horseshoe in the area where it is thrown, a whistle, and the man-overboard pole stowed in a tunnel section integrated into the boat's stern. This is a good clean rig, easily released in an emergency.

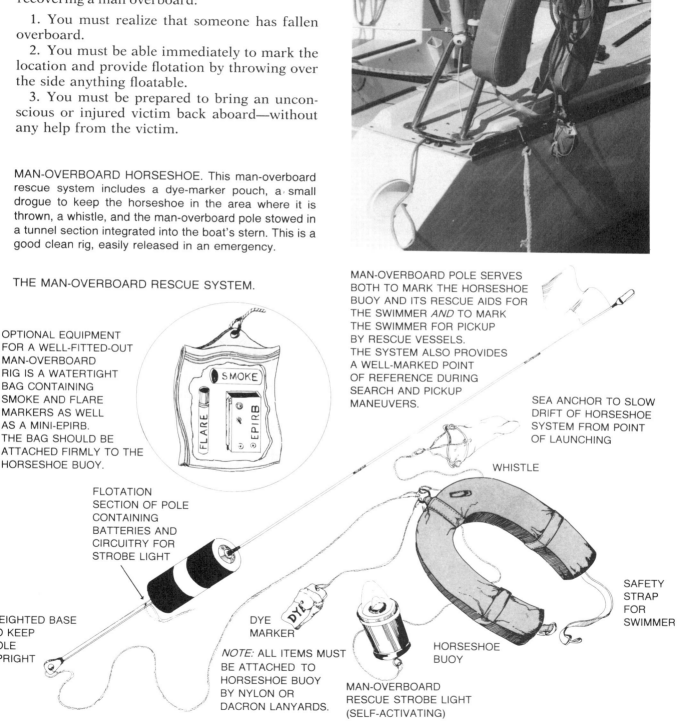

THE MAN-OVERBOARD RESCUE SYSTEM.

OPTIONAL EQUIPMENT FOR A WELL-FITTED-OUT MAN-OVERBOARD RIG IS A WATERTIGHT BAG CONTAINING SMOKE AND FLARE MARKERS AS WELL AS A MINI-EPIRB. THE BAG SHOULD BE ATTACHED FIRMLY TO THE HORSESHOE BUOY.

SMOKE

FLARE

EPIRB

MAN-OVERBOARD POLE SERVES BOTH TO MARK THE HORSESHOE BUOY AND ITS RESCUE AIDS FOR THE SWIMMER AND TO MARK THE SWIMMER FOR PICKUP BY RESCUE VESSELS. THE SYSTEM ALSO PROVIDES A WELL-MARKED POINT OF REFERENCE DURING SEARCH AND PICKUP MANEUVERS.

SEA ANCHOR TO SLOW DRIFT OF HORSESHOE SYSTEM FROM POINT OF LAUNCHING

WHISTLE

FLOTATION SECTION OF POLE CONTAINING BATTERIES AND CIRCUITRY FOR STROBE LIGHT

SAFETY STRAP FOR SWIMMER

WEIGHTED BASE TO KEEP POLE UPRIGHT

DYE MARKER

DYE

NOTE: ALL ITEMS MUST BE ATTACHED TO HORSESHOE BUOY BY NYLON OR DACRON LANYARDS.

HORSESHOE BUOY

MAN-OVERBOARD RESCUE STROBE LIGHT (SELF-ACTIVATING)

A MAN-OVERBOARD SYSTEM contained in a fiberglass launching container. Components include: man-overboard horseshoe, dye marker, whistle, automatic man-overboard light, and sea anchor to keep the system near the point of release. (Forespar)

SELF-RIGHTING AUTOMATIC RESCUE LIGHT. (ACR)

RADAR REFLECTORS are important safety equipment in fog, night, or heavy-weather conditions. This reflector is encased in a protective orange fiberglass container that offers less resistance than the foldout type of reflector. The unit offers thirty-six reflecting surfaces, for a high degree of radar "visibility." The inner array is manufactured of steel and the overall unit weighs four pounds. (Spar)

In regard to the first item, you may see the fall or hear yelling—or perhaps discover that someone is missing, some unknown time after the event. A detailed discussion of the necessary procedures appears in chapter 23. However, to carry out the emergency procedures—which include the second and third points above—you need to be prepared with special flotation and recovery equipment.

Flotation may include the mandatory Type IV PFD for all boats 16 feet or larger: a life ring or horseshoe float mounted near the helm and ready for instant use, supplemented by devices such as buoyant cushions, which may or may not assist the swimmer but will serve as good markers. The best flotation *and* marker is provided by equipping the horseshoe float with a special man-overboard pole—with a float in the middle, a counterbalance weight at the bottom (to keep it upright), and a bright flag and automatic strobe light at the top. Not only does the light help you find the swimmer—it also helps the swimmer find the float. Other equipment—such as a dye marker and a small pen-type flare launcher—can also be included.

Recovery of a disabled victim may require more than brute strength; two or even three people may be unable to lift a deadweight adult out of the water and up three or four feet to the deck without some mechanical assistance. The best solution for such a situation is any one of several commercially available models of lifting slings, which provide additional flotation, keep the victim's head out of the water, and—with some practice—can be used by almost anyone.

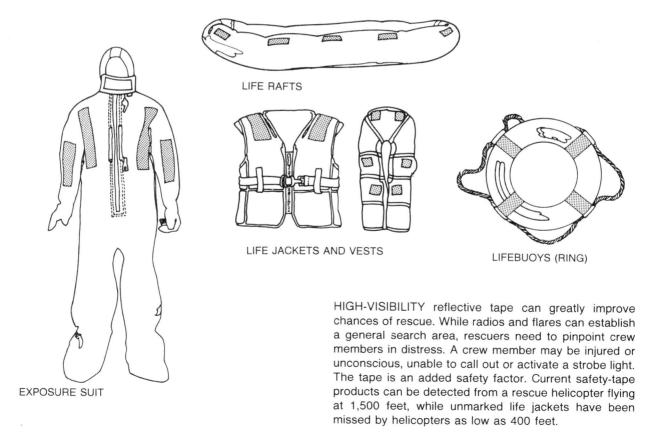

LIFE RAFTS

LIFE JACKETS AND VESTS

LIFEBUOYS (RING)

EXPOSURE SUIT

HIGH-VISIBILITY reflective tape can greatly improve chances of rescue. While radios and flares can establish a general search area, rescuers need to pinpoint crew members in distress. A crew member may be injured or unconscious, unable to call out or activate a strobe light. The tape is an added safety factor. Current safety-tape products can be detected from a rescue helicopter flying at 1,500 feet, while unmarked life jackets have been missed by helicopters as low as 400 feet.

CHAPTER NINE

Emergency Equipment

DISTRESS AND WARNING SIGNALS

Getting help in an emergency situation rests on two basic conditions: (1) Potential rescuers must know that you need help, and (2) rescuers must know where to find you. If you are side by side in an anchorage, there's not much of a problem; when separated by a hundred miles, both conditions might be very difficult to achieve.

Distress signals can be divided loosely into two categories—**NOTIFIERS**, which let people know you're in trouble, and **LOCATORS**, which help would-be rescuers find you. A rocket-type flare is a notifier—the signal clearly means "distress," but the distressed vessel could be anywhere in an area of several square miles; a hand-held flare wouldn't attract much attention beyond a few thousand yards, but when someone is looking for you, it clearly signals, "Here I am."

Some signals are both notifiers and locators, depending on the circumstances. Voice radio is the best-ever notifier, and when monitored by a pair of radio direction finders, it becomes an excellent locator.

ELECTRONIC SIGNALS

Voice radio is the signal method of choice, permitting an explanation of the problem, a report of position, and, usually, an acknowledgment that the message has been received.

The distance over which a voice distress message can be transmitted is determined in advance by the type and condition of radio equipment carried or installed in the boat. Hand-held VHF and most CB radios have a range limited to three or four miles; a good-quality marine VHF will cover 25 miles at sea level, up to 300 miles in communicating with high-flying aircraft; a single-sideband (SSB) unit can span the oceans of the world. Range is also a factor of radio power and antenna height and type. Consult your dealer, and carefully read the unit specifications when making a selection.

An EPIRB—an acronym for Emergency Position Indicating Radio Beacon—is a self-contained floating radio transmitter. There are two main types: older ones and new, high-tech ones.

Class A and class B (water activated and manually activated) EPIRBs send a readily recognized distress signal on one of the standard emergency radio frequencies. These devices do not identify themselves or your boat, but with a range of up to 300 miles and an operational life of as long as seven days, the beacon helps rescue units home in on the signal.

However, these basic EPIRBs offer no guarantee that anything will happen: The signal must be heard by someone before action can be taken, and no one may be listening for that signal. These EPIRBs transmit on VHF frequencies, which are essentially line-of-sight radio. The 300-mile potential range is useful for tracking by high-flying aircraft, but closer to earth, transmission is essentially line-of-sight. If there is no receiver tuned within 25 miles or so, the signal is likely to just keep on going toward infinity.

EPIRB units operate on two frequencies: 121.5 MHz, the civilian aircraft distress channel, and 243 MHz, the military aircraft distress channel. Close inshore—where most boating accidents occur—commercial aircraft are more likely to be concentrating on airport tower and control frequencies, and the aircraft distress channel may be of minimal value.

The latest-model EPIRB—referred to as a "smart" EPIRB—not only sends a distress signal and information about you (such as medical history) and your boat (type, size, name), it also transmits your position to a nearby rescue station. This model is mounted topside and may be

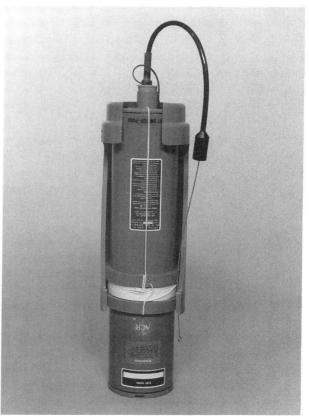

EPIRB RESCUE RADIO held in its mounting rack. This radio has both on/off and test modes of operation for periodic checks. (ACR)

INSULATED RIGGING SCREW. This device isolates a section of the sailboat backstay to create an antenna for radio reception and transmission. Standard turnbuckle shackles are used at each end.

automatically launched and energized by a pressure-sensitive switch.

As a result of a $12 million unsuccessful search for a missing fishing boat, the Coast Guard mandated that all commercial boats (other than charter sportfishermen operating within 20 miles of shore) had to carry the new models by August 17, 1989. Boats that were equipped with older EPIRB models by October 3, 1988, had a six-year grace period.

VISUAL DISTRESS SIGNALS

The Coast Guard classifies visual distress signals for day use only, night use only, and combined day-and-night use. Recreational boats, un-

MINI-EPIRB RESCUE RADIO shown with mounting pouch for use with life jackets, exposure coveralls, or survival suits. (ACR)

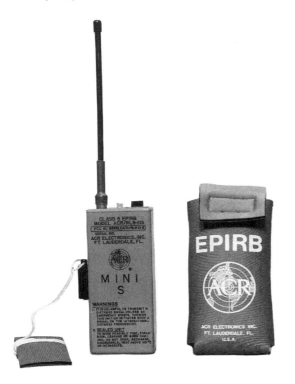

less otherwise exempted, must carry both day and night signaling devices; if pyrotechnic devices are selected, a minimum of three must be carried—three for day use, three for night use, or three day/night devices. Exemptions apply to boats under 16 feet operating in coastal waters, small daysailers, and boats in "marine parades and regattas," which need carry only night signaling devices if operated at night.

Pyrotechnic Flares are fireworks, similar to skyrockets or Roman candles. Some shoot up in the air like meteors and quickly die out; some are attached to parachutes, floating slowly back to earth; some are more like the familiar highway flare, simply a burning stick. Flares are manufactured in a range of colors. Red is the accepted color for distress signals; white and green flares are used as warning signals (see appendix II).

Meteor and parachute flares are available in three sizes, 12-gauge, 25mm, and 37mm, although 37mm is not usually stocked in recreational marine supply stores; hand-held flares come in one basic size. Here are typical characteristics (which may vary somewhat from one manufacturer to another):

- 12-gauge red meteor flares reach altitudes of 200 to 325 feet and burn for six seconds at 10,000 candlepower.
- 25mm red meteor flares reach an altitude of 375 feet and burn for six seconds at 10,000 candlepower.
- 25mm red parachute flares reach an altitude of 1,000 feet and burn for 25 seconds at 10,000 candlepower.
- Red hand-held flares have a two-minute burn time at 500 candlepower.

On a dark, clear night, a flare at a height of 1,000 feet should be visible from a surface location about 40 miles away. It would be half that distance at 250 feet and only three miles if held six feet above the water. The length of time the flare can be seen from any given point depends on burn time and the length of time the flare re-

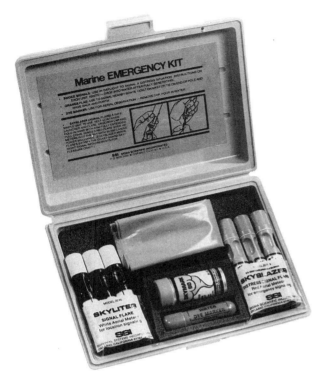

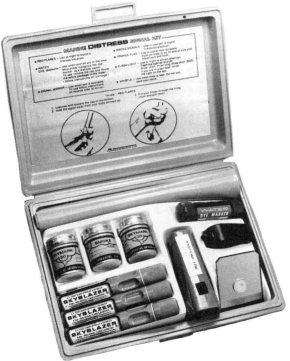

SMALL-BOAT EMERGENCY KIT contains white meteor flares (used best as an "alarm" unit), dye marker (as an "alarm" for aerial search as well as a locator), smoke canister (a locator and for use with rescue helicopters), and red meteors. There is also an orange distress flag. The kit does not contain any long-lasting parachute flares. (Sigma)

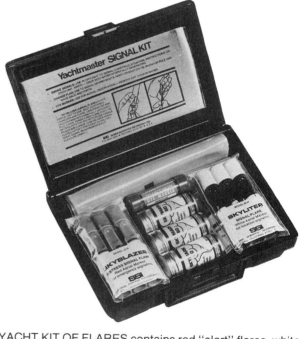

YACHT KIT OF FLARES contains red "alert" flares, white "locators," a distress flag, smoke signals, and dye marker. This kit meets most Coast Guard pleasure-boat requirements but should be supplemented by longer-lasting parachute flares, spare red and white meteors, and, best of all, an EPIRB rescue radio. (Sigma)

EXPANDED SMALL-BOAT KIT contains plenty of red meteors, a dye marker, whistle, smoke signals, a hand mirror, and a distress flag. (Sigma)

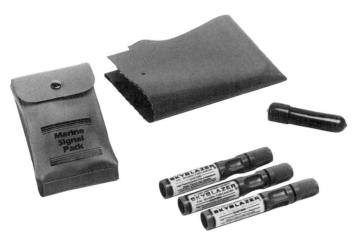

LIFE-JACKET DISTRESS PACK contains red meteors in hand launchers, a dye marker, and a distress panel. This is a useful pack when combined with other packages—such as a small strobe, small EPIRB, smoke signals, and sound signal—in life-jacket systems. (Sigma)

COMPACT FLARE KIT uses minicartridges and a spring-loaded launcher. The kit is small enough to fit in the pocket of a life vest. (Smith & Wesson)

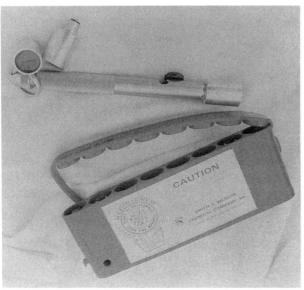

mains above the minimum sighting distance. That 1,000-foot flare would only be seen for a brief moment at 40 miles, regardless of burn time, because it would soon dip below the horizon. But from a distance of 20 miles, the same flare would be seen for the time it would take to fall from an altitude of 1,000 feet to 250 feet—perhaps the full burn time of twenty-five seconds. When it comes to flares, higher and longer-burning ones are better—more expensive, but worth the investment.

Air-launched flares are basically notifiers; they are not particularly useful as locators because they burst at some distance from the launch point and are relatively short-lived. Hand-held flares are not very helpful as notifiers because of the limited range of visibility, but they do serve as locators once a rescue unit is within a few miles.

To be most effective, meteor flares should be fired in bursts of two and spaced not more than a minute apart; an observer is likely to barely notice the first, seen out of the corner of the eye, and will be looking carefully for a few minutes for some sort of reinforcement.

While visible, a flare in daylight is only about 10 percent as effective as a flare at night.

Hand-Held Flares These flares are ignited by a built-in device; they may light with a "pop," which could startle an unwary user into dropping the flare into the boat. In use, these flares should be held out over the water on the downwind side of the boat, to prevent burning slag and noxious fumes from falling back into the boat. Because of the potential hazards, many hand-held flares (such as highway warning flares) do not meet Coast Guard approval and should not be used on boats. On balance, orange smoke in the daytime and an electric strobe at night are both safe and more visible than hand-held flares.

Pistol Launchers These devices are modeled on the wartime Very pistol, but they come in several (usually smaller) sizes. In fact, you should be cautious about purchasing and using a military-surplus flare pistol because you may find it hard to obtain flares. Marine supply stores usually handle flare pistols in two sizes: The smaller one takes 12-gauge meteor flares, the larger takes 12-gauge meteors (with an adapter) as well as 25mm meteor and parachute flares.

Pen Launchers These are just what the name implies—small tubes the size of a fountain pen, with some sort of firing mechanism. They are suitable for attachment to and use in connection with a life jacket, but the flare is too small and short-lived to be counted on for too much.

Cartridge-type Launchers These flares are essentially self-launched; you unscrew the top to expose the firing lanyard, flip it over and point it away, and then pull the lanyard. This is a two-handed operation, one that could be a problem in some circumstances.

Flare Stowage Flares should be ready at hand, not mixed in with miscellaneous junk at the bottom of a locker. Most flare kits come with bulkhead mounting brackets, which should be used. Put the main flare kit just inside the companionway—convenient but out of the weather. Other flares, properly packaged for preservation, should be stowed, as appropriate, in the dinghy, in the bail-out bag, with the life jackets, and—of course—in the life-raft survival package.

Flares absorb moisture, and will likely deteriorate over time even if well packed in waterproof covering. For this reason, all flares are dated and should be considered unsafe or unusable about three years after manufacture or if the flare earlier shows visible signs of deterioration—discoloration, leaking, softness. Flares older than forty-two months (from the date of manufacture) cannot be counted toward Coast Guard minimum requirements.

Disposal Pyrotechnic flares are classed as explosives, and outdated flares must be disposed of in a safe and responsible manner. Do not put them out for the city trash pickup, or dump them

where they are likely to be found by curious children. If possible, turn them over to the Coast Guard.

Nonpyrotechnic signals include smoke flares, smudge pots, fire, dye markers, lights, mirrors, and flags.

Smoke Flares These flares serve two basic purposes: (1) as locators, and (2) to indicate wind direction for rescue aircraft planning to hover or make an air drop. Smoke flares may be hard to notice when looking into the sun, and overall utility is diminished as wind speed increases. They come in various sizes and types; the smaller varieties can be attached to a life jacket. Smoke flares may be hand-held, stand-alone, or floating.

Homemade Smudge Pot An oily rag burning in a bucket is a poor but possibly useful substitute for a smoke flare.

Fire Fire in a "tar barrel" is an ancient distress signal still provided for in international law—but one not likely to be used on a recreational boat, where barrels of any kind are in short supply and where the control of a signal fire may present more of a hazard than whatever distress has prompted the signal. However, be alert for burning tar barrels aboard larger ships.

Dye Markers Brightly colored dye spread in the water with dye markers can be highly visible for a time from the air but less so from a boat unless passing close by. The dye is most useful in calm, windless weather; the color disperses quickly in choppy seas or high current. A handy dye package can be attached to every life jacket so it can be opened easily by a survivor in the water.

Lights On a dark night, even the tiny bulb of a one-cell flashlight can be seen for at least a mile, although it is likely to be overlooked unless a rescue is already in progress. To attract attention, lights should be bright and flashing, either in strobe fashion or transmitting a signal—such

PERSONAL RESCUE LIGHT that meets the SOLAS requirements and can be worn over a foul-weather jacket or survival suit. (Forespar)

WATER-ACTIVATED PERSONAL LIFE-JACKET RESCUE LIGHT. Every life jacket aboard should have a similar light—the type preferred for children's life vests. (ACR)

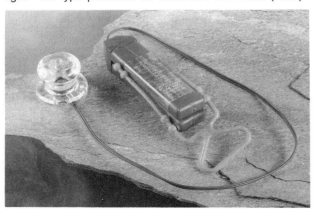

as the Morse code S–O–S (—. . .—). A distress message can easily be sent by flicking the running lights or deck worklights off and on.

Commercially available masthead-mounted strobe lights are internationally recognized distress signals; battery-operated floating models help pinpoint the location of a man overboard—and may last as long as nine hours with fresh batteries. Any crew member working topside in rough weather, day or night, should be wearing a strobe-equipped life jacket.

Signal Mirrors　In daylight, if the sun is in any reasonable position, hand-held signal mirrors transmit a bright flashing light that can be seen for some distance. "Official" signal mirrors have a sighting device, but any flat, shiny object will do in a pinch.

Flags　Flags are a traditional means of maritime communication, but few recreational boaters know the meaning of even the most basic flag distress signals, and most tend to ignore them. However, that does not rule out their use; it only serves as a caution. One important application of a distress flag is not so much to alert someone to your trouble as to help potential rescuers—already summoned by radio—to pick out your boat from the multitudes that might be on the waters.

The international flag distress signal consists of the flags "N" and "C." The flag signal for "man overboard" is the letter "O" ("Oscar" in the phonetic alphabet—and the name given to the life-jacketed dummies thrown into the sea during Navy man-overboard drills). Another generally recognized distress signal is a square orange flag hoisted over or under a black ball; this has evolved into a single orange flag with a black square and a black ball side by side in the center. This is the Coast Guard–approved distress flag, and it can be flown from the mast or a halyard, or laid out on the deck or cabintop, where it could be read more easily by rescue aircraft.

Another distress signal, commonly understood, is to fly the national ensign upside down or (less well known) tied in a knot. A complete listing of distress and other flag signals appears in chapter 21.

AUDIBLE DISTRESS SIGNALS

Sound Sound carries well over water and may reach several miles on a calm, still day. If the wind is blowing, sound will travel downwind perhaps as far as three times the upwind distance—a factor to consider when trying to hail a passing steamer.

International and Inland Rules of the Road provide for an audible distress signal in "the continuous sounding of a fog signal" (which would include a foghorn, a steam whistle, or a bell), or firing a gun "at one-minute intervals." Realistically, you can use any loud noise that might attract attention, including banging on a metal pot and yelling.

Yelling works better if amplified via a loud hailer or a megaphone—which can be improvised from a rolled-up chart or cupped hands. Most loud hailers have an electronic "listening" feature—a great help when trying to carry on a conversation. Megaphones and cupped hands can be used as an ear trumpet, to help focus the sound.

Yelling also is more effective with careful enunciation and simple, easily grasped messages. "Man overboard!" works better than "My wife fell in the water."

All boats of 12 meters (37 feet 3 inches) or larger are required to carry "a whistle and a bell" and to use them in appropriate situations; smaller boats are supposed to have "a means of making an efficient sound signal."

In fog or other restricted visibility, vessels underway use whistle signals and foghorns, and the ringing of a bell at regular intervals signifies a vessel at anchor or aground.

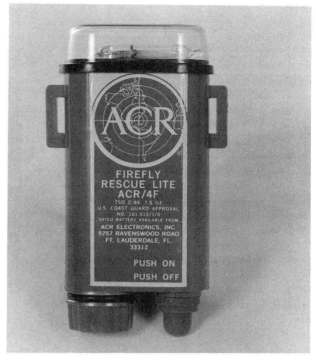

LIFE-JACKET–MOUNTED STROBE LIGHT. (ACR)

SMALL-BOAT HORN powered by a Freon or air cylinder can be carried as an emergency warning, a standard whistle/fog warning, or for use with standard sound signals (for bridges, etc.). Spare canisters should be carried for extended use in fog situations. (Falcon)

FIREFIGHTING

Specific conditions must exist for a fire to start: (1) There must be a fuel (gasoline, oil, wood, cloth, plastic). (2) There must be sufficient heat to bring that fuel to combustion temperature—that is, the temperature at which the fuel begins to vaporize. Wood requires more heat than oil, oil more than gasoline. (3) There must be sufficient oxygen.

Stopping the fire requires blocking the oxygen or lowering the temperature; with many fires, either technique will work: Cover burning wood with a heavy blanket and you'll smother the flame; spray it with water and you'll lower the temperature and the fire will go out. However, not all methods work equally well with all fires; you may be able to smother burning gasoline with a blanket, but dousing with water may not work—the gasoline will float on top of the water, still burning. If you try to put water on an electrical fire, the sparks will fly.

A BURNED-OUT HULK that once was an expensive luxury cruising yacht. This powerboat suffered a galley explosion in Bahamian waters, and heavy flames and smoke caused the crew to abandon the vessel and escape in an inflatable dinghy. Caribbean islands are notorious for their lack of effective Coast Guard patrols and firefighting units.

Because of these differences, and as an aid in selecting the most effective extinguishing agents, fires are classified by fuel type. The extinguishing agent must be matched to the type of fire:

• Class A: Combustible solid materials such as wood, paper, plastics, and cloth. The basic firefighting technique is to cool the fire below the ignition temperature of the materials.

• Class B: Flammable liquids such as oil, grease, gasoline, kerosene. A smothering technique is used to cut off the oxygen necessary for combustion.

• Class C: Fires in, or involving, electrical circuits. The extinguishing agent must not conduct an electric current.

EXTINGUISHING AGENTS

Water The least expensive and most commonly available fire extinguisher, water in most cases should be used only on class A fires. Burning class B liquids might float on top, still burning. Two exceptions: Water can extinguish a small alcohol-stove fire, and a fine spray of water can serve to cool burning oil. But don't use a solid stream; the fire might flash even higher when hit by water. (Most of us have made the mistake—once—of throwing a glass of water on a frying-pan fire.) With a class C fire, water can spread the electric current—and put the firefighter at risk for electrocution.

Water is quite effective in the right place at the right time. It quickly absorbs heat, cooling the fire. When applied as a fine spray, it provides an insulating "curtain" to shield the firefighter from the heat. Delivered under pressure, water penetrates and separates the burning materials, but it can even be delivered by the least sophisticated of firefighting systems—a bucket.

Aboard boats, the use of water is subject to two important limitations:

1. Water is heavy, 10 pounds a gallon. A typical shoreside fire engine can deliver enough water to swamp any boat in a few minutes. The smaller-

HALON PORTABLE FIREFIGHTING UNITS. Halon discharges as a liquefied gas, which lets the firefighter direct the stream. Additionally, Halon does not leave a residue, so equipment and engines can be restarted once the fire is out. The gas does not cool and does not smother the fire—the firefighting values of CO_2 or foam—but attacks the basic combustion process. (Fireboy)

FOUR PORTABLE HALON EXTINGUISHERS FOR CLASS B AND CLASS C FIRES show the range of portable equipment available. Halon can be used to fight class B fires—flammable liquids (fuels)—as well as class C (electrical) fires. The photo at the right shows the instructions found on the back of a typical portable Halon extinguisher. (Kidde)

Fire Extinguishers Recommended by Boat Size

Outboard (Open)	1
Outboard Cruisers	2
Runabouts	2
Cruisers Under 26 feet	2
Cruisers 26–40 feet	3
Cruisers 40–65 feet	4
Auxiliary Sail 26–40 feet	3
Auxiliary Sail 40–65 feet	4

(American Boat and Yacht Council)

capacity pumps normally found aboard ships—or provided by Coast Guard cutters—can move about two tons of water a minute. That's more useful for taking unwanted water out of a boat than for trying to fight a fire in a mattress.

2. Water freezes. In winter, portable water extinguishers may be useless; water lines and valves may become plugged or split; sprayed water may turn to ice, coating the topsides and seriously affecting both the footing of the firefighters and the stability of the now top-heavy boat.

Carbon Dioxide (CO_2)   An inert gas, CO_2 is not chemically active and will not support combustion. Heavier than air, it displaces the oxygen needed for combustion, extinguishing the fire as long as it remains in the area in concentrations of at least 40 percent. Carbon dioxide has a mini-

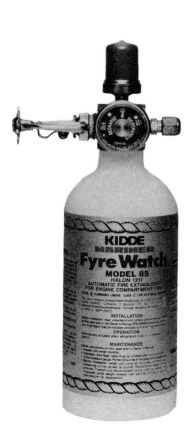

mal cooling effect on a fire, but, paradoxically, it can deliver a damaging thermal shock to hot machinery; the rapid expansion of the gas upon release from an extinguisher produces a severe, but short-lived, temperature drop.

Because it smothers a fire and does not conduct electricity, CO_2 can be used on class A, B, and C fires. However, if the fire is in an open area, the gas will drift away quickly, allowing oxygen to return to the fire site. If the ignition source has not been removed (for example, an overheated wire), or if some burning materials remain above ignition temperature (quite likely with smoldering bedding or trash), the fire will re-flash.

CO_2 will stop a running engine, which could be a problem if you need power to head into the seas to get the wind to blow smoke and flames away from the boat.

Another caution: In a closed space—such as an engineroom—CO_2 can smother the firefighter as well as the fire. Don't trigger a large-capacity installed CO_2 system while anyone is in the space, and never enter a CO_2-filled compartment until ventilation has been restored.

Dry Chemicals Dry chemicals (usually sodium bicarbonate or monosodium phosphate) interfere with the chemistry of combustion while smothering the fire with a fine dust; they can stop an engine and leave a residue that can damage machinery or electronic equipment.

Foam A mixture of water and a chemical foaming agent, foam is most effective with class B fires. It floats on top of the burning liquid, smothering the fire. Foam will work on a class A fire, but it leaves a messy residue. Since it can conduct electricity, it should *not* be used on class C fires.

With sufficient delivery capacity, large quantities of foam can be spread on a fire in a matter of moments—a particularly useful feature for plane crashes and engineroom fires aboard large ships. However, aboard pleasure craft, foam is practical only in portable extinguishers.

Halon Known generically as bromotrifluoromethane, Halon is an odorless gas that interrupts combustion and is effective in concentrations as low as 5 percent. Tests have shown that a Halon system can put out an engineroom fire even while the ventilation blowers are replacing the air at a rate of four times each minute.

While Halon is heavier than air, it readily mixes with air and does not totally displace oxygen (as does CO_2). Halon is not toxic, and in small concentrations can be breathed safely for at least five minutes—the limit recommended by the Coast Guard. Halon will choke a gasoline engine, but a diesel will keep right on running (although the exhaust will contain toxic fumes as a by-product). Halon is expensive, but it will not harm machinery or equipment, and it is the extinguisher of choice for engineroom installation.

Two varieties of Halon are available: Halon 1211 for portable extinguishers and Halon 1301 for fixed systems. Halon 1211 leaves the extinguisher as a liquid, producing a directable stream of about 15 feet before vaporizing. Halon 1301 vaporizes immediately upon release.

Home Remedies A variety of agents, not primarily thought of as fire extinguishers, are readily available and can be used to fight many fires. Baking soda, salt, and flour are effective against galley flareups; sand and blankets will smother any reasonably small fire. Simply throwing a burning object overboard may be quicker, and certainly easier to clean up after, than an extinguishing agent.

Pyrene and Carbon Tetrachloride These chemicals were widely used in the past and may still be found in older extinguishers. They put out fires, but they also generate toxic and potentially fatal phosgene gas. DO NOT USE THESE AGENTS.

FIREFIGHTING EQUIPMENT

Portable Extinguishers These are well suited to small fires in living spaces, where they

INSTALLED ENGINEROOM fire system. The control panel features a power indication light, arming switch, and engine restart indicator. There is also a guarded manual "fire" button. The unit activates automatically from sensors placed near the engine, and a similar panel is mounted at the steering station for remote activation. The control box at right is an interesting safety device: The top switch disables or permits engine start from the helm as a security feature. The lower button permits engine start below as both a backup and a convenience during engine repair and maintenance.

TERMINAL PANEL AND ACTIVATOR SWITCH FOR A HALON SYSTEM. Note that this system has an engine override so you can keep the engine running. The terminal block permits multiple sensors and alarms. (Fireboy)

can be put into action quickly. However, they are of limited use for any but the smallest fire in a closed machinery space, because opening the hatch to gain access to the fire may allow an overwhelming rush of fresh air to fuel the fire.

• Water may be sprayed on a fire from a pressurized tank or a portable tank/pump—a method ideally suited to fires in bedding, waste, or construction debris. Aboard boats, a simple bucket-and-line can be a most useful portable extinguisher; every boat should have one, no matter how elaborate the rest of the firefighting gear.

• Foam extinguishers mix the foaming agent with water; the pressure generated by the chemical action forces the foam out of the container.

• CO_2, dry chemicals, and Halon are packed under pressure in portable cylinders.

• Home remedies such as baking soda, salt, and flour can be applied right out of the box. The galley stowage plan should provide for easy access to these agents.

Installed Systems An installed system is most effective for enclosed compartments; wherever possible, the engineroom should be protected by an installed CO_2 or Halon system. Installed systems have a number of advantages: (1) They quickly deliver a known quantity of the extinguishing agent; (2) they can be triggered by heat-sensitive sensors in the compartment or by hand from a control station; (3) they can be rigged to shut down the engines and turn off ventilation blowers; and (4) they permit you to fight the fire without confronting it. These features are acknowledged by insurance companies, which typically offer premium reductions of 5 to 15 percent for boats with approved installed systems.

Required capacity is determined by matching the net cubic volume of the compartment with the quantity of extinguishing agent needed to obtain the recommended concentration (5 percent for Halon; 40 percent for CO_2). The cubic volume may be approximated by measuring and multiplying the length by the height by the width of the compartment—ignoring any curvatures in the dimensions.

Types of Fires

  A Ordinary Combustibles: Wood, cloth, paper, rubber, many plastics

  B Flammable Liquids: Gasoline, solvents, grease, oil, some paints

  C Electrical Equipment: Wiring, fuse boxes, energized electrical equipment

Types of Fire Extinguishers

	CARBON DIOXIDE	DRY CHEMICAL	HALON
Fire Suitability	①	Ordinary Dry ① / Multipurpose Dry ②	①
Extinguishing Effect	• Smothering. Some Cooling	• Smothering. • Chemical Reaction Interferes With Combustion Process	• Chemical Reaction Interferes With Combustion Process
Suggested Maintenance (Consult maintenance suggestions on extinguisher labels)⁴	• Weigh and Tag, Semi-annually (if 10% weight loss, recharge) • Hydrostatic Test, 5 Years	• With Visual Indicator: Check Pressure Gauge, Monthly • Without Visual Indicator: Weigh and Tag, Semi-annually • Frequently Invert and Solidly Hit the Base to Loosen Extinguishing Agent • Hydrostatic Test, 5 Years	• Check Pressure Gauge, Monthly • Hydrostatic Test, 12 Years
Corrosive/Residue	• None	• On Class C Fires Clean Up Promptly To Prevent Corrosion	• None
Operating Precautions	• Do Not Touch Discharge Horn When In Operation • Use Caution In Unventilated Areas—Depletes Oxygen Supply	• Irritating If Breathed For Long Periods • Use Caution In Closed Areas—Reduces Visibility, Causes Disorientation • On Small Flammable Liquid or Grease Fires, Initial Discharge At Close Range May Cause Spreading	• Avoid High Concentrations⁵ • Do Not Touch Discharge Horn When In Operation (Models Available Without Discharge Horn)
Additional Characteristics	• Not As Effective In Open Areas When There Are Winds Or Drafts	• Suitable For Use In Open Areas	• Strong Wind Currents May Disperse The Extinguishing Agent Too Rapidly

Notes:

¹ Limited use on Class A fires.

² Less effective on deep-seated Class A fires.

³ Intended for use mainly on B:C fires. Some may have Class A rating.

⁴ On all fire extinguishers: Check for leakage, tampering, corrosion or damage. Recharge after use.

⁵ Products from decomposition relatively toxic. Normally, only small quantities of the by-products are formed. Unpleasant, acrid odor serves as a warning of presence.

FIRE EQUIPMENT GUIDE by type of fire. (Courtesy California Dept. of Boating and Waterways)

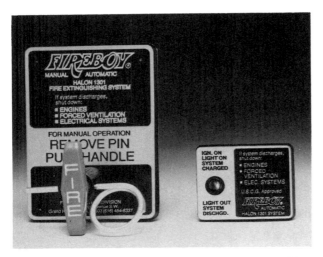

HALON FIREFIGHTING PANEL. This activator panel features both an automatic and a manual release, as well as a charged/discharged light system. Note the safety pin installed in the manual release handle. (Fireboy)

The installed systems may be triggered by any of several means:

• Fusible links, as used in building sprinkler systems, melt and release the extinguishing agent at a preset temperature level. To be effective, a fusible link must be at or near the site of the fire.

• Thermal detectors measure a rise in temperature in the same manner as a home thermostat. They need electricity, however, which could be a problem in some emergency situations.

• Rate-of-rise triggers measure changes in pneumatic pressure within the trigger. The changes are affected by the speed at which the temperature climbs, not by the temperature itself.

Many systems offer a combination of triggers—for backup or to provide different measurements in different parts of the compartment. For example, one Halon system may be set to operate when a heat sensor mounted above the engines hits 212°F, or when the temperature at the bottle—which is mounted off to one side—reaches 180°F.

We recommend that any system also have a manual trigger outside the compartment and away from the fire or explosion. Another recommendation: interconnection with the ignition circuit, preventing engine start until the extinguishing system has been energized. This can be wired in tandem with the circuit that turns on the ventilation blowers.

Water Washdown Systems   These can be rigged for firefighting with the addition of an appropriate spray nozzle. The size and type of nozzle will depend on pump output pressure and the vertical lift. These are not a marine supply item; purchase one from a fire-protection-equipment distributor.

Foam   You can create foam by combining the chemical base (carried to the fire in five-gallon cans) with water (carried under pressure through a hose) in a mixing nozzle similar to those used for spraying paint or garden pesticides. This method is useful for firefighting from the shore or aboard a large ship, but it is not practical aboard a pleasure craft because of storage and water-pressure requirements.

DAMAGE-CONTROL AND EMERGENCY KITS

DAMAGE-CONTROL KIT

When you can't afford to take time to select your weapons for fighting such problems as rapid flooding or dismasting, you need a ready-made damage-control kit. (Details on handling damage-control problems appear in chapter 22.) Suggested contents of the damage-control kit are:

• Heavy, long-handled bolt/wire cutter (suitable for clearing away rigging if the mast goes)
• Smaller one-hand wire cutter
• Crowbar or wrecking bar
• Heavy hammer and/or mallet
• Needlenose pliers
• Several large screwdrivers
• Several cold chisels
• Stillson or pipe wrench large enough to handle the largest nut aboard
• Hatchet
• Crimping tool and lead crimp sleeves
• Two flashlights
• Diver's face mask and snorkel, set of flippers, pair of work gloves, and tending line made up and ready for use
• Small shoulder bag stocked with:
—Tapered wooden plugs in assorted sizes for all through-hull penetrations
—Caulking cotton
—Tube of underwater sealant and caulking gun
—Length of strong braided nylon line
• Collision mat: heavy reinforced canvas, with attached length of line; bronze or stainless nails (for wooden hull)

RIGGER'S BAG

Spare shackles, cotter pins, sail-repair materials, and a few selected tools should be stowed in a special rigger's bag, ready for use on deck or aloft without your having to rummage through the toolbox and spares locker. The bag should be stocked with:

• Sailing needles of various sizes, straight and curved
• Sailmaker's thread
• Wax
• Marline
• Sailcloth patches

• Spare shackles
• Splicing tool
• Hole punch
• Fid
• Sailmaker's palm
• Waxed thread
• Twine
• Monel wire (for securing shackles)
• Marlinespike
• Sailmaker's knife
• Pliers
• Small bronze hammer
• Scraps of leather (for protecting chafe points)

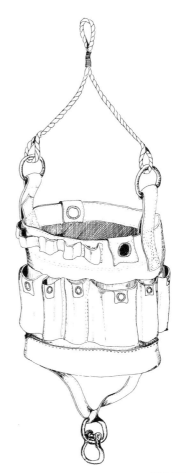

RIGGER'S BAG.

BAILOUT BAG

In the event of an irreversible emergency—fire out of control, flooding beyond any hope of control, capsize of a small outboard—you may be forced to abandon ship. Whether you are going to a life raft, a dinghy, or just into the water with a life jacket, your chances of survival and rescue will be increased by having signaling equipment in addition to whatever may already be stowed in the life raft or dinghy or attached to your life jacket.

The bailout bag, an additional ready-to-go supply of distress signals, should be stowed in a locker having immediate topside access. The bag itself should be a waterproof shoulder bag of the type sold in sporting-goods stores. Stencil the name of your boat and the words EMERGENCY BAG on the outside; attach a dated tag to remind you to make an annual inspection of the contents. The contents should be double-wrapped and sealed in plastic for environmental protection, and a small knife should be included to help you open the wrappings when needed. Suggested contents of the bailout bag:

- Dye marker
- Whistle
- EPIRB
- Flashlight
- Spare batteries
- Signal mirror
- Smoke marker
- Small strobe light
- Length of line
- Space blanket
- Several small flotation devices (inflatable, balloon-type floats or rings)
- Hand-launched small flares (pen-gun type)

DINGHY BAG

Make up a junior version of the bailout bag and stow it permanently in the dinghy: In the event of a catastrophic emergency, you may not have time to grab any other gear. Select the contents based on conditions in your boating area, but at least consider including a flare kit, a signal mirror, a first-aid kit, and some water. Everything should be double-wrapped in plastic, sealed against exposure to the weather.

HEAVING LINE

Be prepared to transfer towing lines, tools, or spare parts from or to other boats by putting in your emergency kit a heaving line—a coil of about 100 feet of very light line with a small weight at one end and a loop at the other. The weight—a heavy ball wrapped in line and traditionally called a monkey's fist—carries the forward end of the line through the air when thrown; the loop is held or hooked onto something to keep the aft end aboard. With the line bridging the distance between the two boats, a heavier line can be attached and pulled across. Small objects to be transferred can be tied on in the middle of the line (along with a life jacket, to prevent loss in case the line breaks or is inadvertently released). All knots used must be firm—the force of passing waves can be strong enough to pull the lines apart.

Throwing a heaving line is an art perfected only with practice, but the skill someday might prove invaluable.

EMERGENCY DRINKING WATER AND MAPS suitable for supplementing standard life-raft supplies. (ACR)

EMERGENCY BILGE PUMPS

The normal bilge-pump installation, as noted in chapter 3, should handle most bilge-pumping requirements—even with some damage-related flooding. However, for the sort of serious flooding that may follow a collision with a submerged rock or the failure of a 2.5-inch intake hose, you may need extra capacity. If your voyage plans call for a high level of security, you might consider any or all of the following:

1. Install an engine-driven pump activated by a V-belt-driven friction clutch; when the clutch is disengaged, the pump is inactive. Engage the clutch and you can move a lot of water. These units are relatively expensive and hard to find— but very effective.

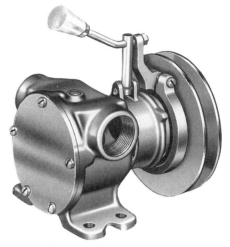

ENGINE-DRIVEN CLUTCH PUMP is one of the most powerful dewatering pumps you can have aboard. The lever engages the belt-driven pulley so you can bring all of the power of your engine to bear on pumping the bilge. Be sure to use a strainer to keep the pump clear of clogging debris. (Jabsco)

ENGINE-DRIVEN CLUTCH PUMP is one of the most powerful pumps. Note the steel belt protection cover. The pump is normally not in use during engine operations. The black-handled lever brings the pulley into contact with the belt and permits the full power of the main engine to be used for bilge pumping. Strainers should be used at the intake of the bilge suction.

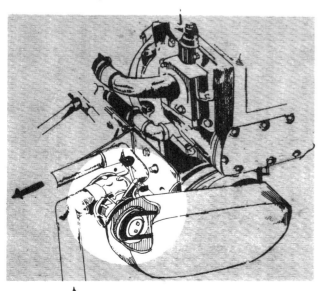

2. Add an auxiliary gasoline-engine-drive pump unit; pumping capacity may approach 4,000 gallons per hour (ten times that of many standard electric bilge pumps).

3. Rig your engine cooling water intake hose with a Y-valve; one arm takes suction at the seacock, the other has a free length of hose that can reach into the bilge. For emergency pumping, shift the Y-valve to the free hose and close the seacock. The bilgewater will circulate through the cooling system and out through the exhaust or discharge. This method poses some jeopardy to the engine and should be used only in a true emergency. At the least, the end of the free hose should be fitted with a strainer, to prevent debris from being sucked into the engine-cooling system.

Keep in mind that with any emergency (or portable) pumping system, you should be prepared to take suction in the forward sections of the bilge. Rapid flooding forward may put the bow too low to allow for a normal flow of water aft to the bilge sump.

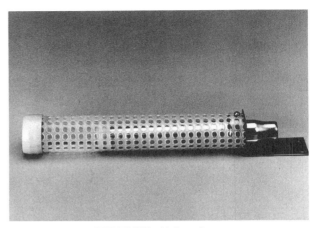

PUMP INTAKE STRAINER. (Jabsco)

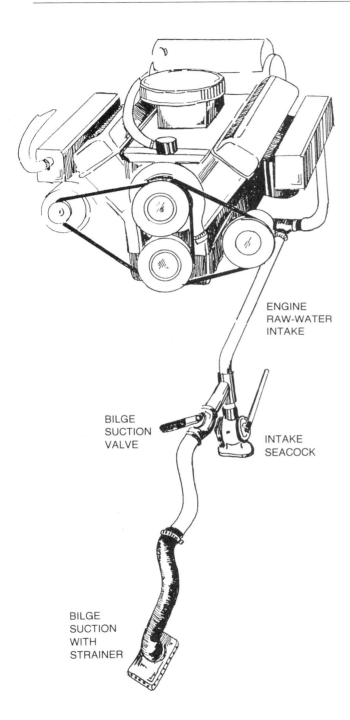

ENGINE
RAW-WATER
INTAKE

BILGE
SUCTION
VALVE

INTAKE
SEACOCK

BILGE
SUCTION
WITH
STRAINER

EMERGENCY BILGE PUMPING USING ENGINE.

FIREARMS

In these days of drug-related lawlessness on the high seas—with tales of murder, kidnapping, and boat theft circulating around the waterfront—many boat owners have added firearms to their safety kit.

If you feel at risk and unprotected without an arsenal, consider the following suggestions:

1. Leave the handguns ashore. They are too easily involved in accidents (especially with children), and, because of their limited range and accuracy, they are not very effective in most probable at-sea situations.

2. A rifle is better suited to long-range warnings than a handgun, and a shotgun is better suited to repelling boarders.

3. If you are going to carry firearms, learn how to use and care for them.

4. If you carry your guns into a foreign port, declare them to customs officials. Your guns might be confiscated for the duration of your stay, but if you *don't* declare them—and they are discovered through any means—your boat might be confiscated. Permanently.

LIFE RAFTS

Our typical image of the life raft, nurtured by too many World War II movies, is a small inflatable boat from which a downed airman fishes for mackerel while awaiting rescue. After the war, many of these rafts were dumped onto the surplus market, at the same time spawning cheap imitations that today can be bought at any discount store but that have little utility outside a swimming pool. Even the original version no longer qualifies as an approved life raft. It was too light in construction, lacked adequate protection from the weather, and came with a minimal "survival kit" consisting largely of a set of fishhooks, a knife, and an ineffective shark repellent.

But experience with the World War II inflatable life raft led to development of some very respectable recreational inflatables—typified by the Avon and Zodiac sport boats and tenders—and a whole new breed of life rafts that provide protection and survival undreamed-of a generation ago.

Do not, however, confuse a recreational inflatable with a life raft. A life raft is not a dual-purpose vessel; it is designed with but one purpose in mind: insofar as possible, to sustain life at sea under the most severe environmental conditions.

A proper life raft will be constructed to standards well beyond those required in a recreational boat. It will have the ability, for example, to retain flotation through a temperature range from −22°F to +150°F.

A proper life raft will have a sturdy canopy with an entry door that can be closed against the weather and a double or insulated bottom to retard hypothermia. It should be designed to resist flipping over in rough seas and high winds.

A proper life raft will be packaged in a protective container that can be mounted securely in an accessible location from which it can be freed quickly upon inflation. The inflation system will be rapid, with both manual and automatic triggers.

And, most important, a proper life raft will be equipped with a carefully planned emergency kit, including signaling devices, first-aid gear, food, and water.

Of course, in this technological age, with instant worldwide communications, satellite surveillance, and electronic gadgets galore, we tend to think of long-term ocean survival as a thing of the past. Not true. Each month brings new tales of sailors who have been adrift helplessly for days and weeks on voyages intended to be one-day, never-out-of-sight-of-land excursions.

Even with instantaneous emergency communications; even with the pinpoint location accuracy that may be possible today; even with the best organized and best operated search-and-rescue services in the world—the victims of maritime mishap, once located, still must wait for rescue. In rough weather, that wait could extend to days. For survivors not equipped with adequate emergency communications, and especially for the independent-minded soul who feels that what he's doing is nobody's business—and therefore has told nobody where he's going or when he expects to return—the waiting could be measured in months.

Whenever possible, the best "place" for waiting is the boat itself. Even if damaged, it still may provide some protection and support: shelter from the weather; food and water; extra clothing and blankets; possible sources of heat for cooking or comfort; the possibility of continued radio communication; a bigger target for search-and-rescue units. Abandoning ship is the last resort in an emergency, and it should be undertaken only in a situation such as uncontrollable fire or sinking, when no options remain.

The next best "place" is a proper life raft, but one veteran life-raft inspector estimates that only 5 percent of yachtsmen have equipped their boats with a raft. Granted, not every boat can or should have one. Most pleasure boating takes place in sheltered waters or within 11 miles of

A VARIETY OF LIFE-RAFT TYPES. Clockwise from left: A simple rescue platform that can be deployed to get crew off a vessel easily. An open, large-capacity coastal type of life raft with a stability bag below. Heavy-duty, offshore, extended-survival raft with a strong dome cover and deep stability bag. Typical yacht-type raft that has stability compartments and is useful in most coastal and some offshore environments. (Switlik)

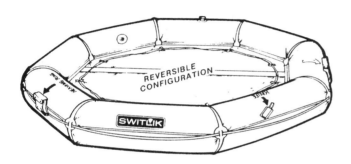

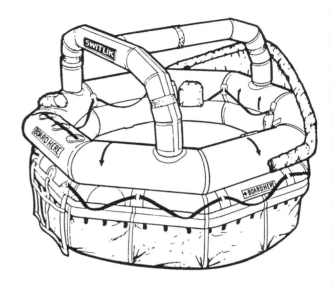

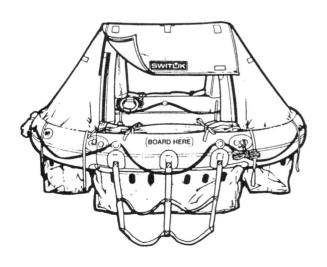

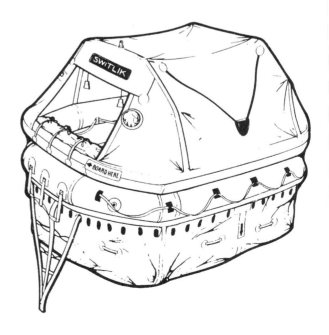

COMMERCIAL-GRADE SIX-MAN LIFE RAFT—partially ballasted type. Note the heavier construction of the lower tubes. (Viking)

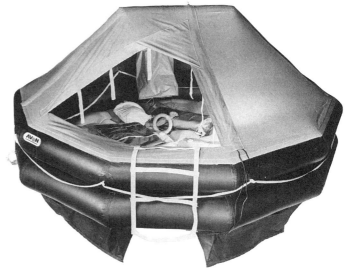

LOW-PROFILE LIFE-RAFT CANISTER mounted on a sailboat foredeck. The canister is a fine, robust design. Note the deck-attached release lanyard. If the canister were used in tropical climates, it could benefit from a fitted canvas case to combat deterioration from the sun. (Viking)

YACHTING-TYPE LIFE RAFT showing the interior and equipment. Note the partial-ballast pockets beneath the raft. The emergency equipment bags packed inside can be supplemented with additional water and survival materials, including an EPIRB. (Avon)

AUTOMATIC LIFE-RAFT RELEASE responds to water pressure to release the raft canister from its boat-mounted cradle. A lanyard then activates the raft. Any vessel active in congested waters (particularly at night) would be well advised to install this as a backup in case of sudden catastrophic collision damage or hull failure. (Viking)

the ocean shore, in fine weather and in the general vicinity of dozens of other boats. Under such conditions, the need for a life raft probably is marginal, and many boat owners rely on a dinghy or an inflatable for emergency backup. That may be a reasonable choice—provided that a few simple steps are taken to improve the emergency capabilities of these small craft (see Alternatives, later in this chapter).

For the offshore fisherman and the long-range cruiser, a life raft should be considered mandatory. The high purchase price (likely to be $2,000 and up) usually is cited as the reason most owners do not buy a life raft—it seems like a lot of money for a piece of gear that probably never will be used. However, most of us buy insurance to protect our families from financial loss; for deepwater sailors, a life raft is insurance against loss of life. Amortized over the period of ownership, with a portion of the cost recovered upon the sale of the boat, this investment can be measured in the "pennies-a-day" range.

LIFE-RAFT STANDARDS

Standards for life rafts are set by periodic Safety of Life at Sea (SOLAS) international conventions, modified or adapted for use in the United States by the Coast Guard. The need for standards grew out of centuries of exploitation of seamen by shipowners, and the standards themselves have been developed primarily for commercial shipping. They establish size and capacity ratings, seaworthiness, sturdiness: Solar specifies that rafts carried on large vessels must withstand a free-fall into the sea from a height of 60 feet without damage to the raft or contents and must be able to operate in any condition of wind and weather for at least thirty days.

Not all craft sold as life rafts for pleasure boats will meet such standards, nor will they carry an official approval from one of these agencies. But this does not necessarily disqualify a raft for pleasure-boat use. For example, a raft of foreign manufacture may not have a U.S. Coast Guard rating but may meet all of the standards. Or, to keep the price within a reasonable range for the pleasure-boat market, a manufacturer may elect to cut a few corners; a life raft designed for a cruising sailboat won't have to survive a free-fall from a helicopter. Or the raft itself may meet the standards, but the equipment in the survival kit may not be USCG– or SOLAS–approved, for similar cost-saving reasons.

Check the manufacturer's specifications against the standards and make a decision based on your own probable requirements; whatever your choice, be prepared to upgrade the emergency kit even if it already meets "official" standards (see below).

TYPES OF LIFE RAFTS

Life rafts may be rigid or inflatable. Rigid, noninflatable rafts are the modern version of the World War I and II cork rings and Carley floats. Consisting of a rectangular plastic ring with a net or webbing floor, they offer basic flotation, no protection, and cost between one-sixth and one-third of comparable-size inflatables. They are useful only in the warmest sheltered waters.

Inflatables come in three basic types:

1. Ballasted. A pouch carried underneath the raft fills with water, creating a heavy ballast to increase greatly raft stability in heavy seas and high winds.

2. Partially ballasted. Water fills small pockets positioned around the raft underbody.

3. Unballasted. The "traditional" form, rapidly becoming obsolete. Stability, such as it is, comes from the weight of the occupants and the drag of a sea anchor.

CAPACITY

Available life-raft sizes range from two-man to twenty-man, with typical pleasure-boat rafts at four-, six-, and eight-man ratings. Those ratings are determined by the number of "men" a half-inflated raft would support; they are not a measure of floor space. Four men in a four-man raft would find themselves quite crowded. In very cold weather, such crowding might amplify body heat to a degree, but the disadvantages of cramped seating space probably would outweigh that advantage.

A MULTIRAFT RESCUE DRILL begins as this Coast Guard H-3 lowers its basket to begin taking off multiple "survivors." Given the large number of people involved and the distance from shore, a second helicopter may be on its way as a backup. As the hoist proceeds and these rafts become lighter, they may tend to blow about or even overturn in the helicopter downwash. Full or partially ballasted rafts will tend to be more stable.

A top-quality four-man raft, case, and equipment will weigh about 70 pounds; an eight-man raft, case, and equipment, over 100 pounds. The raft selected should accommodate the expected crew size, although the weight of the unit should be considered if a slight woman or child might have to handle it. For a large crew, two small rafts might be better than a single large one; they should, however, be tied together with about 30 feet of line.

CONSTRUCTION

Acceptable inflatables are made of nylon or canvas coated with neoprene, rubber, or Du Pont Hypalon; the seams may be sewn or welded. The selection of materials, the design, and the construction methods are a manufacturer's choice—any of these can meet official standards. Inexpensive recreational inflatables are made of polyvinylchloride (PVC) with welded seams, and they meet no standards.

Noninflatable rafts are constructed of polystyrene or a similar foamed plastic.

RECOMMENDED FEATURES

Canopy   A canopy protects against rain and spray and helps conserve body heat. In a 1959 test in the Norwegian Sea, with the outside air and water temperatures below 36°F, the temperature inside a fully loaded twenty-man raft rose to 84°F within an hour. After the lee door was opened for ventilation, the temperature dropped to and stabilized at 74°F.

Most life rafts have canopies; the better models have canopies with double-walled construction to provide increased thermal protection and durability. The canopy will have one or two entrance doors, which can be held closed with Velcro or a similar fastening. Most rafts inflate with the canopy door open, which makes them easy to get into but also a source of unwanted water. Those that inflate with the canopy closed provide a lanyard that can be grabbed easily to pull open the door.

On rafts that meet official standards, the canopies will also offer a method for the collection of rainwater—a desirable feature on any life raft.

Inflated or Insulated Bottom   This slows the flow of heat from the body to the ocean; some models have a sort of corrugated floor to keep water from pooling where the occupants are sitting.

Boarding Net and Handholds   These features aid in climbing aboard from the water, and they provide a grip for survivors who may have to remain in the water because of overcrowding in the raft.

Locator Lights   Mounted on the canopy, locator lights switch on automatically when the raft is inflated and provide a homing beacon for crew members who may be floundering in dark waters.

Identifying Markings   The name or radio call sign of your boat should be marked in large, clear letters on the raft and any item of floating equipment (such as the paddles).

EQUIPMENT AND SUPPLIES

The experiences of countless survivors have contributed to the development of a reasonably standard life-raft emergency package, but recent experiences, and a bit of common sense, suggest some modification even to an officially approved kit. Table 9-1 is a basic equipment list derived from regulation 17 of SOLAS, with some additions we recommend.

When shopping for a raft, make certain that the *listed* equipment and supplies are in fact furnished. Most sales brochures reserve for the manufacturer an option to modify or substitute materials without notice.

When you ask for changes or substitutions—for example, to replace rocket flares with more expensive but more useful parachute flares, or to have everything in the kit double-wrapped in plastic—even though you may be willing to pay the required extra charges, the salesman is likely to resist, on the ground that the kits come "standard." Since you are the person who is likely to be using the raft—not the salesman—and since you are paying for the service, you should be able to have whatever you want included, as long as it will fit, and have it all wrapped with extra care.

PURCHASE OPTIONS

The best option—and the most expensive—is to select and buy a new life raft from a manufacturer or authorized dealer. You can examine display models at any boat show or large showroom. You can obtain the features and equipment best suited to your needs, can be reasonably assured of freedom from flaws and damage, and can have some recourse in the event any flaws are discovered. However, there are other choices.

Remanufactured life rafts are available, usually in the larger commercial sizes, at 20 to 30 percent below the price of a new raft.

Surplus military and commercial rafts sometimes are available; these may be made of obsolete or not-up-to-specifications materials but nonetheless may meet your needs. However, beware of rafts designed for aviation use: To save weight, they may be substantially less sturdy than a shipboard unit. (This is a calculated trade-off, on the assumption that survivors of an aircraft accident at sea will be located and rescued quickly. Aircraft in transit file comprehensive flight plans; overdue or missing status is determined in a matter of hours, triggering the search.)

Rental or Loan may be useful options for that once-in-a-decade transocean race—particularly if expensive SOLAS–approved equipment is required. Rental equipment from a recognized vendor is likely to reflect proper care and timely

---

Table 9-1.   SOLAS Life-Raft Equipment List

1 buoyant rescue quoit attached to at least 100 feet of buoyant line
1 knife and 1 bailer for rafts accommodating fewer than 12 people
2 sponges
2 sea anchors: 1 permanently attached to the raft and 1 spare
2 paddles
1 raft repair kit
1 topping-up pump or bellows
3 can openers
1 approved first-aid kit in a waterproof case
1 rustproof, graduated drinking cup
1 waterproof flashlight suitable for signaling in Morse code, with 1 spare set of batteries and 1 spare bulb in a watertight container
1 daylight signal mirror and 1 signaling whistle
2 parachute distress flares capable of giving a bright red light at a high altitude
6 red hand-held flares

1 set of fishing tackle
Sufficient water, in appropriate containers, to provide 3 pints of fresh water for each person in the raft. A freshwater-producing still may be substituted for 1 pint per person, provided that it has sufficient capacity to produce an equal amount of water.
6 antiseasickness tablets for each person
1 set of survival instructions and a signal chart
1 container of food rations, to include 1 week of food per person for coastal cruising; 3 weeks of food per person for offshore cruising.
Example—4 people for 1 week:
8 cans or packs (14 ounces) sweetened condensed milk
2 boxes (72 packs per box) dextrose
1 bottle, 28 tablets or capsules, of B-complex, minerals-added, high-potency vitamins
5 packages dried fruits and nuts
As much water as can be fitted in the container

inspection; borrowing from a friend might be a mistake. Check the inspection tag and use your best judgment.

If you inherit a life raft with a boat you have bought, get an inspection (see chapter 10) and find out exactly what is inside that neatly stowed case.

MOUNTING

The raft container should be mounted or stowed where it is readily accessible for emergency use but won't get in the way:

Best Mounted on the cabintop or foredeck, centerline, with a clear path to the deck edge, lashed to properly installed and bedded cleats.

Acceptable Under a seat in the cockpit, clear of miscellaneous lines, clothing, cleaning gear, lashed to properly installed and bedded cleats.

Not Acceptable Insecure stowage, lashed to such items as locker lids and seats likely to be washed overboard in a storm, taking along the life raft. A raft placed in a topside locker, cockpit,

CANVAS LIFE-RAFT CANISTER COVER should be used in tropical climates where the sun can adversely affect the canister material.

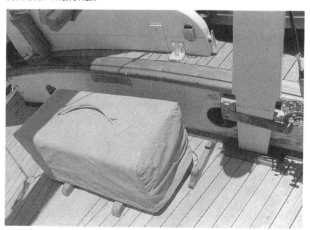

or dinghy, unless securely lashed, can be washed out and overboard; a raft stowed below decks, even at the foot of the companionway, will quite likely still be there when the boat settles to the bottom.

Just Plain Dumb To protect his expensive life raft from theft, one fellow secured it topside with a chain and padlock. At the Moment of Truth, he couldn't find the padlock key.

Since almost any raft may prove too heavy for a slight woman, a child, or an injured man to lift up and out of a locker, a topside location is preferable. With a clear path, even a heavy raft can be slid or rolled to the side.

The lanyard—which triggers the inflation mechanism (see below) and then serves as a painter to keep the raft from drifting away until all crew members are on board—must be secured firmly to the boat.

The raft container should not be used as a seat or stool; the case might crack, or the seal might be broken, allowing water to enter and possibly damage the contents. For the same reason, the attachment point for the lanyard should be below the level at which it enters the container. If not, rain and spray will run down the line and drip, wick, or seep into the container.

The position in which the raft is mounted (especially if it hangs out over the stern) could affect the measurement of a boat for a sanctioned race; check with the race committee before submitting the boat for measurement.

ALTERNATIVES: THE DINGHY OR INFLATABLE AS LIFE RAFT

As alternatives to a proper life raft, dinghies and inflatable tenders leave much to be desired: They lack protection from the weather; they normally lack emergency and survival equipment; and they may lack stability and buoyancy. In any but the calmest weather, it is almost impossible to climb into a dinghy from the water and even more difficult to haul aboard an injured person.

Many sailors think of the tender-in-an-emergency simply as a temporary refuge: Step aboard and row ashore. Unfortunately, in too many reported cases, wind and currents defeat the effort, and the boat is carried out to sea—ill-prepared for its new role as an alternative life raft.

However, dinghies and inflatables have served admirably in place of life rafts—even for people who had had a life raft. Most notable is the case of Maurice and Maralyn Bailey, who in 1973 spent most of a 118-day ordeal in a five-foot inflatable tender after their proper life raft failed.

The survival potential of any dinghy or inflatable can and should be greatly improved, whether intended as a substitute or a backup for a life raft. For example, the buoyancy of a dinghy can be increased with the addition of foam flotation or inflatable bladders. The best suggestion is to use the dinghy for the regular storage of boat fenders. When the fenders are needed, in port, emergency flotation is unnecessary; at sea, fenders are superfluous. They have to be stored *somewhere,* and lashed into a dinghy with bungee cords is a better solution than most.

Inflatables have buoyancy and good stability and are more easily adapted to emergency use than rigid dinghies. One serious limitation, however: the time it takes to inflate the flotation chambers manually. Towing or carrying a fully inflated boat is one solution; another is to keep a partially inflated boat on deck, taking up less room but still available for limited immediate service.

At the very least, all dinghies and inflatables should be equipped with a basic survival kit and limited rations, a tarpaulin that can be rigged as a canopy, and a folding bucket for use as a bailer or a sea anchor. Total additional investment: about $100.

Recommended Additions to Life-Raft Equipment

1 Emergency Position Indicating Radio Beacon (EPIRB)	Dye marker
2 hand-held strobe lights with batteries	Smoke flare
1 foil-type space blanket for each survivor	Additional parachute flares as space allows
	Additional water or Gatorade as space allows

Notes on Equipment and Supplies

• Everything should be double-wrapped in plastic.

• A well-nourished individual can survive up to fourteen days without water, much longer without food, if perspiration and energy expenditure are kept to a minimum. In a survival situation, water is more important than food, and food should not be eaten unless at least two pints of water are available. Gatorade or a similar fortified fluid would be a useful substitute for some (but not more than half) of the water.

• *Do not* add alcoholic beverages to the kit. Alcohol increases thirst and speeds the loss of body heat.

• A comprehensive first-aid kit is vital; more than half of all survivors in pleasure-boat sinkings have been injured, some seriously. Recommendations for first-aid kits, with appropriate additions for life-raft use, appear in chapter 18. You must at least be prepared to stabilize an injury, stop bleeding, prevent infection, and alleviate pain (see chapter 18).

• The instructions with the life raft, the first-aid kit, and any other emergency equipment in the raft may spell the difference between life and death for you and your party. If you require eyeglasses for reading, include a spare pair in the emergency kit.

• It is likely that not all of these items will fit in the container with the life raft; they should be stowed, double-wrapped in plastic, in the emergency bailout bag, which also will contain other emergency supplies and be easily accessible when needed.

CHAPTER TEN

Keeping
the Boat Safe

THE OWNER'S NOTEBOOK

Aboard any well-run U.S. Navy ship on which we ever served, each junior officer was required to develop a notebook, following an established training plan: Trace all steam lines from the boilers to the turbines, and back again, and put a diagram in the book; locate and identify all major pieces of machinery and equipment and put that information in the book, along with a brief description of the function and operation of each; locate each electrical distribution panel and diagram the network of wiring. In other words, study—and document your effort—every major and most minor systems aboard your floating home.

On larger ships, the list may have been attenuated by the sheer magnitude of the task, but the function was the same: to cause the newly assigned officer to become broadly familiar with the inner workings of the ship, no matter what his assignment. To the senior officers of the command and especially to the training and executive officers usually responsible for assigning and

evaluating the results, these notebooks were a vital element in training. To the junior officers, the notebooks frequently were a source of irritation—not because of the work involved, but because "permission to go ashore" for a weekend leave was often held in abeyance pending submission of the weekly notebook installment. Of course, since junior officers are college graduates and therefore presumably clever, many soon discovered the crib sheets hidden away aboard every naval vessel and—well—cheated.

Aboard submarines, the requirements have always been more stringent, and cheating in any form is akin to committing professional suicide. To qualify for a submariner's dolphin, each person—officer and enlisted—must be able to identify each piece of equipment and trace each line or run of pipe while blindfolded. Frequently, to add realism during training exercises, they are also required to do so while standing waist-deep in water underneath a high-pressure stream of water.

Which brings us to the point of this section: Anyone can search out a fuel line or battery cable in a pleasant pierside berth, and repair and replace it as necessary. However, while trapped on a midnight storm-tossed sea without lights, the task may be impossible. Anyone can troubleshoot a malfunctioning bilge pump when the bilges are clean and dry; anyone can follow the step-by-step procedures in the owner's manual for bleeding air from the injectors of a diesel engine while anchored in a sheltered cove. But—pump malfunctions usually are associated with uncontrolled flooding, and air often gets in the injectors when a fuel tank runs dry at the worst possible moment.

Take a leaf from the navy's training program and build your own Owner's Notebook. The time spent will pay off in immediate and intimate knowledge of the boat and its systems. It will quite possibly result in the discovery—and therefore timely repair—of pending trouble: a frayed drive belt hidden behind a safety guard, or an electrical connection corroding quietly out of sight.

A thorough and well-prepared Owner's Notebook by itself will serve several needs: (1) It will provide the owner or any crew member with a vital resource in time of need; (2) it will give outside workers a head start in troubleshooting any number of problems (and, under the general time-tested rubric that "time is money," particularly when billed at $40 or $50 an hour, that head start may quickly repay the owner for his effort); and (3) it will give an eventual new owner not only a head start on learning about his boat, but also tangible evidence that the previous owner was a thorough and thoughtful person who must have maintained his boat accordingly. The well-appointed Owner's Notebook may not add much to the eventual sales price, but it most certainly will be weighed in the choice of one boat over another.

However, one caution if *you* are that new owner: Don't just take the notebook, glance over it, and file it away against a future need. *You* still have to become intimate with the boat's systems, which means you need to crawl around the bilges yourself and trace out the lines.

FORMAT

The Owner's Notebook should be a loose-leaf binder with reinforced pages that won't disintegrate when wet, and all entries should be made in waterproof ink. Beware of most felt-tipped or fineline writing instruments. Pencil is barely acceptable: It is too easily rubbed away, affected by dampness, and almost always difficult to read in dim light.

Obviously, you want to fill the notebook with useful information but also take the time to organize and enter the information in such a manner that almost anyone can read and understand it. Make neat diagrams and use readable handwriting.

CONTENTS

Mechanical Section Make a plan drawing showing the location of each engine, motor, pump, and blower. Make a list of all these items, showing the model and serial number (if appropriate) and the names and addresses of the manufacturer and the nearest agent or supplier. Include telephone numbers—especially for the manufacturer.

All this might seem a bit unnecessary when a call to the local supplier would do the job, but next year, or five years from now, or 5,000 miles from home, a "local" supplier may never have heard of the item and the manufacturer may be the only source of information.

In making your list, be alert to affiliated but nonetheless individual items of machinery. For example, the engine may also include a separately identifiable transmission, water pump, fuel pump, and starter motor.

System Diagrams Diagrams should be prepared for the fuel, electrical, and plumbing systems. Show the location of each line, wire, and pipe, as well as each valve, pump, and switch.

Note the size and type of the piping or wire and obtain some quantity of each for your spares locker. At the least, keep a sample of each on hand to help in matching when you need a supply at a later time. This might prove especially helpful in an area with a language barrier, or in coming reasonable close when the desired size is not available.

Operational Data   Information on operating capacity should be developed and entered. Determine speed curves (determined as rpm over a measured mile); fuel and water capacities; fuel consumption at several levels of operation.

Emergency Equipment   List and locate on a plan drawing fire extinguishers, life jackets, signal flares, flashlights, toolkit, and so forth. Put the same information on an "emergency procedures" card, to be kept near the helm. *You* may remember where all of these items are stowed, but your guests might not, and in an emergency, you might not be able to direct the search.

Problem History File   This might be viewed as the "Dear Diary" section of the notebook: "Today the engine failed to start, and here's how I diagnosed and solved the problem." Over the years, you'll record many problems, large and small, some of which will have been resolved easily and some not. The Problem History File serves as your troubleshooting "memory."

SUPPLEMENTARY MATERIAL

Obtain all appropriate handbooks, manuals, and service bulletins for every piece of equipment you can identify. The typical owner's manual is barely adequate for operation and preventive maintenance. If your sailing plans do not extend much beyond the breakwater, that may well be enough, but if you plan to do extended cruising in more exotic (and mechanically naive) waters, you had better have a complete set of shop and parts manuals aboard. These books can be used by a mechanic to fix your machine when he doesn't have a set of his own; they might be the books *you* use to fix your machine when no mechanic is available. A typical set of shop manuals for a large marine diesel might run to several thousand pages and may cost more than dinner in a good restaurant—but that's inexpensive insurance.

If buying a new boat, use your leverage to obtain a complete set of plans and manuals. If the dealer suggests that such items are not included, you might indicate an interest in seeking another dealer.

HULL AND DECK MAINTENANCE

In the normal course of events, everything wears out or wears down or breaks. Ashore, the deterioration may be gradual and the consequences inconvenient. In the harsh marine environment, particularly along the seacoast, the condition of unprotected and uncared-for equipment goes downhill fast, and the results, none pleasant, may include breakdown at sea, fire and explosion, and sinking.

There are myriad forces that act on and against a boat; the details are discussed, alphabetically, in appendix IV. You should understand each of them; under most conditions, some care and forethought can prevent the consequences of all of them.

The following pages contain guidelines for the routine maintenance of the more critical components of your boat and its systems and present some suggestions on working safely. (It's called "routine" because it must be done on a regular basis, not because it's unimportant.) Here we describe the maintenance actions most directly related to safety, grouped by category: hull and deck, mechanical systems, sails and rigging, electrical systems, and safety equipment.

BOTTOM

To prevent the buildup of marine growth—which can damage the hull, clog intakes, and make emergency repairs difficult—the bottom should be painted with an antifouling formula approximately once a year (depending on environmental conditions and the type of paint used). Most antifouling paints contain copper, which leaches slowly out of the paint and is poisonous to most marine organisms. It can also be harmful to humans; during painting, care must be taken to keep the paint off the skin and to prevent inhalation of paint spray.

GELCOAT (FIBERGLASS HULLS)

The gelcoat should be cleaned regularly to prevent dirt buildup, and it should be waxed two or three times a year to preserve the sheen. This will help in cleaning and also will help preserve the watertight qualities of the gelcoat, thus forestalling the day when painting might be necessary. Do *not* wax deck surfaces, however—they become too slippery.

Check for cracks or crazing in the gelcoat—signs that may warn of hidden damage, a "hard spot," or impending failure. Try to determine and eliminate the cuase; repair the cracks to maintain the watertight surface. Best repair material is a two-part epoxy. Follow the instructions on the package.

Blisters must be cut out and patched; if the apparent damage is extensive, get professional advice.

ZINCS

All sacrificial anodes (zincs) must be inspected regularly—always when the boat is hauled, probably every six months otherwise, with an underwater visit. You can hire a diver for a few dollars, or go down yourself with a face mask. In clear water, you usually can see the zincs from the surface.

Replace any zinc that has deteriorated more than one-third. Mark the replacement date on any new zinc with a waterproof pen. Zincs are inexpensive; propellers, shafts, rudders, and seacocks are not.

THE BOAT OWNER'S TOOLCHEST. While this set would only fit in a large-size yacht, it is complete enough to accomplish even a major overhaul. Note the engine shop manual (which contains valuable exploded views of engine components as well as detailed disassembly and repair sequences). The boat toolchest should be limited only by the amount of available storage space.

SEACOCKS

These vital through-hull valves need lubrication and reasonably frequent use, to keep them from seizing tight. Teflon grease is the lubricant of choice, and it is best inserted from both inside and outside when the boat has been hauled out of the water. Manipulation of each valve should be

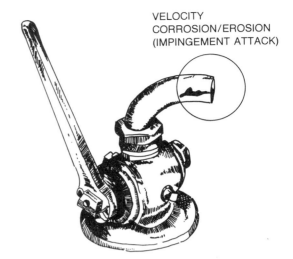

VELOCITY
CORROSION/EROSION
(IMPINGEMENT ATTACK)

CORROSION DAMAGE ON A SEACOCK ELBOW.

part of your regular monthly maintenance routine. Pay particular attention to that one valve that is tucked up out of the way and hard to reach—that's the one most likely to fail becuase it's too easily ignored. Keep a piece of pipe handy—one large enough in diameter to fit over the handles—to gently lever slightly recalcitrant seacocks. Do *not* use too much force—the whole unit could break or pop out of the hull.

LIMBER HOLES

The holes that help bilges drain freely tend to plug up with oil or debris; they must be cleaned out regularly. An easy method: Thread a length of small chain through all of the holes and give it a couple of jerks every now and then.

PROPANE TANK DRAINS

The drains under the propane tank mounting eventually will become clogged with dirt and debris washed in by rain and spray—check them regularly and keep them clear. Unfortunately, they usually are located under the tank and thus are not easily examined. If you open the storage compartment and find the tank floating in a pool of water, you'll know that you have waited too long.

HEAVY CORROSION can be seen on this hard-to-access piping in a New York 32 undergoing a complete restoration. To prevent this type of damage, piping should never be run behind heavy units and out of range of effective cleaning, inspection, and maintenance.

DECKS

All deck surfaces should be kept clean and free of any slippery buildup of dirt; all fittings, lifelines, and railings should be inspected regularly for signs of corrosion or loose mounting.

TOPSIDE LEAKS

When you detect a leak, *fix it*. Topside leaks should never be permitted to continue unchecked for too long. Serious electrical and structural deterioration probably would result.

Leaks can be fixed, but it can become a major project to trace the source of a leak. Water that enters through a tiny gap in the sealant at the base of a bowrail might end up as a drip in the midship galley. Here are some brief instructions for what might be a time-consuming project:

1. First, look for the obvious—loose fittings, dried or missing sealant around porthole frames and between deck planking, cracks in the topside fiberglass, gaps where the cabin structure meets the deck, a loose boot around the foot of the mast on deck.

2. Clean away dirt and debris, and repair these defects.

3. Then, starting at the cabintop at the aft (lower) end, run a stream of water from a freshwater hose pointed aft. Go below and check for a leak. If none appears after a reasonable time, shift the hose a bit forward and repeat the search. By more or less isolating a portion of the topsides for each application, moving from aft to the bow, you eventually may locate the source of the leak.

WATER DAMAGE TO PLANKING can occur from seepage behind a galley sink or icebox. That's what happened to the hull planking on this New York 32.

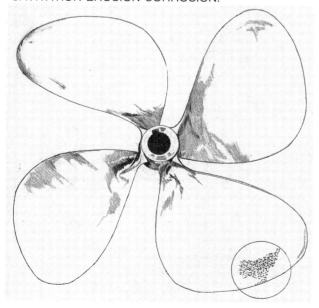

CAVITATION EROSION CORROSION.

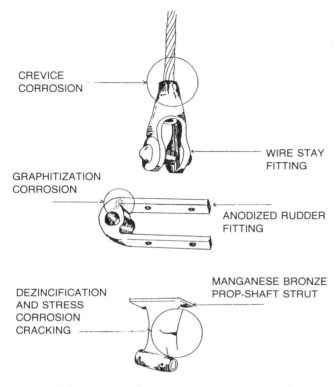

CREVICE
CORROSION

WIRE STAY
FITTING

GRAPHITIZATION
CORROSION

ANODIZED RUDDER
FITTING

MANGANESE BRONZE
PROP-SHAFT STRUT

DEZINCIFICATION
AND STRESS
CORROSION
CRACKING

CORROSION DAMAGE IN THREE VITAL AREAS. Top: crevice corrosion near a turnbuckle toggle attachment on standing rigging. Center: impingement corrosion on a rudder fitting. Bottom: corrosion cracking in the high-turbulence area on a propeller-shaft strut.

GROUND TACKLE

Anchors are very sturdy items—they have to be—but any of the several connections between an anchor and the boat may be, quite literally, the weak link in the chain.

At least once a year—or before any major voyage—break out every set of ground tackle and hose it clean. Lay out the chain and the rode full length and inspect for deterioration (rusting, cracks, frayed or weakened fibers). Check any splices for absolute integrity. (For absolute safety, the *only* splice in an anchor rode should be the one that connects the rode to the thimble by which it is shackled to the chain or anchor.)

Closely examine the anchor swivel, connecting shackle, and pin. The pin should be safety-wired to keep it from working loose, and the safety wire should be replaced during each annual inspection.

Hose down the anchor locker; make sure that the bitter end of the main anchor rode is connected to the boat (to prevent accidental loss of the anchor).

Re-stow all ground tackle carefully so that the main anchor is ready for use and the auxiliary and storm anchors are readily accessible.

MECHANICAL SYSTEMS

ENGINES

The main and auxiliary powerplants need regular, programmed maintenance: the required schedule appears in the owner's manual and should be followed scrupulously. Below are two representative schedules—one for a typical diesel engine, one for a gasoline engine. *These are only samples—not the schedules you should follow for your engines.*

OIL CHANGE

This may be the single most important engine maintenance task—and also may be the one most

easily delayed. That's a particular temptation when the engine has not run many hours, and particularly for a sailboat whose engine is used only around the marina—a full season's operation may put fewer than 100 hours on it. However, carbon and other by-products of combustion combine to produce an aging oil with a high acidic content. This could be as damaging to the engine as running with low oil levels.

One reason oil changes are so often avoided is that they are cumbersome and messy, unlike an automobile oil change. You can't just jack up the engine and let the old oil flow out of a drain plug.

Diesel Engine

Daily
- Check all fluid levels (coolant, oil, fuel).
- Run engine; check oil pressure, operating temperature, charging circuit.
- Check all plumbing and fittings for leaks.

Every 150 Hours
- Examine drive belts for wear; adjust tension.
- Top off water level in batteries.

Every 300 Hours
- Drain and replace oil and transmission fluid.
- Replace oil filter.
- Replace air filter.

Every 600 Hours
- Check fuel filters; clean or replace.
- Drain and refill closed cooling system.

Every 1000 Hours
- Remove and clean injectors.
- Check and adjust valve clearances.
- Inspect and service generator brushes.
- Drain and clean fuel tank.

Gasoline Engine

Daily
- Check all fluid levels (coolant, oil, fuel).
- Check fuel lines for leaks.

Every 25 Hours
- Check transmission fluid.
- Oil all linkages and bearings; fill grease cups.

Every 50 Hours
- Change engine oil and oil filter.

Every 100 Hours
- Change transmission fluid.
- Change fuel filter.
- Clean backfire flame arrester.
- Examine fuel pump and carburetor; clean and adjust.

Every 250 Hours
- Clean and adjust ignition system (plugs, points).
- Check alternator system, regulator; inspect wiring.

Every 500 Hours
- Have the engine checked out by a qualified mechanic.

Some engines may have an installed oil-change system, with valves and pumps arranged for the purpose. But for most of us, the oil comes out the same place the dipstick goes in—through a small length of plastic tubing connected with some sort of pump, either hand operated or powered by an electric drill. These work; the messy part arises when one end of the tubing pops out of place and sprays oil over a wide arc, or when the pump leaks, or when the leaky pump gets slippery and shoots out of your grip, resulting in another dash of oil on the engine or your shirt or in the bilges.

Removing the oil filter (which should be replaced with each oil change) may produce another jolt of unwanted oil; some of the bigger units hold as much as six quarts. Get that oil out of the canister before removing the filter.

THE CLEAN, WELL-LIGHTED ENGINEROOM. Painting an engine white helps pinpoint oil leaks and corrosion. Note the installed Halon firefighting system backed up by a handheld extinguisher mounted near the exit. The round tank at the left is a diesel-fueled Way Wulf marine furnace.

A FITTED DECK BOX divided into appropriate compartments. The large section for fenders, lines, and larger equipment has an open grate for a bottom to permit both drainage and ventilation. Top bins contain spare shackles, pins, winch handles, and related deck equipment. The end-opening compartment is a rigger's section containing sail-repair gear and supplies to make up and repair lines and do other ropework. The flop-down cover doubles as a work surface. The teak box incorporates the same water-protected construction as on any deck hatch.

We mention these hazards by way of warning. In the real world, after you've gone through one engine oil change, you should have accumulated enough experience to avoid future difficulties—or to cause you to turn the chore over to a professional engine service.

ENGINE COLOR

Typical engine colors—green, red, blue, black—present a pleasing sight when the hatch is lifted because they effectively camouflage leaks of oil, fuel, and hydraulic fluid. However, by effectively masking vital warnings of impending failure, these colors may well contribute to unsafe conditions.

It's best to paint your engine (and other machinery) *white* so that any leak or incipient corrosion will be spotted more easily. Changing the color is not very difficult, and the effort will let you become more familiar with some of the hidden-behind-or-underneath lines and controls.

Before painting, follow these steps: (1) Clean the machinery with a commercial engine cleaner, or ammonia and water, to eliminate any dirt, grease, or oil; (2) use a wire brush and sandpaper to get rid of loose and blistered paint (using drop cloths and a vacuum to keep the residue out of the bilges); (3) hit the bare spots with a suitable primer; and (4) spend a reasonable amount of time masking off engine mounts, plumbing, and wires that can't conveniently be removed. Finally, apply two coats of white enamel. For a classic look, color-code the plumbing and polish the copper and stainless steel.

SAILS AND RIGGING

SAILS

Sails are confronted by five major enemies:

1. Sunlight, which works to break down the fibers just as surely as a strong chemical bleach will ruin your best shirt. When sails are not being used, they must be protected from exposure to the damaging ultraviolet (UV) rays by removal or a cover. Roller-furling sails typically will have a blue, UV-proof leech, which covers the rest of the sail when rolled.

2. Salt crystals, which may act like tiny knives, slowly wearing away the fibers. Hose down or wash the sails carefully following saltwater sailing.

3. Embedded dirt and mildew. The one is to be removed by periodic washing in a mild detergent; the other is to be avoided by ensuring that the sails are thoroughly dry when put into storage.

4. Chafing against stays and spreaders. Prevention: Cover stays with a length of soft rubber tubing at the point of contact; put a tennis ball or sheepskin on the ends of the spreaders; sew reinforcements into the sails. Avoidance: Modify the course you are sailing and adjust the trim of the sails, as practicable.

5. Mechanical whipping and flapping under the sometimes-exceptional pressures of the wind. Seams and hems will tend to loosen and fail; frequent inspection and timely repair will forestall irreparable damage.

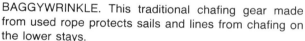

BAGGYWRINKLE. This traditional chafing gear made from used rope protects sails and lines from chafing on the lower stays.

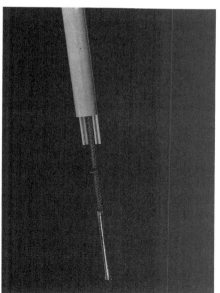

SHROUD ROLLERS.
(Nautical Engineering)

LEATHER CHAFE PROTECTION on turnbuckle stays protects the crew as well as rigging/sail components.

STANDING RIGGING

• At least once a year, examine all metal rigging and fittings for signs of corrosion; remove the covers hiding chainplate fasteners, and inspect and tighten as necessary; remove protective tape from turnbuckles, and inspect and lubricate the threads.

• Ensure that turnbuckles are installed *right side up*—that is, tension is increased by clockwise rotation.

• Look for broken strands of wire ("fishhooks"); if you find any, replace the whole cable.

RUNNING RIGGING

• Lubricate all blocks.

• Once a year, disassemble and clean all winches; relubricate; reassemble (following instructions provided by the manufacturer).

• When a line begins to show signs of wear at the handling end (where it passes through leads and blocks and jam cleats), remove it and reverse it end-for-end. This way, you may avoid early failure and almost double the useful life of the line.

ELECTRICAL SYSTEMS

BATTERIES

Battery maintenance is simple, perhaps so simple that it is too easily forgotten. A neglected battery may soon become a useless battery—at best requiring an expensive replacement and at worst failing to provide needed power at a critical moment. A battery that can't start the engine may transform an afternoon of offshore drift fishing into a nightmare of offshore drifting. As a first step in battery maintenance, be sure to understand how a battery works; review appendix III.

Next, establish a "battery log" as part of your Owner's Notebook. Enter, by date, each significant battery action, starting with the date of delivery.

Basic maintenance begins with checking the level of electrolyte in each of the battery's cells and adding distilled water as necessary. The fluid level should be above the battery plates and below the filler cap—usually, just to the bottom of the filler spout. If the batteries are tucked back under something, making it impossible to look straight down into each cell, use a mirror and a flashlight.

Avoid the temptation to use tap water in your

BATTERY CELL TESTER to evaluate voltage output of individual battery cells.

BATTERY MAINTENANCE EQUIPMENT. From left: Battery corrosion preventative spray and battery cleaner spray; hydrometer to test electrolyte condition; battery cell tester; battery terminal and cell brush combination; safety container for battery acid; bottle containing distilled water to make up lost electrolyte.

batteries; the dissolved minerals will too soon coat the battery plates, reducing and eventually eliminating the surface against which the electrolyte can work. How soon is too soon? A well-maintained marine battery might last for five or six years. Using tap water (and otherwise failing to follow recommended maintenance actions)

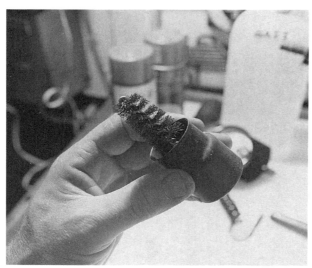

TERMINAL CONNECTOR CLEANING BRUSH.

BATTERY TERMINAL CLEANING BRUSH.

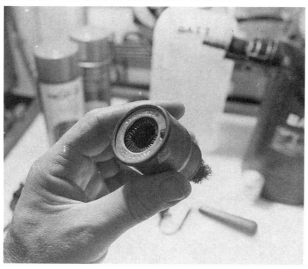

could cut that to two years. Put in real-world terms, that means you'll be replacing $300 worth of batteries every twenty-four months, for an average cost of about $12 a month. A gallon of distilled water costs 50 cents and should last a year.

Periodically determine the level of charge by checking the specific gravity of the electrolyte. (Specific gravity is a measure of the relative heaviness of a substance compared with water, which is assigned a specific gravity of 1.0.) The electrolyte in a storage battery is nominally 75 percent water and 25 percent sulfuric acid, and the specific gravity at full charge should be 1.265. As the battery discharges and the chemical action creates additional water to dilute the solution, the specific gravity will decrease to a level of about 1.120. At this point, the battery cannot deliver a useful current and needs to be recharged. Monitoring the specific gravity will give an indication of the condition of the battery and the adjustment of the charging circuits. It will also reveal the presence of current-draining short circuits somewhere in the electrical system. A healthy battery in a well-adjusted system always should be near full charge.

Specific gravity is measured with a simple device called a hydrometer—a glass tube with a rubber spout at one end, a squeeze-bulb at the other, and a calibrated float in the middle. Squeeze the bulb, put the spout in the battery filler hole, and suck up some electrolyte by releasing the bulb slowly. Hold the hydrometer vertical (bulb end up) and note the level at which the float is riding. Write it in the battery log. Then return the electrolyte to its cell and go on to the next cell.

The device is calibrated against a standard temperature—typically (but not always) 77°F. The reading must be corrected for higher- or lower-temperature electrolyte by adding or subtracting gravity points to the observed result, as specified in the table provided with the hydrometer.

You cannot get a reading unless the cell is properly full of electrolyte, and you cannot get a *proper* reading if you have just filled the cell, because the new water will be floating on top. A thorough mixing will require a period of charging or operation. Also, you won't get an accurate reading right after a period of heavy battery use, such as cranking a recalcitrant engine, because the newly formed water will not yet have mixed with the rest of the solution.

The battery terminals should be inspected for tight connections and for signs of corrosion (white powder around the terminals). Several times a year (or whenever corrosion is evident), the connectors should be removed; if the corrosion buildup is heavy, it can be removed by using a baking-soda-and-water solution. Be careful, however, not to let any of the soda solution get into the battery cells. The connectors and battery terminals should be cleaned to bright metal with a special cleaning tool or a strip of sandpaper (but don't remove any more metal than necessary). Smear the surfaces with petroleum jelly to retard future corrosion and then reconnect them.

Caution: The battery case or the terminals can be irretrievably damaged by improperly removing the connectors; this is not the time to exercise your basic skills as a hammer-and-screwdriver mechanic. Use the appropriate tool—a battery terminal puller. This operates much like a bottle cork puller, lifting the connector straight up off the terminal. First, loosen the nut holding the connector clamp; next, attach the puller; then turn the handle clockwise to apply the lifting leverage. If the connector seems welded to the terminal, squirt some WD-40 or similar lubricant around the post, and, if necessary, *gently* spread the jaws of the clamp with a screwdriver. Don't overdo it; the connector might break. Finally, wipe the surface of the battery to remove any dust, grime, or spilled electrolyte. A minute surface coating of such contaminants can create an electric bridge between the terminals, slowly draining the charge.

In cold weather, keep the batteries fully charged at all times. A discharged battery will freeze at about 14°F, while a fully charged battery will resist freezing until the temperature reaches

A BATTERY HYDROCAP is an optional accessory available from many marine battery manufacturers. It preserves battery-fluid vapors vented during battery charging and discharge cycles, collecting the moisture and permitting it to drop back down into the cells to keep the electrolyte level high.

MAINTENANCE MEANS SPARES. One way of organizing spares is to create kits according to use, as with this compartmented tackle box containing electrical spares. Included are wire terminals, switches, solenoids, fuses, and replacement wire sections.

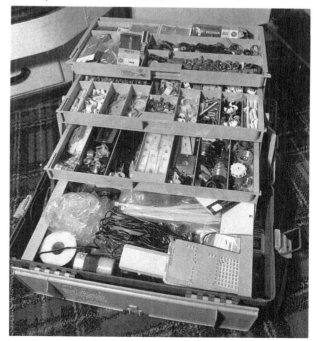

73°F. You'll pay two penalties for letting a battery freeze: (1) You have to buy a new one, and (2) if the case has split (a likely possibility), you'll have to clean up the spilled electrolyte. The best protection is prevention: Take the batteries out of the boat and store them in a warm spot.

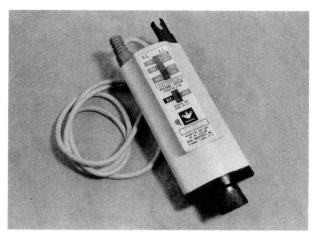

ELECTRICAL TESTER that can read both alternating and direct current.

THREE ELECTRICAL TOOLS. At left is a fuse puller that protects the user. In the center is a plug-in tester for 110V AC circuits to test for ground and wiring. At right is a simple and inexpensive continuity tester to search out power breaks in electrical circuits.

WIRING

• Check the insulation for chafing at hangers or through-bulkhead penetrations; be alert for signs of scorching (dryness, brittleness, wrong color)—probable evidence of an overloaded circuit. *Check it out.*

• Here is a simple four-step method for detecting short circuits or faulty switches: (1) Make sure all switches are off; (2) disconnect the main positive cable at the battery terminal; (3) insert a 12V test light between the terminal and the positive cable (if the light goes on, current is flowing, indicating a short of some kind or a switch inadvertently left on); (4) reconnect the positive battery cable and then move progressively through the circuits—disconnecting at terminal blocks, switches, and so forth, to locate the problem.

CIRCUIT BREAKERS AND FUSES

Circuit breakers should be cycled off-and-on to ensure freedom of movement. Examine each fuse for signs of corrosion; make sure that fuse holders make a tight connection.

MOTORS

Electric motors drive your boat's pumps and blowers, usually in silence. When a motor becomes slow to start, or starts humming or whining, it's asking for help.

• Check the brushes for wear, and buy a replacement set if needed. Next check the commutator against which they rub; the surface may have become rough. If so, lightly rub it with fine sandpaper. Then wrap the sandpaper around the commutator, put the new brush in the brush holder, and rotate the shaft back and forth while putting light pressure on the brush. This will shape the face of the brush to the commutator.

• Lubricate the bearings through the oiler holes or grease cups (if the motor has any) or by running a few drops of oil along the shaft. Be conservative; too much oil or grease may creep into the motor, damaging it.

• Some motors are designed to be maintenance-free: When they start to go sour, they can't be fixed and have to be replaced.

ELECTRONICS

Depth Finder Clean the exposed face of the through-hull transducer monthly (if it can be withdrawn for cleaning), or at least at each haulout. In an area of particularly heavy marine growth, inspect and clean by diving between haulouts. Do not paint the transducer.

Radio Direction Finder (RDF) Check for leaking batteries; always remove batteries for layup and replace them with new ones.

VHF Radio If radio is a battery-operated portable, check for leaking batteries; remove batteries for layup and replace with new ones. Check antenna, antenna connection, and lead. Conduct a radio check. Call on channel 16 to establish contact, then switch to a working channel for a report on your signal strength.

EPIRB Remove batteries during layup; when replacing, ensure that battery contacts are clean and polished. Check the antenna lead and connections for cracks and corrosion. Run a self-test, following instructions on the unit.

Radar Put a warning tag—DO NOT ENERGIZE—on the power switch and then go aloft to examine antenna mounting bolts and connections. Open the antenna cover, inspect for deterioration, and reclose. Remove the warning tag. Operate the radar unit, checking indicated bearings of navigational aids against bearings obtained with a hand-bearing compass. If you note any significant differences, have a trained technician recalibrate the unit.

SAFETY EQUIPMENT

FIRE EXTINGUISHERS

Portable units should be inspected monthly to ensure that each is in its assigned place, has not been used, is fully charged, and shows no signs of corrosion or damage. They should be inspected annually by a qualified technician and tagged with the date of the inspection.

Installed systems should be inspected monthly for corrosion or damage, to ensure that all connections are tight, that the system has not been used, and that access to the control has not been obstructed. Every six months, they should be inspected and tagged by a qualified technician.

Most portable units are equipped with pressure gauges that should indicate the condition of the unit. Usually these are color-coded, with a reading "in the red" indicating a problem. However, these gauges are not fully reliable; each unit should be checked, by weight, every six months, regardless of the gauge reading. A loss of weight is the best way to detect a leak.

The weight at the time of inspection should be equal to the listed weight of the cylinder plus the standard weight for a full charge of the extinguishing agent. Because a difference of a few ounces may be significant, a qualified inspector should do the weighing. A do-it-yourself operation with bathroom-type scales could be a fatal mistake.

Cylinders—both portable and fixed—should be pressure-tested (by a qualified inspector) after use, or when signs of corrosion appear, or every five years. The type and date of each inspection should be listed on an attached tag.

FLARES

Pyrotechnic flares are age-dated and must be replaced after the expiration date. In addition, flares must be examined monthly for signs of leaking or deterioration; if the condition seems questionable, replace them.

LIFE RAFTS

Even the most expensive life rafts will deteriorate over time. That tightly packed container is subject to wide ranges of heat and cold, subject to leaking seals that may let water in or CO_2 out, and always moving up, down, and sideways. Common sense alone dictates some sort of regular inspection; the U.S. Navy and the Coast Guard inspect their rafts on an annual basis. The Royal

A COMPLETE LIFE-RAFT INSPECTION includes pressurization and measurement of pressure-holding capability over time.

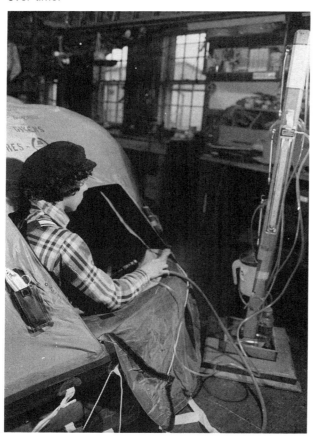

Navy has set the period at three years, but not every raft aboard a given ship is inspected in the same cycle, and perhaps half of the installed rafts will have been inspected within eighteen months. Safety would not be impaired at a well-run naval command, and the government would save money and effort. Aboard your more casually run pleasure boat—with only one life raft to ensure your family's survival—be conservative, not miserly. Have an annual inspection.

In the United States, SOLAS– and Coast Guard–certified rafts must be inspected at a Coast Guard–approved inspection station. To gain approval, these stations must meet basic criteria for inspector training, have demonstrated a commitment to meet stringent inspection standards, and have on hand a stock of recommended replacement parts and supplies. Noncertified rafts may be inspected at stations approved by the raft manufacturer, but, all things considered, a Coast Guard approval is an assurance of top quality. Coast Guard–approved stations may be indicated in Yellow Pages advertisements under "Life Rafts," "Boat Equipment and Supplies," or "Boat Repairing and Service."

Do-it-yourself inspections are false economy. The trained inspector knows what to look for and where—and what to do if he finds it. A certified inspection station will have equipment sensitive enough to measure minute changes in pressure during an inflation test or to detect even the slightest leak in the CO_2 system—and will have on hand the correct parts or supplies to make necessary repairs.

A proper inspection includes (but is not limited to) unpacking the container; a check of all exterior surfaces, valves, webbing, lines, and the survival kit; inflation (with air, not the CO_2 system); thorough inspection of the CO_2 bottle and charging system; and careful repacking.

The annual inspection is an excellent time for you to become familiar with or to refresh your knowledge of the raft and its contents. It offers the opportunity for a three-dimensional rehearsal—getting in and out of the raft, opening and closing the door, locating the contents (for

---

Safety Equipment Checklist

- Verify condition of all flashlight, man-overboard light, and portable radio batteries with a voltmeter or battery tester.
- Cycle EPIRB in test mode.
- Inspect ground tackle (including anchor rode, chain, shackles, and pins) for signs of wear or corrosion.
- Remove storm anchor and other auxiliary anchors from storage; inspect rode, shackles, and pins; replace in highly accessible position.
- Inspect flare kit; check for expiration dates, signs of leaking, or other deterioration.
- Examine man-overboard pole; be sure all connecting lines are in good condition, strobe is operative, horseshoe float is undamaged.
- Examine all life jackets; check for wet spots, fungus, damaged webbing, and fastenings.
- Inspect survival suit for rips or tears, tight seams, smooth-operating zippers.
- Break out the jackline and inspect all fastenings; check each safety harness for tight webbings and smoothly operating hooks and shackles.
- Sound the horn; verify backup supply of compressed gas.
- Test all navigation and running lights; verify location of spare bulbs.
- Examine the medical kit; check contents against contents list; check expiration dates. Add or replace supplies as necessary.
- Verify the location, condition, and ready access of: Distress flag, jury-rigged radio antenna, emergency bailout bag, dinghy bailout bag, emergency tiller, handle for manual bilge pump, heaving line, and stormsail and lines.

---

example, the knife with which you will cut the lanyard/painter). The next time you have the opportunity to do these things, it may be cold and dark, you may be sick or injured, and you most certainly will be terrified.

The inspection also gives you a chance to update the contents of, or make any changes in, the survival kit.

WORKING SAFELY

GENERAL GUIDELINES

1. Working safely means working intelligently. Plan your work before you start: Break out the owner's manual, determine the logical course of action, select the tools, and clear an adequate space.

2. Use the right tool for the job. For example, use the right-size screwdriver: the wrong size may damage the slot on the screw head, complicating removal, or it may slip out of the slot and injure you. Don't use a screwdriver when you need a chisel or a prybar; don't use a pair of pliers when you need a wrench.

3. Avoid using too much force. If screws or nuts are frozen, try freeing them with penetrating oil. But be wary when there is oil on your tools—they quickly become dangerously slippery.

4. Don't end up with leftover parts. When you disassemble a unit, place each part on a bench or a white towel from left to right in the order in which it is removed. Then, during reassembly, go from right to left. Mark electrical wiring with tags or tapes to identify the connection points. When disassembling units mounted in place, keep a pan underneath to catch dropped parts.

5. *Do not work in a poorly ventilated space.* Be sure you have an adequate supply of fresh, clean air. Arrange for blowers or fans to keep air moving through the space, particularly when working with any materials that might be harmful when inhaled.

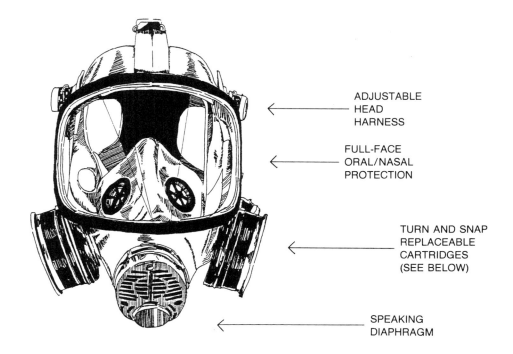

FULL-FACE SKIN AND RESPIRATION PROTECTION.

ADJUSTABLE HEAD HARNESS

FULL-FACE ORAL/NASAL PROTECTION

TURN AND SNAP REPLACEABLE CARTRIDGES (SEE BELOW)

SPEAKING DIAPHRAGM

Filters and Cartridges: A Brief Explanation

Color Code for Cartridges/Canisters

Atmospheric Contaminant	Color Assigned
Acid gas	White
Organic vapors	Black
Ammonia gas	Green
Acid gas and organic vapor	Yellow
Radioactive materials (except tritium and noble gases)	Purple
Dusts, fumes, and mists (other than radioactive materials)	Red
Other vapors and gases not listed above	Olive

Notes:
1. A purple stripe shall be used to identify radioactive materials in combination with any vapor or gas.
2. An orange stripe shall be used to identify dusts, fumes, and mists in combination with any vapor or gas.
3. Where labels only are colored to conform with this table, the canister or cartridge body shall be gray or a metal canister or cartridge body may be left in its natural metallic color.
4. The user shall refer to the wording of the label to determine the type and degree of protection the canister or cartridge will afford.

References: Information for this chart is taken from ANSI K13.1-1973, Identification of Air Purifying Respirator Canisters and Cartridges.

Mechanical Filter Elements

A mechanical filter element provides protection against particulate matter such as dust, mists, or metal fumes. This type of element "filters" particulate matter by physically trapping it in the fibrous filter material.

In addition, the wool-felt filters possess an electrostatic charge that increases filter efficiency by electrostatically attracting the particles to the fibers. Although mechanical filters become more efficient as they are used, they should be changed when breathing resistance becomes excessive.

Chemical Cartridge Elements

Chemical cartridges are elements filled with a specially treated activated carbon with a very high adsorption capacity. Gases and vapors passing through chemical cartridges are attracted and held to the surface of the carbon. In the case of acid and alkaline gases, a chemical reaction and/or absorption occurs.

Unlike mechanical filters, chemical cartridges do not become more efficient with use. Their adsorption capacity is limited; thus when wearers detect any taste, odor, or irritation, they should leave the contaminated areas and change cartridges.

6. Beware of chemicals—cleaning solvents, paint, paint removers, resins, patching compounds, and fuel. Some will damage your skin on contact; some may be absorbed *through* your skin on more prolonged contact; most produce fumes that at the least may prove irritating and at the worst, carcinogenic. *Always read the instructions and precautions on the label before you use any chemical product.*

WORKING WITH HAZARDOUS MATERIALS

Wood Preservatives These are used in treating pilings, pier decks, etc., and may contain PCP, copper, or other poisons.

- Use only when necessary and never in closed spaces.
- Avoid skin contact; wear gloves; use a respirator; ensure adequate ventilation.
- Avoid inhalation of sawdust from treated wood; avoid inhalation of smoke from burning scraps of treated wood.

Solvents These include paints, thinners, resins, cleaners, which typically (but not exclusively) contain petroleum products. Prolonged contact or exposure through breathing may cause brain damage.

- Read and heed label warnings.
- Always use appropriate protective clothing.
- Never use solvents in a confined space without adequate ventilation (blowers or fans); use a respirator.

Fiberglass Tiny bits of glass fiber can be inhaled or get in the eyes; the resins and their fumes are toxic, often resulting in contact burns, dizziness, headaches, and/or nausea.

- Always wear plastic gloves and protective clothing.
- Immediately clean spilled resin from the skin.

- Wear goggles and use a respirator when mixing resins.
- Do not use power sanders until the resins have cured; wear goggles and use a respirator.

Bottom Paints Toxic by their very nature, they are designed to kill living organisms. Most contain compounds of copper; some also contain lead.

- Use only in well-ventilated areas; use a respirator.
- Cover all exposed areas of your body, including your hair.

See appendix V for a more thorough treatment of this subject.

PREFERRED TWO-STRAP FILTER MASK PROTECTION.

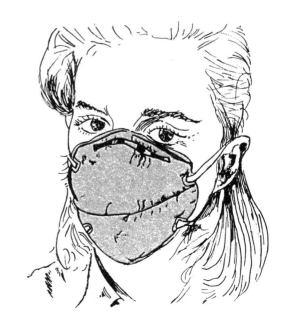

WORKING WITH NOISE

Hearing damage can occur from a combination of hazards. Exposure to dangerous frequencies of noise is a distinct problem. Noise exposure for extended periods of time is another. A third hazard is exposure to loud noise for both short and long terms. The hazard exists to a greater or lesser degree, depending on the relationship between these three elements. High-frequency noise such as the type generated by woodworking machinery can be a hazard during both short- and long-term exposure. And then there are lower-frequency noises that fall in the dangerous acoustic trauma notch. The Deafness Research Foundation has found that hearing damage can occur in the frequency range 3000 to 6000 Hz. Exposure to repetitive hammering, impact machinery, and turbines can cause hearing damage. Greater noise levels can be tolerated with shorter periods of exposure. Low-frequency noise, such as the type generated by marine diesel engines and deck machinery, can be hazardous due to the usually long exposure times.

Besides causing actual damage, excessive frequency, noise level, or long exposure times can produce fatigue and dangerously affect energy levels, as well as a mariner's ability to work with precision (navigate or operate machinery), tolerate hardship (rough seas, hard work, or an emergency), or make judgments.

Earplugs are only an interim measure and do not offer full or long-term protection. Full ear protection with headphone-type "earmuffs" should be used in noise-hazard conditions such as engine spaces, noisy deck areas, and boatyard workshops.

WORKING WITH ELECTRICITY

1. Always assume a circuit is energized until you have personally checked the switch; put a warning tag on the switch—DO NOT OPERATE, REPAIRS IN PROGRESS.

2. If possible, let someone else know you will be working with electricity.

3. Stand or sit on a rubber mat to provide insulation against a flow of current through your body to a ground. If your boat is not already equipped with ground fault circuit interrupters, obtain a portable model for use with power tools.

4. If working with a live or possibly live circuit, try to work with one hand and put the other hand in your pocket. A current flowing from one hand to the other creates a life-threatening cross-chest path. By the same token, don't use your spare hand to hang onto anything metal, such as the mast or the stove.

5. Do not drill into a bulkhead or a partition until you are sure you won't be drilling into a wire on the other side.

6. Beware of capacitors—they may retain a charge even when the current is off.

WORKING OVER THE SIDE

At some point, you may have to go in the water to deal with a problem—plug a hole in the hull or remove a line wrapped around the propeller—or simply to scrub the bottom. In the latter case, we'll assume you're moored in a safe harbor so at least you won't have to worry about the boat sailing off without you.

However, working over the side presents hazards in any event. Being equipped with scuba (self-contained underwater breathing apparatus) gear and a wet suit would be ideal, but that may be too costly (for both the equipment and the necessary training) for casual boating. As a minimum, you should have a face mask, a snorkel tube, and a set of flippers, and heed the following guidelines:

1. Don't go over the side unless you are sure the job is absolutely necessary.

2. Don't go over the side until you are certain you'll be able to get back aboard—boarding ladder in place, crew standing by to help.

3. Plan your work ahead of time. Select the tools and materials and put them in a canvas work bucket; attach everything with lanyards. Wear work gloves.

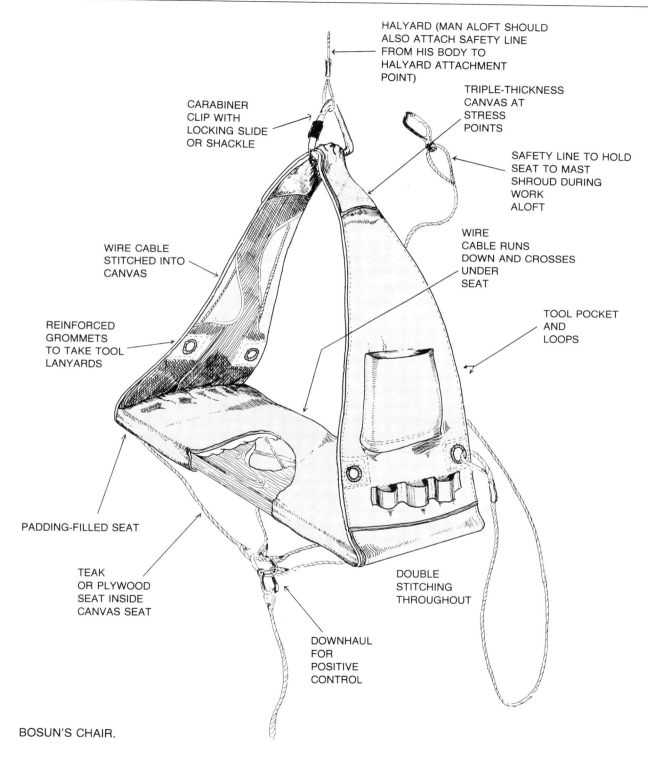

HALYARD (MAN ALOFT SHOULD ALSO ATTACH SAFETY LINE FROM HIS BODY TO HALYARD ATTACHMENT POINT)

CARABINER CLIP WITH LOCKING SLIDE OR SHACKLE

TRIPLE-THICKNESS CANVAS AT STRESS POINTS

SAFETY LINE TO HOLD SEAT TO MAST SHROUD DURING WORK ALOFT

WIRE CABLE STITCHED INTO CANVAS

WIRE CABLE RUNS DOWN AND CROSSES UNDER SEAT

REINFORCED GROMMETS TO TAKE TOOL LANYARDS

TOOL POCKET AND LOOPS

PADDING-FILLED SEAT

TEAK OR PLYWOOD SEAT INSIDE CANVAS SEAT

DOUBLE STITCHING THROUGHOUT

DOWNHAUL FOR POSITIVE CONTROL

BOSUN'S CHAIR.

4. Use a safety line tended by a crew member on deck. Work out hand signals or line signals—one tug for more slack, two tugs for "take in some line," three tugs for "get me out of here."

5. Wear an inflatable life vest (uninflated if you'll be going under the surface) or a regular life jacket if you'll be working on the surface.

6. Watch out for the boat as it rolls and pitches; if the weather is too bad, try to postpone the work.

7. If the water is cold, and you can't postpone the work and you don't have a wet suit, put on heavy clothing and foul-weather gear. This will make it harder to work, but it may delay the onset of hypothermia.

A MODERN BOSUN'S "CHAIR." Most bosun's chairs are time-tested devices for going aloft, but they have the inherent problem of being bulky devices that swing easily and in large arcs in a seaway. They also do not secure the worker effectively, even with safety cables. This canvas web bosun's chair solves the problem—giving security and maneuverability at the same time. (Lirakis)

8. Be alert for the warning signs of trouble: numbness of hands or feet, dizziness, shortness of breath, excessive shivering, inability to concentrate—and *get back aboard.*

GOING ALOFT

Moored alongside a pier on a calm day, you might think that going up the mast would be an interesting way to get a better view of the countryside—rather like a ferris-wheel ride. After you settle into the bosun's chair, a trusted assistant takes the hoisting line to a winch, gives it a few turns, and begins a steady cranking until you're at the top. The line is tied off while you conduct your business. When you are ready for the return trip, the line is eased off slowly with just the right amount of tension to let you descend with proper control.

But this whole procedure becomes a bit more complex when underway and a lot more hazardous in any combination of wind and wave. Of course, if you have an old-fashioned sailing rig

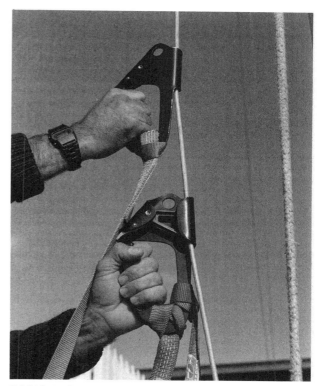

GOING ALOFT. An alternative (or an assist) to a straight hoist aloft in a traditional bosun's chair is this climbing leg and hand set. It is particularly valuable for the single-handed sailor or in a situation where you do not have an able hand to help hoist the working crew member aloft. (Lirakis)

with mast hoops, ratlines, or steps up the mast, getting to the top is easy enough. But for most of us, the bosun's chair is the practical alternative.

A bosun's chair is a simple tool, easily made or commercially available. The least complicated version is a canvas sling that hangs from a hoisting ring. It holds you in what might seem like a secure and comforting grip, but it plays the devil when you want to get something out of a pants pocket.

A wooden seat, suspended from the hoisting ring by four sturdy lines, avoids that problem, but unless it is properly designed and finished, it adds to the natural feeling of insecurity as you are hoisted aloft. The lines should be short, with the hoisting ring at chest level. This will help keep you from sliding off and give you plenty of things to hold onto. The seat must not be varnished—it's too slippery when wet.

The commercial chairs come in a wide variety of models; the best ones incorporate a safety harness and tool pockets or holders. But you can make your own toolholder from a scrub bucket. Just don't use a canvas bag with a drawstring top—it will try to remain closed, complicating tool selection and use when aloft.

Each tool should be secured to the bucket handle or chair hoist with a small line of sufficient length for a full reach. A tool dropped from the masthead is at the least unavailable for use and at the worst a lethal missile to those waiting below.

MAST STEPS provide secure hand- and footholds for going aloft, but remember that use of these steps still requires a safety harness with a double-clip system so the climber is never unhooked.

"Raise the load"

"Lower the load"

"Raise the load slowly"

"Lower the load slowly"

"Stop"

WINCH AND HOISTING HAND SIGNALS have been standardized over time. These are the most commonly needed signals. They are useful in noisy areas or over distances where voices will not carry or can be too easily misunderstood. (U.S. Navy)

The chair is tied or hooked onto the free end of a halyard, which is led to a winch for the motive power. Once aloft, connect a safety line to the lifting ring (or your harness) to keep you from falling should the halyard give way.

Take a trial spin so that you and your crew can check out the system and work out any procedures before you need them. For communication, hand signals are better than yelling, and you can invent your own signals, but using a clenched fist for "stop" and a cranking motion for "go," and pointing up or down for direction is likely to be understood under almost any conditions.

On your first trip aloft, look for sharp projections that could become heavy-weather hazards—and change or pad them as practicable.

Practice hooking your safety line to various points along the way, and practice handling a few tools.

When you need to go aloft while underway, hook a short safety line to a halyard tightened up against the mast. This will help hold the chair in tighter, preventing wide swings and unpleasant collisions. From one corner of the chair, attach a tending line to be handled by a crew member on deck for controlling dangerous gyrations. Better would be two tending lines to two crew members on deck.

Finally—wear a life jacket. Not only will it pad you against bumps and abrasions, but also, should a line fail and you fall, it will keep you afloat even if you are unconscious.

MECHANICAL AND ELECTRICAL SPARES

It should be obvious that backup for certain items of equipment is critical; unless you are an experienced boater, knowing which items to carry could result in an expensive guessing game. Here's a suggested general list:

MECHANICAL SPARE PARTS

- All engine drive belts (alternator, pumps)
- Pump impellers or rebuild kits; spare bilge pump
- Main engine water pump, complete. In an emergency, it's quicker and easier to replace the whole pump than to struggle with impellers and gaskets.
- Starter solenoid
- Injector (for diesel)
- For gasoline engines:
- Spark plugs
- Spark-plug wires
- Distributor cap
- Distributor rotor
- Condenser
- Coil
- Ignition points

- Ignition ballast (older engine models)
- Gasket set or gasket material
- Engine oil
- Transmission fluid
- Nuts and bolts, matched to your engine requirements
- Key stock (for those engine parts that use a key to lock on a shaft)

ELECTRICAL SPARE PARTS

- Light bulbs for all lights, but especially running lights
- Spare fuses, especially for all in-equipment and in-line fuses that are independent of circuit breakers
- Supply of wire, including one run of the largest gauge used aboard, at least double the length of the boat
- Emergency radio antenna
- Kit of terminals and connectors

PART II

Safe Boating

THE SAFE BOATER: YOU

Throughout much of the Western world, you must have a driver's license to operate an automobile and a pilot's license to fly an airplane, and to get either one, you must have demonstrated some measure of skill and understanding to a government official. Throughout most of the world, all you need to operate a boat, large or small, is the money to pay for it. Charter agents may require some proof of skill—their money and liability, after all, are at stake—but a boat dealer may sell you half a million dollars' worth of yacht solely on the strength of your bank account.

Were you to take that big yacht out for a spin without training or professional assistance, you'd be a fool, but fools there are, quickly getting stuck in the mud and unable to call for help because they don't know how to use the radio.

And other fools there are, of course, at the low-price end of the boating spectrum, zipping about the waterways at excessive speed, creating damaging wakes and endangering the lives and limbs of friends and strangers alike. We might assume it to be something in the American psyche—a need to demonstrate independence. Perhaps it's simply that most adults don't like to be told what they can or cannot do, and they assume that boating gives them a freedom not otherwise enjoyed.

However, two inexorable forces oppose that assumption: the laws of man, which seek to impose safety through regulation, and the laws of nature, which demand knowledgeable obedience. Every boat owner and operator, of whatever status, age, or inclination, must understand and heed both.

The good mariner seeks to develop a quiet confidence in everything he does—through training and practice and learning how to deal with his own limits. He knows the limits of his skill and stamina and does not, on purpose, push beyond them. He always knows where he is—and he doesn't get underway until he knows where he's going. He develops a solid routine for everything, from bending on a sail to hauling in a fish. He ensures the safety of his crew and guests by watching over them; he ensures their enjoyment of the cruise by sharing knowledge with them and allowing them to participate in the working of the boat. He is not a loud tyrant, but a calm and steady element—especially in a time of stress. Everything is done in a firm and positive manner: orders are unambiguous; control—of the ship, the helm, a line—is always absolute.

The good mariner frequently checks the broadcast weather forecast but also keeps an eye on the weather itself. Sudden squalls can hit with devastating fury, before the professional weather watchers even know they exist.

The good mariner knows his boat; he's spent hours sitting in the cockpit and mentally working through dozens—no, hundreds—of evolutions: getting underway from a tight slip with a heavy current; actions to take when the engine goes silent in the middle of a crowded channel; putting out a fire in the galley. If he's about to embark on a charter in someone else's boat, which will be *his* for a time, he thoroughly studies the layout and equipment—and spends time going over the same evolutions.

In the spirit of the good mariner, we present in this section a general look at navigation, piloting, and a wide variety of boating operations; offer some specific guidelines on such vital and potentially difficult operations as anchoring and refueling; and offer suggestions on keeping your crew healthy while underway—including safety in the galley and protection from the effects of the sun and the hazards of lightning.

In all of this, we remind you to consider safety foremost. Plan ahead, even for casual recreation—hazards are just as dangerous close to home as a hundred miles away. One example: A routine fair-weather waterskiing trip became a tragedy for a twelve-year-old boy because his father unwittingly chose an area with a high tidal current near a channel-dredging operation. Normal safety rules were followed: A companion was with the father in the boat as a lookout, the boat was handled properly, the boy was a good swimmer and was wearing a life jacket. However—when the boy fell, he was swept downstream by the current, became trapped under the dredge, and drowned. A painful irony in this accident: The father was a policeman, a member of the local rescue squad. It was his team that had to recover the boy's body.

CHAPTER ELEVEN

Getting Ready

Safe boating of course must start with a safe boat, but you can't go very far without a safe crew. Operational safety begins with education, training, and lots of practice, and it includes the care and handling of children and guests, voyage planning (whether for a brief or extended cruise), and careful, orderly, seamanlike handling of the boat.

LEARNING THE RULES

SEAMANSHIP SKILLS

There are innumerable and excellent training courses on basic boating, navigation, and safety; they provide a small reward in the reduction of insurance premiums and a large reward in self-confidence. Courses are offered through high school or junior college adult education programs, by local sailing and yacht clubs, by commercial sailing or maritime schools, and by the U.S. Power Squadrons—a national, nongovernmental organization with more than 400 local branches, each conducting one or more courses a year applicable to both power and sail. Some training courses are basic, some more broadly based; for example, schools affiliated with the American Sail Association offer seven skill levels: basic sailing, basic coastal cruising, bareboat chartering, coastal navigation, advanced coastal cruising, celestial navigation, and offshore cruising.

Some courses may lead to certification, which makes it easier to charter someone else's boat—it validates that you have the skills and knowledge necessary for safe operation of a boat.

Boating Education and Safety Courses

To find a boating course near you,
call BOAT/U. S. FOUNDATION COURSE LINE

1-800-336-BOAT
1-800-245-BOAT (Virginia only)

To find a sailing course near you,
call LEARN-TO-SAIL HOTLINE

1-800-447-4700

COURSES AND SOURCES

U.S. Coast Guard Auxiliary

The USCG Auxiliary offers a variety of boating courses conducted by experienced volunteers.

Boating Skills and Seamanship
Six to twelve lessons covering boathandling, legal requirements, Rules of the Road, navigation, safety, boat terminology, piloting, marine engines, seamanship, sailing, weather, and marine radiotelephone.

Sailing and Seamanship
Seven to twelve lessons. Parallels the above course, but geared to sailors.

Advanced Coastal Navigation
Twelve lessons of advanced instruction in navigation procedures for graduates of the above courses.

U.S. Power Squadrons

This organization offers free instruction for eleven lessons dealing with basic boating taught by experienced volunteers at 500 locations nationwide.

Public Boating Course
Emphasis on power. Includes lessons on safety, equipment, boathandling, seamanship, basic navigation, trailering, weather, engine troubleshooting, and sailing.

Sailboating Course
Lessons cover similar ground as the powerboat course but are specifically oriented toward sailing.

American Red Cross

Various local chapters of the American Red Cross offer on-the-water instructions in canoeing and kayaking, outboard boating, rowing, and sailing. Classes in safe boating and general water safety. Designed for both adults and young boaters.

State Boating Offices

Most states offer boating courses with textbooks and certificates of completion. Many states now have requirements for courses for younger boaters or boaters operating specific types of equipment, such as jet skis. Contact Boat/U.S. or the relevant state boating office (see appendix IX).

Home Study

The Skippers Course
The United States Coast Guard can furnish a textbook-based home-study course for those boaters who cannot attend a course. The course covers basic boathandling, fundamental navigation, trailer boating, basic sailing, and Rules of the Road. Order from: *The Skippers Course,* U.S. Government Bookstore, World Saving Building, 720 North Main Street, Pueblo, Colorado 81003 (Stock # 050012002258 ($6.50), Tel. (719) 544-3142).

Practice Whatever your motivation or path to knowledge, book learning, classroom theory, and written exams merely open the door. Practice makes perfect—or, at the least, helps solidify the benefits of education and training.

Practice in calm weather everything you must be able to do in adverse weather. Learn how your boat responds to heaving-to, or lying ahull, when the wind and waves are at less than gale force.

Practice maneuvering in calm, open water; measure the time your boat takes to do a full circle to the right, then to the left, at several different engine settings. How long does it take to stop, from full ahead?

Put a float in the water, pretend it's a mooring buoy, and practice nudging the bow up close, from different points. Pretend it's the side of a pier, and bring your boarding step smartly alongside. Sail off a hundred yards; pretend there's a man overboard and come back as quickly and accurately as you can.

You can create dozens of different maneuvers, and attempt each in a dozen different ways. Once you have confidence in your own abilities, bring your spouse, children, and neighbors into the game.

If you don't have the time or inclination to learn—or, as is often the case, the time to care for your boat or the inclination to remain apart from your guests while underway, you ought to consider hiring a professional crew. They will have the education, training, and practice needed to provide safe operation under almost any conditions—and they also carry a responsibility to maintain the boat when not underway. A Coast Guard–licensed captain will expect to earn between $25,000 and $100,000 a year, depending on the size, value, and use of your boat, or at least $100 a day on a short-term arrangement. A proper captain provides the owner and guests with the full opportunity to enjoy the cruise or land the big fish.

RULES FOR CHILDREN AND GUESTS

Whatever your relationship with your children at home, do not expect miraculous improvement just because you've bought a boat. The need for discipline (the sort that gets underwear into the laundry or causes the emptying of the garbage) is increased, not reduced, when life and limb may be in jeopardy, and all of the other normal aggravations of living in a house are likely to be magnified many times in the confines of a boat—particularly on a rainy day without a television.

With that understanding, however, your children have as much right to enjoy the boat as you do, and you have a responsibility to help them do it the right way.

Some suggestions follow.

Infants should be left at home. They will not have much fun from the experience; they'll be exposed to too much sun; they're not good swimmers; and their proper care and feeding probably will keep at least one parent from enjoying the cuirse. If you can't find a babysitter and feel that you must take the baby to sea, make sure that the child is securely restrained in an infant seat and that any moving is done with attention to footing.

Toddlers (and children up to kindergarten age) are insatiably curious, mobile enough to get into all kinds of mischief, and not mature enough to understand "danger" or to follow many instructions. Protective nets strung around the lifelines will stop an accidental fall but won't inhibit climbing; topside, a life vest is mandatory. The greatest danger with this age group, we suspect, is not while underway, when supervision is most likely to be close, but alongside the pier or at anchor when adults are relaxed or absorbed in housekeeping or socializing. Control of a toddler—like control of the helm—must be passed from one adult to another in a positive, unambiguous manner. The last words you ever want to hear are "I thought *you* were watching him!"

Older children will most likely want to help too much; well, let them. It may be your boat, but that doesn't mean you get to have all the fun. Realistically, of course, when old enough to participate, the children become part of the crew and should be given as much training and practice as possible. Any child who sails regularly *must* know how to call for help on the radio, how to steer, and how to stop. Beyond that, an ability to execute basic maneuvers is helpful, particularly on that one occasion when you and your teenager go sailing and you do something foolish and fall overboard.

Visiting children should be made to feel a welcome part of the crew. Assign responsibilities: watching for buoys, keeping track of approaching boats, taking bearings, taking a turn at the helm. But don't overdo it—leave plenty of time for sunbathing and eating.

Adult guests may be a joy or a curse, and the choice is more in your hands than theirs. Guests might be aboard for an hour or a month; they might be real guests, with no contingent responsibilities, or they might be considered members of the working crew, with assigned watches and chores. However, *you* have the responsibility for everyone who steps aboard your boat, to ensure

PLASTIC-ENGRAVED SIGN is a clear indicator of where the important first-aid kit is located. Similar signs can be used for life rafts, other safety equipment, or damage-control gear.

the safety and sanity of operation. And that means making sure that each guest is properly prepared for the experience.

Take your guests for a brief tour of the boat; point out the location of the fire extinguishers, life jackets, and signal flares; show them the operating instructions for the radio and the engine controls (which should be posted at the helm), and suggest they take a few minutes to read them.

Give each guest a designated bunk, locker, or cabin; ask that they keep their personal gear in this area, and this area only.

This may be the first voyage for some, who must be warned that boats bounce around—sometimes with unexpected violence. Point out that objects left on tables or bunks are likely to end up on the cabin sole; that some objects might become dangerous missiles; that anything taken from its proper place—books, cooking equipment, a portable radio—must be properly restowed.

Explain the old sailor's adage, "One hand for you, one hand for the boat." Point out the locations of handholds, to help prevent bumps, bruises, and nasty falls. Since the nastiest fall is overboard, each guest should have some man-overboard instruction: Yell for help, then keep calm; don't try to swim after the boat. (More details appear in chapter 23.) Show them what to do if someone else falls overboard—how to launch the man-overboard pole and how to stop the boat.

Discuss other precautions: Stay away from lines under tension—they may break; watch out for the boom—it may swing unexpectedly; be alert for, and report, any unusual smells and noises—trouble may be brewing below.

If you restrict the drinking of alcoholic beverages while underway, inform your guests before the voyage starts.

Go over some of the housekeeping topics more or less peculiar to boats. If you have a limited water supply, explain the need for conservation; explain and demonstrate the operation of the marine toilet; explain and demonstrate proper stove operation. Clearly set forth the responsibility for watching any children; you cannot be a babysitter as well as a captain.

Finally, explain your voyage plan—where you are going and how you expect to get there. Thoroughly discuss assigned chores or watch-standing duties and make sure your guests understand *your* role and responsibilities as well as their own.

Prepare a guest card (see box) that explains the rules and practices aboard your boat. This reinforces—in writing—what you may have explained or demonstrated a bit too hastily.

Sample Guest Card

Welcome aboard *Endeavour*. Here are a few things we'd like you to know about our boat and about cruising with us. Please take a minute and read this card.

RULES FOR EVERYONE

Call the skipper immediately if:

- You see or hear any flare, smoke, emergency signal, or anything you don't understand.
- You see another boat behaving in an unusual or erratic fashion.
- You think we may be in danger of colliding with another boat. One clear indication: the range to another boat is steadily decreasing, while the bearing (that is, the relative direction from our boat to the other) remains about the same.
- You detect any strange or unidentifiable odor.
- Any piece of equipment malfunctions.
- The indicated water depth decreases unexpectedly to 15 feet [or stipulate a depth appropriate to your boat and cruising area].
- There is any accident or injury, however minor.
- You note an abrupt change in wind or sea or clouds or the color of the surrounding water.

Keep the navigator's chart area clear of food and drink; keep heavy metal objects and any electronic gear (such as a portable radio) away from the compass.

Using the head (the bathroom) requires some prior instruction; please ask.

We do not let the helmsman (or anyone likely to become the helmsman) drink any alcoholic beverage while underway.

We have a *zero tolerance* for the use or possession of drugs aboard this boat. If you have *any* with you now, *take them ashore and leave them there.*

If law-enforcement officials board the boat, follow their orders and instructions exactly and immediately. Make no sudden moves and do not leave their presence abruptly or without warning.

When we take on fuel: no smoking at the fuel dock, no getting on or off the boat while fuel is being pumped.

MAN OVERBOARD

If someone falls overboard, yell loudly, "Man overboard," and throw anything that will float into the water. Hold out your arm, pointed toward the person in the water. Do not jump in the water to attempt a rescue.

If *you* fall overboard, yell loudly, "Man overboard," and then try to relax. Don't try to swim after the boat; watch for life rings or floating cushions and swim over to them.

RULES FOR THE HELMSMAN

Know the boat's position before taking the helm, and understand the general plans for your portion of the trip.

Do not deviate from the assigned course without permission from the skipper, except in an emergency or to avoid an object in the water. However, if at any time you are in doubt or feel uneasy about anything, feel free to slow down or stop while waiting for the skipper to come to the helm.

ADDITIONAL RULES FOR NIGHT SAILING

No one is allowed on deck at night unless wearing a life jacket; jackets are stowed in the locker near the galley stove. If the jacklines are rigged, you must have a safety harness as well. We will demonstrate this to you, as appropriate.

Don't turn on bright lights; don't strike a match or use a cigarette lighter topside; don't shine a flashlight in anyone's eyes.

For the helmsman: Check running lights hourly and note in the log; be alert for unexpected lights.

VOYAGE PLANNING

Some planning is required for any voyage, no matter how brief. For example, preparation for a short cruise will include: reviewing the intended route; checking the tides and current; checking the weather forecast; and making sure the boat is fully ready with fuel, navigational, and emergency equipment. Of course, for any extended cruise, you'll need more elaborate preparation: food selection and storage; additional charts and sailing guides; passports or other acceptable identification; a more ambitious toolkit and spare-parts inventory; and sufficient training and experience to give you the confidence that you can embark on extended cruising.

Any voyage plan starts with the chart. How far will you be going? How long will it take to get there? What are the landmarks and hazards and spots of shallow water along the way? And where are the alternative destinations, in the event of trouble or bad weather? Add information on tides and currents and you've planned your basic route.

Or *routes*. There may be choices, and you should study each one. For example, in planning a passage from Jacksonville, Florida, to Charleston, South Carolina, you would consider both the "inside" route through the Intracoastal Waterway and the more direct "outside" route. Inside is long and winding and requires constant control at the helm. Depending on your boat, but assuming (for this example) that you have a slow trawler or sailboat, the inside passage might take four days. Outside, you can get a big push from the Gulf Stream, which, weather permitting, saves a lot of time and effort. But how best to make the outside passage? You might leave Jacksonville in the morning and arrive at Charleston after dark. Unless you're intimately familiar with Charleston Harbor, that's not a very good choice. If you leave Jacksonville in the late afternoon

and make an overnight passage, you can time your arrival in Charleston just at sunrise. You enter with the sun at your back and not in your eyes, and, if visibility is limited, you still have plenty of daylight. You've just saved three days and many gallons of fuel. That's voyage planning.

Voyage planning boils down to posing significant questions and finding satisfactory answers in advance. The greatest planning hazard is to assume that no planning is needed; the best approach to orderly planning is the checklist.

A checklist is a powerful tool: use it right and hazardous or complicated tasks become safe and easy; fail to use it, or do so incompletely, and vital steps may be overlooked inadvertently.

Airline pilots constantly review that lesson. It is a violation of law and common sense for the captain of a commercial airliner to get underway without working through a preflight and takeoff checklist. Each item must be verified. At times, when the pressures of the schedule or the vagaries of human nature intrude, an item or two might have been skipped—and the result too often has been stark headlines, lengthy recriminations, and legal action.

Your responsibilities—to your crew, guests, other boaters, and yourself—are equal to those of an airline pilot. You operate in an equally hazardous environment, and you are equally bound by law and common sense to operate your boat in a safe manner and to protect the lives and property of your pssengers.

And—like the pilot—you should adhere strictly to the checklist. Don't merely review it—check it. Use a new copy for each voyage or evolution. In the next few sections of this book, yu'll find samples of generally applicable checklists. They are offered as guides so you can make your own versions.

HEALTH AND WELFARE

DRUGS AND ALCOHOL

We've noted the *legal* jeopardy in using drugs aboard your boat; if that's not enough to keep your boating straight, what about the hazards added to the operation of a heavy piece of machinery (your boat) in a hazardous environment (the water)? We probably don't have to spend much time making that case.

However, our society doesn't view the possession and use of alcohol with the same concern as other drugs. It's not illegal to have a six-pack of beer or a gallon of gin aboard your boat. It's not even illegal to consume prodigious quantities of the stuff while the boat is underway—although the helmsman can be arrested for operating a boat under the influence of alcohol.

Our principal concern here is not with the law—but with common sense and safety. Alcohol is a depressant, acting quickly to reduce your reaction time and your natural (and learned) inhibitions—long before you reach the point where you legally would be considered "under the influence." After only a couple of beers, you are more likely to take a chance—to try to rush through the bridge opening ahead of another boat, or to enter a narrow inlet with a too-strong following sea. You'll take the chance, but then you might not be able to think or move quickly enough to carry it off.

Military aviators have a rule: no drinking within twenty-four hours of a flight. It cuts down on the time they have available for partying, but they save a lot of lives—including their own. You don't have to be *that* conservative; just be sensible.

Let's assume that you properly save your drinking until you're anchored or tied up for the night. *However,* if you permit your crew and guests freely to imbibe, you (and they) should understand the following:

• Alcohol is alcohol. Beer, wine, and hard liquor, consumed in the normal servings of 12 ounces of beer, four ounces of wine, and 1.5 ounces of liquor, have equal amounts of alcohol and equal impact on your system.

• It takes your system about two hours to process the alcohol from one drink.

• Alcohol increases a sense of disorientation and reduces the sense of balance—hardly an asset aboard a bouncing, rolling boat.

• Alcohol may intensify the additional and acute disorientation caused when water enters the ears; a person who falls overboard may become so disoriented that he or she tries to swim *away from* rather than *toward* safety.

• Alcohol speeds the onset of hypothermia for a person in the water (or constantly wet with spray). In this medical emergency, body temperature is reduced below the level at which the brain and muscles function with any degree of efficiency (see chapter 18). A person who falls overboard may become fatigued so quickly that he can't hold onto the life preserver thrown to his aid.

• Ninety percent of boating fatalities are from drowning.

• Fifty percent of boating fatalities are related to alcohol.

Think about it.

PROTECTION FROM THE SUN

Out on the water, the sun is less filtered by pollution than the sun on land, and, reflected from the dancing waves, is magnified. Too much sun, too quickly, not only results in painful sunburn but also has a debilitating effect on the victim, which can be as insidiously hazardous as the early effects of seasickness.

Protection is easy, although it may require more self-discipline than many people can muster:

1. Use an appropriate sunscreen. If this leaves your hands feeling greasy, be sure to wipe or wash them clean and dry: Slippery hands can't keep a safe grip on steering wheels or winch handles.

2. Wear a hat with a wide brim or visor. The fit should be snug, and an under-the-chin strap is a good idea as a defense against the often-frisky breezes.

3. Take along a long-sleeved shirt and a pair of pants or slacks, and put them on when you've had enough sun. Boating in a bathing suit is great for the image—until the image turns a bright, painful red.

PROTECTION FROM LIGHTNING

The electrical bonding and grounding described earlier should be adequate to protect most large boats from lightning, but there are certain rules for the crew—especially in small, open boats.

During an electrical storm:

1. Everyone should get out of the water and into the boat.

2. Keep arms and legs out of the water.

3. Everyone should remain inside a closed portion of the boat, if possible.

4. Don't touch any part of the rigging, railing, or fittings.

5. And, especially, don't become a conduit between pieces of bonded metal equipment by operating, for example, a winch while holding onto a railing.

GALLEY SAFETY

Cooking at sea presents significant hazards not encountered ashore:

1. As we've noted, a stove should be mounted on gimbals, which help keep the cooking surface more or less level while the boat is rolling, and it should be equipped with a guardrail to prevent pots from sliding off.

2. Because the probability of spills is greatly increased, don't overfill pots—and always wear a shirt when cooking.

3. Be sensible in your selection of cooking methods. On a 1988 South Atlantic passage, a woman was burned seriously when splashed with hot cooking oil. She was deep-frying doughnuts!

4. Any spills on the galley sole seriously interfere with safe footing and must be cleaned up immediately. Keep the stove and cooking utensils clean—free of grease, which might catch fire, and free of any food debris, which will provide a banquet for cockroaches.

5. Be alert to the fire hazards posed by the various cooking fuels; ensure that a proper fire extinguisher is close at hand (and *not* mounted on the other side of a potential fire site). Know the location of the fuel-line shutoff valve (not the same as the burner valves). When lighting the stove, follow the published instructions scrupulously; this is no place for creative shortcuts. Don't leave a lighted stove unattended.

LIGHTING A STOVE

Stove ignition is not a chore for the least experienced crew member. Improper use of stove fuels can lead to explosion or fire.

Propane or butane flow is controlled by valving at the tank (which is mounted outside the living spaces) and at the stove. The tank valve should always be *closed* unless the stove is in use; otherwise, the supply line will be full of fuel just looking for a way to leak through fittings or a partially opened burner valve, settling into the bilges to wait for an igniting spark.

To light the stove: Open the tank valve, activate any electrically controlled valves (from the main electrical panel or a separate panel in the galley), then the stove valve, then the burner valve. Then ignite with a match or mechanical igniter.

When you are almost finished cooking, turn off the valve at the tank *first,* so that the fuel remaining in the supply line will be burned off. *Then* close the burner valves.

Liquid-fuel stoves require priming and pre-heating, which, if not handled properly, can result in a flare-up or flash fire. Stoves should come with appropriate lighting instructions—which you should follow to the letter.

For alcohol stoves, first put some pressure in the fuel tank by pumping the handle until you feel resistance (or until the built-in pressure gauge registers the proper pressure). Then open the burner valve to allow a small amount of fuel to collect in the cup under the burner. Next, close the valve *fully* so that no additional fuel will escape, and light the pool of fuel until it has burned itself out. This may take a few minutes. When you once again open the burner valve (after the fire is completely out), the heated burner should vaporize the escaping fuel (now coming through with a hissing sound), which can be lighted.

If the fuel gurgles rather than hisses, or if drops of unburned fuel begin to collect in the preheating cup, the burner has not been adequately preheated. *Turn off the burner and start over.* Wait until the burner has cooled—otherwise, the heat will evaporate the fresh supply of alcohol you add for a subsequent preheating and *may* cause a flash fire.

Kerosene stoves use somewhat the same system, although the alcohol for preheating is poured into the cup manually. *Never* try to preheat with kerosene—unless you want to create a black, sooty bonfire in your galley.

REFRIGERATION

Since the refrigeration systems on many boats must operate under severe conditions (or must rely entirely upon timely replenishment of ice), spoilage of food is a constant threat. It's not so much the chance that this will make you sick—although that, too, is a possibility—but, rather, the unpleasant reality that spoiled food smells very bad and the odor tends to cling to everything it touches.

If your boat has mechanical refrigeration, your primary concerns will be mechanical, and as long as the system is working, food will stay cold. If, however, you're sailing with an icebox, you'll want to follow a few logical rules:

1. Start with a clean, well-scrubbed box and clean storage containers.

2. Use block ice, not bags of cubes (which melt much too quickly), to fill between one-third and one-half the capacity of the icebox. Fully line the bottom with ice, sculpting the blocks with an ice pick to create a tight fit. Then build a wall up one or more sides of the box (depending on size). Dry ice—if available—is a more efficient cooling agent than block ice, but it's so cold that it can burn the skin, so it must be handled with care.

3. Plan to replenish the ice at a rate of about half-initial-loading every two or three days.

4. As the ice melts, the water should drain out through a hole in the bottom of the box and into the bilges or (better) a gray-water holding tank. (That water will become unavoidably contaminated with food particles and should be pumped out regularly.)

5. In packing the icebox with food, keep the snacks and other often-used items on top, to minimize the amount of time the lid will be open. Wrap food in plastic (preferably Ziploc bags) to keep out water. Don't waste your time on aluminum foil—you'll mostly be wasting food. Store liquids in plastic containers with tight-sealing lids; coated cardboard milk cartons are likely to leak, and merely placing a carton upright is no security during a 40-degree roll.

WATER

Commercially available water fresheners, used at the rate of an ounce per 20 gallons, help control both odor and taste. For water of doubtful parentage, chemical purifiers are available as well. If you want to be absolutely safe, boil any water you intend to drink.

When you are about to take on water in a strange port, it's a good idea to consolidate your remaining supply in one tank, just in case the new supply turns out to be contaminated. If the water tastes or smells bad, or you suddenly have an attack of diarrhea, you'll enjoy the security of having a quantity of unadulterated "good" water on hand.

Of course, *rain* is the ultimate natural source of fresh water, and you can capture it in awnings rigged to drain into jerry jugs or the boat's water tanks. Allow the first few gallons to pass overboard, to ensure that any dried salt has been washed away (check by tasting).

MEDICAL CONSIDERATIONS

Most people out for a day's sail or fishing are better equipped to care for their boat than themselves. They have the knowledge, tools, and spares to fix an engine or a pump or a torn sail, but they don't even have a basic first-aid kit.

And yet, if proper medical care is not applied within the first hour following a serious incident, the risk of complications can double—and survival may even come into question. Many otherwise-good mariners seem to be satisfied that, should a serious medical problem intrude, a Mayday call to the Coast Guard will send help speeding their way.

But the idea that the Coast Guard will come immediately to the rescue in a flurry of whirling chopper blades is a fantasy. Most Coast Guard assistance is given by boat, which may take a long time to reach you. Even if a helicopter is available, it can be tricky business to fly it near enough to a sailboat or a big sportfisherman to provide help. And, while Coast Guardsmen are highly motivated and competent in what they do, they are *not* physicians.

In making your voyage plan, for a daysail close to home as well as for distant travels, you should determine:

1. The general location of, and therefore the distance to, professional medical help;

2. The current medical condition of everyone aboard your boat (heart problems? diabetes? allergies?);

3. The name and telephone number of the physicians who have been treating any of these conditions.

CHAPTER TWELVE

Finding the Way

SOME BASICS

NAVIGATION AND PILOTING

Navigation and piloting are the methods by which you get from here to there without getting lost or bumping into rocks and shoals along the way. Piloting is what you do when close to shore or visible landmarks; navigation involves moving across open waters and may include the use of electronic aids such as Loran or Sat-Nav, celestial measurements, and a lot of educated guesswork.

Reading this section will not make you a competent bluewater navigator, nor will it tell you everything you need to know to become one. That's a subject for entire books and organized classes under the sponsorship of the Power Squadron, the Coast Guard Auxiliary, and various local sailing clubs. Our goal here is, briefly, to demystify the subject as an encouragement to further study.

POSITION

As we have all learned in geography class, any position on the surface of the earth can be defined through the use of latitude and longitude. Rings of latitude circle the earth horizontally, from 0 degrees at the equator to 90 degrees north and south at the poles. The space between each degree is divided into 60 minutes; each minute is further subdivided into 60 seconds. These should not be confused with the minutes and seconds used in measuring time; the terms are similar, but they are not otherwise related.

Rings of longitude circle the earth vertically, each passing through both the North and South poles. The baseline for longitude is the site of the Royal Greenwich Observatory in England, and from this 0 degrees longitude, the lines (also called meridians) are numbered east or west until they meet at 180 degrees on the other side of the world; the spaces between the lines are also divided into minutes and seconds.

With latitude and longitude, a boat's position can be matched precisely with a spot on a chart:

• Chesapeake Bay entrance—latitude 36° 59' north, longitude 76° 00' west;
• Point No Point, Puget Sound—latitude 47° 55' north, longitude 122° 32' west;
• Charleston waterfront—latitude 32° 45' north, longitude 79° 55' west.

NAVIGATION TOOLS can be simple: a well-kept logbook; a traditional taffrail log to gauge speed and distance run; binoculars to identify marks easily, a hand-bearing compass, the basic parallel rules set, dividers—and, in this photo, a digital stopwatch.

For most boating, precise position by latitude and longitude may seem unnecessary. However, should you become wrapped in a sudden fog, knowing your position will help you move cautiously toward home—or, even better, to a safe anchorage to await improved visibility. Even more important: Should you have an emergency requiring assistance, knowing your position may be vital in guiding rescuers to the spot.

DISTANCE

The land, or statute, mile is an arbitrary measure that began as the distance marched in 1,000 paces of a Roman legion and today is set at 5,280 feet. The nautical mile is somewhat longer— 6,076 feet—but represents exactly one minute of latitude.

SPEED

As a measure of speed, the knot is one nautical mile per hour (never use the redundant phrase *knots per hour*). The term comes from an early method of determining speed: A wooden chip, with an attached cord knotted at regular intervals, was tossed overside. The number of knots passing through the fingers in a given time period was equal to the speed in nautical miles.

A useful rule-of-thumb method for determining speed: Throw a floating chip or crumpled ball of paper ahead of the boat and, with a stopwatch, mark the time it takes to pass from the stem to the stern. Then make the following computation:

$$\text{Speed} = .6 \times \frac{\text{(waterline length in feet)}}{\text{time in seconds}}$$

TIDES AND CURRENTS

The *tide* is the vertical movement of the sea under the gravitational pull of the moon. At times it is also influenced by the sun and other heavenly bodies. In most seacoast areas, there are two high and two low tides a day. On any given day, the tide will be at its highest point when the moon is directly overhead (or directly on the other side of the earth) and at its lowest point when the moon is between those positions—roughly, on either horizon. Since the moon circles the earth on an almost twenty-five-hour schedule, the difference between tides is six hours and thirteen minutes.

A flood tide is rising; an ebb tide is falling; slack water is the period of balance before the flow reverses.

The range of the tide will vary globally, depending upon the relative position of the moon and the sun. With a new moon or full moon, the moon and sun are pulling together to create higher (and lower) spring tides; during the first and third quarters of the moon, the sun and moon are in opposition, resulting in reduced neap tides. Also, since the moon's orbit is an ellipse and not a circle, the effect will be greater at the closest point (perigee) and lesser at the farthest (apogee) point of the orbit. These factors, operating in different combinations at different times, produce a continually changing range of high and low water.

The range of the tide will vary locally depending upon weather (an onshore wind will add to the height, an offshore wind will subtract, an area of extremely low atmospheric pressure will literally suck the water higher) and upon geographic features such as slope of the bottom, width of the harbor entrance, and size of the harbor itself. The classic example of an area with an exceptional range of tides is the Bay of Fundy, where spring tides bring a rise-and-fall of more than 40 feet. (In the open ocean, the tidal range is usually only about a foot.) The time of the tide also may vary locally, where the tidal flow enters through a major inlet and then is spread through inland waterways. The time listed in published *Tide Tables* usually will be for a major reference point (e.g., Sandy Hook), with correction factors (e.g., "+ 0.29 minutes") for specific locations.

Note carefully: The published time is standard time, not daylight saving time. In most parts of the country you must convert the tide-table data to daylight saving time during the summer, by adding one hour to the published time.

For a rough estimate of the change of depth at any specific time during a tidal cycle, use the Rule of Twelfths:

First hour	$1/12$ (10 percent) of the range
Second hour	$2/12$ (15 percent) of the range
Third hour	$3/12$ (25 percent) of the range
Fourth hour	$3/12$ (25 percent) of the range
Fifth hour	$2/12$ (15 percent) of the range
Sixth hour	$1/12$ (10 percent) of the range

Current is the horizontal movement of water. In a river, the flow is from higher to lower elevations. In the oceans, currents are created by the spinning of the earth: Some of the water just can't keep up with the equator's eastward speed of 1040 mph, and it appears as a westward-moving current, to pile up on the western shores of the oceans. (Sea level on the Atlantic side of the Panama Canal is several feet higher than on the Pacific side.) Then, in combination with the diversion imposed by the intervening land masses, the Coriolis effect (see appendix VII) flips much of this current to the right (northward in the Northern Hemisphere), creating the Gulf Stream in the Atlantic and the Japan Current in the Pacific.

In coastal areas, current is linked primarily with the flow of the tides, but because of geographic features, it may be offset by several hours from the tide change. The current will not necessarily flow in the opposite direction; the currents associated with high and low tide may be perpendicular or even in the same direction. The direction of current is the set and the speed is the drift. In a channel or a river, the current will be strongest in deep water, reduced in shallow water.

Obviously, it's important to become familiar with the specific conditions in your regular or planned area of boating. Check the charts.

NAVIGATIONAL TOOLS

The basic tools of the navigator's trade include charts, a compass, electronic aids, a few accessories such as parallel rules and dividers—and your eyeballs.

CHARTS AND PUBLICATIONS

Charts come in a variety of styles and scales—from the entire Atlantic Ocean with minimal coastal detail, on down to a harbor chart that shows every smokestack, pier, and piling. For most recreational purposes, the small craft

Charts		
Type of Chart	Typical Scale	Use
Sailing	1:1,200,000	Voyaging between distant ports. Does not show much detail of navigation marks, such as buoys, etc.
General	1:150,000 to 1:600,000	A cruising area such as a portion of coast from Maine to New York. Shows some navigation marks, such as major buoys marking bays.
Coastal	1:150,000 to 1:50,000	A cruising area such as one-half of Long Island Sound. Gives considerable details of buoys, bottom patterns, and channel entrances.
Harbor	1:50,000	Greatest detail. Shows channel details, harbor marks.
Small Craft		These charts differ from the above in that their chief value is not their relative detail but the fact that they are folded into booklets that are handy in small boats.

charts issued by NOAA (or the many commercial derivatives, packaged in regional chart books) work just fine, as long as you have an up-to-date edition.

Charts fill two main purposes: (1) They note prominent landmarks and other features ashore to help you locate your position, and (2) they show the depth of water and underwater obstructions, to help you stay in water deep enough to float your boat. Numbers on the chart reflect the depth at regular intervals or wherever it changes significantly. Measurements are in feet, fathoms (units of six feet), or meters. It is of critical importance to know which system was used to create the chart you are about to use; that information will be noted as, for example, "soundings in feet at mean lower–low water." The "mean lower–low water" part relates to the average level at low tide; in a body of water with a tidal range of many feet, it is also a critical bit of information.

Other vital information also is presented. A compass rose indicates true and magnetic north, quantifies the variation between them, and notes any known annual rate of change. Most charts also show the positions of wrecks or other obstructions to be avoided; the type of bottom (mud, sandy, rocky, etc.); the average strength and direction of current; and—most important—the locations and identifications of various aides to navigation. These aids include buoys, which mark channels or obstructions; beacons and lights, which provide daytime or nighttime reference points; and ranges, pairs of markers that, when viewed in-line, guide you into a channel.

Changes in charted conditions—such as a shoaling inlet, new or relocated buoys—are regularly announced in *Notices to Mariners*, a weekly publication available by subscription if you want to be overwhelmed with paperwork. Fortunately, *Notices to Mariners* are often posted in marine supply stores, yacht clubs, and marina offices. Unfortunately, too few recreational boat operators seem to pay attention to them. When a number of changes have been issued for any given chart, it will be updated and reprinted with a note listing the date of the latest changes.

Orienting the Chart Most but not all charts are oriented with "north" at the top. In fact, the phrase *to orient a chart* is a carryover from the earliest days of mapmaking, when charts were aligned with the lands of the Orient. Today, small craft charts tend to be laid out in the fashion most convenient for the printer, not necessarily for the boat operator. Check the compass rose for compass direction.

Other useful publications include the *Coast Pilot* series, of which each edition provides sailing directions and detailed information for a designated section of the U.S. coast—for example, Cape Cod to Sandy Hook; *Light Lists,* which identify and describe the operating characteristics of such navigational aids as lights, buoys, and radiobeacons; *Tide Tables,* issued annually, providing the predicted time and level of high and low tide for major harbors and the necessary correction factors for other areas; *Tidal Current Tables* and *Tidal Current Charts,* which break out the strength and direction of the current in relation to the state of the tide; and *Sailing Directions,* which give voyage information for offshore passagemaking as well as data on various countries and ports of call.

A well and properly equipped charthouse on a major oceangoing vessel will have all of the publications just described (and more). The recreational boater with some cruising ambition need have none of them, because various publishing houses regularly take advantage of the absence of copyright protection on government publications to package attractive, easy-to-read-and-use "cruising guides" or "waterway guides" containing all of the relevant information. Such publications also often include evaluations and comments on cruising grounds and anchorages, lists of marinas (including facilities and services available), and advertisements for relevant com-

Publications

To order Notices to Mariners:

> Office of Distribution Services
> Defense Mapping Agency
> Washington, D.C. 20315

To order chart catalogs by area:

> Catalog 1   Atlantic, Gulf Stream, Puerto Rico, and Virgin Islands
> Catalog 2   Pacific Coast, Hawaii, Guam, and Samoa
> Catalog 3   Alaska
> Catalog 4   Great Lakes and Adjacent Waterways

> Distribution Division C44
> National Ocean Survey
> Riverdale, Maryland 20840

Each catalog contains a listing of authorized chart agents.

Specialized Charts

Type	Source
Canada	Chart Distribution Office, Department of the Environment, P.O. Box 8080, 1675 Russell Road, Ottawa, Ontario, K1G 3H6, Canada.
Foreign (non–U.S. or Canada)	Defense Mapping Agency Hydrographic and Topographic Center, Office of Distribution Services, Defense Mapping Agency, Washington, D.C. 20315.
Intracoastal Waterway	Army Corps of Engineers, Superintendent of Documents, U.S. Government Printing Office, Washington, D.C. 20402.
Mississippi River	Army Corps of Engineers (available via district offices of the corps, depending on section of Mississippi involved).

mercial enterprises along the way. In addition, monthly reprints of the *Tide Tables* usually can be picked up at marine supply stores and major marinas. A *caution* however: The charts included with many of these cruising guides are usually marked NOT FOR NAVIGATION. They will not reflect the important changes published in the *Notices to Mariners*. Heed that advice.

THE COMPASS

The Chinese discovered that a magnetized iron needle floating in water on a bit of rice paper would align itself on a north-south axis; the Vikings used magnetized material floating on a cork. Today's maritime compass comes in a more attractive package and uses nonfreezing oil

---

United States Coast Pilot Books

These volumes present the channels, anchorages, ports, weather information, hazards, navigation rules, and other key data. The books are to be used as companions to specific charts and are issued in a numbered series.

1. Eastport to Cape Cod
2. Cape Cod to Sandy Hook
3. Sandy Hook to Cape Henry
4. Cape Henry to Key West
5. Gulf of Mexico, Puerto Rico, and Virgin Islands
6. Reserved—no book
7. California, Oregon, Washington, and Hawaii
8. Dion Entrance to Cape Spencer
9. Cape Spencer to Beaufort Sea

(Great Lakes issued on a separate schedule.)

U.S. COAST GUARD LIGHT LISTS

These books, in a set of five, describe specific navigational aids, buoys, seasonal buoys, lighthouses (with their characteristics and electronic beacons, if any), emergency navigational aids, and sound signals.

1. Atlantic Coast from St. Croix River, Maine, to Little River, South Carolina
2. Atlantic and Gulf Coasts from Little River, South Carolina, to Rio Grande, Texas
3. Pacific Coast and Pacific Islands
4. Great Lakes
5. Mississippi River

TIDE TABLES

Times of high and low tides at key harbors and intermediate points. The *Tide Tables* come in four volumes:

1. East Coast of North and South America
2. West Coast of North and South America
3. Europe, West Coast of Africa
4. Central Pacific, Western Pacific, and Indian Oceans

TIDAL CURRENT TABLES

Times of slack water (no current) as well as times and speed of maximum and ebb tidal currents. These are divided into two volumes valid only for the year in which they are issued:

1. Tidal Current Tables, East Coast of North America
2. Tidal Current Tables, West Coast of North America/Asia

TIDAL CURRENT CHARTS

Direction and velocity of the current for specific bodies of water indicated with a series of arrows superimposed on a chart of the waterway for each hour in the tidal sequence. Eleven areas are covered:

Boston Harbor
Narragansett Bay
New York Harbor
Upper Chesapeake Bay
San Francisco Bay
Northern Puget Sound
Narragansett Bay to Nantucket Sound
Long Island and Block Island Sound
Delaware Bay and River
Charleston, S.C., Harbor
Southern Puget Sound

or alcohol rather than water, but it works on the same principle. Even the cheapest magnetic compass is reasonably accurate, although any magnetic compass is subject to certain natural forces that will affect its accuracy unless understood and accommodated.

Variation   A magnetic compass reacts to the local magnetic lines of force, which usually do not run perfectly north-and-south. Variation is the difference in degrees between "true" north and magnetic north, measured in any particular geographic location. In some parts of the world—especially in the higher latitudes—the variation can be quite large, and almost everywhere, the difference is sufficient to cause serious errors in navigation unless taken into account. Check the compass rose for the local variation between true north and that which would be shown by a magnetic compass.

Deviation   This phenomenon is the result of a nearby magnetic influence acting on a particular compass in a particular location. Where the magnet would normally line up with the local magnetic field, this influence will pull it off to one side or the other, giving a false and potentially hazardous reading. Deviation comes in two varieties: (1) permanent, which is the relationship of an installed compass to the rest of the boat, and (2) transient, which can result when a metal toolbox is placed next to the compass.

Permanent deviation can be measured and recorded to provide a correction factor. This deviation is caused by installed equipment such as the engine, the stainless steel rigging, metal handles on drawers in the pilothouse, current-carrying wires running to the flying bridge. If you have more than one compass aboard, you'll have a different deviation for each. Any time you add— or subtract—metal or electronic equipment in the vicinity of a compass, you probably will affect the deviation and will need to recalibrate the compass. Loudspeakers for the radio or a stereo unit are particularly troublesome, because they contain strong magnets that exert an influence even when the equipment is off.

Permanent deviation will vary with the heading or direction of the boat—it may be several degrees to the west on one heading and a similar error to the east on another. The compass is recalibrated by a procedure called "swinging ship," which involves pointing the bow in a series of known directions (at least every 45 degrees through a full 360-degree circle) in an area where you are free of such magnetic disturbances as buried cables, neighboring boats, and passing automobiles. Let the compass steady on the new heading and then mark the reading. Calculate the difference from the actual magnetic heading (True + Variation). This will provide a deviation corrective for each heading, which should be marked on a deviation card kept at or near the compass, ready for use.

"Permanent" deviation, however, is not permanent, and it may change over time, even if you make no changes to your boat. Validate your deviation at least once a year, and certainly before setting out on any extended voyaging.

Transient deviation is more difficult to analyze, since much of the time it will be accidental and may pass unnoticed. Examples are a helmsman wearing a heavy metal belt buckle or carring a rigging knife in his pocket; a portable radio placed for the enjoyment of the crew; even a flashlight tucked in a drawer in the pilothouse. All can influence the compass heading. To find out just how sensitive your compass might be, note the deviation caused when you place various metal objects near it. Always regard the compass much as the ancient mariners did: as a mysterious god of direction. The compass installation should be a shrine kept clear, clean, and uncluttered.

An Electronic Compass   This device overcomes many of the deficiencies of a standard floating compass. Accuracy is increased to within one degree; the compass doesn't bounce around or swing past the reading as a turning boat settles onto a straight course; the unit can be connected to Loran and Sat-Nav systems; the compass is not affected by nearby masses of metal or operating electronic equipment.

The Compass Log　We acknowledge that, much of the time, you won't even be using your compass for recreational daysailing. You'll see where you are and know where you're headed by simply looking around. However—you should develop good habits. Notice the basic compass headings for the most common routes over which you travel, along with the average time for each. Enter this information on your charts, and in your Owner's Notebook. When coming home sometime in rain, haze, or fog, you may find that "looking around" won't be of much value.

The North Star　We would be most remiss if we didn't mention nature's other direction finder (nighttime version). Polaris—the pole star, about which the heavens seem to rotate—stays in the same relative position day to day and year to year. One important attribute of Polaris: It is within a few degrees of true north. If you are in the Northern Hemisphere and can see Polaris, you can steer a broadly accurate course—even without a compass.

ELECTRONICS

The accuracy of navigation has increased remarkably in the years since World War II. In 1945, a typical ship's navigator could count on position accuracy to within a couple of miles—but only at the moment of a good morning or evening star sight. After a few days of cloud-filled skies, he was literally sailing blind. The various electronic aids to navigation—especially Loran and the satellite-based Sat-Nav system—have brought increased accuracy along with convenience.

Loran (short for long-range navigation)
This system uses radio waves from fixed pairs of stations to create an apparent network of radio waves—at least that's what it looks like on the specially printed Loran chart. In fact, the "master" station sends a signal, which triggers a second signal when it reaches the "slave" member of the pair. The Loran unit on your boat measures the difference in the times of receipt of the two signals to compute the distance from each station.

Loran accuracy may be as good as a quarter of a mile, and daytime reception *may* be available as far out to sea as 500 miles; nighttime range might be double that of the daytime range. Some units are advertised as accurate within an eighth of a mile, with daytime reception to 700 miles. These claims might be true, but the range and accuracy of any Loran unit depend first on the

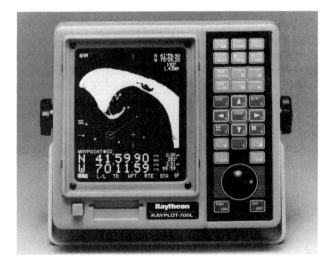

LORAN PLOTTER is one of the newest systems available to boaters. The system uses the outputs of the Loran navigation beacons matched to programmed chart cards digitized for computer memory. The trackball permits the operator to position the screen cursor at any point on the displayed chart to develop position-finding bearings. The navigator can place and move buoys on the chart cards. The system represents one of the closest syntheses of the "radar" type of display and actual action video of boat movement. (Raytheon)

boat's location, the quality and placement of the antenna, and the elimination of any local interference. And of more concern than long-range accuracy (which is, after all, of interest to a minuscule portion of the boating community) is the accuracy close to shore, where moonless nights and sudden fogs are not romantic, but traumatic. Loran is subject to anomalies; the signals may be affected by the weather; the time of day (especially dawn and dusk) and the proximity of land may produce unreliable readings. Sometimes—as in the case of land nearby—the error may be constant. Once determined, it may be used on subsequent passages as a cautious correction to the signal.

The convenience of the various Loran units varies, usually with the price of the unit. With the least-sophisticated, lowest-cost units, you can't determine your position until you plot the readouts on a Loran chart. More sophisticated units (increasingly prevalent) give a direct reading in latitude and longitude. And—such is the march of technology—units just now reaching the market use computer chips to create a video-display chart of your sailing area—with a flashing cursor marking your location. Also displayed are your latitude and longitude, your course and speed, and the bearing and distance to any of a hundred selected waypoints. Further, should you want to know the range and bearing from your boat to a geographic feature on the chart, just position the cursor and press a button. The software responsible for this bit of magic is available for every cruising ground in the continental United States (including much of Alaska and even the Mississippi River).

Satellite Systems Long-range cruisers have been blessed with the introduction of the satellite navigation system—Sat-Nav—which is accurate to within 100 feet. Unlike Loran, which provides a continuously updated position, a Sat-Nav fix can be obtained only when the satellites pass overhead—perhaps every ninety minutes (although most satellite navigation systems will

SATELLITE GLOBAL POSITIONING NAVIGATION SYSTEM can track up to five satellites simultaneously. The display will give the boat's latitude/longitude position, bearing and range to an upcoming waypoint, speed and course, and actual course made good in terms of the sea bottom, adjusting for current. This system is programmable for up to ninety-nine different waypoints and can be installed to interface with Loran and radar display units. (Raytheon)

SMALL-BOAT RADAR has a seven-inch screen (as opposed to the larger nine-inch screens). The radar is capable of displaying Loran and latitude/longitude readouts on its screen. This highly flexible unit also has an adjustable range ring with an audible alarm that warns of potential collision. The unit can also freeze its picture for more intensive study. (Raytheon)

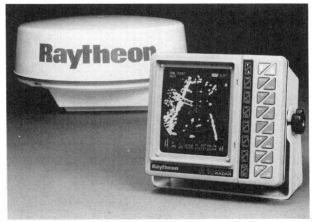

update themselves between satellite fixes using actual or inputted course and speed data). Close inshore, the comparative utility of Sat-Nav thus is diminished; offshore, where Loran is marginal or not available, Sat-Nav is a lot better than star sights twice a day and a sun line or two—if the weather permits. And, between fixes, the Sat-Nav unit will compute and display estimated positions based on your known course, speed, and recent experience with set and drift. Sat-Nav signals can be received almost anywhere in the world, and, unlike Loran, are not affected by weather or the time of day.

Loran and Sat-Nav units can be teamed with an autopilot, which will steer your boat with considerable accuracy toward any selected destination or waypoint along the route.

RASTER SCAN HIGH-DEFINITION RADAR with a 14-inch screen and a built-in interface for linkage to external navigation systems such as Loran, geopositioning systems, and SatNav. The radar features an audible alarm warning of a possible collision. This is a relatively expensive unit that has rugged construction with flexible big-ship features. (Raytheon)

Radar This is both a short-range navigational tool and a method for avoiding collisions with other boats, especially when visibility has been reduced by rain, fog, or darkness. The radar transmitter sends out a series of energy pulses, which bounce from the surface of a "target"—a nearby channel buoy, a distant freighter, a high building, or a shoreside cliff—to be picked up by the receiving circuit and converted into a TV-like display. With radar, you can pick your way up a marked channel in the densest of fog; you can avoid a collision with a lumbering tanker; and you can plot your boat's position—using prominent geographic features—with fair accuracy.

Radio Direction Finders (RDFs) These devices use a highly sensitive rotating antenna to tune in on radiobeacons, or even commercial radio towers (identified on charts), to establish an electronic line of position (LOP). For a beacon, you dial up the frequency, then turn the antenna until the signal disappears. Called the "null," this actually provides the reading. For a commercial radio, you tune in the station, then use a built-in strength meter to find the bearing with the highest reading. The unit gives relative bearings—that is, a bearing relative to the unit, which is not related to the real world until the unit itself is oriented. Normally, you set the unit on the cabintop or a table, aligned fore-and-aft with the boat, and then translate the reading from the bearing ring to the boat's compass reading. An RDF is particularly useful in finding a fog-shrouded inlet if it is marked with a radiobeacon—you can literally home in on the null.

A caution: Any electronic device can break down. A prudent sailor will acquire, in addition to these laborsaving marvels, a basic understanding of navigation to be able to provide emergency backup. A prudent sailor will also regularly compare the electronic fixes with information obtained from more conventional means.

PLANNING THE ROUTE

Using the appropriate charts and guidebooks, study the route to your destination. With a pencil, draw a line along your intended track, making sure that it is clear of any hazards and runs through water deep enough for your boat. As you do this, note key aids to navigation (buoys, lighthouses, smokestacks) and other landmarks along the way. Determine the nearest point of approach to any hazard; if it seems too close to allow a margin of error or maneuvering room in the event of trouble, adjust your course. Look for alternative destinations, in case of trouble or changes in the weather.

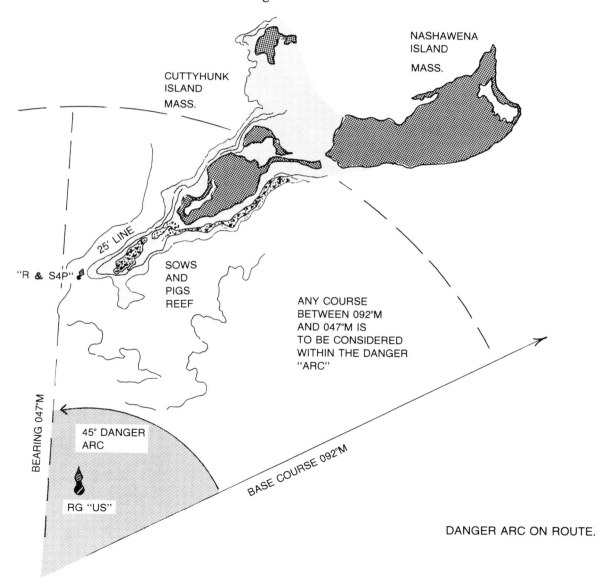

DANGER ARC ON ROUTE.

Some Tips
on Plotting Your Track

All navigators work out their own procedures, based on their training, experience, and knowledge of local conditions. Here's one navigator's approach to laying down a track:

1. Start with a rough track, based on your probable average speed. This will give you a quick approximation of the time of transit (not adjusted for current or weather). Add 30 percent—and use that result to determine a rough time of arrival at your destination. If this turns out to be at night, you may want to adjust your time of departure or speed (or both) to arrange for a daylight arrival.

2. Calculate the state of tide and current at your estimated time of arrival. If too adverse, adjust. Then, by checking tides and currents along the route during the time of passage, fine-tune your track.

3. Work along your track on the chart and identify *and mark* significant hazards, landmarks, and other navigational aids.

4. Don't plot a track directly to your destination; build in a measure of offset to one side or another of your track. Then, if visibility is reduced and you miss your expected mark, you'll already know that you're probably to the right (or left) and can turn in the proper direction. Offset to which side? If sailing along a coastline, always offset to seaward; if sailing toward a coastline, offset in the direction that wind and current will most likely be taking you.

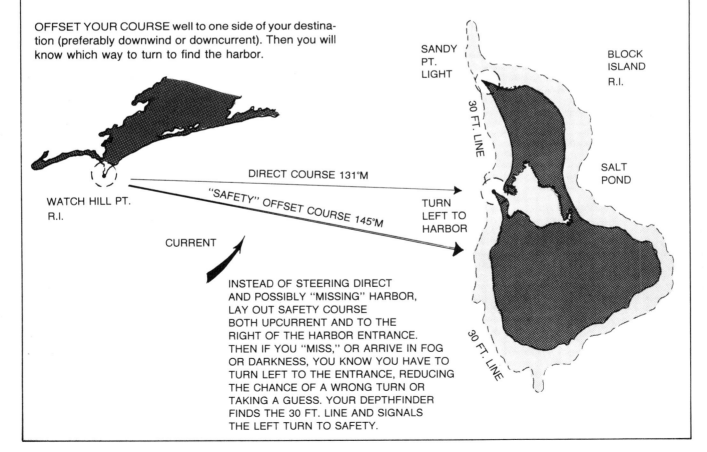

OFFSET YOUR COURSE well to one side of your destination (preferably downwind or downcurrent). Then you will know which way to turn to find the harbor.

SANDY PT. LIGHT

BLOCK ISLAND R.I.

30 FT. LINE

SALT POND

DIRECT COURSE 131°M

WATCH HILL PT. R.I.

"SAFETY" OFFSET COURSE 145°M

TURN LEFT TO HARBOR

CURRENT

INSTEAD OF STEERING DIRECT AND POSSIBLY "MISSING" HARBOR, LAY OUT SAFETY COURSE BOTH UPCURRENT AND TO THE RIGHT OF THE HARBOR ENTRANCE. THEN IF YOU "MISS," OR ARRIVE IN FOG OR DARKNESS, YOU KNOW YOU HAVE TO TURN LEFT TO THE ENTRANCE, REDUCING THE CHANCE OF A WRONG TURN OR TAKING A GUESS. YOUR DEPTHFINDER FINDS THE 30 FT. LINE AND SIGNALS THE LEFT TURN TO SAFETY.

30 FT. LINE

Next, using tide and current tables, determine the probable height of the tide and the direction and speed of the current at key points along the route. Under some fixed bridges, the water may be too high, at times, to let you pass. In some channels, the speed of the current may be too great: A 6-knot boat headed into a 7-knot current simply won't make it. In some waters, tidal current and rips (the point where an incoming and an outgoing body of water meet) create extremely hazardous conditions for recreational boaters.

Using tide and current tables, double-check the charts for adequate water depth over any stretch of the route during low tide. Make notes on the chart for ready reference during the trip.

Compute your probable speed-made-good (see appendix VII) over the route, considering your preferred boat speed and the effect of the current. Depending on whether it's with you or against you, it might make a significant difference. This will give you the timing of waypoints, approximate course changes, and arrival. This information should also be included in your float plan. (More information on voyage planning appears in chapter 13.)

FINDING YOUR POSITION

PILOTING

Determining your position underway (in sight of land) is a simple matter of establishing your relationship, in direction and distance, to a known object or position. This can be accomplished with visual bearings (using a compass to provide the direction), radio bearings, a radar plot, electronic signals from Loran stations or orbiting satellites, or good old-fashioned observation and measurement of celestial bodies.

Compass bearings are best obtained with a hand-held portable compass with a built-in sight. Wait until the compass has steadied before taking a reading, and, if the boat is bouncing around

QUICK REFERENCE CHARTS for key navigation symbols and the Rules of the Road are useful additions near the helm. You should know the Rules however—you will rarely have time to check the official regulations in an actual at-sea encounter. But these sturdy waterproof charts can provide a quick reminder when kept on the chart table.

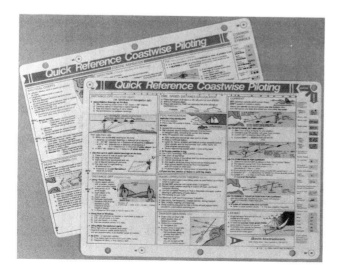

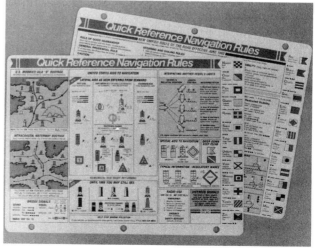

too much, take three readings of the same object and use the average. Overall, take readings of three different landmarks (e.g., a smokestack, the edge of an island, the peak of a mountain) that are 60 to 90 degrees apart, if possible. To increase accuracy, take the bearings as close together in time as possible.

If a hand-bearing compass is not available, you can take approximate readings by pointing your bow at the object, or by sighting along your hand or a straightedge.

If you're ready for the latest electronic aid, use a flux-gate magnetometer instead of a hand compass. About the size of a pocket calculator, the unit is pointed at the object (using a built-in sight) and the bearing is recorded by pressing a button. Several bearings can be memorized, for later ease in plotting the position.

You can use your RDF unit to get one or more additional bearings. However, avoid the temptation to set the RDF on top of the compass to facilitate reading the bearing; the electronics are likely to induce a serious deviation error in the compass.

Your depth finder is another tool for determining location, by comparing the reading with the depth recorded on the chart. This may not be too revealing over a broad, flat bottom, but it can provide an accurate line of position when crossing a major change in depth or unusual configuration noted on the chart.

Finding the Range to a Light at Night

Lights used as navigational aids will be noted on the chart, included in the *Light List*, and described in the *Sailing Directions, Coast Pilot,* or commercial cruising guide. By checking the height of the light—and knowing your own "height of eye" above the water—you can fix the distance to the light at the moment it appears on the horizon.

1. Plan ahead. Know what lights you are likely to be sighting, and when.

2. When the light first appears, bob your head up and down a few feet to verify that the light is just coming over the horizon. The light should disappear as you lower your head, then reappear as you return to normal height.

3. Pick the appropriate height and range information from the table below. Your "height of eye" is the actual height above the water, and it is something you ought to measure and remember (or record); "distance to horizon" is from your boat. "Height of object" comes from the chart or other published information; "distance from horizon" is the measure to the object from the horizon. Add these last two figures to obtain the total distance.

(Continued)

Height of Eye (feet)	Distance to Horizon (nautical miles)	Height of Object (feet)	Distance from Horizon (nautical miles)
6	2.8	30	6.3
8	3.2	32	6.5
10	3.6	34	6.7
12	4.0	36	6.9
14	4.3	38	7.1
16	4.6	40	7.2
18	4.9	42	7.4
20	5.1	44	7.6
22	5.4	46	7.8
28	6.1	48	7.9
		50	8.1

At night, you might be able to measure visually and use the distance to a navigational aid such as a lighthouse to provide a range arc, to intersect the bearing lines (see box). On a clear, cool day, it is possible to use such visual information in daylight; however, atmospheric haze and heat waves usually intrude except for relatively short distances.

Plotting the Fix Using the parallel rules and the chart, create a pencil line of position (LOP) measured *from* each sighted object—or radio transmitter—*to* your boat. These lines of position will cross at some point, indicating your position. Because of probable inaccuracies in taking compass bearings, the intersection is likely to be a small triangle rather than a pinpoint; assume your position to be in the center of the triangle.

With a draftsman's compass, draw any range arcs. Set the compass arms to the distance scale on the chart; put the point on the designated navigational aid (or identifiable tall building, tower, and so on) and swing the pencil end through your probable position.

Check the water depth with your depth finder, and match with your probable location on the chart. Make a notation of the time of this fix.

If the fix is not on (or very near) your planned track, it's likely you are being offset by wind or current or faulty steering. Determine the cause, and adjust your track accordingly.

CELESTIAL NAVIGATION

Away from sight of land, position-finding involves a different set of skills and equipment. The classic, time-honored method is celestial navigation—which formerly involved the exercise of trigonometry and other skills that you were supposed to have learned in high school but probably don't remember. That's okay, because most of the real work has already been done by publishers of books and tables, and all you have to do now is fill in some numbers on a form, work

some simple arithmetic, and then plot the results on the proper chart.

Of course, with today's electronic navigational marvels, few boaters need rely on celestial-navigation skills. However, an understanding of the method someday may help you through a tight spot.

Briefly, celestial navigation is merely a system for determining your position relative to a heavenly body of a precisely known location, relative to the earth. Just as twilight is falling, pick out a bright star—say, Betelgeuse—so that you can see both the star and the line of the horizon. Using a sextant—a simple device incorporating a telescope, a mirror, and a scale—measure the angle from the horizon up to the star. Mark down the precise time of this measurement, then, working quickly before the horizon disappears into blackness, measure the angle for two or three more selected stars.

Precise time is important, because seconds count: An error of one minute will produce a geographic error of seventeen miles at the equator.

SEXTANT.

In the old days—and the not-so-old days, for that matter, before the advent of quartz-crystal timepieces—a ship's chronometer was one of the most precise instruments known to man. Mounted on gimbals in a sturdy box, kept away from extremes of temperature and humidity, and lovingly cared for by the quartermaster, the chronometer was treated with even more veneration than the compass. The secret of the chronometer's power was consistency. The thing wasn't necessarily all that precise, but it would drift off at a predictable rate as long as it was wound regularly, and as long as there were careful records of this rate. Woe betide the quartermaster or apprentice who wound the clock at the wrong time (thus screwing up the rate) or—a court-martial offense—failed to wind it at all. Fortunately for ships with slovenly quartermasters in this century, they could always verify the real time by radio signal from the U.S. Naval Observatory.

Each measured angle represents the side of an imaginary cone, the apex of which is at the star, the bottom edge of which forms wide circle. Your position is somewhere on that circle. Since you already know, for example, that you're probably off the coast of California, you can eliminate most of the circle. You pick the computed tables for the part of the world you know you are in, select the figures that represent the position of that star at the time you took your reading, do the simple computation, and then mark a short line of position on a plotting sheet, which lets you do the rough work without mucking up the chart.

After you compute and create the LOPs for the other stars—*voilà!*—you should have created a small triangle where the edges of the cones overlap. Your position, for most purposes, would be at the center of the triangle. The smaller the triangle, the more confidence you can have in the accuracy of the position; a pinpoint intersection of five LOPs is a captain's joy and a navigator's pride.

By the way, the effort of computation—even the effort of finding the right tables and filling in the forms—has effectively disappeared for any navigator willing to spend a few hundred dollars on a pocket-size computer with all of the necessary tables stored in its memory.

DEAD RECKONING

In spite of good training, steady practice, and the best equipment that money can buy, you won't always be able to get a fix. It's hard to take compass bearings in the fog, for example; you can't get a star sight through a heavy overcast; your electronic marvels might inexplicably go dark. That's when the best skills of the navigator come into play—in developing the DR plot.

DR—which actually stands for "deduced" *(ded,* not *dead)* reckoning—develops positions deduced from information obtained solely from the boat and its occupants. Speed, time run, course, probable effect of wind and current—all combine to keep a running plot of uncertain but nonetheless useful accuracy.

Helpful instruments include wind speed and direction indicators, speedometers (with a distance-traveled display), and the depth finder. These come in a wide variety of models, but all help you keep track of your position by updating the DR plot.

THE LOG

Finally, you should keep a log. It has legal utility in the event of accident, and it may serve as a pleasant memento of voyages past, but a well-kept log also may help ensure that you'll reach your destination by providing a running record of where you've been. Even if your sailing plans involve nothing but fishing or water-skiing—keep a log.

Some log-keeping suggestions:

• If possible, use a preprinted logbook; it's easier.

• Typical entries include names of embarked crew and guests, quantities of fuel and water taken aboard, description of the weather, destination, time underway, course and speed, position (periodically, as firmly established).

• Mandatory entries: hearing, answering, responding to any emergency radio transmission.

• Intelligent entries: full description of any unusual event or accident, or of illness or injury to crew, guests, or others.

• Make entries whenever there are significant changes in the weather, your course, your speed, or the condition of your boat and crew.

CHAPTER THIRTEEN

Getting Underway

A MENTAL JOURNEY

In the next few chapters, we'll mentally go through a logical series of boating operations, from getting underway to returning to port. You may be a beginner or you may be a well-experienced boater: if the former, we hope to give you a broad sense of what should be involved in safe operations; if the latter, we hope this review will help you focus on some points you may have overlooked or forgotten.

And—once again we emphasize—safe boating involves a continuing review of what should or what might come next; it involves thinking through an action *before* you're committed to doing it, and knowing what you must do when the unexpected occurs.

Put that another way: You want to be able to *expect* the unexpected.

PREPARATIONS FOR GETTING UNDERWAY

The act of getting underway seems simple enough to observers and guests: You climb aboard, start the engines, untie the mooring lines, and pull out of the slip. Perhaps that deceptive simplicity is why so many new boat owners get into trouble before they have even begun their first solo cruise.

We've touched on this subject in several earlier chapters; here we put it all together as a series of questions you should answer and steps you should work through before heading out from the pier.

1. Do you have an up-to-date marine chart and a working compass? You may know the local waters as well as you know your own backyard, but what if you, the operator, should become disabled? Someone else will have to find the way home or to safe haven and will need the chart

that you never bother to check. When all visibility is lost in a solid, sustained downpour, or when a sudden fog rolls in—which direction is home or safe haven? You need a compass to match up with the chart. You've been out longer than planned and—surprise!—it's dark. Which of the myriad lights along the shore are meaningful and which merely misleading? Now you need a pair of binoculars to go with the chart and the compass—and a small flashlight as well, so that you can see the chart and the compass.

2. Have you checked the weather? The best source of weather information is the National Weather Service, broadcasting on the VHF weather channels around the clock, with regular updates and timely warnings.

3. Have you checked the tide? Not just for your departure, but for critical points along the route *and* at the expected time of your arrival at your destination.

4. Do you have enough fuel? This seems so obvious, yet thousands of out-of-fuel boaters need assistance each year.

5. Is safety equipment aboard and ready for use? A life jacket left in the garage will be of little value at sea; an anchor buried under a pile of old line and buckets won't be of much help when the engine cuts out just before you pile up on the rocks. Check the radio; the navigation equipment; the running lights. You may be planning a daytime trip, but adverse weather or mechanical problems could extend it past sunset.

6. Is the boat ready for safe operation? Any signs of damage from recent thunderstorms? Sail covers torn, hull banged up or floating at an awkward angle, mooring lines rubbed down to a few useless strands? Is the water around the boat clear of trash and garbage that could clog the cooling water intake or foul the propeller? Any unusual odors—a hint of leaking engine or stove fuel? Since most fuel vapors are heavier than air, this is best checked by sniffing in the bilges and along the galley deck. Check the bilges for water level, and for proper operation of the main bilge pump, by manipulating the float switch.

7. Is the boat ready for sea? Is it ready for

bouncing around in wave or wake and ready for emergency and not about to be loaded—with passengers and supplies—beyond the safe limits noted on the Coast Guard loading plate. Passenger limit is established not by the number of seats available, but by the number of 150-pound people, engine, fuel, and equipment, which all adds up to the determined safe limit.

Any gear that is not properly stowed or secured undoubtedly will end up crashing to the deck or slipping overboard. All emergency gear must be at hand before an emergency erupts: fire extinguishers in place; anchor ready to let go (and not stowed below or lashed down with a lot of fancy knots); life jackets and distress signals on top, not on the bottom, of the other supplies in the locker.

8. Is the engine ready to go? Too many boat owners treat their marine propulsion systems the same way they do an automobile: Jump in and turn it on. In a gasoline-powered boat, that could be a fatal mistake; the engine compartment must first be ventilated to clear out any potentially explosive fumes that may have accumulated. Levels of engine oil and transmission and coolant fluid should be checked. Top off all that are necessary; open seacock for the raw-water inlet and inspect the strainer for debris that could clog it.

9. Are you completely ready for your intended voyage? Food and beverages must be stowed aboard; guests must be briefed on normal and emergency procedures. Are adequate protective clothing and sunscreen on hand?

10. Have you filed a float plan? Neither the experience of the skipper and crew nor the sophistication of the boat and equipment will *guarantee* a safe and timely return. At the very least, *someone* should know where you are going and when you expect to return. Give a copy of your float plan to your spouse or your next-door neighbor or your dockmaster. This plan might be elaborate or simple, written or oral, but it will put someone on alert that you are going out on your boat, headed for someplace, and that you expect to arrive or return at an approximate time.

11. Check all alarms and detectors for normal readings. Make a final check to be sure that the

FLOAT PLAN

Vessel _____ Home Port _____ Reg. # _____
Master _____ Master's Home Phone _____
Address _____
Radio Call Sign _____ Frequency guarded _____
Type of Vessel _____ Rig _____ Length _____ Maker _____
Color of topsides _____ Color of superstructure _____ Color of deck _____
Propulsion Power Plant _____ Gasoline _____ Diesel _____
Number in Crew _____ Number Passengers _____ Of Whom _____ Are Under 12 Years
Total Aboard _____ Dinghy _____ Inflatable Boat _____
Departure Date _____ Time _____ Place _____
Destination Date _____ ETA _____ Place _____
Possible Intermediate Stops _____
Remarks _____

( ) True   SKETCH OF PROPOSED ROUTE   ( ) Magnetic

A SAMPLE FLOAT PLAN, which can be used as a guide
to design one of your own that suits both your boat and
your cruising plans.

Float Plan Filed With _____ Date _____ Sig. Master _____

CHECKLIST

__(1) Fuel	__(7) Food	__(11) Life Jackets	__(18) Steering System	__(23) Navigational instruments
__(2) Lube Oil	__(8) Water	__(12) Navigational Lights	__(19) Rigging	__(24) Radio Check
__(3) Engine Check	__(9) Ice	__(13) Flashlight	__(20) Bilge Pump	__(25) Weather Check
__(4) Engine Cooling	__(10) Stove Oil	__(14) Foghorn	__(21) Sanitary System	__(26) Charts
__(5) Electrical System		__(15) Signal Flares	__(22) Ground Tackle	__(27) Float Plan Filed
__(6) Tools		__(16) First-Aid Kit		
		__(17) Fire Extinguisher		

Note: Official agencies recommend the completion of this information and the filing of the duplicate copy with an "interested party
ashore" prior to departure. The term "interested party" is defined as "family, neighbors, or a friend." Then, when or if a call to the official
agency is required, this person will be able to supply information that is correct and adequate.

bilges have in fact been ventilated.

12. Check for lines and debris in the water. The examination you conducted when you arrived at the boat is now obsolete; you or your crew may have allowed a loose line to dangle overside; the current may have carried some garbage right up to your engine intake. A final check is essential before you start the engine.

13. Start the engine. Immediately check the gauges for oil pressure and alternator output. If none is indicated, shut down and investigate. If you have a water-cooled exhaust, look over the side to ensure that the cooling-water output is correct; a "dry" exhaust is a sign of blocked coolant flow, and the engines must be shut down immediately. Also, watch the temperature gauge for a too-rapid rise in temperature—another indication of blocked flow.

Let the engines reach operating temperature before getting underway; it's better for the engines and it's also the best way to ensure that everything is working properly. For example, a diesel might run for about five minutes on the fuel in the lines, with the tank supply valves closed. It's better to run out of fuel at the pier rather than just as you reach the channel.

14. While the engines are warming up, you can take in the telephone line and disconnect the shore power. Turn off the shore power at the control panel, then on the pier. Next, disconnect one end or the other of the power cable. If you're taking the cable with you, disconnect both ends, so that you can stow it out of the way. Many boaters, going on short cruises, will leave the cable coiled neatly on the pier. We suggest that you always take it with you—not so much for theft prevention, but because you never know where you might have to spend the night. Mechanical problems with your boat, adverse weather, a stuck highway bridge—all could divert you to another marina, where you'll be glad you have your power cable.

We feel much the same way about mooring lines. You can leave them hanging on the pilings, ready for an easy snatch upon return, but if you get stuck away from home, you probably will wish you had brought them with you. At least have a spare set aboard.

15. Have your anchor ready for use any time you're maneuvering in a harbor. (You'll notice that large ships, even when being assisted by tugboats, will have an anchor let down almost to the waterline. Should something go wrong, they can get the anchor on the bottom in seconds.)

16. At this point, you're *almost* ready to get underway. Cycle the engine controls; operate the steering, lock to lock; make a last-minute check of the bilges. Spend a few minutes mentally going over your plans for the next few hours

Boathandling in Tight Quarters

When you steer an automobile, the front wheels lead the way; when you steer a boat, the hull swings around a pivot point (typically, but not always, about two-thirds of the distance back from the bow). The bow swings in the direction of the turn, and the stern swings out the other way. When maneuvering through a tight spot, such as a group of anchored boats or a narrow channel, you must allow for this stern movement. You counteract the swing by using opposite rudder, with an extra burst of power.

A common error in getting underway from a pier is use of the rudder to swing the bow out—which swings the stern in to bang against the pier (or another boat). This effect is particularly pronounced with an outboard boat. The best solution is to *push* the bow out until it is pointed in the intended direction of travel, then go slowly ahead with the rudder (or outboard) amidships.

This pivoting factor can be used to good advantage when trying to get the hull lined up with a slip or narrow passage. With the boat more or less dead in the water, a burst of propeller wash against the rudder will swing the boat before you gain much headway. This technique is even more useful when trying to *back* into a narrow slip, especially with an ungainly single-screw sailboat or trawler. Put the rudder full over to the side *opposite* the desired direction of swing (in other words, turn the wheel far right to swing the stern to the left); with the engine at idle, shift *ahead*, give the throttle a boost, and then go back to idle before shifting astern. Repeat the cycle as many times as necessary; with practice, you should be able literally to back around a corner.

Checklist for Getting Underway

- ☐ Charts and navigational gear ready for use.
- ☐ Weather forecast obtained, and suitable.
- ☐ State of the tide checked.
- ☐ Fuel supply verified.
- ☐ Safety equipment checked and ready for use.
- ☐ Boat in safe condition; bilges checked for fuel vapors and excess water.
- ☐ Ready for sea, all gear stowed properly.
- ☐ Engine ready for operation: oil, transmission, coolant checked; fuel and water intake valves open.
- ☐ Supplies aboard; crew and guests briefed; float plan filed.
- ☐ Ventilate bilges (gasoline engines).
- ☐ Check all alarms and detectors for normal readings.
- ☐ Check for lines and debris in the water.
- ☐ Start and warm up engine(s); check gauges, exhaust discharge.
- ☐ Anchor ready to let go.
- ☐ Take in all lines: telephone cable first, shore power next, then mooring lines.

UNDERWAY

- ☐ Move out slowly, watching out for other boats; assess effect of wind and current.
- ☐ Note time of departure in log.
- ☐ Close lifeline boarding gate; stow all service and mooring lines.

and—after checking the direction and force of the wind and the current—the steps you will take in the next few minutes to get the boat out of the slip and on the way.

Do not assume that any helpful people on the pier—including the dockboys—actually know what they are doing. Put first reliance on your own crew, with whom you should practice getting underway (and returning to the berth). If you do accept assistance from others, provide friendly but clear instructions. You don't want them to let go all of the lines at once; you don't want them to throw your lines in the water; you need to take in the mooring lines in a progression that leaves you some control. Getting underway singlehanded—with no help from crew or neighbors—can be a challenging experience; if the wind and current are at all adverse, have an extra cup of coffee while you plan your moves.

17. When ready to go, *keep everything simple*. Let go the mooring lines or take them aboard; touch the throttle lightly; be calm and purposeful.

Note the time of departure in your log. Also note the basic course you are taking (to help you find your way back, especially in fog or at night). As quickly as possible, get all mooring lines coiled and stowed to ensure a clear and uncluttered deck; close the lifeline boarding gate.

You're now underway, but you're not yet cruising. It's likely you're in an area of high traffic, with boats entering and leaving the marina, stopping at the fuel dock, funneling into narrow channels. This may be a major shipping channel, with large commercial traffic barreling along. A big ship does not have to be moving very fast to create enough wake or turbulence to push your boat around; an unwary guest, not yet prepared for pitching and rolling, could be thrown down or overboard. Be alert, and warn your crew and guests likewise.

REFUELING

Having left your slip, your next move may be a short trip to the nearest fuel dock—or this might be handled later in the voyage. Or, particularly on a sailboat with a small auxiliary engine that uses little fuel, this might be almost an annual event.

In *any* case, refueling requires special attention and care to prevent it from becoming spectacularly dangerous. Of the 379 incidents of fire and explosion reported to the Coast Guard in 1986, almost 10 percent occurred while taking on fuel.

Remember: Gasoline vapors are heavier than air and will settle toward the bottom of the boat. Try to tie up with the bow pointed into the wind, or perpendicular to the wind, to keep vapors from being blown into the cabin. Close all hatches and windows. Turn off any pilot lights. Turn off the engine.

Take any portable tanks onto the pier and fill them there, not aboard the boat. Wipe off any spilled fuel before taking the tanks aboard again.

Don't smoke. That may seem obvious, but we have seen some dockboys handling fuel lines while cigarettes were stuck firmly between their lips. Don't let *anyone* around you smoke while you are at the fuel pier.

Don't operate any electrical equipment. Don't let anyone get on or off while fueling is underway—the rocking of the boat could pull the fuel hose out of the fill pipe, spilling fuel. Make sure there is metal-to-metal contact between the fuel nozzle and the filler plate; the movement of the fuel through the hose and piping can build up a static charge just looking for a chance to turn into a spark. Since the filler plate *should* be electrically bonded to the fuel tank, the static charge will be drained off harmlessly.

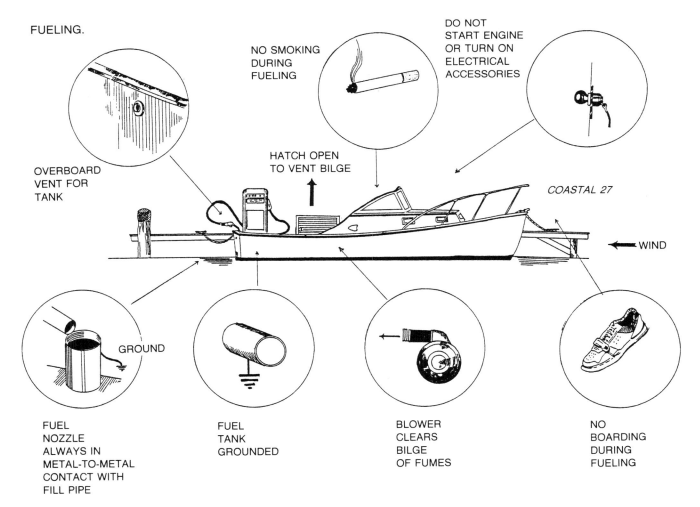

FUELING.

NO SMOKING DURING FUELING

DO NOT START ENGINE OR TURN ON ELECTRICAL ACCESSORIES

OVERBOARD VENT FOR TANK

HATCH OPEN TO VENT BILGE

COASTAL 27

WIND

GROUND

FUEL NOZZLE ALWAYS IN METAL-TO-METAL CONTACT WITH FILL PIPE

FUEL TANK GROUNDED

BLOWER CLEARS BILGE OF FUMES

NO BOARDING DURING FUELING

Listen to the sound of the fuel going into the tank. When you hear an increase in pitch—indicating fuel rising in the fill pipe—stop pumping. Don't wait until fuel starts running out of the overflow tube and into the water. Not only is it dangerous to be floating in a pool of gasoline, it also is a violation of the law against discharge of fuel and oil into navigable waters.

When finished, open the hatches and windows and run the engineroom or bilge blower until you're certain no gasoline odor remains—for this, your nose is a simple but effective tool.

Taking on diesel fuel is not as touchy as taking on gasoline, but it still should be handled with care. The vapor is not explosive, but any fuel spilled in the bilges will be a fire hazard—and, as we have said, fuel spilled into the water is illegal.

The quality of diesel fuel may vary widely from one part of the country to another; we've encountered some that appeared more suited to a home furnace than an engine. You can check your engine data for the recommended fuel specifications, and you can ask the dealer for the specifications of his fuel, but, all things considered, you may be stuck with whatever he has. This is another element of voyage planning—time your fuel stops for major, not minor, locations.

To counteract water that may be mixed with the fuel—which will impede starting, particularly in cold weather—use a commercial additive such as dry gas. To prevent the growth of fungus in the fuel—which would clog the fuel strainer or injectors—use a commercial fuel additive such as Bio-Bor.

CHAPTER FOURTEEN

Underway

BASIC CONSIDERATIONS

Being underway on a bright, warm spring morning with just enough breeze to fill your sails or blow away your cobwebs—this is the reward for all of the preparations.

However, this is *not* the time to lean back and enjoy liberty: Eternal vigilance, we might say, is the price of safety. Below are some suggestions to enhance the safe, normal, fair-weather operation of your boat:

1. Keep a good lookout. Watch for other boats in your path, or heading for the same apparent point, and be prepared to take the appropriate action mandated by the Rules of the Road (see appendix I). Watch for large floating objects (which may barely show at the surface), and steer to avoid them. Watch for patches of floating garbage or seaweed and try to keep away from them, lest something be sucked into your engine cooling-water intake or become wrapped around the propeller shaft.

2. Watch for changes in the weather; be alert for a sudden drop in the temperature, which might signal the onset of fog. Take action before that distant squall line passes over your position.

3. Keep track of your position. We doubt that many boaters out for a Sunday cruise will keep a position track and plot, yet if an emergency strikes, you should be able to be more precise than "a couple of miles offshore north of Fort Lauderdale." *Always* have some sense of the direction back home—or to an alternative harbor.

4. Be aware of the state of the tide and the probable effect of current on your boat, particularly when operating in confined waters.

5. Monitor channel 16 on your VHF radio; be prepared to respond to an emergency request and to record the transmission in your log.

6. Be aware of, and respect, wildlife sanctuaries.

7. Don't drink and drive; if you go ashore for a beach picnic, don't drink if you will be getting underway later.

8. Be alert to the condition of your guests and crew; watch for signs of seasickness, sunburn, fatigue.

Heavy-duty elastic suspenders with quick release buckles

Velcro-sealed storm collar for full neck protection

Deep waterproof envelope patch pocket with velcro

Attached, hood with cap

Double outside storm flap velcro-sealed closure with plastic inside zipper

Seamless shoulders

Full cut for free movement

Storm cuffs with elastic inside plastic snaps outside

Nylon draw cord

Snug-fitting elastic waist

420D nylon oxford reinforced seat and knees

100% waterproof, Hypalon-coated nylon fabric

Two deep front storm-proof pockets with velcro flap closures

Plastic adjustable snaps

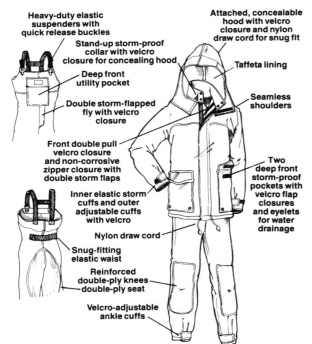

Heavy-duty elastic suspenders with quick release buckles

Stand-up storm-proof collar with velcro closure for concealing hood

Deep front utility pocket

Double storm-flapped fly with velcro closure

Front double pull velcro closure and non-corrosive zipper closure with double storm flaps

Inner elastic storm cuffs and outer adjustable cuffs with velcro

Nylon draw cord

Snug-fitting elastic waist

Reinforced double-ply knees double-ply seat

Velcro-adjustable ankle cuffs

Attached, concealable hood with velcro closure and nylon draw cord for snug fit

Taffeta lining

Seamless shoulders

Two deep front storm-proof pockets with velcro flap closures and eyelets for water drainage

FEATURES OF HIGH-QUALITY FOUL-WEATHER GEAR. Coastal foul-weather gear (top); Offshore foul-weather gear (bottom). (Achilles)

SAILING GLOVES not only protect your hands, but also provide that critical extra measure of holding power when you just cannot afford a slip. Use them when handling sheet winches, halyards, hoisting crew members aloft, or in important maneuvers like anchoring or docking. (Davis Instruments)

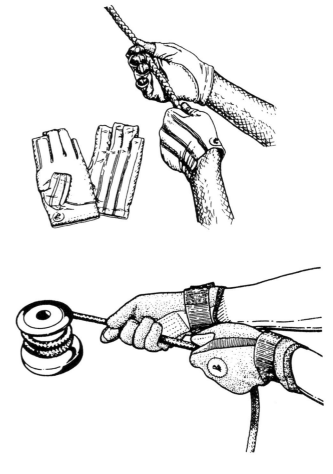

9. Enforce a safe boating "dress code"—deck shoes with nonslip soles; gloves for handling lines and the anchor rode; a hat, a jacket, or long pants, as appropriate; life jackets for children when topside; life jackets and safety harness for adults at night or in bad weather.

10. Enforce safe boating procedures: no sitting or leaning on lifelines; no running on deck; hands and feet well clear of running rigging and winches; crew well braced against pitch and roll when standing to handle sails or the anchor, or landing a fish; Clear and uncluttered deck; lines stowed when not in use.

11. Honor speed limits and "no wake" zones; show courtesy to other boaters; don't impede the passage of large, less maneuverable ships, particularly when they are in a marked channel.

12. Always be alert to all potential hazards and provide a timely warning: waves and wakes about to hit the boat; a boom about to swing; a gust of wind approaching.

RULES OF THE ROAD

Ashore, operations of motor vehicles are largely controlled by paved (or at least graded) roadways, stop signs, lights, posted speed limits, and the general concept of "right-of-way" at otherwise-unmarked intersections: Give way to any vehicle approaching from the right.

Afloat, the controls are just as precise but their application may be less clear to the operator. Certainly, marked channels are similar to roadways, but they occur only in shallow and/or crowded waterways. Speed limits may be posted in mph or as "no wake" zones, which mean what they say.

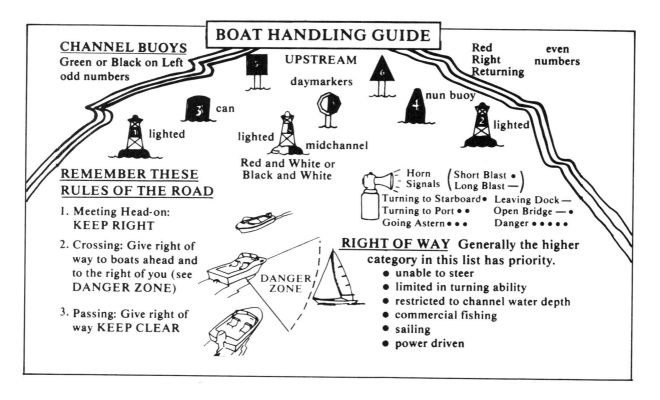

However, there are no stop signs on the waterways; in open water, there are no clearly defined pathways or intersections, and boats may move around willy-nilly in any and all directions. To compound the potential for disaster, boats can't stop or change direction as easily as automobiles can—indeed, some larger ships can't turn in less than a mile or stop short of three or four miles.

If you are the average recreational boater, the maneuvering characteristics of an oil tanker or aircraft carrier become important only when both of you are headed for the same patch of water at the same time—in which case, you are likely to be smart enough to turn aside and stay out of the way. However, recreational boaters frequently face less clear-cut but nonetheless hazardous situations involving decisions of who gives way to whom, and when.

Over the centuries, a series of international agreements have prescribed the rules under which mariners should maneuver their vessels to avoid collision. Also, there are rules for the display of identifying lights (or many equivalent "dayshapes"), which help other mariners to determine the heading of another ship, or to determine if it is a powerboat or a sailboat, or if it is at anchor or aground, or to understand any peculiarities of operation—tugboat with tow, fishing trawler dragging a net, and so forth.

The most recent codification of the rules was adopted in 1972 as the *International Regulations for Preventing Collisions at Sea* (usually called the COLREGS—see appendix I). These rules apply in most international waters around the globe, and they generally are applied also in the inland waters—lakes and rivers—of the United States. There are some exceptions: A few nations (including Japan, Italy, the Philippines) still adhere to an earlier (1960) version, which differs in some specifics, and additional rules apply in some areas within the United States—for example, on certain major rivers, where boats traveling with the current have the right-of-way over boats headed upstream. There is one other major rule applicable within U.S. inland waters: Law-enforcement vessels may display a flashing blue light (not provided for in the COLREGS). As you enter the world of boating in any area, make a prudent check with the local Coast Guard (or other boaters with local knowledge) for any specific peculiar rules; if you are doing long-distance cruising, your planning should be thorough enough to include a determination of the rules in effect wherever you travel.

APPLICATION OF THE RULES

All boats are subject to the Rules. Although small daysailers, rowboats, and dinghies are exempt from some of the regulations (such as requirements for permanently installed lights), the *operators* are not exempt from *operating* according to the rules.

While heeding the Rules, any skipper is at the same time required to exercise common sense: specifically, "nothing in these Rules shall exonerate any vessel . . . from the consequences of any neglect to comply with these Rules or of the neglect of any precaution which may be required by the ordinary practice of seamen or by the special circumstances of the case." In other words, you can't find an excuse for inappropriate behavior by sorting through the Rules.

SOME SPECIFICS

- You must keep a good lookout.
- You must operate at a safe speed appropriate to the weather, state of visibility, other traffic in the area, and the capabilities of your boat.
- You must take every precaution to avoid collision with another boat.
- You must not get in the way of larger vessels, which cannot so easily stop or turn, especially those operating in a narrow, restricted channel. A 30-foot sailboat, for example, does *not* have the right-of-way over an oil tanker.
- Whenever possible, stay to the right side of a narrow channel.
- When crossing a channel, do so at a right angle to the channel and as quickly as possible.

Maneuvering and Warning Signals

These signals are almost always used by professionally operated vessels, but—unfortunately—almost never by recreational boaters. Any boat operator can and should use the appropriate signals, especially when there is any doubt about the intentions of the other boat, and most especially when expected to respond to a signal from another.

The signals are made by whistle or horn (with a "short blast" lasting one second and a "prolonged blast" lasting four to six seconds) *and,* if at night and if considered necessary, by flashing light (lasting one second at one-second intervals).

One short blast/flash	"I am altering my course to starboard."
Two short blasts/flashes	"I am altering my course to port."
Three short blasts/flashes	"I am operating stern propulsion."

Five short blasts/flashes	"I do not understand your intentions"—the danger signal.

For a boat overtaking another:

Two prolonged blasts and one short blast	"I intend to overtake you on your starboard side."
Two prolonged blasts and two short blasts	"I intend to overtake you on your port side."

For the boat being overtaken, if in agreement: One prolonged, one short, one prolonged, one short blast.

If not in agreement: sound the danger signal.

Any boat nearing a bend in a channel or an area of obscured visibility, where another boat may be approaching unobserved, shall sound one prolonged blast. This must be answered by any approaching vessel within hearing.

For signals to use in fog or restricted visibility, see chapter 20; for distress signals, see chapter 21.

MANEUVERING RULES

• A powerboat (which can maneuver easily) should give way to a sailboat under sail (which cannot). A sailboat moving under engine power, whether or not sails are hoisted, is to be considered a powerboat.

• Any recreational boat should keep out of the way of a vessel "not under command" (that is, broken down), a vessel restricted in its ability to maneuver (by size or type of operation, such as in towing or pushing another vessel), or a vessel engaged in fishing.

• When two sailboats are approaching each other: If each has the wind on a different side, the boat with the wind on the *port* side keeps out of the way of the other; if both have the wind on the same side, the boat to *windward* keeps out of the way of the boat to *leeward.*

• When one boat is overtaking another, it must keep out of the way of the boat being overtaken. To prevent misunderstanding, the boats should exchange signals (see box).

• When two power-driven boats are about to meet head-on, each must alter course to *starboard* so that they will pass each other port-to-port.

• When two power-driven boats are in a crossing situation that involves the risk of collision, the boat with the other on its own starboard side is called the "give-way" vessel and must keep out of the way of the other.

• In the above situation, the "other" boat is known as the "stand-on" vessel, and it must continue on its present course and speed so that the give-way boat can make sensible movements to stay out of the way. If the give-way boat does *not* take proper action, and the risk of collision is imminent, the stand-on boat can take whatever action seems necessary. Normally, this should *not* mean turning to *port* with the other boat on her port side.

The specific Rules, which add some flesh to this bare-bones summary, appear in appendix I.

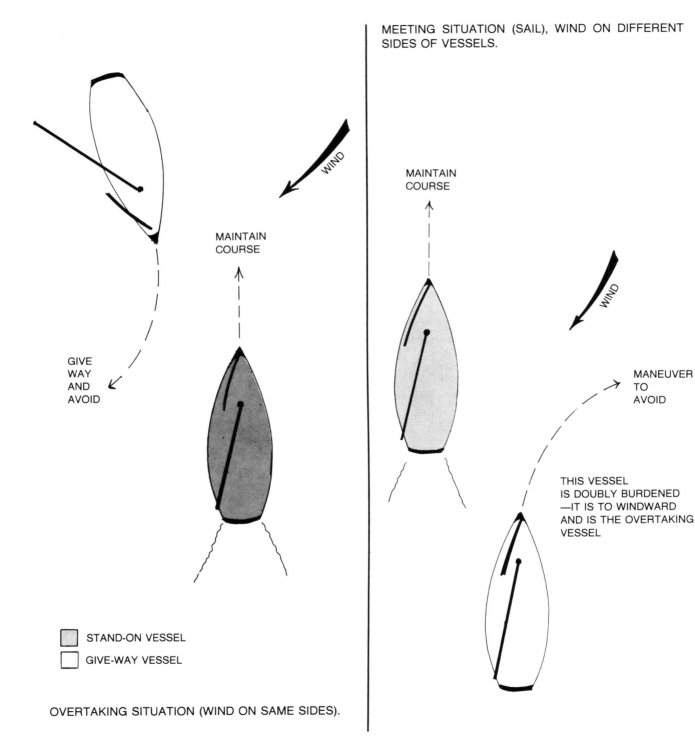

MEETING SITUATION (SAIL), WIND ON DIFFERENT SIDES OF VESSELS.

WIND

MAINTAIN COURSE

MAINTAIN COURSE

GIVE WAY AND AVOID

MANEUVER TO AVOID

THIS VESSEL IS DOUBLY BURDENED —IT IS TO WINDWARD AND IS THE OVERTAKING VESSEL

STAND-ON VESSEL

GIVE-WAY VESSEL

OVERTAKING SITUATION (WIND ON SAME SIDES).

MEETING SITUATION.

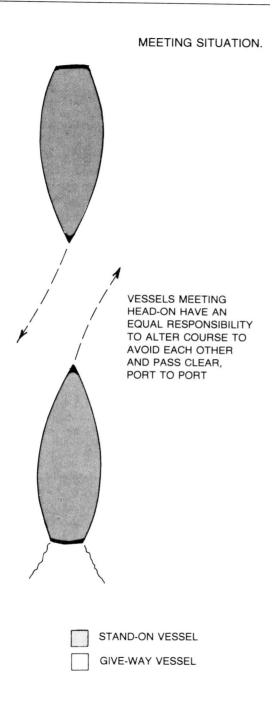

VESSELS MEETING
HEAD-ON HAVE AN
EQUAL RESPONSIBILITY
TO ALTER COURSE TO
AVOID EACH OTHER
AND PASS CLEAR,
PORT TO PORT

STAND-ON VESSEL

GIVE-WAY VESSEL

CROSSING SITUATION.

MAINTAIN
COURSE

VESSEL TO PORT
ALTERS COURSE
TO CLEAR

LIGHTS

At sunset, you should turn on the running lights appropriate to your mode of operation (see appendix I). For a motorboat (or a sailboat with the engine running), that means port and starboard sidelights, a masthead light, and a stern light. For a sailboat under sail, sidelights and stern light; if the boat is less than 20 meters (65 feet) long, these lights may be combined in one three-lens lantern mounted aloft for clear visibility unblanketed by the sails. For a boat at anchor, an anchor light at the masthead (unless anchored in a designated area, as noted on the chart, in which case no lights are required). Rowboats and dinghies should be prepared to show some light (even a flashlight) whenever another boat is approaching.

Special lighting schemes apply to special circumstances: boats towing or pushing other boats or barges; boats engaged in commercial fishing operations; boats aground or not under command. While most of these probably will never apply to your own boat, you should be aware of the differences and be prepared to look them up when necessary. You certainly do not, for example, want to inadvertently cut between a towboat and its tow because you thought they were two separate boats. Whenever you see an unfamiliar light pattern, *check it out.*

DAYSHAPES

Just as special information is conveyed by lights at night, so too do dayshapes alert other mariners to special circumstances.

Dayshapes include balls, cones, cylinders, and diamonds hung from the rigging to indicate a boat at anchor, or aground, or drifting, or engaged in diving operations or commercial fishing. One dayshape too often unused: an inverted cone, which signifies a sailboat, with sails set, that is also operating under power.

BRIDGES

Bridges that cross navigable waterways fall into two categories—fixed, and opening. With a fixed bridge, boats obviously are limited to an overall height that permits passage under the bridge, the only variation being afforded by the range of the tide. This is particularly critical for powerboats with fishing towers and all sailboats. Check the chart for the designed clearance of any bridges along your planned route before starting out; don't assume anything. (For example, the "controlling height" of bridges along the Intracoastal Waterway is supposed to be 65 feet—except for one bridge in Miami that sits, stubbornly, at 55 feet.)

Opening bridges may swing, or lift, or be lifted. The chart usually will list the type; it also may list the opening schedule. Some bridges open according to a schedule intended to accommodate heavy automobile traffic, such as during rush hour or in the midst of high tourist season—typically, on the hour and the half-hour. At other times, or in less congested areas, bridges will open at any time upon signal.

The signal to use: one long and one short blast. The bridge tender will answer with the same signal when the bridge is about to open; don't be impatient if your signal is not answered immediately. After you've passed through, you'll hear five short blasts, indicating that the bridge is about to close.

Some bridgetenders monitor VHF radio; check the local cruising guide for details.

SAFE SAILING

Most of the material in this book applies equally to power and sail, and most of the powerboat guidance is also applicable to engine-powered sailboats. However, when it comes to the safe enjoyment of being under sail, much of the discussion will be of interest only to sailors.

This is not to suggest that other boaters should ignore the subject of sailing. Even in this final quarter of the twentieth century, with every sophisticated device that technology allows, the rudiments of the maritime craft are best learned in a sailing vessel—an example set by both the U.S. Naval Academy and the Coast Guard Academy. Under sail, you are more perfectly aligned with nature—and more easily grasp the hard lessons of seamanship—than under power.

What follows is not a primer on sailing; rather, it focuses on those aspects of sailing that may be dangerous if done improperly.

SAILING HAZARDS

Sailboats offer the same general operational hazards as powerboats, but there are a few additional factors to consider.

INCREASED ON-DECK OBSTACLES

Always wear shoes on deck. There are too many opportunities to stub (or break) an unprotected toe on deck. Also, bare feet are more likely to slip on wet decks than shoes with proper nonskid soles.

Keep unused lines off the deck and out of the way. The hazard is not so much in being tripped (although that can happen) but in having the line roll under your foot with almost the same result as if you'd stepped on a marble.

Watch out for sails underfoot. Any piece of sailcloth on deck can be as slippery as a pool of oil.

THE BOOM

The boom may run into you or you may run into it; in either case, the result may be at least a splitting headache. It runs into you because you're not watching out for it. The hazard of the boom is as good a reason as any for establishing and enforcing procedures. The orders "stand by to jibe" and "prepare to come about" are intended not only to alert winch- and sailhandlers but also to serve as fair warning for everyone to beware of the boom.

At anchor, when the boat is likely to be rocked by the wake of passing boats, the boom should be parked firmly in the gallows or secured with tightly set sheets, preventers, vangs. (A fuller discussion of preventers and boom vangs appears later in this chapter.) Any and every line that is used to control movement of the boom also can be used to keep that movement to a minimum (although not as effectively as a gallows or crutch).

Running into the boom usually is a consequence of being in too much of a hurry to get somewhere. There is a lesson here: The bump *may* put you out of action for a while, so if you must be in a hurry, make it a controlled and cautious hurry. Watch both your step and your head.

Incidentally, watching your head will be complicated by the otherwise laudable act of wearing a hat with a sun visor. It may also put the boom out of your line of sight.

USING A WINCH SAFELY

Start with the minimum number of turns around the winch drum needed for the job, usually two or three. Wrap the line clockwise by hand, from the bottom up. (The winch handle should be removed and out of the way, but be sure it is in no danger of sliding overboard.) *Keep your fingers out from under the line.* Pull the line through by hand until the load is too great, then take a final turn through the self-tailing jaws, insert the winch handle, be sure you have good footing, and crank.

With a two-speed winch, turning the crank in one direction will produce one power ratio and in the other direction, another—which may be two or three times as great. Use the highest ratio until, as before, the load becomes too great; then shift to the lower ratio for the rest of the job.

Be sure that the tail of the line—the part that is coming off the winch—*keeps* coming off the winch. A self-tailing winch does this for you; otherwise, a second crew member should keep the tail in hand and guide it. With either type of winch, be sure to keep the tail out from underfoot.

When the job is finished, remove and stow the winch handle and take the line to a cleat or stopper.

Beware of overwraps: A tangle around the winch drum may jam the line, preventing its release. To prevent an overwrap, keep excess slack out of the line and don't be overzealous with your cranking. Keep the line moving steadily, all the while keeping the tail out of the way. If you develop an overwrap that cannot be unwound by hand or winched through, head to windward to take pressure off the sail and then try again. If the line is still too tight, you may have to unrig the sail; if it's a roller-furled headsail, cranked aft as tight as the sheet winch operator could make it, there may be no recourse but to cut the line. If so, cut just aft of the cringle (to avoid shortening the line too much) and keep the sail under control with the other sheet. Get the winch cleared, retie the sheet to the cringle, and sail on—with a bit more caution.

POLES

A spinnaker pole serves to get the spinnaker out, to take best advantage of the wind; a whisker or reaching pole is often used to hold the clew of a genoa jib out to the side, particularly when sailing downwind, wing-and-wing (i.e., boom and mainsail out to one side, pole and genoa out to the other).

Poles should be handled with care. Whisker or reaching poles are fairly light (some sailors just use a boathook); spinnaker poles are sturdier—and heavier. Make sure that connections are made firmly; watch out for your fingers (and head). When changing course, take in the pole first, then reset on the new course.

ROUTINE PROCEDURES

There is no room for doubt. The skipper is in charge, and the crew must be alert to, and quickly respond to, any commands. Routine procedures *must* be established. Sails must be raised and lowered in coordination with the action of the helmsman; if the crew acts too soon—or too late—the boat may be caught by too much wind, or with too little speed.

Crew members (and passengers) who ignore the skipper's commands also may find themselves in danger of a nasty collision with the boom, of being caught by line, or of flipping overboard as the boat takes a sudden heel.

Also, each crew member should have specifically assigned duties (port sheet winch, starboard sheet winch, mainsheet, and so forth) to keep them from running into each other—and each should *understand* his or her duties to keep them from making mistakes that could range anywhere from minor to fatal.

SAILHANDLING

As with the handling of engines, smooth, steady control is the key to safe sailhandling. You start with an organized plan—to set certain sails in a certain order. For casual cruising, with a roller-furling headsail, that usually means heading into the wind, setting the mainsail, then pulling out the headsail as rigged (typically, a genoa-cut sail, fuller than a jib but better suited to average sailing conditions). At the other end of the sail-planning scale, preparing for a race, you'll line up a range of sails and have them ready to bring on deck in the order you think you might need them. In between, you may plan to use two or three different headsails along with your main, although few sailors with roller-furling headsails usually bother to do that.

You don't need to work with the sails one at a time in heel-and-toe order: You can have one sail hoisted but not unfurled—that is, wrapped and held by light-line stops, which can be broken with a pull on the sheet, releasing the sail in an instant. Another sail can be lashed to the toerail or the base of the pulpit with bungee cords, ready to be hanked on at a moment's notice. (*Do not* lash any sail to the lifelines—it will add a penalty of windage and may block the helmsman's view.)

To prepare sails (other than roller-furling ones) for safe handling, fold and pack each so that the three attachment points (head, luff, and leech) are all together at the mouth of the sail bag. Otherwise, the sail may too easily be blown away while you're grubbing around in the bag, hank in hand, looking for a cringle. (Hank? Cringle? See appendix VII.)

SETTING SAIL

Heading into the wind and waves without the steadying effect of any sails presents one of the potentially more hazardous aspects of sailing. The crew members, working valiantly to get the sails ready on the pitching foredeck, must devote as much attention to their own security as to the job at hand. The amount of time they are thus exposed can be minimized to a large extent if the basic set of sails is hanked on and ready for hoisting before the boat gets underway.

SETTING THE MAIN

1. Loosen the mainsheet.
2. Attach the halyard to the sail head; sight up along the line to ensure that it is free and not fouled on a stay or spreader.
3. Pull up the topping lift to get the boom out of its cradle.

4. Helmsman brings the bow to within 45 degrees of the wind.
5. When ready, or on command, hoist the sail and cleat the halyard.
6. As soon as the halyard is cleated, tighten the sheet or fall off, depending on your course.
7. As the wind takes the sail, slack off the topping lift.
8. Set your course; trim the sail with the mainsheet; adjust the halyard and outhaul tension as necessary.

SETTING THE JIB

When ready to hoist:

1. Helmsman brings bow into the wind (if necessary to reduce the initial pressure on the sail);
2. Sight up along the halyard to make sure that it is clear of stays and spreaders;
3. When ready, or on command, hoist the sail;
4. Cleat the halyard; trim the sail.

SETTING A ROLLER-FURLED SAIL

The order of setting (main, then headsail) and the course to be steered (generally into the wind) are the same as for other sails. The principal caution: You must keep slight tension on the inhaul while you are unrolling the sail by pulling the *outhaul* (for the main or staysail) or the leeward sheet (for a jib or genoa). The inhaul, which lets you roll the sail up again, wraps around a drum as the sail unwinds. Should the inhaul develop an overwrap or tangle, you might be unable later to pull it out to refurl the sail. In light winds, that's not much of a problem; in heavy winds, it's a different story. In order to depower the sail, you have to release the sheets while simultaneously trying to gather up the billowing cloth, keep it from flapping, and get it under control.

SETTING THE SPINNAKER

The spinnaker is that big, parachutelike sail that adds so much to the visual beauty of sailing.

Spinnakers offer a large surface area—it's their reason for being—but can become powerful adversaries if handled carelessly. Perhaps the most common error is to fly a twisted spinnaker, producing an hourglass rather than a balloon shape. You can avoid this by making sure the sail is rigged properly before hoisting. Should it occur, however, the sail must be taken down, unhooked, untwisted, and rehoisted.

The more hazardous aspects of using a spinnaker: dipping the pole (and corner of the sail) in the water; leaving the sail up too long as the wind rises from light to heavy; getting wrapped in the sail as you try to take it down.

RACING

Racing under sail may be *the* classic example of teamwork. Each crew member is assigned specific tasks, which must be carried out with skill and precision. It is not enough to know *how* to perform the task—that knowledge must be reinforced with both training and practice; for many sailors, half the fun of racing is getting ready for it. However, racing brings added hazards to the crew. Some of these we've touched on, involving boat design and construction; others are easily enough imagined in terms of pushing the limits of wind, weather, and man. The guidelines and cautions we present in this book certainly apply to racing, but many racers may consider our boundaries overcautious and may want to push beyond them.

DOWNWIND SAILING

Running before the wind can be pleasant—and deceptive. It's pleasant because the relative wind is reduced—you're running along with the wind, rather than pushing into it; this makes the course warmer and drier. It's deceptive for the same reason—the wind seems to be less than it actually is. It can be dangerously deceptive, however, when you decide to reverse course and turn into the wind. This usually is not much of a problem on a powerboat, but on a sailboat, you can be heeled

sharply and, without warning (putting crew members in jeopardy of being launched overboard), face possible damage to unprepared sails and rigging.

BOOM VANG can be made up of block-and-tackle arrangements. A rigid spar such as the one shown here can also be incorporated. Used to help control the boom during downwind sailing, the vang also helps maintain sail shape.

SAIL HAZARDS

Uncontrolled Flapping　This hazard is hard on the sail, looks lubberly (i.e., unseamanlike), and, most significant, can be hazardous to the crew. At the least, it can deliver a stinging slap to the head or hand; at worst, it can become a potentially lethal weapon if a shackle or other piece of hardware is attached to the flapping end. Then, too, if the sail is big enough and the flapping strong enough, a crew member could be knocked overboard.

You avoid uncontrolled flapping, obviously, by keeping the sail under control with tension on the halyard and sheets. The easiest way to lose control is to lose a line—either through failure of the line or a fitting (poor maintenance is the most likely reason) or because (1) the line was not properly cleated and (2) you had neglected to tie a stopper knot in the end of the line to prevent it from running loosely through any fairlead or block.

Blown-Out Sail A blown-out sail may be the result of a rip, a failed seam, a broken fitting, or a parted line; whatever the cause, the sail is out of control and should be taken in as quickly as possible to prevent further damage. In so doing, be sure to keep the sail out of the water.

Sail in the Water While the lines are still attached to it, a sail in the water can become a giant scoop—very hard to handle and exhibiting a malevolent desire to pull someone into the water with it. The sail will also resist any logical straightforward efforts to haul it in. Solution: Release a sheet and let the sail streamline to the flow; this gets the pressure off (but be careful not to let the sail or any lines become fouled around the propeller). Then pull in the sail and bring it aboard from forward.

CHANGING COURSE: TACKING AND JIBING

TACKING

Tacking is a maneuver for changing course by swinging the bow through (across) the wind. On the new course, the wind and sails have swapped places and what was on the port side is now on the starboard side, and vice versa.

The most likely hazard in tacking is that a crew member may be hit by the boom as it moves from one side of the boat to the other. The second most likely hazard is that the boat stops in the middle of the turn, in "irons," and heads into the wind, sails flapping and bow pitching.

The first hazard is avoided by scrupulous adherence to procedures. When getting ready to change course, the helmsman sings out, "Prepare to come about," and the crew members take their assigned stations. At the command, "Ready about!" the helmsman starts the turn, the foresheet handlers slack off and haul in as necessary to let the foresail come across to the new side, the boom swings over, and *everyone* keeps a wary eye on it.

The second hazard is avoided by having enough speed before starting the turn—often achieved by first falling off (see appendix VII) slightly to build speed, then reversing rudder to make the turn. In this, don't jam the rudder hard over at the beginning of the turn—it may act more like a brake than a rudder.

If the seas are building, wait for a series of low waves to make the turn, and time the turn so the bow is at the top of a wave as it goes through the wind.

JIBING

A jibe is a maneuver for changing course by swinging the stern through the wind. Properly controlled, a jibe is a perfectly acceptable evolution; improperly controlled or accidental, a jibe can be a disaster as the boom slams from one side to the other with potentially damaging force—a hazard to the rigging and any crew member caught unaware.

The secret to a controlled jibe is simple: Alert the crew with a "prepare to jibe" command, send them into action with a "jibe-ho!" and keep the boom under steady control with the sheet, pulling it in quickly as the helmsman changes course and easing it out smoothly as the wind takes the sail on the new heading. The foresheets are slacked off just before the jibe, and the reaching or spinnaker pole (if rigged) is taken in. The poles are replaced and the sheets retensioned once the foresail has come over to the downwind side.

One caution: Do *not* cleat the mainsheet tightly as the boom swings through. A gusty wind could catch the sail—now firmly held at the centerline—and blow the boat around into a broach (see below).

An accidental jibe usually is the unwanted consequence of downwind sailing, particularly when sailing wing-and-wing. While it is unintended, it usually does not happen without some warning. Be sensitive to the first signs of a shift in the wind—you may feel it on the back of your neck or detect it in the flapping of the telltale on the backstay. The boom may rise and the main start luffing. Don't wait for anything else to happen; immediately change course *toward* the wind—that is, bring the wind more on the beam opposite the side on which the main is set. Get everything under control and settle back on a better course for the new wind direction.

In light winds, the boom may have a tendency to swing a bit aimlessly and then, suddenly, the boat takes a roll and the boom slams over to the other side. Do not sail downwind with the wind and the boom on the same side of the boat; adjust course so that the wind is coming over the quarter opposite the boom. This keeps pressure on the sail to stay in position even in very light winds.

All of the above having been said, the best pre-vention against an accidental jibe is to rig a pre-venter or a vang. The preventer is a line hooked to the boom and run forward to a fitting on deck, to hold the boom out to the side. The vang typically is a block-and-tackle arrangement run down from the boom to a fitting on the deck or cabintop, to hold the boom down. These lines must be released immediately before making a controlled jibe, and then reattached (on the other side of the boat) on the new course. Be aware that these devices can become dangerous liabilities in higher winds and seas. If your position changes in relation to the wind (by a wind shift to leeward or the force of the waves), the lateral push on the restricted sail could cause the boat to broach.

AS THE WIND INCREASES

When the wind begins to rise to the point where it threatens to take control, you must reduce the sail area upon which the wind is acting. This keeps the boat sailing and keeps the sails from being torn apart. At 15 knots, the wind pressure is about one pound per square foot of sail area; double the wind speed and the pressure is increased four times.

A sail under too much pressure is a hazard to itself and to the boat, so you actually must reduce the sail area *before* the wind takes over. A weak seam may fail; a worn-out line may part; the excessive pressure may heel the boat beyond the point of prudence, where the lee rail is churning along under the surface of the water. Forget all of those dramatic photos of racing boats dipping the rail; that's not *you* unless you are experienced well past the level of this book. If the wind pressure becomes too great, the shrouds or stays may fail, with a catastrophic ultimate result: dismasting.

How much wind is "too much"? The answer depends upon the size of your boat, the type and condition of the rig. It might be 12 to 15 knots for a daysailer, 18 to 20 knots for a racer-cruiser, higher for a world-class open-ocean cruising boat. One good sign of the need to reduce sail: increased weather helm. If there's too much wind pressure on the mainsail, the boat will be twisting into the wind and require constant heavy rudder to stay on course.

Incidentally, reducing sail does not necessarily mean reducing speed; under many conditions, you'll actually sail faster because the boat will be in better balance, using and not fighting the wind.

You can reduce sail area in one of several ways. For the main, you reduce the area by reefing. To keep the headsail in balance with the reduced main, you can change the sail, rigging a smaller and sturdier jib, and/or reef the sail as conditions require. (Reefing gear is described in chapter 8; steps to take when the weather has deteriorated well beyond normal safe levels are detailed in chapter 20.) In *this* section, we'll walk through the methods for reducing sail when the wind level rises unexpectedly during an otherwise routine day of sailing and before you are into heavy weather.

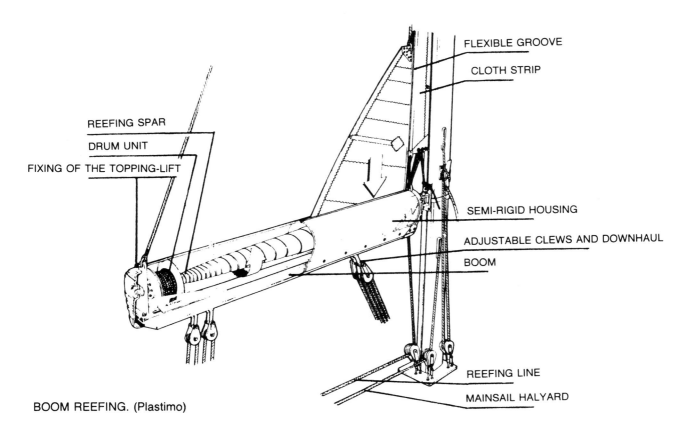

REEFING SPAR

DRUM UNIT

FIXING OF THE TOPPING-LIFT

FLEXIBLE GROOVE

CLOTH STRIP

SEMI-RIGID HOUSING

ADJUSTABLE CLEWS AND DOWNHAUL

BOOM

REEFING LINE

MAINSAIL HALYARD

BOOM REEFING. (Plastimo)

REEFING

PREPARATIONS

When headed out of port and into a wind that you know—or suspect—might be too high, reef before you reach the open waters. If your caution proves unnecessary, it is far easier to shake out the reef than to try to put one in during a stiff breeze.

• Wear a safety harness, clipped to a jackline or deck structure, to allow free use of both hands while reefing.

• Stand to windward of the sail.

• With a single-masted boat (sloop or cutter), reef the main first: It presents the greater area and therefore the more urgent need.

• With a divided rig (ketch or yawl), begin by reducing the mizzen, then the main. In heavy weather, you are likely to fly a storm jib and storm mizzen, without a main.

• Aboard a schooner, reduce the mainsail first.

REEFING THE MAIN

1. Get the wind off the sail and align the boom with the centerline by heading almost into the wind, if possible.

2. Avoid heading dead into the wind to prevent coming about unintentionally; luff the sail only as necessary to get the reef points secured.

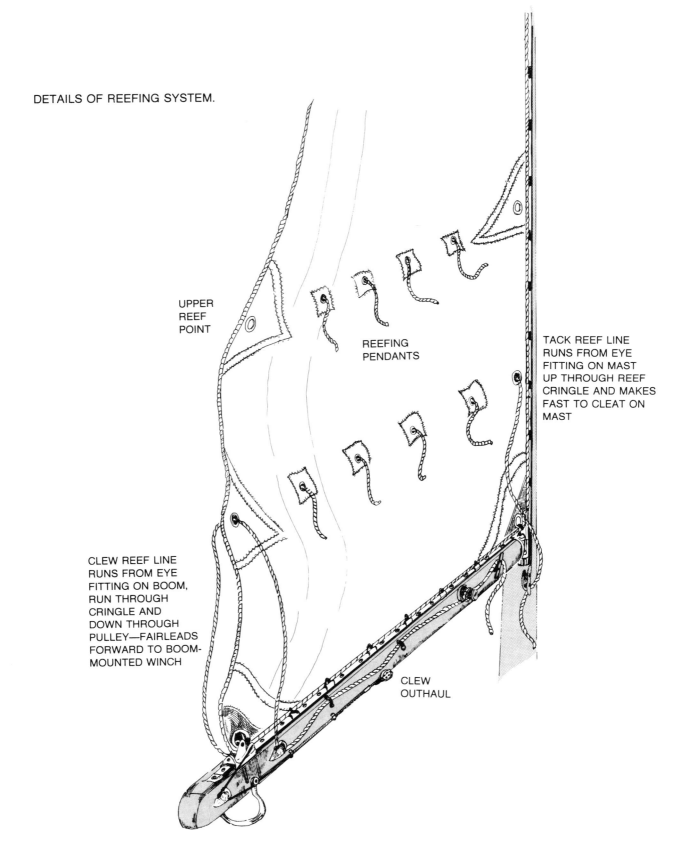

DETAILS OF REEFING SYSTEM.

UPPER
REEF
POINT

REEFING
PENDANTS

TACK REEF LINE
RUNS FROM EYE
FITTING ON MAST
UP THROUGH REEF
CRINGLE AND MAKES
FAST TO CLEAT ON
MAST

CLEW REEF LINE
RUNS FROM EYE
FITTING ON BOOM,
RUN THROUGH
CRINGLE AND
DOWN THROUGH
PULLEY—FAIRLEADS
FORWARD TO BOOM-
MOUNTED WINCH

CLEW
OUTHAUL

3. Work quickly before the boat loses too much speed.

Traditional Reefing

1. Take up on the topping lift.
2. Slack the halyard.
3. Pull down on the downhaul or reefing pendants to bring the reef cringles to the boom.
4. Attach the forward pendant to the gooseneck and tie the after pendant around the boom.
5. Use the reef points to secure the belly of the sail; if possible, tie them under the sail itself, and *not* under the boom.

Jiffy Reefing

1. Take up on the topping lift.
2. Slack the halyard.
3. Take in on the downhaul or reefing line; this will pull the aft reefing cringle to the boom, then the forward reefing cringle to the boom. Hook each one to the boom.
4. Use the reef points to secure the belly of the sail.
5. Tighten the halyard; slack off the topping lift.

Jiffy reefing can largely be handled from the cockpit—a great advantage for shorthanded or singlehanded sailors.

CHANGING A HEADSAIL WHILE UNDERWAY

With a pair of forestays, it's easy to have a second jib already clipped on, tied down to the toerail, and ready for use. Get the first sail down; shift the halyard; transfer the sheets; hoist the new jib; get the "old" one under control.

If there is only one forestay, you will need to follow these procedures:

1. Attach the tack.
2. Unclip the bottom two hanks of the drawing jib and fasten all of the hanks for the new sail (bottom hank first).
3. Lower the drawing sail, unclipping hanks as you go.
4. Transfer the sheets to the new jib.
5. Switch the halyard from the head of the old sail to the head of the new one. When ready, or upon command, hoist and trim.
6. Finish securing the old jib, either to stow it below or ready it for reuse.

REEFING A HEADSAIL

1. Take a downwind course, if practicable, to steady the boat and keep the deck drier. Otherwise, head into the wind.
2. Bring the luff cringle down to the bow fitting and shackle.
3. Bring the leech cringle down to the bottom of the sail and tie it.
4. Transfer the sheets to the leech cringle.
5. Don't leave the belly of the sail lying on the deck; secure with reef points.

Spinnaker The spinnaker is only for light to moderate winds; it can't be reefed and must be taken down early—before the wind builds up and makes removal both difficult and dangerous.

DROPPING SAIL

The key: Get the wind out of the sail and then let it fall, under control of the halyard, as the crew gathers it in at the foot—unless an emergency requires an immediate dousing, which means you let the halyard go quickly and hope for the best. In such an event, it will be helpful to have a set of lazyjacks rigged to catch the billowing cloth as the sail drops.

To take in a headsail when sailing downwind or nearly so, the best course is to come around into the wind. Taking in the genoa on a downwind course can be particularly tricky: Unless the sail is blanketed by the main (or unless the winds are particularly light), it will tend to be blown forward and may fall into the water.

To take in any sail with roller furling, lead the inhaul to the winch and take two or three turns; get the wind out of the sail; slack the sheets and take in on the inhaul (by hand while you can, then using the winch). Maintain slight tension on the sheet to keep the sail from wrapping itself around the wrong way.

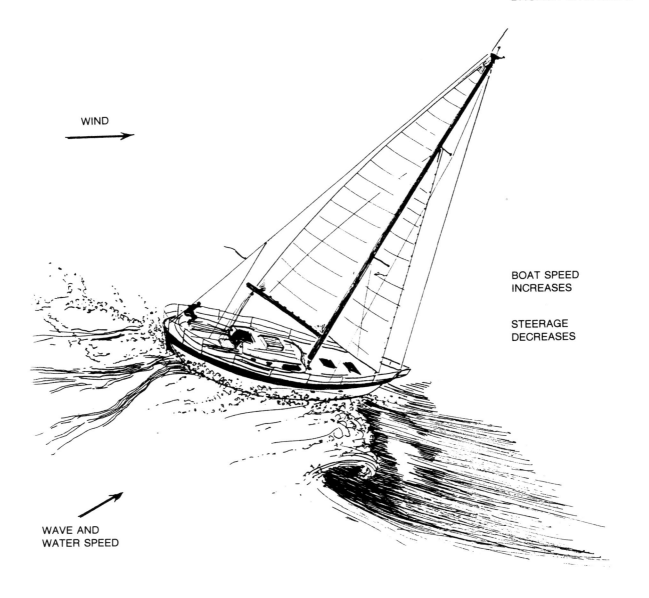

BROACH SITUATION.

WIND

BOAT SPEED
INCREASES

STEERAGE
DECREASES

WAVE AND
WATER SPEED

BROACHING

Broaching occurs when your boat is caught at right angles to the waves (and usually the wind as well) without the forward speed or available power to continue turning away. This puts the boat in danger of, at the least, unmerciful rolling, and at the worst, being capsized.

The condition most likely to result in a broach: sailing downwind with a strong following sea just off the quarter. A wave can literally pick up the stern and swing it around into a broach. If running downwind, try to keep the seas square astern; be sensitive to any shift in the wind or waves away from aft, and follow them around. If wind and waves are rising, reduce or take in the mainsail, using only headsails; this will offset the twisting moment of the following seas.

For specific guidance on heavy-weather seamanship and tactics, see chapter 20.

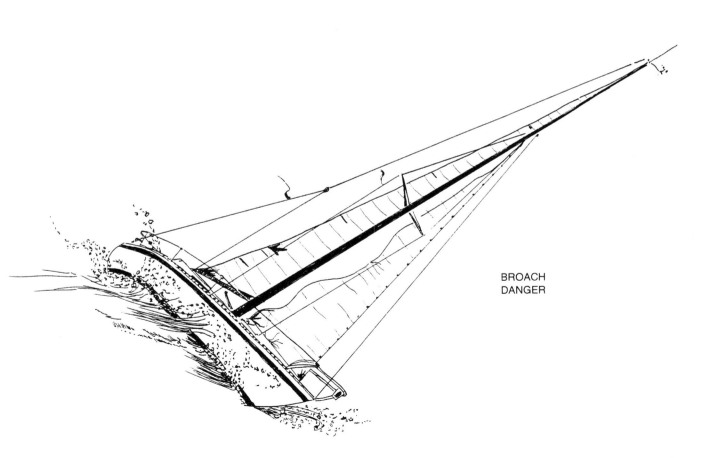

BROACH
DANGER

CHAPTER FIFTEEN

Anchoring

The selection of ground tackle was described in chapter 8; in this section, we take a look at where and how to use the anchor.

SELECTING AN ANCHORAGE

For a bit of fishing or swimming on a clear day, almost any spot might do for an anchorage, provided that: the water is not too deep or too shallow; the area is not subject to overwhelming wave or current action; you're not in the middle of a shipping channel or harbor entrance; and the bottom is free of entangling obstructions. Any spot might do, that is, as long as you *check it out thoroughly.*

Your chart will indicate depth of water and type of bottom and will note any known wrecks or obstructions. The presence of other boats anchored nearby may be a good sign; the total absence of such may—or may not—be meaningful, but it should suggest some caution. In any event, don't play follow-the (possibly inept)-leader; use *your* best judgment.

Explore a proposed anchorage by slowly circling the spot where you expect to place the anchor, checking the depth finder for any uncharted shoals or obstructions. If you have a reasonably sensitive unit—particularly a "fishfinder" type, which displays the bottom and indicates depth—you can spot such hazards as rocks and abandoned mooring anchors.

For an overnight (or longer) stay at anchor, where the tide and current and wind are all likely to change, you'll need to take a closer look at the chart. You'll want good holding ground—a bottom in which your anchor will take a firm bite. In general, anchors hold best in sand or mud, not well at all in heavy grass, and they can get fouled up in rocks and coral. Therefore, try to pick a spot with a sand or mud bottom; failing that, use the best type of anchor for the situation (as described in chapter 8).

You'll want a sheltered area such as a small cove or a protected harbor—sheltered from both wind and wave, if possible. If you have to make a choice between those two devils, try to avoid the waves and heavy swells—they make for an uncomfortable night and may dislodge the anchor. On the other hand, a steady wind might not be bad: It could keep flying insects at bay, and the slight strain will ensure that the anchor is dug in. However, don't take the wind for granted: A wind blowing onshore in the afternoon may reverse

after sunset; the passage of a weather front can bring a radical wind shift.

Try to find an area that is not subject to heavy tidal currents, because the shifting tide may pull the anchor free. More nerve-racking is an anchorage near a heavily traveled channel or a ferry crossing. The anchorage will prove more interesting for you and the crew if there is an easy landing spot close by—for a bit of sightseeing or a stroll on the beach or for reaching shore-side services. All of these features will be indicated on the chart.

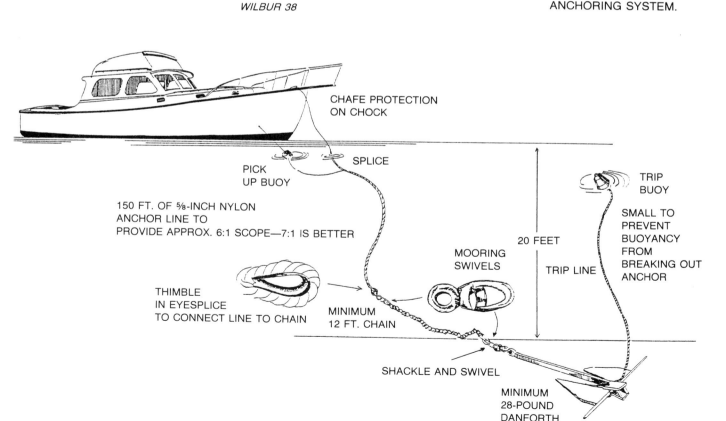

WILBUR 38

ANCHORING SYSTEM.

CHAFE PROTECTION ON CHOCK

SPLICE

PICK UP BUOY

150 FT. OF ⅝-INCH NYLON ANCHOR LINE TO PROVIDE APPROX. 6:1 SCOPE—7:1 IS BETTER

TRIP BUOY

SMALL TO PREVENT BUOYANCY FROM BREAKING OUT ANCHOR

20 FEET

MOORING SWIVELS

TRIP LINE

THIMBLE IN EYESPLICE TO CONNECT LINE TO CHAIN

MINIMUM 12 FT. CHAIN

SHACKLE AND SWIVEL

MINIMUM 28-POUND DANFORTH ANCHOR

ANCHORING

1. Verify that the anchor is ready for use and that the anchor rode is free to run.

2. Make sure that the foredeck crew and the helmsman (assuming you will be one or the other) have discussed the procedures and have worked out a set of simple hand signals.

3. Having picked the spot, head slowly into the wind or current until the bow reaches the point where the anchor should be let go. This is *not* where the boat will be when at anchor—it's perhaps two or three boatlengths upwind.

4. Stop the boat and lower the anchor. Let the boat move back with the wind or current, and aid it by backing the engine slowly to keep the boat pointed upwind/upcurrent.

5. Allow the anchor rode to pay out until it reaches the proper scope. This can be determined in advance by laying out the rode on deck to the correct length, or by using distance markers on the rode. The length of the rode will be determined by the depth of water expected at high tide, the expected weather, and the type of rode itself. Typically, a nylon rode with 10 to 12 feet of chain should be set at a length between five and seven times the depth of the water—more in time of wind and wave, less if you have an all-chain rode.

6. Snub the rode on a cleat or samson post, and allow the anchor to set itself on the bottom by continuing to back down slowly until the boat stops.

7. Then, increase engine speed somewhat, to ensure that the anchor truly has set. To verify this, notice your position in relation to landmarks or anything floating nearby on the surface.

8. When you are satisfied that the anchor has set, reduce speed gradually to idle, shift to neutral, and stop the engine. If you shift to neutral or stop the engine abruptly, the boat might spring forward—pulled by the tension in the rode—and dislodge the anchor.

9. Unless you are in a special anchorage area, as designated on the chart, you must next hoist the daytime black anchor ball, or turn on your anchor light. In one fatal accident on a dark, moonless night in the Florida Keys, a woman sleeping aboard a houseboat was killed when a speeding runabout cut straight through her bedroom. If the houseboat was displaying an anchor light—which seems doubtful—the operator of the runabout apparently did not see it; or, if he did, he didn't know what it meant.

SPECIAL CONDITIONS

In a crowded anchorage where the boats cannot swing without fouling or colliding, or in an area where a full swing would put your boat up on the beach, you should use two anchors, bow and stern (or tie your stern to a tree ashore). In an area with a heavy tidal current, however, the stern anchor might not hold—the force of water working sideways against the keel, rudders, and stern can overpower the anchor. The "Bahamian moor" is a two-anchor alternative that allows the boat to swing with the tides—but only within its own length, thus not endangering other boats in a crowded anchorage. With this system, both anchors are set from the bow, equidistant from the

boat along the axis of the current. The boat is thus centered between them, swinging from the bow but not going anywhere.

Some boats have an annoying habit of sailing back-and-forth in any sort of a wind, and the oscillating sideways pull can reach the anchor and break it loose. This danger can be minimized by using two anchors set about 45 degrees apart, with the lighter anchor about two boatlengths farther to windward.

Before setting a second anchor—whether from the bow or from the stern—make sure the *first* anchor is well set. Then mark the rode at the proper scope, slack off that rode, and move over to the spot for laying the second anchor (or drop back to the spot for the stern anchor). Drop the second anchor and back down (or go forward) until it, too, is set. Finally, cleat the first anchor rode at the mark; adjust and cleat the other rode.

If you must anchor with an unacceptably short scope—in a particularly crowded anchorage or one with unusual geographic constraints—you can improve holding power by using a catenary weight along the rode. The weight will slide down the rode to the bottom, holding more of it along the bottom and thereby increasing the lateral pull. The weight also dampens the upward jerking of the rode that otherwise can pull the anchor free. These weights are commercially available with a sliding shackle, or you can improvise with a *sturdy* scrub bucket filled with heavy tools or chain—all firmly attached to prevent spilling. Attach a length of light line to the sliding shackle (or bucket handle) so that you can control the position of the weight and also retrieve it before hauling in the anchor. A catenary weight also can be used with a rode of normal or long scope to increase holding power against wind and waves. (For information on anchoring in heavy weather, see chapter 20.)

Anchor Buoy

Easily made from a fender or a plastic detergent or bleach bottle, an anchor buoy is a handy accessory. Attach it to the anchor with a piece of small line a bit longer than the depth of the water (allowing for tidal changes). The buoy will float right over the anchor, helping you to head toward it when getting ready to leave, and alerting other boats not to drop their anchors on top of yours. If the line is sturdy enough, it also can be used to help break the anchor free, should it become dug in too firmly.

Things That Can Go Wrong—and How to Avoid Them

Anchoring is a skill best honed on a calm day when no other boats are in the vicinity. As a friendly warning, here is a list of things that can go *wrong*:

1. The anchor isn't ready—it's still lashed to the foredeck—when the skipper signals, ''Let go!''
2. The rode becomes intermingled with stray mooring lines (which should have been stowed the moment you left the dock) or gets wrapped around the ankle of a crew member who is too intent on checking the position of the anchor.
3. The backward speed of the boat—from wind, current, or power—is too high; the rode is whistling over the bow too fast to be snubbed off. (Don't hesitate to throttle back and shift from astern to ahead to control the speed.)
4. A crew member tries to grab the rode—and gets painful rope burns. (A pair of gloves is a piece of safety gear too often overlooked.)
5. The bitter end of the rode (which is supposed to be secured in some fashion in the chain locker) does not hold, and it follows the anchor to the bottom.
6. The helmsman, too intent on the foredeck action, neglects to check astern and fouls his propeller on the anchor rode of another boat. Or he smashes into another boat.
7. The anchor doesn't set because:

• The scope was too short, not permitting a good parallel pull along the bottom.
• The anchor landed upside down or on its side—or even in an ideal orientation—and wasn't given the necessary setting pull.
• You're using the wrong type of anchor for the bottom, or the anchor is simply too small to do the job.
• You've got the right anchor, but during an aborted first attempt, the flukes dredge up a good load of mud or clay. Unless the anchor is hauled all the way up and dunked to remove that cargo, the mud balls may keep the flukes from digging in.
8. With an anchor finally set, the boat settles into place—too far back from the intended position because of one or more of the following: (1) The anchor was not put in the right spot; (2) the boat was moving back before the anchor touched bottom; (3) the scope is too long; (4) the anchor was dragged back a distance before setting. The anchor must be raised and reset.
9. You have used the right anchor, and it's now properly set—and halfway through the night you notice that the boat doesn't seem to be floating. You have committed the cardinal anchoring sin: You didn't check the depth around the anchorage and didn't verify the tide. Until the tide returns, you are now as well set on the bottom as your anchor.

THE ANCHOR AS A TOOL

The sturdy anchor that helps you stay in place can also help you get *out* of a place where you don't want to stay. A grounded boat can use an anchor—taken by dinghy as far back as line and depth allow—to provide a solid point against which to pull. You can provide the pulling power by hand with a halyard winch or—if so equipped—an anchor windlass. (If it's electric, keep a wary eye on the state of the battery charge.) This kedging operation is explained in more detail in chapter 22.

WEIGHING THE ANCHOR

Pulling up the anchor usually is easier than setting it. First, slowly move up on the anchor while a crew member hauls in the rode. When the rode is straight up-and-down, the anchor should have broken free of the bottom. At this point, of course, the boat is no longer anchored and the helmsman needs to pay closer attention to navigation than to the activity on the foredeck. This is particularly important in an area of high current, where you can be swept into danger before you realize it. High current also requires a closer coordination between helm and foredeck; unless your boat speed matches or slightly exceeds the force of the current, the foredeck crew will be unable to haul in the anchor rode. Crew members also will become good candidates for painful rope burns if they try to use brute strength to hold the boat in position.

What if the anchor won't come off the bottom? First try using engine power to break the anchor free. Move ahead slowly, taking in the rode as you go, until the bow is right over the anchor. Snub the rode down tight and go forward slowly. The foredeck crew should stand clear and not try to pull on the rode. If nothing happens, shift to neutral—the anchor may be hooked on an object or on another boat's anchor line, and added power won't necessarily help the situation. You may need to unfoul the anchor—or be prepared to cut it loose and leave it.

Unfouling is relatively easy in the crystal-clear waters of the Bahamas, where you can see the problem and watch your progress as you use boathooks or grappling hooks, or carefully manipulate the rode. In most parts of the world, however, you're operating blind. Carefully work the anchor rode, try to assess the cause, and do your best. A closeup inspection using diving or snorkeling equipment may offer the only chance to save the anchor.

Here's one more abnormal situation: Let's assume that, because of an earlier emergency, you had to drop anchor without time to thoroughly check the water depth and the state of the tide. Now you must get underway, but the water over the anchor has become too shallow for your boat to ride up to it, and the anchor, well set, will not work free. So you launch the dinghy and try to work the anchor from that platform, without success. A possible solution: You and any other crew members move to the bow of the dinghy and take in as much rode as possible. Snub it so tight that the bow is dipping well down. Then, everyone move aft. The lever action just may do the job.

CHAPTER SIXTEEN

End of the Voyage

RETURNING TO PORT

The transition from open-water boating to a congested channel, and from a relatively relaxed operation to a potentially high-stress one, tends to make the end of a voyage the most hazardous phase. Think about these factors:

1. You may be tired—the cumulative effects of hard work, several hours of standing, and exposure to the sun or rain or spray (or all three).

2. You may have violated common sense and consumed a couple of beers. Most certainly, *some* of the boaters crowding into the channel with you will have consumed more than a few, but you won't know which ones. Sail defensively.

3. The light of day may be failing fast.

4. The hazard of grounding is greatly increased.

5. Tidal currents and weather-driven waves may create dangerous conditions, especially in any narrowing waterway, such as an inlet from the ocean.

PREPARATIONS FOR ENTERING PORT

Before you reach the point where considerations may turn into crisis, *prepare* for the end of the voyage:

- Recheck the tide and current tables.
- Break out the harbor chart and have it handy.
- Clean the windshield.
- Be sure that the radio is set on channel 16, with the volume at the right level.
- Check the air horn for pressure.
- Check the depth finder, the wind indicator, and the radar for proper settings.
- Have all loose gear—including personal and recreational equipment—off the decks and stowed.
- Verify that the anchor is ready for instant use.

• If you are racing sunset into port, test the running lights.

Aboard a sailboat, get your sails under control while still offshore. Don't get caught in the middle of the channel trying to drop and furl all sails, particularly on a gusty day.

Finally, have the crew and guests *sit down,* or at least be sure they are not blocking your line of sight. If any children are aboard, they must be totally under the control of someone other than the skipper.

RADAR INSTALLATION in a substantial cruising sailboat cockpit solves a continuing problem—where to put sensitive electronics in open cockpits. This radar can be moved below easily but is available for easy viewing by the cockpit crew during fine weather conditions.

Now, the above comments apply when returning to a familiar port in relatively good weather. If visibility is reduced by heavy fog or an opaque tropical downpour, *stop,* anchor, sound your fog signals, and wait.

For an unfamiliar destination, the hazards increase geometrically and preparation must be even more focused. Review the *Waterway Guide* or *Sailing Directions;* double-check the charts; verify the position and markings of the channel; locate any hazards to navigation; find your destination—whether an anchorage or a marina—and recheck the route.

A voice radio call to the marina in advance of arrival not only will verify a berth for the night but also may provide some useful "local knowledge" to ease your way:

Bluewater Marina, this is *Endeavour* Whiskey Bravo 5730 passing the Bay Bridge and requesting confirmation of berth. We are a 65-foot motorsailer drawing six and a half feet and require shore power. Our ETA your location is 1430 hours. . . .

Endeavour, this is Bluewater Marina. Your slip will be outboard at the near end of A dock; we'll be watching for you. Be sure to take a left turn just past the Moran dredge and come in by the back channel. The railroad bridge over the main channel has been jammed shut all day. . . .

Bluewater has given you some useful advice—which should send you back to the *Waterway Guide* and the chart and prompt increased vigilance as you pick your way along. That detour may not be as well marked or maintained as the main channel: Markers may be missing, the depth may be less than advertised, the dredge may have set an anchor right at the edge of the channel.

MAKING A NIGHT APPROACH

1. Protect your night vision; avoid bright lights in the cockpit; beware of spotlights from passing boats—especially patrol boats of customs agents or law enforcement officials.

2. Have your own spotlight or a good flashlight ready for use in picking out unlighted daymarks—both for identification and for avoidance.

3. Make an absolute identification of the entrance buoy to ensure that you are where you think you are when starting up the channel.

4. If you have radar, use it—both as an aid to navigation and to help signal your presence to other shipping. Your radar sweep may throw an interference pattern on the other guy's scope.

5. Keep a good log: course, speed, time of changes, and time of passing marks and buoys. Some approaches may take several hours; should you become confused, or should anything irregular occur, you can stop and review your progress in the log.

6. Be alert for any passing, crossing, or overtaking traffic. Don't trust the other guy to follow the Rules of the Road—particularly small fishermen, who may not even know there *are* Rules of the Road.

7. Be prepared to identify any "unusual" pattern of running lights—those that mark tugs and tows, dredges, and disabled vessels are there to keep you out of danger.

8. Be particularly concerned about sorting out the meaningful lights from the clutter. Blinking traffic lights ashore—even the car brake lights—can be easily mistaken for channel markers.

RETURNING TO A SLIP

Getting back into the slip may not be as easy as the departure from it a few hours earlier. At the end of a jolly day's sail, the judgment and skill of too many skippers have been impaired by fatigue generated from standing up at the wheel all day, cranking winches, yelling at errant children, and drinking too much beer. At the same time, the weather so often seems to have turned sour—with a fresh breeze where before there were only lazy zephyrs, and a strong current seemingly determined to set the boat across the bows protruding from several adjacent slips.

The sound of a skipper in trouble is an engine racing ahead, then crash-shifted astern—still at full rpm—and then again ahead with such stunning swiftness that the boat barely moves in any direction.

If the wind and current have gotten the best of you, stop fighting. Tie up somewhere; hook onto a piling. Relax while you plan a more useful strategy. From this point, it may be easiest to pull the boat into the slip by hand (using the mooring lines you have thoughtfully taken along on your afternoon's cruise). As long as you have a line fast to something solid, you're not going to drift into danger or into other boats.

TYING UP

You are not yet safe. Remember that if the skipper is tired, the crew and guests—less accustomed to boating, less cautious about becoming fatigued—will be even more so. There are new hazards to avoid: getting hands or feet crushed between the boat and a piling; being struck by a line that snaps under too much tension; moving too quickly to be helpful and then slipping and falling overboard.

Have your fenders out; have a "portable" fender ready for use. The first line ashore should be amidships, for use as a springline; if you put the bow line over first, you may lose control of the stern; with the stern line over, the bow may swing out—and into the boat alongside.

Keep control of the lines on your boat; don't trust the judgment or experience of dockboys or helpful strangers.

If your berth is alongside a floating pier, you need not worry about adjusting your mooring lines for the tidal range. Otherwise, based on your experience in your own home port, you should have marked your lines at the make-fast point with a strip of cloth, for example, tucked into the lay of the line. If you do so, you'll be able to tie up in exactly the right position every time.

At the point where it passes through a chock or over a rail, each line should be protected against chafing with some chafing gear. This can be a rubber hose (split along its length, for easy placement on the line) or a wrapping of heavy canvas or leather; whichever, it must be secured with some small line to prevent it from being worked out of position by the movement of the boat.

If the weather looks threatening, put out a double set of lines for extra security.

Turn off your engine and hook up the shore-power connector. Flip the switch on the pier and then the one on the boat (watching or listening for the "reverse polarity" warning).

SECURING THE BOAT

When leaving your boat for a time, your routine should be as distinct as the one you followed when preparing to get underway. Some suggestions:

1. Make a quick check of the bilges for an unexpected level or a flow of water. You may have unknowingly bumped into something or strained a seam, putting the boat in a sort of silent jeopardy.

2. Extinguish all pilot lights and close all fuel valves.

3. Turn off all unneeded electrical equipment; disconnect all unneeded circuits at the main distribution panel. Turn off the main battery switch. Make sure that the bilge-pump switch is in the automatic position.

4. Close all seacocks. "All" means *all:* main intake valve, plumbing, overboard waste-discharge lines, refrigerator cooling-water intake, generator cooling-water intake. This is an area about which we all tend to become too complacent.

Modern marine seacocks, we assume, are virtually indestructible, and modern marine plumbing is designed to last virtually forever. However, every year a handful of boats sink alongside piers when a seacock or line gives way, unnoticed. A handful is not many—unless one of them was yours. Regular exercise of the seacocks also keeps them unfrozen, ensuring that they can be closed quickly in an emergency.

5. If your boat is not well ventilated, take ashore any wet clothing and damp bedding. With adequate ventilation, these items could be left aboard, if properly spread out to dry. *Do not* leave wet items piled in a corner or stuffed in a locker.

6. Sink, stove, and icebox must be clean and free of random bits of food; all trash and garbage must be taken ashore. If any food is being left aboard, it must be stored in tightly sealed containers, such as those made by Tupperware. The cockroach has an appetite for almost anything, and the sturdy varieties in the Caribbean or South Florida, for example, will easily cut through plastic wrapping to get at the goodies inside.

7. Removable topside equipment should be stowed below, to prevent anyone else from removing it.

8. Lockers should be *locked.*

9. Make a final check of the mooring lines. Think "tides" and think "storm," and determine whether your mooring lines are set and in proper condition for both.

10. Cancel your float plan. You're home safe; don't trigger an expensive and possibly hazardous search for your "overdue" boat.

CHAPTER SEVENTEEN

Small Boats

Throughout most of this book, our focus is on boats of moderate size and above—that is, boats capable of weekend cruises or realistic offshore operation. This is not the result of preference or prejudice; rather, it grows out of an inherently wider range of equipment, operating conditions, and potential for trouble. However, the overwhelming majority of boats in use are smaller—more than half are under 16 feet—and 75 percent of reported accidents and personal injury involve boats under 26 feet. In this chapter, we'll take a closer look at small-boat safety.

We'll start with a proposition: Small boats are not inherently more dangerous, but the people who operate them may be inherently less concerned. To many people—operators and passengers alike—rowboats, canoes, outboard runabouts, and fishermen are simply outside the rules. These are for recreation; larger boats—for which you need training and skill—are too much like work.

Of particular concern: Many small boats are operated by children, who have little training and less maturity and therefore require supervision. Too many people send their kids off to play in the boat—with tragic consequences.

Much of the material in this book applies to all boats, large or small; the points that follow are more specifically directed at small-boat operations.

SMALL-BOAT AQUATIC SAFETY

According to the National Safety Council, drowning is the second leading cause of accidental death for Americans between the ages of one and forty-four. Most of these victims did not intend to be, or were unprepared to be, in the water.

In chapter 23, we cover the subject of "man overboard" in some detail, but in that section, we presume that the individual will have fallen from a boat operating in open water, often in heavy weather. In small-boat operations, people often

---

Mounting an Outboard

- Never step from the pier to the boat while carrying the motor. Get in the boat first and then take the motor aboard—preferably with an assist from someone on the pier.
- Fasten the safety line before horsing the motor into position on the transom.
- Tighten the motor mounting clamps as securely as possible, to minimize the effect of engine vibration.
- Make sure the motor is mounted straight-up-and-down. If the shaft is tilted aft, the propeller will force the bow up when underway; if the shaft is tilted forward, the bow will be forced down. Either condition interferes with efficient operation and increases the danger of swamping.

---

go overboard on purpose—for swimming, for waterskiing, for wading ashore—and they may be in as much jeopardy as the storm-tossed bluewater sailor knocked overboard by a wave.

Here are some key points to remember in order to keep "safety" in the overboard aspects of your boating.

1. Know whether there are any nonswimmers in your boat; if they fall overboard, they'll require special help—quickly.

2. Do not leave small children unattended, even for a moment.

3. When swimming in unfamiliar water, *always* enter the water feet first; *do not dive.* Someone capable of operating the boat should remain in the boat; that person should also be a capable swimmer.

4. When operating (particularly with an engine) near swimmers, exercise *great* caution.

5. Be alert for the signs of any swimmer in trouble. A drowning victim may be too busy trying to breathe to call for help.

6. If you spot a problem, you have both a legal and a moral obligation to help; you do not have an obligation to risk your own life.

7. To provide assistance:

- Get some flotation device to the swimmer as quickly as possible, but be aware that he may be unable—because of panic, confusion, injury, or total lack of swimming ability—to grab the device.
- If feasible, get your boat alongside the swimmer (transmission in neutral, slow approach).
- Get a line to the swimmer and bring him aboard over the stern.
- Put someone else in the water *only* if necessary, and provide that person with any available flotation—an air mattress, a surfboard, a life jacket.
- Be wary of a terrified victim who may fight, rather than welcome, assistance.

In our judgment, anyone who operates a boat not only should know how to swim but also should have the benefit of Red Cross–sponsored lifesaving training, readily available from many local schools, municipal swimming pools, and organizations such as the YMCA and YWCA.

LOADING

Just because a boat has ten places to sit does not mean it will carry ten people safely. The Coast Guard loading plate specifies the maximum number of passengers, which must *not* be exceeded. A common violation of this commonsense (and legal) limit: hauling passengers in a dinghy between boat and shore, and vice versa. Trying to save an extra round-trip by crowding in an extra passenger or two may prove to be a fatal mistake.

The load—of passengers *and* equipment— should be distributed evenly so that the boat floats on an even keel.

Safety equipment should be accessible but attached to the boat; in the event of capsize, you don't want your signaling gear headed for the bottom and your life jackets scudding away downwind. Make it a practice to rig an "equipment line" with all safety gear snapped onto it.

You can carry this line between home and the boat, along with your fishing gear and other "removables."

When renting a small boat, take nothing for granted (especially the assurances of the dockboys). All too often, small-boat operators do not adequately inform themselves about their cruising waters. Take along a marine chart or similarly detailed inland water chart no matter what the size of your boat. Local advice is a supplement, not a substitute. Check the condition of the boat and equipment; examine the loading plate to verify the maximum allowable outboard-motor size and load limit. Assemble your own safety gear (see above)—the rental operator no doubt will provide life jackets, but you should also have a flashlight, signaling gear, and a first-aid kit.

WATERSKIING

A boat used for waterskiing must have a towing rig designed to prevent the towline, when slackened, from fouling the prop. It also must have sufficient power to keep the skier moving smartly, and not just slogging along. (That puts a strain on the boat, limits maneuverability, and probably isn't much fun anyway.) The ski equipment should be well made and made for the purpose—no homemade rigs or inner tubes.

In choosing an area for waterskiing, don't just pick a place that's convenient to the launching ramp: You'll just be crowding in with all of the other unsafe boat operators. Avoid areas of high traffic, fast currents (better, no current at all), popular fishing grounds, and such obstructions and obstacles as bridges and construction equipment.

WATERSKIING.

Know the skill level of the skier and adjust your maneuvers accordingly. For teaching beginners, find a spot with shallow water for the take-off. Don't try launching any skier from a pier.

Never operate with fewer than two people in the boat: one to drive and one to observe. The observer should be facing aft, with only one assignment—watch the skier; the driver should keep his attention forward, on the lookout for swimmers and floating debris. (The operator *can* watch the swimmer, however, if the boat is equipped with a special water-ski rear-view mirror.)

The boat operator is responsible for safe operation and is in charge.

The skier must be wearing appropriate flotation gear—a vest or, at the minimum, a ski belt. Don't use a regular life jacket; it can be torn loose too easily during an impact with the water, particularly in higher-skill-level maneuvers such as jumping a ramp. Use flotation gear rated for waterskiing.

ACCEPTED HAND SIGNALS BETWEEN WATER-SKIER AND TOWBOAT: (1) Speed up; (2) Slow down; (3) Turn the boat; (4) Return to the starting dock; (5) Stop, cut the motor; (6) OK, i.e., the speed is OK, the course is satisfactory, etc.; (7) OK (after a fall). (American Water Ski Association)

Be sensible, not inventive. For example, a skier trying to work his way forward and into the boat while underway risks serious injury. Leave stunts to the water-show specialists.

Ensure that the operator, the observer, and the skier are absolutely clear on the meaning of hand signals.

The towline must be top quality, inspected each day, and it must be equipped with a brightly colored float near the handle. This helps a skier in the water to spot the handle as it comes around. It also keeps other boaters from running over the towline.

If the skier falls, throttle back and turn back sharply (but not so sharply that a prop leaves the water) to check the skier (unless he signals okay). The observer can bring the towline aboard, or, if you're going to continue, can let the towline swing around in a wide, looping arc, to bring the handle close to the skier.

The drop-off is critical—the skier should *not* go slamming spectacularly toward the beach or a pier but should settle back slowly into the water. When the signal for "drop-off" has been exchanged, the operator should look carefully to make sure that the approach to the drop-off point is free of swimmers and other boats and that his route away from that point also is clear.

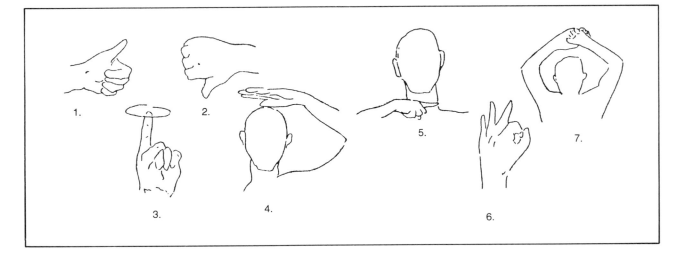

Water Skier's Safety Code

All skiers should be well versed in the fundamental safety rules. These fundamentals as well as other safety procedures are available from AWSA Headquarters in poster format. Whenever possible learn to water ski by taking instruction from a certified instructor.

Rule 1: Always wear a flotation device.

A properly fitted personal flotation device is designed to fit snugly so that it won't slip up on the body during a fall. The recommended type is a jacket or vest which covers the chest, abdomen and back.

Rule 2: Always be sure your equipment is in good condition.

Your personal safety and enjoyment depends on the equipment used. Check your equipment regularly. Be sure the skis do not have sharp or protruding surfaces that could cut or scrape the skier, check towlines for frayed areas or broken bridles and handles. Repair or replace damaged or unsafe articles.

Rule 3: Don't give the signal to start until the slack has been taken out of the line and you are sure you are clear. Keep your ski tips up.

Rule 4: Do not ski near docks, pilings, other boats or swimmers.

Always look ahead and be sure you are aware of your surroundings and where you are going at all times. This may sound silly but the predominance of water ski injuries result from collision with docks or other solid objects.

Rule 5: Never put any part of your body through the handle-bridle or wrap the line around yourself in any way.

Rule 6: Never ski in shallow water or in an area where there may be obstructions above or just beneath the surface.

Rule 7: When a fall is inevitable, try to fall backward or to either side. A forward fall increases the chance of contacting a ski.

Rule 8: Know and use the skier signals; particularly important is the skier's OK signal if you are all right after a fall.

Rule 9: If you fall in an area where there is other boat traffic, lift one ski more than halfway out of the water as a signal to other boaters.

Rule 10: Never ski to the point of excessive fatigue.

Rule 11: Always ski during daylight from sunrise to one-half hour after sunset.

Rule 12: Never ski directly in front of another boat.

Rule 13: Always use equal length ropes when skiing doubles.

Rule 14: Always ensure that the boat's motor is "off" when a skier is entering the boat from the water.

Rule 15: Always have an observer in the towboat.

Enjoy the sport by being courteous to others using the waterways. Courtesy is contagious.

(American Water Ski Association)

SMALL CENTERBOARD SAILBOATS

Small sailboats are especially sensitive to sudden changes in the wind, are easily capsized, and never should be operated by people who are not competent swimmers—particularly children, who also should be required to *wear* life jackets.

Chapter 14 covered some of the hazards of sailing, most of which apply to smaller boats as well as larger ones, but here are some specific points to keep in mind:

• Distribution of weight is essential, and in a small boat, that means distribution of the *crew*. The crew should be considered movable ballast:

Sitting on the rail to windward will help keep the boat on an even keel; hanging out over the side to windward will help the boat sail closer to the wind; hanging *way* out to the side in a trapeze is even more effective. This increases the physical challenge of sailing, particularly when racing, but it also increases the probability of getting wet. Be prepared.

• The helmsman should sit forward of the tiller and on the upwind wide. In this position, his body won't block tiller movement and he can hike out over the rail quickly, for balance.

CATAMARAN RIGHTING SYSTEM for singlehanded sailors. The Cat-Righter (TM) uses a vinyl bag to scoop up water and a system of ropes and pulleys to pull the hull upright in the water. The bag provides from 150 to 500 pounds of self-righting force. Current models are available for catamarans up to 21 feet in length. (Lake Enterprises)

HIKING HARNESS. There are specialized harnesses for varying angles and levels of loading. This is a well-built harness for use with catamarans and light daysailers requiring active hiking by the crew. (The Spinnaker Shop)

• If everyone sits aft, on the downwind side, a small boat caught by a puff of wind could take water over the stern and capsize.

• A close-hauled small boat caught by a puff of wind may heel too far and capsize anyway; if the wind is variable, with relatively strong puffs, the helmsman should keep the mainsheet *in hand*, ready for instant adjustment (i.e., letting the mainsail out more parallel to the wind). Do *not* cleat the sheet under these conditions.

• Heading up into the wind will also reduce the heel, although not as quickly as slacking the mainsheet; it will, however, help maintain the speed of the boat.

• Speed is important: A boat moving along smartly is less vulnerable to capsize.

If the boat *does* capsize, quickly do the following:

• Try to keep it from going belly-up, a position from which it is much harder to recover. Get out immediately and stand on the centerboard, to provide lever action. Have a crew member (if there is one) get some flotation, such as a life jacket, to the end of the mast.

• All crew members should don life jackets (if not already wearing them). You may be in the water for some time.

• Stay with the boat. Don't try to swim for shore; it may be much farther than you think, and your boat will continue floating, even if it is upside down.

• Grab any gear that should have been tied down in the cockpit but was not, and is now floating away.

• If the boat is in danger of drifting into a bridge or a heavily traveled shipping channel, try to get an anchor down; otherwise, let it drift while you work at getting it upright.

• Take in on the mainsheet to get the boom secured. Release the main and jib halyards (in turn) and get the sails to the boom (and deck) and furled loosely. On very small boats, you may not need to strike the sails to get the boat upright, but you need to slack the sheets so that the sail will streamline as the hull comes up.

• In all of this, take your time. You're already subject to the debilitating effects of hypothermia induced by being in the water (see chapter 18).

• When all is ready, stand as far out on the centerboard as possible, hanging onto the gunwale, and let the lever action of your weight slowly but surely bring the boat back to vertical.

• Boarding over the stern, climb into the cockpit and bail out as much water as possible before getting underway again.

• If accepting help from another boat, beware of letting your straying lines foul its propeller.

TRAILERING

Many small boats are transported on a trailer, the handling of which requires both special equipment and special skill—neither of which is conferred automatically with the purchase of the rig. The "equipment" includes your automobile or truck plus the hitch you use to pull the trailer: All must be large enough and strong enough for the task. Before making a purchase, check with the dealers of both trailer and automobile to be sure of their suitability.

Some boats, sold with trailers, are too large for casual launching and recovery at a local boat ramp. In such a case, "trailerability" means it provides an alternative (other than a boatyard) for winter storage and it facilitates transfer from one locale to another.

Getting Underway (with Trailer) Checklist

1. Make sure that all rollers and other contact points are adjusted to the contour of the boat.

2. Secure any loose gear on the boat; check all lashings and tiedowns.

3. Make sure that the battery and the gas tanks are secure and capped tightly.

4. Be sure the motor is mounted tightly.

5. Make sure that all trailer mechanical devices, such as winches and tilt cradles, are locked.

6. Check the hitch. The trailer should be balanced so that the weight at the coupler is no higher than about 75 pounds. Grease the ball. Check the safety chain to make sure it's in good condition, well connected to both the trailer and the pulling vehicle, and long enough to permit turns without binding but short enough to take up the load quickly should the hitch fail.

7. Check all moving parts for lubrication, but especially the wheel bearings. This item is too easily affected if the wheel hubs become submerged during launching or recovery, and too easily overlooked.

8. Check all tires for proper inflation and lug nuts for tightness.

9. Check the lights and brakes for proper operation.

10. While driving, stop periodically (preferably every hour) and make a check of tires and wheels, tiedowns, and position of the boat on the trailer; look inside the boat for any gear that may have come adrift; check around the hull for any signs of wear or chafing at points where contacted by the trailer.

11. In launching the boat, the method will vary with the size of boat and type of trailer, so you should have the dealer (or previous owner) walk you through the steps involved. However, there are some cautions that apply to all trailer launchings:

• Back slowly down the ramp, stopping before the trailer wheel hubs are in the water.

• Put an automatic transmission in park (*not* in drive or reverse) and a manual transmission in first gear.

• Set the emergency/parking brake.

• Leave the driver's door *open*.

• Set a pair of sturdy chocks under the rear wheels. Even if the car is properly braked and in gear, the rig might slide down a wet, muddy, grassy, or mossy launching ramp. Chocks will also help when pulling the boat and trailer back up the ramp. You can easily make a pair of chocks by sawing an 8 × 8 × 15 inch timber along the diagonal (have the lumberyard cut it for you when you buy the wood). Cut some grooves across the bottom of each chock to increase holding power.

Towing a trailer with a car or truck takes patience and practice. The patience keeps you from driving faster than you should (thus keeping the trailer from whipping back and forth dangerously and permitting controlled stops when necessary). The practice teaches you how to maneuver in tight places. Two things to keep in mind: (1) When going forward, the trailer will turn "inside" the pulling vehicle, so make your turns extra wide to avoid clipping the curb or hitting barriers; (2) when going backward, the trailer will turn in the *opposite* direction.

CANOES

TYPES

Canoes come in two basic types—for lakes and for rivers—although each will work in the other situation. However, if you have a choice, here are some points to consider:

CANOEING/KAYAKING VEST. Vests have been designed for virtually every water sport and activity. In this case, the paddler's vest combines ease of action with flotation and head support. (Mustang)

• Canoes with flat bottoms and straight keels are best for lakes; they are quite stable and can carry reasonably heavy loads.

• Canoes with round bottoms and keels raised at bow and stern are best suited for running a river; they're highly maneuverable, can spin on a dime (an asset in white water, a liability when trying to steer a straight and steady course in calm water), but are tippy and not well suited to moving cargo.

• As with any boat, a canoe with a narrow bow and stern is faster, but wetter, than a bluffer shape.

• A flat stern—for mounting an outboard—adds drag when paddling.

SIZES

Small (about 11 feet) This size will adequately carry only one person and is harder to paddle in a straight line than longer canoes.

Medium (17 to 18 feet) Well suited for two or three persons; handles easily both in and out of the water. Weight: about 60 to 80 pounds.

Large (20 feet) The canoeing equivalent of a cruising boat. Good capacity for equipment for extended operations for two people. Weight: 125 pounds.

Too Large There may be some old cargo boats around, 25 feet or longer. They can carry 2,000 pounds—which is hardly recreational.

MATERIALS

Aluminum is the most popular material for canoes. It is strong, light in weight, and easily maintained. It does, however, get hot in the sun. Wood-and-canvas is the traditional material, and subject to such traditional ills as punctures and rot. Fiberglass is easily shaped into more exotic hull designs, relatively maintenance-free, and tends to make a faster hull.

PADDLES

Length Bow paddles should reach to the chin of a standing bow paddler; stern paddles (which also are used for steering) are comparatively longer, reaching to the eyes of the stern paddler or slightly higher.

Width Wide blades give more bite to the stroke but use more energy; narrow blades are the opposite. This choice is primarily related to the paddler's stamina.

Grip This is a matter of personal choice—whatever will feel comfortable after hours and hours of paddling.

Quantity One per paddler, plus at least one backup in the event of loss.

Double-bladed Paddles Usually associated with kayaks, these are also very efficient with small canoes.

Poles Not exactly paddles, of course, poles can be useful when paddles are lost or when maneuvering through tangled water plants. They can be improvised easily but must be long enough to reach the bottom.

TECHNIQUE

Avoid the temptation to make long, slow, powerful strokes. They'll wear you out too soon and are not very efficient. Short, quick strokes are better, at a tempo of one every 1.5 to 2 seconds.

SOME TIPS

Safety Gear Never get underway without some sort of bailing bucket or scoop. Never get underway without an acceptable life jacket (the cushion you kneel on for paddling is *not* acceptable).

Loading Heaviest items should be on the bottom. Provide your gear with flotation and a tether unless you fancy watching your goods settle to the bottom of the lake or go bouncing off downstream.

Boarding The canoes should be fully floating and boarded with care but not temerity. The stern paddler should steady the boat while the passengers and the bowman get in. Then the bowman holds the canoe steady while the stern man gets aboard.

Landing Watch out for sharp stones and shells; tie a length of mooring line to a tree or rock to keep the canoe from drifting away.

Standing While not forbidden, this posture should certainly be adopted with care. In fact, standing is one way to catch a good look at the rapids ahead before you get there, and it is the only way to maneuver with a pole.

Changing Positions It's not a good idea to change positions—and, with a typical double-ended canoe, not necessary. Just turn around and keep going.

ROUGH-WATER CANOEING

For a canoe, rough water can mean waves of a foot or higher. The bow tends to push into the waves, rather than ride up and over, and the canoe takes on water. Do the following:

1. Shift cargo away from the ends and into the center of the canoe; this will help the bow and stern rise with the waves and will increase maneuverability.

2. Sit or kneel low down, on the bottom of the canoe. Use the seats only in the calmest of waters.

3. Stay near the edges of the body of water, and do not try to strike out across open water.

4. Go *with* the waves rather than *into* them.

5. If you capsize while running a river, stay away from the bow (which now becomes a dangerous weapon). Grab the stern and let the boat pull you along until you reach calmer water.

CANOE FILLED WITH WATER

When a canoe fills with water, you have several options:

• You can get aboard and paddle a swamped canoe (with your hands, if necessary). You won't move very fast, but you'll move.

• You can swim alongside, pushing the canoe into shallower water.

• You can try to empty out as much water as possible by first holding one end under water so that the high end will drain; then, with the canoe back level, rock it sharply from side to side to slosh the remaining water over the sides.

The *greatest* canoeing hazard is shock or a heart attack caused by sudden immersion (or hypothermia caused by continued immersion) in very cold water. While the air temperature may indicate "summer," many of the popular canoeing waters consist of runoff from high mountain snow and can be brutally cold. Get out of cold water as soon as possible.

DAMS AND LOCKS

The dams and locks that often intrude on lakes and rivers present hazards too often overlooked (or ignored) by small-boat operators.

Fixed-crest low-level dams, only a few feet in height, are designed to keep a constant level of water above the dam for industrial or municipal water intakes. Because the dam structure is so low, a canoeist or kayaker may think it's simple and safe to ride over the dam. *Don't try it.* The water flow tends to trap a boat against the downstream face of the dam and hold it there; the force can even be strong enough to pull a lifejacketed person under water—and hold him there.

Conventional dams (built to control flooding, preserve water supplies, generate electrical power, and/or create a recreational boating area) present dangerous currents and strong turbulence both above and below. Stay well clear of them.

Locks are designed to allow commercial traffic to pass from one water level to another, avoiding rapids or connecting separate bodies of water; they are also designed to move a large quantity of water in a short time (which sets up powerful currents and turbulence). The small-boat operator going through a lock, alone or in company with other boats, must exercise particular caution:

1. Read and heed posted instructions and wait for the lockmaster's signals. These may be by light or sound.

2. Have a mooring line (at least 150 feet) ready for use.

3. Have all persons on deck don life jackets.

4. Hang fenders from both sides of the boat.

5. On signal, enter the lock slowly; follow the attendant's instructions for tying up, either to the lock or to another boat.

6. Turn off the motor.

7. No smoking.

8. Follow the attendant's instructions for slacking off the mooring line, or taking up slack, as the water level changes.

9. Upon signal, start the motor and leave the lock slowly.

OTHER SMALL-BOAT HAZARDS

Small-boat operations usually are carried out in an area crowded with many other small boats, and they call for extra vigilance and caution: More than 25 percent of small-boat accidents involve inattention or carelessness.

Other accidents may be attributed to such conscious violations of safety and common sense as drinking-and-driving, speeding, and operating in unsafe waters. Here are some typical problems:

• Passengers leaning too far over the side, particularly in rough waters (or where the wakes of passing boats amount to the same thing); the passenger may be bounced overboard, or unwanted water may come pouring in over the gunwale.

• Too many people gathering at the stern to help pull in a fish or tinker with the motor; in this case, the unwanted water will come pouring in over the transom.

• Turning abruptly at high speed and flipping over.

• Being caught in a squall; trying to enter a narrow inlet with a strong following sea; operating in any body of water for which the boat is not suited.

• Failure to be on the alert for swimmers, water-skiers, and other boats.

• Failure to check the chart for submerged rocks, hidden remnants of ancient piers, shoaling water.

PART III

Facing Problems and Handling Emergencies

You've carefully selected the right boat for your type of sailing; you've ordered the survey, negotiated the price, arranged the financing and insurance.

You've taken the time to go through your boat, carefully modifying or replacing unsafe equipment or conditions.

You've learned how to handle your boat well, having taken a course or weathered a self-taught program of learning and practice.

You're not planning a solo circumnavigation, or even a two-week excursion to the Caribbean. Your typical day of sailing—perhaps occasionally extended to a weekend—keeps you within a dozen miles of home. You have confidence in your abilities to handle your boat under the conditions you normally encounter, and you've already been through a few minor—but anticipated—problems.

But . . . should you be hit by a true emergency, the complacency engendered by all of the above actions and attributes may be your greatest danger. When an emergency hits, it is likely to hit hard, without warning; if you're not already prepared—with the right equipment and, more important, with the right knowledge and attitude—you may not be able to deal with it.

In the following sections, we present suggested actions that encompass the range of maritime or medical problems you might encounter. We've tried to be comprehensive, but these are not rules to be followed; every situation will be different and require different actions. However, these general suggestions should serve as the starting point for your own mental preparation. Sitting on your boat, in a calm harbor or slip, is the best time to plan ahead for the unplanned. Take one problem or emergency at a time and determine how you might best handle it.

CHAPTER EIGHTEEN

Medical Problems and Emergencies

Most medical conditions aboard your boat will be more like the human equivalent of fender-benders than emergencies, but they nonetheless can ruin a cruise. Be prepared to cope with virtually all of these minor problems—and learn how to handle the critical first moments of more serious medical situations.

There are certain medical supplies you should carry, and there is a certain mental attitude you must adopt. For the supplies—you don't need to convert your boat to a floating ambulance, but you need some basics for close-in cruising and some additions for long-range voyaging. For the attitude—you need the same sense of confidence in your own skill and ability as you bring to handling the boat.

Legally speaking, you have the time-honored responsibility of a captain for the welfare of his crew. Practically speaking, you don't have much choice.

MINOR MEDICAL PROBLEMS

SEASICKNESS

Mal de mer—sickness of the sea—is an almost-universal malady. There are few mariners, of whatever age, sex, nationality, or boating persuasion, who have not become ill at one time or another. A very few people seem immune; some people get sick at the mere sight of light shimmering on the surface of the water. Aside from individual differences, the likelihood and probable severity of an attack are related to several factors:

- Length of time since last at sea;
- Length of time at sea on any given voyage;
- Overall health and level of fatigue;
- Alcohol, or the residual effects of alcohol remaining from last night's party;
- Type of seas—generally those that produce an unaccustomed pattern of motion (wave size is not necessarily a factor, although here we get back to individual differences);
- Fear, or, especially, anxiety about getting sick.

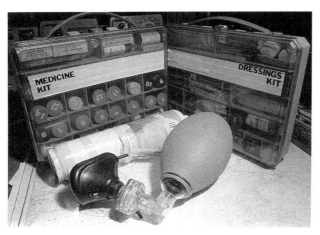

THE BOAT'S MEDICAL GEAR. A protective tackle box can be used to divide medical supplies for a basic onboard medical kit. The two items in the foreground are an air splint for broken or sprained limbs and an Ambu-Bag to help in restoring and maintaining breathing.

THE SOURCE OF SEASICKNESS. A detailed anatomy of the inner ear shows the semicircular canals that help you maintain a sense of balance. Abnormal or uncommon stimuli (such as wave action) cause neural overloading in the canals, which cannot keep up the body's response to motion. This is why reestablishing a point of reference (by looking at the horizon) can help a seasick crew member. Staying below in a pitching cabin without an obvious reference frame aggravates the situation. (U.S. Navy)

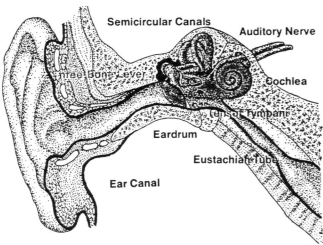

For most people, seasickness is largely transient (that is, once they become accustomed to the motion of the boat, the problem evaporates) and is generally avoidable with preventive medication and/or sensible precautions.

Seasickness usually begins with slight feelings of drowsiness, nausea, dizziness, or general anxiety. In the early stages, seasickness may be little more than a mere annoyance. However, from a safety standpoint, a slightly ill crew member, with the edge taken off judgment and coordination, may be more of a hazard than a really sick one: The sick one knows he's sick, and so does everyone else. In its full-blown stage, seasickness may interfere so seriously with motor control and concentration as to render the sick crew member useless at best and dangerous on average.

While seasickness generally takes the form of nausea, it's not the stomach's fault but, rather, the passages in the inner ear that normally tell your brain which way you're moving and which way is up—your built-in gyroscope. However, the brain too easily becomes confused on a bouncing boat. Just at the point where it has accepted and adjusted to one motion, the motion changes abruptly, the signals pass each other coming and going, and the brain stops trying to cope and starts ringing your internal alarms.

On a boat, there is no quick relief from the motion, and the negative effects of other sensory inputs become greatly magnified. A swaying lamp, food sloshing around in the stomach, any unusual odors—all are insistent reminders that something is wrong.

Prevention centers on delaying the onset of seasickness until the body has adjusted to the motion and the threat has passed. The classic medications for delaying seasickness have been Dramamine, Bonine, and related antihistamines, which keep the signals from reaching the brain and need to be taken some time—several hours, anyway—before getting underway. A probable side effect: drowsiness. The warning label on the package may say, "Do not operate machinery or drive while taking this medication." Somehow, that seems at cross purposes with the boater's need to handle his vessel in an alert manner. At any rate, be forewarned.

These medications are available as pills, capsules, and suppositories. If you postpone taking the medication until you're already sick, you'd better have a supply of suppositories—the pills won't stay down long enough to work. Other remedies—available by prescription—include the scopolamine adhesive patch, which slowly releases medication through the skin and into the bloodstream. For some people, these patches solve the seasickness problem; for others, they provoke nausea. The best source of information and guidance on this subject, of course, is your friendly local physician.

The "normal" method for using a patch is to place it behind an ear: The blood vessels are close to the surface and the surface is close to the brain, where the medication does its job. However, it is better to put the patch where it is not likely to be touched, perhaps behind a knee. The drug comes off easily onto a finger, even from a casual touch to check that the patch is tight. Should the finger then touch the eye—say, to wipe away some spray—the result might be several days of blurred sight and dizziness. The same result could come from taking a shower with the patch behind the ear, unless you exercise great care.

With or without medication, seasickness may be avoided (or the severity greatly reduced) by minimizing any disorienting factors:

1. Provide your brain with a steady element—look out at the horizon. Even better, do so standing up and keep your head as level as possible by flexing your legs. Don't turn your head unless you have to—and do so slowly, keeping your ears level with the horizon. Don't bend over; if you have to pick up something, bend your knees, not your back.

2. Should you be eating or abstaining? Eating is an individual choice; some people swear by soda crackers and hard-boiled eggs, others recommend constant sipping of water or soft drinks. Do what you feel comfortable doing, but *don't* add to your brain's confusion by imbibing alcoholic beverages during or before a voyage. And don't smoke—or allow anyone nearby to do so.

3. Keep your head in the fresh air. Stay away from fuel, food, fishing-bait, or bathroom smells. If at all possible, stay away from the head, where you'll find no horizon, no fresh air, and unpleasant odors. Also, you usually have to bend over to pump the thing, bringing your face even closer to disaster.

4. Another place to avoid: a forward bunk, where the motion is most pronounced. Boats tend to pitch (up-and-down) and yaw (side-to-side) around a point that is roughly two-thirds of the way back from the bow. The best place to be, logically, is right at that center and on the centerline.

5. Stay away from the smell of sickness—yours and anyone else's. At the same time, you must be sensitive to your fellow voyagers and try to minimize any effects from your illness. As long as you're able, clean up after yourself. A can of air freshener should be mandatory on any boat with an enclosed cabin space—although the smell of some air fresheners can also trigger a wave of nausea through an already queasy stomach.

6. Sailing well heeled over tends to exacerbate the problem: It's more visually disorienting and requires considerable muscle power to keep from sliding off the deck at a time when you may not have much muscle power available. Take in some sail or shift to a less dramatic course.

7. Being under power on a downwind course may smooth out the pitching, but it increases the yawing. It also guarantees that much of your engine exhaust will be traveling right along with you. Change course.

8. Unless you have become too ill to concentrate on anything, take a turn at the helm. This will keep you looking out at the horizon and force you to focus your attention on something other than your queasiness. It would be thoughtful, however, to have a bucket nearby.

Illness Kit

(Many of the following medications require a doctor's prescription. Consult your family physician before planning or assembling a personalized medical kit.)

Drug/Material (Date on Board)	Form/ Concentration	Adult Dosage (Children Similar Unless Specified)	Use
Wounds			
Betadine skin cleanser	Skin soap solution	Surface use	Lather your hands and the wound with ample water. Allow a second application to dry in air. With burns, wash off with water after cleansing.
Burns			
Furacin ointment	Ointment, also available in impregnated gauze	Surface use	Apply after cleaning area and cover with gauze dressing. Change dressing once per day or if wet.
Antibiotics			
Penicillin*	Solution 250 mg/5 ml. Tablets 250 mg each	Dose every 6 hours Adult—250–500 mg Child—25mg/kg	Some few individuals are allergic to penicillin. Use alternate antibiotic.
Erythromycin	Tablets 200 mg/tab	Dose every 6 hours Adult—400 mg Child—10–15mg/kg	For adults allergic to penicillin. Can be used for children upon advice. Often produces nausea and vomiting.
Ampicillin	Solution 250 mg/5 ml Capsule 500/mg	Dose every 6 hours Adult—500 mg Child 10–20 mg/kg	A penicillin derivative
Dicloxacillin	Suspension 62.5 mg/15 ml Capsule 250 mg	500 mg every 6 hours Child—20mg/kg	For skin infections. Use erythromycin if allergic to penicillin.
Poisoning			
Spirit of Ipecac	Elixir	Tablespoon every 20 minutes until vomiting occurs	Give with water. *Do not use in poisoning involving solvents, iron tablets, petroleum products, fuels, kerosene, polishes.*
Eye			
Sulfacetamide ophthalmic solution	10% solution	2 drops every 2–3 hours	For infection. Wash eye gently and apply drops.
Ophthaine Anesthetic (Eye)	0.5% solution	1–2 drops	For *severe* eye pain only. Use eye patch after application. *Do not touch or rub eye after use.*
Ear Problems			
Cortisporin Otic Solution	Drops	3–4 drops in each ear, 2 to 3 times per day	For severe pain due to swimmer's ear with no fever.
Auralgan Otic Solution	Drops	1–2 drops in affected ear, 2–3 times/day	For middle-ear infection with fever usually present. Use with antibiotic.

*Note: Certain individuals are either allergic or sensitive to specific medicines. Always consult a physician before using prescription medications. Remember, your first task or obligation in any medical situation is to do no harm.

Drug/Material (Date on Board)	Form/ Concentration	Adult Dosage (Children Similar Unless Specified)	Use
Nose and Throat			
Neosynephrine	Spray 0.25% solution	As needed	For nasal congestion. Do not overuse or nasal irritation can result.
Robitussin-DM	Solution	Dose every 3–4 hours Adult—1 teaspoon Child—¼–½ teaspoon	For cough that interrupts sleep
Sudafed Syrup	Syrup	As directed	For congestion in upper respiratory areas in children.
Digestive Problems			
Pepto-Bismol	Solution	As directed	Upset stomach with diarrhea.
Lomotil	Tablets	2 tablets every 6–8 hours; do not use for children	Severe diarrhea
Skin			
Benadryl	Elixir solution. 12.5mg in 5cc. Prescription.	Dose every 6–8 hours Adult—2–4 teaspoons Child—1.5 mg/kg	For allergic reactions that develop over several hours. Drowsiness may result.
Epinephrine	Solution 1 mg/1 ml purchased in 5, 1 ml ampules w/syringe. Prescription.	Adult—0.2–0.3cc subcutaneous injection, repeat in 30 minutes Child—0.01 mg/kg per dose	For severe allergic reactions only. USE ONLY AFTER RADIO CONSULTATION AND ADVICE OF PHYSICIAN.
Kwell shampoo & lotion	Liquid	As directed	For lice and other small parasites in hair and eyebrows.
Pain Management			
Codeine sulfate	½ grain tablets	½–1 grain every 6 hours; do not use for children	Do not overmedicate. Ease pain to a tolerable level. Do not give to anyone having breathing problems, to anyone unconscious, or after intake of alcohol.
Ethylene-chloride	Spray bottle	As directed	For local anesthetic to dress wounds or burns, remove hooks or splinters, etc.

Other Items

Aspirin	Boric acid solution	Ammonia inhalants	Paba sun screen
Contac cold pills	Tums	Bonine (Dramamine)	Calamine lotion
Thermometer	Castor oil	Cotton wool	Eugenol or oil of cloves
Sodium bicarbonate	Paba-Gel lip screen	Eyewash cup	Blistex
Q-tip applicators	Salt tablets	Povidone iodine	Boric acid ointment
Eye patches	Tylenol	Tongue depressors	Adolph's meat tenderizer
Measuring spoon	Liquiprin children's aspirin	Afrin spray	

Injuries Kit

Material/Drug/or Equipment	Qty/Size	Use
Neosporin ointment	1 ½-oz tube	For burns
Nupercainal cream	1 2-oz tube	For anesthetic ointment treatment of burns
Sodium chloride bacteriostatic sol.	1 30-ml jar	General cleansing
Foille ointment	1 tube	Burn ointment
Gauze bandage roll	2 3″ × 6 yd	General dressing
Safety pins	1 package	General dressing
Surgical scissors	1	General dressing
Cotton Q-tip applicators	6	General dressing
Safety razor and blades	1	General dressing
Steri-Drape surgical towels	2	General dressing
Steri-strip suture strip skin closures	5 ½″ 4″	Wound closure
Absorbable hemostats	2-in bottles	Help stop bleeding
Gauze pads	2 4″ × 4″	General dressing
Compress bandages	2 4″	General dressing
Triangular bandages	1 40″	General dressing
Vaseline gauze dressings	1 package	Burn dressing
Alcohol	1 jar (small)	General dressing
Vaseline Petrolatum packs	3 packs	For burns
Tourniquet	1	Stop bleeding
Wire splint	1	Immobilize limbs
Betadine skin cleanser	1 4-oz jar	Clean hands and wounds
Gauze bandage	1 2″ × 10 yd	General dressing
Gauze bandage	1 3″ × 10 yd	General dressing
Gauze bandage	3 2″ × 6 yd	General dressing
Band-Aids	14 assorted	Small cuts, etc.
Povidone iodine	1 bottle	General dressing
Gauze pads	2 3″ × 3″	General dressing
Gauze pads	2 2″ × 2″	General dressing
Alcohol wipes	9	General dressing
Disposable skin swabs	6	General dressing
Bandage compresses	4 2″	General dressing
Gauze bandage	1 3″ × 6 yd	General dressing
Sterile surgical gloves	1 pair	General dressing
Medium dressing pack	1, sterile	Contains: 1 drape, 2 3″ × 3″ sponges, 2 8″ × 4″ sponges, 1 5″ × 9″ Surgipad
Tincture of green soap	1 4-oz bottle	General cleaning
Surgical tape	1 roll	General dressing
Adhesive tape	1 roll	General dressing
Ambu-Bag and mask		
Oxygen tank		
Air splints		

Everyday Care Kit

Material/Drug/or Equipment	Qty/Size	Use
Povidone iodine	1 small jar	General dressing
Small scissors	1	General dressing
Tweezers	1	General dressing
First-aid cream	1 2-oz tube	Burns, scrapes, etc.
NoDoz tablets	1 small jar	
Laxative tablets	1 small jar	For minor stomach problems
Tums	1 roll	For minor stomach problems
Aromatic ammonia inhalants	12	For dizziness or fainting
Airway	1 Adult; 1 child	For resuscitation
Salt tablets	1 small jar	For heat exhaustion
First-aid tape	1 roll	General dressing
Foille ointment	2 small tubes	Burns
Kleenize eyewash	1 jar	Eye problems
Butterfly closures	1 box, medium	To stop bleeding and close wounds
Paba-Gel skin screen	1 bottle	For sun protection
Thermometer	1	
Q-tips	1 box	General dressing
Bonine (Dramamine)	1 package	Seasickness
Aspirin/Tylenol/Liquiprin	1 bottle	Mild pain
Gauze compresses	Various	General dressing
Neosporin ointment	Small tube	Mild burns
Cepacol throat lozenges	1 package	Sore throat
Eye dressing	1, packaged	Eye injury
Vaseline gauze dressings	1 pack	Burns
Triangular bandage	1	General dressing
Bandage compresses	Various	General dressing
Band-Aids	Various	General dressing

How to Calculate Dosages for Children

Occasionally you may be in a situation where you need a particular medication in a child's dosage but only have adult prescriptions aboard. While it is not good practice to be free and easy with any prescription drug, it *is* useful to understand how to cut back an adult prescription and use it for a child (this is particularly true for penicillin, etc.).

Prescriptions are developed based upon body weight and that is the key to understanding how to prescribe for a child. Let us say that your child has an infection and you want to use an adult prescription for penicillin. The adult dose is 250 to 500 milligrams (mg) given every four hours. This would be a total daily input of 1,500 to 3,000 milli-grams per day. First take your child's weight in pounds and convert that to kilograms. One kilogram equals 2.2 pounds. A 22-pound child would weigh 10 kilograms: The child dosage is given as 100mg/kg/day, dosed every six hours. This means 100mg $\times$ 10kilos = 1,000mg per day. This is divided into four doses (250mg) given six hours apart.

The important concepts to remember are weight, that 1 kilogram = 2.2 lbs, and that the daily limit is divided into specified doses. You can give children doses on a weight basis until their dosages reach the adult dose size.

9. Think about almost anything other than your queasiness. For many people, the anticipation and fear of seasickness are greater problems than the actual disorientation.

10. If you *are* becoming ill, in spite of all precautions, don't hesitate to say so. It's not a sign of weakness, and some of the greatest mariners of all time were sick for a great portion of their professional lives. Any sailor who gamely tries to hang in without telling the skipper that he's not operating at full capacity becomes a hazard, not an asset. Additionally—particularly on long voyages—symptoms assumed to be those of seasickness (headache, cold sweat, weakness, constipation, and nausea) *may* signal a variety of other maladies, ranging from flu to appendicitis.

FIRST-AID SITUATIONS

Bumps or Blows to the Head Keep a close watch on the victim for signs of concussion (vomiting, cloudy eyes, dilated pupils, lack of orientation). Generally, it's not a good idea to let someone take a nap right after a good headbanger. A big "egg" or black-and-blue mark should not be as much of a worry—the swelling represents a collection of blood or other fluids in the damaged area. A cold pack applied as soon as possible should help reduce the swelling; if swelling persists, shift to a warm pack. If swelling remains overnight, it may be time to see a doctor.

Burns Cell death from thermal injury continues for some time after an accident; for minor burns, try to cool the area with water (fresh, *not* salt water) or an ice pack. For serious burns, see below.

Constipation Constipation can become a problem on longer cruises; it can be largely prevented by a diet heavy on fruit, bran, and fluid and light on the bulky stuff, like potatoes.

Dental Problems These usually fall into one of two categories—an exposed nerve (generally from a lost or broken filling) or an infection. If the pain is aggravated by a rinse of cold water, it's a nerve problem. If warm water produces pain and there is visible swelling, it's an infection.

To provide temporary relief, start with aspirin or Tylenol. For the exposed nerve, cover with a pellet of cotton soaked in oil of cloves or Eugenol. If your first-aid kit includes some dental cement, you can make a temporary filling to hold the pellet in place. For an infection, use cold compresses and antibiotics, if available.

Diarrhea Treat diarrhea by stopping all food intake for at least six hours and beginning the intake of large amounts of fluids such as Coca-Cola, Gatorade, and weak tea. To prevent dehydration, try to ensure that as much fluid is going

---

Supplements to Standard First-Aid Kit

PABA-based sunscreen lotion	2-inch bandage compress
Aspirin	4-inch bandage compress
Wire splint	Eye dressing and cup (prepackaged)
Vaseline gauze bandages or prepackaged Burn-paks	Iodine swabs
Additional seasickness pills	Antidiarrhea pills
Furacin ointment	Hexachlorophene ointment
Ammonia inhalants	First-aid book
No-Doz tablets	*With physician's advice:* Pain-killer and antibiotics
Adhesive bandage	

in as is coming out. This is particularly important with small children, who tend to dehydrate more easily than adults. Pepto-Bismol, Kaopectate, or Immodium may be helpful. The prescription drug Lomotil, if available, may be used to control *severe* cases in adults (never in children, in whom it may cause serious side effects).

Earache This may be the result of an infection, or "swimmer's ear," where trapped water will not drain. To tell the difference, look for indications of infection in other parts of the body (fever, cough, runny nose). If the external ear is red and painful, without a fever or other symptom of infection, it's probably swimmer's ear.

Swimmer's ear may be treated with Cortisporin Otic Solution, followed by periodic washing of the ear with alcohol to help remove residual water. The victim should avoid swimming for a time.

Earache can be treated with antibiotics and Auralgan ear drops; the pain can be mollified with aspirin or Tylenol.

Eye Problems Most eye problems fall into one of three categories: inflammation from infection, contamination with a foreign body, or damage from a blow or penetration.

To remove foreign material:

1. Pull down the lower lid to see if the object is on the inner surface; if so, lift it out gently with the corner of a clean tissue. Do not use dry cotton.

2. If the object seems to be under the upper lid, have the patient look down while you hold the lash of the upper lid. Pull the upper lid down over the lower one. The resultant tears may wash out the contaminant.

3. If the overlapping-eyelid technique does not work, place a small, smooth stick (such as a matchstick or a Q-tip shaft) on the edge of the upper lid, and depress the lid gently. Then, grasping the upper lash, roll the lid back up and over the stick. You should be able to see the offending object then and lift it out with the corner of a tissue.

4. If none of these techniques work, *do nothing further.* Put a clean protective dressing on the eye and seek professional help.

Other eye contamination can be treated by using an eyewash in a washing cup. A sulfacetamide ophthalmic solution is a good choice for the eyewash.

If an accident has caused severe eye pain, anesthetize the area with Ophthaine and then cover the eyes. Caution: Do *not* let the patient rub or touch an anesthetized eye. Since there is no feeling, the patient could cause corneal damage. Don't leave a young patient alone.

For a penetration of the eye:

1. Lay the person on his back and keep him still.

2. Do not wash, medicate, clean or anesthetize the eye.

3. Cover *both* eyes loosely with a sterile dressing. Do not create any pressure on the eye. Covering both eyes helps prevent movement of the injured eye.

4. Get professional help as soon as possible.

EYE CARE for foreign material in the eye involves lifting the upper eyelid up, out, and then down over the lower lid and softly massaging with almost no pressure, letting eye fluids wash away the debris. If this does not work quickly, use an eye cup and appropriate eyewash.

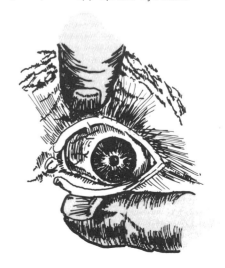

Fever Fevers are an indication of infection and a sign the body's natural defenses are at work. Aspirin and Tylenol will help relieve some of the fever symptoms, and mild fevers usually clear up when the underlying problem goes away. High fevers—approaching 104°F—must be treated by lowering the body temperature to avoid convulsions. A sponge bath in lukewarm (not cold) water usually helps. If fever persists, you must determine the reason for it, and deal with that.

Insect Bites and Animal Stings These can be serious, possibly triggering an allergic reaction. Watch for unusual signs of swelling, complaints of lightheadedness, or difficulty in breathing. Calamine lotion or baking soda will soothe most insect bites; commercial meat tenderizer may help counter the toxins from jellyfish stings.

Minor Wounds Remove every bit of what caused the damage—all splinters, battery acid, fishhooks (unless deeply embedded, in which

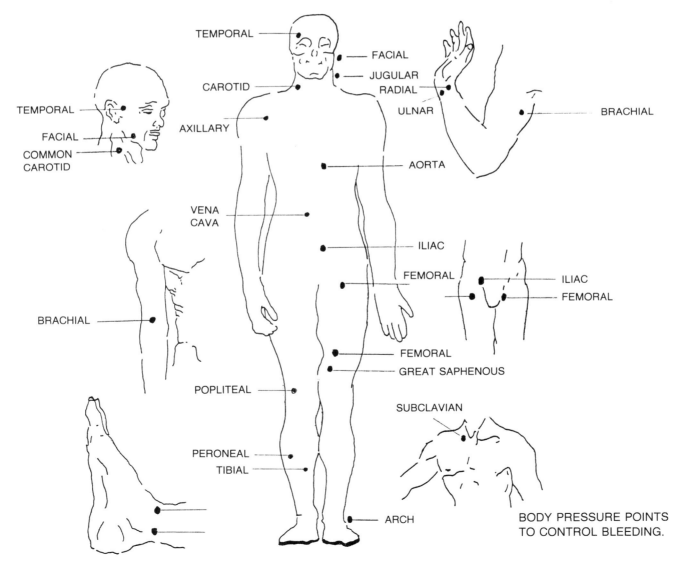

BODY PRESSURE POINTS TO CONTROL BLEEDING.

case, leave it for a doctor to remove). If a wound is not bleeding heavily, let it bleed a bit to help flush out dirt and debris.

If the bleeding does not soon stop, apply pressure or cold—or both—right over the wound, after covering the opening with plastic wrap. (For a nosebleed, tip the head back and apply a cold compress.)

Next, clean the area with soap and water (fresh if possible), and/or any common antiseptic such as alcohol, hydrogen peroxide, or a proprietary antibacterial spray or cream. (If necessary, use salt water. It will add some antiseptic value but may sting like the dickens.)

Vomiting Treat by stopping all food intake for three or four hours (for adults; less for children) and then starting small quantities—a teaspoon at a time—of fluids or a mild sugar solution. Too much liquid taken too quickly will trigger more vomiting.

MEDICAL EMERGENCIES

Burns Remove the burning agent immediately and flush with cool water. Remove loose clothing; loosely cover the burn with a clean cloth. Do not use ointments, creams, or butter. Guard against infection; administer fluids (in large quantities with a serious burn, to prevent shock and dehydration caused by fluid loss through the burn). *No alcohol.* Keep the patient warm and lying down, with feet elevated. In case of an electrical burn, the damage may be internal, with no apparent injury. Treat as above.

DEGREES OF BURNS. Since treatment of burns varies dramatically according to the severity of the wound, knowledge of burn degree is important. First-degree burns are red and have minor swelling. Initial pain passes quickly. Second-degree burns are redder, often mottled with white areas and blisters. There is often some loss of skin area and longer, more severe pain. Third-degree burns are charred, black-and-white tissue. Most of the outer skin area is gone. Ironically, in this most severe burn situation, there is little pain, since most nerve endings have been destroyed.

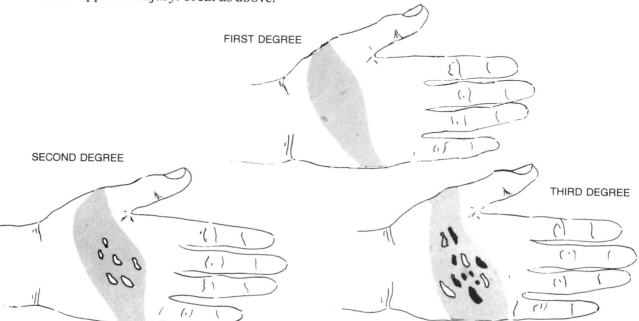

FIRST DEGREE

SECOND DEGREE

THIRD DEGREE

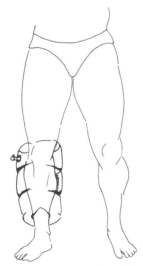

AIR SPLINTS for broken or sprained limbs are easy to stow and use. They can be inflated to varying degrees of hardness.

FIRST-AID books and documents should include a good first-aid manual (ideally, one created for the marine boating environment); a book on dangerous marine animals (including suggested action and antidotes); an book on the International Code of Signals containing a section on medical radio signals and treatment codes; and a small medication log listing onboard medicines, shelf life for dated prescriptions, inventories, and dosages.

Eye Burns　Most burns to the eye come from acid or alkalis.

- For an *acid burn:*

1. Wash the face and eyes with fresh water for at least five minutes. Hold the eyelid open and pour water into the eye, from the inner to the outer corner. Take care not to wash the burning chemical from one eye to the other.

2. Prepare a weak solution of baking soda and water (one teaspoon to a quart) and flush the eye, following the initial treatment.

3. Cover the eye with a clean dressing (do not use cotton) and bandage.

- For an *alkali burn* (detergents, cleaners, and so on):

1. Flush the eye with fresh water for at least fifteen minutes, from the inner to the outer corner. Take care not to wash the alkali into the other eye. Do *not* use a baking-soda solution.

2. Begin treatment immediately, even if the pain or damage appears slight. These burns can become worse over time.

Choking　Use the Heimlich maneuver immediately; without oxygen entering the lungs, a victim will lose consciousness in seconds and die in minutes.

Diabetes　Diabetes can present conflicting complications—one caused by too much sugar in the blood, the other by too little sugar. Either one can lead to coma, but the symptoms are different:

- Too much sugar: thirst; excessive urination; nausea and vomiting; rapid deep breathing; hot, flushed skin; cracked lips; an odor of acetone on the breath. These symptoms develop slowly, over a period of days.
- Too little sugar: cool, moist skin; sweating; pallor; fast but weak pulse; loss of appetite; headache; visual disturbances; mental confusion. These symptoms could develop in less than an hour.

These conditions can be life-threatening, but the more serious one is low blood sugar. Administer orange juice or candy. If the patient lapses

Special Equipment

Any special equipment you carry on board usually deals with emergency situations. This will include oxygen for drowning, diving, and general resuscitation treatment—and an "Ambu-Bag" to aid in resuscitation. In addition, you should carry a number of air splints (which have several uses).

AMBU-BAG

Most sailors know the general technique of mouth-to-mouth resuscitation. However, many do not realize that you may have to give mouth-to-mouth for forty-five minutes to an hour before you get best results (or have to give up). This can be a tremendous physical strain. Also, once you have started some independent lung movement, you would have to stop mouth-to-mouth to give oxygen (two things cannot go in the same place at the same time). The Ambu-Bag solves this. The device looks like a child's play football with a mask and valve on it. You simply place this over the nose and mouth of the patient (having cleared his airway) and then squeeze in and out in the mouth-to-mouth rhythm. This forces air in and out of the lungs and you are freed from some of the physical strain. The Ambu-Bag can be kept in operation with oxygen tapped into the valve from an oxygen tank. Thus, it helps force oxygen into the lungs and then into the bloodstream, aiding recovery.

OXYGEN

Easy to obtain, small to stow, oxygen is of tremendous value in cardiac situations as well as in drowning and diving accidents. In any interruption of breathing, the greatest fear is a lack of oxygen that will cause brain damage or cell death. Oxygen can only be given to people who have started to breathe again on their own, even if they have difficulty breathing. It can also be administered with the Ambu-Bag. The important point is to get enough oxygen on board to be able to provide a four-liter-per-minute flow rate for at least 1½ hours. A flow-control valve is important so you can extend the supply. Several lightweight, inexpensive, and very well-made oxygen kits are available at hospital and surgical supply houses. Beware of too-small, free-flow, short-duration bottles. They cannot do the job.

AIR SPLINTS

You can splint breaks and sprains with small pieces of wood or other items in your boat's equipment, but air splints are even better. These plastic "envelopes" can be inflated by a locking valve and fit over a hand, arm, foot, or leg. As the inner wall of the splint inflates, it increases pressure on the affected limb, and eventually it develops enough pressure to immobilize the leg or arm.

---

into a coma, keep the airway open and get immediate help. Do *not* try to force fluids on an unconscious or semiconscious person; he might choke. Be alert for respiratory arrest and the need for CPR. If the patient is a known diabetic and has an insulin kit, do *not* assume that he forgot to take the shot and do it for him.

Epileptic Seizure Prevent head injury by easing the victim to the floor, but don't restrain movements. With a padded tongue blade, try to keep the tongue from obstructing the airway, but don't put your hand in the victim's mouth and don't try to force anything between the teeth. After the seizure has run its course, keep the victim lying on his side (to avoid aspirating vomit or mucus) until he is fully conscious.

RADIO MEDICAL ADVICE can be obtained either with direct voice or by special coded signals established for use with the International Code of Signals.

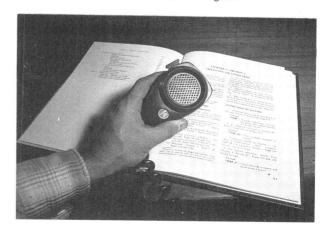

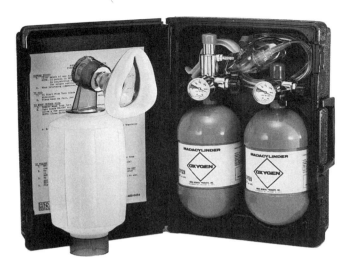

EMERGENCY RESUSCITATION EQUIPMENT. The Ambu-Bag shown in the foreground is used in restoring breathing and maintaining respiration as well as in force-feeding oxygen to victims whose breathing has stopped or is not fully operative. Man-overboard victims, drowning casualties, and victims of heart attacks can all benefit from this equipment. (Mada Medical Products)

If You Suspect a Heart Attack, Follow This Procedure

1. Immobilize the patient immediately to ease the demands on the heart. A sitting position is best. If the patient has a known heart problem, administer medication. If not, provide reassurance that help is on the way.

2. Make sure that help *is* on the way; call the Coast Guard. The primary danger in the first hour is cardiac arrest; with medical treatment, the chances of survival are greatly increased.

3. Pain medications probably won't help, but you can try them if you wish.

4. Don't let the patient drink any fluids except a few sips of room-temperature tap water.

Heart Attack   A heart attack often is called "coronary" because there is a loss of blood flow to the heart, caused by a clot blocking the coronary arteries. A stroke occurs when a blood vessel bursts in the brain or a clot forms in the circulatory system.

Early symptoms of a heart attack include:

• Dizziness or disorientation;
• Pain in the neck or jaw;
• Shortness of breath;
• Pain or numbness in the left arm, gradually spreading to the right arm;
• Chest pains beneath the breastbone.

The most common symptom is "denial," passing off the other symptoms as indigestion, heartburn, or muscle aches. For a patient above the age of thirty-five, don't let these signals be ignored, even if they seem to disappear; for anyone, if the symptoms persist—pay attention. The degree of pain is not a good indicator of the seriousness of the problem. Some heart problems even occur without any warning.

Until help arrives for a heart-attack victim, keep a close watch for any change in condition; should the heart fail, you must take immediate action to deal simultaneously with both the heart stoppage and the loss of breathing.

The technique you should use is called cardiopulmonary resuscitation (CPR). This is *not* something you learn from a book. Instruction is readily available through the American Red Cross, the American Heart Association, and your local health and emergency agencies. Take a course *now*, before you need it—by which time, it will be too late.

Hyperthermia   This condition results from a body temperature *above* the normal range, presenting a risk of seizures or convulsions. Symptoms include flushed skin that is warm to the touch, and increased pulse and respiratory rate. Treatment: Get the victim out of the sun; loosen clothing; apply cool, moist towels to the skin. If the victim is conscious, administer cool fluids.

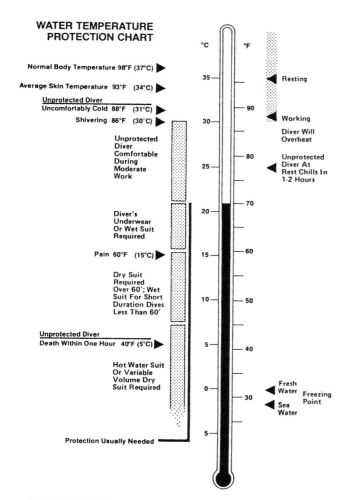

WATER TEMPERATURE PROTECTION CHART

Normal Body Temperature 98°F (37°C) ▶

Average Skin Temperature 93°F (34°C) ▶

<u>Unprotected Diver</u>
Uncomfortably Cold 88°F (31°C) ▶

Shivering 86°F (30°C) ▶

Unprotected Diver Comfortable During Moderate Work

Diver's Underwear Or Wet Suit Required

Pain 60°F (15°C) ▶

Dry Suit Required Over 60'; Wet Suit For Short Duration Dives Less Than 60'

<u>Unprotected Diver</u>
Death Within One Hour 40°F (5°C) ▶

Hot Water Suit Or Variable Volume Dry Suit Required

Protection Usually Needed ▬

°C °F

Resting

Working

Diver Will Overheat

◀ Unprotected Diver At Rest Chills In 1-2 Hours

Fresh Water Freezing Point
Sea Water

HYPOTHERMIA is a function both of water temperature and length of exposure. Note that even 80°F water eventually will cause chilling.

Hypothermia

This condition results from a cooling of the body *below* the normal temperature range of 97 to 99°F, due to immersion in water or prolonged exposure on deck. The water itself need not be cold to bring on hypothermia; body heat is transferred away very quickly in water. The symptoms include mental confusion, decreased pulse and respiration, and cool skin. Treatment: Warm *slowly* with blankets or towels. Do *not* use hot water. If the victim is conscious, administer heated (not hot) fluids. *No alcohol;* forget all those stories of a shot of brandy given to shipwreck victims. Alcohol dilates the blood vessels, causing further loss of body heat.

Respiratory Arrest

Heart stoppage may result from electrocution or drowning, for example. Administer CPR, and do so as quickly as possible. Permanent brain damage may result if the flow of oxygen has been cut off for as little as *four minutes*. If the victim has been submerged in cold water, that critical period may be extended somewhat; the body's natural defense mechanisms slow everything down. This may be the only time when being submerged in cold water has an advantage.

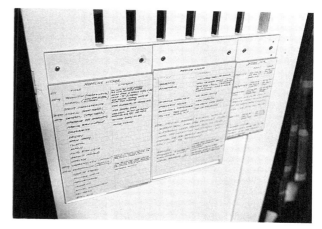

MEDICAL INVENTORIES, including shelf life and dosage data, should be readily at hand—for use in medical emergencies as well as for inspection by customs and other government officials. Remember, the most medically skilled person on board may be the one injured or sick—and the boat's medical instructions should be aimed at the least skilled person.

Marine Animals That Bite

SHARKS

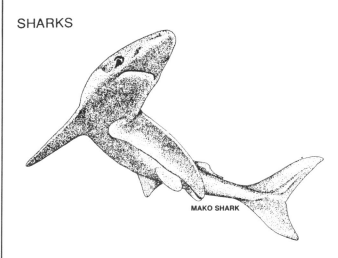

MAKO SHARK

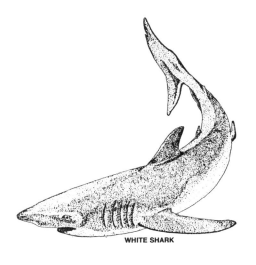

WHITE SHARK

Mako Shark
Distribution—Oceanic species found in tropical waters or warmer waters of the Atlantic. Varieties of species are found in the Pacific.

Appearance—Teeth are prominent. Slender form. Color is deep blue grey, bright blue, or deep blue above. White underneath. Up to 13 feet long.

Hazard—Savage and dangerous. Fast. History of human attack, classified as a game fish, and has been known to attack boats.

Tiger Shark
Distribution—Widespread in all tropical and warm belts of all oceans. Inshore and offshore. Most common shark in tropics.

Appearance—Prominent teeth, short snout, sharply pointed tail. Grey or greyish brown, darker above. Striping usually only on smaller fish. Up to 15–20 feet long.

Hazard—Mostly a scavenger. Fast in pursuit, usually sluggish otherwise. Some human attacks.

Porbeagle Shark
Distribution—Continental waters of the North Atlantic, Mediterranean, N. W. Africa, North Sea, Northern British Isles, Atlantic coast of U. S. and some Scandinavian regions.

Appearance—teeth are prominent. Dark, bluish grey above. Lower sides change to white. Anal fin is white or dusky. Dusk tips on pectoral fins. Up to 12 feet long.

Hazard—Active when in pursuit. Otherwise sluggish.

White Shark
Distribution—Widespread oceanic distribution, mostly in tropical, subtropical or warm water temperature areas. Numerous in Australian waters.

Appearance—Slate brown, slate blue, dull grey, or almost black above. Dirty white underneath. Small black spots with black fin tips. Larger white sharks are sometimes dun-colored or leaden white.

Hazard—One of the most dangerous and has even been known to attack boats. Aggressive and fast, with a history of numerous attacks on humans.

White-Tipped Shark
Distribution—Tropical and subtropical Atlantic and Mediterranean. Also found along Iberian Peninsula. Found in deep offshore waters.

Appearance—short snout, rounded dorsal fin. Light grey to pale brown to slate blue above. Whitish color below. Some spotting, and in some species white tips on fins. 13 feet or longer.

Hazard—Fearless in contact with man. Indifferent. Record of human attack.

Dusky Shark
Distribution—Often found in shallow waters in warm temperature zones on both sides of the Atlantic.

Appearance—Back and upper sides are usually leaden grey or bluish. Lower parts are white. Up to 14 feet long.

Hazard—Unpredictable. Fearless.

HAMMERHEAD SHARK

Lemon Shark

Distribution—Often found in inland waters, saltwater creeks, bays and sounds. Commonly active near docks. Inshore Western Atlantic, Carolinas, Northern Brazil, tropical West Africa.

Appearance—Second dorsal fin that is almost as large as the first. Broad, round snout. Prominent teeth. Yellowish brown above, occasionally dark blue grey above, sides and belly yellow. Up to 11 feet long.

Hazard—Unpredictable, with some history of human attack.

Sand Shark

Distribution—Shore species living on or near the bottom. Inhabits the Mediterranean, West Africa tropical zones, Canaries and Cape Verdes in North Atlantic, South Africa, Western Atlantic from Maine to Florida, Southern Brazil. Similar species in Pacific Indian areas and Argentine waters.

Appearance—Five gill openings in front of fins. Two fairly equally-sized dorsals. Teeth are prominent. Bright color, grey brown above, dark along back. Pale on sides, with grey white on belly and lower sides of fins. Rear body often marked with spots. Up to 10 feet.

Hazard—Fairly sluggish but with an active appetite. North American species are generally harmless, but sharks in Indian Ocean and some tropical areas can be dangerous.

Hammerhead Shark

Distribution—Both in offshore and inshore waters. Often seen swimming on surface. Found in varying species in all tropical and warm zones of all oceans and seas.

Appearance—Obvious hammer head shape. Eyes on outer edges. Ashen grey above fading to white below. Up to 15 feet long.

Hazard—Powerful, known to attack man.

Prevention

1. Making noise, blowing bubbles, etc. are of questionable value. Some noise attracts sharks.
2. Slow, purposeful movements should be used. Often, remaining absolutely still is best.
3. Often sharks can be "shoved" away with a large stick or "shark billy."
4. Attempts to kill or wound a shark are usually more dangerous than effective.
5. In striking a shark, concentrate on snout, eyes or gills.
6. Dark colored clothing and instruments are preferable.
7. Explosions, flashing lights, noise, or thrashing all can attract sharks.
8. Do not swim with open wounds. Do not dangle legs or arms in water. Enter and leave boats quickly.
9. Do not throw food, waste, or any food refuse overboard if sharks are suspected to be in the area.
10. The use of firearms by "swim-sentries" should be with extreme caution. Automatic weapons or hand guns should never be employed.

11. Avoid situations of an isolated swimmer. Groups of divers are in a better position to ward off attack.

Treatment

1. Bites from sharks are severe, with an extremely high rate of fatality (50–80%). Abrasions can result from contact or brushing up against a shark.
2. Bites result in large amount of bleeding and tissue loss. Immediate action should be taken to control bleeding using large gauze pressure bandages. Wounds should be filled with gauze and material held in place by elastic bandages.
3. Treat for shock immediately after (or while) bleeding is being managed.
4. Hospitalization and transfusions are required in virtually all cases.
5. Wounds should be cleaned as soon as possible, and advanced surgical procedures, such as primary closure and skin-grafting accomplished within as rapid a time as possible.

Marine Animals That Sting

Zebrafish
Distribution—Found throughout the world, most common in tropical waters.

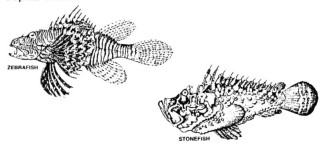

Stonefish
Like the Catfish and Toadfish, the Stonefish is spiny in appearance, found in warm tropical waters and is extremely poisonous.

Catfish
Distribution—Usually fresh water, found worldwide.
Appearance—Varies, but lips usually equipped with long barbels; skin is thick, no scales.
Hazard—Venom in spines in dorsal and pectoral fins.

Toadfish
Distribution—Warmer coastal waters, worldwide.
Appearance—Broad, depressed heads, large mouths, repulsive looking.
Hazard—Dorsal and gill cover venomous spines; fish often camouflaged.

Weever Fish
Distribution—Temperate zone, Europe to North Africa.
Appearance—Small fishes (to 18"), usually seen buried in the mud with only the head exposed.

VENOMOUS FISH

Hazard—Spine on cheek, used as a weapon in hunting for food. Aggressive.

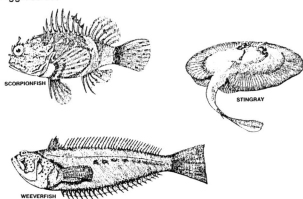

Scorpionfish (including Zebrafish and Stonefish)
Distribution—Widely distributed in temperate and tropical seas; some in arctic waters. Shallow water, bottom dwellers.
Appearance—Gaudy, ugly, ornate.
Hazard—Stings in fins; fearless; some venom is deadly.

Stingrays
Distribution—Common in all tropical, subtropical, warm and temperate regions i varying species. Usually favor sheltered water, burrow into sand with only eyes and tail exposed.
Appearance—Bat-like with a long spine or tail.
Hazard—Wounds are either of the laceration or puncture type. Symptoms can include a fall in blood pressure, vomiting, diarrhea, sweating, rapid heart beat, muscular paralysis, and extreme pain. Death has occasionally been reported.
Prevention and Treatment
No known antidote.

Prevention and Treatment

1. Avoid handling fish.
2. Get victim out of water; watch for possibility of fainting.
3. Observe for signs of shock.
4. With large sting, wash wound with salt water (cold) or sterile saline.
5. Try to remove venom by sucking; make small incision to open wound if necessary.
6. A tourniquet may be of help to prevent spread of the venom; if used, it should be placed between the wound and the heart, as near the wound as possible. It must be released frequently to avoid cutting off circulation.
7. Soak wound in hot water for 30–60 minutes.
8. Water heat may break down the venom—have the water as hot as the victim can tolerate. Use hot compresses if wound is on the face.
9. Addition of magnesium sulfate or Epsom salts to water may help.
10. Local injection of 0.5 to 2% procaine may help; if this fails, intramuscular or intravenous Demerol may help.
11. When pain has subsided, cover wound and elevate if possible. Get medical assistance.

More Fish That Bite:

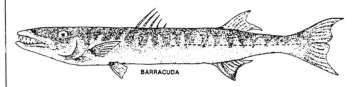

BARRACUDA

Barracuda

Distribution—West Indies, tropical waters, Brazil, north to Florida, and in the Indo-Pacific from the Red Sea to the Hawaiian Islands.

Appearance—Long, thin fish with prominent jaws and teeth. Silver to blue in color. Large head. V-tail. Small to large size which can be from 6 to 8 feet long.

Hazards—20 odd species that vary in their danger. In some regions these fish are more dangerous than sharks. Exceedingly fast swimmers, striking rapidly and fiercely at anything that enters the water. Will follow swimmers but will seldom attack an underwater swimmer. Known to attack surface swimmers and limbs dangling in the water.

Prevention and Treatment

1. Barracuda wounds can be differentiated from those of a shark by their tooth pattern. Barracuda leave straight cuts, while those of a shark are curved like the shape of their jaws.
2. Barracuda are attracted by any bright object, and will also strike a speared fish carried by a diver. Splashing or any flurry of activity can also stimulate a Barracuda to attack.
3. Treatment is the same as for shark bits.

KILLER WHALE

Moray Eels

Distribution—Confined to tropical and subtropical waters. Some temperate zone species are known. Bottom dwellers. Commonly found in holes, crevices, under rocks or coral.

Appearance—Snake-like in appearance and swimming. Tough leathery skin. Can attain a length of 10 feet. Teeth are prominent.

Hazard—Extremely hazardous. Will attack readily and easily provoked. Powerful and vicious biters.

Prevention and Treatment

1. Bites from Moray Eels are of the tearing jagged type.
2. Extreme care should be used when diving in rocky areas, entering caves or reaching into blind holes.
3. Treatment is the same as for shark bits.

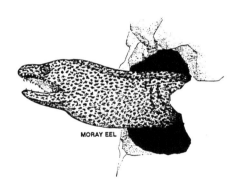

MORAY EEL

Killer Whales

Distribution—Found in all oceans, tropical and polar.

Appearance—Large mammal, with a blunt, rounded snout. High black dorsal fin. Usually, a white patch can be seen behind and above the eye. Sharp contrast between jetblack head and back, and snowy white undersides. Usually observed in packs of from 3-40 whales.

Hazard—Killer whales are extremely ferocious. They have powerful jaws, great weight, speed, and interlocking teeth. They will attack anything in the water without hesitation.

Prevention and Treatment

If killer whales are spotted everyone should immediately leave the water. In addition, extreme care should be taken on shore areas, docks, barges, ice floats, etc. when the whales are in proximity.

Octopus

Distribution—Widespread in tropical and temperate zones. Species vary as to region. Grouping includes, nautilus, cuttlefish and squid.

Appearance—Large sac surrounded by eight or ten tentacles. Head sac is large with well-developed eyes. Horny jaws on mouth. Movement is made by jet action produced by expelling water from the mantle cavity through the siphon.

Hazard—Octopus hide in caves and crevices. They possess a well-developed venom apparatus, and sting by biting.

Prevention and Treatment

Octopus bites consist of two small punctures. Burning or tingling sensation results, and will soon spread. Bleeding is often severe. Clotting ability of the blood is often retarded. Swelling, redness and heat.
General treatment for controlling bleeding. No specific treatment.

Distribution—Widespread species vary according to oceanic region. Hazardous types include: Sea Wasp, Sea Nettle, Sea Blubber, Sea Anemone, Rosy Anemone and Portuguese Man-Of-War.

Appearance—Blue, green or transparent in appearance. Balloon-like floats with tentacles dangling down into the water. The Sea Wasp and Portuguese Man-Of-War are the most dangerous types.

Hazard—Hazardous jellyfish can come into direct contract with a diver in virtually any ocean region. When this happens, the person is exposed to literally thousands of minute stinging organs in the tentacles.

Prevention and Treatment
Jelly fish stings usually result in painful local skin irritations. However, ulceration of the skin can be severe. The Sea Wasp's sting can produce death in from 3–8 minutes. Symptoms can range from itching to blistering, to abdominal pain, to convulsions. Diluted ammonia and alcohol should be applied as soon as possible, and further medical attention sought.

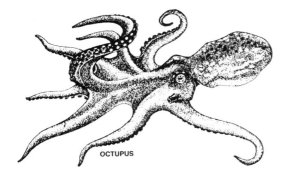

OCTUPUS

Sea Urchins
Distribution—Widespread in varying species.
Appearance—radial shape with long spines.
Hazard—Penetration of the sea urchin spine can cause immediate debilitating affects; lead to numbness and partial paralysis.

Prevention and Treatment

The sting can produce faintness, pain, loss of speech, respiratory disability and in severe cases death. Generally, these stings should be treated in much the same way as any venomous sting (see fish stings). However, particular care should be taken in removing the spine from the wound. This should be done immediately since the spine can continue to inject venom. The spines are particularly brittle, and can break off during removal.

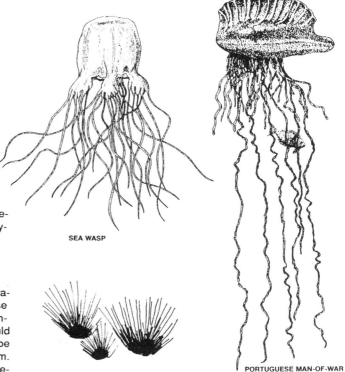

SEA WASP

PORTUGUESE MAN-OF-WAR

Sea Snakes

Distribution—Mostly Indo-Pacific area, warm, sheltered waters; have been observed 150 miles from land.

Hazard—Some species have highly toxic venom; snakes swim forward or backward with ease, can remain submerged for several hours. Disposition: unknown.

Appearance—True snakes, usual length 3–4 feet but may reach 9 feet. Flat, paddle-shaped tail. Markings: various, generally banded.

Prevention and Treatment

1. Symptoms develop gradually, usually taking about an hour. No pain at the bite. May show euphoria or general aching and anxiety. Thickness of tongue and muscle stiffness develop, leading to paralysis.
2. Keep victim still. Apply tourniquet to thigh or upper arm, if indicated.
3. Get the victim to a hospital but don't make him walk.
4. Try to capture the snake for positive identification. It may be a harmless variety.
5. Do not use normal snake bit procedure of incision/suction of venom.
6. Administer anti-venom therapy as soon as possible.
7. Keep victim under observation for at least 24 hours.

SEA SNAKE

Cone Shells

Distribution—Widespread in all regions with varying species. Usually found under rocks, coral, or crawling along sand.

Appearance—Usually a single shell or lack of shell. Body is usually symmetrical in a spiral coiled shell. Shells are usually colorful. Usually a distinct head, one to two pairs of tentacles, two eyes, and a large flattened foot.

Hazard—Highly developed venom apparatus. Have caused some deaths. Paralysis or coma may insue, and death is by cardiac arrest.

Prevention and Treatment

1. Numbness and tingling usually begin at the wound site (a puncture).
2. Symptoms spread rapidly, soon involving the entire body but pronounced near the lips and mouth.

3. There is no specific Treatment, and cone shell poisoning should be dealt with similarly to fish bites and stings.

OTHER ANIMALS

Corals (various)

Distribution—Tropical and subtropical waters.

Appearance—Porous, rock-like formation.

Hazard—Extremely sharp. The most delicate appearing corals are often the most dangerous, having razor sharp edges. Coral cuts, while usually fairly superficial, are very long in healing. Can cause a temporary disability. Some varieties of coral can actually "sting" a diver much like a jelly fish. Whether a cut or sting, the smallest wound, if left untreated, can develop into an ulcer coupled with an extensive sensitive red area.

CONE SHELL

Prevention and Treatment

1. **Promptly cleanse the wound.**
2. **Remove all foreign particles.**
3. **Apply antiseptic agents.**
4. **Bed rest, elevation of the affected limb, and/or further medication is often required.**
5. **Extreme care should be used in working around coral. Often coral is located in a reef formation which is subjected to heavy surface water action, and both surface and bottom current. Surge also develops in reef areas. For this reason, it is easy for the unprepared diver to swept or tumbled across coral with serious consequences.**
6. **Coral should not be handled with bare hands. Completely soled swim fins should also be used.**

Trauma Trauma involves any serious injury to flesh and muscle. Your first step is to stop any heavy bleeding using direct pressure on the wound. At this stage, don't worry about infection; that can be treated later. Do not use a tourniquet except as a last resort. According to the American Red Cross, ". . . the decision to apply a tourniquet is in reality a decision to risk sacrifice of a limb in order to save life." Then:

* For a *mangled hand:*
1. Cover it with a clean cloth and leave it alone until the doctor arrives.
2. If a finger has been severed, save it in sea water or a saline (salt) solution.

* For *broken bones:*
1. Do no further harm. Do not try to reset the fracture; do not touch or try to push back any exposed bone. You could cause irreparable damage to blood vessels and nerves.
2. Cover any open wound, then splint the fracture, taking great care not to rearrange anything.
3. Do not move the patient unless necessary.
4. To reduce swelling, put ice bags around, but not on top of, the fracture.

* For a *deep puncture wound:*
1. Wash with hydrogen peroxide or other disinfectant.
2. If the agent is still in the wound (a fishhook, for example), leave it there.

CHAPTER NINETEEN

Troubleshooting and Repairs Underway

YOUR ENGINE: PRIMARY SAFETY EQUIPMENT

An engine failure can do a lot more than ruin your day of waterskiing or fishing, and an engine out of commission is more than an inconvenience. That iron powerpack nestled in the bilge or hanging off the stern is what might bring you home ahead of the weather, keep your bow headed into heavy seas, get you safely through a tricky inlet, or help get an injured crew member ashore.

Every boater should know what to do in the event of engine failure—and that doesn't mean call the Coast Guard. The Coast Guard is not a maritime "Triple-A." Their job is to save lives, not start engines. The Coast Guard *will* take you off a sinking boat, lend you a pump to help control flooding, take you in tow if your boat is in danger, and turn you over to a commercial salvor or tow operator (see chapter 22), if one is available.

In other words, you'd better be prepared to deal with your own stalled engine. If yours is a sailboat, you also should develop your sailing skills to a point where you don't need to rely on the engine. If that seems too hard, remember that there are thousands of small sailboats that don't have engines and never will, and somehow their owners manage quite nicely.

THE FIRST RULE OF ENGINE REPAIR

Maintaining the engine is cheaper, easier, and safer than fixing it. Know your engine; follow the maintenance schedules in the owner's manual; keep track of the work in your Owner's Notebook (see chapter 10).

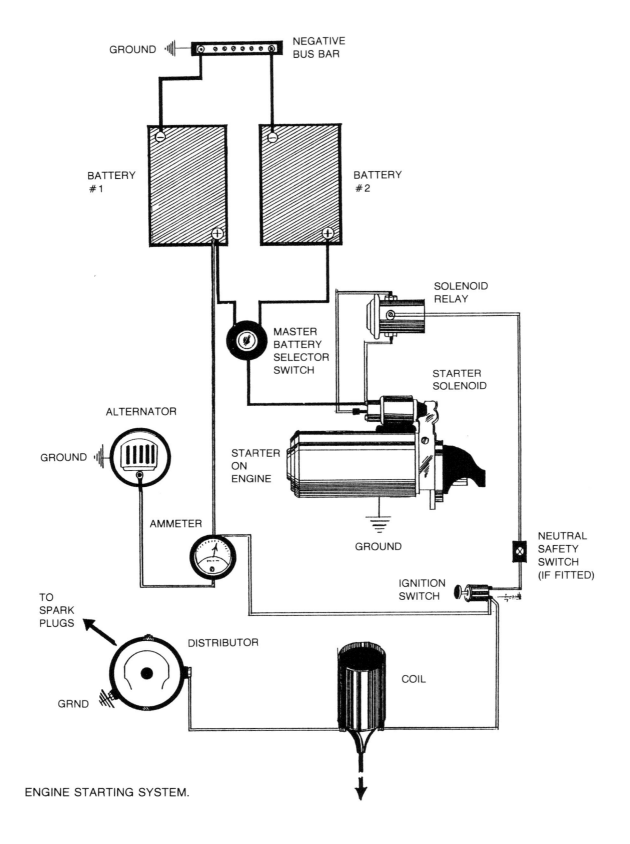

GROUND

NEGATIVE
BUS BAR

BATTERY
#1

BATTERY
#2

SOLENOID
RELAY

MASTER
BATTERY
SELECTOR
SWITCH

STARTER
SOLENOID

ALTERNATOR

GROUND

STARTER
ON
ENGINE

AMMETER

GROUND

NEUTRAL
SAFETY
SWITCH
(IF FITTED)

IGNITION
SWITCH

TO
SPARK
PLUGS

DISTRIBUTOR

GRND

COIL

ENGINE STARTING SYSTEM.

ENGINE FAILURE

In the event of engine failure, immediately stabilize the situation. If you're in the middle of a busy channel and still have some headway, steer over to the side or get out of the channel. Sound the five-blast danger signal on your horn to let other boaters in the vicinity know you're not in control. Hoist the "D" flag (should you have one aboard) to signal, "Keep clear of me, I am maneuvering with difficulty," or the "F" flag, which says, "I am disabled; communicate with me."

When (and if) conditions permit, drop the anchor.

Quickly note the readings on your instrument panel: A high-temperature indication might be a clue to the problem. If you wait too long to take the reading, the gauge might merely be showing the increase in the temperature of the noncirculating coolant, which occurs in a stopped engine.

ENGINE TROUBLESHOOTING

The first step in engine troubleshooting is to understand your engine basics: The operation of any internal-combustion engine depends upon three elements—fuel, air, and fire.

The fuel is pulled from a fuel tank and through a filter by the fuel pump; it is then mixed with air and sprayed or injected into the engine through a carburetor or fuel injector; it is ignited either by an electrical spark (in a gasoline engine) or by high pressure (in a diesel).

If the engine will not start, one of these three elements most likely is missing. With a gasoline engine, chances are the problem is in the ignition circuits; with a diesel, look first to the fuel supply.

If the engine has stopped, the symptoms of the stoppage may give the clue to the problem:

• If stoppage was preceded by coughing or surging, check the fuel supply and in-line fuel filters. Switch to a full fuel tank. Then clean and/or replace fuel filters. With a diesel engine, air will be sucked into the lines from an empty tank and you'll have to bleed the air out of the system before it will restart. Follow the instructions for this in the owner's manual.

• An engine that *quietly* "stops" without warning is most likely the victim of an electrical problem. With a gasoline engine, check the leads to the distributor. With a diesel, check the shutoff

solenoid. It may have short-circuited and closed off the air supply.

• If the engine stops with a thump, you may have hit something in the water or you may have wrapped a line around the propeller. Try to ascertain the nature of the problem before you try to correct it. If you've merely bumped up against something, the engine may restart readily; however, if the propeller shaft or blades have been bent or nicked, you are likely to note vibration, which will become more distressing as speed is increased. Run the engine just below the critical speed. Don't run it at all if additional damage to the mounting struts and shaft bearings seems possible.

• Before trying to restart any engine that has stopped mysteriously, check the oil and transmission levels and look for signs of water: a milky color in the oil, a frothy texture in the transmission fluid. If the levels are too low: Did you check them before starting out or is this a sudden development?

• If you do start and run an engine without fully understanding the cause of the stoppage, use power sparingly and keep a constant watch on all fluid levels, pressures, and temperatures until a qualified mechanic can check over the engine.

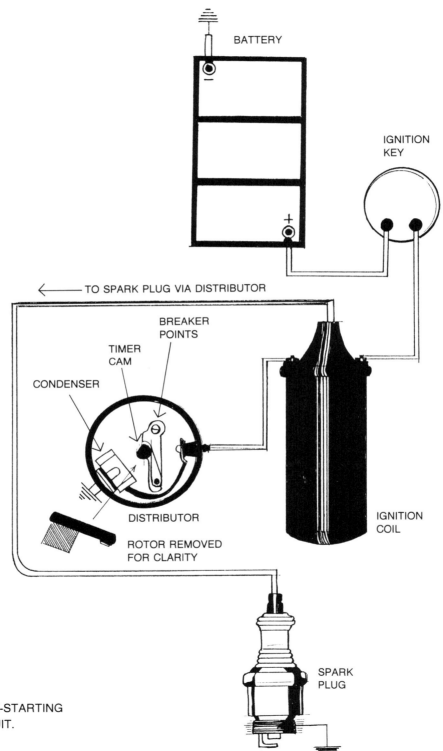

BATTERY

IGNITION
KEY

TO SPARK PLUG VIA DISTRIBUTOR

BREAKER
POINTS

TIMER
CAM

CONDENSER

DISTRIBUTOR

ROTOR REMOVED
FOR CLARITY

IGNITION
COIL

SPARK
PLUG

THE BASIC ENGINE-STARTING
ELECTRICAL CIRCUIT.

KEY MAINTENANCE POINTS
ON TYPICAL OUTBOARD
ENGINE. (Evinrude)

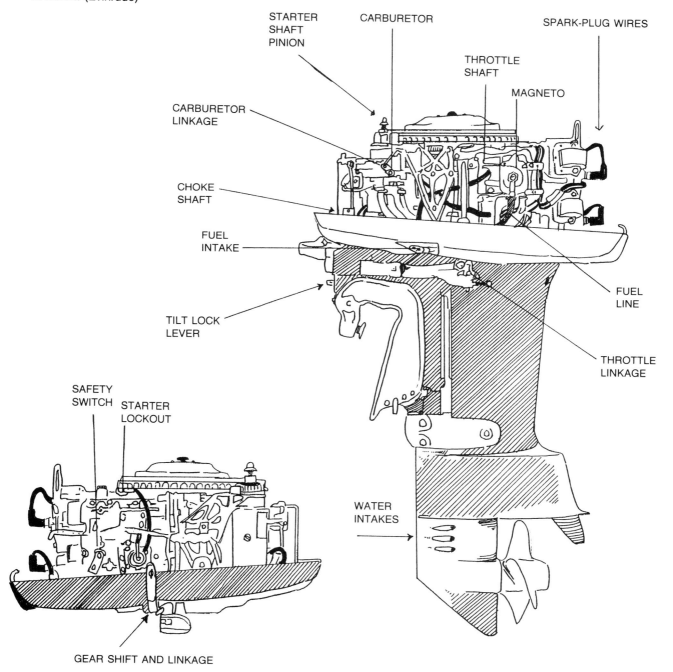

TROUBLESHOOTING TREES

The following Troubleshooting Trees walk you through a problem—or a series of problems—in logical, step-by-step fashion, then suggest a solution for each problem as located. Try these out before you *need* to use them, and work through a few examples while everything is operating properly. Troubleshooting for electrical problems is discussed at the end of this chapter.

Engine Warning Signs and Troubleshooting

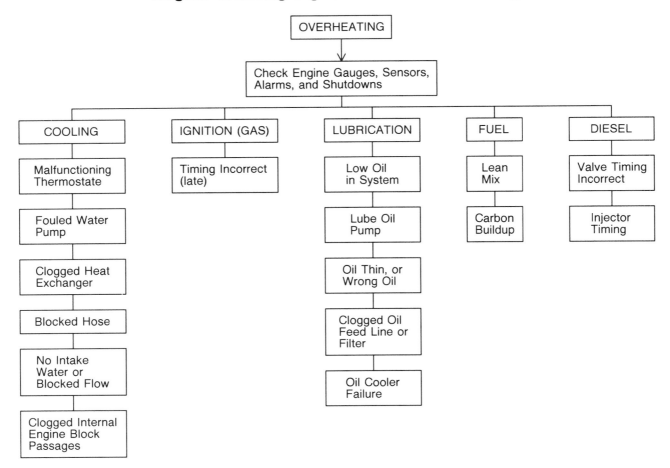

Troubleshooting the Diesel Engine

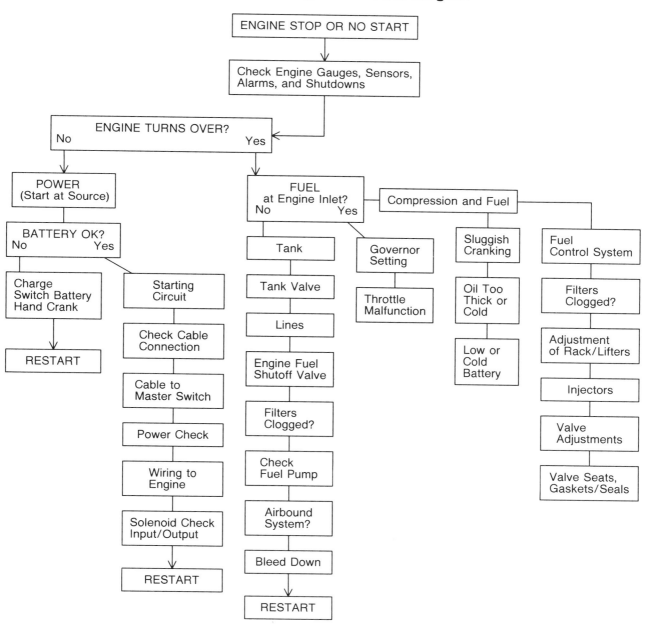

Troubleshooting the Gasoline Engine

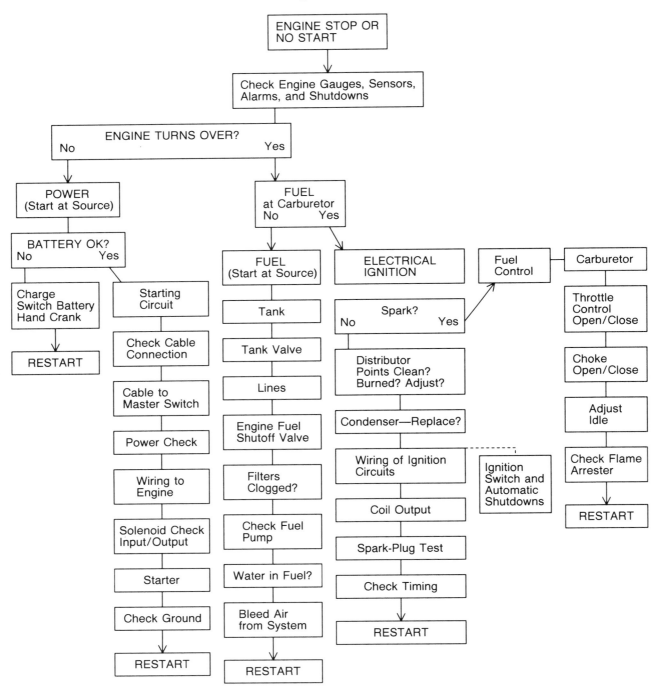

CLEARING A FOULED PROPELLER

Wrapping a line around the prop is perhaps the universal boating accident: It happens to almost everyone. But it doesn't have to happen, because prevention is quite simple:

- Keep all your lines out of the water.
- Secure the ends of all sheets and halyards and never allow mooring lines to drape or trail over the side.
- Make sure your anchor rode is properly stowed when not in use.
- Don't back down on your dinghy while you're maneuvering for an anchorage or other mooring—and don't let it drift up astern unnoticed.

Getting the line off the prop is not nearly as easy as getting it on; if you're lucky, it's just a couple of turns, which can be teased off or unwrapped. However, don't just grab at a free end of the line and pull without (1) turning off the ignition and (2) putting the transmission in neutral. You might remember that all early automobiles were started with a crank; what else, indeed, is a line wrapped around the shaft but a potentially efficient starting crank?

You could uncouple the shaft from the transmission, to allow freewheeling while you work the line loose. This *might* let you free the line without your having to go over the side.

If the line is *really* wrapped around the prop or shaft, or if the frictional heat developed in the wrapping has melted the line into a solid mass, you'll have to cut it loose—which means going over the side with a knife. At the least, you must have a face mask to enhance visibility, a snorkel to enhance breathing, and a sharp, sturdy knife (attached with a lanyard) to make the cut. A knife with a serrated edge provides a sawing effect and is more effective than one with a straight edge. Do not go over the side without a safety line: You don't want to complicate the fouled-prop problem with a man-overboard emergency. If the water is cold and you don't have a wet suit or other "professional" diving equipment, at least put on some heavy clothing, including socks and long underwear. Then don foul-weather gear or oilskins. Harder to swim this way? Sure, but better than suffering a quick, severe, and debilitating case of hypothermia. Your safety line to the surface will help keep you out of trouble.

LOSS OF STEERING

Rudder control can be lost in any of several ways: (1) The rudder hits bottom or is damaged when mooring stern-to; (2) the rudder is thrown too hard over when backing or is hit by a stern wave; (3) the control cables come loose, or break, or get fouled and won't run through the guiding sheaves; (4) any part of the steering gear breaks. The cause may have been poor seamanship or poor maintenance; the solution may be difficult.

First, check out the damage. If it is simply a matter of a slipped control cable, you should be able to put it back in the groove, adjust the ten-

sion so it won't slip again, and go on your way. *A caution,* however: Don't overtighten or you'll be inviting other problems. If the cable is broken, it can be repaired using a short length of spare cable and some cable fasteners.

EMERGENCY STEERING

Using one or more of the following methods, you might at least be able to move closer to a safe haven and assistance—or even get all of the way home.

• If the rudder is not damaged, use the emergency tiller.

• You can steer a twin-engine powerboat with the throttles.

• With single engine power or under sail, use a drogue or a sea anchor to provide drag, aft, to port or starboard. To jury-rig a sea anchor, bundle a fender with a spare anchor, or drag a bucket, from a V-shaped bridle—one end to the port quarter, the other to the starboard quarter. By slacking off one line or the other, you transfer the drag to the opposite quarter and turn the boat in that direction. Two cautions, however: (1) With any sort of speed, the force on the lines can be enough to damage your fittings; (2) when slowing down, beware of letting those lines settle down into your prop.

• Under sail, careful shifting and trimming of the sails (particularly with a two-masted rig) will give you some control.

• Jury-rigging a rudder can be a very iffy proposition. Granted, you can steer a small boat with an oar (or even a broom stuck out astern), but creating an emergency rudder—and mounting it in some sort of useful fashion—becomes geometrically more difficult as boat size increases. Look over your boat and plan how you *might* do it in time of need.

PROBLEMS WITH A SAILING RIG

HALYARD OR SAIL FOULED ON STAY OR SPREADER

First, slack off and try to shake off the sail or halyard. If this doesn't work, try increasing tension slightly; when pulled, the line or sail may unwrap itself from the stay.

If a halyard has slipped off the masthead sheave, someone may have to go up the mast to put it back on (see chapter 10).

BROKEN HALYARD

Trying to replace a halyard while underway might be next to impossible; a spare halyard, rigged and tied off on a cleat, is a good backup for a broken halyard. It can also be used as a jury-rigged shroud or stay and to help rig a bosun's chair.

If no spare is available, try using the topping lift or the halyard from the genoa; if the sail won't go all the way to the top, reef the sail to maintain a reasonable shape.

BROKEN STAY OR SHROUD

Immediately slack, then lower all affected sails to get the lopsided tension off the mast as quickly as possible—and to avoid breaking the mast. Get on the opposite tack or otherwise adjust course so that the pressure of the wind will pull the mast against the remaining wire. Jury-rig the spare halyard (or other line) as a temporary replacement. Proceed under power if you can; if not, sail very conservatively with minimum pressure on the sails.

TORN OR RIPPED SAIL

Get the sail down (or out of the water, as the case may be), taking care that you are not knocked about or pulled overboard. With the sail safely on deck, you may be able to effect temporary repairs with rough stitching or emergency patches secured with contact cement or even good-quality duct tape.

TROUBLESHOOTING THE ELECTRICAL SYSTEM

Most electrical problems can be traced to one of three causes: (1) The circuit is interrupted by a broken wire or loose connection; (2) the current is being dumped out through a short circuit—typically, where the insulation has been worn away as the wire rubs against some piece of metal equipment, or (3) the electrical unit (light bulb, motor, whatever) has failed. Locating the problem usually is fairly simple.

First, you want to make sure that power is in fact reaching the nonfunctioning element. Is the control-panel switch on? Check the fuse or circuit breaker.

If the switch is on and the fuse is intact, is power reaching the panel? If other equipment seems to work fine, the problem probably is in the connection at the switch, in the line from the panel to the equipment, or in the equipment itself. Here's where a simple 12V test lamp comes in handy. You can buy one or make one—rig a light bulb with test leads attached to the positive and negative contacts. Hook one lead to the engine block and use the other as a probe, working your way along the system at each connection point. If that portion of the circuit is complete, the bulb will light. This is most useful in checking for broken wires or loose connections.

Another handy tool is the multimeter, which, among other features, can put a small current into the circuit to check for continuity—to ensure that the current is flowing to the equipment, through the equipment, and back to the meter. This is particularly helpful when trying to evaluate a hard-to-reach problem, such as a nonfunctioning masthead light. Is the problem a burned-out bulb or something more abstract? A burned-out bulb (or corroded socket) will not pass the current.

A continuity check can also help find a short-circuited wire hidden somewhere up an aluminum mast. Attach one probe to the mast and touch the other, in turn, to the wires running up the mast. Continuity between any wire and the mast reveals a short circuit to the mast—most likely, insulation rubbed away—and indicates the need for repair or replacement of the wire. Before you go to the trouble of pulling a new wire through the mast, check for the short at any points where the wire exits the mast.

Full instructions on the use of a multimeter come with the unit; work through them one step at a time and you'll soon be an expert.

ELECTRICAL TROUBLESHOOTING THE ENGINE

The weakest link in the maritime powerplant chain is the electrical system. The exposure to moisture, salt air, and vibration is constant, and each works to defeat the steady flow of electricity that is vital to the operation of a gasoline engine and necessary (at the least) for starting most diesels.

Table 19-1.
Engine Electrical Troubleshooting

Symptom	Action	Symptom	Action
Starter will not turn over	Close the switch.	Engine turns over but will not start	Do not keep turning over the engine. Once you have determined that the engine (gas or diesel) is getting fuel to the cylinders, begin to check ignition.
	Using a test light or voltmeter, test for voltage at the battery (12V in most boats).		Remove the high-voltage wire from the coil, hold it close to the engine block, and attempt to start the engine. You should see a spark jump to the block.
	Be sure battery connections are clean and tight.		
	Check the ground strap.		If there is no spark, look to the distributor. Make sure that the points are opening and closing as the shaft turns in the distributor. You can open and close the points manually to see whether, when the points open, a spark jumps from the coil's high-voltage lead to the ground.
	Using a voltmeter, test for power on the starter side of the solenoid (small can-type switch usually mounted on the starter).		
	Test for power on the starter terminal itself.		
	Since the starter grounds itself via its mounting plate and the mount bolts on the engine, make sure this mount is clean and tight.		If there is no spark, then: (1) Check for short circuits or corrosion on the moving point; (2) change the condenser; or (3) change the coil.
	If starter will not start after these tests, remove it for repair or replacement.		
Starter pinion gear moves but will not turn over completely	Using the voltmeter, test the battery voltage while the starter attempts to turn. Low voltage (anything below 8V) means the problem is in the battery.	If there is spark to the block but engine still will not fire, then:	Reconnect the coil high-voltage wire.
	If battery voltage is between 10 and 12V, the problem may lie in the conductors and connections between the battery and the starter.		Remove a spark-plug wire and hold the end near the engine block. Turn over the engine. A spark should jump to the block.
	If the voltage at the starter is at least 9V and is close to the battery measured voltage, the problem lies within the starter itself. Remove, repair, or replace.		If there is no spark, and you have already tested for power between distributor and coil—then the problem lies between the distributor and the plugs. There is a short to ground in the distributor rotor or cap. This can be a crack in the rotor body or the cap itself, or it could be moisture buildup. If cracked, replace the cap
Engine starts briefly and then stops when key is released	Check for an open circuit at the ballast resistor.		
	Use spare wire to create a temporary bypass to the ballast resistor.		

Table 19-1. *(Continued)*

Symptom	Action	Symptom	Action
	and rotor; if whole, thoroughly dry these components.		gap. One hint: To aid starting, dip the ends of the spark plugs in gasoline before installation. Do not overtighten the plugs in their sockets. Check the plug specifications (in the box) for the correct setting to use on your torque wrench when installing new plugs.
	If in doubt, install a new cap and rotor.		
	If there is a spark and still no ignition, remove and replace the spark plugs with the proper heat range and		

Engine Component Electrical Checks

Symptom	Action
Generator low charging power out	Check all connections as well as drive-belt tension. To pinpoint the trouble, disconnect the connector between the voltage regulator and the generator field terminal. With the engine running, touch the wire to the engine block. If the generator is operating properly, it will make voltage flow to the frame. Your problem, therefore, lies in the voltage regulator. Make this a momentary test, since excessive operation with a grounded generator can cause damage.
Alternator charge power	First, disconnect the voltage regulator. Make up a wire jumper from fairly substantial insulated wire. Connect the alternator field terminal to the positive (+) terminal on the battery. Run the engine. If the alternator furnishes charging power then the problem is in the voltage regulator.

For individual components, most of your tests will be for continuity (or lack of it) between two connections. This will mean a resistance test using a voltage-ohmmeter.

Tests with a VOM (Voltage–Ohm–Milliammeter)

Component	Connection	Reading
Spark plug	Shell to hot terminal	Infinite. If reading occurs then plug is fouled, clean or replace.
Ballast resistor	Measure when warm	Use X1 scale; should read less than 2 ohms.
Distributor points	Across closed points	Zero
	Across open points	Infinite
	Pivot (hot point) to engine	Infinite
	Ground point to engine	Zero
Condenser	Metal case to wire pigtail	Set ohmmeter on high range. As test leads touch, the meter should momentarily go to infinite and then return to zero.
		Reverse leads and look for the same result.
Coil	Between two primary terminals.	Should read 1 to 2 ohms.
	Primary terminal to metal case	Infinite
	Hot terminal to primary terminal	5,000 to 10,000 ohms
	Hot terminal to case	Infinite

CHAPTER TWENTY

Weather

YOUR NEED TO UNDERSTAND THE WEATHER

Two events of the mid-twentieth century stand as stark evidence of the need to understand, and be prepared for, the power of the weather at sea.

On December 18, 1944, a U.S. Navy task force was hit by a typhoon about 300 miles east of the Philippines. Three destroyers capsized and sank; twenty-eight other ships were damaged; and 790 men were lost. The commanding officers had placed too much reliance on radio weather forecasts, which proved to be inadequate, and they failed to heed clear signs of the approaching storm in time to take evasive action. In the words of the official report: "There was a lack of appreciation . . . that really dangerous weather conditions existed, until it was too late to make the preparations for security that might have been helpful."

On August 14, 1979, the 303 boats entered in the Fastnet Race off the coast of Britain were hit by a massive storm that continued for twenty hours. Weather forecasting was inadequate, and when the early signs of the storm became appar-ent, race officials did not warn the boats. The in-dividual skippers—too intent on running the race—thus did not prepare their boats for the storm.

When the storm hit, it was too late. Even though manned by some of the most skilled sail-ors in the world, seventy-seven boats capsized; twenty-four were abandoned by their crews on the assumption that they were sinking; five did sink. More than 100 of the boats were knocked down until their masts touched the water. Six sailors were lost when their safety harnesses broke, and nine others either drowned or died of hypothermia.

Notwithstanding the above examples, mari-time weather should be viewed in relative, not absolute, terms. To a boy in a sailing dinghy, a passing thundershower may be just as hazardous as a monster hurricane is to a destroyer.

To most recreational boaters, the weather becomes a problem when the winds are above 20 knots and the seas at six feet or higher. What was supposed to be "fun" now becomes work; just holding on uses a great deal of energy.

In a really heavy blow, you'll find visibility as low as zero; your boat heeled far over just by the force of the wind, with little margin to accommodate the force of the waves; and water trying to pour in through any and all openings. The normal preparations for going to sea are not enough; if you might be caught in a storm you can't avoid, you need to take additional precautions—and have additional knowledge.

THE SOURCE

The phenomenon we call "weather" is caused by the sun's bombardment of the earth and the subsequent movement of heat from one area to another. You can think of the earth as a giant heat pump, absorbing energy from the sun and moving it around the planet's surface. Most of the energy from the sun hits near the equator, which presents a broad, direct target. The sun has an increasingly reduced effect farther north and south as the rays strike at an increasingly oblique angle—until, at the poles, most of the energy doesn't reach the surface but is deflected away by the atmosphere. If there were no "weather" to keep things in balance, the equator would become impossibly hot and the temperature at the poles would continue to sink toward absolute zero.

In this chapter, we'll look at weather in the general sense, but also with particular focus on weather as it affects boating in the United States and Europe.

AIR PRESSURE

At the equator, the heated air rises to an altitude of about 50,000 feet and spreads out in a broad horizontal flow until it becomes cool enough to sink back to earth. This occurs at about 30 degrees north (and south) latitude—roughly, the middle of the United States. The downward-flowing air creates a band of high pressure around the earth (which actually takes the form of a series of high-pressure cells), and the airflow at the surface spreads out north and south, creating relatively constant winds.

However, these planetary winds don't flow straight north and south; they are deflected to the right by the Coriolis effect. This means that the winds originally headed north are bent to the northeast; those headed south are now twisted toward the southwest. A New York–based sailing ship of the nineteenth century, for example, could count on westerly winds in the north Atlantic for a crossing to Europe; then, riding the back of the "Bermuda high," it could drop down to the west coast of Africa, there to pick up the prevailing easterlies for the voyage home.

The vast areas of rising and falling air create variations in the weight of the air—the atmospheric pressure—at any given spot on the earth's surface. The "standard" weight of the atmosphere is pegged at 14.7 pounds per square inch, and the nominal pressure anywhere on the earth's surface should be equivalent to 29.92 inches of mercury in a barometer (or 1013.2 millibars), since 14.7 pounds per square inch will push a slim column of mercury to that height in the glass tube of a traditional barometer. The actual pressure varies from one part of the world to another and from one season to another. However, it is not the specific pressure, but the relative change and rate of change in pressure, that is the key to the analysis and prediction of weather.

For the boater, "pressure" is easily translated into practical terms: high pressure generally means good weather; low pressure, the opposite. The old seaman's phrase, "The glass is falling fast," refers to a rapid drop in the level of mercury in the barometer, and the more rapid the fall, the more serious may be the approaching weather.

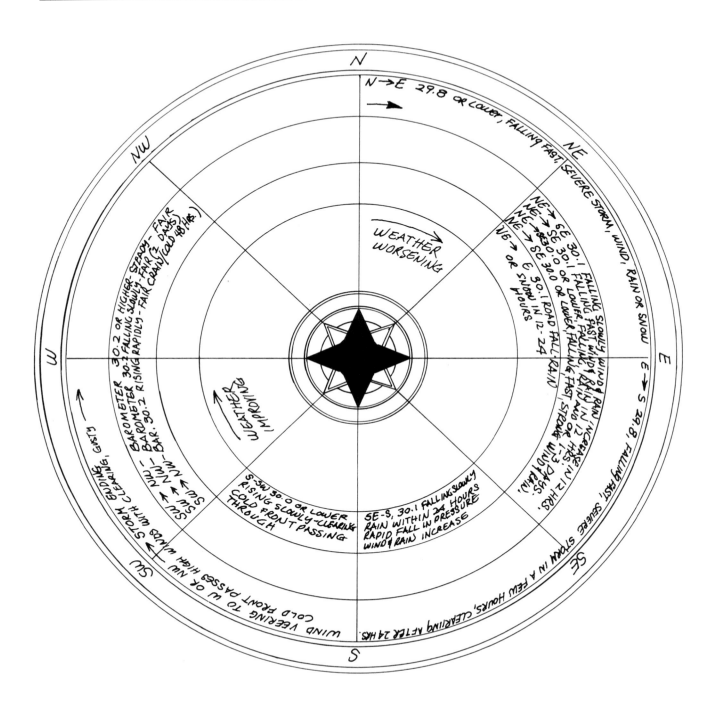

READING WIND AND BAROMETRIC PRESSURE.

WIND

Wind is the movement of air from an area of higher to an area of lower pressure. This movement may be part of the global weather system, or it may be generated locally. For example, onshore and offshore winds generally are created by the relative temperature of the land and its adjoining body of water. The sun beating down on a bare sandy beach or a cluster of buildings will create an upflow of warm air; when the cooler air offshore is drawn in by the reduced pressure caused by this rising air, we have an onshore wind, normally an afternoon phenomenon. In the evening, no longer being warmed by the sun, the air piled up over the land begins to cool and flow back out over the water as an offshore or land breeze.

WEATHER FRONTS

Most changes in weather are associated with the passage of weather fronts. A cold front is a mass of cooler air pushing behind a mass of warmer air; a warm front is a mass of relatively warmer air following along behind a mass of cooler air.

Cold fronts tend to act like snow shovels, forcing their way under the warmer air and creating quickly passing and often violent thunderstorms, squalls, tornadoes.

Warm fronts ride up over a departing mass of cooler air and usually take several days to pass. A warm front may bring steady drizzle, fog, overcast skies.

A stationary front is one that has become stalled when the pressure differentials are almost in balance—it rarely brings much wind but usually results in sustained rainfall. An occluded front may bring the worst of both worlds, so to speak: A warm front has been overtaken, and forced upward, by a cold front. The cold front provides heavy winds; the warm front, heavy and steady rain.

OTHER WEATHER SYSTEMS

Some weather patterns are local, peculiar to a particular part of the world. The weather in San Francisco, for example, is controlled largely by the interaction of the hot inland desert and the cold offshore current. The strong upward movement of air over the desert sucks moist air from farther out to sea over the cold water; the moisture condenses to fog; the continued inland "vacuum" pulls the fog into the city. You can almost guess the temperature inland by the distance the fogbank has moved.

Another example: Cape Hatteras is known for frequent and violent storms. The cape is the crossroads for cold, dry air swinging down from Canada and warm, damp air moving along the 80°F waters of the Gulf Stream.

FOG

At any given temperature, air will hold a certain percentage of water vapor. The ratio of the level of water vapor to the amount the air *could* hold at that temperature is called humidity. Warm air can hold more moisture than cool air. For example, when the humidity is 30 percent, the air is very dry (typical of the desert, with very warm air and not much water around, or of the interior of a home in winter where cold outside air has been heated with no additional moisture); when the humidity is 98 percent, the water content is so high you can feel it.

When the humidity reaches 100 percent, there is so much water vapor that you can see it—and that is fog.

How does the humidity reach that point—called the dew point? Usually it occurs when the moist body of air is cooled below the temperature at which it can support the moisture it already contains, and sometimes when warmer moist air mixes with cooler air. Here are the basic conditions under which fog will form:

Steam Fog Cold air moves over warm water, as in a swamp at night.

Advection Fog Warm, moist air moves over cold water and is cooled from below. The San Francisco story.

Radiation Fog Loss of heat from the ground at night cools the adjoining layer of air. If the air stays over the land, this is not much of a problem for boaters, but the resultant fog can drift out over the river or harbor.

Up-slope Air currents carry warm, moist air up a hillside to a higher elevation, where the air becomes cooler. Not a problem for boaters except, perhaps, on mountain lakes.

Frontal Rain falling from cooler higher elevations cools the warmer air through which it falls; or rain falling from warmer higher elevations hits cold air below, raising the humidity to the dew point.

Note that in most fog formations, warm (or cold) air must move over a colder (or warmer) surface. If the air is stationary, it will be at about the same temperature as the surface below; by the same token, if it is moving too fast, it won't have time to change temperature. Fogs will lift— or be dissipated—if the air is heated past the dew point. The engine for this heating, typically, is the

---

Sound Signals in Fog

Patterns of *long* (–) and *short* (.) blasts on horn:

–	Power vessel making way
– –	Power vessel underway but stopped
– ··	Sailing vessel underway. Vessel not under command, restricted in ability to maneuver; towing, pushing, or fishing
– ···	Vessel under tow
Bell	Rapid ringing for five seconds—vessel at anchor—followed by five-second gong for vessel more than 300 feet long

---

Actions to Take in Fog

Always be alert for conditions leading to fog. If you are operating in an area known to be subject to frequent or sudden fog, keep better track of your position than you might otherwise. Once a fog hits, visual position finding becomes impossible, and you're forced to rely on Loran (possibly inaccurate inshore) or on radio direction finding (a rarity—but all the more reason to equip your boat with an RDF). If you have a radar set, well, these are the conditions under which it pays off. However else you may be equipped, use your depth finder to help match your position with the recorded depths on the chart, but be sure to compensate for the state of the tide.

As you become wrapped in fog:

1. Fix your position as accurately as possible.
2. Begin sounding fog signals and listening for fog signals from buoys, lighthouses, and other boats. Stop your engine as necessary to listen for faint or distant signals. If you have a fog-signal loud hailer that functions also as a listening device, switch to the "listen" mode often.

3. If you know where you are and where you're going, proceed slowly. Put a lookout on the bow. Use your RDF and your best dead-reckoning skills to keep an accurate plot. Double-check tide and current tables and account for set and drift.

4. If you don't know where you are, anchor and wait for the fog to clear. If you are in the middle of a crowded channel or in water too deep to anchor, move carefully to a safer spot. Begin sounding the "at anchor" fog signal— ringing the bell for five seconds every minute.

5. Above all, don't be in a hurry to go anywhere. Use your VHF radio to contact the marina and advise of your delay, or use the marine operator to make a telephone call to the person who has your float plan.

HEAVY WEATHER

Heavy weather is the sailor's term for weather that is beyond fun and moving into the area of positively dangerous. There are two basic forms of heavy weather: (1) the fast-moving, tightly packed, unpredictable, short-lived squall and (2) the large, powerful storm (usually classified as a gale or hurricane). A line of squalls may accompany the passage of a cold front, or individual squalls may be generated by local geography. For example, wide beaches or steep coastal hills may help create unstable movement of air—typically, late on a hot summer day. Gales and hurricanes are "cyclonic" storms, close cousins of the tornado and the cyclone; the winds whirl counter-clockwise around the center in the Northern Hemisphere and clockwise in the Southern Hemisphere.

Squalls may come boiling along from any direction. Gales of the temperate zone—called extratropical storms—tend to move in a generally west-to-east direction. Storms of the tropics—called tropical storms—are erratic and will spin, twist, and double back without warning. And even though tropical storms are *born* in the tropics, they don't necessarily *stay* there.

HURRICANES AND TYPHOONS

They're called hurricanes in the Atlantic and typhoons in the Pacific. The storms are identical, except in name and seasonal variation.

These tropical storms are not just one big wind; they vary from point to point in intensity and danger. In general, the right side of the storm (viewed looking down the track in the Northern Hemisphere) is the dangerous semicircle; the pressure gradients are steep, the winds intense, and the seas tend toward the catastrophic. The left side of the storm (viewed looking down the track in the Northern Hemisphere) is known as the "safe" or navigable semicircle; the pressure gradients are spread out, and so are the effects of the storm.

The maximum winds of a hurricane or typhoon have never been measured, because the manmade measuring instruments have all blown away at some point. We know of sustained winds above 150 knots, and suspect gusts as high as 225 knots.

The name *hurricane* was borrowed by the Spanish from the Indians of the Caribbean. Interestingly, tribal variations of the word all meant much the same thing: *huracan* was an evil spirit, *hurakan* was the god of thunder and lightning, *hyroacan* was a devil. Hurricanes are summer storms, as the old sailor's rhyme attests:

> June, too soon
> July, stand by
> August, don't trust
> September, remember
> October, all over.

The derivation of the word *typhoon* is not as clear. It might come from the Cantonese *t'ai fung* (great wind), but the Greek philosopher Aristotle used the word *typhon* (monster) to mean a wind-containing cloud.

Typhoons can occur at any time of year, although 90 percent happen between June and December. Typhoons in the western Pacific are more numerous than hurricanes in the eastern Atlantic, in a ratio of about 8:1. A particularly vicious Pacific phenomenon is the Fujiwahara effect (first described by a Japanese scientist named Fujiwahara), the synergism of two independent but proximate typhoons. Fortunately, it rarely occurs.

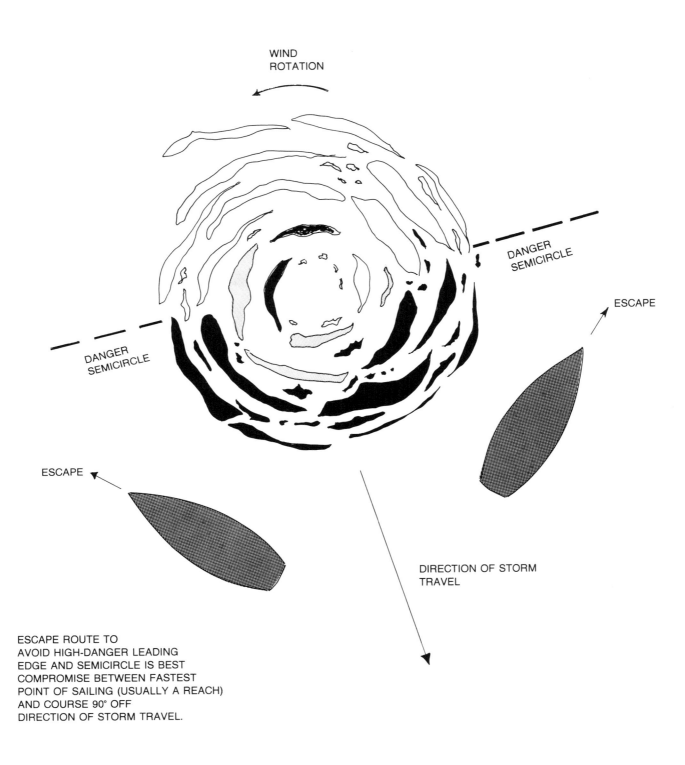

WIND
ROTATION

DANGER
SEMICIRCLE

DANGER
SEMICIRCLE

ESCAPE

ESCAPE

DIRECTION OF STORM
TRAVEL

ESCAPE ROUTE TO
AVOID HIGH-DANGER LEADING
EDGE AND SEMICIRCLE IS BEST
COMPROMISE BETWEEN FASTEST
POINT OF SAILING (USUALLY A REACH)
AND COURSE 90° OFF
DIRECTION OF STORM TRAVEL.

STORM ARC OF DANGER.

WEATHER FORECASTING

In the modern world, we can hardly escape the weather forecasts even if we wanted to: Commercial radio and television keep us posted from moment to moment; the daily newspapers present short- and long-range forecasts; and the National Oceanic and Atmospheric Administration (NOAA) operates twenty-four-hour weather channels on VHF.

However—a good mariner learns the rudiments of weather prediction for himself. There will be times when the professional forecasts will be in error; when sudden storms hit without public warning; when Mother Nature pulls a fast one and shifts things around. And the rudiments, as practiced by mariners from time immemorial, are not all that complicated.

In North America, weather tends to move from west to east at about 20 to 25 mph, and, even without the aid of a barometer, the visible characteristics of approaching cold and warm fronts permit relatively accurate short-range weather forecasting. Larger storm systems (see below) are signaled by falling barometric pressure (see boxes).

SQUALLS

Squalls can develop without warning, and therefore may or may not be reported on commercial weather broadcasts or even the NOAA weather channel. The best "prediction" for squalls is to *expect* them any afternoon in the summer and any time a cold front is expected to pass through.

Squalls move quickly—as fast as 40 knots—but can be seen at a great distance as towering thunderheads boil up into the sky with a mean, almost black, base. You can measure the distance to a squall by noting the time it takes for the thunder to reach you after you see the lightning, and dividing by five. This will give you some measure of the time you have left to ready the boat—sails down, hatches and ports closed, fishing lines in, and so on.

GALES, HURRICANES, AND TYPHOONS

By their very nature, these are areas of low barometric pressure. Thus, a falling barometer is an indication that a storm may be approaching; a rapidly falling barometer is almost a guarantee of a storm, and the faster the rate of fall, the more powerful the event. One small consolation: The warning usually will come far enough in advance to permit adequate preparation: to return to port (or remain in port) and properly secure the boat or, if caught too far out at sea, to head away from the most dangerous part of the storm.

Barometric Changes and Weather Prediction

Rate of Fall	Warning	Rate of Fall	Distance to Storm Center
.06 inch in three hours	Impending storm	.02 to .06 inch per hour	250 to 150 miles
.15 inch in three hours	Strong storm	.06 to .10 inch per hour	150 to 100 miles
.30 inch in three hours	Extreme storm	.10 to .12 inch per hour	100 to 75 miles
		.15 to .19 inch per hour	Under 50 miles

Barometer Forecasting

Pressure (inches)	Wind	Weather
30.2 or higher, steady	SW to NW	Fair, small temperature change
30.2 or higher, falling	SW to NW	Fair for a few days, rising temperatures
30.1 or higher, falling	NE to E	Summer—light winds, rain in 3 days; winter—rain in 1 day
30.1 or higher, falling fast	NE to E	Summer—rain in 1 day; winter—rain or snow in 12 hours
30.1 to 30.2, steady	SW to NW	Fair for 1 or 2 days, temperatures steady
30.1 to 30.2, rising	SW to NW	Fair, but rain coming in 48 hours
30.1 to 30.2, falling	SE to S / NE to SE	Rain in 1 day / Wind and rain in 12 hours
30.1 to 30.2, falling fast	SE to S / NE to SE	Wind and rain in 12 hours / Wind and rain in 12 hours

Pressure (inches)	Wind	Weather
30.0 or lower, falling	NE to SE	Rain in a few days
30.0 or lower, falling fast	NE to SE	Rain and strong wind soon, followed in a few hours by fast clearing
30.0 or lower, rising	S to SW	Clearing, fair weather coming
29.8 or lower, falling fast	N to E	Heavy storm and rain warning; winter—snow and cold temperatures
	E to S	Severe storm warning (hours), fast clearing (1 day)
29.8 or lower, rising fast	Veering wind to W or NW	Storm ending, clearing weather with gusty winds if coming from sea, steady winds if from land

Clouds and Weather Forecasting

Cloud Types	Description	Weather Prediction
Cirrus	High, wispy, white	Approaching warm front, fine weather
Cirrostratus	High sheets of cloud, sometimes gray haze with sun/moon halo	Generally fair weather, but haze can mean storm coming if halo present
Cirrocumulus	Puff-type balls, "fish-scale" mackerel sky	Good weather, weather is changing
Altostratus	Medium altitude, slightly thicker and darker	Rain may be coming
Altocumulus	Cottony puffs	Good weather in summer; beware if they darken

Cloud Types	Description	Weather Prediction
Stratocumulus	Puffballs in tight layers, medium altitude	Weather changing
Cumulonimbus	Dark, tightly packed balls	Weather worsening, storms, possible thunder/lightning
Cumulus	Puffy/white	Fair weather unless clouds darken
Nimbostratus	Heavy, low, gray, and dense masses	Fog, rain, and drizzle
Stratus	Higher and gray in flat planes	Some drizzle

MARITIME WEATHER CLASSIFICATIONS: THE BEAUFORT SCALE

Devised in 1805 by Admiral Sir Francis Beaufort, Royal Navy, and modified somewhat since then, the scale describes the relationship between wind speed and sea condition and codifies the terms. Otherwise, one man's "near gale" might be another man's "spanking breeze," and how could mariners, therefore, ever agree and understand what was meant? Beaufort brought some precision to the language, and a reliable method for determining the approximate wind speed from the state of the sea.

Here are some points to remember about the chart that follows:

1. "Sea state" numbers, used at times in weather forecasts, equate to the Beaufort wind numbers 0 to 10. You don't need extra numbers to indicate a sea state worse than 10. A quick rule of thumb for converting Beaufort number to wind speed: subtract 1 and multiply by 5.

2. In sheltered or restricted waters, the Beaufort force will likely be one number higher than indicated by sea conditions. For example, wind streaks are clearly apparent on open waters at Beaufort 7 but might not show up on a small lake until the wind hits Beaufort 8. On a river with the wind blowing at right angles, wind streaks might not be generated at all. Let's keep this example purely academic: You do *not* want to be out on any body of water above force 6.

3. The wind descriptions should not be confused with the weather patterns discussed in weather forecasts and reports. Near-gale winds might be generated by a weather front or in a tropical depression; the winds in a tropical storm might cover the range from force 8 to force 11. However, if sustained winds are above 63 knots, it's typically classified as a hurricane or its Far Eastern cousin, a typhoon.

Marine Weather Information

A complete source of information on marine weather is the NOAA marine weather chart, which lists marine weather broadcast times and frequencies; National Weather Service office telephone numbers; phone numbers for marine weather recordings; coastal warning display sites; and locations of weather transmitters of the National Oceanic and Atmospheric Administration (NOAA).

The marine weather charts are divided by area, cost $1.25 each, and are available from: NOAA, Herbert Hoover Building, Washington, DC 20230.

Marine Weather Service Charts

Number	Area Covered
MSC-1	Eastport, ME, to Montauk Point, NY
MSC-2	Montauk Point, NY, to Manasquan, NJ
MSC-3	Manasquan, NJ, to Cape Hatteras, NC
MSC-4	Cape Hatteras, NC, to Savannah, GA
MSC-5	Savannah, GA, to Apalachicola, FL
MSC-6	Apalachicola, FL, to Morgan City, LA
MSC-7	Morgan City, LA, to Brownsville, TX
MSC-8	Mexican border to Point Conception, CA
MSC-9	Point Conception, CA, to Point St.George, CA
MSC-10	Point St. George, CA, to Canadian border
MSC-11	Great Lakes—Michigan and Superior
MSC-12	Great Lakes—Huron, Erie, and Ontario
MSC-13	Hawaiian waters
MSC-15	Alaskan waters

SEA STATE CHART
Wind and Sea Scale for Fully Arisen Sea

Sea State	Sea—General Description	(Beaufort) Wind Force	Wind Description	Range (Knots)	Wind Velocity (Knots)	Wave Height Feet Average	Wave Height Feet Average 1/10 Highest	Significant Range of Periods (Seconds)	T (Average Period)	l (Average Wave Length)	Minimum Fetch (Nautical Miles)	Minimum Duration (Hours)
0	Sea like a mirror	0	Calm	Less than 1	0	0	0	—	—	—	—	—
	Ripples with the appearance of scales are formed, but without foam crests.	1	Light Airs	1–3	2	0.05	0.10	up to 1.2 sec.	0.5	10 in.	5	18 min.
1	Small wavelets, still short but more pronounced; crests have a glassy appearance, but do not break.	2	Light Breeze	4–6	5	0.18	0.37	0.4–2.8	1.4	6.7 ft.	8	39 min.
	Large wavelets; crests begin to break. Foam of glassy appearance. Perhaps scattered white horses.	3	Gentle Breeze	7–10	8.5	0.6	1.2	0.8–5.0	2.4	20	9.8	1.7 hr.
					10	0.88	1.8	1.0–6.0	2.9	27	10	2.4
2	Small waves, becoming larger; fairly frequent white horses.	4	Moderate Breeze	11–16	12	1.4	2.8	1.0–7.0	3.4	40	18	3.8
					13.5	1.8	3.7	1.4–7.6	3.9	52	24	4.8
3					14	2.0	4.2	1.5–7.8	4.0	59	28	5.2
					16	2.9	5.8	2.0–8.8	4.6	71	40	6.6
4	Moderate waves, taking a more pronounced long form; many white horses are formed. (Chance of some spray.)	5	Fresh Breeze	17–21	18	3.8	7.8	2.5–10.0	5.1	90	55	8.3
					19	4.3	8.7	2.8–10.6	5.4	99	65	9.2
					20	5.0	10	3.0–11.1	5.7	111	75	10
5	Large waves begin to form; the white foam crests are more extensive everywhere. (Probably some spray.)	6	Strong Breeze	22–27	22	6.4	13	3.4–12.2	6.3	134	100	12
					24	7.9	16	3.7–13.5	6.8	160	130	14
					24.5	8.2	17	3.8–13.6	7.0	164	140	15

Sea State	Force	Name	Wind (knots)	Description								
6				foam from breaking waves begins to be blown in streaks along the direction of the wind. (Spindrift begins to be seen.)	30	14	28	4.7–16.7	8.6	250	280	23
					30.5	14	29	4.8–17.0	8.7	258	290	24
7					32	16	33	5.0–17.5	9.1	285	340	27
	8	Fresh Gale	34–40	Moderately high waves of greater length; edges of crests break into spindrift. The foam is blown in well-marked streaks along the direction of the wind. Spray affects visibility.	34	19	38	5.5–18.5	9.7	322	420	0
					36	21	44	5.8–19.7	10.3	363	500	34
					37	23	46.7	6–20.5	10.5	376	530	37
					38	25	50	6.2–20.8	10.7	392	600	38
					40	28	58	6.5–21.7	11.4	444	710	42
	9	Strong Gale	41–47	High waves. Dense streaks of foam along the direction of the wind. Sea begins to roll. Visibility affected.	42	31	64	7–23	12.0	492	830	47
					44	36	73	7–24.2	12.5	534	960	52
					46	40	81	7–25	13.1	590	1110	57
8	10	Whole Gale	48–55	Very high waves with long overhanging crests. The resulting foam is in great patches and is blown in dense white streaks along the direction of the wind. On the whole, the surface of the sea takes on a white appearance. The rolling of the sea becomes heavy and shocklike. Visibility affected.	48	44	90	7.5–26	13.8	650	1250	63
					50	49	99	7.5–27	14.3	700	1420	69
					51.5	52	106	8–28.2	14.7	736	1560	73
					52	54	110	8–28.5	14.8	750	1610	75
					54	59	121	8–29.5	15.4	810	1800	81
	11	Storm	56–63	Exceptionally high waves. (Small and medium-sized ships might for a long time be lost to view behind the waves.) The sea is completely covered with long white patches of foam lying along the direction of the wind. Everywhere the edges of the wave crests are blown into froth. Visibility affected.	56	64	130	8.5–31	16.3	910	2100	88
					59.5	73	148	10–32	17.0	985	2500	101
9	12	Hurricane	64–71	Air filled with foam and spray. Sea completely white with driving spray. Visibility very seriously affected.	>64	>80	>164	10–(35)	(18)			

Courtesy U.S. Navy

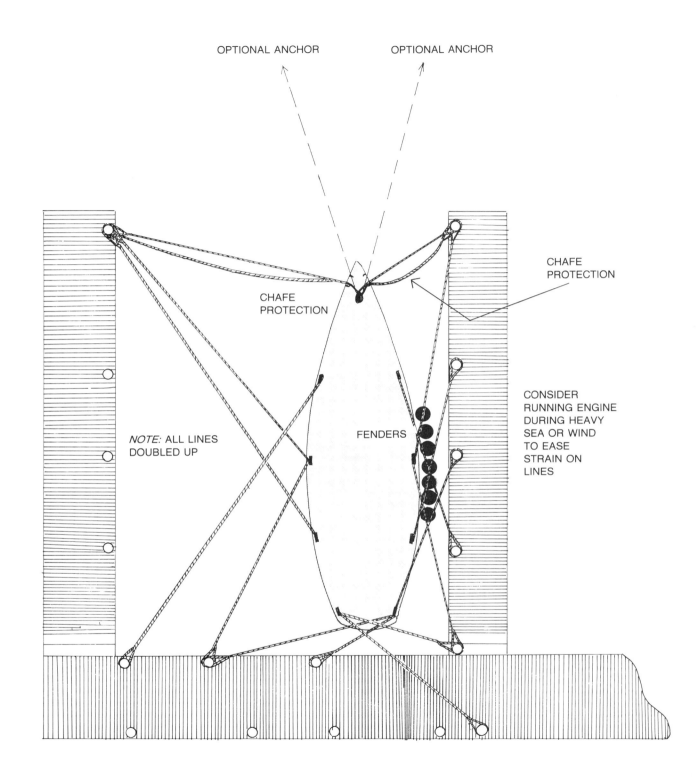

OPTIONAL ANCHOR   OPTIONAL ANCHOR

CHAFE PROTECTION

CHAFE PROTECTION

NOTE: ALL LINES DOUBLED UP

FENDERS

CONSIDER RUNNING ENGINE DURING HEAVY SEA OR WIND TO EASE STRAIN ON LINES

RIGGING A BOAT IN A SLIP FOR HEAVY WEATHER.

STORM PREPARATIONS WHEN *NOT* UNDERWAY

It may seem, perhaps, that we are emphasizing the underway aspects of boating safety, but since most safety problems, accidents, and emergencies happen while underway (or while getting underway), that emphasis is not inappropriate. However, it certainly should not be exclusive. More boats are damaged by storms when in harbor or in their owners' backyards than when at sea. Suggestions for preventive measures follow.

TRAILERED BOAT

- Put it in the garage, if possible.
- Remove the outboard(s), electronic equipment, and canvas covers and put them in the garage, the basement, or your living room.
- Tie down the boat and trailer securely; use trees, fences, or stakes pounded into the ground as anchors.
- Avoid parking in the slot between two structures (your house and garage, or your house and that of a near neighbor), because such an area could become a high-speed wind tunnel.
- Avoid parking under trees and power lines.
- Smaller boats not on trailers (unless equipped with inboard engines) can be "ballasted" with water from the garden hose.

BOATS IN THE WATER

- Many coastal marinas have a standing rule that all boats must be evacuated in the event of a major storm; a storm surge of 10 or 20 feet would make it virtually impossible to keep a boat on its mooring. Locate and negotiate for (well in advance of need) an appropriate storm refuge to which the boat probably can be moved before the storm hits. It should be in a sheltered waterway, as far inland from the coast as feasible. If you seek last-minute storm refuge in an inland marina, be prepared to pay $400 to 500 a day—*if* space is even available.

- Alongside a pier (or in a proper slip), all lines must be doubled or tripled, led to solid pilings or trees, and long enough to accommodate a storm surge well above normal high tide. Use chafing gear to protect lines at any point where they cross your deck edge or a pier. Take in sails, covers, and cushions, and stow them below. Disconnect your shore-power cable and bring it aboard. Don't use fender boards—they tend to break. Put out all your fenders, all around—not just for protection from hitting the pier, but from other boats that may be blown into your boat.
- If mooring in a canal, you may be rafting up with other boats. Use plenty of fenders, lines, and anchors to ensure that you're all protected from each other and that you will stay in the water and not be deposited on someone's lawn. By the same token, be wary of such flying debris as lawn chairs and barbecue grills.
- Don't block a canal by mooring near the entrance while plenty of room remains inland. In an area such as South Florida, for instance, there's precious little safe haven for all the boats as it is, without some unthinking captain cutting off the supply.
- Once the storm has largely passed, possibly having cut off water and electricity for many hours or even days, you may find that your boat is a more hospitable refuge than your house. Therefore, the boat should be stocked with emergency supplies of food, full tanks of fuel and water, batteries in good condition and at full charge, plenty of towels, several changes of clothes, as well as a radio and/or TV for weather and local condition reports.
- You might elect to ride out the storm, either in a slip or anchored. Being aboard does give you some measure of control: You can use your engines to hold your position and you can adjust or replace lines. As the water recedes, you may be able to prevent your boat from settling on top of a pier or some pilings.
- If you choose to anchor out, take the time to do it *right*:

1. Use at least two anchors set over the bow with a 45-to-60-degree angle between them, the boat headed into the wind.

2. A third anchor can be attached to the scope of the larger, storm anchor, at about one-third the distance back.

3. Attach an anchor buoy to each anchor, with a stout line to a fluke. This will serve two vital needs: (1) To warn other boats of the location of your anchor, and (2) to help you retrieve what will most likely be a very firmly set hook.

4. Lay the anchors. Drop the first anchor at the desired spot and set it by backing down; mark the rode at the desired scope and then take in any slack as you move over to the spot for the second anchor. Drop the second anchor and back down to set it firmly. Adjust both rodes.

5. Firmly fasten the anchor rodes to a samson post, sturdy cleats, or the base of the mast. It's best to have each rode fastened to a different piece of hardware, as a hedge against failure.

6. Use plenty of chafing gear at every point where the rodes touch the boat.

7. Take a round of bearings and mark your position on the chart; follow up regularly to verify that you are not dragging anchor.

8. Take in sails, covers, and cushions, and stow them below, but have your stormsail ready for use.

9. Be prepared, with fuel, water, and food, for a blow of at least two or three days.

10. Be prepared to reset the anchors if there is any sign of dragging; this is likely to follow a major wind shift. Use your engines to take the strain off the rode before you try to handle it.

11. If the eye of a hurricane passes over your position, quickly reset the anchors in anticipation of a 180-degree shift in the wind.

12. Once you commit to staying aboard at anchor, *stay aboard.* Don't change your mind and try to take the dinghy ashore; it could be a fatal mistake.

OTHER CONSIDERATIONS

Selecting a safe haven is one thing; getting there might be quite another. With a storm in the offing, the highway bridges across any local waterways will be turned toward the evacuation of people from low-lying or coastal areas and will *not* open for boats. You must move before the emergency is declared, or be prepared to leave your boat wherever it is.

Of course, if your clearance is less than that of the intervening bridges, you might sail on under to safe haven without difficulty—unless you have waited too long and the storm surge has made the water level too high. Think about it: An increase in water level of five feet *lowers* the bridge clearance by five feet; the storm surge from a hurricane can be as much as 20 feet.

STORM PREPARATIONS FOR A BOAT UNDERWAY

Preparation really begins ashore—by equipping the boat properly and ensuring that the equipment remains serviceable and available. You won't be able to do too much about heavy-weather stability: It's pretty much designed (or not designed) into the boat. Boats that are basically unstable—such as small, open fishermen and top-heavy motorboats—simply have no business at sea in heavy weather. Boats that *are* sta-

ble—such as midsize cruising sailboats—can ride out almost any weather.

For the recreational boater, the normal precautions for offshore sailing will not be adequate in a real storm, where safety and survival depend on specific, thorough preparation. We must assume that you will not be out when heavy weather threatens unless you are an experienced boater with an experienced crew—in which case, much of what we suggest will (should be) second nature. However, any boater should periodically run through storm preparations as part of a safety training regimen. Walk through your boat with the following lists in hand, and mentally rehearse each action.

PRECRUISE HEAVY-WEATHER CHECKLIST

Before starting any major cruise, and otherwise every six months, you should:

☑ Check all batteries in flashlights, strobes, and portable radios.

☑ Check flares for date and condition. Verify location of the distress flag.

☑ Test the EPIRB (as outlined on its case).

☑ Examine all life jackets, survival suits, foul-weather gear, and safety harnesses for signs of deterioration; pull at the seams; work the zippers. Restow all for ready access.

☑ Break out the jackline; make sure it's in good condition and complete with all fittings.

☑ Check all lifelines for corrosion; make sure stanchions are mounted securely.

☑ Check the man-overboard pole; ensure that all lines and fittings are intact and strong.

☑ Check the anchor, storm anchor, anchor rode, and all connections. Make sure the rode is free to run; make sure the anchor is secure on deck.

☑ Verify the location of the emergency tiller or steering-cable repair materials.

☑ Check and test manual bilge pumps; verify condition of spare-parts kits.

☑ Verify the location and condition of the emergency radio antenna.

☑ Check emergency spare parts and toolkit for completeness.

☑ Check the condition of all sails, especially the little-used stormsail, which should be ready at hand.

☑ Check all navigation lights; verify supply of spare bulbs.

☑ Examine the radar reflector; if it is already aloft, make sure that the mounting has not deteriorated.

☑ Inventory the medical kit; verify shelf life of dated materials.

☑ Remove, repair, or replace any items that don't pass muster.

SAFETY NET AND FOOTROPES give the foredeck crew on this traditional gaff cutter secure footing when working the headsails. Note the foresail furled on the bowsprit stay and ready for quick release.

A STORM ANCHOR (folding-stock type) stowed with its lead chain near the bowsprit on this traditional, heavily built sailboat. The anchor can be set up and easily handed overboard without digging through lockers or the recesses of the engine room . . . and it does not have to be manhandled long distances down a heaving deck before use.

UNDERWAY CHECKLIST

☑ Double-check to ensure that *all* household goods and equipment are stowed and secure. Tape or tie shut all drawers and doors. When going through the boat, keep thinking "upside down"—think what would happen to any piece of gear or equipment if the boat should take an exceptional roll or suffer a knockdown. Ensure clear and quick access to all damage-control and emergency equipment.

☑ Break out the distress signal and emergency toolkit and have them ready at hand just out of the weather, but be sure they are secure from loss.

☑ Pump the heads dry and close the seacocks.

☑ Close all other seacocks; on a sailboat, close the engine intake as well, since you'll most likely use shortened sail to hold your course through the blow. Remember to reopen the seacock if you need to use the engine. However, if you forget, a rapid rise in engine temperature should give you a warning before the engine is damaged.

☑ Food will become vital to keep up energy levels and forestall fatigue. Take advantage of whatever time you have and get food prepared; at the least, have hot soup and coffee in Thermos bottles. You may not be able to use the stove once the storm hits. Put other food in watertight plastic containers. Stow the booze and beer for consumption *after* the storm.

☑ Check the bilges, bilge pumps, and deck drains for debris that may produce unwanted clogging. Check the float switches. Test all bilge pumps—*especially* the hand pump—and have emergency pumping gear ready.

☑ Ensure that the appropriate charts and lists of lights are handy and out of the weather.

☑ Test the running lights and horn.

☑ Get a radio check. Announce your position and condition as an update to the float plan you filed when you left home.

☑ Make sure all topside lines and equipment are secure. Ensure that all hatch, locker, and lazarette covers are closed and secured.

☑ Double-check the lashing of the life-raft container—and quickly refresh your memory on deployment and operation.

☑ If you have a storm anchor, get it on deck, lashed down but ready for use. If not, check that the normal anchor is stowed securely—but be sure you can deploy it in a hurry, if necessary. Have other anchors, the sea anchor, or a drogue ready for use (but protected from waves washing over the deck).

☑ Close ventilators and dog down ports and hatches.

☑ Topside, all hands should be in life jackets with attached single-cell or strobe light (tested for operation), wearing safety harnesses properly secured. Below decks, life jackets also are a good idea—in an emergency, there may be precious little time to get togged out for topside work. All crew members should dress warmly and don foul-weather gear, even in warm climates: The onset of hypothermia or exposure-induced fatigue can be insidious. The helmsman at the least, and others if possible, should wear survival suits (if they are the type that permits free movement; if not, have the suits broken out and ready).

☑ Rig leecloths or bunkboards (if so equipped) to facilitate sleeping.

A WELL-PROTECTED AND COMPLETE ENGINE PANEL in an open-cockpit cruising sailboat. The gauges can be clearly seen behind this Lexan fascia. The plate Plexiglas is vented to prevent gauge fogging.

☑ Have all hands, especially the skipper and the navigator, get as much rest as possible before the storm hits.

☑ Prepare to get wet, above and below decks. Wrap spare clothing and bedding in plastic bags.

☑ Rig protection for windshields or large glass windows. An oversize sheet of Lexan, cut to fit and provided with mountings, is ideal, but you may have to improvise.

☑ Cut all electrical consumption to a minimum to conserve battery power; if there is more than one battery, keep one isolated for engine starting and emergency use.

☑ Reduce sail to a minimum required to maintain steerageway; if possible, get unneeded sails off the rig and stowed below.

☑ Get all other unneeded equipment, awnings, cushions, and covers off the deck and below. One exception: If you have them, put storm covers *on* hatches and skylights, securely lashed in place. This will help preserve watertight integrity below.

☑ If you have been towing the dinghy, get it aboard. Equip it with fenders for additional flotation; be sure the dinghy bag is aboard. Lash the dinghy upside-down on deck wherever it will be most secure and least in the way.

☑ Rig the jackline.

☑ Tape or wire shut all pelican hooks on lifelines and gates.

☑ Review the principles of heavy-weather seamanship.

HEAVY-WEATHER SEAMANSHIP

The first move, of course, would be to try to avoid the storm. You should not be caught out in heavy weather on purpose, and a timely return to port should be your first choice. Should you be heading for port, continue to make *all of the storm preparations* described above. You might get caught short, but you *don't* want to get caught unprepared.

However, a return to port might be impossible and avoidance may be difficult; by the time you see indications of an approaching major storm, it may already be too late to get far enough away. In that case (see diagram p. 322), do the following:

1. Using broadcast weather data, plot the location of the storm. Update the plot as frequently as possible.

2. If broadcast information is unavailable, you can determine the approximate bearing of the storm center by adding 115 degrees to the direction from which the wind is blowing. If the result is greater than 360, subtract 360 to get the bearing. If arithmetic was not your best subject in school, put your back to the wind and hold your left arm out to the side; don't force it back, but let it hang comfortably. It will be pointing generally toward the center of the storm (in the Northern Hemisphere).

3. If the wind shifts gradually to the right, or clockwise, you are in the dangerous semicircle; if the wind shifts to the left (counterclockwise), you're in the more-or-less-"safe" semicircle. If the wind is steady in direction but increasing in speed as the barometer falls, you're in the path of the storm. If the wind direction remains steady, with decreasing speed and a rising barometer, you're on the storm track but safely behind the center.

4. Your next step is to move as best you can—without capsizing or running into reefs, islands, or continents—away from the storm:

• If you are dead ahead of the storm, directly in its path, put the wind on your starboard quarter almost astern (160 degrees relative) and make the best possible speed.

• If you're in the safe semicircle, put the wind on the starboard quarter (at 130 degrees relative) and make the best speed.

• If you're in the dangerous semicircle, put the wind on your starboard bow (45 degrees relative) and make the best speed possible.

• If you are dead astern of the storm, choose the best riding course that takes you away from the center.

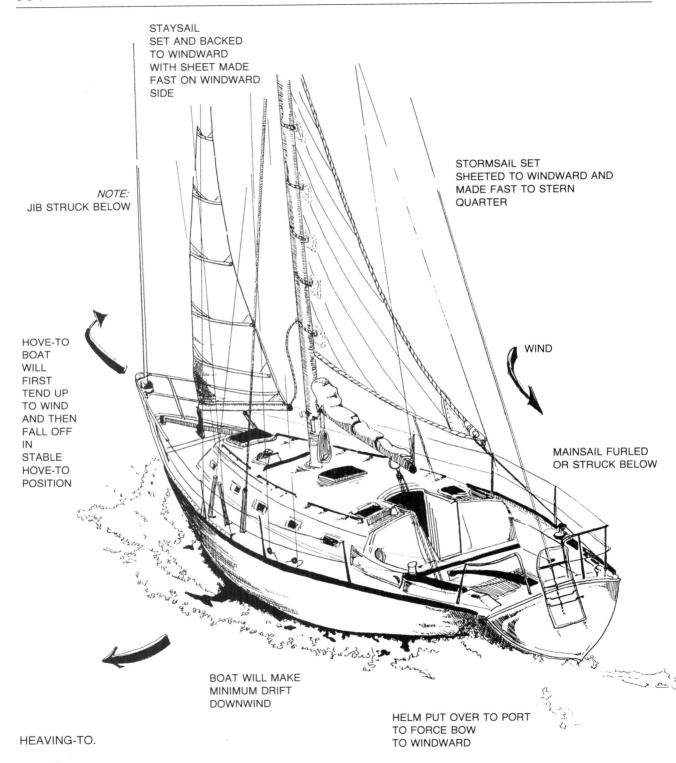

STAYSAIL
SET AND BACKED
TO WINDWARD
WITH SHEET MADE
FAST ON WINDWARD
SIDE

NOTE:
JIB STRUCK BELOW

STORMSAIL SET
SHEETED TO WINDWARD AND
MADE FAST TO STERN
QUARTER

HOVE-TO
BOAT
WILL
FIRST
TEND UP
TO WIND
AND THEN
FALL OFF
IN
STABLE
HOVE-TO
POSITION

WIND

MAINSAIL FURLED
OR STRUCK BELOW

BOAT WILL MAKE
MINIMUM DRIFT
DOWNWIND

HELM PUT OVER TO PORT
TO FORCE BOW
TO WINDWARD

HEAVING-TO.

OTHER STORM TACTICS

Heavy-weather sailing might be considered the "graduate level," well beyond the scope of this book. And yet, since our goal is to be as comprehensive as possible, here's a brief overview of heavy-weather tactics.

Depending upon the type of boat, and as determined by the weather conditions, you have these options:

1. *Heading into the seas* with bare steerageway: just enough water flowing past the rudder to give you directional control or at some slightly higher speed easily tolerated by hull and passengers. This is an appropriate tactic for all types of boat, and the preferred tactic as long as the ride is bearable. This is not a time for thrill-seeking. At any speed, avoid plunging the bow into larger waves, which brings the risk of smashed windows and skylights.

2. *Heaving-to:* maintaining a heading into the seas, but without much headway. The boat will drift to leeward somewhat; be sure that you're not in dangerous proximity to the shore. This technique is most useful for sailboats, because a minimum of sail can be used to keep the boat in balance; it might work for some powerboats on which the superstructure provides "sail" area, thus conserving fuel. Test this with the transmission in neutral before you stop the engines.

A sea anchor run out from the bow will help keep the bow pointed into the seas. This may be a commercially produced item or something improvised with a fender or sail bag. The sea anchor may be subjected to considerable jerking force from the waves, so use a stout line, and adjust its length for the most comfortable ride. Ideally, it should be let out *two wave lengths* forward of the bow; if it is out only one wave length, the sea anchor and the boat will be moving at almost the same speed, and the slowing effect will be minimal. Make sure that the line is well secured to a part of the boat, such as a samson post, that will not easily give way under the strain.

3. *Lying ahull:* all sails down, helm lashed to leeward, allowing the boat to take her own position relative to wind and weather. As with heaving-to, the boat will drift to leeward, requiring added vigilance. The boat may lie in the trough between the waves and be subjected to heavy and uncomfortable rolling, but in moderate seas, it should not be in any danger. As the seas increase, so does the possibility of being damaged or capsized by the waves. With a top-heavy shallow-draft powerboat, that possibility might become an inevitability.

4. *Running with the storm* requires constant effort at the helm, but it may be the best course in truly heavy weather, unless you're in danger of being driven up on a beach, and until you're too tired to keep up the active steering necessary for doing this. Greatest danger: pitchpoling or broaching. A pitchpole is a nautical somersault: As the boat is flung along by the onrushing waves, the bow digs in and the stern is thrown up and over. A broach is being thrown sideways and possibly capsized by a wave from astern. Towing a long line or even putting out a stern anchor may help keep the boat under control.

Running is not a useful option for small-to-medium-size powerboats with an open stern cockpit or salon, which would be in critical danger from flooding by an overtaking wave. They should point into the seas and make the best of it.

5. *If caught at sea in a storm,* it's best to stay at sea until it passes. For one thing, the traffic jam in a storm-tossed inlet will be more hazardous than most combinations of wind and waves offshore. For another, it is a well-known fact that boats ride out a storm better in the water than on a rock jetty or a beach.

6. *If for any reason you must anchor*—to prevent being blown onto a beach, for example—try putting out two anchors in a Y shape, with as much scope as possible and a catenary weight at the midpoint (*not* free to run along the rode). If at all possible, be heading into the seas with your

boat under control; when you drop the anchors, you may even have to keep your engines going forward to prevent the boat from moving backward too quickly. This will prevent *you* from being hurled to the deck (or overboard) when the anchors grab, and it keeps your cleats from being ripped out of the deck and the bitter end of the anchor rode from being torn loose.

7. *If you have been caught ahead of the storm,* you'll likely experience the eerie calm of the "eye" as it passes over your position. Do not be lulled into complacency: The storm is far from over. This is not the time to romp about the deck taking photographs; rather, use the few minutes of calm to check the safety and security of your boat.

GALERIDER DROGUE for heavy-weather boat stabilization. This device (in an appropriate size) should be deployed from the stern and fastened to a secure fitting capable of handling extreme loads. If no such fitting exists at the stern, the attachment line can be led forward to a suitable fastening point (or around the mast). However, the pulling point must be at the stern. The drogue provides resistance to control boat speed and eliminate surfing beyond hull speeds, which can imperil steering control. The drogue also can slow progress toward a lee shore. Four sizes are available (according to boat displacement): 30 × 36 boats to 10,000 pounds; 36 × 42 boats 10–30,000 pounds; 42 × 48 boats 30–55,000 pounds; 48 × 56 boats 55–90,000 pounds. Be aware that all drogues and sea anchors develop extreme drag weights. (Hathaway, Reiser & Raymond)

SEA ANCHOR. Upper picture shows a large, parachute-type sea anchor deployed to stabilize and slow a vessel in heavy seas. The middle picture shows the considerable strain set up by the sea anchor, pointing up the need for firm fastening on deck. The lower drawing shows details of the trip rig used to manipulate the anchor, and its effect. (Shewmon Co.)

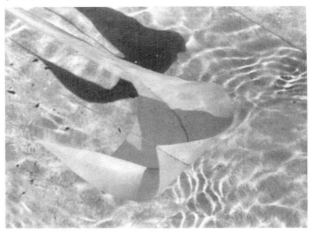

SOME FINAL THOUGHTS

In assessing the 1944 disaster in the Philippines, Fleet Commander Admiral Chester Nimitz offered these observations to his sailors—and to all of us:

A hundred years ago, a ship's survival depended almost solely on the competence of her master and on his constant alertness to every hint of change in the weather. To be taken aback or caught with full sail on even by a passing squall might mean the loss of spars and canvas; and to come close to the center of a genuine hurricane or typhoon was synonymous with disaster. While to be taken by surprise was thus serious, the facilities for avoiding it were meager. Each master was dependent wholly on himself for detecting the first symptoms of bad weather, for predicting its seriousness and movement, and for taking the appropriate measures, to evade it if possible and to battle through it if it passed near to him. There was no radio by which weather data could be collected from over all the oceans and the resulting forecasts by expert aerologists broadcasted to him and to all afloat. There was no one to tell him that the time had now come to strike his light sails and spars, and snug her down under close reefs or storm trysails. His own barometer, the force and direction of the wind, and the appearance of sea and sky, were all that he had for information. Ceaseless vigilance in watching and interpreting signs, plus a philosophy of taking no risk in which there was little to gain and much to be lost, was what enabled him to survive.

The mariner of today is certainly well ahead of that game, with myriad weather forecasts and warnings available to him, including the local newspaper, commercial radio and television, and continuous weather reports on the NOAA frequencies.

No prudent boat operator would set out on a voyage or excursion in the face of dire warnings of storm, yet each year, more than 200 boating fatalities can be attributed directly to bad weather.

Sudden squalls can hit almost without warning, shredding sails and tossing unprepared deckhands into the water; swells generated by distant, unseen storms can overwhelm a shallow inlet, swamping small boats and pushing large craft up on the rocks. Lightning can fry unprotected electronic equipment—and operators.

Thus, just like the mariners of old, you must *be prepared.* Keep your boat and its equipment in good order. Don't get underway, *ever,* with gear adrift above or below decks. Practice storm seamanship—practice lowering sails in a hurry, practice reefing sail, practice streaming and recovering the sea anchor.

Become a weather watcher, with one eye on the sky and the other on the waves, and take action well before you're hit by a storm. If that means heading for home while the fish are still biting, leave the fish for another day.

As Admiral Nimitz summed up in his advice to fleet sailors: "The time for taking all measures for a ship's safety is while still able to do so. Nothing is more dangerous than for a seaman to be grudging in taking precautions lest they turn out to have been unnecessary. Safety at sea for a thousand years has depended on exactly the opposite philosophy."

CHAPTER TWENTY-ONE

Calling for Help

RECOGNIZE THE NEED

Not every problem will be an emergency, and many will be handled easily within your own resources. However, the prudent boater will not be reluctant to seek assistance when it seems needed. If your engine cuts out and you are drifting with the Gulf Stream, it's far better to call for help than to end up in Newfoundland. That small galley fire you're certain can be handled may just get out of hand. The guest with an ashen pallor and chest pain who insists, "I'm all right" *may* indeed be all right—or may be suffering a heart attack. When in doubt, there should be no doubt: Send a distress signal or a "Mayday" call. Your help is likely to come from other boaters in your vicinity, and you want to get that help on the way—sooner, rather than too late. In the meantime, you should be doing everything you can, within the limits of your skill and resources. You can always cancel the call if you get the situation under control.

Let's make the point as strongly as we can: The Coast Guard has reported that in 85 percent of

fatal boating accidents, it could find no evidence that distress signals had been used—even if there were some aboard.

To be of any value, of course, the message sent must also be *received* by someone in some fashion. Certain signaling methods carry greater assurance of this than others, even though—as with an Emergency Position Indicating Radio Beacon (EPIRB—see chapter 9)—the method might not provide for acknowledgment of the message. A signal that would seem most compelling, such as a rocket flare fired across the bridge of a passing merchantman, might be seen by no one. Shipwreck survivors, adrift in open ocean, frequently have reported not being sighted by ships passing as close as two miles, even with the repeated use of flares.

Unfortunately for the drifting castaway, merchant ships sail with a minimum crew. Under normal conditions, this may translate into one or two people on the bridge. The ship is most likely on autopilot, with the bridge watch paying more attention to what shows up on the radar plot 20 or 30 miles ahead than to whatever might be happening off to the side. Even within a passing distance of a few miles, the chances of being spotted by a merchantman are minimal. You *might* have better luck with a military ship, which typically mans its bridge with at least six—including port and starboard lookouts whose only job is to look out.

RECOGNIZED DISTRESS SIGNALS

The following are some of the signals that are recognized as indicating distress and need of assistance.

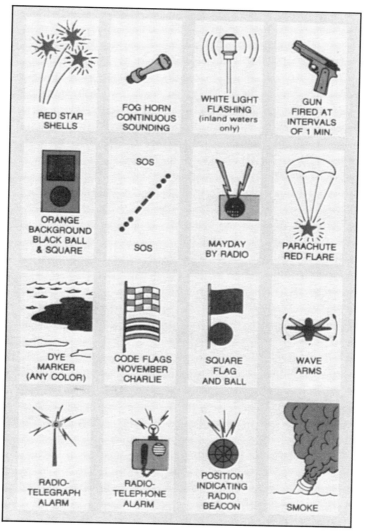

RECOGNIZED DISTRESS SIGNALS.

METHODS

VOICE RADIO

Voice radio is the best method for sending a distress signal. VHF channel 16 (156.8 MHz) has been designated the basic calling and emergency channel. All boats so equipped must monitor channel 16 whenever the set is operating. Because channel 16 will be serving a large number of boats and shore stations at any given time, it should be used to establish contact with another boat but not for extended conversations—both boats should shift to an agreed working channel.

RADIO USER INSTRUCTIONS, as well as distress frequencies, should be mounted on a protected card near the boat's VHF radio. A sample distress message can be a great help to someone unfamiliar with marine radios.

When trying to establish contact, you are limited to three attempts, spaced two minutes apart, and then must wait fifteen minutes before calling again.

The widely accepted alerting call is the word "Mayday," repeated three times in succession. Derived from the French *m'aidez,* the call means, literally, "help me."

Strictly speaking, "Mayday" should be reserved for emergencies where life and property are in imminent danger. The international voice signal "pan" is reserved for less dramatic situations—such as a simple stranding on a mud bank—where assistance is required but the full resources of Coast Guard Search and Rescue need not be mobilized. Another international signal—"security"—should be used to alert listeners to potential hazards, such as large floating logs or malfunctioning lighted buoys. *Panne* (breakdown) and *securité* (safety) also come from the French.

The format for a voice distress message is also internationally recognized. The alerting word should be repeated three times, followed by the identification of the sender, the nature of the emergency, position, and relevant medical information. For example:

> Mayday Mayday Mayday, this is the motor yacht *Endeavour, Endeavour, Endeavour,* on fire, 12 miles southeast of Cape May, two injured. Send help. . . . Over.

Technically, you should also include your FCC radio call sign, but in an emergency, we suggest you establish contact and get the right kind of help on the way before you worry too much about the bureaucratic niceties.

On VHF, you'd make the call on channel 16. With a life-threatening emergency, don't switch to another channel until after your basic message has been sent—and acknowledged. *Then* you can move to a less-crowded channel.

Every radio aboard should have an "emergency procedures" card that clearly outlines—even for young children, as long as they can read—the steps to follow in making a distress call.

Incidentally, interfering with emergency transmissions is a serious violation of the law—and broadcasting bogus distress calls equally so. Penalties can range as high as a $10,000 fine and two years' imprisonment. Nor is this a toothless law: In 1986, an eighteen-year-old Massachusetts man was sentenced to one year in prison, ordered to submit to psychological counseling, and ordered to repay the Coast Guard in part for the almost $700,000 estimated cost of a twenty-hour search precipitated by his prank distress call.

A MINI-EPIRB RESCUE RADIO in a suitable size for use with an individual life jacket or in a small life raft. (ACR)

FIVE METHODS OF RESCUE USING THE EPIRB EMERGENCY RESCUE RADIO.

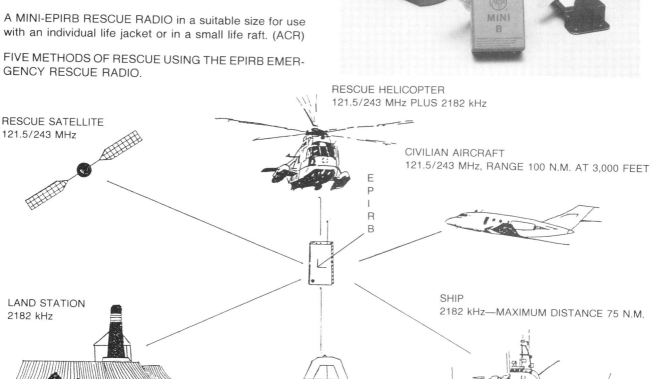

RESCUE HELICOPTER
121.5/243 MHz PLUS 2182 kHz

RESCUE SATELLITE
121.5/243 MHz

CIVILIAN AIRCRAFT
121.5/243 MHz, RANGE 100 N.M. AT 3,000 FEET

E
P
I
R
B

LAND STATION
2182 kHz

SHIP
2182 kHz—MAXIMUM DISTANCE 75 N.M.

INTERNATIONAL MINIMUM 121.5/243 MHz
RECOMMENDED: 121.5/243 MHz AND 2182 kHz

Using Flares Safely

- Never fire or ignite a flare in the presence of gasoline fumes.
- Keep flares out of reach of curious children; in port, keep flares in a locked cabinet.
- Never launch a flare directly toward a rescuing boat or helicopter.
- A flare launcher can be as dangerous, at close range, as any other firearm; in some localities, pistol launchers may carry the same restrictions as firearms. Check with local authorities. Always assume the launcher is loaded, and *never*—whether in jest or out of carelessness—point it at any person.

SIGNAL FLARES

Coast Guard requirements for recreational distress signals are discussed in chapter 9; however, having the proper signals aboard and knowing when and how to use them are different matters entirely.

Hand-held flares are ignited by a built-in device; don't be startled by the "pop" when they light. In use, these flares should be held out over the water on the downwind side of the boat, to prevent burning slag and noxious fumes from falling back into the boat. Use them if you must, but orange smoke in the daytime and an electric strobe light at night are both safer—and more visible—than hand-held flares.

Pistol launchers are easy to use: Release the barrel catch, allowing the hinged barrel to drop down. Then insert the shotgunlike shell, close the barrel, point toward the sky, . . . and pull the trigger.

Pen launchers and cartridge-type launchers are easy enough to use—just follow the simple directions—but they are not very effective. Use them if you have them, but don't count on them for much. On the other hand—*any* device that helps attract attention, as long as it is not aboard in place of a more effective unit, is of some value.

OTHER METHODS OF SIGNALING DISTRESS

Internationally recognized distress signals include:

- Flying the national ensign upside down or tied in a knot.
- The continuous sounding of a fog signal (which would include a foghorn, steam whistle, or bell) or firing a gun at one-minute intervals.
- Masthead-mounted strobe lights.
- Signal mirrors.
- Flags: The international flag distress signal consists of the flags "N" and "C." The flag signal for "man overboard" is the letter "O." The Coast Guard–approved distress flag is orange, with a black square and a black ball side by side in the center.

Other emergency messages:

"V" flag (Morse code . . .–) I require assistance.
"CB" flags (Morse code –.–. –. . . .) I require immediate assistance.
"W" flag (Morse code .––) I require medical assistance.
"AN" flags (Morse code .– –.) I need a doctor.

The boxes that follow include the radio alphabet and numbers as well as samples of communications for reporting your vessel in distress, reporting another vessel in distress, and acknowledging a Mayday call. Use these samples to make up a placard to mount near your VHF radio as a quick-reference guide in the event of an emergency.

You should be ready to accept assistance when it arrives; this is covered in chapter 23.

Radio Alphabet and Numbers

A	Alpha	**N**	November	**1**	one
B	Bravo	**O**	Oscar	**2**	two
C	Charlie	**P**	Papa	**3**	thuh–ree
D	Delta	**Q**	Quebec	**4**	four
E	Echo	**R**	Romeo	**5**	fi–yuv
F	Foxtrot	**S**	Sierra	**6**	six
G	Golf	**T**	Tango	**7**	seh–vun
H	Hotel	**U**	Uniform	**8**	eight
I	India	**V**	Victor	**9**	niner
J	Juliet	**W**	Whiskey	**0**	zee–roh
K	Kilo	**X**	X-ray		
L	Lima	**Y**	Yankee		
M	Mike	**Z**	Zulu		

Reporting Your Vessel in Distress

Procedure	Sample
1. Call on channel 16.	
2. Transmit. (Use Mayday only when severe life-threatening emergency.)	**"Mayday, Mayday, Mayday."**
3. Give call sign (3 times).	**"Whiskey Bravo 5-6-3-zero; Whiskey Bravo 5-6-3-zero; Whiskey Bravo 5-6-3-zero."**
4. State vessel name (3 times).	**"This is the vessel *Endeavour* . . . *Endeavour* . . . *Endeavour*. . . ."**
5. State position—in latitude and longitude, Loran position, or bearing and distance in miles from a known navigational mark.	**"We are three miles due east of Race Point Light."**
6. State condition.	**"We are taking water fast and sinking."**
7. Give number and condition of persons on board.	**"This is *Endeavour*. . . . We have five people on board. One is burned badly."**
8. State seaworthiness of craft.	**"We had an explosion here and there is a hole on the port side and we are sinking fast."**
9. Give description.	**"We are a white hull with an orange distress flag on the cabin."**
10. Give channel.	**"This is the yacht *Endeavour* standing by on channel 16."**
11. Repeat.	**". . . Mayday, Mayday, Mayday. . . . We are sinking three miles east of Race Point Light. . . . Over."**

Reporting Another Vessel in Distress

Procedure	Sample	Procedure	Sample
1. Transmit on channel 16.	"Mayday relay, Mayday relay, Mayday relay."	5. Give complete details of vessel.	"I say again, he is a white sailboat with an orange flag on the cabintop. He says there are five aboard with one injured . . . burn I think."
2. Give your name and call sign three times.	"This is the motor yacht *Pilgrim,* Yankee Papa 4-6-2-niner. I say again, this is motor yacht *Pilgrim,* Yankee Papa 4-6-2-niner. . . . motor yacht *Pilgrim* Yankee Papa 4-6-2-niner."	6. State your intentions.	"I am proceeding west at 15 knots. My ETA *Endeavour*'s reported position is 45 minutes."
3. Give your position.	"I am approximately 13 miles due east of Race Point, 10 miles east of a vessel that is calling Mayday."	7. Give standby channel.	"I will guard channel 16 for further traffic."
4. State nature of distress.	"The Mayday vessel is a white sailboat called *Endeavour.* I think his call sign is Whiskey Bravo 5-6-3-zero. He says he is sinking fast about three miles east of Race Point Light."		

Acknowledging a Mayday Call

Procedure	Sample	Procedure	Sample
1. Listen; do not transmit. (Another vessel closer to the emergency may want to respond and you do not want to block the channel.)	——	3. Give your name and call sign.	"This is the motor yacht *Pilgrim,* Yankee Papa 4-6-2-niner. . . ."
		4. Acknowledge Mayday.	". . . received your Mayday. . . ."
2. Transmit on channel 16 and repeat name and call sign of calling vessel—if you determine that you may be the closest vessel.	"Calling *Endeavour,* Whiskey Bravo 5-6-3-zero. . . ."	5. Give your position and the estimated time of your arrival at distress scene.	"I am 10 miles east of your position and coming to you . . . ETA 45 minutes."

CHAPTER TWENTY-TWO

Seamanship in an Emergency— Saving the Boat

GROUNDING AND STRANDING

As a practical matter, being grounded is being stuck in less water than it takes to float your boat, and being stranded is being washed up on the beach. They have several common attributes: You can't move the boat; you may need assistance; and you or members of your crew may be in jeopardy, particularly in trying to swim ashore or deal with the problem from *in* the water.

However, most groundings are not serious— most of us have gotten stuck a few times by straying into shallow water, or bumping up against an uncharted sandbar, or not being alert to the state and range of the tide when anchoring. Some groundings are serious, indeed—running hard into a submerged rock, for example, or being caught on a steep slope with a falling tide.

Strandings have a strong tendency to become fatal (to the boat) and are better studied in the context of avoidance rather than rescue.

For the purists among you, we will acknowledge that stranding also applies to a solid grounding—particularly one that might have been initiated deliberately to keep a boat from sinking—and may or may not involve a beaching.

GROUNDINGS

Groundings can be benign or damaging, depending upon the nature of the bottom, the speed at which you hit it, the type of boat you do it in—and how well built the boat may be.

Bottom qualities are obvious and don't need much explanation: Rocks will do more damage than mud, but mud can put a lock on a boat and make it very difficult to move off the ground.

Speed of contact also is pretty obvious, and obviously related to the type of bottom. At zero speed—settling with an outgoing tide—you'll encounter little damage unless you happen to settle on top of a sharp rock or a metal rod. At great speed, you could tear the bottom out of the boat and inflict considerable harm on the passengers, who will be thrown into the windshield. In between, at even 5 knots, a heavy boat has so much momentum that it can sustain a great deal of damage.

Some boats can handle groundings better than others: Trawlers and full-keeled sailboats will rest on the bottom reasonably well. In some parts of the sailing world, boats sit on the bottom of a harbor twice a day when the tide goes out.

With most powerboats, getting the bow stuck is no problem, but since the propellers hang down below the keel, you need to be very careful with the stern. And fin-keeled sailboats with spade rudders should never be sailed out of deep water: Something is sure to break off or bend.

Prevention Be conservative; know your cruising area; don't go zipping around in unfamiliar waters. If you're uncertain of your location, stop and figure it out before proceeding. Study the chart and mark danger areas with a big circle. Be aware of the state and range of the tide—don't get trapped in questionable waters at high tide. Check your depth finder frequently, and if it has an alarm, set it at a depth about 30 percent greater than your draft. This might give you time to respond, but don't forget that your depth finder shows only the depth under the transponder and not ahead of the boat. Learn to "read" the depth of the water by color. In many parts of the country, it never changes from a murky brown, but in most areas there are color differences related to depth. In the ideal turquoise waters of the Florida Keys, deeper blue means deeper water, lighter green to yellow indicates shallow water—and a sudden patch of black may indicate a coral head rising from the bottom.

Getting Off the Ground If you're still moving, bumping along the bottom, try to stop your forward motion and back away. With a sailboat under sail (depending on the shape of your keel), you might be able to spin around and head back the way you came. If you've hit hard while under power, your first action should be to shut down the engine in order to keep muck and debris from being sucked into the intake. Next, quickly check the bilges for any sudden rush of water. If the bottom has been damaged, you're better off staying put and plugging the leaks while you are at least protected from sinking.

Check the chart to find the best route to deeper water. Quite likely, it is back the way you came in, but the chart may show other problem spots nearby.

Next (if your intakes appear to be clear of the bottom), start the engine and make a single good attempt to back off. Swing your rudder back and forth as you do so: This may help break the boat free, particularly in mud or sand. Don't race your engine from full astern to full ahead, as you might do in trying to free a car from sand or snow. This action may get you off the ground, but it also may ruin your transmission.

If there are any waterskiing boats in the vicinity, get one to run in circles around your boat at high speed—depth of water permitting. The wash from the wake, combined with your engine power, may break you free.

If these first attempts don't work, review the situation. If you're grounded at or near low tide, you may have to display seamanlike patience and wait for the turn of the tide. If this means sleeping on sharply canted bunks, well, so be it.

If the tidal range is great (particularly with a sailboat), you may find your boat canting *very* sharply as the water level recedes. With such a condition, make every effort, as early as possible, to heel the boat toward the shallower, rather than the deeper, water, to avoid flooding as the tide returns. Shift all possible weight to the "shallow" side of the boat and get some lines out to the side (see below, under Kedging). If the bottom is rocky or otherwise rough textured, try to put some fenders or other protective buffers between the low side of the hull and the bottom.

If the wind is high, beware of the possibility of being floated as the tide comes in and gradually blown into even shallower water. Get an anchor out to keep you in place.

Set an anchor out as far astern as possible, and, using the anchor windlass (should you be fortu-

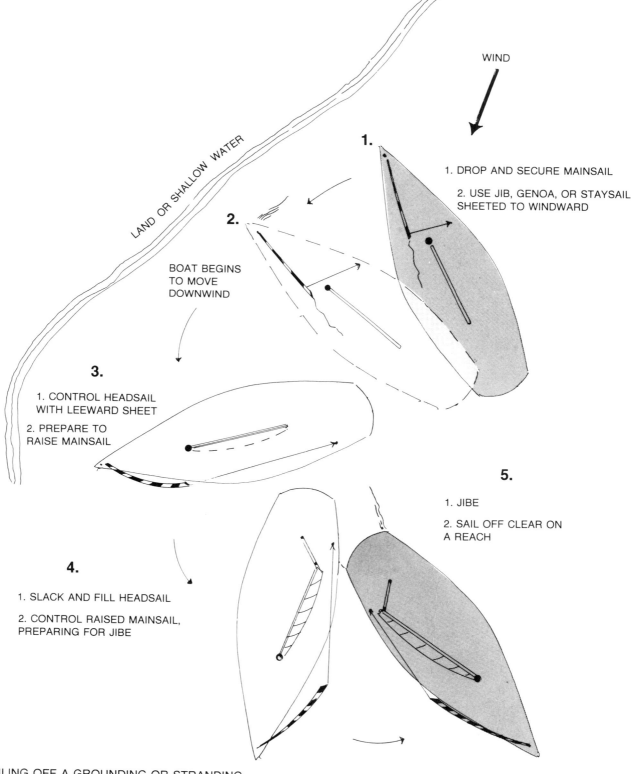

WIND

1.

1. DROP AND SECURE MAINSAIL

2. USE JIB, GENOA, OR STAYSAIL
SHEETED TO WINDWARD

LAND OR SHALLOW WATER

2.

BOAT BEGINS
TO MOVE
DOWNWIND

3.

1. CONTROL HEADSAIL
WITH LEEWARD SHEET

2. PREPARE TO
RAISE MAINSAIL

5.

1. JIBE

2. SAIL OFF CLEAR ON
A REACH

4.

1. SLACK AND FILL HEADSAIL

2. CONTROL RAISED MAINSAIL,
PREPARING FOR JIBE

SAILING OFF A GROUNDING OR STRANDING.

nate enough to have one) or muscle power, try to kedge the boat back off the ground. Pulling against the anchor, while working the engines and/or sails, may add enough extra power to help you move off. *A caution:* Any operation where a winch is used to multiply human power may put tremendous stress on the line. A good winch doesn't know when to stop—it just keeps winding. When a highly stressed line breaks, it becomes a lethal weapon, and if the fittings give way before the line does, *they* become deadly missiles.

To carry the anchor into position, put the anchor and the coiled rode in the dinghy; pay out the line as you go. (Don't try to pull the rode along behind you.) If the anchor is particularly heavy, let it rest on or hang over the stern. Don't get in a position where you have to stand up in the dinghy to wrestle with a big anchor.

A sailboat might be able to use various sets of sails to pivot the boat, however slowly, back toward deeper water—and then sail off. And a sailboat might be able to take advantage of the fact that heeling reduces the effective draft, possibly even enough to float free. Here's how to make it work:

• With the wind ahead of or on the beam, hoist the mainsail and sheet it in. With luck (and enough wind), you can heel, turn, and slowly inch your way back into deeper water.

• With sails down, set the boom as far out as possible (toward the low side, if the boat is heeling at all). Have some crew members slide out to the end, thus setting up a lever action. Start the engine and try to motor off.

• Send a crew member up the mast (wearing safety harness and life jacket) to sit out as far as possible on the spreader. Try to sail or motor off.

• Set an anchor as far out to the low side as possible and tie a halyard from the masthead as far out as possible along this anchor line. Using winches, take in on the anchor rode and the halyard at the same time to pull the boat into a heel. As with kedging, don't overstress the line—it could result in a broken mast in addition to injuries to the crew. Try to motor into deeper water.

• If necessary—and if practical—you might be able to use a combination of pivoting, heeling, and kedging.

A later section covers towing.

STRANDING

In the inadvertent, rather than deliberate, context, stranding usually is the result of inattention or engine failure or some combination of the two. If a grounding can at times be treated with a certain jocularity, a stranding is no joke, no matter what the cause. The combination of onshore wind, changing tides, and onrushing surf can either set a boat so high on the beach that removal becomes an engineering feat, or pound it to pieces so quickly that removal is not even an option.

Prevention Take all measures possible to prevent a stranding:

1. If you beach your boat for a picnic—or anchor just a few yards offshore—be satisfied that you're on a sheltered beach on a small lake or river with a minimal or nonexistent tidal range.

2. When picnicking on a beach that might be subject to heavy surf (even if the water is placid at the time), be wary of sudden changes in the weather. The wind accompanying even a distant squall might go from 0 to 20 knots in just a few minutes—often not enough time for you to notice the change, grab your picnic gear, get in the boat, and get beyond the surf line.

3. When under power anywhere near an exposed shoreline, expect an engine failure. That will keep you on your toes and ensure that you always have an anchor ready. Each year, too many boats are irrevocably washed up on an otherwise-unthreatening shore because of a power or transmission failure, accompanied by a failure to stop the boat by putting out the anchor. Once "on the beach," even the most gentle surf, especially if matched with an incoming tide, will slowly, wave by wave, move your boat farther up the sand.

Controlling the Situation At this stage, your options narrow quickly:

1. Get an anchor out as far into deeper water as possible and set it as firmly as possible. Keep the rode under tension to prevent the boat from being moved slowly farther ashore. Try to kedge the boat toward deeper water.

2. Enlist the aid of passersby, if there be any. If there are enough volunteers and your boat is not too large, you may be able to refloat by timing a big push to match the flotation effect of each incoming wave. BUT WATCH OUT: Almost any boat being knocked around in the surf can be classed as a lethal weapon.

3. Enlist the aid of a passing boat, or send for a commercial tow service, to pass you a line and try to pull you off; first, read the comments below under Salvage.

Assisting a Stranded Boat Pulling a stranded boat off a surf-wracked beach is almost as hazardous to the assisting boat as to the stranded one; it can too easily get caught in the surf, bang the bottom, become unmaneuverable, and end up on the beach itself.

The rescuer should remain as far out of the surf line as possible and send a messenger line floating ashore attached to a life jacket, fender, or horseshoe float. Once the stranded boat has picked up the float (with a boathook, or off the beach), the heavier towing line, attached to the messenger, can be pulled over.

If the stranded boat is broached, lying sideways on the beach, it will be easier to pull the *bow* than the stern. Then, once the bow starts to lift with each incoming wave, a few inches of progress might be made.

SAFE TOWING

Towing involves two vessels—the one being towed and the one towing—and at any time, you might find yourself in the position of one or the other. Our suggestions encompass both.

The international signal for "I require a tug" is the letter "Z"—Zulu. It may be displayed by flag, semaphore, or blinking light—although it is unlikely that most yachtsmen will have either the equipment or the knowledge to do that. The captain of a boat in need of a tow is most likely to wave his arms a lot and yell, "Can you give me a hand?"

If you're that captain asking for help, it's likely you're doing so on the assumption that any fellow yachtsman, as a courtesy, will gladly render the needed assistance. However, be aware that the towing vessel may try to claim salvage rights (see below).

SALVAGE

Salvage is the attempt by someone other than the owner or crew member to save (or conserve from damage) a vessel in danger—in expectation

of reward. That friendly stranger who offers you a tow when your engine conks out may be just that—friendly, and wishing nothing more than your thanks. However, should you be in imminent danger of smashing on the rocks, his assistance might give rise to a salvage claim in admiralty court.

Salvage claims apply to property, not people. The master or person in charge of any vessel is obligated by law and custom (with the force of law) to provide whatever assistance can safely be given to any individual at sea in danger of being lost—and may be subject to fine and/or imprisonment for failure to do so. Having expended all reasonable efforts to save the crew, however, the rescuer has no responsibility whatever to try to save the vessel, and if he does so, he may qualify as a salvor.

For a salvage claim to be valid, three conditions apply: (1) The vessel must actually have been in distress, in the judgment of the owner; (2) the salvor must be a volunteer; (3) the salvage must be successful.

The owner cannot be forced to accept assistance, no matter how imminent the danger; if the owner agrees to accept help, and he and the potential salvor agree on a price in advance (by the hour, day, or event), the salvor becomes a contractor. His pay is limited to the agreed amount and he is not eligible to file a salvage claim. If a valid salvage effort is undertaken, the salvor may—or may not—qualify for a claim. Under an admiralty concept of "no cure, no pay," an unsuccessful salvor is not entitled to payment unless his contribution significantly improved the situation. The amount of a salvage award would be determined by the courts and takes the form of a maritime lien of high priority.

Should you think that, in case of emergency, the good old United States Coast Guard will come to the rescue free of charge—think again. The Coast Guard, caught between its own budget constraints and complaints of unfair competition from commercial services, has been revising the rules of the game. Unless a request for assistance involves injuries or imminent disaster—that is, unless a true emergency exists—the request may be denied. A sailboat with a dead engine may be refused help if the sail rig is in good working order and the crew is in no danger. A boat hard aground on an offshore reef—deemed in no immediate peril—may be turned over to a commercial towing service. Even if the Coast Guard begins a tow, they may pass it over to a commercial salvor should one appear on the scene. You can expect to pay at least a dollar a minute for towing and mechanical service, with a one-hour minimum.

On a more positive note: A recent development applies the concept of "automobile-club service" to boating. In addition to locally operated services that are found in many parts of the country, national membership in Boat US carries a $50 towing allowance; extra coverage may be purchased.

To avoid any doubt, before passing any lines, ask whether there will be a charge for the service, and if so, agree upon the amount. To play it even safer, stay aboard your boat to forestall the possibility of a claim of abandonment.

If the towing vessel is not a commercial salvor, you will need to furnish the towing line. Your anchor rode should be the longest and strongest line aboard—and the best one to put into towing service.

The Coast Guard or a commercial towing service will provide their own lines. A towline from a merchant ship or large commercial tug is likely to be a wire rope—strong enough to pull almost anything under almost any conditions but almost impossible to handle. You need to jury-rig an "adapter" out of your own line to permit attachment to any fitting on your boat.

The towline can be passed directly—weather permitting—or pulled across with the use of a heaving line (see chapter 9).

Before starting out, discuss the specifics of the operation with the captain of the towing vessel. For example, if you're aground on a sandbar, do you want only to be pulled free or do you also want to be towed to safe harbor? How will the two boats communicate—by VHF (if so, pick the channel and test it) or by hand signals (agree on their meaning)?

RIGGING FOR THE TOW

The magnitude of the forces generated in towing can be considerable. As long as the towing and towed boats are moving along smoothly in calm waters, there should be no problem, but any degree of pitching and yawing will jerk lines and fittings, and the force necessary to nudge a stranded boat off a sandbar may be more than the boat's hardware can withstand. Cleats may be broken or pulled bodily from the deck; a towline may snap and whip back on a crew member, with serious consequences.

The best piece of hardware for use in towing is a samson post—designed to take the strain but too seldom found on pleasure boats. Any hardware used must be adequate to the task. You may not know until you've tried it, but you can be sure that anything merely screwed to the deck will not hold up under the strain—it must be through-bolted and also should have a backing plate. A

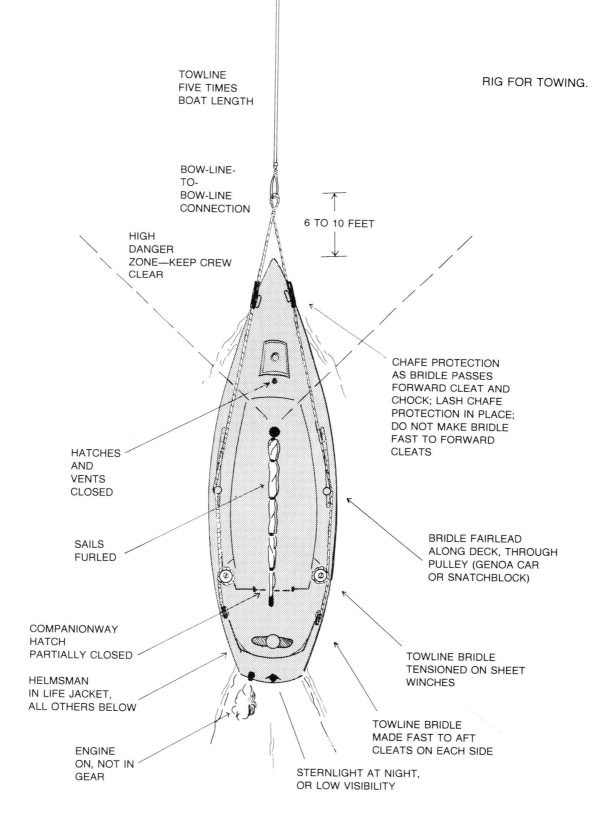

TOWLINE
FIVE TIMES
BOAT LENGTH

RIG FOR TOWING.

BOW-LINE-
TO-
BOW-LINE
CONNECTION

6 TO 10 FEET

HIGH
DANGER
ZONE—KEEP CREW
CLEAR

CHAFE PROTECTION
AS BRIDLE PASSES
FORWARD CLEAT AND
CHOCK; LASH CHAFE
PROTECTION IN PLACE;
DO NOT MAKE BRIDLE
FAST TO FORWARD
CLEATS

HATCHES
AND
VENTS
CLOSED

BRIDLE FAIRLEAD
ALONG DECK, THROUGH
PULLEY (GENOA CAR
OR SNATCHBLOCK)

SAILS
FURLED

COMPANIONWAY
HATCH
PARTIALLY CLOSED

TOWLINE BRIDLE
TENSIONED ON SHEET
WINCHES

HELMSMAN
IN LIFE JACKET,
ALL OTHERS BELOW

TOWLINE BRIDLE
MADE FAST TO AFT
CLEATS ON EACH SIDE

ENGINE
ON, NOT IN
GEAR

STERNLIGHT AT NIGHT,
OR LOW VISIBILITY

small boat can be towed with the bowring used when trailering the boat.

Small sailboats may have no deck hardware worthy of holding a towline. Avoid the temptation to attach the line to the forestay—which is not meant to handle a fore-and-aft pull—and take the line to the mast.

If you want to tow a small sailboat that has capsized, first get it upright. Otherwise, it will have a tendency to bury the bow, increasing the tension on the line. Also, as you approach shallower water, the mast will at some point hit the bottom, causing damage to the rig that could have been avoided.

On larger sailboats, the mast may—or may not—provide a secure attachment point. A mast stepped on deck might be pulled off, and therefore should not be used as a towing point unless it's supported by a strong tabernacle. A towline passed around a secure mast must also be tied down on deck—if not, the line could ride up the mast and reach a point where it pulls the boat over on its side.

On a larger boat—lacking proper fittings—you can rig a towing bridle by passing a line *around* the boat, provided it crosses no sharp edges or anything likely to be damaged, such as a boarding ladder.

All of the foregoing comments about attachment and fittings also apply to the towing boat; if the towboat has no fittings adequate to the task, it should use a bridle as well.

To keep some reserve of maneuverability, the towing boat should attach the line at some point forward of the rudder. A large knife—or an axe—should be handy in the event of an emergency that requires the line to be cut.

If the towing line is passed straight over the bow, pitching and yawing can yank out the bow pulpit. If time permits, rig a Y-shaped bridle so that its ends pass outside the hull through the bow chocks—provided these contain no hard edges, which would quickly cut the line under tension.

Wherever the towline crosses a deck edge or goes through a chock, it should be protected adequately with chafing gear.

THE TOW

The tow itself should begin with a gradual pull, as much to test the strength of the line and fittings as to get moving. Keep an eye on the rig but keep well out of the way; always remember that a line under tension can snap with great force.

The speed should be adjusted to conditions of wind and weather and to the safe towing speed for the hull design—not to exceed hull speed. The reasons:

• Nonplaning hulls pulled faster than hull speed will start dragging a lot of water. The bow rides up on the large bow wave while the stern squats down just under an unaccustomed stern wave. Overwhelmed, the boat sinks, stern first.

• Towing a planing hull at too high a speed may have the opposite effect with the same result: The extra-large bow wave might merge with a naturally large wave crest and the boat would be pulled into, rather than be allowed to ride over, the mound of water.

The best speed is a relatively slow one, regardless of the type of hull. This is not the time to be worried about missing an appointment ashore.

The towline should be at least ten times the length of the towed boat. In heavy seas, try to adjust the length of the tow to match the distance

---

Towing a dinghy is a common practice that should be done with more care than often is used. A quick squall—or even a subtle increase of wave activity—can swamp a towed dinghy. When towing, make sure the towline is fastened firmly at both ends; set the length of the line so that the dinghy rides up on your stern wave. When coming to a stop, you *must* tend that line quickly—the dinghy will continue forward and the towline can easily become wrapped around a propeller. A polypropylene floating line will help avoid this; a nylon line with a few small floats attached may also help—if the floats aren't torn loose sooner by the passing wake.

This caution applies in any astern towing situation; when ending a tow, both boats must be alert to keeping the now-slack towline out of the water.

between wave crests. An anchor or any heavy object slung from the center of the towline will act as a shock absorber.

In towing a small boat with a centerboard, beware of its tendency to heel sharply at higher towing speeds, when the centerboard tries to act like an airplane wing. An unexpected capsize is a logical result. Raise the centerboard.

Alongside towing may be an expedient in waters where maneuvering room is restricted or where neither boat has a long-enough towline, but the two boats will be in constant danger of banging against each other. Put every available fender between the two boats; attach and adjust bow and stern lines so that the fenders are just touched by both boats, leaving little play between them. A springline from the towing boat provides the towing force. The paired boats will be cumbersome and will tend to turn toward the towed boat. Turning in the other direction may be difficult.

While involved in a tow, both boats are regarded as a single unit (see Chapter 14 for a description of the relevant lights and dayshapes required under the Rules of the Road). The captain of the towing vessel is in charge, but the skipper of the towed vessel still has full responsibility for the safety of his boat and crew.

1. BOW LINE

2. BOW SPRING

3. BREASTLINE—MAIN TOWING LINE; BE SURE LINE IS DOUBLED UP; TENSION ON WINCH.

4. STERN SPRING (WHEN TOWING POWERBOAT GOING ASTERN)

5. STERNLINE

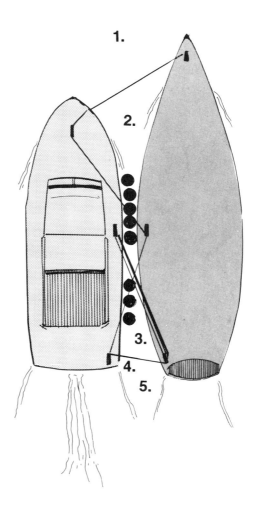

TOWING ALONGSIDE.

CONTROLLING DAMAGE

Damage control begins well before the damage. Preparation starts with a thorough knowledge of your boat, continues through the acquisition of appropriate tools and repair supplies, and ends with a series of "what if" drills in which you mentally work through a range of possible problems: a hard grounding with possible hull damage, a dismasting in a storm, or a fire in the galley.

In these drills, you should have imagined damage in different parts of the boat and mentally worked through the problems you would face and the actions you would take. One of the first problems might have been locating the damage; one of the first actions, cutting electrical power to the area. Here's one time when your Owner's Notebook will pay off; you will have explored every hidden nook, you will have diagrammed every through-hull fitting, and you will have

charted the location and purpose of every run of wire and every switch. You may even have transferred some of this information to a set of data cards, readily available for use by any crew member.

Having been thus prepared, dealing with the actual emergency can proceed in a logical, not panicky, fashion.

HULL DAMAGE AND FLOODING

Most damage-control problems will deal with watertight integrity; the less integrity, the bigger the problem.

Water usually will flood in from one or all of the following sources:

- A failed through-hull fitting;
- A broken intake line;
- A hole in the hull from grounding, stress, or collision;
- Over the side or through hatches and ventilators.

Your immediate defense is a high-capacity bilge pump powered by a fully charged battery, which may help you keep ahead of the problem . . . for a while. You have to make every effort to stop or minimize the leak as quickly as possible—and this may not be as hard as you might think.

The pressure of the incoming water is not great; you can hold it back with the palm of your hand—provided your hand can cover the opening. This low pressure permits you to stuff something into the hole from inside the hull—rags, clothing, or a tapered wooden plug (one of which should be stowed alongside each through-hull fitting). In a pinch, you can improvise with a screwdriver: Wrap the handle in a rag and jam it into the opening.

The plugs (and the screwdriver, if jammed in tight enough) should stay in position; rags by themselves probably will not, and they must be held in place with some sort of prop.

HEAD-ON COLLISION. This German-built motorsailer was run down by a steel fishing dragger in a fog off Cape Cod. The motorsailer lost about 15 feet of its bow, but luckily, an internal bulkhead forward held. The bulkhead, a full section, managed to keep the boat from sinking during the slow trip back to port. Quick damage-control action by the crew in shoring up the bulkhead saved the vessel. Training, tools, and spare material, including collision mats and lumber, were the keys to survival.

If the flooding comes from a broken intake hose or one that has come loose from the seacock, your first action is to close the seacock. If the handle won't move freely, use the spare length of pipe from your damage-control kit for leverage, but do not overstress, or you might pull the seacock out of the hull, creating a larger hole.

Damage of any significant size—a hole punched through by a rock or floating log, for instance—will require some fast engineering. If you can get to the damage from the outside, do so: Apply a professional collision mat if you have one, or stuff a life jacket into the hole or lash a mattress over the hole. With a wooden hull, don't hesitate to nail the material in place; in any event, outside water pressure will help hold the stuffing until you can make more substantial repairs. This sort of bandage may not stop the water, but it should effectively decrease it.

In warm and relatively calm water, you can send someone over the side to plug the hole, but this should not be considered a casual undertaking. Any person who goes in the water should:

• Wear a lifeline tended from the deck by another crew member;
• Use a face mask, snorkel, and flippers, if possible;
• If trained and properly equipped, use scuba gear.

A boarding ladder should be down and ready for use; flotation gear—the larger the better—should be ready in case the diver becomes adrift or needs a rest. A set of signals should have been arranged and agreed to: one tug on the line, "stop"; two tugs, "give me slack"; three tugs, "take up slack"; rapid tugging, "help, haul me in." (See chapter 10.)

In less than calm/warm conditions, or if it is not safe to put someone in the water, you can use a sail, tarpaulin, or even a heavy blanket to rig a sort of pressure bandage: (1) Secure one end at the deck edge and attach a small anchor to the other; (2) let the weight of the anchor pull the material into the water; (3) lead the free end of

the anchor line to the bow or stern and then under the hull; (4) work the line back (or forward—but the rudder and screws will impede your progress from astern; use a boathook to keep the line clear). Then pull the line aboard, drawing the underwater end of the "bandage" tight against the leak.

If you need to handle a substantial leak from inside the boat, you *may* need to clear away cabinets or decking—and may need to do so quickly, even violently. A hatchet and a prybar should be included in your emergency toolkit, and a willingness to use them must be part of your emergency mindset.

Once you can get at the leak, use cushions, pillows, or a mattress to hold back the water, and use portions of the removed cabinetry to rig shoring to hold the stuffing in place.

A commercially available "leak umbrella" might prove a valuable addition to your kit. You thrust the folded device through the hole from inside the hull, open the umbrellalike fabric cover, and secure the handle inside. It's a quick

COLLISION DETAILS from the head-on collision in fog between the motorsailer and the fishing dragger. This temporary plywood false bow was added in port to enable the motorsailer to cross Nantucket Sound for extensive repairs. The collision induced distortions throughout the hull, causing drawers to jam in bureaus and doors to jam shut. Damage estimates exceeded $120,000.

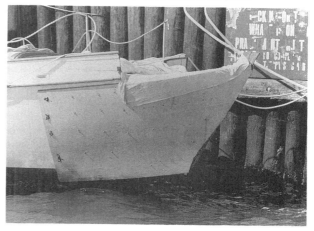

and efficient method for covering a relatively large opening, although it will not necessarily stop all of the leaking.

Relatively small leaks can be filled temporarily with underwater patching compounds or sealants applied with a putty knife or a cartridge gun.

Of course, all of the above suggestions apply to open holes in the hull. Older wooden boats, working in a seaway, may start leaking through every seam. In such an event, you must try to minimize hull action by adjusting course and speed, hope that your pumps and power are adequate to the task, and bail like a sonofagun if they are not—until you can reach sheltered, shallow water.

PUMPING OUT THE WATER

When the flooding exceeds the capacity of your bilge pumps, you'll need to put the emergency backup into service. This may be a high-capacity manual pump or an engine-driven or auxiliary

RESCUE-EQUIPMENT READY RACK at a Coast Guard rescue air unit. Rescue stretchers are visible at the top of the rack. The drumlike containers hold droppable pumps and dewatering equipment.

unit; don't overlook the possibility of pumping through your engine cooling water intake, as described in chapter 9.

When operating electric bilge pumps, keep your engine running if at all possible. Otherwise, the drain on the batteries may too soon render the pumps useless, and they will barely turn over under increasingly reduced current.

If additional pump capacity is required, the Coast Guard is your best bet; cutters and auxiliaries are equipped with high-capacity pumps and helicopters can drop portable gasoline-powered units. You may, of course, have to accept the assistance of a commercial salvor—and may have no option but to honor his claim (see chapter 22).

DISMASTING

A mast might be lost for any or a combination of several reasons: too much or too little tension on the standing rigging; deterioration of the mast, particularly at the step. You just might be pushing the limits of the boat. Whatever the cause, quick action is required:

1. While you are breaking out the heavy bolt cutters from the damage-control kit, get the crew in life jackets.

2. You have two basic options—to try to save the mast and tow it home, or to cut it loose and get away. A mast surging with the waves can become a potent battering ram directed at your hull.

3. Whichever your choice, don't start the engine until you are certain that all stray lines, shrouds, sails, and loose gear have been cleared and secured. Having lost your main wind power, you don't want to foul up your engine power as well.

4. If you feel you can save the mast, maneuver it into a position where it can be cinched tight up against the hull—preferably protected with a mattress or pillow cushion to keep it from pounding against (and possibly holing) the hull.

5. If you can't save the mast, get it free as quickly as possible.

6. Depending upon conditions and your own ingenuity, you can probably fashion a jury rig from the mast stump, the boom (if it's still aboard), any part of the mast you can salvage, a spinnaker pole, even a boathook—and whatever bits of cloth you can hang in the wind.

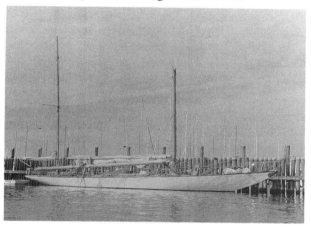

DISMASTED SLOOP shows both the damage and the jury rig. The aluminum mast fractured just below the spreaders, but there was little damage to the hull, cabin, or watertight integrity. The skipper has set up the boat's main boom as a jury-rigged mast, running stays from the outhaul fittings at the boom end to the deck. The jury-rigged sail was hoisted loose-footed for the sail back into Nantucket Harbor.

CATASTROPHIC MAST FAILURE on this large yawl occurred just above the lower stay supports. The crew managed to bring back aboard the mast's fractured section and lash it next to the boom.

MAST FRACTURES TEND TO OCCUR IN THE VICINITY OF STAY TERMINAL POINTS. This mast fractured just above the lower stays. One of the lower spreaders can be seen still attached to the section that was brought back aboard with a tackle system set up to the mast stub. The sheer bulk and weight of this mast section sends the clear message that dismasting at sea is always a catastrophe.

JURY RIG.

FIREFIGHTING

The average pleasure boat carries minimal fire-fighting equipment—which, once installed, is taken for granted. Few boat owners have ever practiced using a fire extinguisher, let alone run their weekend guests through emergency drills; among the most common defects noted in marine surveys are expired inspection tags on fire extinguishers. When it comes to firefighting, the opportunities for preparation and training end the moment *before* a fire starts.

About 90 percent of boat fires begin in the engine spaces and involve fuel or fuel vapors; most can be avoided by preventing the escape of fuel and by the early detection of potentially explosive vapors. Of those fires that do get started, a majority could be controlled quickly by automatically triggered extinguishing systems in the engine spaces. Clearly, the most important step in fire prevention is the proper installation, maintenance, and operation of fuel systems; next, a wise investment in fire control would be an engine-room extinguishing system.

However, the prudent boat owner will be prepared, with both equipment and knowledge, to handle anything from a smoldering mattress to a distribution-board short circuit—and to do so in a timely and appropriate manner. Pausing to read the instructions on a fire extinguisher does not count toward timely, and using an extinguishing agent that may make intensify the fire is certainly not appropriate.

Remember that fire depends on three factors—a combustible substance, a source of ignition, and oxygen. The prevention of fire involves keeping combustible substances away from heat; the extinguishing of fire involves either cooling the burning materials below ignition temperature or interfering with the chemical process of combustion—typically, by keeping oxygen from the flames. (Review the section on firefighting equipment in chapter 9.)

ACTION

Class A Fires   Drench the fire with water; open up the burning material to expose any hidden fire; drench again.

Class B Fires   Direct the extinguisher discharge at the base of the fire, with a sweeping motion; if the fire is from a drip or leak in a fuel line or tank, start at the lower part of the fire and work upward. Try to shut off the supply of fuel.

Class C Fires   Immediately cut off the supply of electricity; extinguish burning materials by smothering with the agent.

ENGINEROOM FIRE

- Stop the engines.
- Stop feeding oxygen to the fire: Shut off all blowers.
- Avoid opening the engine compartment for the same reason. If possible use a portable extinguisher to direct the discharge into the compartment through an access port. With a fixed system, manual or automatic control will trigger the extinguisher.

Fire Classifications

The following definitions from chapter 8 are repeated here for clarity and convenience.

Class A.   Combustible solid materials such as wood, paper, plastics, and cloth. The basic firefighting technique is to cool the fire below the ignition temperature of the materials.

Class B.   Flammable liquids such as oil, grease, gasoline, kerosene. A smothering technique is used to cut off the oxygen necessary for combustion.

Class C.   Fires in, or involving, electrical circuits. The extinguishing agent must not conduct an electric current.

• Allow the extinguishing agent to remain in the compartment as long as possible before opening, ventilating, and entering.

• While ventilating, stand by with a portable extinguisher and be alert for a reflash.

• Determine the cause of the fire before restarting the engine.

With all fires: Take nothing for granted. The fire you *think* is out may just be lying low, waiting to strike again. After all fires, replace or recharge extinguishers *at once*.

HOME REMEDIES

• Baking soda, salt, and flour: Sprinkle heavily on galley flareups.

• Sand and blankets: Smother a small fire.

• Throw the burning object overboard.

CHAPTER TWENTY-THREE

Seamanship in an Emergency— Saving the Crew

MAN OVERBOARD

A man-overboard situation is not an extemporaneous swim call to be treated as a joke; it is a life-threatening emergency and must be handled as such. Even in ideal weather, with the water at bathtub temperature, the person in the water may be a nonswimmer, may be panicking, or may have been stunned or injured in the fall. For example, in trying to stop a fall, we instinctively grab for the lifelines and might end up with a dislocated shoulder. In less than ideal weather, the jeopardy is greatly increased by the difficulty in maneuvering the boat and the increased danger of hypothermia. In particularly cold water, the shock may trigger a heart attack.

This is one accident against which you must exercise constant vigilance. Prevention is the best solution, and that means enforcing rules topside: not letting children run free, putting all crew members in life jackets when necessary. That means developing standard procedures for handling anchors and sails, especially for heavy-weather and night sailing. That means, for exam-

ple, that the helmsman on watch alone should *always* wear a safety harness, and he should make a signed log entry at least once an hour, noting the time, course, and speed; should he disappear, you'd have some idea of how far back to start the search.

Vigilance also means letting someone else know where you are and what you're doing. A few years back, on a delightfully calm, clear day, while slowly sailing into a protected harbor, an experienced lifelong sailor went to the foredeck to furl a sail. The boat took a roll and a free-swinging staysail club caught him behind the knees, knocking him off balance and overboard. His wife was below in the galley; by the time she realized something was amiss, the boat had drifted well off the spot. The Coast Guard recovered his body two days later.

Rescue while underway requires quick thinking and coordinated action—all enhanced by mental preparation. In the U.S. Navy, neophyte bridge watch-standers are regularly tested on the proper actions to be taken at the moment of a "man overboard!" call. The crew is run through periodic man-overboard drills to recover a floating dummy thrown—without warning—into the water. (The dummy is affectionately known as "Oscar"—named for the "O" flag, the international signal for "man overboard.")

On a private pleasure craft, the helmsman must be as ready to respond as the navy officer-of-the-deck, and the crew—frequently untrained landlubbers out for a Sunday outing—should have been given some orientation. It goes without saying that, should you become the man overboard, you'll want to have some confidence that the crew will be able to take appropriate action.

STEPS FOR RESCUE

The procedures below, for the most part, assume that someone saw the accident or you know it happened within the previous few minutes; when the time of the fall is uncertain, your response would start at step 6.

1. Whoever sees the crew member fall calls out, as loudly as possible, "Man overboard, [port] [starboard] side!" and points toward him and he—or someone—*keeps pointing.*

2. Throw the life ring or horseshoe float toward the swimmer, along with any other floatable object (such as cushions and fender) at hand. Be aware, however, that anything floating on the surface may drift at a speed greater than that of a swimmer moving along only with the current. Make allowances for the force of the wind. This is a time when you'll want to be equipped with a ballasted man-overboard pole.

3. Get the boat headed back for the swimmer; if under sail, lower the sails and start the engine. If you've launched a buoy with an attached line, be sure to keep the line from fouling your propeller.

4. Ensure that one or several crew members keep the swimmer in sight at all times. This is not always easy: In heaving, storm-whipped seas,

STERN-MOUNTED MAN-OVERBOARD RIG can be released easily without danger of fouling lifelines or rigging.

MAN-OVERBOARD LIGHT begins to flash as soon as it rights itself after launch. (Forespar)

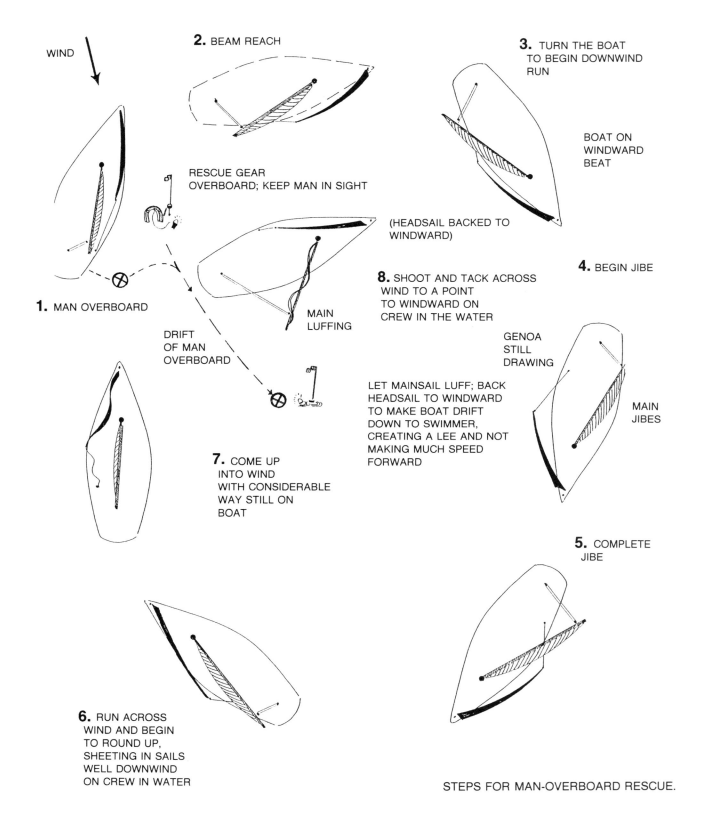

WIND

2. BEAM REACH

3. TURN THE BOAT TO BEGIN DOWNWIND RUN

BOAT ON WINDWARD BEAT

RESCUE GEAR OVERBOARD; KEEP MAN IN SIGHT

(HEADSAIL BACKED TO WINDWARD)

8. SHOOT AND TACK ACROSS WIND TO A POINT TO WINDWARD ON CREW IN THE WATER

4. BEGIN JIBE

MAIN LUFFING

GENOA STILL DRAWING

1. MAN OVERBOARD

DRIFT OF MAN OVERBOARD

LET MAINSAIL LUFF; BACK HEADSAIL TO WINDWARD TO MAKE BOAT DRIFT DOWN TO SWIMMER, CREATING A LEE AND NOT MAKING MUCH SPEED FORWARD

MAIN JIBES

7. COME UP INTO WIND WITH CONSIDERABLE WAY STILL ON BOAT

5. COMPLETE JIBE

6. RUN ACROSS WIND AND BEGIN TO ROUND UP, SHEETING IN SAILS WELL DOWNWIND ON CREW IN WATER

STEPS FOR MAN-OVERBOARD RESCUE.

with the boat maneuvering for a pickup, the lookouts can too easily become disoriented. They should continue to point with outstretched arms, even when they can't see him, and they should try to adjust to the change in heading by aligning with the waves or a star or any stable element. If the accident occurs at night, the searchlight will help you find the man and help give him some confidence that you're looking.

5. Do *not* let anyone, any time, jump into the water to help the man overboard unless there is no other choice.

6. At night or in reduced visibility, when the man overboard is not in sight, and particularly when you don't know exactly how much time has elapsed, use the Williamson turn to get headed back along your track: Put the helm hard over, turning *toward* the side (if known) over which the man fell until your heading has changed 60 degrees. Then quickly reverse the rudder and come around 240 degrees. You'll be headed back, almost running down your own wake. (Practice a few times in good weather, and fine-tune the maneuver to match the characteristics of your own boat.)

7. With a boat under sail, the procedure will vary, depending upon the direction of the wind.

8. If you can spare a crew member, send out a radio call for help; it's far easier to cancel the request when the man is back aboard than to have to explain what might become a fatal delay. If you've really lost sight of the man, or are not certain as to when he went overboard, send out a call *immediately*. Provide a good fix of your position, the course you were on when the man went overboard, and a clear identification of your boat; searchers need to be able to sort you out from all of the other traffic.

9. With the man in sight, try to approach upwind, so your boat will drift toward him and at the same time provide a lee shelter.

10. As you near the swimmer, stop the engine.

11. Get a line on the swimmer before you do anything else; you don't want to lose him while trying to get him aboard. *That* step may not be easy.

12. If your boat is equipped with a good boarding ladder that can be let down into the water, an uninjured person may be able to climb aboard easily. Otherwise, see step 14.

13. Climbing aboard a smaller boat can be tricky, as the boat can capsize easily. Entry should be made from the stern.

14. However, don't assume that even an uninjured person will be able to help himself get out of the water. The combined effects of hypothermia (not just in cold water), waterlogged clothing, and fatigue may have robbed him of any strength. Getting a weakened or unconscious person aboard will pose additional problems, and this is likely to require that another crew member go overboard to assist. Hook a line to the safety harness (if worn) or run a sling under the arms, chest upward. You can use the boom and a winch, or rig a sling from the jib, but these operations presume some familiarity with rigging skills. Learn how to do it—and practice—before you ever need to do it.

ADVICE FOR THE PERSON IN THE WATER

You won't have this book for a reference, so you should review this section frequently enough to remember the key points at the moment of crisis. They are:

1. Don't try to swim after the boat. You'll never catch it and you'll waste valuable energy. Let the boat come to you. *Do* swim to any float or life ring thrown in the water; it will provide valuable flotation and also give your companions a more visible target.

2. Don't panic if the boat seems to have sailed away over the horizon; the horizon from water level isn't very far, and it is a lot closer when the waves get in the way.

3. When the boat has sailed out of sight, don't waste a lot of energy by shouting. Use the whistle attached to your life jacket for signaling, and turn on the light (unless it's already been activated by the dunking). This assumes, of course,

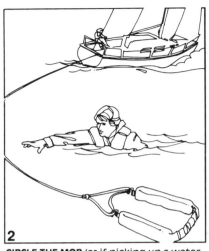

STOP THE BOAT IMMEDIATELY near MOB. Sailboats head into wind. Luff all sails. Maintain visual contact with MOB at all times.

DEPLOY LIFESLING. Throw off transom of boat. It will trail behind boat to end of floating tether line.

CIRCLE THE MOB (as if picking up a water skier). Lifesling or tether should reach MOB within first or second circle. Sailboats should maneuver under sail to eliminate risk of fouling propeller in overboard sheets and other lines. Do not sail over tether and avoid hitting MOB.

WHEN LIFESLING REACHES MOB, STOP THE BOAT IMMEDIATELY. Sailboats head into wind and drop all sails, jib first. Powerboats: stop all engines completely. **MOB PLACES LIFESLING UNDER ARMS** and connects plastic buckle. Built-in floatation helps float MOB. Do not tow MOB behind boat. He could drown in his own wake.

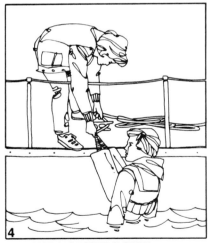

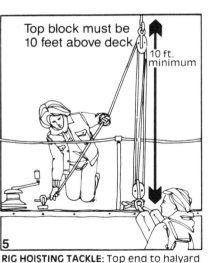

PULL MOB ALONGSIDE SLOWLY, preferably on windward side of boat (however, either side will do). Lift MOB as far as possible and **TIE TETHER TO CLEAT.** MOB is secured out of immediate drowning danger while hoisting tackle is rigged. **MAINTAIN TENSION ON TETHER SO MOB WILL NOT SLIP OUT.**

RIG HOISTING TACKLE: Top end to halyard **A MINIMUM OF TEN FEET ABOVE DECK** to allow MOB to clear lifeline. Main halyard recommended, but any halyard will do. Bottom end to loop in tether. Lead tail through jib lead block and to winch.

HOIST MOB ABOARD

LIFESLING SYSTEM is a fairly recent development for use in a man-overboard (MOB) situation. The sequential diagram shows the general operating principles, which should be discussed with the entire crew in advance. (Lifesling MOB)

that you're wearing a life jacket and that it's appropriately equipped.

4. Keep your clothes on; they'll provide sufficient insulation to keep your skin temperature about 5°F above the water temperature.

5. Curl up into the fetal position, and float. Move your arms and legs as little as possible—every movement will flush colder water through your clothing, reducing the insulating value.

MAN-OVERBOARD SYSTEM consists of a horseshoe buoy, man-overboard pole, attachment line, man-overboard light, and dye marker—all assembled on a rail-mounted system ready to let go. Assembly should be near the cockpit or mounted with pole in tube integral to the hull.

RESCUE AND EMERGENCY TRANSFER AT SEA

On a calm and placid day—the sort upon which we always hope our emergencies might intrude, if intrude they must—passing a sick or injured crewman from your boat to some other, for treatment or further transportation, is accomplished easily. You tie up briefly side by side and hand the ailing soul over the deck edge.

But wait. Even on a calm and placid day, what if one of the deck edges is attached to a merchant ship and is separated from yours—vertically—by a distance of 20 or 30 or 40 feet? Suppose that—even on a calm and placid day—a gentle, rolling swell is adding and subtracting a dozen feet a dozen times a minute? You must then worry not only about the ability of your crew member to scramble up a ladder (or be hoisted in a sling), but also about *your* ability to keep your small and fragile boat from being smashed into (or literally erased by rubbing up against) the impassive steel wall of your maritime companion. And this is in *good* weather.

An emergency transfer at sea is not as clear-cut as many other emergency operations, and in fact may pose the greatest risk of injury (other than with fire and explosion). Some suggestions:

1. It is easier to put a healthy, medically trained person aboard your boat under any conditions than to try to remove an injured crew member.

2. For transfer to another boat (for example, from your slow-moving sailboat to a high-speed powerboat for a quick trip ashore), have the powerboat, which most likely will be the most maneuverable, approach the sailboat's quarter with caution to the set of the sails; have fenders ready on both boats; lash the boats tight enough so that they won't suddenly separate during the transfer.

3. For transfer between sailboats, a stern-quarter-to-stern-quarter approach might be a difficult maneuver, but it presents the least danger of get-

ting the rigs (masts, booms, bowsprits, stays, whatever) fouled as the boats roll and pitch in the seaway.

4. For transfer to a large ship: Hope for a flat calm, which will permit the safe use of a litter and sling, or hope that the ship has a small boat and qualified crew who can be launched to come to your aid. With most merchant ships, that's not a likely possibility; for almost all naval and Coast Guard vessels, it's a certainty. *However,* the conditions under which a boat can be launched and recovered safely are not open-ended. One possible alternative when an auxiliary boat is not available or feasible: the larger ship can set a life raft or float between the hull and your boat, to act as a buffer.

HELICOPTER RESCUE should occur only in critical situations, since these rescues always hold some danger for both boat and helicopter crews. Sketch shows key elements of a successful helicopter rescue: (1) Helicopter is pointed directly into wind, giving pilot maximum control. Boat is headed off 45 degrees and maintains good steerageway. (2) Port-side lifelines have been lowered clear of basket. (3) Mainsail is furled and lashed, with boom firmly secured to starboard. (4) Both boat crewmen are wearing life jackets. Note that, in this position, the pilot has a somewhat limited view of the boat and must depend on his doorway hoist crewman for final positioning instructions. (U.S. Coast Guard)

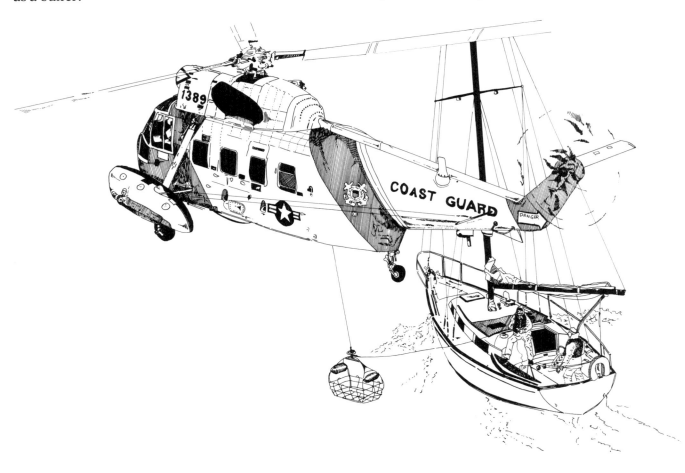

5. For transfer by helicopter:

• From a small powerboat, the helicopter might be able to hover directly overhead, lowering a lifting sling or basket and a crewman to assist; however, the downwash of the rotor blades will tend to shove the boat away, so careful maneuvering is required of both the copter and the boat.

• From a boat with a high tower or mast, the copter will more likely stay off to one side to avoid fouling the lifting rig. Transfer would be facilitated by putting the injured crewman in your small boat (especially an inflatable—most stable under the downwash), which you *must* keep on a tether to prevent uncontrolled drifting. Should a lift from the deck of a sailboat be the only feasible route, get the sails down and out of the way, set the boom in the boom crutch or lash it to the side, and try to unrig the backstay to provide the best open space.

• A metal cable lowered from the helicopter will most likely carry a charge of static electricity. Do *not* touch this cable until it has been grounded in the water or on deck. (You can, however, handle a rope without first grounding it.)

• Do *not* attach any line from the copter to your boat. The pilot must be free for instant maneuvering.

6. The person being transferred, by whatever means, must be wearing a life jacket. If possible, to assist in treatment, provide a brief written summary of the circumstances of the illness or injury. Wrap it in plastic, if you can, to keep it dry; stuff it in the victim's pocket and pin it shut (to keep the memo from popping out in the wind or the helicopter downdraft); tell rescuers about the memo and its location.

7. Good communications is the key to a safe and successful transfer, by whatever means. If VHF radio is not available, try hand signals, messages written with a felt marker on a bunk sheet or sail, and yelling.

RESCUE BASKET ON DECK. Note key elements in this sketch: (1) Crewman is wearing his life jacket. (2) He has permitted basket to reach the deck before touching it, letting static-electricity buildup discharge. (3) Lifelines on port side have been dropped clear of basket. (4) Sail is furled and boom lashed clear to starboard. (5) Distress flag is displayed prominently on cabintop.

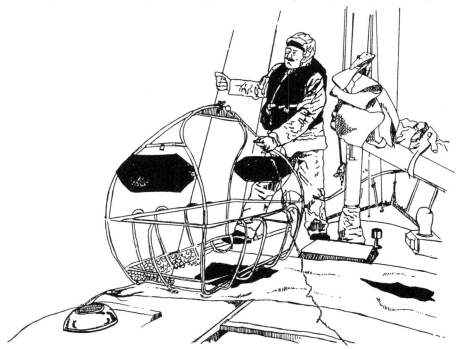

Helicopter Rescue Checklist

This checklist covers most items that are of concern to rescue helicopter and vessel crews. Extraordinary conditions may require deviation from the norm, so be sure to *pay attention* to the helo crew during briefing, and be sure to let them know of any special circumstances on board your vessel.

Initial Distress Call
- Use VHF/FM Channel 16 or other emergency frequency
- Activate EPIRB for location and homing
- Give: Boat name and radio call sign
    Your situation (indicating degree of emergency and any problems
    Your position
    Description of boat and any special markers
    Number of people on board

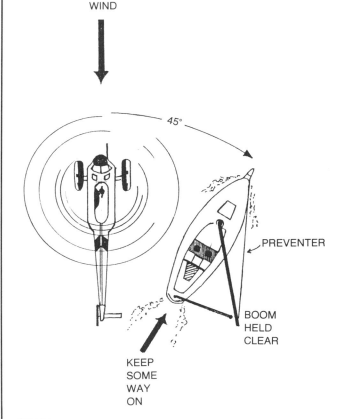

WIND

45°

PREVENTER

BOOM
HELD
CLEAR

KEEP
SOME
WAY
ON

Preparing the Boat
- Lower, furl, and lash all sails
- Remove all unnecessary sheets, halyards, and lines
- Remove all gear from deck
- Remove (or cut) port lifelines and remove stanchions from bases
- Remove all gear from cockpit
- Remove all unused antennae from pulpits as well as fishing rods and man-overboard poles
- Place flares in a dry, accessible place (near companionway)
- Locate and check radio jury-rig antennas
- Rig cabintop marker flag or make reflective-tape marker
- Rig boom to starboard and secure with vang or lashing

Maneuvering the Boat
- Head 30 to 45 degrees off the wind on port tack
- Keep sufficient way on to permit effective steering; be prepared to handle boat in heavy winds

Communications
- Do not change channels once communication is established
- Use proper radio procedure to avoid confusion
- Repeat instructions to guarantee understanding
- Find out how many people are aboard helicopter
- Ask for instructions to be repeated if you do not understand helo briefing

Hoisting
- Tag patient, indicating medication given or other conditions that should be known by doctor (time tourniquet applied, for example)
- Have crew in life jackets; put life jacket on patient and strap in litter with hands inboard, clear of sides
- Determine crew hoisting order, injured first; be sure flotation chest pad is in place on stretcher victim
- Allow stretcher or basket to contact metal part of boat firmly to discharge static electricity; wear gloves to grab basket
- Do not secure trail line, cable, basket, or stretcher to boat
- Use trail line to steady stretcher or basket; keep line clear of rigging, pulpits, and crew; keep tension on line
- Do not use any of your boat's equipment except on instructions of helo crew
- Do not try to assist cabin crewman; keep hands in basket and stay in basket until secure in cabin

- Do not lunge at basket
- Do not ever tie off cable, trail line, stretcher, or basket
- Do not let your hands come out of basket or stretcher

Don'ts
- Do not shine lights at helicopter cockpit or fire flares at aircraft
- Do not jerk trail line

(U.S. Coast Guard)

ABANDONING SHIP

Leaving the boat is the last line of defense, a step to be taken only if there is no further hope of staying afloat. This must not be a casual decision: Many boats, even if half full of water or fully swamped, even if capsized, will still float and thus at least provide something to hang onto, and, in most cases, some degree of habitability. Remember that your boat is your basic safety and survival package. Abandon it only in the event of dire peril.

USING A LIFE RAFT

LAUNCHING

Getting the life raft into the water and inflated may be accomplished manually by untying or cutting the lashings and then sliding, rolling, or heaving the container overboard; the lanyard, yanked by the motion or with an extra tug by hand, will initiate inflation. A handy knife, mounted next to the container, will help ensure a timely launch; another knife, stored aboard as part of the raft equipment, can be used to cut the lanyard/painter after survivors are aboard. *Never* try to inflate the raft on deck before launching. It will become almost impossible to handle even if it doesn't get jammed between the cabin and the lifelines or rigging.

The raft can be fitted with a supplementary automatic release mechanism, which is triggered by water pressure when a sinking boat (with raft still attached) reaches a preset depth—typically, between 8 and 15 feet. The container—designed to have some buoyancy even when tightly packed—will then float free until the lanyard activates the inflation system. The tension established between the greatly increased buoyancy of the inflated raft and the weight of the sinking boat will either snap the lanyard or pull it loose without damage to the raft.

Automatic release mechanisms are of greatest value in the type of catastrophic sinking where the crew has little time to realize what is happening, let alone follow any sort of regular emergency procedures. There is always a danger, however, that the raft can become trapped in wreckage or rigging, so whenever possible, the raft should be launched manually.

INFLATION

The lanyard-activated CO_2 system will inflate the flotation chambers within about thirty seconds; the pressure will force open the container, freeing the raft. (The hissing sound you may hear during and for some time after inflation is excess pressure being bled off through a preset safety valve.)

As the CO_2 expands, it cools well below the freezing point; frost may appear on the surface of the flotation chambers. In cold weather, the freezing effect of pure CO_2 could also clog the valve orifice, preventing inflation. For this reason, rafts carried in northern latitudes are charged with a mixture of CO_2 and nitrogen, while in southern waters, only CO_2 is used. If a boat is being moved from the South to the North for cold-weather operation, the gas mixture should be checked and possibly replaced. The temporary freeze may induce microscopic stress fractures in the life-raft fabric. This, however, was taken into account when the raft was designed and should have no effect on flotation unless the material has already been damaged by previous freeze-and-thaw cycles. The CO_2 system should be used for inflation one time, and one time only—in an emergency. Never "test" the raft with the automatic inflation system.

For a short time after inflation, some of the CO_2 may be absorbed into the chamber fabric; the hand pump is used to restore pressure. The actual pressure within the chambers is quite low—typically, 1.5 to 3 pounds per square inch. You could jab one with an ice pick and only get a slow leak, which is easily offset by the hand

LIFE RAFT AND RESCUE BASKET. Note that this partially ballasted raft is remaining stable despite the heavy downdraft from the hovering helicopter. The basket is the standard unit used by the Coast Guard. People in life rafts should swim to the basket and not attempt to enter the basket directly from the raft. (Avon)

pump. While the undamaged chambers keep the raft afloat, large holes, rips, and tears can be repaired readily with the clamshell clamps or other tools carried in the repair kit.

LIFE-RAFT BOARDING AND USE

The raft should inflate right side up, but if not, it should be an easy matter to turn it over. The strongest uninjured survivor should get aboard first, to help others in boarding. If possible, hold the raft alongside to permit dropping or handing over additional supplies and equipment, and if possible to allow boarding directly from deck. Under most conditions, however, survivors are likely to have to board from the water, climbing up the net or ladder and being helped by the first person aboard. Since a free-floating life raft will drift much faster than a life-jacketed swimmer, the raft should be kept connected to the boat as long as possible.

Once settled inside the raft, survivors should bail or sponge out the bottom, sort out their equipment and supplies, switch on the EPIRB, tend to injuries—and start planning ahead.

APPENDIXES

APPENDIX I

Rules of the Road: International Regulations for Preventing Collisions at Sea (COLREGS), 1972

PART A—GENERAL

Rule 1.—Application

(a) These Rules shall apply to all vessels upon the high seas and in all waters connected therewith navigable by seagoing vessels.

(b) Nothing in these Rules shall interfere with the operation of special rules made by an appropriate authority for roadsteads, harbours, rivers, lakes or inland waterways connected with the high seas and navigable by seagoing vessels. Such special rules shall conform as closely as possible to these Rules.

(c) Nothing in these Rules shall interfere with the operation of any special rules made by the Government of any State with respect to additional station or signal lights, shapes or whistle signals for ships of war and vessels proceeding under convoy, or with respect to additional station or signal lights or shapes for fishing vessels engaged in fishing as a fleet. These additional station or signal lights, shapes or whistle signals shall, so far as possible, be such that they cannot be mistaken for any light, shape or signal authorized elsewhere under these Rules.

(d) Traffic separation schemes may be adopted by the Organization for the purpose of these Rules.

(e) Whenever the Government concerned shall have determined that a vessel of special construction or purpose cannot comply fully with the provisions of any of these Rules with respect to the number, position, range or arc of visibility of lights or shapes, as well as to the disposition and characteristics of sound-signalling appliances, without interfering with the special function of the vessel, such vessel shall comply with such other provisions in regard to the number, position, range or arc of visibility of lights or shapes, as well as to the disposition and characteristics of sound-signalling appliances, as her Government shall have determined to be the closest possible compliance with these Rules in respect to that vessel.

Rule 2.—Responsibility

(a) Nothing in these Rules shall exonerate any vessel, or the owner, master or crew thereof, from the consequences of any neglect to comply with these Rules or of the neglect of any precaution which may be required by the ordinary practice of seamen, or by the special circumstances of the case.

(b) In construing and complying with these Rules due regard shall be had to all dangers of navigation and collision and to any special circumstances, including the limitations of the vessels involved, which may make a departure from these Rules necessary to avoid immediate danger.

Rule 3.—General Definitions

For the purpose of these Rules, except where the context otherwise requires:

(a) The word "vessel" includes every description of water craft, including non-displacement craft and seaplanes, used or capable of being used as a means of transportation on water.

(b) The term "power-driven vessel" means any vessel propelled by machinery.

(c) The term "sailing vessel" means any vessel under sail provided that propelling machinery, if fitted, is not being used.

(d) The term "vessel engaged in fishing" means any vessel fishing with nets, lines, trawls or other fishing apparatus which restrict manoeuvrability, but does not include a vessel fishing with trolling lines or other fishing apparatus which do not restrict manoeuvrability.

(e) The word "seaplane" includes any aircraft designed to manoeuvre on the water.

(f) The term "vessel not under command" means a vessel which through some exceptional circumstance is unable to manoeuvre as required by these Rules and is therefore unable to keep out of the way of another vessel.

(g) The term "vessel restricted in her ability to ma-noeuvre" means a vessel which from the nature of her work is restricted in her ability to manoeuvre as required by these Rules and is therefore unable to keep out of the way of another vessel.

The term "vessels restricted in their ability to mano-euvre" shall include but not be limited to:

(i) A vessel engaged in laying, servicing or picking up a navigation mark, submarine cable or pipeline;

(ii) A vessel engaged in dredging, surveying or underwater operations;

(iii) A vessel engaged in replenishment or transferring persons, provisions or cargo while underway;

(iv) A vessel engaged in the launching or recovery of aircraft;

(v) A vessel engaged in mineclearance operations;

(vi) A vessel engaged in a towing operation such as severely restricts the towing vessel and her tow in their ability to deviate from their course.

(h) The term "vessel constrained by her draught" means a power-driven vessel which because of her draught in relation to the available depth of water is severely restricted in her ability to deviate from the course she is following.

(i) The word "underway" means that a vessel is not at anchor, or made fast to the shore, or aground.

(j) The words "length" and "breadth" of a vessel mean her length overall and greatest breadth.

(k) Vessels shall be deemed to be in sight of one another only when one can be observed visually from the other.

(l) The term "restricted visibility" means any condition in which visibility is restricted by fog, mist, falling snow, heavy rainstorms, sandstorms or any other similar causes.

PART B—STEERING AND SAILING RULES

SECTION I—CONDUCT OF VESSELS IN ANY CONDITION OF VISIBILITY

Rule 4.—Application

Rules in this section apply in any condition of visibility.

Rule 5.—Look-out

Every vessel shall at all times maintain a proper look-out by sight and hearing as well as by all available means appropriate in the prevailing circumstances and conditions so as to make a full appraisal of the situation and of the risk of collision.

Rule 6.—Safe Speed

Every vessel shall at all times proceed at a safe speed so that she can take proper and effective action to avoid collision and be stopped within a distance appropriate to the prevailing circumstances and conditions.

In determining a safe speed the following factors shall be among those taken into account:

(a) By all vessels:

(i) The state of visibility;

(ii) The traffic density including concentrations of fishing vessels or any other vessels;

(iii) The manoeuvrability of the vessel with special reference to stopping distance and turning ability in the prevailing conditions;

(iv) At night the presence of background light such as from shore lights or from back scatter of her own lights;

(v) The state of wind, sea and current, and the proximity of navigational hazards;

(vi) The draught in relation to the available depth of water.

(b) Additionally, by vessels with operational radar:

(i) The characteristics, efficiency and limitations of the radar equipment;

(ii) Any constraints imposed by the radar range scale in use;

(iii) The effect on radar detection of the sea state, weather and other sources of interference;

(iv) The possibility that small vessels, ice and other floating objects may not be detected by radar at an adequate range;

(v) The number, location and movement of vessels detected by radar;

(vi) The more exact assessment of the visibility that may be possible when radar is used to determine the range of vessels or other objects in the vicinity.

Rule 7.—Risk of Collision

(a) Every vessel shall use all available means appropriate to the prevailing circumstances and conditions to determine if risk collision exists. If there is any doubt such risk shall be deemed to exist.

(b) Proper use shall be made of radar equipment if fitted and operational, including long-range scanning to obtain early warning of risk of collision and radar plotting or equivalent systematic observation of detected objects.

(c) Assumptions shall not be made on the basis of scanty information, especially scanty radar information.

(d) In determining if risk of collision exists the following considerations shall be among those taken into account:

(i) Such risk shall be deemed to exist if the compass bearing of an approaching vessel does not appreciably change;

(ii) Such risk may sometimes exist even when an appreciable bearing change is evident, particularly when approaching a very large vessel or a tow or when approaching a vessel at close range.

Rule 8.—Action to Avoid Collision

(a) Any action taken to avoid collision shall, if the circumstances of the case admit, be positive, made in ample time and with due regard to the observance of good seamanship.

(b) Any alteration of course and/or speed to avoid collision shall, if the circumstances of the case admit, be large enough to be readily apparent to another vessel observing visually or by radar; a succession of small alterations of course and/or speed should be avoided.

(c) If there is sufficient sea room, alteration of course alone may be the most effective action to avoid a close-quarters situation provided that it is made in good time, is substantial and does not result in another close-quarters situation.

(d) Action taken to avoid collision with another vessel shall be such as to result in passing at a safe distance. The effectiveness of the action shall be carefully checked until the other vessel is finally past and clear.

(e) If necessary to avoid collision or allow more time to assess the situation, a vessel shall slacken her speed or take all way off by stopping or reversing her means of propulsion.

Rule 9.—Narrow Channels

(a) A vessel proceeding along the course of a narrow channel or fairway shall keep as near to the outer limit of the channel or fairway which lies on her starboard side as is safe and practicable.

(b) A vessel of less than 20 metres in length or a sailing vessel shall not impede the passage of a vessel which can safely navigate only within a narrow channel or fairway.

(c) A vessel engaged in fishing shall not impede the passage of any other vessel navigating within a narrow channel or fairway.

(d) A vessel shall not cross a narrow channel or fairway if such crossing impedes the passage of a vessel which can safely navigate only within such channel or fairway. The latter vessel may use the sound signal prescribed in Rule 34(d) if in doubt as to the intention of the crossing vessel.

(e)(i) In a narrow channel or fairway when overtaking can take place only if the vessel to be overtaken has to take action to permit safe passing, the vessel intending to overtake shall indicate her intention by sounding the appropriate signal prescribed in Rule 34(c)(i). The vessel to be overtaken shall, if in agreement, sound the appropriate signal prescribed in Rule 34(c)(ii) and take steps to permit safe passing. If in doubt she may sound the signals prescribed in Rule 34(d).

(ii) This Rule does not relieve the overtaking vessel of her obligation under Rule 13.

(f) A vessel nearing a bend or an area of a narrow channel or fairway where other vessels may be obscured by an intervening obstruction shall navigate with particular alertness and caution and shall sound the appropriate signal prescribed in Rule 34(e).

(g) Any vessel shall, if the circumstances of the case admit, avoid anchoring in a narrow channel.

Rule 10.—Traffic Separation Schemes

(a) This Rule applies to traffic separation schemes adopted by the Organization.

(b) A vessel using a traffic separation scheme shall:

(i) Proceed in the appropriate traffic lane in the general direction of traffic flow for that lane;

(ii) So far as practicable keep clear of a traffic separation line or separation zone;

(iii) Normally join or leave a traffic lane at the termination of the lane, but when joining or leaving from either side shall do so at as small an angle to the general direction of traffic flow as practicable.

(c) A vessel shall so far as practicable avoid crossing traffic lanes, but if obliged to do so shall cross as nearly as practicable at right angles to the general direction of traffic flow.

* * *

(j) A vessel of less than 20 metres in length or a sailing vessel shall not impede the safe passage of a power-driven vessel following a traffic lane.

* * *

SECTION II–CONDUCT OF VESSELS IN SIGHT OF ONE ANOTHER

Rule 11.—Application

Rules in this Section apply to vessels in sight of one another.

Rule 12.—Sailing Vessels

(a) When two sailing vessels are approaching one another, so as to involve risk of collision, one of them shall keep out of the way of the other as follows:

(i) When each has the wind on a different side, the vessel which has the wind on the port side shall keep out of the way of the other;

(ii) When both have the wind on the same side, the vessel which is to windward shall keep out of the way of the vessel which is to leeward;

(iii) If a vessel with the wind on the port side sees a vessel to windward and cannot determine with certainty whether the other vessel has the wind on the port or on the starboard side, she shall keep out of the way of the other.

(b) For the purposes of this Rule the windward side shall be deemed to be the side opposite to that on which the mainsail is carried or, in the case of a square-rigged vessel, the side opposite to that on which the largest fore-and-aft sail is carried.

Rule 13.—Overtaking

(a) Notwithstanding anything contained in the Rules of Part B, Sections I and II, any vessel overtaking any other shall keep out of the way of the vessel being overtaken.

(b) A vessel shall be deemed to be overtaking when coming up with another vessel from a direction more than 22.5 degrees abaft her beam, that is, in such a position with reference to the vessel she is overtaking, that at night she would be able to see only the sternlight of that vessel but neither of her sidelights.

(c) When a vessel is in any doubt as to whether she is overtaking another, she shall assume that this is the case and act accordingly.

(d) Any subsequent alteration of the bearing between the two vessels shall not make the overtaking vessel a crossing vessel within the meaning of these Rules or relieve her of the duty of keeping clear of the overtaken vessel until she is finally past and clear.

Rule 14.—Head-on Situation

(a) When two power-driven vessels are meeting on reciprocal or nearly reciprocal courses so as to involve risk of collision each shall alter her course to starboard so that each shall pass on the port side of the other.

(b) Such a situation shall be deemed to exist when a vessel sees the other ahead or nearly ahead and by night she could see the masthead lights of the other in a line or nearly in a line and/or both sidelights and by day she observes the corresponding aspect of the other vessel.

(c) When a vessel is in any doubt as to whether such a situation exists she shall assume that it does exist and act accordingly.

Rule 15.—Crossing Situation

When two power-driven vessels are crossing so as to involve risk of collision, the vessel which has the other on her own starboard side shall keep out of the way and shall, if the circumstances of the case admit, avoid crossing ahead of the other vessel.

Rule 16.—Action by Give-Way Vessel

Every vessel which is directed to keep out of the way of another vessel shall, so far as possible, take early and substantial action to keep well clear.

Rule 17.—Action by Stand-on Vessel

(a) (i) Where one of two vessels is to keep out of the way, the other shall keep her course and speed.

(ii) The latter vessel may, however, take action to avoid collision by her manoeuvre alone, as soon as it becomes apparent to her that the vessel required to keep out of the way is not taking appropriate action in compliance with these Rules.

(b) When, from any cause, the vessel required to keep her course and speed finds herself so close that collision cannot be avoided by the action of the give-way vessel alone, she shall take such action as will best aid to avoid collision.

(c) A power-driven vessel which takes action in a crossing situation in accordance with subparagraph (a)(ii) of this Rule to avoid collision with another power-driven vessel shall, if the circumstances of the case admit, not alter course to port for a vessel on her own port side.

(d) This Rule does not relieve the give-way vessel of her obligation to keep out of the way.

Rule 18.—Responsibilities Between Vessels

Except where Rules 9, 10 and 13 otherwise require:

(a) A power-driven vessel underway shall keep out of the way of:

(i) A vessel not under command;

(ii) A vessel restricted in her ability to manoeuvre;

(iii) A vessel engaged in fishing;

(iv) A sailing vessel.

(b) A sailing vessel underway shall keep out of the way of:

(i) A vessel not under command;

(ii) A vessel restricted in her ability to manoeuvre;

(iii) A vessel engaged in fishing.

(c) A vessel engaged in fishing when underway shall, so far as possible, keep out of the way of:

(i) A vessel not under command;

(ii) A vessel restricted in her ability to manoeuvre.

(d) (i) Any vessel other than a vessel not under command or a vessel restricted in her ability to manoeuvre shall, if the circumstances of the case admit, avoid impeding the safe passage of a vessel constrained by her draught, exhibiting the signals in Rule 28.

(ii) A vessel constrained by her draught shall navigate with a particular caution having full regard to her special condition.

(e) A seaplane on the water shall, in general, keep well clear of all vessels and avoid impeding their navigation. In circumstances, however, where risk of collision exists, she shall comply with the Rules of this Part.

SECTION III–CONDUCT OF VESSELS IN RESTRICTED VISIBILITY

Rule 19.—Conduct of Vessels in Restricted Visibility

(a) This Rule applies to vessels not in sight of one another when navigating in or near an area of restricted visibility.

(b) Every vessel shall proceed at a safe speed adapted to the prevailing circumstances and conditions of restricted visibility. A power-driven vessel shall have her engines ready for immediate mano-euvre.

(c) Every vessel shall have due regard to the prevailing circumstances and conditions of restricted visibility when complying with the Rules of Section I of this Part.

(d) A vessel which detects by radar alone the presence of another vessel shall determine if a close-quarters situation is developing and/or risk of collision exists. If so, she shall take avoiding action in ample time, provided that when such action consists of an alteration of course, so far as possible the following shall be avoided:

(i) An alteration of course to port for a vessel forward of the beam, other than for a vessel being overtaken;

(ii) An alteration of course toward a vessel abeam or abaft of the beam.

(e) Except where it has been determined that a risk of collision does not exist, every vessel which hears apparently forward of her beam the fog signal of another vessel, or which cannot avoid a close-quarters situation with another vessel forward of her beam, shall reduce her speed to the minimum at which she can be kept on her course. She shall if necessary take all her way off and in any event navigate with extreme caution until danger of collision is over.

PART C—LIGHTS AND SHAPES

Rule 20.—Application

(a) Rules in this Part shall be complied with in all weathers.

(b) The Rules concerning lights shall be complied with from sunset to sunrise, and during such times no other lights shall be exhibited, except such lights as cannot be mistaken for the lights specified in these Rules or do not impair their visibility or distinctive character, or interfere with the keeping of a proper look-out.

(c) The lights prescribed by these Rules shall, if carried, also be exhibited from sunrise to sunset in restricted visibility and may be exhibited in all other circumstances when it is deemed necessary.

(d) The Rules concerning shapes shall be complied with by day.

(e) The lights and shapes specified in these Rules shall comply with the provisions of Annex I to these Regulations.

Rule 21.—Definitions

(a) "Masthead light" means a white light placed over the fore and aft centreline of the vessel showing an unbroken light over an arc of the horizon of 225 degrees and so fixed as to show the light from right ahead to 22.5 degrees abaft the beam on either side of the vessel.

(b) "Sidelights" means a green light on the starboard side and a red light on the port side each showing an unbroken light over an arc of the horizon of 112.5 degrees and so fixed as to show the light from right ahead to 22.5 degrees abaft the beam on its respective side. In a vessel of less than 20 metres in length the sidelights may be combined in one lantern carried on the fore and aft centreline of the vessel.

(c) "Sternlight" means a white light placed as nearly as practicable at the stern showing an unbroken light over an arc of the horizon of 135 degrees and so fixed as to show the light 67.5 degrees from right aft on each side of the vessel.

(d) "Towing light" means a yellow light having the same characteristics as the "sternlight" defined in paragraph (c) of this Rule.

(e) "All-round light" means a light showing an unbroken light over an arc of the horizon of 360 degrees.

(f) "Flashing light" means a light flashing at regular intervals at a frequency of 120 flashes or more per minute.

Rule 22.—Visibility of Lights

The lights prescribed in these Rules shall have an intensity as specified in Section 8 of Annex I to these Regulations so as to be visible at the following minimum ranges:

(a) In vessels of 50 metres or more in length: A masthead light, 6 miles; A sidelight, 3 miles; A sternlight, 3 miles; A towing light, 3 miles; and A white, red, green or yellow all-round light, 3 miles.

(b) In vessels of 12 metres or more in length but less than 50 metres in length:

A masthead light, 5 miles; except that where the length of the vessel is less than 20 metres, 3 miles;

A sidelight, 2 miles;

A sternlight, 2 miles;

A towing light, 2 miles; and

A white, red, green or yellow all-round light, 2 miles.

(c) In vessels of less than 12 metres in length:

A masthead light, 2 miles;

A sidelight, 1 mile;

A sternlight, 2 miles;

A towing light, 2 miles; and

A white, red, green or yellow all-round light, 2 miles.

(d) In inconspicuous, partly submerged vessels or objects being towed:—a white all-round light, 3 miles.

Rule 23.—Power-Driven Vessels Underway

(a) A power-driven vessel underway shall exhibit:

(i) A masthead light forward;

(ii) A second masthead light abaft of and higher than the forward one; except that a vessel of less than 50 metres in length shall not be obliged to exhibit such light but may do so;

(iii) Sidelights; and

(iv) A sternlight.

(b) An air-cushion vessel when operating in the non-displacement mode shall, in addition to the lights prescribed in paragraph (a) of this Rule, exhibit an all-round flashing yellow light.

(c) A power-driven vessel of less than 7 metres in length and whose maximum speed does not exceed 7 knots may, in lieu of the lights prescribed in paragraph (a) of this Rule, exhibit an all-round white light. Such vessel shall, if practicable, also exhibit sidelights.

(i) A power-driven vessel of less than 12 metres in length may in lieu of the lights prescribed in paragraph (a) of this Rule exhibit an all-round white light and sidelights;

(ii) A power-driven vessel of less than 7 metres in length whose maximum speed does not exceed 7 knots may in lieu of the lights prescribed in paragraph (a) of this Rule exhibit an all-round white light and shall, if practicable, also exhibit sidelights;

(iii) The masthead light or all-round white light on a power-driven vessel of less than 12 metres in length may be displaced from the fore and aft centreline of the vessel if centreline fitting is not practicable, provided that the sidelights are combined in one lantern which shall be carried on the fore and aft centreline of the vessel or located as nearly as practicable in the same fore and aft line as the masthead light or the all-round white light.

Rule 24.—Towing and Pushing

(a) A power-driven vessel when towing shall exhibit:

(i) Instead of the light prescribed in Rule 23(a)(i) or (a)(ii), two masthead lights in a vertical line. When the length of the tow measuring from the stern of the towing vessel to the after end of the tow exceeds 200 metres, three such lights in a vertical line;

(ii) Sidelights;

(iii) A sternlight;

(iv) A towing light in a vertical line above the sternlight; and

(v) When the length of the tow exceeds 200 metres, a diamond shape where it can best be seen.

(b) When a pushing vessel and a vessel being pushed ahead are rigidly connected in a composite unit they shall be regarded as a power-driven vessel and exhibit the lights prescribed in Rule 23.

(c) A power-driven vessel when pushing ahead or towing alongside, except in the case of a composite unit, shall exhibit:

(i) Instead of the light prescribed in Rule 23(a)(i) or (a)(ii), two masthead lights in a vertical line;

(ii) Sidelights; and

(iii) A sternlight.

(d) A power-driven vessel to which paragraph (a) or (c) of this Rule applies shall also comply with Rule 23(a)(ii).

(e) A vessel or object being towed, other than those mentioned in paragraph (g) of this Rule, shall exhibit:

(i) Sidelights;

(ii) A sternlight;

(iii) When the length of the tow exceeds 200 metres, a diamond shape where it can best be seen.

(f) Provided that any number of vessels being towed alongside or pushed in a group shall be lighted as one vessel, (i) a vessel being pushed ahead, not being part of a composite unit, shall exhibit at the forward end, sidelights; (ii) A vessel being towed alongside shall exhibit a sternlight and at the forward end, sidelights.

(g) An inconspicuous, partly submerged vessel or object, or combination of such vessels or objects being towed, shall exhibit:

(i) If it is less than 25 metres in breadth, one all-round white light at or near the forward end and one at or near the after end except that dracones need not exhibit a light at or near the forward end;

(ii) If it is 25 metres or more in breadth, two additional all-round white lights at or near the extremities of its breadth;

Red

 Green   Yellow

LIGHTS AND SHAPES

VESSEL UNDER OARS.

POWER-DRIVEN VESSEL of less than 7 meters in length whose maximum speed does not exceed 7 knots.

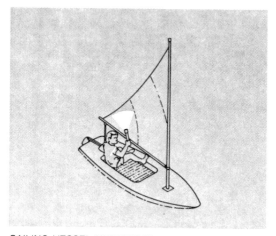

SAILING VESSEL UNDERWAY—less than 7 meters in length.

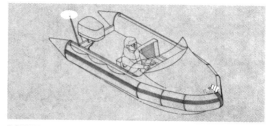

POWER-DRIVEN VESSEL of less than 12 meters in length.

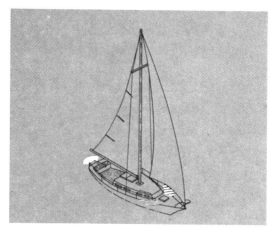

SAILING VESSEL UNDERWAY.

SAILING VESSEL UNDERWAY—less than 20 meters in length.

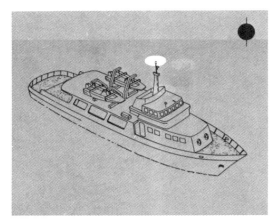

VESSEL AT ANCHOR—less than 50 meters in length.

POWER-DRIVEN VESSEL UNDERWAY—less than 50 meters in length.

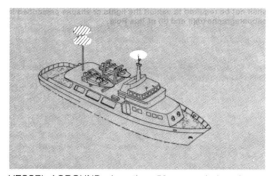

VESSEL AGROUND—less than 50 meters in length.

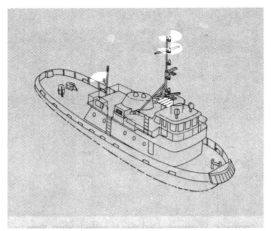

POWER-DRIVEN VESSEL PUSHING AHEAD OR TOWING ALONGSIDE—towing vessel less than 50 meters in length.

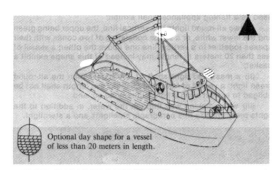

Optional day shape for a vessel of less than 20 meters in length.

VESSEL ENGAGED IN TRAWLING—making way; vessel less than 50 meters in length.

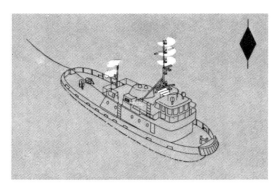

POWER-DRIVEN VESSEL TOWING ASTERN—towing vessel less than 50 meters in length; length of tow exceeds 200 meters.

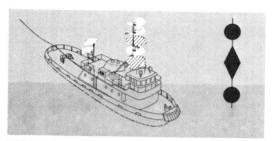

VESSEL ENGAGED IN TOWING OPERATION that severely restricts towing vessel and her tow in their ability to deviate from their course—length of tow does not exceed 200 meters; towing vessel less than 50 meters in length.

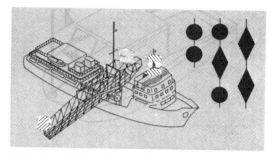

VESSEL ENGAGED IN DREDGING OR UNDERWATER OPERATIONS when restricted in ability to maneuver—not making way, with an obstruction on the starboard side.

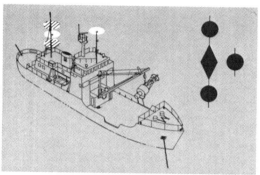

VESSEL RESTRICTED IN HER ABILITY TO MANEU-VER—at anchor; vessel less than 50 meters in length.

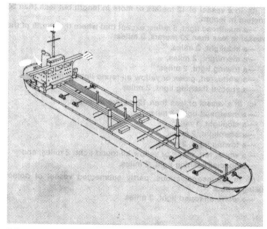

POWER-DRIVEN VESSEL UNDERWAY.

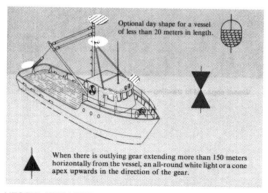

Optional day shape for a vessel of less than 20 meters in length.

When there is outlying gear extending more than 150 meters horizontally from the vessel, an all-round white light or a cone apex upwards in the direction of the gear.

VESSEL ENGAGED IN FISHING OTHER THAN TRAWL-ING—making way.

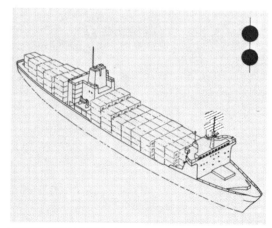

VESSEL NOT UNDER COMMAND—not making way.

(iii) If it exceeds 100 metres in length, additional all-round white lights between the lights prescribed in sub-paragraphs (i) and (ii) so that the distance between the lights shall not exceed 100 metres;

(iv) A diamond shape at or near the aftermost extremity of the last vessel or object being towed and if the length of the tow exceeds 200 metres an additional diamond shape where it can best be seen and located as far forward as is practicable.

(h) Where from any sufficient cause it is impracticable for a vessel or object being towed to exhibit the lights or shapes prescribed in paragraph (e) or (g) of this Rule, all possible measures shall be taken to light the vessel or object towed or at least to indicate the presence of such vessel or object.

(i) Where from any sufficient cause it is impracticable for a vessel not normally engaged in towing operations to display the lights prescribed in paragraph (a) or (c) of this Rule, such vessel shall not be required to exhibit those lights when engaged in towing another vessel in distress or otherwise in need of assistance. All possible measures shall be taken to indicate the nature of the relationship between the towing vessel and the vessel being towed as authorized by Rule 36, in particular by illuminating the towline.

Rule 25.—Sailing Vessels Underway and Vessels Under Oars

(a) A sailing vessel underway shall exhibit:
(i) Sidelights;
(ii) A sternlight.

(b) In a sailing vessel of less than 20 metres in length the lights prescribed in paragraph (a) of this Rule may be combined in one lantern carried at or near the top of the mast where it can best be seen.

(c) A sailing vessel underway may, in addition to the lights prescribed in paragraph (a) of this Rule, exhibit at or near the top of the mast, where they can best be seen, two all-round lights in a vertical line, the upper being red and the lower green, but these lights shall not be exhibited in conjunction with the combined lantern permitted by paragraph (b) of this Rule.

(d) (i) A sailing vessel of less than 7 metres in length shall, if practicable, exhibit the lights prescribed in paragraph (a) or (b) of this Rule, but if she does not, she shall have ready at hand an electric torch or lighted lantern showing a white light which shall be exhibited in sufficient time to prevent collision.

(ii) A vessel under oars may exhibit the lights prescribed in this Rule for sailing vessels, but if she does not, she shall have ready at hand an electric torch or lighted lantern showing a white light which shall be exhibited in sufficient time to prevent collision.

(e) A vessel proceeding under sail when also being propelled by machinery shall exhibit forward where it can best be seen a conical shape, apex downwards.

Rule 27.—Vessels Not Under Command or Restricted in Their Ability to Manoeuvre

(a) A vessel not under command shall exhibit:
(i) Two all-round red lights in a vertical line where they can best be seen;
(ii) Two balls or similar shapes in a vertical line where they can best be seen;
(iii) When making way through the water, in addition to the lights prescribed in this paragraph, sidelights and a sternlight.

(b) A vessel restricted in her ability to manoeuvre, except a vessel engaged in mineclearance operations, shall exhibit:
(i) Three all-round lights in a vertical line where they can best be seen. The highest and lowest of these lights shall be red and the middle light shall be white;
(ii) Three shapes in a vertical line where they can best be seen. The highest and lowest of these shapes shall be balls and the middle one a diamond.
(iii) When making way through the water, a masthead light or lights, sidelights and a sternlight, in addition to the lights prescribed in subparagraph (i);
(iv) When at anchor, in addition to the lights or shapes prescribed in sub-paragraphs (i) and (ii), the light, lights or shape prescribed in Rule 30.

(c) A power-driven vessel engaged in a towing operation such as severely restricts the towing vessel and her tow in their ability to deviate from their course shall, in addition to the lights or shapes prescribed in Rule 24(a), exhibit the lights or shapes prescribed in subparagraphs (b) (i) and (ii) of this Rule.

(d) A vessel engaged in dredging or underwater operations, when restricted in her ability to manoeuvre, shall exhibit the lights and shapes prescribed in subparagraphs (b) (i), (ii) and (iii) of this Rule and shall in addition, when an obstruction exists, exhibit:
(i) Two all-round red lights or two balls in a vertical line to indicate the side on which the obstruction exists;
(ii) Two all-round green lights or two diamonds in a vertical line to indicate the side on which another vessel may pass;

(iii) When at anchor, the lights or shapes prescribed in this paragraph instead of the lights or shape prescribed in Rule 30.

(e) Whenever the size of a vessel engaged in diving operations makes it impracticable to exhibit all lights and shapes prescribed in paragraph (d) of this Rule, the following shall be exhibited:

(i) Three all-round lights in a vertical line where they can best be seen. The highest and lowest of these lights shall be red and the middle light shall be white;

(ii) A rigid replica of the International Code flag "A" not less than 1 metre in height. Measures shall be taken to ensure its all-round visibility.

(f) A vessel engaged in mineclearance operations shall in addition to the lights prescribed for a power-driven vessel in Rule 23 or to the lights or shape prescribed for a vessel at anchor in Rule 30 as appropriate, exhibit three all-round green lights or three balls. One of these lights or shapes shall be exhibited near the foremast head and one at each end of the fore yard. These lights or shapes indicate that it is dangerous for another vessel to approach within 1000 metres of the mineclearance vessel.

(g) Vessels of less than 12 metres in length, except those engaged in diving operations, shall not be required to exhibit the lights and shapes prescribed in this Rule.

(h) The signals prescribed in this Rule are not signals of vessels in distress and requiring assistance. Such signals are contained in Annex IV to these Regulations.

* * *

Rule 30.—Anchored Vessels and Vessels Aground

(a) A vessel at anchor shall exhibit where it can best be seen:

(i) In the fore part, an all-round white light or one ball;

(ii) At or near the stern and at a lower level than the light prescribed in sub-paragraph (i), an all-round white light.

(b) A vessel of less than 50 metres in length may exhibit an all-round white light where it can best be seen instead of the lights prescribed in paragraph (a) of this Rule.

(c) A vessel at anchor may, and a vessel of 100 metres and more in length shall, also use the available working or equivalent lights to illuminate her decks.

(d) A vessel aground shall exhibit the lights prescribed in paragraph (a) or (b) of this Rule and in addition, where they can best be seen:

(i) Two all-round red lights in a vertical line;

(ii) Three balls in a vertical line.

(e) A vessel of less than 7 metres in length, when at anchor, not in or near a narrow channel, fairway or anchorage or where other vessels normally navigate, shall not be required to exhibit the lights or shape prescribed in paragraphs (a) and (b) of this Rule.

(f) A vessel of less than 12 metres in length, when aground, shall not be required to exhibit the lights or shapes prescribed in sub-paragraphs (d) (i) and (ii) of this Rule.

* * *

PART D—SOUND AND LIGHT SIGNALS

Rule 32.—Definitions

(a) The word "whistle" means any sound signalling appliance capable of producing the prescribed blasts and which complies with the specifications in Annex III to these Regulations.

(b) The term "short blast" means a blast of about one second's duration.

(c) The term "prolonged blast" means a blast from four to six seconds' duration.

Rule 33.—Equipment for Sound Signals

(a) A vessel of 12 metres or more in length shall be provided with a whistle and a bell and a vessel of 100 metres or more in length shall, in addition, be provided with a gong, the tone and sound of which cannot be confused with that of the bell. The whistle, bell and gong shall comply with the specifications in Annex III to these Regulations. The bell or gong or both may be replaced by other equipment having the same respective sound characteristics, provided that manual sounding of the prescribed signals shall always be possible.

(b) A vessel of less than 12 metres in length shall not be obliged to carry the sound signalling appliances prescribed in paragraph (a) of this Rule but if she does not, she shall be provided with some other means of making an efficient sound signal.

Rule 34.—Manoeuvring and Warning Signals

(a) When vessels are in sight of one another, a power-driven vessel underway, when manoeuvring as authorized or required by these Rules, shall indicate that manoeuvre by the following signals on her whistle:

One short blast to mean "I am altering my course to starboard";

Two short blasts to mean "I am altering my course to port";

Three short blasts to mean "I am operating astern propulsion."

(b) Any vessel may supplement the whistle signals prescribed in paragraph (a) of this Rule by light signals, repeated as appropriate, whilst the manoeuvre is being carried out:

(i) These light signals shall have the following significance:

One flash to mean "I am altering my course to starboard";

Two flashes to mean "I am altering my course to port";

Three flashes to mean "I am operating astern propulsion";

(ii) The duration of each flash shall be about one second, the interval between flashes shall be about one second, and the interval between successive signals shall be not less than ten seconds;

(iii) The light used for this signal shall, if fitted, be an all-round white light, visible at a minimum range of 5 miles, and shall comply with the provisions of Annex I to these Regulations.

(c) When in sight of one another in a narrow channel or fairway:

(i) A vessel intending to overtake another shall in compliance with Rule 9(e) (i) indicate her intention by the following signals on her whistle:

Two prolonged blasts followed by one short blast to mean "I intend to overtake you on your starboard side";

Two prolonged blasts followed by two short blasts to mean "I intend to overtake you on your port side."

(ii) The vessel about to be overtaken when acting in accordance with Rule 9(e)(i) shall indicate her agreement by the following signal on her whistle:

One prolonged, one short, one prolonged and one short blast, in that order.

(d) When vessels in sight of one another are approaching each other and from any cause either vessel fails to understand the intentions or actions of the other, or is in doubt whether sufficient action is being taken by the other to avoid collision, the vessel in doubt shall immediately indicate such doubt by giving at least five short and rapid blasts on the whistle. Such signal may be supplemented by a light signal of at least five short and rapid flashes.

(e) A vessel nearing a bend or an area of a channel or fairway where other vesels may be obscured by an intervening obstruction shall sound one prolonged blast. Such signal shall be answered with a prolonged blast by any approaching vessel that may be within hearing around the bend or behind the intervening obstruction.

(f) If whistles are fitted on a vessel at a distance apart of more than 100 metres, one whistle only shall be used for giving manoeuvring and warning signals.

Rule 35.—Sound Signals in Restricted Visibility

In or near an area of restricted visibility, whether by day or night, the signals prescribed in this Rule shall be used as follows:

(a) A power-driven vessel making way through the water shall sound at intervals of not more than 2 minutes one prolonged blast.

(b) A power-driven vessel underway but stopped and making no way through the water shall sound at intervals of not more than 2 minutes two prolonged blasts in succession with an interval of about 2 seconds between them.

(c) A vessel not under command, a vessel restricted in her ability to manoeuvre, a vessel constrained by her draught, a sailing vessel, a vessel engaged in fishing and a vessel engaged in towing or pushing another vessel shall, instead of the signals prescribed in paragraph (a) or (b) of this Rule, sound at intervals of not more than 2 minutes three blasts in succession, namely one prolonged followed by two short blasts.

(d) A vessel engaged in fishing, when at anchor, and a vessel restricted in her ability to manoeuvre when carrying out her work at anchor, shall instead of the signals prescribed in paragraph (g) of this Rule sound the signal prescribed in paragraph (c) of this Rule.

(e) A vessel towed or if more than one vessel is towed the last vessel of the tow, if manned, shall at intervals of not more than 2 minutes sound four blasts in succession, namely one prolonged followed by three short blasts. When practicable, this signal shall be made immediately after the signal made by the towing vessel.

(f) When a pushing vessel and a vessel being pushed ahead are rigidly connected in a composite unit they shall be regarded as a power-driven vessel and shall give the signals prescribed in paragraph (a) or (b) of this Rule.

(g) A vessel at anchor shall at intervals of not more than one minute ring the bell rapidly for about 5 seconds. In a vessel of 100 metres or more in length the bell shall be sounded in the forepart of the vessel and immediately after the ringing of the bell the gong shall be sounded rapidly for about 5 seconds in the after part of the vessel. A vessel at anchor may in addition sound three blasts in succession, namely one short, one prolonged and one short blast, to give warning of her position and of the possibility of collision to an approaching vessel.

(h) A vessel aground shall give the bell signal and if required the gong signal prescribed in paragraph (g) of this Rule and shall, in addition, give three separate and distinct strokes on the bell immediately before and after the rapid ringing of the bell. A vessel aground may in addition sound an appropriate whistle signal.

(i) A vessel of less than 12 metres in length shall not be obliged to give the above-mentioned signals but, if she does not, shall make some other efficient sound signal at intervals of not more than 2 minutes.

(j) A pilot vessel when engaged on pilotage duty may in addition to the signals prescribed in paragraph (a), (b) or (g) of this Rule sound an identity signal consisting of four short blasts.

Rule 36.—Signals to Attract Attention

If necessary to attract the attention of another vessel any vessel may make light or sound signals that cannot be mistaken for any signal authorized elsewhere in these Rules, or may direct the beam of her searchlight in the direction of the danger, in such a way as not to embarrass any vessel. Any light to attract the attention of another vessel shall be such that it cannot be mistaken for any aid to navigation. For the purpose of this Rule the use of high-intensity intermittent or revolving lights, such as strobe lights, shall be avoided.

Rule 37.—Distress Signals

When a vessel is in distress and requires assistance she shall use or exhibit the signals described in Annex IV to these Regulations.

* * *

ANNEX IV

DISTRESS SIGNALS

1. The following signals, used or exhibited either together or separately, indicate distress and need of assistance:

(a) A gun or other explosive signal fired at intervals of about a minute;

(b) A continuous sounding with any fog-signalling apparatus;

(c) Rockets or shells, throwing red stars fired one at a time at short intervals;

(d) A signal made by radiotelegraphy or by any other signalling method consisting of the group ...---... (SOS) in the Morse Code;

(e) A signal sent by radiotelephony consisting of the spoken word "Mayday";

(f) The International Code Signal of distress indicated by N.C.;

(g) A signal consisting of a square flag having above or below it a ball or anything resembling a ball;

(h) Flames on the vessel (as from a burning tar barrel, oil barrel, etc.);

(i) A rocket parachute flare or a hand flare showing a red light;

(j) A smoke signal giving off orange-coloured smoke;

(k) Slowly and repeatedly raising and lowering arms outstretched to each side;

(l) The radiotelegraph alarm signal;

(m) The radiotelephone alarm signal;

(n) Signals transmitted by emergency position-indicating radio beacons.

2. The use or exhibition of any of the foregoing signals except for the purpose of indicating distress and need of assistance and the use of other signals which may be confused with any of the above signals is prohibited.

3. Attention is drawn to the relevant sections of the International Code of Signals, the Merchant Ship Search and Rescue Manual and the following signals:

(a) A piece of orange-coloured canvas with either a black square and circle or other appropriate symbol (for identification from the air);

(b) A dye marker.

APPENDIX II

Warning Signals

While the average boater need not become familiar with the full range of international and special-purpose signals likely to be overheard or seen, he should at least be aware of the following:

A white flare acts as a warning of imminent danger, such as collision, or as acknowledgment of a distress signal.

Green flares are used by navy ships and aircraft engaged in training exercises.

Whistle signals are always used by large ships—and too infrequently by recreational boaters—to indicate maneuvering intentions. These are prescribed by the Rules of the Road; see appendix I.

Flag	Morse Code	Meaning
A (or, *commonly in U.S. waters*, the "diving" flag)	.-	"Diving operations are in progress. All boats should keep clear and at a slow speed and be alert for surfacing divers.
L	.-..	"You should stop your vessel immediately."
M	--	"My vessel is stopped and making no way through the water."
J	.---	"I am on fire and have dangerous cargo on board; keep well clear of me."
D	-..	"Keep clear of me; I am maneuvering with difficulty."
F	..-..	"I am disabled; communicate with me."
U	..-	"You are running into danger."
PS	.--. ...	"You should not come any closer."
Y	-.--	"I am dragging my anchor."

APPENDIX III

The Marine Battery

CONSTRUCTION AND OPERATION

Batteries are made up of a series of individual cells contained in a hard-rubber or plastic outer case. Each cell generates about 2V, and the number of cells determines the nominal output of the battery: three cells for a 6V unit, four for 8V, and six for 12V.

Each cell is a sandwich of alternating metal plates; the positive plates are composed of lead dioxide (PbO_2) and the negative plates are lead of a spongy texture (which increases the effective surface area of the plate). The plates are immersed in a sulfuric acid/water (H_2SO_4 and H_2O) solution—called an electrolyte because it stimulates galvanic (or electrical) activity. Here's how it works:

When dissimilar metals (even those as slightly dissimilar as lead and lead dioxide) are submerged in an electrolyte, an electric current may be the result.

In the typical storage battery, some of the oxygen in the lead dioxide (PbO_2, positive) plate combines with some of the hydrogen in the sulfuric acid to produce more water (H_2O); sulfate (SO_4) combines with the residual lead to form lead sulfate ($PbSO_4$), while sulfate ions at the same time move to the spongy lead (negative) plate, also forming lead sulfate and releasing electrons to move out through the open circuit.

However, the action will remain suspended, potential rather than actual, unless there is an open circuit—someplace for the electrons to go. If all switches are off and there are no electrical leaks, the electrons stay put and no electricity will be generated.

However, once the current begins to flow, the dissimilar metals become more and more alike (both are being converted into lead sulfate), the electrolyte becomes more and more diluted (with water), and the current is reduced and finally stops.

MARINE BATTERIES are not auto batteries. These are heavy-duty batteries set up in a series to provide high amperage for engine starting. (Surrette)

Typical Specifications for 12-Volt Marine Batteries

Type of Battery	Ampere Hours (20-Hour Rate)	Reserve Capacity* (In Min.)	Cold Cranking Capacity** (At 0°F in Amps)	Net Weight, Wet (Lb.)	Net Weight, Dry (Lb.)	Length (All in Inches)	Width (All in Inches)	Height (All in Inches)	Electrolyte Per Battery (Qts.)	Electrolyte Per Battery (Oz.)
Heavy-Duty Marine	62	100	325	48	35	10.25	6.75	8 13/16	5.1	192
Small Craft	100	160	450	52	37	11.75	6.75	9 1/8	5	176
Heavy-Duty Marine	105	160	420	80	68	18	7 9/16	9 5/8	8	256
Diesel	130	215	520	105	84	20 7/16	7.5	9 5/8	10	320
Extra Heavy-Duty	140	224	535	120	95	16	7.25	11.25	9	288
Diesel	165	285	775	135	108	20.25	8.75	9.75	12	384
Diesel	193	310	855	148	118	20.25	9 15/16	9 5/8	13	416
Diesel	230	368	900	165	132	20.25	11	9.75	14	448
Extra Heavy-Duty	221	430	920	165	134	20.25	11	9.75	14	448
12-Volt Marine "Compact" Types										
Marine Standard	115	—	—	75	—	13 5/8	6.75	11	7	224
Heavy-Duty	195	—	—	160	—	14 3/8	10 5/8	14	14	448
6-Volt "Compact" High Capacity—Two Batteries in Series for 12 Volts										
Engine Starting	195	—	—	65	—	10.25	7 1/8	10.25	6	192
Heavy-Duty	225	—	—	80	—	10.25	7 1/8	11.25	6.5	208
Heavy-Duty	262	—	—	90	—	11 23/32	7	11.25	7.5	240
Heavy-Duty	375	—	—	129	—	11 23/32	7	16.75	10.5	336

*Reserve Capacity defined as number of minutes a fully charged battery at 80°F can be discharged at 25 amperes and maintain a voltage of 1.75 volts per cell or higher.

**Cold Cranking Capacity defined as the discharge load in amperes that a battery at 0°F can deliver for 30 seconds and maintain a voltage of 1.2 volts per cell or higher. (Note: For diesels, cranking test is longer and terminal voltage lower.)

RECHARGING

Here's the magic part: Thanks to the reversible nature of the chemical action, an electric current applied from the outside will restore the capacity of the battery. The water breaks down into hydrogen and oxygen; the oxygen recombines with lead in the positive plate; the hydrogen recombines with the sulfate from both plates as sulfuric acid. The plates are once again dissimilar, the electrolyte is strong, and the electric potential is restored.

When the battery nears the fully charged state, the chemical reaction attenuates and no further charging benefit will accrue. However, as long as the outside current is being pumped in, water will continue to break down into hydrogen and oxygen, which, having nowhere else to go, now escape up and out of the solution as bubbles of gas. Hydrogen and oxygen form a highly explosive mixture; if you recall seeing photographs of the destruction of the hydrogen-filled dirigible *Hindenburg,* you have some idea of what that could mean. *Batteries can explode.* Never use a match or open flame around a battery. Battery compartments must be ventilated, to dilute and carry away the explosive gas.

The recharging current may be provided by an engine-driven alternator or generator, which uses magnets to convert mechanical energy into electrical energy, or a battery charger, which converts 110V AC power into 12V DC before it reaches the battery.

A well-designed charging circuit will sense the state of charge and taper off and then stop the charge when it's no longer needed. With alternators and generators, that's accomplished by a voltage regulator. On a battery charger, a built-in sensor turns the circuit off when the battery is fully charged, and on as the charge is depleted.

A typical automobile battery charger is *not* suited to marine use. In a marine charger, the 110V circuit *must* be isolated from the charging circuit to prevent unwanted and dangerous stray currents in the boat, and the on-off control of the charge must be absolute. Many automobile chargers have a "trickle" charge feature, with some current always flowing; in the cheapest models, automobile chargers just keep pumping away as long as they are plugged in. With either device, your boat batteries would become overcharged, adding to the hazard of explosion while leading to a shorter battery life.

Because of internal resistance within the battery, the charging circuit must deliver about 2V more than the nominal level (12.6V) of a fully charged battery. Thus, if your control panel includes a battery meter, you'll note a reading of 14V or more while a charging circuit is in operation. Batteries that get hot during charging are being overcharged.

BATTERY COMBINATIONS are ways of either building voltage or building starting power in terms of amperage, or of isolating a battery for specific uses (starting versus boat service, for example). (Ah=amp/hours in table.)

Temperature Rating for Conductor Cable Suitable for Battery Applications

Size of Wire Conductor (AWG Sizes)		Maximum Allowable Rated Continuous Current (Amps) Matched to Temperature		
		140°F (60°C)	167°F (75°C)	194°F (90°C)
2		81	128	144
1		96	146	168
0	Welding	113	173	196
00*	cable	131	199	228
000*	type of	151	233	264
0000	conductors	174	270	289

Notes: 1. Cable smaller than #2 AWG is not recommended for battery applications.
*2. 00 and 000 are usually recommended for battery applications.
3. If any part of battery cable run exceeds 3 feet, go to next larger size.
4. Use only single conductors, i.e., one multistrand copper conductor in each cable.
5. The above table was developed by the authors from information from battery manufacturers and the American Boat and Yacht Council.

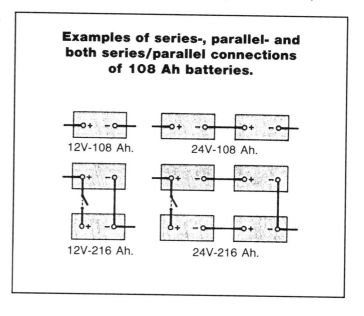

Examples of series-, parallel- and both series/parallel connections of 108 Ah batteries.

12V-108 Ah.   24V-108 Ah.

12V-216 Ah.   24V-216 Ah.

BATTERY RATING

When you buy a battery for your automobile, you simply look on a chart at the dealer's to determine the proper size (both in dimensions and power output) for your particular model. Beyond that, your choice will center on price, which is proportional to the manufacturer's warranty expressed in months. A "48"-month battery will cost more than a "24"-month version.

Buying a boat battery may be a bit more involved. Logically, of course—assuming that your boat already has a battery that has done well—you can replace it with a similar unit. But, if the battery has been barely adequate, or should you have added or plan to add new electrical equipment, you'll need to determine the appropriate size—in terms of capacity—to meet your requirements.

Batteries are rated according to measures of capacity that describe their ability to deliver a large jolt of power in a short time or a steady flow of low power for a longer period of time.

"Battery cold cranking rating" is the discharge load, in amperes, that a battery at 0°F can deliver for thirty seconds. Since few of us worry about starting our boat engines at 0°F, you might think that this rating is more

directly useful in selecting automobile batteries. However, it is a relative indication of power output at any temperature and is the one measure that relates to your engine starting requirements.

"Battery reserve capacity" is the number of minutes a fully charged battery, at 80°F, can be discharged with a load of 25 amperes. The "twenty-hour rate" is the number of amps that can be withdrawn at a steady rate, at 80°F, for a period of twenty hours. These ratings apply to the ability of the battery to supply your housekeeping power needs—lights, radios, pumps.

CRANKING POWER AT DIFFERENT STATES OF CHARGE AND VARYING TEMPERATURES. (Graph from Battery Council International)

BATTERY CRANKING POWER AT DIFFERENT TEMPERATURES. (Graph from Battery Council International)

Power required to crank engine with 10W–30 SAE crankcase oil at different temperatures

0°F · 210% Required

32°F · 155% Required

80°F · 100% Required

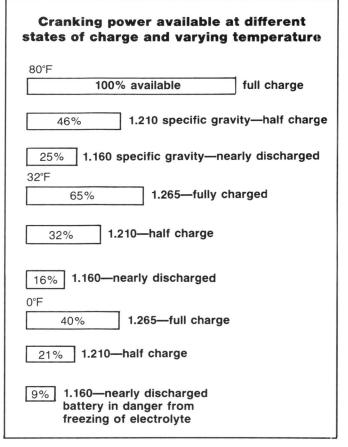

Cranking power available at different states of charge and varying temperature

80°F
100% available · full charge

46% · 1.210 specific gravity—half charge

25% · 1.160 specific gravity—nearly discharged

32°F
65% · 1.265—fully charged

32% · 1.210—half charge

16% · 1.160—nearly discharged

0°F
40% · 1.265—full charge

21% · 1.210—half charge

9% · 1.160—nearly discharged battery in danger from freezing of electrolyte

MARINE VERSUS AUTOMOBILE BATTERIES

Because of the marked difference in the cost of automobile batteries compared with marine batteries, you may be tempted to use automobile-type batteries in your boat. That is *possible*—but you should first understand the reasons for the difference. Batteries intended for use in starting automobiles are designed with waffle-textured plates, which greatly increase the effective surface area and produce a large jolt of power. These batteries normally would be recharged quickly once the engine is running; in fact, they cannot long withstand longer-term discharge and recharge. Batteries intended to provide such longer-term power—for navigation and accommodation lights, for example—are built with thicker lead plates to provide modest quantities of power while withstanding several hundred complete discharge-recharge cycles. The extra surface area needed to generate the power for engine starting

is produced by having more plates in each cell. These "deep-cycle" marine batteries are significantly heavier (and therefore significantly more expensive) than automobile batteries.

Even though an automobile battery of the proper capacity *can* be used for starting boat engines, we don't recommend it. Unlike a marine battery, an automobile battery will discharge slowly when not in use; five or six weeks of idleness inside a hot boat may produce a dead battery. Also, because of the lack of deep-cycle capability, it would be false economy to use an automobile battery for "house power." Even so, reserved just for starting, but under the heavy demands of the boat engine and the difficult conditions of the marine environment, the battery might last at best for two seasons. And—you should check this out—the manufacturer's warranty probably will be invalidated.

"MAINTENANCE-FREE" BATTERIES

The so-called "maintenance-free" batteries now being touted for automotive use are just not suitable for marine applications. These lead-calcium type of batteries supposedly do not need topping up with makeup water. Whatever the advertising may say, these units are still basically automotive batteries with high starting power and low service life. They are designed for a car that will average about 12,000 miles a year (approximately 300 to 400 hours of driving)—and the battery will be constantly charged by the engine alternator when in use. Definitely not your basic marine working cycle. Three hundred hours is about two weeks' steady cruising in a pleasure boat, with the engine on intermittently (less in sailboats). However, there is almost always some sort of current discharge going on.

The lead-calcium battery does suppress hydrogen and oxygen gassing, but this has a corresponding effect on charging (since part of the final charging process *is* the release of hydrogen and oxygen). The "maintenance-free" battery needs 15V of charge instead of the average 13.8 used for lead-acid types, and often the input voltage can only get the battery to an 80 percent charge level.

Since the main aim of the maintenance-free battery is high initial cranking power, it consists of many thin

plates. The calcium component (which is often less than 1 percent of the alloy) is there mostly to give strength to the plate grid. The remainder of the battery structure does not have sufficient substance to take the vibration, corrosion exposure, and other rigors of the marine environment. Also, these are not deep-cycling batteries, and you can "flat-out" the battery in discharge. When this happens with the lead-calcium auto type, it is usually impossible to bring back the battery in any satisfactory way.

ALKALINE BATTERIES

These are the nickel-cadmium and nickel-iron types. There are three classes:

1. Nickel-Iron Tubular. Not generally used on yachts except for heavy-duty or regular continuous cycling on larger vessels. These batteries tend to lose a lot of power when they are not in use and will not retain a charge for long periods.

2. Nickel-Cadmium Flat Plate (High Performance). Capable of very high discharge rates and therefore quite good for engine starting, particularly in cold-weather environments. Often used for combined service in the United Kingdom. The self-discharge loss is

quite low and a fully charged battery can last for months.

3. Nickel-Cadmium Flat Plate (Normal Resistance). Not suitable for engine starting, best for "house" service only. Fairly low self-discharge rate.

There are some peculiarities with alkaline batteries. The normal charge rate in amps is calculated as 0.25 of the total battery capacity in ampere-hours applied over a period of six hours. A higher charge rate can be used, but the battery must be kept cool (below 135°F). Gassing does not indicate a charged condition.

The chief advantage of alkaline batteries is their ability to stand idle for long periods without special treatment. If they are at least 80 percent charged, you can leave them in the boat without any sort of trickle charging. They also have a fairly long life.

But there are disadvantages that are very significant for the American boat owner:

• They are *very* expensive (about 10 times the price of lead-acid types).
• They will not take abuse in charging and some of the containers are quite fragile.
• The electrolyte is potassium hydroxide in distilled water and can be hard to find.
• It is quite hard to regulate the charging cycle. Aircraft, which use alkaline batteries, have several thousand dollars' worth of control gear.

CALCULATING BATTERY REQUIREMENTS

The proper size of battery for starting your engine—under ideal conditions—will be specified by the engine manufacturer. Since conditions are rarely ideal, you should install a battery of higher-than-specified capacity.

For your housekeeping requirements, you'll need to determine probable daily consumption by multiplying the name-plate power requirement for each appliance (pumps, radio, reading lights, running lights, etc.) by the number of hours used each day. This requires a bit of guesswork, but—for example—you know you'll need to use the anchor light from sunset to sunrise, which is a specific length of time. Or you'll need to run all of the running lights for an overnight passage. If you read before going to bed, include that time in your calculations.

If the name-plate data on some equipment notes *watts* rather than *amps,* convert to amps by dividing the rating in watts by the number of volts. A 40-watt, 12V light bulb will consume 3.3 amps per hour of operation.

Add up the requirements in ampere-hours: That's the amount of 12V current you'll need to have available, with no engine running or no dockside replenishment, for a day of sailing or (for a powerboat) sitting at anchor. Double that number and you'll have a safe approximation of your housekeeping needs.

Then—to be well prepared—buy a pair of batteries of the proper size for starting the engine (cold cranking power) and for maintaining housekeeping service (the twenty-hour rate). Either battery can then be selected for starting or for housekeeping, alternating usage to balance out the number of discharge-recharge cycles. For cold-morning starts—or as the batteries deteriorate and loose effectiveness—use the batteries together. When you replace them, do it at the same time.

COMPARATIVE SIZES OF 12-VOLT BATTERY CABLE CONDUCTORS.

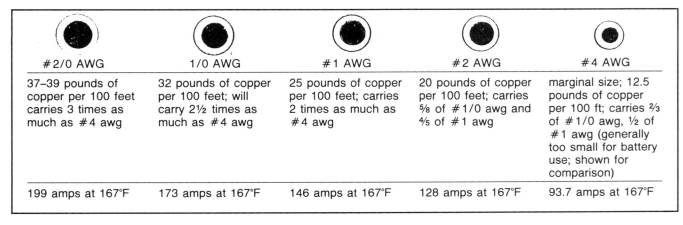

#2/0 AWG	1/0 AWG	#1 AWG	#2 AWG	#4 AWG
37–39 pounds of copper per 100 feet carries 3 times as much as #4 awg	32 pounds of copper per 100 feet; will carry 2½ times as much as #4 awg	25 pounds of copper per 100 feet; carries 2 times as much as #4 awg	20 pounds of copper per 100 feet; carries ⅝ of #1/0 awg and ⅘ of #1 awg	marginal size; 12.5 pounds of copper per 100 ft; carries ⅔ of #1/0 awg, ½ of #1 awg (generally too small for battery use; shown for comparison)
199 amps at 167°F	173 amps at 167°F	146 amps at 167°F	128 amps at 167°F	93.7 amps at 167°F

"Maintenance-Free" Batteries

The so-called "maintenance-free" batteries now being touted for automotive use are just not suitable for marine applications. These lead-calcium type of batteries supposedly do not need topping up with makeup water. Whatever the advertising may say, these units are still basically automotive batteries with high starting power and low service life. They are designed for a car that will average about 12,000 miles a year (approximately 300 to 400 hours of driving)—and the battery will be constantly charged by the engine alternator when in use. Definitely not your basic marine working cycle. Three hundred hours is about two weeks' steady cruising in a pleasure boat, with the engine on intermittently (less in sailboats). However, there is almost always some sort of current discharge going on.

The lead-calcium battery does suppress hydrogen and oxygen gassing, but this has a corresponding effect on charging (since part of the final charging process *is* the release of hydrogen and oxygen). The "maintenance-free" battery needs 15V of charge instead of the average 13.8 used for lead-acid types, and often the input voltage can only get the battery to an 80 percent charge level.

Since the main aim of the maintenance-free battery is high initial cranking power, it consists of many thin plates. The calcium component (which is often less than 1 percent of the alloy) is there mostly to give strength to the plate grid. The remainder of the battery structure does not have sufficient substance to take the vibration, corrosion exposure, and other rigors of the marine environment. Also, these are not deep-cycling batteries, and you can "flat-out" the battery in discharge. When this happens with the lead-calcium auto type, it is usually impossible to bring back the battery in any satisfactory way.

ALKALINE BATTERIES

These are the nickel-cadmium and nickel-iron types. There are three classes:

1. Nickel-Iron Tubular. Not generally used on yachts except for heavy-duty or regular continuous cycling on larger vessels. These batteries tend to lose a lot of power when they are not in use and will not retain a charge for long periods.

2. Nickel-Cadmium Flat Plate (High Performance). Capable of very high discharge rates and therefore quite good for engine starting, particularly in cold-weather environments. Often used for combined service in the United Kingdom. The self-discharge loss is quite low and a fully charged battery can last for months.

3. Nickel-Cadmium Flat Plate (Normal Resistance). Not suitable for engine starting, best for "house" service only. Fairly low self-discharge rate.

There are some peculiarities with alkaline batteries. The normal charge rate in amps is calculated as 0.25 of the total battery capacity in ampere-hours applied over a period of six hours. A higher charge rate can be used, but the battery must be kept cool (below 135°F). Gassing does not indicate a charged condition.

The chief advantage of alkaline batteries is their ability to stand idle for long periods without special treatment. If they are at least 80 percent charged, you can leave them in the boat without any sort of trickle charging. They also have a fairly long life.

But there are disadvantages that are very significant for the American boat owner:

• They are *very* expensive (about 10 times the price of lead-acid types).
• They will not take abuse in charging and some of the containers are quite fragile.
• The electrolyte is potassium hydroxide in distilled water and can be hard to find.
• It is quite hard to regulate the charging cycle. Aircraft, which use alkaline batteries, have several thousand dollars' worth of control gear.

INSTALLATION

The first step in installing a marine battery is getting it aboard the boat. A better-grade 12V marine battery, for a medium-to-large boat, may weigh 150 pounds. Unless you are a professional weight lifter, moving one of these may simply be beyond your solo capabilities. Get someone to help you; better yet, have the battery delivered and installed by the dealer.

There are lighter batteries, of lesser capacity but well suited to smaller installations, but even these will weigh in at around 75 pounds and might be just as hard for one person to haul aboard. If you anticipate a need to shift your batteries while cruising alone in remote locations, there is one other alternative: Buy and install two 6V batteries for each replaced 12V unit. Connected in series (the negative terminal of one to the positive terminal of the other), they deliver the same 12V power; however, you are adding another connection that might fail later, and you may find that 6V batteries are not commonly available when it comes time for replacement.

APPENDIX IV

The Adverse Forces of Nature and Man

The forces that work on, in, and against boats have not changed much over the centuries, and even in this technological age of ours, they still remain as serious problems. Animal, vegetable, mineral, and physical—the forces are varied, but unless countered, the end result is the same: the piece-by-piece deterioration and eventual destruction of your boat.

The hazards are obvious: sudden openings in the hull when fittings give way or hoses burst; a mast crashing down when rigging pulls loose; a handhold that rips out just as you climb aboard in a storm-tossed sea.

Of course, not all consequences are that dramatic or life-threatening. Most of the time, only your bank account will suffer when you repair the damage—or when you try to sell the boat and find that the best offers are many thousands of dollars below your asking price.

In most instances, the damage can be prevented first by understanding these underlying forces and then by taking appropriate action. This might be nothing more complicated than following a routine maintenance schedule; it might involve repairing a defect, replacing an inadequate component—or simply walking away from the purchase of a particular boat.

The following discussion presents the range of forces at work; a brief background on the physics, chemistry, or biology involved; and some examples of typical preventive measures.

ACCIDENT

Boats often bump into pilings, piers, rocks, and other boats. Because hulls are designed to flex under stress, the external signs of damage may be limited to scrapes, scratches, or slight surface ripples; the real damage may be severe but remain hidden for years. What appears to be localized damage at the bow, for instance, may be evidence of a blow hard enough to misalign structural components all the way to the stern. Any external hint of damage should be regarded as fair warning and should prompt a thorough internal examination by a qualified marine surveyor.

AGE

By itself, the age of a boat is not a defect. Most of the materials of which boats are made have been known to last for generations, and many boats of yachting's "Golden Age" are still going strong at the half-century mark. However, the conditions under which they have survived usually are quite different from those of most operating boats. Few boats are so well built or so well maintained that they remain seaworthy more than twenty years. The classified ads are full of listings for "ideal live-aboards"—a term that may serve less as a description of the accommodations than as a subtle warning never to get underway.

However, the age of a boat should be measured not so much in years, but as the total of all the factors, good and bad, discussed in this appendix.

As a general rule, however, a novice should avoid the temptation to find "more boat for the money" by shopping the antiques.

CHAFING

Wear and tear on sails and lines can be accelerated by rubbing against the rigging or the side of the boat. Salt crystals, caught in the weave of a sail, can act as microscopic knives as the sail works in the wind. Protection includes the use of chafing gear (wrappings to cushion the friction or absorb the wear); care in setting sails and mooring lines; and timely freshwater washdowns after saltwater sailing.

CHEMICALS

Unless used properly, otherwise-beneficial chemicals will destroy materials and can injure humans. Familiar examples: A rag used to wipe up spilled battery acid will soon crumble to dust; petroleum products and cleaning solvents dissolve many plastics and adhesives and may cause skin rashes, breathing problems, or serious illness in humans. Less obvious examples: Some powdered detergents will increase the ultraviolet sensitivity of polyester sails and lines, hastening deterioration; the acid in heavily polluted air can have the same effect on nylon.

Always read and *heed* label warnings and instructions for use.

CORROSION

Corrosion is a generic term for galvanic or chemical deterioration. Even rust—the most common form of corrosion—is a galvanic process. A tiny electrical charge is generated by, and flows between, dissimilar

metals in contact with each other, or between portions of the *same* metal when the surface oxygen levels are different. As the current flows, it carries away electrons, leading to the eventual destruction of the metal (see Electrolysis, below). Chemical corrosion (which may also be partly galvanic) is largely influenced by the levels of sulfur, chlorine, oxygen, and carbon dioxide in the air (see Pollution, below).

Aluminum and stainless steel work well in the marine environment because under normal conditions, they corrode to the point where a protective oxide coating is built up, resisting further corrosion—unless they come in contact with each other, in which case the galvanic process continues.

On aluminum, the natural corrosion is noticeable as the bright metal surface changes to a dull lead color. Anodized aluminum has been electrolytically corroded deliberately to create a thicker-than-natural coating of oxide; color is often added for appearance.

Trailered aluminum boats must be protected from the accelerated corrosion produced by salt compounds used on roads in winter (traces of which will remain in the spring) and from the alkali found in most soil. Hose down a trailered boat after use and do not allow an aluminum boat to rest directly on the ground.

DEZINCIFICATION

Brass is an alloy of zinc and copper; in a saltwater environment, the zinc may be slowly dissolved out of the alloy, leaving only spongy copper. Telltale signs of this problem include reddish copper-color spots on the otherwise-yellow brass or a dull (rather than ringing) sound when hit by a hammer. Some brass alloys are not so vulnerable: those with a zinc content below 15 percent and those with a trace of tin, such as admiralty brass. However, brass is best left for interior decoration; bronze, stainless steel, and Monel should be the metals of choice for exterior fittings and fastenings.

ELECTROLYSIS/GALVANIC CORROSION

All metals have the potential to generate a small electric current when in contact with a dissimilar metal in the presence of an electrolyte. The metals might be as different as brass and iron, or the "dissimilarity" may come from different oxygen levels on the same piece of

THE GALVANIC SERIES.

The Galvanic Series

Table One — Recommended Maximum Allowable Potential Difference
Exposed Position — 0.2V
Interior Position — 0.25V

Givers
Anodic End
Least Noble

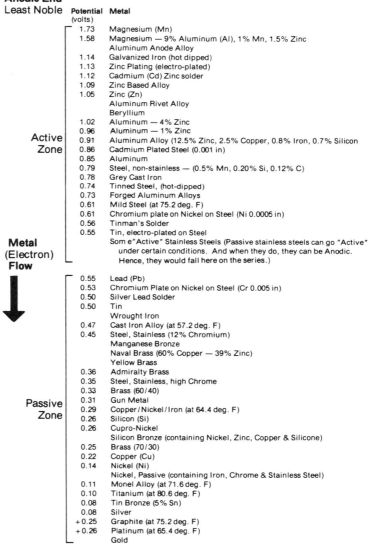

Potential (volts)	Metal
1.73	Magnesium (Mn)
1.58	Magnesium — 9% Aluminum (Al), 1% Mn, 1.5% Zinc
	Aluminum Anode Alloy
1.14	Galvanized Iron (hot dipped)
1.13	Zinc Plating (electro-plated)
1.12	Cadmium (Cd) Zinc solder
1.09	Zinc Based Alloy
1.05	Zinc (Zn)
	Aluminum Rivet Alloy
	Beryllium
1.02	Aluminum — 4% Zinc
0.96	Aluminum — 1% Zinc
0.91	Aluminum Alloy (12.5% Zinc, 2.5% Copper, 0.8% Iron, 0.7% Silicon
0.86	Cadmium Plated Steel (0.001 in)
0.85	Aluminum
0.79	Steel, non-stainless — (0.5% Mn, 0.20% Si, 0.12% C)
0.78	Grey Cast Iron
0.74	Tinned Steel, (hot-dipped)
0.73	Forged Aluminum Alloys
0.61	Mild Steel (at 75.2 deg. F)
0.61	Chromium plate on Nickel on Steel (Ni 0.0005 in)
0.56	Tinman's Solder
0.55	Tin, electro-plated on Steel
	Some "Active" Stainless Steels (Passive stainless steels can go "Active" under certain conditions. And when they do, they can be Anodic. Hence, they would fall here on the series.)

Active Zone

Metal (Electron) Flow

Potential (volts)	Metal
0.55	Lead (Pb)
0.53	Chromium Plate on Nickel on Steel (Cr 0.005 in)
0.50	Silver Lead Solder
0.50	Tin
	Wrought Iron
0.47	Cast Iron Alloy (at 57.2 deg. F)
0.45	Steel, Stainless (12% Chromium)
	Manganese Bronze
	Naval Brass (60% Copper — 39% Zinc)
	Yellow Brass
0.36	Admiralty Brass
0.35	Steel, Stainless, high Chrome
0.33	Brass (60/40)
0.31	Gun Metal
0.29	Copper/Nickel/Iron (at 64.4 deg. F)
0.26	Silicon (Si)
0.26	Cupro-Nickel
	Silicon Bronze (containing Nickel, Zinc, Copper & Silicone)
0.25	Brass (70/30)
0.22	Copper (Cu)
0.14	Nickel (Ni)
	Nickel, Passive (containing Iron, Chrome & Stainless Steel)
0.11	Monel Alloy (at 71.6 deg. F)
0.10	Titanium (at 80.6 deg. F)
0.08	Tin Bronze (5% Sn)
0.08	Silver
+0.25	Graphite (at 75.2 deg. F)
+0.26	Platinum (at 65.4 deg. F)
	Gold

Passive Zone

Takers
Cathodic End
Most Noble

Notes: All temperatures are at approximately 77°F unless otherwise noted. All potentials are negative (unless noted). Potentials are shown only to illustrate relative position of materials in the series. Potential values are only valid when taking full environmental aspects of the solution into consideration. This would include variables such as temperature, velocity, and oxygen content. Table developed from various data in French.

Table developed from various data in French, LaQue, Miller, Zadig, Duffet & Pretzer (see bibliography of further reading).

metal. The electrolyte may be seawater, brackish water in a coastal bay, polluted water in an inland lake, even morning dew that has dissolved some dried salt spray from the previous day's sail. The electric current may be barely measurable, but it can lead to the destruction of one of the metals as it gives up electrons—and some of its very substance—to the galvanic partner.

The galvanic potential of all metals can be ranked, high to low (see Galvanic Series table, below). The position on the list determines which metal in a pair will be the active partner—the anode—and which will be the passive partner—the cathode. The relative distance between the two metals on the list indicates the probable degree of activity; the interaction between bronze and nickel would be slow, whereas a pairing of zinc with stainless steel will lead to the rapid destruction of the zinc. Zinc is used in "sacrificial anodes" because it is at the active end of the scale, and by giving up electrons, it will protect any other metal to which it is likely to be attached or bonded. At the other end of the scale, gold and platinum are so passive that they remain virtually unchanged under any conditions.

The mass of metal may be a factor. Fasten a bronze fitting with iron screws and the screws will quickly "rust" away; put bronze screws through an iron fitting and the iron will still give up electrons, but the effect will barely be evident.

The dissimilar "metals" do not have to be cast or machined solids; bottom paints that contain mercury or copper can have a disastrous effect on aluminum. Unless you choose a bottom paint with care, your aluminum outdrive unit might become a very expensive sacrificial anode.

Crevice Corrosion

This is a special case involving different portions of the same metal. Electrolyte is trapped in the crevice between a loosely bedded fitting and the deck. The difference in oxygen levels between the exterior and the hidden surface is sufficient to set up electrolytic deterioration of the hidden surface. The process is similar to what occurs when dew leaves rust spots on the surface of an untreated iron plate; in that instance, however, evaporation of the dew halts the galvanic activity. With crevice corrosion, the action may be continuous and result in failure of the fitting.

Stress Corrosion

This occurs when the microscopic elongation or separation of the grains of a metal under stress results in "crevice corrosion" between the grains. Stress corrosion can be a particular problem with alloys, because the crystals are also of dissimilar metal.

Stray-Current Corrosion

This results when electric circuits are wired improperly and current "escapes" and damages metal components. The current may be escaping because the grounding circuit is wrong or because the shore-power polarity is reversed, or it even may be coming from another boat in the marina. The stray current accelerates any other galvanic activity and also can affect wood mounts with what looks much like rot—the wood fibers become soft and spongy.

GRAPHITIZATION

A process similar to dezincification but applied to cast iron rather than brass. The iron content is carried away, leaving spongy carbon. Cast iron is not often used in boats, but it may show up in older plumbing systems.

FIRE

According to insurance statistics, fire is the most frequent cause of boat destruction; as cited in Coast Guard reports, fire results in twice the annual property loss (in dollars) of any other category of boating accident. In most cases, fire is the consequence of hazardous conditions or careless practices, all of which can be avoided.

FREEZING

Most materials become brittle and lose strength when frozen, so take caution when putting stress on lines in the winter. However, the main freezing problem is with water, which expands with exceptional force, cracking and splitting anything in the way. Freezing water can turn tiny cracks into gaping crevices, loosen joints, split plumbing, and crack engine cooling systems. Unless a storage battery is kept fully charged, water in the electrolyte can freeze, bursting the case.

Keep joints tight and seams filled; use antifreeze; blow freshwater lines clear with compressed air; put batteries on trickle charge or store them in a heated space.

IGNORANCE

Yours—and that of the person who owns the boat you want to buy. The most difficult lesson for novice boaters is to accept the fact that almost everything connected with boating must cost so much. After one dose of price-tag shock, most of us at first avoid marine supply stores and shop for tools, paint, fittings and accessories at automobile supply houses, hardware stores, and chain drugstores, where the prices seem better—but where most of the materials simply are not suited to the marine environment. We learn from our mistakes and, sooner or later, pay the inevitable price and buy a proper replacement. But we must learn to recognize—and thereby avoid—these mistakes when they are made by others, particularly those who may have done a quick-and-dirty "fix-up" to improve the appearance of a boat put up for sale.

MILDEW

Mildew is a fungus that grows on, and slowly destroys, cloth, leather, and paint. It especially loves such dark, damp places as hanging lockers. A burning light bulb, low in the locker, will raise the temperature and thus reduce the humidity below the mildew point. Sunlight and fresh air are the natural enemies of mildew; chemicals used for control are effective, but they may damage the materials on which they are used.

POLLUTION

Unfortunately, too many marinas are located adjacent to such other waterfront industries as powerplants and shipyards; the air- and water-borne chemical stew can ruin sails, lines, and paint—and even eat holes in the baked-enamel finish of an automobile. Boat covers and frequent washing will help prevent damage. Best advice: Find a better parking spot.

RODENTS

Mice and rats love to nest in sails stored for the winter; while they don't actually *eat* the material, they chew it into tiny pieces to make soft bedding.

ROT

Long regarded as the boater's nemesis, the prevalence of rot in boats has been declining steadily as more and more boats are constructed primarily of fiberglass. But rot itself has not disappeared: In field and forest, rot is the primary mechanism through which organic materials return to nature.

Rot is caused by fungi that digest cellulose fibers. These fungi are spread by spores, billions of which can be released by a single fungus. The rot fungus thrives only under certain conditions—within a temperature range, for example, of about 50°F to 80°F. But the most critical factor in the development of rot is the moisture content of the wood: If too wet (such as living wood, or hull planking covered with bilgewater), there's not enough oxygen; if too dry—a moisture content under 20 percent (about that of wood stabilized in air)—the spores lie dormant. For most rot fungi, the ideal moisture content is about 40 percent. That level is easily achieved when rain-wet wood has partially dried. Once the digestive process has begun, moisture is a by-product, and the rotting may proceed without additional wetting. Rot lives in a freshwater environment and is killed by salt; it is rarely found in the hulls of boats operated in salt water—but above the waterline, wherever fresh rainwater can seep, watch out!

Rot in boats usually is detectable by the soft, spongy texture of the affected wood; by a darker surface color; by peeling or blistering paint. Rot may be hidden under an intact paint surface, in which case tapping and/or careful probing with a screwdriver should reveal the affected areas. Or rot may be attacking the center of a timber where the endgrain is exposed to wetting, such as on the stem of a wooden boat; here, the damage might go unnoticed until the hull fastenings begin to pull out.

Small patches of rot might be amenable to chemical treatment and patching with wood putty; some commercial nostrums entomb the rot in plastic while at the same time making the diseased fibers stronger than the original wood. These measures may be expedient, but truly sensible treatment of rot involves radical surgery: Cut out and replace the diseased wood.

Rot prevention centers, first, on the selection of rot-resistant woods such as teak, oak, longleaf yellow pine; second, on keeping fresh water out of wood fibers by closing open seams and cracks, capping exposed endgrain, and ensuring an unbroken covering of paint. There are chemical remedies of limited utility: (1) Wood can be soaked in or painted with creosote, but this is messy and smelly and won't take paint; (2) wood can be pressure-treated with fungicidal chemicals such as copper naphthanate, but treated wood is hard to work with; (3) cutting usually exposes untreated sections; (4) chemicals reject paint. Treated wood is best used in the construction of sundecks, pilings, and piers.

ULTRAVIOLET DETERIORATION

Objects can be sunburned just as people can. Those faded displays in the window of your local barbershop show typical ultraviolet damage, because they were printed with the wrong type of ink. You've seen the same sort of problem with the dyes used in cheap furniture. However, not all such damage is merely cosmetic—as you may have realized when your plastic lawn chairs disintegrated after one season in the sun.

If such vulnerable materials have been used on your boat—in sails, rigging, mooring lines—you'll not only suffer economic loss but also may face serious safety hazards. Avoid polypropylene lines; make sure that Dacron sails are stored under a sunproof cover; in general, don't let anything lie in the sun any longer than it has to be there.

WARPING

A wooden plank with a homogeneous moisture content usually will run straight and true; if one side becomes dehydrated from exposure to the sun, the plank will warp in that direction. Lumber is best used only after an aging process that allows the moisture to evaporate slowly and evenly; that process frequently is accelerated by running the lumber through a drying kiln.

Some varieties of wood will warp more easily than others, just as some are harder, or softer, or lighter, or more or less vulnerable to rot. Because of the harshness of the marine environment, the woods used in boatbuilding must be selected carefully and prepared properly. And they should come from a specialty wood dealer. A nice-looking piece of white pine from your neighborhood lumberyard is *not* the wood to use for hull repair; the plywood you would use to panel your recreation room will self-destruct aboard a boat.

WORMS

Wooden hulls are vulnerable to rapid destruction by the teredo (shipworm) and *Limnoria* (gribble)—saltwater shellfish that eat wood fibers. From eggs laid on exposed wood, newly hatched infants burrow inside and feast their way to maturity. The outer shell of the hull may appear normal, with small entry holes the only visible evidence of severe damage.

The nickname "shipworm" notwithstanding, the teredo is not a worm but a mollusk, kin to the snail and the octopus. A shell on its head works like a drill as the animal tunnels through the banquet of life.

The gribble is a crustacean, related to shrimp and lobsters. Whereas teredos work deep and out of sight, gribbles work close to, and may even break through, the surface, leaving telltale spots of sawdust.

Both of these pests thrive in warm, still salt water; they can't get a mouthhold on a moving boat, and a mooring in a current seems to be a deterrent. Frequent trips to fresh water may help, but the best defense includes proper bottom paints as well as regular hauling and inspection.

Hazardous Materials and Environments

As noted in chapter 10, boat owners and maintenance personnel often are exposed to unusual hazards in working with various solvents, paints, and materials. While unusual—in the sense that most of these hazards are not normally encountered in the home or office—the hazards are not unknown. In this appendix we offer an elaboration of the information in chapter 10—although it still is limited to a bare-bones summary.

The manufacturers of potentially hazardous products are required not only to post a warning on the label of the container, but also to publish a materials safety data sheet, which must be available to the consumer—you—on request from the seller. These sheets describe the hazards, recommend the methods of protection, and note the probable symptoms of injury. Few consumers ask for the data sheets; you *should*—and you should maintain a file of them alongside your Owner's Notebook. You should also check OSHA requirements for boatyard workers.

WORKING SAFELY WITH HAZARDOUS MATERIALS

WOOD DUST

Plain old dust from boat-repair or boatbuilding operations can be hazardous to boat workers and boat owners. The hazard grows with repeated and lengthy exposure to wood dust. Consider this:

The Recommended Standard for Exposure to Wood Dust, according to the American Council of Governmental Hygienists, is 5 mg per cubic meter of air.

Hand sanding in an unventilated area (such as a boat cabin or small shop) will produce about 15 mg per cubic foot of air. Power sanding in the same area will produce about 150 mg per cubic foot of air. Wood-dust exposure has been linked to asthma, bronchitis, skin irritation (particularly with exotic or other hardwoods such as teak), and cancer.

Hazardous Materials

Solvents	Where Found	Protection	Danger/Symptoms	Treatment
(Plant-based)	paints, treatments, teak oils, cleaners, turpentine	ventilation, gloves, protective clothing	flammable/skin rash, dizziness	extinguish; soap and water, fresh air
(Ammonia)	cleaners, some paints, window cleaner	ventilation, protective clothing, eye protection, gloves	irritant to skin and eyes	water flush, soap and water
	some epoxy hardeners (polyamine)	respirator with ammonia filter	can damage larynx and respiratory system	see a doctor

Caution: Never mix ammonia with chlorine product; result can be toxic mustard gas.

Solvents	Where Found	Protection	Danger/Symptoms	Treatment
Toluidines Nitroaniline Nitrobenzene (Aniline)	paints, paint remover	ventilation, protective clothing, gloves, respirator with organic filter	can be absorbed by skin; heavy exposure can cause convulsions or coma; dizziness, headache	light exposure—wash with water; heavy exposure—see a doctor
Benzyne Styrene Toluene Aliphatics Xylene Aromatics Ethanes Methanes (Petroleum)	gasoline, lubricants, kerosene, diesel fuel, paints, coatings, thinners, waxes fiberglass construction systems	ventilation, eye protection, gloves, respirator with organic vapor filter fully protective clothing	flammable/nervousness, excitement, dizziness, irritability; serious long-term exposure can cause memory loss, or brain, liver, kidney, or nervous-system damage	extinguish; do not wash; if swallowed, do NOT induce vomiting; see a doctor

Caution: Benzyne should be avoided—the chemical can cause anemia and leukemia.

Solvents	Where Found	Protection	Danger/Symptoms	Treatment
Methanols Ethanol Acetones Ketones (Alcohol)	paints, strippers, cleaners, thinners	ventilation, eye protection, gloves, respirator, protective clothing	flammable and volatile/euphoria, dizziness, skin irritation	extinguish; wash any exposed skin with isopropyl alcohol
Isocyanates (Cyanide)	2-part foams, urethane paint, spray-paint systems	ventilation, gloves, eye protection, disposable overalls; for spray application, use positive-pressure respirator with appropriate filter	toxic/respiratory difficulty, serious asthmatic illness	Do *NOT* use near water; the combination of these chemicals with water can produce cyanide gas

Caution: Isocyanates can be toxic below odor levels.

Solvents	Where Found	Protection	Danger/Symptoms	Treatment
(Fluorides)	bottom paints	ventilation during sanding and painting, protective clothing, gloves, eye protection; when sanding, use a toxic dust mask; when painting, use respirator with filter and disposable coveralls	nausea, respiratory difficulty, vomiting, muscle cramps, abdominal pain	fresh air; see a doctor
(Phenols)	glues, adhesives, sealants, coatings, creosote, wood preservative	ventilation, toxic dust mask, gloves, protective clothing	respiratory difficulty, headache	fresh air; see a doctor

Caution: PCP (pentachlorophenols) in wood preservatives such as creosote-preserved woods can be carcinogenic. Avoid such wood or products. Linseed oil can be substituted as a preservative.

Other Materials	Hazard and Protection	Treatment
Paint and varnish strippers Methylene chloride Ethylene chloride Methanole Toluene Xylene Acetone	highly irritating to skin and eyes; gloves, protective clothing, eye protection, respirator with organic vapor filter	fresh air at first sign of dizziness, nausea, or lightheadedness; flush eyes with water (at least 20 minutes); see a doctor; if skin affected, flush with water

Caution: Avoid methylene chloride formulations if you have lung disease or a heart condition.

Other Materials	Hazard and Protection	Treatment
Topside paints Alkyd Silicone alkyd Oil/polyurethane Acrylic/polyurethane	most not seriously toxic when applied in brush form; toxic dust mask for sanding old paint or between coats; dangerous when sprayed—full clothing protection, gloves, eye protection, positive-pressure respirator	
Bottom paints Soluble-matrix diffusion type	toxic even in brush form; dizziness, nausea, respiratory difficulty	gloves, eye protection, disposable overalls
Copolymers	often contain acrylic resins, aromatic solvents, xylol, biocides, and polyisocyanates—eye protection, gloves, and positive-pressure respirator for spray application	fresh air; see a doctor

A further word on paints:

Lead components in marine paints and preservatives can cause abdominal cramps and rigidity. This can be further aggravated by consumption of alcohol.

Zinc chromates are serious eye irritants, can adversely affect respiration, and are suspected carcinogens.

Copper (most widely used antifouling material in bottom paint) is the least damaging of the metal materials, but it can cause some poisoning with repeated skin contact. Certain individuals are allergic to metallic compounds.

Mercuric materials should be avoided.

Varnishes are paints without pigment and should be used with proper precautions according to their component materials.

Other Materials	Hazard and Protection	Treatment
Polyester and epoxy resins	includes strong solvent material—esters, ethyl, methol ketone perioxide (MEKP); accelerator mixed with catalyst can be explosive; eye protection, gloves, disposable overalls, combination filter respirator	cleaning with solvent can increase skin sensitivity; thorough ventilation of work area
Fiberglass and fairing compounds (including microballoon compounds)	itching, contact dermatitis, respiratory problems; disposable clothing, toxic dust mask for sanding	

PROTECTIVE PRACTICE

1. Whenever possible, use planes and other edged tools such as cabinet scrapers instead of sandpaper.

2. Ventilate the area.

3. Use a dust-collection system or device at the source of dust.

4. Be particularly careful of hardwoods and exotic woods (frequently used in boat interiors).

5. Use a protective face mask when sanding, sawing, or operating a router, jointer, or planer. A nuisance-type filter mask will help; a toxic dust mask is preferable.

WOOD PRESERVATIVES

The goal of any wood preservative is to kill organisms that attack and deteriorate wood. Any poison holds potential hazard to humans, but the preservative that is hazardous to anyone working in and around boats is one that contains penta, or PCP (pentachloro-phenol). This preservative is often contaminated with dioxins. Pressure-treated lumber is always suspect as having been treated with hazardous preservatives. It should *not* be used in marine applications or in closed areas. Also, creosote-containing products have been linked to cancer. Other preservatives include metallic compounds, such as CCA (chrome, copper, and arsenic) and ACA (ammonium, copper, and arsenic), which are potentially hazardous. Such products as Cuprinol, zinc naphthanate, and tributylin seem to be less hazardous but should be used with care.

PROTECTIVE PRACTICE

1. Use preservatives only when absolutely necessary, and be aware of their potential health hazard. Do not use them in enclosed living areas or galleys—and never use them on surfaces involved in food preparation.

2. Use a properly rated and prepared respirator when applying preservatives or working in areas

Gloves

Gloves are one of the most important ways of preventing skin problems because the hands and fingers are the areas most commonly exposed to hazards. However, no single type of glove will protect against all chemicals. So be sure to choose the type of glove that will protect you from the chemicals with which you are working.

Chemical	Natural Rubber or Latex	Neoprene Rubber	Latex/ Neoprene	Butyl Rubber	Buna-N or NBR Rubber	Nitrile	Polyvinyl Chloride
Acetic acid	G	G	G	G	G	G	G
Acids (dilute)	G	G	G	G	G	G	G
Acids (concentrate)	NR	G	G	G	NR	NR	NR
Alkalis	G	G	G	G	G	G	G
Alcohols	G	G	G	G	G	G	G
Aromatic hydrocarbons (toluene, xylene)	NR	NR	V	NR	G	G	NR
Chlorinated hydrocarbons (methylene chloride, methyl chloroform)	NR	V	V	V	NR	G	NR
Ketone (e.g., acetone)	G	G	G	G	NR	NR	NR
Lacquer thinner	NR	NR	V	NR	G	NR	NR
Paint and varnish remover	NR	V	V	V	V	G	NR
Paint thinner	NR	G	G	NR	G	G	NR
Petroleum distillates	NR	G	G	NR	G	G	NR
Phenol (carbolic acid)	NR	G	G	G	G	G	G
Polyester resin	NR	NR	V	NR	V	G	NR
Turpentine	NR	G	G	NR	G	G	NR

G=good; V=variable; NR=not recommended

Note: The information in this table on gloves is based on material that originally appeared in *WoodenBoat* magazine. It comes from interviews conducted at the Marine Trades Center of the Washington County Vocational Technical Institute in Eastport, Maine. Further information was gathered from the Art Hazards Project of the New York Center for Occupational Hazards.

where preservatives have been applied and are still drying.

3. Provide adequate ventilation.

4. Wear gloves.

5. Avoid all skin contact.

6. Avoid frequent and prolonged inhalation of sawdust generated from treated wood. Use a respirator when working with such wood, wear gloves, and protect your eyes with goggles.

7. Wash thoroughly after working with preservatives.

8. Do not burn preservative-treated wood or scraps suspected of having preservative treatment.

9. Seal wood after preservatives have been applied. Some woods will not take finishes after preservative treatment, so check all labels before preservative treatment.

Note: Some of the above information on wood dust and wood preservatives originally appeared in *WoodenBoat* magazine.

Safety Equipment

Note: Before selecting protective equipment, be sure to consult the materials safety data sheet for each product you plan to use.

Equipment	Buyer's/User's Guide
Protective clothing	Properly rated protective overalls, either permanent or disposable, are well worth their minor cost. Bottom paint can cost up to $100 per gallon, while disposable overalls go for as little as $4 a pair. Short of buying rated equipment, when working with materials that could irritate your skin, wear a long-sleeved shirt and keep your shirt buttoned. Sweatshirts and pants can be useful protective clothing since they are absorbent and keep material from penetrating (for a while). Do not postpone removing those products that get onto skin. Any delay will not match the time you spend at a doctor's office or hospital.
Barrier creams	Barrier creams can be useful on face, hands, and arms when painting or grinding. They are *not* a substitute for properly rated protective clothing and equipment. Creams can offer some protection against some solvents and hazardous dusts. Vaseline is a minimal barrier cream, but it is better than nothing. Be sure that any material you are using as a barrier cream has products that are FDA-approved.
Dust masks	Dust masks are not respirators. A dust mask protects only against dust (when properly fitted). A respirator is specifically for vapors, fumes, gases, or smoke. Dust masks are cheap (about $2 each); buy the best. Buy only the type with two elastics: One elastic cannot give you a tight-enough fit. After fitting and first use, check the interior of the mask for dust tracks, which indicate the fit is not correct and should be adjusted. Toxic dust masks are even more refined and should be used if you expect any involvement with hardwoods or exotic woods. Remember: Using a dust mask instead of a respirator can be hazardous, since the dust mask can absorb dangerous fumes and vapors, thus concentrating them and creating an even higher hazard level.
Respirators	When buying any respirator, be sure it is NIOSH/MSHA–approved and rated for the specific type of material you expect to encounter. Hazardous vapors usually are measured in parts per million of air—which means your exposure may be significantly higher for the same material when you work in a confined or nonventilated space, as opposed to open air. Nor is your sense of smell a dependable warning system. For instance, certain ingredients of popular marine urethane paints cannot be smelled until you already have been overexposed. Be aware that facial hair (beards and mustaches) can seriously hamper a true seal with any respirator. To test for fit: Place your hands over the cartridge inlets and inhale gently. The face piece should collapse slightly. Hold your breath for about ten seconds. If the face piece stays collapsed, the seal probably is okay. If not, adjust for a better fit. Be sure to use the proper cartridge for the hazard involved, and do not use the cartridge beyond its rated useful life.
Goggles	Remove contact lenses before working with potentially hazardous chemicals. Lenses usually cannot be cleaned of toxic materials. Soft lenses can absorb such material and become toxic. Safety splash goggles and/or face masks are inexpensive and should be worn before you open any containers holding potentially hazardous materials.

APPENDIX VI

Miscellaneous Legal Considerations— Documentation, International Travel, Boarding by Law-Enforcement Officials

DOCUMENTATION

A boat intended solely for recreational (not business) use may be documented in the United States, under the following conditions:

1. The boat must be owned by a U.S. citizen; if there is more than one owner, all partners must be citizens; if owned by a corporation, controlling interest (51 percent or more) must be held by citizens. Any hired captain also must be a U.S. citizen.
2. The boat must be a net five tons or more.

A discussion of the advantages and purposes of documentation appears in chapter 7.

The ownership criteria are easy to understand; the "net five tons" can be confusing. This refers to a theoretical cargo capacity measured in 100-cubic-foot units—which have nothing to do with either the dry or the loaded displacement of the boat. The method for determining this capacity is called "admeasurement"; if done with precision, it would first require a computation of hull volume, from which the space occupied by machinery would be subtracted to yield the net tonnage.

With pleasure craft not intended for carrying passengers for hire, the Coast Guard permits the owner to use a simplified computation method:

- With a *sailboat*, multiply the length times the breadth times the depth, divide the result by 100, then divide by two. This provides the *gross* tonnage. The *net* tonnage—which counts for documentation—is recorded as nine-tenths of the gross figure unless there is no inboard engine, in which case the net will be the same as the gross.
- With a *powerboat*, multiply the length times the breadth times the depth, divide the result by 100, and take two-thirds of that number for the *gross* tonnage; the *net* will be recorded as eight-tenths of the gross.
- Length is measured from the foremost part of the stem to the aftermost part of the stern, excluding bowsprits and davits. Breadth is measured side-to-side at the widest part of the hull (excluding rubrails). Depth is measured from the main deck straight down to the (outside) bottom of the hull; if the keel is enclosed in the skin of the hull, it is included in the measurement. Depth should not be confused with draft—which is

measured from the waterline to the deepest projection under the hull.

• With a multihull design, the figure for each hull is computed and then both or all are added together; for a boat with a disproportionately large deckhouse—such as a houseboat—deckhouse volume is computed in 100-cubic-foot units (length times width times height divided by 100) and added to the gross tonnage of the hull as determined above.

In general, a boat shorter than 25 feet probably won't measure up, but if it has an exceptionally broad beam (or is a houseboat), it may; in any event, it takes only a few minutes for a determination under this simplified method. If you wish, you can ask the Coast Guard to conduct a formal measurement (the normal procedure for commercial vessels), but chances are that if the boat is under five net tones by the simplified procedure, it will not become larger after Coast Guard scrutiny.

To start the audit trail of ownership established by documentation, the Coast Guard requires that you produce adequate evidence of origin and title, including the original builder's certificate or master carpenter's certificate and verifiable bills of sale for each subsequent change of ownership. Should these records not be available, a waiver might be granted or alternate documents accepted.

Once the boat has been approved for documenta-tion, but before the final certificate will be issued, the boat must be properly marked. First, the assigned official number must be marked permanently on a major interior hull member. The traditional method is to carve the numbers in a wooden beam or outline them with a metal punch on a steel or aluminum frame; the advent of so many fiberglass hulls presented some problems, so the rules were modified a few years back to permit the use of stick-on plastic numbers coated with clear epoxy to render them unalterable. Official numbers should be three inches high, unless there simply isn't enough room, in which case they should be as large as possible.

Next, all documented boats must show the boat name and the home or hailing port in a "conspicuous place"—typically, on the stern. The letters should be at least four inches high and easily read. You have your choice of home port—the location of the Coast Guard marine inspection office where the documentation is recorded—or hailing port—the place within the same marine inspection zone where the boat was built *or* where one of the owners lives. The place where the boat normally is docked or moored is irrelevant.

The fees for documentation are quite reasonable, and even if you hire an agent to handle all of the paperwork (including searching for liens and preparation of a bill of sale), the total cost should only be a few hundred dollars. Renewal is annual, and it can be handled by mail.

INTERNATIONAL TRAVEL

International travel can be one of the most rewarding of boating activities—and also one of the most frustrating, as the captains of three U.S. fishing boats discovered when they transferred supplies among themselves while in harbor in the Caribbean island of Sint Maarten. The fact that they had entered port to escape a storm and repair some damage meant little to the local authorities: Transferring "goods" without first clearing customs was a violation of law, and the skippers languished in a local jail for more than sixty days—until fines had been paid and apologies made.

Clearly, when a boat enters the territorial waters of a sovereign nation, it—including passengers and crew—becomes subject to the laws of that nation. The captain has a responsibility to understand the usual requirements of international travel and to be fully in-formed—in advance—of any peculiar local rules that may affect his stay. This is not much different from the situation of any international traveler, who must pass in and out of customs and be alert to local laws, but most boaters will need to learn the procedures without the more or less automatic help and counsel of a friendly travel agent.

Customs and immigration clearance is a universal practice that should, in most cases, be routine. The foreign jurisdiction has the right to determine the identity and nationality of each visitor; the passport is the internationally accepted form of identification.

The normal form of "permission to visit" is the visa, which may be obtained in advance from embassies or consular offices—or, for many nations, granted on the spot upon arrival. Most nearby nations—such as Canada, Mexico, Bermuda, and the Bahamas—require neither passport nor visa, but a traveler must have some proof of citizenship, such as a birth certificate or a voter's registration card. The same identification will be required to reenter the United States.

A foreign jurisdiction has as much right to determine a *vessel*'s nationality as a *crew*'s nationality. For U.S. boaters, federal documentation offers the best proof of nationality, although state registration papers are readily accepted in those nations closest to the United States.

Each nation is likely to have specific customs rules—largely designed to protect local industries or to inhibit the movement of illegal materials. The average traveler, arriving by air, is unlikely to be bothered by customs, or even to be searched. Arrival on a boat capable of carrying large quantities of contraband may be a different matter. Firearms, alcoholic beverages, prescription medications—all may be subject to control. The basic rule: *Always* list *everything* on the declaration form. To make that practical, have copies of your loading plan available. An "unacceptable" item may be confiscated and returned on departure; that's preferable to having yourself or a crew member confiscated and jailed for making a false declaration.

Upon returning to the United States after a visit to a foreign port, members of a boat's crew have the same responsibility to clear customs as if they were reentering through an airport. In most major international boating areas, customs clearance can at least be initiated by a telephone call from designated locations. If your voyage was routine and you have little or nothing to declare, clearance may even be granted over the telephone. If you've visited many ports, have a complex declaration—or, for whatever reason, fit a suspect profile, you may be asked to stand by for a visit from a customs official.

Vessels that have visited Puerto Rico—and *only* Puerto Rico, not very logical voyage planning—need not clear customs, since Puerto Rico is treated, for this purpose, as another U.S. state.

Health screening of visitors has been practiced, in varying degrees, at least since the days of the Black Plague. However, today, when such classic scourges as plague and smallpox seem to have been all but eliminated, proof of immunization normally is not required. Nonetheless, it would be wise for yachtsmen planning extended international voyages to be protected against possible exposure to disease—however remote that possibility may be—and to carry personal immunization records.

One important exception to today's simplified health clearance procedures: They might not apply to pets. While smallpox has almost disappeared, rabies has not. There are some nations that have escaped this disease—and they hope to maintain that situation by imposing strict entry and quarantine regulations against applicable pets. In the case of dogs, for instance, this might be *six months*. Check it out.

BOARDING BY LAW-ENFORCEMENT OFFICIALS

Law-enforcement officials, Bureau of Alcohol and Firearms agents, customs agents, and members of the U.S. (*and* foreign) Coast Guard—all have the right to board your boat to search for contraband, check for safety violations, and inspect your papers and your log. How often is this likely to happen? The U.S. Coast Guard alone conducts about 85,000 such inspections a year—in more than half, some violations are reported.

If the inspectors determine that an unsafe condition exists or that you are engaged in hazardous operation (which might include speeding, too many passengers, not enough life jackets, leaking fuel, or a "manifestly unsafe voyage"—such as an attempt to sail to Hawaii in a bathtub), they may issue an order to cease and desist or return immediately to port. Such orders have the full force of law, and a failure to comply may provoke charges in addition to those that might be lodged for the cited offense.

Boarding parties do not need a search warrant, nor do they need your permission. They may not always be friendly and may not always follow what might seem to be either common sense or common decency.

You might even find yourself hailed by a U.S. Navy ship. While U.S. military units traditionally have been legally prohibited from active law enforcement, they can—and do—provide support to other government agencies, particularly in the interdiction of drug traffic. Many U.S. Navy ships operating in known drug-trafficking areas carry a Coast Guard law-enforcement detachment, which has full powers of search, seizure, and arrest.

Coast Guard and other law-enforcement vessels are clearly marked; if making a nighttime boarding, the Coast Guard will shine a spotlight on its flag and, if possible, on the distinctive red stripe on its bow. Coast Guard and law-enforcement officials are not likely to be confused with pirates: They wear distinctive uniforms. If asked by such a vessel to heave-to and permit a party to come aboard, do so. Remember that while the party is aboard, and unless—and until—you have been placed under arrest, you are still fully responsible for the safe operation of your boat.

How should you behave? As though you understand that these folks have an important and difficult job to do. Be open and friendly. Present all requested documents, open any cabinets or storage compartments as requested. Don't make jokes; boarding parties are not selected for their sense of humor. Don't argue, don't claim your "rights," don't threaten to write your congressman.

You can, of course, contact your congressman, your lawyer, or anyone else to discuss a complaint . . . *after* you've been released and allowed to proceed. If you feel you have been treated unreasonably, document everything as soon as you can. Take a photograph of the departing ship. Fill your log with a chronology, direct quotations, names (which you usually can get from the name tags on the uniforms).

You can—and should—also contact the Coast Guard itself; if you're not comfortable calling the local commander, you may write or telephone Coast Guard headquarters:

Special Assistant for Consumer Affairs (G-BC)
U.S. Coast Guard Headquarters
Washington, DC 20593
Tel. (202) 472-2384

How do you avoid being boarded in the first place? The flip answer: Don't get underway in the first place. A somewhat more realistic answer: Don't do anything to attract attention and certainly don't sail at night without proper lights. Don't ignore a radio call or a hail from a government vessel. Don't own a boat that resembles the types most favored by the drug trade—i.e., very fast ocean racers, converted freighters, large commercial fishing trawlers. Should you happen to be a commercial fisherman, expect to join a growing fraternity of boat operators who are boarded with regularity.

The Coast Guard does put a closer watch on some boats than on others, and it circulates descriptions of likely suspects. If you're unfortunate enough to have purchased a boat previously suspected of trafficking in drugs, you can expect a period of repeated boardings. One innocent boat was boarded three times in the same day by representatives of three different agencies—none of whom were impressed by the fact that the skipper was a retired naval officer and the boat had been given clearance just a few hours earlier. The boat matched a suspect profile, and the officials had no intention of taking chances.

APPENDIX VII

A Working Glossary of Sailing Terms

ABACK—when the wind has shifted around and hits the sail on the lee side.

ABAFT—toward the stern.

APPARENT WIND—the direction and speed of the wind as felt aboard a moving boat; the result of a combination of the boat's heading and speed with the actual (or "true") wind.

BACK A SAIL—to sheet a sail to windward (on the opposite side of the boat you would normally set a sail); this provides a braking or steadying force on the boat, a tactic usually reserved for heavy-weather sailing.

BACKSTAY—the stay that supports the mast from aft.

BATTENS—flexible strips of wood or plastic inserted into pockets along the leech of a sail to provide support for the roach.

BEAR AWAY, BEAR OFF—to steer away from the wind.

BEAT—to sail close-hauled on alternate tacks in order to make good a course as much into the wind as possible.

BOBSTAY—a stay run from the waterline to the bowsprit to counteract the pull of the forestay.

BOOM—a spar used to spread a fore-and-aft sail.

BOOM CRUTCH. *See* GALLOWS

BOWSPRIT—a spar extending forward from the bow to hold the forestay.

BREAK OUT—to open or unfurl a sail or flag; *also,* to free the anchor from the bottom when heaving it in.

BROACH—to be caught by a following sea and spun sideways into the trough of the waves.

BROAD REACH—a point of sailing, with the wind blowing over the quarter.

CLEAT—a fitting around which a line is wrapped to hold it in place; the act of thus securing a line.

CLEVIS PIN—a locking pin secured with a cotter pin or split ring to prevent accidental removal.

CLEW—the after, lower corner of a sail.

CLOSE-HAULED—sailing into the wind as much as possible.

CLOSE REACH—a point of sailing when the wind comes from forward of the beam (but not as far forward as when close-hauled).

COME ABOUT—to turn; to change direction; to tack.

CORIOLIS EFFECT—the deflection of wind and water at the surface caused by the spinning of the earth—to the right in the Northern Hemisphere, to the left in the Southern.

COTTER PIN—a metal pin inserted through two parts to hold them together; its split ends are then bent back to keep the pin in place.

CRINGLE—an eye (or grommet) stitched into a sail.

CUNNINGHAMS—grommets in the luff and foot of a sail that can be pulled, by lanyards, toward the tack to adjust the shape of the sail.

DOUSE A SAIL—to lower a sail suddenly.

DOWNHAUL—a rope for pulling down a sail or boom.

DOWNWIND—sailing with the wind coming from astern.

DROGUE—a sea anchor or drag made of planks, a bucket, etc., and towed to slow the movement of a boat.

EYE OF THE WIND—the direction from which the wind is blowing.

FAIRLEAD—a fitting through which a line runs to change the direction of the line or to keep it clear of other equipment.

FALL OFF—to change course away from the wind.

FOOT—the bottom edge of a sail.

FORESTAY—the forward stay, running from the top of the stem to the masthead to support the mast and to which the headsail is hanked.

GALLOWS—a deck fixture for supporting the boom when it is not in use.

GENOA—a large headsail that overlaps the mainsail.

GIMBALS—an arrangement of swivels that lets gravity keep an object level despite the motion of the boat.

GO ABOUT—to swing the boat through the eye of the wind to the opposite tack.

GOOSEWING. See WING-AND-WING

GUY—a steadying rope for a boom or spinnaker pole.

GYBE. See JIBE

HALYARD—a rope used for hoisting and lowering sails and flags.

HANK—a clip that attaches the luff of a sail to a stay; "to hank on" is to attach the sail in this fashion.

HARDEN A SAIL—haul in on the sheet to flatten the sail.

HEAD-TO-WIND—pointing the bow straight into the wind.

HEADWAY—forward movement of a boat through the water.

HEADWIND—a wind blowing from the direction in which you want to travel, requiring the boat to beat.

HEAVE-TO—to back the jib with the rudder full into the wind; a heavy-weather tactic.

HEEL—listing far to one side under pressure of the wind.

IN IRONS—to be stuck head-to-wind, unable to fall off on either tack.

JIB—the foremost headsail.

JIBE—to shift the wind from one quarter to the other by swinging the stern through the wind.

KEDGE—to move a boat by means of a line attached to an anchor laid out in the direction desired.

KICKING STRAP. See VANG

LAZYJACKS—a set of light lines, run from the topping lift to the boom on each side of the sail, to catch the billows as the sail is lowered.

LEECH—the aft edge of a triangular sail; the side edges of a square sail. See also ROACH

LEE HELM—the tendency of a boat to head away from the wind. See also WEATHER HELM

LEE SHORE—the shore toward which the wind is blowing and upon which a boat might be driven by the wind.

LEEWARD—the direction toward which the wind is blowing; thus, the downwind side of a boat. See also WINDWARD

LET FLY—to release a sheet instantly, spilling the wind from a sail.

LUFF—the forward edge of a sail; "to luff" is to bring the bow into the wind until the luff shakes.

MAINMAST—the principal, heaviest mast.

MAINSAIL (OR MAIN)—the fore-and-aft sail set on the after side of the mainmast.

MIZZEN—the fore-and-aft sail set on the after side of the mizzenmast.

MIZZENMAST—the after mast in a ketch or yawl.

MIZZEN STAYSAIL—a triangular sail set on the forward side of the mizzenmast.

OFF THE WIND—sailing into the wind but with the sheets slacked off; not close-hauled.

ON THE WIND—sailing close-hauled.

OUTHAUL—a rope used to tighten the foot of a sail.

PAY OUT—to let a line out gradually.

PINCH—to sail too close to the wind.

POINT—one of thirty-two equal divisions of the compass, or 11¼ degrees.

POINTS OF SAILING—the various angles from the wind on which a boat may sail.

PORT TACK—a boat is on the port tack when the wind is coming over the port side and the boom is out to starboard.

PREVENTER—a rope set to limit the movement of a boom.

QUARTER—that portion of a boat midway between the beam and the stern.

REACH—to sail with the wind generally on the beam.

REEF—to reduce sail area by rolling or folding part of the sail.

REEFING PENDANT—a rope hanging from the luff or leech cringle, used to pull the sail down to the boom when reefing.

REEF POINT—a short length of line, attached to the sail, to gather and hold the folds of the sail when it is reefed.

RIGGING—"running rigging" comprises the movable lines that control the sails; "standing rigging" comprises the shrouds and stays that hold the masts in place and normally do not move while sailing.

ROACH—the outward curve along the leech of a sail.

ROLLER FURLING—a mechanical system for reducing and storing sails by wrapping them around a stay.

ROLLER REEFING—a mechanical system for reducing sail area in which the boom is turned along the horizontal axis so that the foot of the sail rolls around it.

ROUND UP—to come into the wind from a run or a reach.

RUN—to sail with the wind aft.

RUN BEFORE—to run with the wind in a gale or squall.

SAIL OFF—to turn away from the wind.

SET—to hoist or make sail (not to be confused with the direction of tidal flow).

SHAKE OUT—to let out a reef.

SHEAVE—a grooved wheel—in a block or at the masthead or the end of the boom—around which a rope will run.

SHEET—a rope for trimming the sail, attached to either the clew of the sail or the end of the boom.

SPAR—the general term for any pole (such as a mast or boom) used to carry or give shape to a sail.

SPEED-MADE-GOOD—actual speed over the ground, accounting for the effects of wind and current on the boat's speed through the water.

SPINNAKER—a large, lightweight, balloon-shaped sail used when reaching or running.

SPINNAKER POLE—a pole used to hold the foot of a spinnaker to best catch the wind.

STARBOARD TACK—a boat is on the starboard tack when the wind is coming over the starboard side and the boom is out to port.

STAYSAIL—a triangular fore-and-aft sail, typically set on a stay between the jib and the main, as in a cutter rig.

STEERAGEWAY—sufficient movement through the water to permit the rudder to act.

STERNWAY—motion backward through the water.

STOP—a light binding of small line used to secure a sail that is hoisted but not broken out; a sharp tug on the sheet releases the sail.

TACK—the lower forward corner of a sail. *See also* PORT TACK; STARBOARD TACK. "To tack" is to sail a zigzag course into the wind. *See* BEAT

TELLTALE—a short length of twine secured to a sail or stay to provide a visual clue to the direction of the wind.

TOPPING LIFT—a line from the masthead to the end of the boom, used to support the boom.

TRAVELER—a fitting that slides along a track and is used to adjust the angle of the sheets.

TRIM—adjustment of the helm and the sheets to allow the sails to take the best advantage of the wind.

VANG—a rope used to haul down the boom to flatten the sail.

WEATHER HELM—the tendency of a boat to head up into the wind. *See also* LEE HELM

WHISKER POLE—a light pole used to hold the clew of a headsail out to one side when running.

WINDWARD—the direction from which the wind is blowing; toward the wind. *See also* LEEWARD

WING-AND-WING—sailing downwind with the mainsail out to one side and the headsail out to the other, presenting the appearance of a bird with wings outstretched.

APPENDIX VIII

Valuable Further Reading

There are literally thousands of books on maritime subjects ranging from Anchors to the Zen of Sailing. Listed below are books that have two criteria: (1) that they are relevant to safety at sea; and (2) that the authors have read each book and found it to be outstanding in its field.

An additional note: Many of these books may be found in libraries or at your local booksellers'. Some are out of print, but they can still be obtained via libraries and used-book stores. In addition, there are five major mail-order sources for many of these titles (both in and out of print).

SOURCES

THE ARMCHAIR SAILOR offers an extensive catalog of books and videos covering a full range of boating and related maritime subjects. It is also a stocking center for worldwide chart and navigation publications:

> The Armchair Sailor
> Lee's Wharf
> Newport, RI 02840
> 1-800-292-4278

DOLPHIN BOOK CLUB (a division of Book-of-the-Month Club) books may be ordered through club membership, which is offered in advertising found in the major boating magazines, or by writing directly to:

> Dolphin Book Club
> Camp Hill, PA 17012

INTERNATIONAL MARINE PUBLISHING COMPANY is a general boating-subject publisher and distributor:

> International Marine Publishing Co.
> P.O. Box 220
> Camden, ME 04843
> 207-236-4837

THE NAVAL INSTITUTE PRESS has the most significant collection of books for the professional mariner, merchant mariner, or naval officer. Despite this official description, many of the institute's books are of great value and interest for the recreational boater. Books on navigation, construction, boathandling, sailing, as well as works of fiction, tales of voyaging, and maritime history, are part of the library. A catalog can be obtained from:

> Naval Institute Press
> U.S. Naval Academy
> Annapolis, MD 21402
> 301-268-6110

THE WOODENBOAT CATALOG offers more than books and covers more than wooden boats:

> The WoodenBoat Catalog
> P.O. Box 78
> Brooklin, Maine 04616
> 207-359-4652
> Or, toll-free, 1-800-225-5205

BOOKS

DESIGN AND CONSTRUCTION

Boatman's Guide to Modern Marine MATERIALS, Ernest A. Zadig. Motor Boating & Sailing Books, New York, NY.
Desirable and Undesirable Characteristics of Offshore Yachts, John Rousmaniere. W.W. Norton, New York, NY.
From a Bare Hull, Ferenc Maté. W.W. Norton, New York, NY.
How to Build a Wooden Boat, David C. McIntosh. WoodenBoat Publications, Brooklin, ME (1987).

ELECTRICITY AND ELECTRONICS

The Complete Book of Marine Electronics, Ernest Zadig. Motor Boating & Sailing Books, New York, NY.
Electrical and Electronic Equipment for Yachts, John French. Dodd Mead, New York, NY.
Electronic Corrosion Control for Boats, John D. Lenk. Howard Sams & Co., Indianapolis, IN.
Your Boat's Electrical System, Conrad Miller and E.S. Maloney. Hearst Marine Books, New York, NY.

ENGINES

The Complete Book of Pleasure Boat Engines, Ernest A. Zadig. Prentice-Hall, Englewood Cliffs, NJ (1980).
Engines for Sailboats, Conrad Miller. Yachting Books, Ziff-Davis, New York, NY.

EQUIPMENT

Marine Products Directory (September 1988, and previous directories by subject). Underwriters Laboratory, Publications Stock, 333 Pfingsten Rd., Northbrook, IL 60062.

MAINTENANCE

Shipshape: The Art of Sailboat Maintenance, Ferenc Maté. W.W. Norton, New York, NY.

MEDICAL

Advanced First Aid Afloat, Peter F. Eastman, M.D. Cornell Maritime, Centreville, MD.
Dr. Cohen's Healthy Sailor Book, Michael M. Cohen, M.D. International Marine Publishing, Camden, ME.
The Ship's Medicine Chest and Medical Aid at Sea. U.S. Department of Health and Human Services, Public Health Service, U.S. Government Printing Office, Washington, DC.

NAVIGATION

American Practical Navigator, Nathaniel Bowditch, Vol. I. Defense Mapping Agency Hydrographic Center, Washington, DC.
Dutton's Navigation and Piloting, Elbert S. Maloney. Naval Institute Press, Annapolis, MD.

Piloting and Dead Reckoning, H.H. Shufeldt & G.D. Dunlap. Naval Institute Press, Annapolis, MD.

SAFETY STANDARDS

Lightning Protection Code, N.F.P.A. No. 78. National Fire Protection Association, 60 Batterymarch St., Boston, MA 02110.

Rules and Regulations for Recreational Boats, 1 July 1989, previously published as COMDTINST M16752.2 (old CG-497). American Boat and Yacht Council, Inc. P.O. Box 747-405 Headquarters Drive, Suite 3, Millersville, MD 21108; 301-923-3932.

Safety Standards for Small Craft. American Boat and Yacht Council, Inc., 15 East 26th St., New York, NY 10010

SAILS, SAILING, AND SEAMANSHIP

The Annapolis Book of Seamanship, John Rousmaniere. Simon & Schuster, New York, NY.

The Elements of Seamanship, Roger C. Taylor. International Marine Publishing, Camden, ME.

Heavy Weather Sailing, Adlard Coles. John de Graff, Inc., Clinton Corners, NY.

Mariner's Guide to the Rules of the Road, William H.A. Tate. Naval Institute Press, Annapolis, MD.

The Marlinspike Sailor, Hervey Garrett Smith. John de Graff, Inc., Clinton Corners, NY.

The Ocean Sailing Yacht, Vols. I and II, Donald Street. W.W. Norton, New York, NY.

Practical Yacht Handling, Eric Tabarly. David McKay, New York, NY.

Sail Power, Wallace Ross. Alfred A. Knopf, New York, NY.

Sea Sense, Second Edition, Richard Henderson. International Marine Publishing, Camden, ME.

Seawise, Donald M. Street, Jr. W.W. Norton, New York, NY.

This Is Sailing, Richard Creagh-Osborne. Sail Books, Boston, MA.

WEATHER

Instant Weather Forecasting, Alan Watts. Dodd, Mead, New York, NY.

The Sailor's Weather Guide, Jeff Markell. W.W. Norton, New York, NY.

Weather for the Mariner, 3rd Edition, William J. Kotsch. Naval Institute Press, Annapolis, MD.

OTHER SOURCES

SAFETY REPORTS

Boating Safety Circular. United States Coast Guard, Department of Transportation Publication. Monthly. Various safety-oriented reports, consumer information. Topics in March 1989 issue: Answers to safety questions on visibility, unsafe watercraft, ventilation systems, safe loading limits, fuel systems, risks of bareboat chartering, recalls on specific boats and marine products by company, electrical system standards.

INFORMATION ON EQUIPMENT

Boat Buyer's Guide
Yachting Publishing Corp.
50 W. 44th St.
New York, NY 10036

Sailboat and Equipment Directory
38 Commercial Wharf
Boston, MA 02110

VIDEOS

Heavy Weather Sailing, 95 min. VHS Product #350-17S, Beta Product #350-17B. Available from WoodenBoat Catalog, P.O. Box 78, Brooklin, ME 04616.

Safety at Sea, 95 min. VHS Product #350-18S, Beta Product #350-18B. Available from WoodenBoat Catalog, P.O. Box 78, Brooklin, ME 04616.

Radar Navigation & Collision Avoidance, Jens Jacobs. North Sea Navigator Company, 220 Rt. 25-A, Northport, NY.

Marine Hurricane Preparedness. Bennett Marine Video, 730 Washington St., Marina del Rey, CA 90292.

Abandon Ship. Bennett Marine Video, 730 Washington St., Marina del Rey, CA 90292.

Using Loran. Magic Lamp Productions, 4220 Glencoe, Marina del Rey, CA 90292.

The Annapolis Book of Seamanship: Powerboat Navigation, by John Rousmaniere, Available from The Armchair Sailor, Newport, RI. NOTE: This is one in a series of five well-produced videos, some done with the assistance of the United States Coast Guard. Other titles include: *Cruising Under Sail, Heavy*

Weather Sailing (see above), *Safety at Sea* (see above), and *Daysailers: Sailing & Racing.*

Navigation, Robin Knox Johnston. Available from The Armchair Sailor, Newport, RI.

Small Boat Engine Maintenance, Jim Storey. Available from The Armchair Sailor, Newport, RI.

COMPUTER SOFTWARE

East and West Coast (U.S.) Voyage Computer Simulation, Dolphin Marine Systems. Available from The Armchair Sailor, Newport, RI.

APPENDIX IX

Useful Addresses

UNITED STATES COAST GUARD DISTRICTS

District Offices	Jurisdiction	District Offices	Jurisdiction
First Coast Guard District 408 Atlantic Ave. Boston, MA 02210-2209 (617) 223-8310	All New England to Toms River, NJ, and part of NY	Ninth Coast Guard District 1240 East 9th St. Cleveland, OH 44199-2060 (216) 522-4422	MI, parts of OH, IL, IN, MN, WI, NY, and PA
Second Coast Guard District 1430 Olive St. St. Louis, MO 63103-2378 (314) 425-5971	Mississippi River system (except south of Baton Rouge) and the Illinois River north of Joliet	Eleventh Coast Guard District 400 Oceangate Long Beach, CA 90822-5399 (213) 499-5310	CA, AZ, NV, and UT
Fifth Coast Guard District 431 Crawford St. Portsmouth, VA 23704-5004 (804) 398-9505	MD, DE, Washington, DC, VA, NC, and parts of NJ and PA	Thirteenth Coast Guard District 915 Second Ave. Seattle, WA 98174-1067 (206) 442-7355	OR, WA, ID, and MT
Seventh Coast Guard District 51 S. W. First Ave. Miami, FL 33130-1608 (305) 536-5698	SC, GA, and most of FL and Puerto Rico and adjacent US islands	Fourteenth Coast Guard District 300 Ala Moana Blvd. Honolulu, HI 96850-4982 (808) 546-7130/546-7109	Hawaii and the Pacific islands beling to the US west of latitude 140°W and south of latitude 42°N
Eighth Coast Guard District 500 Camp St. New Orleans, LA 70130-3396 (504) 589-2972	Western Florida, parts of AL and MS, and LA, TX, and NM	Seventeenth Coast Guard District P.O. Box 3-5000 Juneau, AK 99802 (907) 586-7467	Alaska

STATE BOATING SAFETY OFFICES

ALABAMA
Marine Police Division
Dept. Conservation
  & Natural Resources
Folsom Administrative Building
Montgomery, AL 36130
(205) 261-3673

ALASKA
U.S. Coast Guard
Federal Building
P.O. Box 3-5000
Juneau, AK 99802-1217
(907) 586-7467

ARIZONA
Game & Fish Dept.
2222 West Greenway Rd.
Phoenix, AZ 85023
(602) 942-3000

ARKANSAS
Game & Fish Commission
Boating Safety Section
No.2 Natural Resources Dr.
Little Rock, AR 72205
(501) 223-6377
Boat Registration:
(501) 371-2824

CALIFORNIA
Dept. of Boating & Waterways
1629 "S" St.
Sacramento, CA 95814
(916) 445-6281
Boat Registration:
(916) 732-7844

COLORADO
Div. of Parks & Outdoor Recreation
13787 So. Highway 85
Littleton, CO 80125
(303) 795-6954

CONNECTICUT
Dept. of Environmental Protection
Bureau of Law Enforcement
Marine Patrol Division
333 Ferry Rd.
Old Lyme, CT 06371
(203) 434-8638
Boat Registration:
(203) 566-3781

DELAWARE
Division of Fish & Wildlife
Richardson & Robbins Building
P.O. Box 1401
Dover, DE 19903
(302) 736-3440

FLORIDA
Dept. of Natural Resources
3900 Commonwealth Blvd.
Tallahassee, FL 32399-3000
(904) 487-3671
Boat Registration:
(904) 488-1195

GEORGIA
Dept. of Natural Resources
Game & Fish–Law Enforcement
205 Butler St., SE
East Tower, Suite 1366
Atlanta, GA 30334
(404) 656-3534/656-3510

HAWAII
Harbors Division
Dept. of Transportation
79 S. Nimitz Highway
Honolulu, HI 96813
(808) 548-2515/548-2838

IDAHO
Dept. of Parks & Recreation
Statehouse Mail
Boise, ID 83720
(208) 334-2284
Boat Registration:
(208) 334-3810

ILLINOIS
Dept. of Conservation
Division of Law Enforcement
524 South Second St.
Springfield, IL 62701-1787
(217) 782-6431

INDIANA
Law Enforcement Division
Dept. of Natural Resources
606 State Office Building
Indianapolis, IN 46204
(317) 232-4010

IOWA
State Conservation Comm.
Wallace Building
Des Moines, IA 50319
(515) 281-5919
Boat Registration:
(515) 281-4508

KANSAS
Kansas Dept. of Wildlife & Parks
Rt. 2, Box 54A
Pratt, KS 67124
(316) 672-5911, ext. 108

KENTUCKY
Dept. of Natural Resources
Kentucky Water Patrol
107 Mero St.
Frankfort, KY 40601
(502) 564-3074

LOUISIANA
Louisiana Dept. Wildlife & Fisheries
7389 Florida Blvd., 3rd Floor
P.O. Box 15570
Baton Rouge, LA 70895
(504) 925-4912

MAINE
Dept. Inland Fisheries & Wildlife
284 State St., Station 41
Augusta, ME 04333
Boat Registration:
(207) 289-2043
Law Enforcement:
(207) 289-2766
Boat Safety:
(207) 289-5220

MARYLAND
Dept. of Natural Resources
Tawes State Office Building
Annapolis, MD 21401
(301) 974-2240
Boat Registration & Titles:
(301) 974-3211

MASSACHUSETTS
Division of Law Enforcement
100 Cambridge St.
Boston, MA 02202
(617) 727-1614

Boat Registration:
(617) 727-3905

MICHIGAN
Dept. of Natural Resources
Steven T. Mason Building
P.O. Box 30028
Lansing, MI 48909
(517) 373-1650/373-1230
Boat Registration & Titles:
(517) 322-1528

MINNESOTA
Boat & Water Safety Section
Dept. of Natural Resources
Box 46, 500 Lafayette Rd.
St. Paul, MN 55155-4046
(612) 296-3310
Boat Registration:
(612) 296-4507
Public Water Access:
(612) 296-6413

MISSISSIPPI
Mississippi Dept. of Wildlife
  Conservation
P.O. Box 451
Jackson, MS 39205
(601) 961-5300

MISSOURI
Dept. of Public Safety
Missouri State Water Patrol
P.O. Box 603
Jefferson City, MO 65102-0603
(314) 751-3333
Boat Registration:
(314) 751-4509

MONTANA
Boating Safety Division
Dept. of Fish, Wildlife & Parks
1420 East 6th St.
Helena, MT 59620
(406) 444-4046
Boat Registration:
(406) 846-1424

NEBRASKA
State Game & Parks Commission
2200 North 33rd St.
P.O. Box 30370
Lincoln, NE 68503
(402) 464-0641

NEVADA
Nevada Dept. of Wildlife
Division of Law Enforcement
P.O. Box 10678
Reno, NV 89520
(702) 789-0500

NEW HAMPSHIRE
Dept. of Safety Marine Patrol
Hazen Dr.
Concord, NH 03305
(603) 271-3336/293-2037

NEW JERSEY
New Jersey State Police
Marine Law Enforcement Bureau
Box 7068
West Trenton, NJ 08628-0068
(609) 882-2000, ext. 2530
Boat Registration:
(609) 292-2452

NEW MEXICO
Natural Resources Dept.
State Park & Recreation Division
Boating Safety Section
P.O. Box 1147
Santa Fe, NM 87504-1147
(505) 827-3986
Boat Registration:
(505) 827-7465

NEW YORK
Office of Parks, Recreation
  & Historic Preservation
Marine & Recreational Vehicles
Agency Building No. 1
Empire State Plaza
Albany, NY 12238
(518) 474-0445

NORTH CAROLINA
Wildlife Resources Comm.
Archdale Building
Raleigh, NC 27611
(919) 733-7191

NORTH DAKOTA
ND Game & Fish Dept.
100 N. Bismarck Expressway
Bismarck, ND 58501-5095
(701) 221-6300

OHIO
Division of Watercraft
Dept. of Natural Resources
Fountain Square
Columbus, OH 43224
(614) 265-6480

OKLAHOMA
Dept. of Public Safety
P.O. Box 11415
Oklahoma City, OK 73136
(405) 424-4011, ext. 2143
Boat Registration:
(405) 521-2439

OREGON
State Marine Board
3000 Market St., NE, #505
Salem, OR 97310
(503) 378-8501

PENNSYLVANIA
Pennsylvania Fish Commission
3532 Walnut St.
P.O. Box 1673
Harrisburg, PA 17105-1673
(717) 657-4538

PUERTO RICO
Dept. of Natural Resources
Commission of Navigation
P.O. Box 5887
Puerto de Tierra, PR 00906
(809) 724-2340

RHODE ISLAND
Dept. of Environmental Mgt.
Boat Registration Office
22 Hayes St.
Providence, RI 02908
(401) 277-6647
Law Enforcement:
(401) 277-2284

SOUTH CAROLINA
Division of Boating
Wildlife & Marine Resources Dept.
P.O. Box 12559
Charleston, SC 29412
(803) 795-6350/734-3997

SOUTH DAKOTA
Dept. of Game, Fish & Parks
Anderson Building
445 E. Capitol
Pierre, SD 57501
(605) 773-3630/773-4506

TENNESSEE
Tennessee Wildlife Resources
  Agency
P.O. Box 40747
Ellington Agricultural Center
Nashville, TN 37204
(615) 360-0500

TEXAS
Parks and Wildlife Dept.
4200 Smith School Rd.
Austin, TX 78744
(512) 389-4850

U.S. VIRGIN ISLANDS
Dept. of Planning
  & Natural Resources
179 Altona & Welgunst
Charlotte Amalie
St. Thomas, VI 00802
(809) 774-3320

UTAH
Division of Parks & Recreation
1636 West North Temple St.
Salt Lake City, UT 84116
(801) 533-4490

VERMONT
Vermont State Police HQ
Marine Division
103 S. Main St., Rm. 221
Waterbury, VT 05676
(802) 244-8778

VIRGINIA
Commission of Game
  & Inland Fisheries
P.O. Box 11104
Richmond, VA 23230-1104
(804) 367-1000

WASHINGTON
State Parks & Rec. Comm.
7150 Cleanwater Lane (KY-11)
Olympia, WA 98504
(206) 586-2165
Boat Registration & Titles:
(206) 753-6920

WASHINGTON, DC
Metropolitan Police Dept.
Harbor Patrol
550 Water St., SW
Washington, DC 20024
(202) 727-4582

WEST VIRGINIA
Law Enforcement Division
Dept. of Natural Resources
1800 Washington St. E
Charleston, WV 25305
(304) 348-2783

WISCONSIN
Bureau of Law Enforcement
Dept. of Natural Resources
P.O. Box 7921
Madison, WI 53707
(608) 266-0859

WYOMING
Game & Fish Dept.
5400 Bishop Blvd.
Cheyenne, WY 82002
(307) 777-7605

CANADA
ONTARIO
Ministry of Natural Resources
Room 3423
Whitney Block, Queen's Park
Toronto, Ontario M7A 1W3
(416) 965-3238

BOATING ORGANIZATIONS

The organizations and government agencies listed (alphabetically) below serve a wide variety of functions for recreational boaters.

American Boat and Yacht Council, Inc., P.O. Box 747, 405 Headquarters Dr., Suite 3, Millersville, MD 21108, (301) 923-3932. Develops and publishes *Standards and Recommended Practices For Small Craft* on designing, building, equipping, and maintaining pleasure and commercial craft. Also publishes *Boating Information: A Bibliography and Source List,* which lists over 1,300 books, pamphlets, articles, and videos on boating topics.

American Boat Builders and Repairers Association, 715 Boylston St., Boston, MA 02116, (617) 266-6800. A national trade association of 300 boatyards, manufacturers, and marinas working to improve boating-industry repair and maintenance practices. Conducts Dispute Response Process to adjudicate disputes between member boatyards and their customers without litigation.

American Canoe Association, 8580 Cinderbed Rd., Suite 1900, P.O. Box 1190, Newington, VA 22122-1190, (703) 550-7523. National nonprofit organization offering comprehensive training in canoeing, kayaking, and instructor certification. Maintains rental film library, bookservice, free brochures.

American Power Boat Association, 17640 E. Nine Mile Rd., East Detroit, MI 48021, (313) 773-9700. National member organization and sanctioning body for powerboat events and professional racing in the U.S. Monthly publication: *Propeller.*

American Red Cross (national HQ), 17th & D Sts. NW, Washington, DC 20006, (202) 639-3686. Sponsors basic boating, rescue, swimming, and water safety courses. Teaches paddling, canoeing, kayaking, outboard boating, sailing, and rowing. Contact your local chapter. Publishes *Safe Boating* and *Safe Boating: A Parent's Guide.* Maintains audio-visual loan library at Frank Stanton Production Center, American Red Cross, 5816 Seminary Rd., Falls Church, VA 20041.

American Sail Training Association, 365 Thames St., Newport, RI 02840, (401) 846-1775. A national service organization and clearinghouse for sail training. Publishes a bimonthly newsletter and biennial directory of sail training ships and programs.

American Sailing Association, 13922 Marquesas Way, Marina del Rey, CA 90292, (213) 822-7171. Trains and certifies professional sailing instructors, offers public instruction through 150 affiliated sailing schools nationwide. Publishes *American Sailing* newsmagazine.

American Water Ski Association, P.O. Box 191, Winter Haven, FL 33880, (813) 324-4341. Organizing, sanctioning, and governing body for competitive U.S. water skiing. Promotes broader participation in the sport, certifies instructors, maintains legislative coordination and oversight and skier rating system. Publishes *Water Skier* magazine and instructional booklets on safety and water recreation.

Boat Owners Association of the United States (BOAT/U.S.), 880 S. Pickett St., Alexandria, VA 22304, (703) 823-9550. A national membership organization that represents the interests of its members before Congress and the federal agencies and publishes the authoritative newsjournal *BOAT/U.S. Reports.* Provides a wide variety of services including a Consumer Protection Bureau to help solve problems between boaters and the marine industry.

BOAT/U.S. Foundation, 880 S. Pickett St., Alexandria, VA 22304, (703) 823-9550. National nonprofit boating safety organization with toll-free CourseLine for information on free boating courses (800-336-BOAT; in VA, 800-245-BOAT). Researches boating accidents and safety issues; produces and distributes free safety literature; maintains national recreational boating reference library; promotes boating education.

Canadian Coast Guard, Canada Building, Minto Place, 344 Slater St., Ottawa, ONT K1A ON7, (613) 991-3119. Enforces boating restrictions and regulations for small vessels and pleasure boats. Publishes *Safe Boating Guide* (free) and other boating safety publications. For information on boating courses or to obtain copies of publications, call (613) 990-3116.

Defense Mapping Agency (DMA), Office of Distribution Services, Code: IMA, 6500 Brookes Lane, Washington, DC 20315, (202) 227-3048. Collects data to chart the world's navigable waters. Provides charts for U.S. defense effort and for recreational and commercial boaters.

Federal Communications Commission (FCC), Aviation & Marine Division, 2025 M St. NW, Washington,

DC 20554, (202) 632-7197. Regulates interstate and foreign radio and wire communications; prescribes qualifications and classifications for operators; issues operator and station licenses.

Insurance Information Institute, 110 William St., New York, NY 10038, (212) 669-9200. A national clearinghouse for information and research on property and casualty insurance. Provides financial ratings of companies, assists consumers in purchasing insurance and handling disputes with insurance companies. Sponsors a national hotline (1-800-221-4954) for insurance information.

Marine Retailers Association of America, 155 N. Michigan Ave., Suite 5230, Chicago, IL 60611, (312) 938-0359. National trade association of boat and equipment retailers.

National Boating Federation, Inc., 1000 Thomas Jefferson St. NW, Suite 525, Washington, DC 20007, (202) 338-5718. An alliance of state and regional boating organizations and boat clubs, chartered as a nonprofit corporation. Publishes bimonthly newsletter *Lookout.*

National Fire Protection Association, Batterymarch Park, Quincy, MA 02269, (617) 770-3000. Independent, nonprofit organization that develops and publishes fire safety standards and codes, and educational materials. Publishes two marine-related booklets, *Pleasure and Commercial Motor Craft* and *Marinas and Boatyards.* Toll-free ordering: 800-344-3555.

National Marine Manufacturers Association, 401 N. Michigan Ave., Chicago, IL 60611, (312) 836-4747. Trade association representing 1,400 boat, motor, and equipment manufacturers in legislative and industry-related matters. Sponsors major national boat shows. For 72-page booklet, *Boating Basics . . . Blueprint for Safe Boating,* send $1 for postage to above address.

National Oceanic and Atmospheric Administration (NOAA), National Ocean Service, Public Affairs Office, Room 5805 Herbert C. Hoover Building, Washington, DC 20230, (202) 377-4190. Collects, analyzes, and disseminates data and information on physical properties of oceans, U.S. coastal waters, estuaries, and Great Lakes. Publishes charts, tide and current tables, Coast Pilots, etc. To order NOAA/NOS charts and other publications, call or write: Distribution Branch, (N/CG33), National Ocean Service, Riverdale, MD 20737-1199. For credit card orders, call (301) 436-6990.

National Safe Boating Council, 2550 M St. NW, Suite 425, Washington, DC 20037, (202) 296-4588. National nonprofit organization with over 60 affiliated boating and boating safety groups. Annually sponsors National Safe Boating Week (begins first Sunday in June) and the National Boating Education Seminar (March). Publishes a Media Kit/Action Manual annually for National Safe Boating Week, and proceedings of the Education Seminar.

National Sailing Industry Association, 401 N. Michigan Ave., Chicago, IL 60611, (312) 836-4747. A trade association of sailing schools, sailboat and hardware manufacturers, and charter companies that promotes sailing and sailing education. Publishes the booklet *Community Sailing Programs.* Sponsors the Learn-to-Sail Hotline, 1-800-447-4700 for information on on-the-water commercial sailing instruction.

National Sea Grant Marine Advisory Service, 6010 Executive Blvd., Rockville, MD 20852, (301) 443-8886. A division of NOAA supporting a national network of over 200 universities and marine research institutions. Provides information to help improve productivity of marine resources through public education workshops, seminars, TV, and publications on Sea Grant research findings on marine resources, boating, coastal engineering, and environmental and economic impacts.

National Weather Service, Public Affairs Office, 8060 13th St., Silver Spring, MD 20910, (301)443-8910. Provides reporting, forecasting, broadcast, and warning services to promote navigation safety among private and commercial boaters.

Personal Watercraft Industry Association, 401 N. Michigan Ave., Chicago, IL 60611, (312) 836-4747. A trade association of personal watercraft manufacturers that sets performance and safety standards and promotes personal watercraft safety. Publishes the free booklet *Fun with Safety on your Personal Watercraft.*

Underwriters Laboatories, Inc., P.O. Box 13995, 12 Laboratory Drive, Research Triangle Park, NC 27709, (919) 549-1565. Nonprofit independent organization testing for public safety. Tests marine products; develops marine safety standards. Publishes *Marine Products Directory* and *Standards for Safety for Recreational Boats.* Order publications from: Underwriters

Laboratories, Inc., Publications Stock, 333 Pfingsten Rd., Northbrook, IL 60062.

U.S. Army Corps of Engineers, HQUSACE (DAEN-CWO-R), 20 Massachusetts Ave. NW, Washington, DC 20314-1000, (202) 272-0247. Improves navigation, reduces flood damage, protects environment, and promotes safe boating on nation's waterways and other civic works. Call for address and phone of your district office.

U.S. Coast Guard (Boating Safety), Commandant (G-NAB), 2100 Second St. SW, Washington, DC 20593-0001, (202) 267-0972. Minimizes loss of life and property on high seas and U.S. waters through search and rescue, assures safety and security of vessels, installs and maintains aids to navigation, enforces laws, promotes safety among commercial and recreational boaters. Publishes consumer fact sheets for boaters, *Federal Requirements for Recreational Boats,* and more. Toll-free Boating Safety Hotline: 1-800-368-5647.

U.S. Coast Guard Auxiliary, Commandant (G-NAB), 2100 Second St. SW, Washington, DC 20593-0001, (202) 267-0972. Voluntary civilian arm of the U.S. Coast Guard. Sponsors free boating courses, conducts Courtesy Marine Exams (CMEs), patrols marine events and regattas, assists boaters in distress. For boating course information: 1-800-336-BOAT (in VA, 1-800-245-BOAT).

U.S. Customs Service, Carrier Rulings Branch, Washington, DC 20029, (202) 566-3962. Controls importation and reporting requirements for vessels entering the U.S. Publishes *Pleasure Boats,* describing reporting and U.S. entry requirements for recreational boaters.

U.S. Fish & Wildlife Service, Division of Federal Aid, 18th and C Sts. NW, Washington, DC 20240, (703) 235-1526. Provides grants through federal Sport Fishing Restoration Trust to states to construct and improve boating access facilities. Also provides grants through Hunter Education and and Aquatic Resources to states to encourage safe boating practices.

U.S. Power Squadrons (National Headquarters), 1504 Blue Ridge Rd., P.O. Box 30423, Raleigh, NC 27622, (919) 821-0281. Private nonprofit national member organization of boating enthusiasts. Over 500 local squadrons offer free public boating courses. For USPS boating course information: Call 1-800-336-BOAT (in VA, 1-800-245-BOAT).

U.S. Yacht Racing Union (USYRU), Box 209, Newport, RI 02840, (401) 849-5200. Official governing body and national authority for offshore, one-design, sailboard, and multihull sailboat racing in the U.S. Trains sailing instructors, produces learn-to-sail manuals and videotapes. Publishes monthly *American Sailor* and *International Yacht Racing Rules* rulebook.

STANDARDS, TESTING, REGULATIONS

Chief, Office of Boating Safety (G-8)
United States Coast Guard
Washington, DC 20590

American Boat and Yacht Council
15 E. 26th St.
New York, NY 10010

Lloyd's Register of Shipping
Yacht and Small Craft Department
69 Oxford St.
Southampton S01 1DL, England

Underwriters Laboratory
12 Laboratory Dr.
P.O. Box 13995
Research Triangle Park, NC 27709-3995
(919) 549-1400

Underwriters Laboratory publishes a *Marine Products Directory* containing listed and classified marine products as well as recognized marine components.

International Maritime Consultative Organization
Publications Section
4 Albert Embankment
London SE1 75R
(01) 735-7611

RADIO AND COMMUNICATIONS INFORMATION

Radio Technical Commission for Maritime Services
P.O. Box 19087
Washington, DC 20036

Federal Communications Commission
Public Services Division
Field Operations Bureau
1919 M St. NW
Washington, DC 20554

FCC Private Radio Bureau
Licensing Division
P.O. Box 1040
Gettysburg, PA 17325

TRAVEL AND CUSTOMS

U.S. Customs Service
Department of the Treasury
Washington, DC

NAVIGATION

National Oceanic & Atmospheric Administration
(NOAA)
Herbert Hoover Bldg.
Washington, DC 20230

New York Nautical Instrument Co.
140 West Broadway
New York, NY 10013
(212) 962-4522

Southwest Instrument Co.
235 W. Seventh St.
San Pedro, CA 90831
(213) 519-7800

Marine Educator Textbooks
124 North Van Ave.
Houma, LA 70360-3866
(504) 879-3866

HAZARDOUS MATERIALS, POLLUTION, AND HAZARD PROTECTION

National Institute for Occupational Safety and Health
(NIOSH)
4676 Columbia Parkway
Cincinnati, OH 45226

Occupational Safety and Health Administration
(OSHA)
U.S. Department of Labor
200 Constitution Ave.
Washington, DC 20246

National Clearinghouse for Poison Control Centers
Food and Drug Administration
Department of Health & Human Services
5401 Westbard Ave.
Bethesda, MD 20016

SOLAS—Safety of Life at Sea
Regulations can be obtained from
International Maritime Consultative Organization
Publications Section
4 Albert Embankment
London SE1 75R, England

SOURCES AND RESOURCES:
SAFETY AND RELATED EQUIPMENT

Alarms, Monitors, and Warning Equipment

Anchor and Off-Course Alarm
First Mate
41 Kindred St.
Stuart, FL 34994
(407) 286-4480

Battery Alarms
Balmar
1537 N.W. Ballard Way
Seattle, WA 98107
(206) 789-4970

Battery Alarm (Low Power)
Spa Creek Div., Landmark Marine
612 Third St.
Annapolis, MD 21403
(301) 267-6565

Bilgewater Alarm
Sensatron
7551 Convoy Ct.
San Diego, CA 92111
(619) 268-0099

Burglar Alarms

Sentry Devices
33 Rustic Gate Lane
Di Hills, NY 11746
(516) 491-3191

Brisson Development
13845 Nine Mile Dr.
Warren, MI 48089
(313) 778-3038

Electrolysis Indicator and Electrical Condition Alarms
Professional Mariner
1565 Callens Rd., Suite A
Ventura, CA 93003
(805) 644-1886

Fire, Engine Oil, Engine Water Flooding Alarms
Aqualarm
1151 D Bay Blvd.
Chula Vista, CA 92011
(619) 575-4011

Flooding Alarm
Datasonic
255 E. Second St.
Mineola, NY 11501
(516) 248-7330

Gas Vapor and Carbon Monoxide Alarms
Rule Industries
Cape Ann Industrial Park
Gloucester, MA 01930
(508) 281-0440

High- and Low-Voltage Alarms
Professional Mariner
1565 Callens Rd., Suite A
Ventura, CA 93003
(805) 644-1886

Man-Overboard Alarm
MSTS, Marine Safe Telemetry Systems
800 Del Grove Ave.
Newark, DE 19713
(302) 366-8073

Remote Telephone Boat Monitors
Metro Auto and Marine Accessories
P.O. Box 3629
Annapolis, MD 21403
(301) 263-7608

Reversed-Polarity Indicators
Raritan Engineering
530 Orange St.
Millville, NJ 08332
(609) 825-4900

Smoke and Fume Alarms
Insta-Sniff Div. of Kercheval Ind.
7390 Pasadena Blvd.
St. Louis, MO 63121
(314) 385-7470

Strobe Alarms
ACR Electronics
5757 Ravenswood Rd.
Fort Lauderdale, FL 33312
(305) 981-3333

Tank Level Alarm
Modern Automation
3209 Rymal Rd.
Mississauga, Ont. L4Y 3B8, Canada

Anchors and Mooring Equipment

Anchors and Rollers
A&B Industries
415 Tamal Plaza
200 Tamal Vista Blvd.
Corte Madera, CA 94925
(415) 924-1300

Chafe Guards
Samson Ocean Systems
P.O. Box 1127
Anniston, AL 36202
(800) 722-2673

Chain, Claw-Type Anchors
Wilcox-Crittenden
699 Middle St.
Middletown, CT 06457
(203) 632-2600

CQR Plow Anchors
Simpson-Lawrence
Jay Stuart Haft
Box 11210
Bradenton, FL 34282-1210

Danforth-Type Anchors
Rule Industries
Cape Ann Industrial Park
Gloucester, MA 01930
(508) 281-0440

Mooring Snubbers
Avon Seagull Marine
1851 McGaw Ave.
Irvine, CA 92714
(714) 250-0880

Windlasses/Capstans

Jay Stuart Haft
Box 11210
Bradenton, FL 34282-1210
(813) 746-7161

W.H. Denouden (USA)
P.O. Box 8712
Baltimore, MD 21240
(301) 796-4740

Ideal Windlass
P.O. Box 430
Dept. 7
E. Greenwich, RI 02818

Lunenburg Foundry & Engineering
Lunenburg, Nova Scotia B0J 2C0
  Canada

*Yachtsman's Anchors
(including hard-to-find Herreshoff
  Anchor)*
Paul E. Luke
Box 816
E. Boothbay, ME 04544
(207) 633-4971

Charts and Navigation Publications

Books and Charts (Navigation)
Armchair Sailor International
126 Thames St.
Newport, RI 02840
(401) 847-4252

Boating Almanac
203 McKinsey Rd.
Severna Park, MD 21146

Celestial Products
10 W. Washington St.
Box 801-B
Middleburg, VA 22117
(703) 687-6881

Kleid Navigation
443 Ruane St.
Fairfield, CT 06430
(203) 259-7161

C. Plath N. America,
  Div. of Litton Systems
222 Severn Ave.
Annapolis, MD 21403
(301) 263-6700

Navigation Texts
Naval Institute Press
Annapolis, MD 21402
(301) 268-6110

Tide Books ("Eldridge's")
Robert E. White Instruments
34 Commercial Wharf
Boston, MA 02110
(617) 742-3045

Waterproof Charts
Better Boating Association
P.O. Box 407
Needham, MA 02102
(800) 242-7854

International Sailing Supply
320 Cross St.
Punta Gorda, FL 33950
(813) 639-7626

Damage-Control Equipment

Rigging Cutters
Bay Sailing Equipment
986 Cherry St.
Fall River, MA 02720
(508) 678-4419

Loos & Co.
One Cable Rd.
Pomfret, CT 06528
(203) 928-7981

Norseman Marine
516 W. Olas Blvd.
Fort Lauderdale, FL 33312
(305) 467-1407

*Water-Activated Fiberglass Cloth
  for Emergency Repairs*
Neptune Research
2611 Old Okeechobee Rd., Suite 3
W. Palm Beach, FL 33409
(407) 683-6992

Davits

Aluminum Davits
"Vetus," W.H. Denouden (USA)
P.O. Box 8712
Baltimore, MD 21240
(301) 796-4740

*Polyurethane-Coated
  Aluminum Davits*
Edson
Ten Industrial Park Rd.
New Bedford, MA 02745
(508) 995-9711

Stainless Quick-Release Davits
A&B Industries
415 Tamal Plaza
200 Tamal Vista Blvd.
Corte Madera, CA 94925
(415) 924-1300

Stainless Steel Davits
Stonington Stainless
RD2, Box 142
Taugwonk Rd.
Stonington, CT 06378
(203) 535-1355

Dayshapes and Other Signals

Anchor Ball and Steam Cone
Basic Designs
5815 Bennett Valley Rd.
Santa Rosa, CA 95404
(707) 575-1220

Black Ball and Cone Shapes
Plastimo USA
6605 Selnick Dr.
Rte. 100 Business Park
Baltimore, MD 21227
(301) 796-0002

Dayshapes
Atlantic Pacific
200 Mt. Pleasant Ave.
Newark, NJ 07104
(800) 526-1293

Deck Fittings

Boom Gallows Fittings
A&B Industries
415 Tamal Plaza
200 Tamal Vista Blvd.
Corte Madera, CA 94925
(415) 924-1300

Bowsprit and Gallows Fittings
New Found Metals
240 Airport Rd.
Port Townsend, WA 98368
(206) 385-3315

Deckplates and Scuppers
Lunenburg Foundry & Engineering
P.O. Box 1240
Lunenburg, Nova Scotia B0J 2C0,
    Canada

*Helmsman Seats, Pedestal
    Accessories*
Edson
Ten Industrial Park Rd.
New Bedford, MA 02745
(508) 995-9711

Safety Horseshoe Holders
S&J Products
P.O. Box 2099
Chicago, IL 60690
(312) 935-6210

Steering Pedestal Accessories
Merriman Yacht Specialties
301 Olive St.
Grand River, OH 44045

Winch Handle Holders

Beckson Marine
P.O. Box 3336
Bridgeport, CT 06605
(203) 333-1412

Nicro-Fico
675 Brannan St.
San Francisco, CA 94107
(415) 283-3335

Desalinators and Emergency Watermakers

*Hand-Operated Reverse-Osmosis
    Emergency Watermaker*
Recovery Engineering
1204 Chestnut Ave.
Minneapolis, MN 55403
(612) 333-6828

Survival Still
W.L. Gore Assoc.
4747 Beautiful Lane
Phoenix, AZ 85044
(602) 431-0077

Dinghies

Fiberglass Dinghies
The Anchorage
65 Miller St.
Warren, RI 02885
(401) 245-3300

Folding Dinghies
Britannia Boats
P.O. Box 5033
Annapolis, MD 21666
(301) 269-6617

Inflatable Dinghies

Achilles Inflatable Craft
390 Murray Hill Parkway
E. Rutherford, NJ 07073
(201) 438-6400

Avon Seagull Marine
1851 McGaw Ave.
Irvine, CA 92714
(714) 250-0880

IMTRA
30 Sam Barnett Blvd.
New Bedford, MA 02745
(508) 990-2700

Sailing Inflatables
Sea Dory Rigid Inflatable Boats
P.O. Box P-48
S. Dartmouth, MA 02478

Zodiac of North America
P.O. Box 400
Thompson Creek Rd.
Stevensville, MD 21666
(301) 643-4141

Wooden Whitehall Skiffs
Shew & Burnham
S. Bristol, ME 04568
(207) 644-8120

Wood Sailing-Type Prams
WoodenBoat Catalog
P.O. Box 78
Brooklin, ME 04616

Distress Signals and Equipment

Distress Flag

Annin & Co.
55 Locust Ave.
Roseland, NJ 07068
(201) 228-9400

Flares and Smoke Signals

Bristol Flare
P.O. Box 540
Bristol, PA 19007
(215) 788-3001

Kilgore
Rte. 138
Bradford Rd.
Toone, TN 38381
(901) 658-5231

Olin Signal Products Operation
East Alton, Il 62024
(618) 258-3130

Revere Survival Products
603 W. 29th St.
New York, NY 10001
(212) 736-5400

Sigma Scientific
1830 S. Baker Ave.
Ontario, CA 91761
(714) 947-6600

Light Signals

ACR Electronics
5757 Ravenswood Rd.
Fort Lauderdale, FL 33312
(305) 981-3333

Light Sticks

American Cyanamid
Chemical Light Dept.
One Cyanamid Plaza
Wayne, NJ 07470
(201) 831-2000

Morse Code Flasher

Aqua Signal
33 W. 480 Fabyan Pkwy.
W. Chicago, IL 60185
(312) 232-6425

Electrical Equipment and Supplies

Alternators

C.E. Niehoff and Co.
4925 W. Lawrence St.
Chicago, IL 60603

Auto-Gen
Mercantile Manufacturing Co.
Box 895
Minden, LA 71055

*Automatic Alternator
Charge Controller*

Spa Creek Div., Landmark Marine
612 Third St.
Annapolis, MD 21403
(301) 267-6565

Automatic Switches, Solenoids

Automatic Switch
50-60 Hanover Rd.
Florham Park, NJ

Batteries

General Battery
P.O. Box 14205
Reading, PA 19612-4205
(215) 378-0500

Surrette America
P.O. Box 249
Tilton, NH 03276
(603) 286-8974

*Battery Chargers, Converters,
Inverters*

La Marche
106 Bradrock
Des Plaines, IL 60018
(312) 299-1188

Marine Development
P.O. Box 15299
Richmond, VA 23227
(804) 746-1313

Newmar
P.O. Box 1306
Newport Beach, CA 92663
(714) 751-0488

Battery Charge Indicators

Sea-Air
Route 16, Box 338
Chocorua, NH 03817
(603) 323-8102

SSI (Sailing Specialties)
P.O. Box 99
Commerce Ave.
Hollywood Ind. Pk
Hollywood, MD 20636
(301) 373-2372

Battery Switches

Cole Hersee
20 Old Colony Ave.
S. Boston, MA 02127
(617) 268-2100

Guest
48 Elm St.
Meriden, CT 06450
(203) 238-0550

Marinetics
P.O. Box 2676
Newport Beach, CA 92663
(714) 646-8889

*Circuit Breakers/Overcurrent
Protections*

Heinemann Electric
P.O. Box 6800
Lawrenceville, NJ 08648-0800
(609) 882-4800

Current Limiting Converter
Raritan Engineering
530 Orange St.
Millville, NJ 08332
(609) 825-4900

*Electrical/Electronic Measurement
 and Test Equipment*

Burton Rogers
220 Grove St.
Waltham, MA 02154
(617) 894-6440

John Fluke
P.O. Box C9090
Everett, WA 98206
(206) 356-5400

Electrical Panels
Bass Products
50 Grove St.
Salem, MA 01970
(508) 744-7003

Electrical Supplies

Belden Corporation
2200 Kensington Ct., Suite 300
Oak Brook, IL 60521

Allied Radio
12311 Industry St.
Garden Grove, CA 92641

Generators
Onan
1400 73rd Ave., N.E.
Minneapolis, MN 55432
(612) 574-5000

Ground Fault Interruptors
Pass & Seymour
50 Boyd Ave.
Syracuse, NY 13221

Isolation Transformers
La Marche
106 Bradrock
Des Plaines, IL 60018
(312) 299-1188

Isolator Charge Dividers
RGM Industries
3342 Lillian Blvd.
Titusville, FL 33714
(407) 269-4720

Panel Switches
Perko
P.O. Box 64000D
Miami, FL 33164
(305) 621-7525

Shaft-Driven Alternator
Sail Charger
2895 46th Ave.
N. St. Petersburg, FL 33714
(813) 522-9471

Shore-Power Cable and Fittings
Hubbell
P.O. Box 3999
Bridgeport, CT 06605
(203) 333-1181

*Shore-Power Cable Connection
 Alarm*
Omnifac
1700 E. Whipp Rd.
Dayton, OH 45440
(513) 434-8400

*Shorepower/Onboard
 Transfer Switches*
Onan
1400 73rd Ave., N.E.
Minneapolis, MN 55432
(612) 574-5000

Solar Panels

AEG
P.O. Box 3800
Somerville, NJ 08876-1269
(201) 722-9800

Atlantic Solar Products
P.O. Box 70060
Baltimore, MD 21237
(301) 686-2500

Solar-Powered Battery Chargers

Energy Sciences
16728 Oakmount Ave.
Gaithersburg, MD 20877
(301) 544-1404

Haines Solar Energy
Dept. M15
2720 N. 68th St.
Scottsdale, AZ 85257
(602) 481-6974

Portable Solar Chargers
Solar Electric Engineering
175 Cascade Ct.
Rohnert Park, CA 94928
(800) 832-1986

Solar Modules
Solarex
1335 Piccard Dr.
Rockville, MD 20850
(301) 948-0202

Solar Regulator Monitor
Solmate Solar Products
11648 Manor Rd.
Glen Arm, MD 21057
(301) 661-9880

Switchpanels
Marinetics Corp.
P.O. Box 2676
Newport Beach, CA 92663

Switches and Outlets
Cole Hersee
20 Old Colony Ave.
S. Boston, MA 02127
(617) 268-2100

*Water-/Explosion-Proof
 Starter Switches*
Nartron
5000 No. U.S. Rte. 131
Reed City, MI 49677
(616) 832-5525

Watertight Electrical Connectors
Aqua Signal
33 W. 480 Fabyan Pkwy
W. Chicago, IL 60185
(312) 232-6425

Waterproof Plugs and Sockets
Jay Stuart Haft
Box 11210
Bradenton, FL 34282-1210
(813) 746-7161

Windlass Heavy-Duty Breakers

South Pacific Assoc.
4918 Leary Way N.W.
Seattle, WA 98107
(206) 782-7700

Marinetics
P.O. Box 2676
Newport Beach, CA 92663
(714) 646-8889

Professional Mariner
1565 Callens Rd., Suite A
Ventura, CA 93003
(805) 644-1886

Wiring Accessories

Accel Performer Products
P.O. Box 142
Branford, CT 06405
(203) 481-5771

AMP Industrial Div.
Valley Forge, PA 19482
(215) 647-1000

Emergency Equipment

Catamaran Righting System
Lake Enterprises
76 Pinon Heights Rd.
Sandia Park, NM 87047
(505) 281-5601

Collapsible Anchor
Nav-X
1386 W. McNab Rd.
Fort Lauderdale, FL 33309
(305) 978-9988

Survival Cards
P.O. Box 1805
Bloomington, IN 47402
(812) 336-8206

Emergency Rations, Survival Food

Emergency Water (Flexipaks)
ACR Electronics
5757 Ravenswood Rd.
Fort Lauderdale, FL 33312
(305) 981-3333

Freeze-Dried and Dehydrated Foods

Food Reserves
P.O. Box 456
Dania, FL 33004
(305) 733-9578

Stow-A-Way Industries
P.O. Box 967 Hwy.
E. Greenwich, RI 02818
(401) 885-6899

EPIRBs (Emergency Position Indicating Radio Beacons)

ACR Electronics
5757 Ravenswood Rd.
Fort Lauderdale, FL 33312
(305) 981-3333

Emergency Beacon
15 River St.
New Rochelle, NY 10801
(914) 235-9400

Guest
48 Elm St.
Meriden, CT 06450
(203) 238-0550

Fenders and Buoys

Buoys
Cal-June
5238 Vineland Ave.
N. Hollywood, CA 91601
(213) 761-3516

Fenders and Buoys

W.H. Denouden (USA)
P.O. Box 8712
Baltimore, MD 21240
(301) 796-4740

Jabsco Products ITT
1485 Dale Way
Costa Mesa, CA 02626
(714) 545-8251

Fenders and Fender Guards
Nelson A. Taylor
10 W. 9th Ave.
Gloversville, NY 12078
(518) 725-0661

Firefighting Equipment: Extinguishers

American LaFrance
P.O. Box 6159
Charlottesville, VA 22906
(804) 973-4361

Ansul Fire Protection
One Stanton St.
Marinette, WI 54143
(715) 735-7411

Falcon Safety Products
1065 Bristol Rd.
Mountainside, NJ 07092
(201) 233-5000

Fireboy
P.O. Box 152
Grand Rapids, MI 49502-0152
(616) 454-8337

Walter Kidde
1394 S. Third St.
Mebane, NC 27302
(919) 563-5911

Sea Fire Extinguishing
   Marine Products
Div. of Metalcraft
718 Debelius Ave.
Baltimore, MD 21205
(301) 485-0882

First-Aid Equipment

Dental Emergency Kit
Dental Aide Products
P.O. Box 1164
Rahway, NJ 07065
(201) 381-8969

Emergency Oxygen Kits
General Scientific Equipment
1821 J.F. Kennedy Blvd.
Philadelphia, PA 19103
(800) 523-0166

First-Aid Kits and Supplies
North Health Care
1515 Elmwood Rd.
Rockford, IL 61103
(815) 877-2531

General First-Aid Kits
Sentinel Consumer Products
7750 Tyler Blvd.
Mentor, OH 44060
(216) 974-8144

Oxygen and Resuscitation Units
Mada Marine Oxygen
60 Commerce Rd.
Carlstadt, NJ 07072
(201) 460-0454

Flag Signals

*International Code of
   Signals Flag Set*
Import Marine
P.O. Box 3214
Norfolk, VA 23514
(804) 622-7859

Flags and Signals
Annin & Co.
55 Locust Ave.
Roseland, NJ 07068
(201) 228-9400

Visual Distress Flags
ACR Electronics
5757 Ravenswood Rd.
Fort Lauderdale, FL 33312
(305) 981-3333

Flotation Materials

Flotation Systems
Myriad Marine Sales
P.O. Box 201
Crystal Lake, IL 60014
(815) 455-0405

Flotation Bags
Switlik Parachute
P.O. Box 1328
Trenton, NJ 08607
(609) 587-3300

Fog Signals

Hailer/Foghorn Combination
Cybernet/Kyocera
100 Randolph Rd., CN 6700
Somerset, NJ 08873

Power Megaphone
ACR Electronics
5757 Ravenswood Rd.
Fort Lauderdale, FL 33312
(305) 981-3333

Galley Equipment

Nonskid Pads
Medof Marine
5320 Derry Ave., Suite N
Agoura Hills, CA 91301
(818) 707-2991

Nonskid Tableware
Yachting Tableware
P.O. Box 546
Wilmington, DE 19899
(302) 655-9168

Nonslip Locker Lining Material
Dycem
P.O. Box 6920
83 Gilbane St.
Warwick, RI 02887
(800) 458-0060

Unbreakable Storage Bottles
Dry Top
610-C Bicycle Path N.
Port Jefferson, NY 11776
(516) 473-1231

Waterproof Matches

Coghlan's
121 Irene St.
Winnipeg, R3T 4C7, Canada

Davis Instruments
3465 Diablo Ave.
Hayward, CA 94545-2746
(415) 732-9229

Ground Plates and
Lightning Protection

Guest
48 Elm St.
Meriden, CT 06450
(203) 238-0550

Lightning Electronics
Box 1207
Cabot, AR 72023
(501) 843-6561

Harnesses and Related Gear

Harnesses and Tethers
Survival Technologies Group
Marine Challenge
101 16th Ave.
St. Petersburg, FL 33701
(800) 525-2747

Heavy-Duty Offshore Harness
Lirakis Safety Harness
18 Sheffield Ave.
Newport, RI 02840
(401) 846-5356

Safety Harnesses

Cal-June
5238 Vineland Ave.
N. Hollywood, CA 91601
(213) 761-3516

Forespar
22322 Gilberto Rd.
Santa Margarita, CA 92688
(714) 858-8820

Safety Hooks (Double-Acting)
Bay Sailing Equipment
986 Cherry St.
Fall River, MA 02720
(508) 678-4419

Hatches

Acrylic, Aluminum, Plastic Hatches
W.H. Denouden (USA)
P.O. Box 8712
Baltimore, MD 21240
(301) 796-4740

*Aluminum Hinged and
   Sliding Hatches*
Bomar
P.O. Box W
Charlestown, NH 03603
(603) 826-5794

Fiberglass Hinged Hatches
Plastimo USA
6605 Selnick Dr.
Rte. 100 Business Park
Baltimore, MD 21227
(301) 796-0002

*Glass-Reinforced,
   Plastic-Hinged Hatches*
Forespar
22322 Gilberto Rd.
Santa Margarita, CA 92688
(714) 858-8820

Stainless Hinged Hatches
Hood Yacht Systems
Maritime Drive
Portsmouth, RI 02871
(401) 683-2900

Horns, Bells, and Sound Signals

Horns
Buell
P.O. Box 303
8125 W. 47th St.
Lyons, IL 60534
(312) 447-6320

Megaphones and Foghorns
Fanon/Courier
14281 Chambers Rd.
Tustin, CA 92680
(800) 345-1354

Mouth-Operated Foghorns
Gem Marine Products
140 Industrial Loop
Orange Park, FL 32073
(904) 264-0173

Jay Stuart Haft
Box 11210
Bradenton, FL 34282-1210
(813) 746-7161

Portable Push-Button Horns
Falcon Safety Products
1065 Bristol Rd.
Mountainside, NJ 07092
(201) 233-5000

Inspection Ports (Plastic)

Beckson Marine
P.O. Box 3336
Bridgeport, CT 06605
(203) 333-3412

Forespar
22322 Gilberto Rd.
Santa Margarita, CA 92688
(714) 858-8820

Nicro-Fico
675 Brannan St.
San Francisco, CA 94107
(415) 283-3335

Ladders (Boarding Type)

Aluminum Folding Ladders
Sea-Link
P.O. Box 637
St. Joseph, MI 49085
(616) 429-4463

Boarding Ladder Hardware
A&B Industries
415 Tamal Plaza
200 Tamal Vista Blvd.
Corte Madera, CA 94925
(415) 924-1300

Folding Boarding Ladder
American Ladder
2120 S.W. 58th Ave.
Hollywood, FL 33023
(305) 962-0077

Hinged Transom Ladder
High Seas
4861 24th Ave.
Port Huron, MI 48060
(313) 385-4411

Ladder Hardware
Buck Algonquin Marine Hardware
1565 Palmyra Bridge Rd.
Pennsauken, NJ 08110
(609) 665-9405

Stainless Ladders
Seabrite Stainless Steel of Florida
424 DeLeon Ave.
Titusville, FL 32796
(407) 269-7812

Transom Ladders
Garelick
644 2nd St.
St. Paul, MN 55071
(612) 459-9795

Life Jackets and Life Vests

Automatic and Inflatable Gear
Quality Marine Products
4880 Church Lane
Galesville, MD 20765
(301) 867-1462

"Fastnet" Inflatable Vest/Harness
Switlik Parachute
P.O. Box 1328
Trenton, NJ 08607
(609) 587-3300

Viking Life-Saving Equipment
38 N.W. 11th St.
Miami, FL 33136
(305) 374-5115

*Standard Life Jackets, Vests, and
    Other Personal Flotation Devices*

Atlantic Pacific
200 Mt. Pleasant Ave.
Newark, NJ 07104
(800) 526-1293

Douglas Gill USA
Div. Weathermark
6087 Holiday Rd.
Buford, GA 30518
(404) 945-9463

Mustang
P.O. Box 5844
2171 E. Bakerview Rd.
Bellingham, WA 98227
(800) 533-5628

Omega
130 Condor St.
East Boston, MA 02128
(617) 569-3400

Stearns
P.O. Box 1498
St. Cloud, MN 56302
(612) 252-1642

Lifelines, Stanchions, Pulpits, and Related Equipment

Aluminum Handrail Fittings
Hollaender
10285 Wayne Ave.
P.O. Box 156399
Cincinnati, OH 45215-6399
(513) 772-8800

Bronze Stanchion Hardware
Buck Algonquin Marine Hardware
1565 Palmyra Bridge Rd.
Pennsauken, NJ 08110
(609) 665-9405

Fittings
Merriman Yacht Specialties
301 Olive St.
Grand River, OH 44045
(216) 352-8988

Fittings and Vinyl-Coated Lifelines
MacWhyte Wire Rope
2906 14th Ave.
Kenosha, WI 53141
(414) 654-5381

Lifeline Wire, Fittings, Safety Net
C. Sherman Johnson
Industrial Park
East Haddam, CT 06423
(203) 873-8697

Pulpits
Fortress Marine Design Prod. Div.
P.O. Box 6102
Clearwater, FL 34618
(813) 581-9991

Pulpits, Stanchions, and Rails
Ocean Engineering
232 Branford Rd.
Branford, CT 06471
(203) 488-4552

Stainless Stanchions
W.H. Denouden (USA)
P.O. Box 8712
Baltimore, MD 21240
(301) 796-4740

Life Rafts

Avon Inflatables (East Coast)
IMTRA
30 Sam Barnett Blvd.
New Bedford, MA 02745
(508) 990-2700

Avon Inflatables (West Coast)
Avon Seagull Marine
1851 McGaw Ave.
Irvine, CA 92714
(714) 250-0880

Givens Ocean Survival Systems
1741 Main Rd.
Tiverton, RI 02878
(800) 328-8050

B.F. Goodrich Engineered
    Rubber Products
1555 Corporate Woods Pkwy.,
    Suite 500
P.O. Box 1299
Uniontown, OH 44685-1299
(216) 374-4269

Survival and Safety Designs
1 Fifth Ave.
Oakland, CA 94606

Switlik Parachute
P.O. Box 1328
Trenton, NJ 08607
(609) 587-3300

Viking Life-Saving Equipment
38 N.W. 11th St.
Miami, FL 33136
(305) 374-5115

Winslow
928 S. Tamiami Dr.
P.O. Box 917
Osprey, FL 34229
(813) 966-2114

Zodiac of North America
P.O. Box 400
Thompson Creek Rd.
Stevensville, MD 21666
(301) 643-4141

Life Rings and Horseshoes

*Circular-Type, Horseshoe, and
   Rescue Floats*
Atlantic Pacific
200 Mt. Pleasant Ave.
Newark, NJ 07104
(800) 526-1293

Horseshoes
Cal-June
5238 Vineland Ave.
N. Hollywood, CA 91601
(213) 761-3516

Horseshoes and Holders
Forespar
22322 Gilberto Rd.
Santa Margarita, CA 92688
(714) 858-8820

Traditional Life Rings
Hinckley Shipstore
Southwest Harbor, ME 04679
(207) 244-5531

Lightning Rods and Ground Devices

Ground Plates
Guest
48 Elm St.
Meriden, CT 06450
(203) 238-0550

Lightning Rods
Lightning Electronics
Box 1207
Cabot, AR 72023
(501) 843-6561

Lights

Anchor Lights
Wilcox-Crittenden
699 Middle St.
Middletown, CT 06457
(203) 632-2600

Chart Lights
Bass Products
P.O. Box 901
Marblehead, MA 01945

Guest
48 Elm St.
Meriden, CT 06450
(203) 238-0550

Emergency Strobe Light
Brisson Development
13845 Nine Mile Dr.
Warren, MI 48089
(313) 778-3038

Foredeck Lights
A&B Industries
415 Tamal Plaza
200 Tamal Vista Blvd.
Corte Madera, CA 94925
(415) 924-1300

Halogen Lights
Hellamarine
P.O. Box 1064
42 Jackson Dr.
Cranford, NJ 07016
(201) 272-1400

Interior and Running Lights
Wilcox-Crittenden
699 Middle St.
Middletown, CT 06457
(203) 632-2600

Running and Signal Lights
Aqua Signal
33 W. 480 Fabyan Pkwy.
W. Chicago, IL 60185
(312) 232-6425

Sail Illumination Lights
Barnegat Light Marine Products
10 W. College Ave.
Yardley, PA 19067
(215) 493-2777

Searchlights
ACR Electronics
5757 Ravenswood Rd.
Fort Lauderdale, FL 33312
(305) 981-3333

Spreader Lights
Perko
P.O. Box 64000D
Miami, FL 33164
(305) 621-7525

Maintenance and Repair

Crack-Detector Kit
Ameritech Industries
Redding Municipal Airport
Redding, CA 96002
(916) 221-2225

Knives
Lirakis Safety Harness Co.
18 Sheffield Ave.
Newport, RI 02840
(401) 846-5356

Leather (Chafe Guards)
Edson
Ten Industrial Park Rd.
New Bedford, MA 02745
(308) 467-8325

Rigging Knives
Murphy Co.
13 Groton-Harvard Rd.
Ayer, MA 01432
(508) 772-3481

Sealing and Waterproof Tapes
S & J Products
P.O. Box 2099
Chicago, IL 60690
(312) 935-6210

Swage and Nicopress Tools
S & F Tools
1245 Logan Ave.
P.O. Box 1546
Costa Mesa, CA 92626
(714) 546-8073

Winch Maintenance Kit
Barient (IMI)
P.O. Box 308
New Whitfield St.
Guilford, CT 06437
(203) 453-4374

Man-Overboard Lights

ACR Electronics
5757 Ravenswood Rd.
Fort Lauderdale, FL 33312
(305) 981-3333

Cal-June
5238 Vineland Ave.
N. Hollywood, CA 91601
(213) 761-3516

Forespar
22322 Gilberto Rd.
Santa Margarita, CA 92688
(714) 858-8820

Guest
48 Elm St.
Meriden, CT 06450
(203) 238-0550

Man-Overboard Poles and Systems

Standard, Strobe-Type, Stern-Tube

Forespar
22322 Gilberto Rd.
Santa Margarita, CA 92688
(714) 858-8820

Jay Stuart Haft
Box 11210
Bradenton, FL 34282-1210
(813) 746-7161

Strobepole
Plastimo USA
6605 Selnick Dr.
Rte 100 Business Park
Baltimore, MD 21227
(301) 796-0002

Man-Overboard Rescue Systems

Heaving Line
Schaefer Marine
186 Industrial Park
New Bedford, MA 02745
(508) 995-9511

Lifesling Rescue System
Port Supply
500 Westridge
Watsonville, CA 95076
(408) 728-4417

Man-Overboard Alarm
MSTS, Marine Safe
  Telemetry Systems
800 Del Grove Ave.
Newark, DE 19713
(302) 366-8073

Man-Overboard Breathing Air Tank,
  Abandon-Ship Bag
Survival Technologies Group
Marine Challenge
101 16th Ave S.
St. Petersburg, FL 33701
(800) 525-2747

Rescue Throwrope
Omega
130 Condor St.
E. Boston, MA 02128
(617) 569-3400

Throwable Inflatable Horseshoe
Survival Technologies Group
Marine Challenge
101 16th Ave.
St. Petersburg, FL 33701
(800) 525-2747

Mechanical Equipment

Ball Valves and
  Through-Hull Fittings
Buck Algonquin Marine Hardware
1565 Palmyra Bridge Rd.
Pennsauken, NJ 08110
(609) 665-9405

Cooling Water Strainers
Raritan Engineering
530 Orange St.
Millville, NJ 02832
(609) 825-4900

Drain Antisurge Valves
Edson
Ten Industrial Park Rd.
New Bedford, MA 02745
(508) 995-9711

Electric Tank Gauges
VDO Yazaki Instruments
P.O. Box 2897, 980 Brooke Rd.
Winchester, VA 22601
(703) 665-0100

Engine Controls

Edson
Ten Industrial Park Rd.
New Bedford, MA 02745
(508) 995-0711

Morse Controls
21 Clinton St.
Hudson, OH 44236
(216) 653-7702

Engine Water Cooling Systems
A&B Industries
415 Tamal Plaza
200 Tamal Vista Blvd.
Corte Madera, CA 94925
(415) 924-1300

Engine Water Pumps and Spares
Jabsco Products ITT
1485 Dale Way
Costa Mesa, CA 92626
(714) 545-8251

Fittings
Perko
P.O. Box 64000D
Miami, FL 33164
(305) 621-7525

Fuel Filters and Water Separators

Racor Industries
Div. Parker Hannifin
P.O. Box 3208
Modesto, CA 95351
(209) 521-7860

Perko
P.O. Box 64000D
Miami, FL 33164
(305) 621-7525

Wix Filters
1301 E. Ozark Ave.
Gastonia, NC 28052
(704) 864-6711

Fuel Tank Gauges
Hart Systems
4041C Ruston Way, Suite 2-A
Tacoma, WA 98402
(206) 759-3791

Garboard Drain Plugs, Seacocks
Perko
P.O. Box 64000D
Miami, FL 33164
(305) 621-7525

Heat Exchangers, Strainers,
Freshwater Cooling Systems
Sen-Dur Products
25 Moffitt Blvd.
Bay Shore, NY 11706
(516) 665-0689

Hose and Fittings
Hecht Rubber
6161 Phillips Hwy.
Jacksonville, FL 32216
(800) USA-3401

Mufflers and Exhaust System
Manifolds
Marine Manifold
134 Verdi St.
E. Farmingdale, NY 11735
(516) 694-0714

Oil Coolers
Sen-Dur Products
25 Moffitt Blvd.
Bay Shore, NY 11706
(516) 665-0689

Plastic Fittings (Plumbing)
Forespar
22322 Gilberto Rd.
Santa Margarita, CA 92688
(714) 858-8820

Plastic Through-Hull Fittings
Rule Industries
Cape Ann Industrial Park
Gloucester, MA 01930
(508) 281-0440

Pump Intake Strainers
and Marine Hose
Beckson Marine
P.O. Box 3336
Bridgeport, CT 06605
(203) 333-1412

Recessed Engine Panels
SSI (Sailing Specialties)
P.O. Box 99
Commerce Ave.
Hollywood Industrial Park
Hollywood, MD 20636
(301) 373-2372

Seacocks
Jay Stuart Haft
Box 11210
Bradenton, FL 3482-1210
(813) 746-7161

Strainers
Wilcox-Crittenden
699 Middle St.
Middletown, CT 06457
(203) 632-2600

Through-Hull Accessories
and Seacocks
Jabsco Products ITT
1485 Dale Way
Costa Mesa, CA 92626
(714) 545-8251

Waterlocks
W.H. Denouden (USA)
P.O. Box 8712
Baltimore, MD 21240
(301) 796-4740

Water-Protected Exhaust Systems
Allcraft
55 Border St.
West Newton, MA 02165

Navigation Equipment

Celestial Navigation Forms
Kleid Navigation
443 Ruane St.
Fairfield, CT 06430
(203) 259-7161

Plotters
C. Plath N. America,
    Div. of Litton Systems
222 Severn Ave
Annapolis, MD 21403
(301) 263-6700

*Tools, Protractors, Calculators,
    Rulers, Sextants*
Davis Instruments
3465 Diablo Ave.
Hayward, CA 94545-2746
(415) 732-9229

Nonskid Deck Surfacing

Antislip Tape
3M Center
223-6 NW
St. Paul, MN 55144
(612) 733-3300

Sure-Foot Industries
6519 Lorain Ave.
Cleveland, OH 44102
(216) 631-5788

Protective Safety Equipment

*Disposable Clothing, Respirators,
    Gloves, Dust Masks, Safety Gear*

MSA
600 Penn Center Blvd.
Pittsburgh, PA 15235

Norton Safety Products
200 Plainsfield Pike
Cranston, RI 02920

3M Company
P.O. Box 119
Bristol, PA 19007

Wilson Safety Products
P.O. Box 622
Reading, PA 19603

Safety Equipment Supply Houses

Interex
520 West County Rd.
St. Paul, MN 55112

Lab Safety Supply
P.O. Box 1368
Janesville, WI 53547

Rockford Medical & Safety Co.
P.O. Box 5166
Rockford, IL 61125

Pumps

Avon (IMTRA)
30 Sam Barnett Blvd.
New Bedford, MA 02745
(508) 990-2700

Dart Union Co.
Marine Division
134 Thurbers Ave.
Providence, RI 02905

Edson
Ten Industrial Park Rd.
New Bedford, MA 02745
(308) 467-8325

Gross Mechanical Labs (Groco)
7240 Standard Dr.
Hanover, MD 21076
(301) 796-5242

ITT Jabsco Products
1485 Dale Way
Costa Mesa, CA 92626
(714) 545-8251

Lovett Pumps
Shore Rd. & Ocean Ave.
Somers Point, NJ 08244
(609) 927-4144

Oberdorfer Pumps
6237 Thompson Rd.
Syracuse, NY 13201
(315) 437-0351

Raritan Engineering
530 Orange St.
Millville, NJ 08332
(609) 825-4900

Rule Industries
Cape Ann Industrial Park
Gloucester, MA 01930
(508) 281-0440

*Pump Switches, Sensors,
    and Flooding Alarms*

Sensatron
7551 Convoy Ct.
San Diego, CA 92111
(619) 268-0099

Raritan Engineering
530 Orange St.
Millville, NJ 08332
(609) 825-4900

Jabsco Products ITT
1485 Dale Way
Costa Mesa, CA 92626
(714) 545-8251

Radar

Reflectors

Davis Instruments
3465 Diablo Ave.
Hayward, CA 94545-2746
(415) 732-9229

Jay Stuart Haft
Box 11210
Bradenton, FL 34282-1210
(813) 746-7161

Radio

Licensing
Federal Communications
    Commission
Public Services Division
Field Operations Bureau
1919 M St. NW
Washington, DC 20554

Marine Radio Information
Radio Technical Commission
    for Maritime Services
P.O. Box 19087
Washington, DC 20036

Rigging and Sails

Bosun's Harness,
    Mast Climbing System
Lirakis Safety Harness Co.
18 Sheffield Ave.
Newport, RI 02840

Folding Mast Steps
A&B Industries
415 Tamal Plaza
200 Tamal Vista Blvd.
Corte Madera, CA 94925

Folding Mast Rungs
Damage Control
7670 Bay St.
Pasadena, MD 21122
(800) 543-6315

Grommet Replacement Kit
Lord & Hodge
P.O. Box 737
Middletown, CT 06457
(203) 347-2636

Masthead Halyard Locks
Hall Spars
7 Burnside St.
Bristol, RI 02809
(401) 253-4858

Roller Reefing
Cables Unlimited/Famet Marine
2900 Main St.
Alameda, CA 94501
(415) 522-2191

Rubber Spreader Boots
Tempo Products
6200 Cochran Rd.
Cleveland, OH 44139
(216) 248-1450

Sail-Furling Gear
Norseman Marine
516 W. Olas Blvd.
Fort Lauderdale, FL 33312
(305) 467-1407

Sail Repair Kits
Hayden-Schreiber
57 Compton Ave.
E. Greenwich, RI 02818
(401) 885-4565

Sail Repair Tape
Spartan Plastics
1845 S. Cedar
Holt, MI 48842
(517) 694-3911

Spar and Deck Fittings

Forespar
22322 Gilberto Rd.
Santa Margarita, CA 92688
(714) 858-8820

Jay Stuart Haft
Box 11210
Bradenton, FL 34282-1210
(813) 746-7161

Harken Yacht Fittings
1251 E. Wisconsin Ave.
Pewaukee, WI 53072
(414) 691-3320

Kenyon Spar (IMI)
P.O. Box 308
New Whitfield St.
Guilford, CT 06437
(203) 453-6109

Merriman Yacht Specialties
301 Olive St.
Grand River, OH 44045
(216) 352-8988

Sea Anchors and Drogues

Anchors & Drogues
Hathaway, Reiser & Raymond
164 Selleck St.
Stamford, CT 06902
(203) 324-9581

Custom-Made Sea Anchors
Dow Canvas Products
4230 Clipper Dr.
Manitowoc, WI 54220
(800) 558-7755

Parachute-Type Anchor/Drogue

Para-Tech Engineering
10770 Rockville St., Suite B
Santee (San Diego), CA 92071
(619) 448-1189

Shewmon
1000 Harbor Lake Dr.
Safety Harbor, FL 34695
(813) 447-0091

Sea Anchors
Cal-June
5238 Vineland Ave.
N. Hollywood, CA 91601
(213) 761-3516

Spars

Interlocking Spar Components
Sheerline Spars
Alexander-Roberts Co.
1851 Langley Ave.
Irvine, CA 92714

Spar Kits, Spares, Replacements
LeFiell Marine Products
13700 Firestone Blvd.
Santa Fe Springs, CA 90670

Steering and Controls

Geared Steerers
Lunenburg Foundry & Engineering
P.O. Box 1240
Lunenburg, Nova Scotia B0J 2C0,
    Canada

Lightweight Wheels
Harken Yacht Fittings
1251 E. Wisconsin Ave.
Pewaukee, WI 53072
(414) 691-3320

Pedestal Steerers
Merriman Yacht Specialties
301 Olive St.
Grand River, OH 44045
(216) 352-8988

Steering and Controls
Edson
Ten Industrial Park Rd.
New Bedford, MA 02745
(508) 995-9711

Stoves

Gas Alarms and Controls

Bass Products
50 Grove St.
Salem, MA 01970
(508) 744-7003

Marinetics
P.O. Box 2676
Newport Beach, CA 92663
(714) 646-8889

Newmar
P.O. Box 1306
Newport Beach, CA 92663
(714) 751-0488

Gas Cylinders & Exchange Service
Gas Systems
5361 Production Dr.
Huntington Beach, CA 92649
(714) 891-2411

Gas Safety Valves
Xintex Products
P.O. Box 152
Grand Rapids, MI 49501-152
(616) 235-2360

Gas Shutoff Valves
Marinetics
P.O. Box 2676
Newport Beach, CA 92663
(714) 646-8889

LP Gas Cylinders
Worthington Cylinders
1085 Dearborn Dr.
Columbus, OH 43085
(614) 438-3013

Propane Gas Storage Lockers

Marine Energy Systems
P.O. Box 968
104 Epping Rd.
Exeter, NH 03833
(603) 772-5091

Seaward Products
15600 Salt Lake Ave.
City of Industry, CA 91745
(818) 968-2117

Stoves

Paul E. Luke
East Boothbay, ME 04544
(207) 633-4971

Shipmate Stove Division
Richmond Ring Co.
Richmond Rd.
Souderton, PA 18964

Survival Suits

Bayley Suit
900 S. Fortuna Blvd.
Fortuna, CA 95540
(707) 725-3391

Mustang
P.O. Box 5844
2171 E. Bakerview Rd.
Bellingham, WA 98227
(800) 533-5628

Parkway/Imperial
241 Raritan St.
S. Amboy, NJ 08879
(201) 721-5300

Stearns
P.O. Box 1498
St. Cloud, MN 56302
(612) 252-1642

Testing Equipment

*Testing Fluids (for welds and
    other metal joints)*
Magnaflux Corp.
7300 W. Lawrence Ave.
Chicago, IL 60656

Tools and Supplies

*Note: The following names and
    addresses represent tool and
    supply organizations and outlets
    where the authors have specific
    knowledge of quality and service.
    Local chandleries and
    high-quality hardware stores often
    carry the same materials, and the
    wise buyer should check prices. In
    addition, many marine
    distributors maintain their own
    catalogs that include tools and
    boating supplies. The sources
    listed below are specific tool and
    supply mail-order houses that
    either cater specifically to boaters
    or offer extremely high-quality
    materials.*

*Cabinet and Marine-Grade
  Hardwoods; Woodworking Tools
  and Hardware*
Constantine
2067 N. Eastchester Rd.
Bronx, NY 10461

General Marine Chandlery Products
Merritt Marine Supply, Inc.
2621 N.E. 4th Ave.
Pompano Beach, FL 33064
(303) 946-5350

General Marine Supplies

Hamilton Marine
Main St.
Searsport, ME 04974
(207) 548-2985

Fisheries Supply Co.
1900 N. Northlake Way
Seattle, WA 98103

Cook Marine Products
101 Rowayton AVe.
Rowayton, CT 06853
(203) 866-0164

J.J. & J. Read
327 Shirley Rd.
Southampton, England

Sailmaker's and Rigger's Tools

Howe and Bainbridge
220 Commercial St.
Boston, MA 02109

Ratsey and Lapthorn
E. Schofield St.
City Island, NY 10464

Topping Brothers
4405 S. Clinton Ave.
Plainfield, NJ 07080

Tools

Garrett Wade Co. Inc.
161 Avenue of the Americas
New York, NY 10013
(800) 221-2942

Woodcraft Supply Corp.
Dept. B118
41 Atlantic Ave.
P.O. Box 4000
Woburn, MA 01888
(617) 935-5860

Valves

Seacocks

Apollo Valve Division
Consolidated Valve Industries
P.O. Box 125
Pageland, SC 29728

Buck Algonquin
1565 Palmyra Bridge Rd.
Pennsauken, NJ 08110
(609) 665-9405

Wilcox-Crittenden
699 Middle St.
Middletown, CT 06457
(203) 632-2600

Ventilators

Aluminum Cowl Vents
Paul E. Luke
Box 816
E. Boothbay, ME 04544
(207) 633-4971

Blowers and Fans
Jabsco Products ITT
1484 Dale Way
Costa Mesa, CA 92626
(714) 545-8251

Blowers
Wilcox-Crittendon
699 Middle St.
Middletown, CT 06457
(203) 632-2600

Chrome and Brass Ventilators

A&B Industries
415 Tamal Plaza
200 Tamal Vista Blvd.
Corte Madera, CA 94925
(415) 924-1300

Beckson Marine
P.O. Box 3336
Bridgeport, CT 06605
(203) 333-4412

Cowl and Mushroom Vents
W.H. Denouden (USA)
P.O. Box 8712
Baltimore, MD 21240
(301) 796-4740

*PVC, Stainless, Solar Ventilator
  Systems*
Nicro-Fico
675 Brannan St.
San Francisco, CA 94107
(415) 283-3335

Stainless Cowl Vents
Hood Yacht Systems
Maritime Dr.
Portsmouth, RI 02871
(401) 683-2900

Windscoops
Davis Instruments
3465 Diablo Ave.
Hayward, CA 94545-2746
(415) 732-9229

Watermakers (Emergency)

Reverse-Osmosis Watermaker
Recovery Engineering
1204 Chestnut Ave.
Minneapolis, MN 55403
(612) 333-6828

Windows and Portlights

Aluminum, Bronze, Plastic Windows
Bomar
P.O. Box W
Charlestown, NH 03603
(603) 826-5794

Clearview Windshield Screen
W.H. Denouden (USA)
P.O. Box 8712
Baltimore, MD 21240
(301) 796-4740

Deadlights
Jay Stuart Haft
Box 11210
Bradenton, FL 34282-1210
(813) 746-7161

Stainless Portlights
Hood Yacht Systems
Maritime Dr.
Portsmouth, RI 02871
(401) 683-2900

Zincs, Sacrificial (Anodes)

Outboard Motor Anodes
OMC Parts & Accessories
Seahorse Dr.
Waukegan, IL 60085
(312) 689-5653

Zincs

W.H. Denouden (USA)
P.O. Box 8712
Baltimore, MD 21240
(301) 795-4740

Essex Machine Works
West Ave.
Essex, CT 06426
(203) 767-8285

Wilcox-Crittenden
699 Middle St.
Middletown, CT 06457
(203) 632-2600

Index